PICTURING CANADA
A History of Canadian Children's Illustrated Books and Publishing

Working within the scholarly framework of studies in book and print culture, the history of publishing and the book trade, and concepts of childhood, *Picturing Canada* explores the changing geographical, historical, and cultural aspects of Canadian identity through the lens of children's illustrated book publishing over two centuries.

Gail Edwards and Judith Saltman illuminate the connection between children's publishing and Canadian nationalism, analyse the gendered history of children's librarianship, identify changes and continuities in narrative themes and artistic styles, and explore recent developments in the creation and consumption of children's illustrated books. Over 130 interviews with authors, illustrators, editors, librarians, booksellers, critics, and other contributors to Canadian children's book publishing document the experiences of those who worked in the industry.

An important and original work, *Picturing Canada* is fundamental to our understanding of publishing history and the history of childhood itself.

(Studies in Book and Print Culture)

GAIL EDWARDS is the chair of the Department of History at Douglas College.

JUDITH SALTMAN is an associate professor in the School of Library, Archival and Information Studies and the chair of the Master of Arts in Children's Literature Program at the University of British Columbia.

PICTURING CANADA

A History of Canadian Children's Illustrated Books and Publishing

GAIL EDWARDS and JUDITH SALTMAN

UNIVERSITY OF TORONTO PRESS
Toronto Buffalo London

ISBN 978-0-8020-3759-6 (cloth)
ISBN 978-0-8020-8540-5 (paper)

Printed on acid-free and 100% post-consumer recycled paper with vegetable-based inks.

Library and Archives Canada Cataloguing in Publication

Edwards, Gail, 1957–
    Picturing Canada : a history of Canadian children's illustrated books and
publishing / Gail Edwards and Judith Saltman.

(Studies in book and print culture)
Includes bibliographical references and index.
ISBN 978-0-8020-3759-6 (bound)   ISBN 978-0-8020-8540-5 (pbk.)

1. Illustrated Children's books – Publishing – Canada – History.   2. Children's
literature, Canadian – History and criticism.   3. Children – Canada – Books and
reading.   I. Saltman, Judith   II. Title.   III. Series: Studies in book and print culture

Z483.E39 2010   381'.450020971   C2010-900553-8

Illustration details on page iii and chapter openers: [David Boyle]. *Uncle Jim's Canadian
Nursery Rhymes: For Family and Kindergarten Use*. Illustrated by C.W. Jefferys. London
and Toronto: Musson, 1908. Reproduction from the Arkley Collection of Early and Historical Children's Literature, Rare Books and Special Collections, University of British
Columbia Library.

University of Toronto Press acknowledges the financial assistance to its publishing
program of the Canada Council for the Arts and the Ontario Arts Council.

 Canada Council   Conseil des Arts    ONTARIO ARTS COUNCIL
for the Arts   du Canada   CONSEIL DES ARTS DE L'ONTARIO

This book has been published with the help of a grant from the Canadian Federation
for the Humanities and Social Sciences, through the Aid to Scholarly Publications
Programme, using funds provided by the Social Sciences and Humanities Research
Council of Canada.

University of Toronto Press acknowledges the financial support for its publishing
activities of the Government of Canada through the Book Publishing Industry Development Program (BPIDP).

Contents

List of Illustrations

COLOUR PLATES

(Colour plates follow page 136)

Acknowledgments

This book has been published with the help of a grant from the Canadian Federation for the Humanities and Social Sciences, through the Aid to Scholarly Publications Program, using funds provided by the Social Sciences and Humanities Research Council of Canada. We wish to acknowledge the support of the Social Sciences and Humanities Research Council of Canada through a research grant for the years 2000 through 2003, and the University of British Columbia Hampton Fund Research Grant for the years 2003 through 2005. The funding has enabled us to travel to archives and libraries across Canada, complete an extensive series of interviews, and recruit graduate student assistants.

We also acknowledge the support of the University of British Columbia Faculty of Arts Humanities and Social Sciences Research Grant for the years 2008 through 2009, Steve Koerner and the Moss Rock Park Foundation for the years 2008 through 2009, the Bibliographical Society of Canada Marie Tremaine Fellowship for the years 2008 through 2009, and the International Board on Books for Young People – Canadian Section, Frances Russell Research Award for the years 2008 through 2009, all for support toward dissemination of research.

We gratefully acknowledge a wide range of individuals, associations, organizations, and libraries without whose assistance and support this book could not have been completed.

We thank everyone who agreed to be interviewed. One hundred and thirty-six writers, illustrators, editors, designers, publishers, booksellers, reviewers, critics, librarians, teachers, children's literature specialists, and academics generously shared their time and knowledge with us. They participated in interviews on audio tape, and by email, correspondence, and telephone, some of them more than once. Thirty-four individuals declined to be interviewed or did not reply to our requests.

Not every individual interviewed was quoted in this book, but all provided substantive information, background, and context for the research. Their experiences, memories, and reflections have created an oral history of Canadian children's publishing and illustrated books.

Archival information was provided to us by individuals working within associations and organizations. We thank: Charlotte Teeple, Executive Director of the Canadian Children's Book Centre, and librarians Brenda Halliday and Naseem

Hrab; Judy Green, Marketing and Communications Officer, the Canadian Library Association; James McCann, President of CWILL (Children's Writers and Illustrators of British Columbia); Susan Shipton, President of IBBY Canada (the Canadian national section of the International Board on Books for Young People); and Ann Montanaro, Director of the Movable Book Society.

Libraries and archives provided access to archival papers, historical and rare books, and contemporary materials. We thank: Josiane Polidori, Head, Library and Archives Canada's Canadian Children's Literature Service, and assistants Alfonsina Clemente and Daniel St.-Hilaire; Leslie McGrath, Head, The Toronto Public Library's Osborne Collection of Early Children's Books; Dr Richard Virr, McGill University's Rare Books and Special Collection Division; Ralph Stanton, Head, the University of British Columbia Library's Rare Books and Special Collections, and librarians Katherine Kalsbeek and Frances Woodward, and library assistant Weiyan Yan; Christopher Ball, Head, the University of British Columbia's Education Library and librarians Linda Dunbar and Jo-Anne Naslund; Judi Walker, Head, Children's Library, Vancouver Public Library.

Grateful acknowledgment is made to Kenneth Marantz, professor emeritus of Ohio State University, and Sylvia Marantz for permission to model our interview questions on their books of interviews.

Many graduate research assistants from the University of British Columbia's School of Library, Archival and Information Studies' Master of Library and Information Studies Program, PhD Program, and the University's Master of Arts in Children's Literature Program contributed. They helped with research, interviews, and the creation of the website and database of the Canadian Children's Illustrated Books project, available online at http://www.canadianchildlit.ca. A special thank you is extended to three graduate student assistants for their invaluable contributions: Brian Hornberg, Merinda McClure, and Kathryn Shoemaker. Grateful thanks to:

Research: Desiree Baron, Shailloo Bedhi, Lian Beveridge, Marilynne Black, Joanne Canow, Marcia Fuller, Carol Gladstein, Derek Gratsby, Rina Hadziev, Elizabeth Heideman, Brian Hornberg, Merinda McLure, Noreen Ma, Richard Matiachuk, Carmen Merrells, Michelle Purdon, Randi Robin, Jonathan Scop, Kathryn Shoemaker, Tanya Thiessen, Emily Tufts, Ginger Warden, Stephen Warren, Anne Marie Weiss, Michele Wiens, Mei-Mei Wu.

Website: Manuela Boscenco, Joanne Boucher, Virginia Chan, Nicholas Chang, Annette DeFaveri, Sarah Donald, Julie Friel, Nicole Gjertsen, Peggy Holm, Kristina McDavid, Marilyn McPherson, Michelle Mallette, Anne Martin, Patty Montpellier, Tom Richardson, Sion Romaine, Karen Sharkey, Kathryn Shoemaker, Kevin Stranack.

Database: Carolyn Casenas, Tanya Goos, Sean Hannan, Teresa Lee, Julie Michaud, Karim Tharani, Peter Tyrrell, Kelly Woods.

Interview transcription, editing, and indexing: Kirsten Andersen, Shauna Barry, Maryn Brown, Erin Creak, Allison Davis, Paul Evans, Kathryn Foley, Jing Jiang, Stephanie Karnosh, Marilyn McPherson, Michelle Mallette, Heather Marker, Hugh Morrison, Danielle Russell, Carolyn Sin, Annette Tellis, Alyssa Uecker, Lindsay Ure, Donna Waye, Diana Wilkes, Linda Yan.

Interviews: Camille Callison, Cherie Givens, Kathryn Shoemaker.

Technical support was provided by Shelley MacDonald Beaulieu of To The Letter, Montreal, Justin Beckett of TR Trades in Vancouver, and Al Karim and staff at Copies Plus in Vancouver.

We thank our colleagues at Douglas College and the School of Library, Archival and Information Studies, University of British Columbia, for their support during the lengthy process of research and writing. Thanks in particular are owed to Kathy Denton, Dean of Humanities and Social Sciences, Douglas College; to Ken Haycock and Edie Rasmussen, past Directors, and Terry Eastwood, Interim Director, the School of Library, Archival and Information Studies, University of British Columbia; and to Mary Grenier, Administrator at SLAIS, who provided assistance in managing our grant accounts. We also thank our undergraduate students in Canadian History at Douglas College and UBC, and our graduate students at SLAIS in LIBR 522D Contemporary Canadian Children's Literature, LIBR 522E Illustrated Books for Children, and LIBR 523 Canadian Literature and Other Materials for Children, who continually challenge us to clarify and revise our ideas.

At various critical points, friends and colleagues provided invaluable feedback and encouragement. We thank Keith Bunnell and David Swan, Ann Curry, Ron Jobe, Rick Kopak, Patricia McLean, Frank Leonard, Kit Pearson, Joanne Richardson, Mary Sue Stephenson, and Toshiyuki and Yukiko Tosa for their invaluable professional expertise and support. In particular, we would like to express our gratitude to Ronald Hagler, Keith Niall, and Guy Robertson for their generous assistance with editing and proofreading. Any remaining mistakes, of course, are all ours. We also thank the peer reviewers of the manuscript for their insightful comments.

We thank our editors, Siobhan McMenemy, Ryan Van Huijstee, Frances Mundy, and the University of Toronto Press for their sustained and patient assistance in moving the project forward to completion. Thanks to James Leahy for his copyediting of the manuscript, and to Annette Lorek for preparing the index.

We thank our families, who have provided their support and encouragement and exercised patience throughout the project. Special thanks are owed to Judi's daughter, Anne Barringer, who has shared the pleasures of reading picturebooks with her mother since infancy.

Finally, we remember and honour Sheila Egoff and Alixe Hambleton, our first mentors and guides, who inspired us with their commitment to Canadian children's literature.

A Chronology of Children's Print History in Canada

1846   *Little Grace, or, Scenes in Nova Scotia*, with two engraved plates, published in Halifax.

1847   *The Snow Drop, or, Juvenile Magazine* begins publication in Montreal, issued until 1853.

1856   Robert M. Ballantyne, *Snowflakes and Sunbeams; or, the Young Fur Traders. A Tale of the Far North* published in the UK.

1859   Amelia Frances Howard-Gibbon illustrates the manuscript of *An Illustrated Comic Alphabet Book*.

1898   Ernest Thompson Seton, *Wild Animals I Have Known* published in New York.

1908   [David Boyle], *Uncle Jim's Canadian Nursery Rhymes for Family and Kindergarten Use*, illustrated by C.W. Jefferys, published in Toronto by the Musson Book Company.

1908   L.M. Montgomery, *Anne of Green Gables* published in Boston.

1912   Toronto Public Library institutes annual display of books suitable for holiday gifts.

1912   Toronto Public Library's Boys' and Girls' Division established, headed by Lillian H. Smith, the first trained children's librarian in Canada.

1917   A 'Round Table of Librarians interested in work among Boys and Girls' formed as a group within the Ontario Library Association.

1918   Cyrus Macmillan, *Canadian Wonder Tales* published in London and New York.

1921   Canadian Book Week established by the Canadian Authors' Association.

1922   Boys and Girls House, Toronto Public Library, opens the first separate children's library in the British Empire.

1927   *Books for Boys and Girls*, edited by Lillian Smith, published by the Toronto Public Library.

1931   R.K. Gordon, *A Canadian Child's ABC*, illustrated by Thoreau MacDonald, published in Toronto by Dent.

1939   Canadian Association of Children's Librarians formed.

1946   Canadian Library Association formed.

1947   Children's Book of the Year Award inaugurated by the Canadian Association of Children's Librarians.

1948   William Toye joins Oxford University Press, Toronto.

1949   Edgar Osborne, a British librarian, donates his collection of rare children's books to the Toronto Public Library.

1949   *Young Canada's Book Week / La Semaine du livre pour la jeunesse canadienne* organized by the Canadian Library Association.

1951   Royal Commission on National Development in the Arts, Letters and Sciences report recommends the creation of the Canada Council and the National Library.

1952   Canadian Retail Booksellers Association (later renamed the Canadian Booksellers Association) established.

1952   Senate Special Committee on Sale and Distribution of Salacious and Indecent Literature begins hearings.

1953   National Library of Canada established by Parliament.

1954   Frank Newfeld, illustrator and graphic designer, arrives in Toronto, sets up design studio.

1957   Canada Council established by Parliament (later renamed Canada Council for the Arts).

1957   Scholastic Books expands its publishing operations into Canada.

1959   *Canadian Literature* begins publication.

1959   Governor General's Literary Awards administered by Canada Council.

1962   Sheila Egoff joins the School of Librarianship at the University of British Columbia as the first tenured professor of children's literature at a Canadian university.

1965   *Literary History of Canada* published, including essay on children's literature.

1965   Peter Martin Associates (PMA) founded in Toronto.

1966   Oberon Press in Ottawa and Fitzhenry and Whiteside in Toronto are founded.

1967   *In Review*, a reviewing journal of Canadian children's literature, begins publication.

1967   Sheila Egoff, *The Republic of Childhood: A Critical Guide to Canadian Children's Literature in English* published by Oxford University Press.

1967   The National Library building in Ottawa opened.

1967   Tundra Books founded in Montreal by May Cutler.

1968   Mary Alice Downie and Barbara Robertson, *The Wind Has Wings: Poems from Canada,* illustrated by Elizabeth Cleaver, published by Oxford University Press.

1969   William Toye, *How Summer Came to Canada* and *The Mountain Goats of Temlaham*, illustrated by Elizabeth Cleaver, published by Oxford University Press.

1970   Ryerson Press sold to McGraw-Hill.

1970   Scholastic Books institutes Canadian publishing program of original and reprinted Canadian titles, issued as Scholastic-TAB Publications.

1970   The Ontario Royal Commission on Book Publishing appointed.

1971   Amelia Frances Howard-Gibbon Illustrator's Award inaugurated by Canadian Library Association.

1971   Ann Blades, *Mary of Mile 18* published by Tundra Books; May Cutler opens Tundra Books of Northern New York in Plattsburgh, New York.

1971   *Books in Canada* begins publication.

1971   *Canadian Materials (CM)* begins publication.

1971   Communication-Jeunesse established in Montreal to promote children's literature published in Quebec.

1971   Independent Publishers' Association established.

1972   Canada Council Block Grant funding introduced.

1972   Canadian Women's Educational Press founded in Toronto; issues books as Women's Press.

1972   Janet Lunn appointed children's editor at Clarke, Irwin.

1972   Ontario Arts Council block grants to publishers introduced.

1973   Association for the Export of Canadian Books established.

1973   Before We Are Six publishing collective founded.

1973   Breakwater Books founded in St John's, Newfoundland.

1973   *Emergency Librarian* begins publication.

1973   Kids Can Press founded in Toronto as a ten-person collective.

1973   *Notable Canadian Children's Books / Un Choix de livres canadiens pour la jeunesse* exhibition the National Library of Canada, with catalogue by Sheila Egoff and Alvine Bélisle.

1973   Ontario Royal Commission on Book Publishing final report issued.

1973   The Canadian Library Association and the Association canadienne des bibliothécaires de langue française present a brief to the Secretary of State requesting the appointment of a children's librarian/consultant at the National Library.

1973   Writers' Union of Canada established in Toronto.

1974   Children's Book Store opened in Toronto by Judy Sarick.

1974   Dennis Lee, *Alligator Pie* and *Nicholas Knock* published by Macmillan.

1974   Foreign Investment Review Agency established by Government of Canada.

1974   Marilyn Fisher appointed children's editor at McClelland and Stewart.

1975   Books by Kids founded by Anne Millyard and Rick Wilks.

1975   Canada Council Children's Literature Prizes inaugurated.

1975   *Canadian Children's Literature / Littérature canadienne pour la jeunesse* begins publication at the University of Guelph.

1975   Irene Aubrey appointed Chief of the Canadian Children's Literature Service at the National Library of Canada.

1975   The 8th International Loughborough Conference on Children's Literature held at the University of Toronto.

1976   Annick Press founded by Anne Millyard and Rick Wilks in Toronto (incorporated in 1979).

1976   Canadian children's publishers begin to exhibit at Bologna Children's Book Fair.

1976   Children's Book Centre established in Toronto, with Irma McDonough as interim director.

1976   *Illustration of Books for Children: An Historical Sampling* exhibition at the Norman Mackenzie Art Gallery in Regina.

1976   Independent Publishers' Association renamed Association of Canadian Publishers.

1976   John P. Wilkinson, *Canadian Juvenile Fiction and the Library Market* published.

1976   *Notable Canadian Children's Books / Un Choix de livres canadiens pour la jeunesse* supplements begin publication.

1976   *Owl* magazine begins publication.

1976   Pacific Rim Conference on Children's Literature held at the University of British Columbia.

1976   Ruth Schwartz Children's Book Award established by the Canadian Bookseller's Association.

1977   CANSCAIP (Canadian Society of Children's Authors, Illustrators and Performers) established.

1977   Children's Book Centre appoints Phyllis Yaffe as Executive Director.

1977   Children's Book Festival organized by the Children's Book Centre; author tours begin.

1977   Children's Literature Roundtable in Edmonton established.

1977   Firefly Books founded by Lionel Koffler.

1977   Kaleidoscope, Canadian Rockies Conference on Literature for Children and Youth in Calgary, sponsored by the Alberta Learning Resources Council.

1977   *Our Choice*, a selection guide to Canadian books for children by the Children's Book Centre begins publication.

1978   Groundwood Books founded in Toronto by Patsy Aldana.

1978   Nimbus Publishing founded in Nova Scotia.

1978   Vancouver Children's Literature Roundtable formed by Ronald Jobe and colleagues in the Department of Language Education, University of British Columbia.

1978   Woozles children's bookstore in Halifax opened by Ann Connor Brimer and Liz and Brian Crocker.

1979   Books By Kids changes name to Annick Press; Robert Munsch, *Mud Puddle* and *The Dark*, illustrated by Michael Martchenko, published by Annick.

1979   Canadian Book Publishing Development Program established by Government of Canada.

1979   *Chickadee* magazine begins publication.

1979   *Emergency Librarian* published by Ken Haycock and Carol-Ann Haycock.

1979   *Pictures to Share / Images pour tous* exhibition at the National Library of Canada, with catalogue by Irene Aubrey.

1979   Valerie Hussey joins Kids Can Press.

1980   IBBY Canada (International Board on Books for Young People) established.

1980   Pemmican Publishing founded in Winnipeg by the Manitoba Métis Federation.

1980   Theytus Books founded by Randy Fred as a wholly Aboriginal-owned and -operated publisher.

1980   University of British Columbia's Creative Writing Department offers a course in writing for children, developed by Sue Ann Alderson.

1981   Alcuin Society Book Design Awards inaugurated.

1981   Annick Press releases its first print run of Annikins, miniature format reprints.

1981 Claude Aubry Award for distinguished service in children's literature inaugurated by IBBY Canada.

1982 Frances E. Russell Award for research in Canadian children's literature inaugurated by IBBY Canada.

1982 *Images of Childhood – The Art of the Illustrator* exhibition at Toronto's Harbourfront.

1982 Janet Lunn named Regina Public Library's Writer in Residence for 1982–3.

1982 L'Association des illustrateurs québécois established in Montreal.

1982 *Serendipity* children's literature conference inaugurated by Vancouver Children's Literature Roundtable.

1982 Theytus Books purchased by the Okanagan Tribal Council and the Nicola Valley Indian Administration.

1983 Vancouver Kidsbooks opened in Vancouver by Phyllis Simon.

1984 Annick Press named Publisher of the Year by the Canadian Booksellers Association.

1984 Canadian Children's Book Centre establishes positions for regional officers in Alberta, Saskatchewan, and Manitoba.

1984 CANSCAIP Packaging Your Imagination workshop inaugurated.

1984 Orca Book Publishers founded by Bob Tyrrell in Victoria.

1984 Stoddart Publishing develops children's book list.

1985 CANSCAIP-West established as a Vancouver branch of the Canadian Society of Children's Authors, Illustrators and Performers.

1985 Children's Book Festival includes illustrators in the tours.

1985 Elizabeth Mrazik-Cleaver Picture Book Award inaugurated by IBBY Canada.

1986 Ann Connor Brimer selected as the first Atlantic regional officer for the Children's Book Centre.

1986 *Canadian Images Canadiennes* bilingual conference on Canadian children's literature inaugurated by the Manitoba School Library Association.

1986 Granny Bates Children's Books opened in St John's, Newfoundland, by Margie McMillan and Nora Flynn.

1986 Kids Can Press restructures from a collective to a privately held company, with Valerie Hussey and Ricky Englander as co-publishers.

1986 Parent-Child Mother Goose Program established in Toronto by Barry Dickson and Joan Bodger, in cooperation with author Celia Barker Lottridge and Katherine Grier.

1987 Canada Council Children's Literature Prizes renamed the Governor General's Literary Awards for Children's Literature.

1987 Children's Book Centre renamed Canadian Children's Book Centre.

1987 Eve Orpen Award for Publishing Excellence awarded to May Cutler of Tundra Books.

1987 Information Book Award inaugurated by the Children's Literature Roundtables of Canada.

1987 Sheila A. Egoff Children's Literature Prize inaugurated by the British Columbia Book Prizes.

1988 Children's Book Festival renamed Children's Book Week.

1988   Mabel's Fables bookstore opened by Eleanor LeFave and Susan McCul-
        loch in Toronto.
1988   *Once Upon A Time* exhibition at the Vancouver Art Gallery.
1988   Second Story Press founded in Toronto.
1988   *The Secret Self: An Exploration of Canadian Children's Literature / Le moi
        secret: une exploration de la littérature de jeunesse canadienne* exhibition at the
        National Library of Canada.
1988   Vancouver International Writers' Festival founded by Alma Lee.
1989   Kids Can Press awarded Publisher of the Year by the Canadian Booksell-
        ers Association.
1989   Mr Christie's Book Award inaugurated.
1989   *Word on the Street* book and magazine fair begins in Toronto.
1990   *Canada à Bologna / Canada at Bologna* exhibition of Canadian children's
        book illustration at the Bologna Children's Book Fair.
1990   International Board on Books for Young People (IBBY) elects Ronald Jobe
        as President.
1990   *Read Up On It / Lisez sur le sujet* kit begins publication by National Library
        of Canada.
1991   Ann Connor Brimer award for Children's Literature inaugurated by the
        Nova Scotia Library Association.
1991   *La Griffe Québécoise dans l'illustration du livre pour enfants* exhibition and
        catalogue organized by Communication-Jeunesse.
1993   Children's Writers and Illustrators of British Columbia (CWILL)
        established.
1993   Irene Aubrey retires from the National Library of Canada.
1995   Amazon online bookstore launched in the United States.
1995   Canadian Children's Book Centre in Toronto organizes art auction of work
        by Canadian children's book illustrators.
1995   Chapters, formed from a merger of SmithBooks and Coles, begins to open
        mega-bookstores.
1995   Kids Can Press licenses the film, video, and merchandising rights to the
        Franklin series to Nelvana, a Toronto-based animation company.
1995   Oxford University Press closes all its international children's trade
        divisions.
1995   *Resource Links: Connecting Classrooms, Libraries and Canadian Learning
        Resources* reviewing journal begins publication.
1995   Tundra Books purchased by McClelland and Stewart.
1996   Guadalajara Book Fair in Mexico exhibits original illustrations from Cana-
        dian children's books.
1996   Indigo Books and Music launches a chain of mega-bookstores in competi-
        tion with Chapters.
1996   Lester Publishing suspends operations.
1996   Tradewind Books founded by Michael Katz in Vancouver.
1996   Tundra Books moves to Toronto.
1997   Blue Metropolis International Literary Festival organized in Montreal.
1997   *Creating the Mosaic: A Celebration of Canadian Children's Literature*, exhibition

of 300 Canadian children's books, travels to ten cities in Japan; symposium in Nagoya on Canadian children's literature.

1997   *The Art of Illustration: A Celebration of Contemporary Canadian Children's Book Illustrators / L'art d'illustrer: un éloge des illustrateurs canadiens contemporains de livres pour enfants* exhibition opens at the National Library of Canada, featuring 29 contemporary Canadian children's book illustrators.

1998   *Emergency Librarian* renamed *Teacher Librarian: The Journal for School Library Professionals.*

1998   Kids Can Press purchased by Nelvana Limited animation studios. Ricky Englander retires and Valerie Hussey remains CEO, president and publisher.

1999   Annick Press opens a west coast office with Colleen MacMillan as associate publisher.

1999   Canadian Children's Book Centre begins to seek corporate sponsors to stabilize funding.

1999   Chapters Online begins internet book ordering in Canada.

1999   Canadian Children's Literature Symposium organized by University of Ottawa, in conjunction with National Library of Canada.

1999   Master of Arts in Children's Literature program established at the University of British Columbia.

1999   Norma Fleck Award inaugurated by the Canadian Children's Book Centre.

1999   University of Alberta offers online course, *Canadian Literature for Young People in Schools and Libraries.*

2000   Children's Book Store closed in Toronto when Judy and Hy Sarick retire.

2000   Eastern Horizons conference on Canadian Children's Literature organized in St John's by Newfoundland and Labrador Teachers' Association.

2000   Kids Can Press and Nelvana sold to multimedia company Corus Entertainment.

2000   Avie Bennett, owner of McClelland and Stewart sells 25 per cent of the company to Random House of Canada, and donates 75 per cent of the publishing arm of the company to the University of Toronto.

2000   National Library of Canada appoints Josiane Polidori Head of the Canadian Children's Literature Service.

2000   Red Deer Press affiliates with the University of Calgary.

2000   Standing Committee on Canadian Heritage holds hearings into the Canadian book industry.

2000   TD Canadian Children's Book Week renamed, with sponsorship from TD Bank Financial Group.

2001   Indigo takeover of Chapters; launches chapters.indigo.ca online bookstore.

2001   Simply Read Books founded in Vancouver.

2002   Amazon.ca website launched.

2002   Canadian Coalition for School Libraries organized.

2002   *Internationales Illustratorenforum* exhibition at the International Youth Library in Munich, Germany.

2002   *Read To Me!* program launched by the Nova Scotia Family Literacy Program.

2002   Stoddart Publishing and General Distribution Services enter receivership; Fitzhenry and Whiteside purchases Stoddart's children's list.

2002   *This Magical Book* exhibition at the Toronto Public Library.

2003   *Beyond The Letters: A Retrospective of Canadian Alphabet Books / Au-delà des lettres: Rétrospective des abécédaires canadiens* exhibition at the National Library of Canada.

2003   *Children's Book News* renamed *Canadian Children's Book News*.

2003   Christie Harris Illustrated Children's Literature Prize inaugurated by the British Columbia Book Prizes.

2003   *Fun of Reading: An International Forum on Canadian Children's Literature / Lire me sourit: Forum international sur la littérature canadienne pour la jeunesse* organized by the National Library of Canada.

2003   Ken Haycock, *The Crisis in Canada's School Libraries: The Case for Reform and Re-Investment* published.

2003   School Library Summit organized by Canadian Coalition for School Libraries in Ottawa.

2004   Library and Archives Canada created by merger of the National Library and the National Archives.

2004   *Show and Tell: Outstanding Canadian Picture Books, 2000–2003 / Montre et Raconte: albums illustrés canadiens remarquables 2000–2003* travelling exhibition organized with accompanying catalogue launched by IBBY Canada.

2004   TD Canadian Children's Literature Award inaugurated by Canadian Children's Book Centre.

2005   *ALOUD: A Celebration for Young Readers* inaugurated as part of Authors at Harbourfront Centre program in Toronto.

2005   Bratislava Illustrations Biennale (BIB), Slovakia, includes Canadian illustrators.

2005   *Canadian Children's Literature / Littérature canadienne pour la jeunesse* moves to the University of Winnipeg.

2005   Groundwood Books purchased by House of Anansi Press.

2005   Mavis Reimer named Canada Research Chair in the Culture of Childhood at University of Winnipeg.

2005   Red Deer Press purchased by Fitzhenry and Whiteside.

2005   *Writing for Young Readers* workshop at Toronto's Humber School for Writers begins.

2006   Centre for Research in Young People's Texts and Cultures established at the University of Winnipeg.

2006   Kids Can Press announces retirement of Valerie Hussey as CEO, President and Publisher; Karen Boersma appointed as publisher.

2006   Libris awards given by the Canadian Booksellers Association adds two new children's book categories for authors and illustrators.

2006   Lieutenant Governor's Aboriginal Literacy Camps inaugurated by the Ontario government, in collaboration with Frontier College, to provide literacy enrichment and outreach activities to Aboriginal children.

2006   Marilyn Baillie Picture Book Award inaugurated by Canadian Children's Book Centre.

2007   International Board on Books for Young People (IBBY) elects Patsy Aldana President.

2007   Kids Can Press appoints Lisa Lyons as President.

2007   Orca Book Publishers owner Bob Tyrrell sells 50 per cent interest to Andrew Wooldridge.

2007   *Picture Perfect!* exhibition at the TD Gallery of the Toronto Reference Library featuring original picturebook art from the Osborne Collection of Early Children's Books.

2007   Red Deer Press announces resignation of Dennis Johnson as publisher, and Peter Carver as children's editor.

2008   Orca Book Publishers appoints Andrew Wooldridge as publisher; Bob Tyrrell continues as president and editorial director.

2008   *Our Choice* renamed *Best Books for Kids and Teens*.

2008   Raincoast Books halts its publishing program to focus on distribution and wholesaling.

2009   *Canadian Children's Literature / Littérature canadienne pour la jeunesse* reconfigured and renamed *Jeunesse: Young People, Texts, Cultures.*

PICTURING CANADA
A History of Canadian Children's Illustrated Books and Publishing

CHAPTER ONE

Introduction

In a 1996 article, 'Margaret K. McElderry and the Professional Matriarchy of Children's Books,' the American scholar Betsy Hearne discusses the secondary place given to children's literature and children's publishing in literary, publishing, and educational histories. She described children's publishing as 'a matriarchy of cultural activity that has received little recognition outside a small professional circle,' whose stories about their professional practice are used as reference points to define kinship structures.[1] This study traces the genealogies of children's book publishing in Canada through the particular lens of children's illustrated books in order to explore the histories of the communities of creators, publishers, disseminators, critics, and readers who directly shape the communications circuit of children's literary production in Canada.

Our research begins with a series of seemingly straightforward questions about the interaction of image and text in children's books; about the relationship between creators, disseminators, and readers; and about nationalism and identity in Canadian children's illustrated books. What do Canadian children see when they pick up an illustrated Canadian children's book? How have creators and publishers shaped the image of Canada presented in children's books? Have those images changed over time, and why? What role do illustrated books play in the creation of communities of readers? And finally, why have critics argued that Canadian children need Canadian children's books in order to develop a Canadian cultural identity?

When we began the project, we knew that the literature was sparse, and that we would be engaged in considerable primary research, using the books issued by Canadian publishers as evidence of the material culture of children's literary production. As we conducted interviews and amassed the documentation to contextualize the information presented by our interviewees, a new and more robust picture emerged of the development and maturation of indigenous children's publishing in Canada. Our study traces the vital role of kinship networks among creators, publishers, critics, and readers, and the ways in which debates over Canadian cultural identity and the nature of childhood play a critical role in determining what is written, published, and read.

Illustrated Books and Picturebooks

The picturebook, a relatively recent development within the history of children's publishing, is the only book format that is the exclusive domain of children's literature. The picturebook is a separate, unique and particular form of the illustrated book, shaped by particular ideas about childhood and child development. As a form, the picturebook shares a territorial boundary with the illustrated book, but the differences between the two are as critical as their similarities.

In the illustrated book, the pictures are usually limited in number, spatially separated from the text, and subordinate to it, often dispersed throughout the book at distinct intervals as partial pages, spot illustrations, or head and tail pieces. The text, which may vary in length from a brief narrative to multiple chapters of dense prose, is the predominant carrier of meaning and exists independently from the illustrations. In turn, the images add to the narrative, reiterate and reinforce textual meaning, decoratively set off the text, capture a visual response to a single moment in the text, or enhance and symbolize the spirit of the text, but are not essential and inseparable to understanding the meaning of the text.[2] Illustrations in illustrated books, therefore, are static, unlike the cinematic unfolding of the picturebook.[3] And because there is no inherent collaboration between author and illustrator, it is not uncommon for a classic text to be republished in successive editions with different illustrators who are working decades or, in some cases, centuries after the author.

In contrast to the illustrated book, in a picturebook, the visual and textual narratives are integrated and interdependent, creating a metatext through the interplay and counterpoint of image and word. In the picturebook, neither words nor images exist in isolation but are integrated into a complex synthesis in which all parts of the book are crucial to understanding.[4] Text and image cannot stand alone, but must be seen in relationship to each other.

In the picturebook, text and images both describe, but may confirm or contradict each other.[5] The two elements, visual and verbal, employ separate sign systems, each with its own conventions, and require the reader to engage in a process of dual decoding.[6] These sign systems may be symmetrical, complementary, or contradictory. The images may illuminate the text or expand it or subvert it. The potential slippage between the unidirectional linearity of the text and the descriptive non-linearity of the images can create a fruitful tension that encourages the picturebook reader to assemble meaning from two different modes of communication.[7] It is this simultaneous and doubled experience, the reading of words and the viewing of images, that gives picturebooks their imaginative power and expressiveness, drawing the reader into what critic Margaret Meek has called 'a distinctive kind of imaginative looking.'[8]

The picturebook, as a doubled medium of communicating meaning, also employs a range of what the French scholar Gérard Genette describes as paratexts, a set of codified practices and discourses that further the reception and consumption of a text by mediating between the book, the author, the publisher, and the reader.[9] He distinguishes between peritexts, things within the confines of the covers of the book, including tables of contents, page design, typography, and format, and epitexts, things outside the volume, including reviews and interviews. Together, peritexts and epitexts make up the book's paratext. As Lawrence Sipe argues, the picturebook is not a single genre of literature but a format for a variety of narrative genres, characterized by the synergy of multimodal relationships between text and images in combination with the peritext. In a picturebook, the fusion of text and images interacting with peritextual elements of typeface, page design, endpapers, and cover create 'an aesthetic whole that is greater than the sum of the individual parts.'[10] As Kenneth Marantz has stated, the art of the picture book is in the totality of the book.[11]

Although Sipe privileges narrative trajectory as the defining feature of the picturebook, or picture storybook, other heavily illustrated genres of children's literature, including alphabet and counting books and information books, may also share the same aesthetic unity and synergy that characterize the picturebook. More recently, picturebooks have also been influenced by conventions of the graphic novel, in which a series of images and words are arranged in a sequence of panels to represent successive moments in a narrative, in the same way that the successive individual frames of a film are connected temporally. The reader's task is to make meaning by connecting the sequential art of images and text, and by linking the individual panels into a narrative whole.[12]

Canadian Children's Illustrated Books

Any discussion of Canadian illustrated books for children must begin by interrogating what seems at first to be self-evident. The definition of what constitutes a book for children has been rigorously contested by children's literature scholars, depending, in part, on how they define what constitutes a child reader, and what they believe to be the function of reading.[13] Harvey Darton, whose 1932 *Children's Books in England* was the first systematic study of children's literature, defined them as 'printed works produced ostensibly to give children spontaneous pleasure, and not primarily to teach them, nor solely to make them good, nor to keep them profitably quiet.'[14] The author and critic John Rowe Townsend's definition excluded pleasure to focus on pragmatics: a children's book was a book that appears 'on the children's list of a publisher.'[15] Similarly, Roderick McGillis focuses on the age of the implied reader, defining children's literature as all books published and marketed for infants, children, adolescents, and teenagers.[16] In contrast, Peter Hunt makes a distinction between 'live' books, that is, those read by contemporary children, and 'dead' books, which may have been read by children in the past, but are no longer applicable to a contemporary child audience, adding that the definition must include the idea that constructions of childhood change over time. For Hunt, then, 'particular texts … written expressly for children who are recognisably children, with a childhood recognizable today,' are children's books.[17]

Carole Gerson has identified the problem of defining the parameters of a children's book by attending to the issue of readership, and whether it is the intended reader or the actual reader that determines the conceptual category in which an author's work is placed. She argues that one way to overcome the historical marginalization of the genre is to apply the definitions inclusively rather than exclusively. Her model suggests that a 'children's book' includes work not explicitly written for young children, while simultaneously excluding genres of material clearly intended for an adult audience, even when read by children.[18]

The related problem of the definition of 'Canadian' is bound up in the particular histories of authorship, publishing, and book distribution in this country. As a robust, indigenous publishing industry for children was slow to develop, children's Canadiana, prior to the mid-twentieth century, necessarily refers not only to Canadian-authored and Canadian-published materials, but also to those titles created for children by expatriates, by non-Canadians who briefly visited Canada, by arm-chair travellers, by foreign illustrators who researched Canadian visual images, and by foreign publishers, all reflecting views of the Canadian hinterland from a distant metropole. Few of these books were directly intended for Canadian audiences. They were written for British or American readers, who gained their first textual and visual images of the perceived Canadian reality through a filtered sensibility.

Leslie McGrath, Head of the Osborne Collection of Early Children's Books at the Toronto Public Library, comments that in Canada, 'most of the early children's books were imported. What was available depended on the child's circumstance and background, the family's taste, how close they were to distribution points and what they had to choose from, of imported works.'[19] Imported children's books continued to make up the basic core of Canadian reading materials for children well into the 1970s, and arguably still form the majority of children's books read in this country. Thus generations of Canadian child readers found themselves looking back through their books to Britain or the United States for an interpretation of images of their own land, society, and self long before there were Canadian books created by people who had experiential knowledge of this country, its geography, history, and particular cultural diversity.

Approaches to the Criticism of Illustration and Picturebooks

The creation of a robust body of scholarly literature equally devoted to the analysis of picture and text was relatively slow to develop. The critic and author John Rowe Townsend distinguishes between 'book people,' or authors, publishers, public librarians, and critics who focus on literary criticism and analysis, and 'child people,' or parents, teachers, and school librarians who focus on the use of books with children. He characterizes the tensions in the evaluation of children's literature as a division between a 'book-centred' focus on the application of critical principles based on comparatively stable standards of literary quality, and a 'child-centred' functional approach based on the personal response of the reviewer and the imagined purpose of the literature under review, applied to descriptive reviews of individual books, aids to book selection, and general surveys.[20]

Academic study and research in children's literature began in the fields of education and librarianship in the first half of the twentieth century. 'Book-centred' historical overviews of the development of children's books, bio-critical surveys of individual writers, and prescriptive bibliographies to guide teachers and librarians in the selection of books predominated. Books were evaluated almost entirely on their aesthetic and literary merit, based on absolute criteria of perceived quality and suitability for entry into the canon of the 'best' children's literature. 'Child-centred' approaches included textbooks that introduced the genres of children's literature for classroom use, functional reviewing of children's literature that emphasized the uses of books with children, including the values and morals inculcated, the appropriateness of individual titles for developmental stages of childhood, and the pedagogical application of books.

Critical scholarship began to change as scholars introduced broader thematic and analytical approaches to the literature. Barbara Bader's important study, *American Picturebooks from Noah's Ark to the Beast Within* (1976) attempts to define a specific country's themes and patterns in its literature for the very young. Bader was one of the first scholars to discuss the complex nature of the picturebook, describing it as 'text, illustrations, total design; an item of manufacture and a commercial product; a social, cultural, historical document; and foremost, an experience for a child. As an art form it hinges on the interdependence of pictures and words, on the simultaneous display of two facing pages, and on the drama of the turning of the page.'[21]

Other national approaches to the historical development and genealogy of a particular country's illustrated books for children were published in the 1970s. In *Looking at Picture Books* (1973), Brian Alderson assesses the range of British titles and defines a set of critical standards by which aesthetic judgments can be made about children's picturebooks. Marcie Muir's *History of Australian Children's Book Illustration* (1982), and chapters on illustration and picturebooks in Judith Saltman's *Modern Canadian Children's Books* (1987), and Sheila Egoff and Judith Saltman's *The New Republic of Childhood: A Critical Guide to Canadian Children's Literature in English* (1990), also focus on particular national traditions of illustration, while Joyce Irene Whalley and Tessa Rose Chester's *A History of Children's Book Illustration* (1988) provides an overview of children's book illustration of the English-speaking world.

At the same time, the new critical approaches to children's illustrated books extended bio-critical and historical analysis to include the discipline of art history. Diana Klemin, in *The Illustrated Book: Its Art and Craft* (1970), evaluates illustrated books by the criteria and standards of gallery art, with classification according to media, technique, style, and art movement. This approach is also utilized by Lyn Ellen Lacy in *Art and Design in Children's Picture Books: An Analysis of Caldecott Award-Winning Illustrations* (1986). Responding to the new focus on the visual aesthetics of the illustrated book, illustrators began to write of their philosophies of illustration, of their growth and development as artists, their understanding of the particular ways that an artist uses the grammar of illustration, colour, shape, and composition to establish meaning through visual codes. In *Picture This* (1991; 2000) author-illustrator Molly Bang explores the design process, influenced by Rudolf Arnheim's visual communication theories. Jane Doonan also approaches aesthetic analysis through a personal codification of the grammar of art in *Looking at Pictures in Picture Books* (1993), in which she examines the formation of meaning and perception through the illustrator's choices of shape, colour, line, framing, and other artistic conventions. Kenneth and Sylvia Marantz also draw on art criticism and visual analysis in their collections of published interviews with illustrators, children's literature scholars, and members of the publishing and book trade community. They published the first annotated bibliography related to picturebook illustration, *The Art of Children's Picture Books: A Selective Reference Guide* (1988).

Although picturebooks have been used in the classroom for decades to help inculcate textual literacy, it was only in the 1970s that academics from faculties of education began to design curriculum around visual literacy instruction. Patricia Cianciolo's *Illustrations in Children's Books* (1970; 1976), John Stewig's *Looking at Picture Books* (1995), and Barbara Kiefer's *The Potential of Picturebooks: From Visual Literacy to Aesthetic Understanding* (1995) explore instructional ideas, lesson plans, and classroom activities to help guide children through the analysis, classification, and comparison of images to gain an understanding of elements of design and construction of visual image. Other critics of children's literature, including Margaret Meek, Aidan Chambers, Morag Styles, Evelyn Arizpe, and Victor Watson have explored the children's reading practices through participant observation and critical ethnography, informed by theories of reader response. There is now a growing body of professional literature that explores the ways in which children's responses to words, pictures, and the relationship between the two allow them to actively engage in the creation of meaning in their reading experiences.

A major development in picturebook scholarship took place in the late 1980s and 1990s as scholars from the disciplines of English, linguistics, and communications explored the semiotics of visual grammar, the sign systems of illustration as means of communication. In so doing, they bridged the gap between the evaluation of words and evaluation of pictures. Joseph Schwarcz's *Ways of the Illustrator: Visual Communication in Children's Literature* (1982) focuses on visual communication and the interaction of word and image, describing a continuum of interaction between text and art from congruency to deviation. In *Words about Pictures: The Narrative Art of Children's Picture Books* (1988), Canadian children's literature critic Perry Nodelman applies semiotic and linguistic theory to picturebook evaluation, acknowledging the hybrid nature of the picturebook as a dual pictorial and textual narrative in which 'the words tell us what the pictures do not show, and the pictures show us what the words do not tell.'[22] The dual interaction of visual and verbal is also central to Maria Nikolajeva and Carole Scott's *How Picturebooks Work* (2001), in which they develop a typology of picturebooks by a close examination of setting, characterization, narrative perspective, time and movement, mimesis and representation, metafiction and intertextuality, and the peritext, developing a scale of relationships between art and text from symmetry to contradiction. David Lewis, in *Reading Contemporary Picturebooks: Picturing Text* (2001), emphasizes the interaction of word and image, surveys previous scholarship of the picturebook, and develops a critical taxonomy of the visual and verbal that follows semioticians Gunther Kress and Theo van Leeuwen on the path towards the full articulation of a visual grammar. His approach to what he calls the ecology of the picturebook turns away from rigid classification and instead responds to the heterogeneity of the form and the variety of readings of pages and images dependent on the reader. For Lewis, the flexibility and mutability of the picturebook results from its ability to hybridize not only words with text, but the book with other artefacts of the popular culture of childhood, including toys, games, chapbooks, and comic strips.

The role of reader response theory in making meaning from the multimodal metatext of word and image is also central to Scott McCloud's *Understanding Comics: The Invisible Art* (1993), which explores the importance of the gutter or closure, the crucial space between images in which the reader's/viewer's imagination is engaged. Michèle Anstey and Geoff Bull's *Reading the Visual: Written and Illustrated Children's Literature* (2000) draws on a wide range of theoretical approaches, including semiotics and reader response, to help readers develop analytic frameworks for visual and textual analysis of picturebooks and other children's illustrated books, bridging theory and practice.

Critics and the Peritext of the Picturebook

Good picturebook design involves every aspect of the book arts. The illustrator and designer deliberately choose a particular design aesthetic to communicate with the viewer, shaped by the artist's style in combination with the peritext. The formal elements of pictorial construction, including colour, compositional elements of line, shape and texture, the medium used to create the images, and the particular artistic style employed by the illustrator all affect the reader's aesthetic response to the textual narrative and help to establish the emotional context of the picturebook.[23] The cover, endpapers, typeface, and paper on which the book is printed – in other words, the peritextual elements – also play a role in the ultimate success of the picturebook experience by further shaping the reader's interaction with image and text. In the words of Canadian art director and designer Michael Solomon, the art of design brings 'a rich, literary, and illustrative art to life through the book.'[24]

Aesthetic criticism and a new focus on the dynamics of the metatextual possibilities of the picturebook eventually superseded the pure historical and biographical analyses of the early twentieth century. Nonetheless, well into the 1980s, and in contrast to the emerging scholarly literature on the semiotics of the picturebook, general studies of children's literature and reviews of individual books published in the reviewing journals have been reticent to adopt a more comprehensive and theoretical understanding of the ways in which pictures and text interact and the role of the peritext in shaping the reader's experience. Most published reviews of picturebooks, written by reviewers whose expertise is in the literary rather than the visual sphere, devote the majority of reviews to the textual, focusing on narrative and character, and on pedagogical utility rather than the analysis of image or image and text, and demonstrate a rather limited understanding of the interplay between image and text in the construction of meaning.

All too often, the pictures in picturebooks are discussed perfunctorily as adjuncts to the text that aid the emergent reader in the decoding of words on the page, or as decorative ornamentation subordinate to the text, isolated from any narrative function. The language used to describe the illustrations is often limited and repetitive, focusing on attributes like 'bright and lively,' or 'subtle and soft,' rather than engaging in a sustained analysis of the visual. In English-speaking Canada, the mimetic function of the images in picturebooks to show the reader a representation of reality has been particularly valorized, and images in picturebooks are often praised for their lifelike fidelity of the reproduction in the 'real.'[25]

In the last decade, the discourse of picturebook criticism has shifted and changed continuously as different academic disciplines turned their attention to the genre. As the picturebook itself changes through the absorption of new styles and genres and through the impact of technological change and cultural and commercial influences, so too has the criticism of children's literary production incorporated postmodernism, feminism, queer theory, and postcolonialism. Newer approaches to literary criticism and aesthetic criticism have extended the analysis of picturebooks beyond a straightforward pedagogical assessment of the genre as tools for textual and visual literacy acquisition. The introduction of semiotics to the critical mix added the beginnings of a new grammar to explore the role of the visual image in meaning-making. Critics of the picturebook now consider how meaning is negotiated in the space between words and image.

What Happens When a Child Looks at a Picturebook?

Exposure to language, story, and books in a child's early years through the shared activities of reading picturebooks, storytelling, conversation, and singing are generally believed by most child development experts to be fundamental in the development of textual and visual literacy skills in children. Children learn to decode print and make meaning of text and image through their exposure to books that are read aloud to them in a variety of formal and informal settings.[26]

Through picturebook reading with adults, children internalize what Catherine Snow and Anat Ninio term the 'contracts of literacy,' a set of basic rules that emphasize the stability of the text on the page and the mimetic function of images. According to Snow and Ninio, children who are introduced to picturebooks learn that books are not toys; that the reader is led by the text; that pictures are not things but representatives of things; that pictures are linked to the names of things; that pictures, although static, can represent events; that book events occur outside real time; and that books constitute an autonomous fictional world.[27]

The storyteller and author Celia Barker Lottridge argues that children need to have reading modelled for them. In the process of being read to by an adult, a child sees that stories are contained in books, that words connect with pictures, and that images on the printed page are stable and unchanging from reading to reading.[28] Children who share books with adults and have the opportunity to engage in talk about the pictures and words gain familiarity with the book as a physical object and with the printed page as a carrier of meaning. In the shared experience of reading aloud, children become familiar with the conventions of the printed page. They become aware of how English text moves from top to bottom and left to right, how the book is held with the opening facing the reader, and they become dexterous in the process of page turning.[29] As children's eyes move across the page to view the illustrations, they hear and are informed by the reading voice and begin to discern that the pattern of text on the page has meaning.[30] They are introduced to the diversity of language and develop skills in listening and comprehending text. They absorb narrative patterns and begin to take pleasure in anticipating and predicting the repetition of familiar words and phrases. They explore the interaction of the pictures with the words and develop verbal fluency while discussing pictures and text with the adult reader.

The multiple layering of the picturebook, comprising a text that may be read aloud and images that convey narrative simultaneously with and independently from the text, acts as a conduit to textual and visual literacy. Despite the fixity of the image on the page, and the belief in the mimetic power of images to accurately and unambiguously represent the text for the young child who is learning the names of things, the decoding of images is a learned skill. Learning to read pictures involves mastering specific cultural norms about representation, just as the belief that realistic pictures show what is 'really real' is a cultural construct.[31]

In learning to read the pictures in picturebooks, children are introduced to the conventions of semiotic codes and signifiers. In exploring the slippages between the temporal and spatial, they learn that images have a sequence that relates to the narrative.[32] Through the interplay of pictures and text, they begin to understand the multiple ways that images can convey information, and that 'stories include what the reader knows and the text needn't say.'[33] The picturebook can encourage children to develop a personal visual and aesthetic repertoire, although some critics have argued that the images in picturebooks, like the images in films, can limit the child's imaginative encounter with the narrative.[34]

Through the medium of the picturebook, children can gain an awareness that reading is an interactive process of meaning-making.[35] Thus, children who come to literacy through the experience of daily book sharing with adults have a familiarity with the printed page and the contracts of literacy and have been introduced to the 'pleasure of a parallel life … a separate magically imaginative world' represented by literary production.[36] The particular nature of the picturebook, in which images and text can be read separately or in concert, may encourage readers 'to reflect on the act of reading itself.'[37]

Cultural Identity and the Illustrated Children's Book

Complex and contested ideas about nation, community, and the importance of cultural identity are embedded in any discussion of a national children's literature. How nations define themselves and construct, deconstruct, and reconstruct their cultural identities inevitably changes over time in response to changes in political and social alignment, especially in countries with a history of colonization. In Canada, competing notions of 'home,' and debate over the relative value of indigenous and colonial cultural production, indeed, of the viability of the very idea of a 'national literature,' are further complicated by the role of language as a disputed terrain for discourses of belonging.[38]

The interaction of children and texts is bound to geographies and histories of childhood. Critics have argued that the function of literacy and engagement with printed texts is to inculcate morality, furthering the goals of civil society by teaching right attitudes and beliefs. The pedagogic function of the picturebook in aiding textual decoding and encouraging the acquisition of literacy is seen as another of its critical roles. Critics have valorized illustrated books and picturebooks for their ability to show children the world in which they live, and judged literary and visual creation by the degree of fidelity in reproducing the 'real.'

Children's literature, however, can also articulate the 'values, tensions, myths, and psychology that identify a national character,' both shaping and responding to dominant discourses and counter-discourses.[39] The mimetic role of children's illustrated literature in both reflecting and constructing ideas of nationhood has been summarized by critic Jeffrey Canton, who believes that Canadian children's literature 'gives our young readers a unique chance to see their lives as Canadians reflected back at them through the artistic perspectives of our writers and artists. Ultimately in trying to define what it is, it defines who we are.'[40] Of course, Canton's comments also raise questions of who are 'our young readers' and 'our writers and artists,' and whether a sense of national identity and belonging are uniformly experienced.

British critic Margaret Meek raises the question of the role that children's literature plays in helping children to understand what she calls 'the social sameness and difference that constitute "national identity,"' arguing that through reading, children can gain self-understanding about belonging and differentiation.[41] The creation of a national literature for children, therefore, is part of a subtle, ongoing dialogue about belonging and differentiation, in which adults seek to inculcate desired social and cultural norms by reinforcing valued social identities in the places called 'home.'

Children's literature and, more particularly, the visual images in children's books can do the ideological work of extending hegemonic discourses within a society about collective identity, memory, and normative social practices. As Jerry Diakiw notes, 'Story is a powerful and traditional way to provide a common bond for members of a society and to familiarize children with a culture.'[42] At the same time, the discovery of selfhood is a strong narrative theme in writing for children, which may incorporate questioning one's 'cultural address' in the process of self-individuation. Thus, children's literature constructs, reflects, and questions particular social realities that articulate wider national and cultural concerns.

The study of historical reading experiences poses particular challenges, especially when the subject of study is children's literature and children as readers.[43] Adult creators and readers construct the abstracted idea of the 'child reader' as they define the capabilities of children as readers and listeners to engage with art and text.[44] As Australian scholar Clare Bradford explains, children's books are not passively mimetic, but actively formulate and produce ideologies and articulate beliefs by adult creators about 'what children should know and value.'[45] By attending closely to chronologies, to the contexts of creation, to the imagined communities of readers, and the materiality of the book as a physical object, it is possible to bring into sharper focus the changing views of childhood and children's ability to interpret visual experience.[46]

The histories of illustrated children's books in Canada reveal contested ideas about whether there can, and should, be a distinction between culture and commerce in children's publishing. The Australian scholar Robyn Sheahan-Bright has described the insistence with which some critics divide publishers into mutually exclusive binaries, those driven by altruistic, cultural, literary, and aesthetic objectives, and those driven by profitability. As she notes, such an unproblematized view of publishing as meeting either altruistic and cultural goals or profit-driven commercial goals erases the creative tension in which publishers necessarily negotiate both culture and commerce.[47] A history of children's publishing needs to locate publishers and creators as partners in the creation of culture within the context of ownership, production, technology, distribution, and consumption, rather than seeing marketing as 'an activity distinct from the production of culture.'[48]

Considering the illustrated book as a physical object makes it possible to begin to document changes in the ways that creators and producers have set about the task of creating culture within the marketplace.[49] It also allows a more nuanced exploration of the intersection of fine art, commercial art, and popular culture within the publishing industry and the changing aesthetic preferences among publishers, retailers, and consumers. Tracing the working lives of illustrators helps to identify and make clear the boundary work that divides artists into a tightly controlled distinction between creators of fine, or high, arts and creators of commercial, or popular, arts.[50]

Following developments across time, it is also possible to trace prevailing trends and preferences in cultural iconography, and changes and continuities in narrative themes and artistic styles in English Canadian children's illustrated books and picturebooks, from an intensely pragmatic, realist explication of text to the current preference for an interweaving of textual and visual narratives in a variety of artistic styles. Attending to the ways that creators and disseminators of children's books discuss artistic production also explicates the visual canon of design, in which aesthetic affinities are placed in their historic, social, economic, and professional context.[51]

The history of children's publishing in Canada is relatively undocumented. At present, no research study has attempted a comprehensive assessment of Canadian children's illustrated books from a scholarly perspective. There is a striking need for an interdisciplinary perspective that integrates literary and visual analysis within sociocultural and historical frameworks from a variety of methodological and theoretical perspectives. Exploring what Robert Darnton famously called the communications circuit, in which texts circulate from creators to publishers to the marketplace to readers and back again to creators, begins the process of documenting children's literature communities in Canada.[52] Acknowledging the marginalization of children's literature creators and disseminators within the broader Canadian publishing industry and attending to the role of gender in patrolling those boundaries allow a more nuanced understanding of the particular histories of Canadian children's publishing. By drawing on theories of print history, we can bring into focus the constructedness of texts and the processes of cultural production for children.[53] By tracing commonalities and differences in educational and work histories, artistic and design philosophies, visual media, style and technique, experiences of collaborative work, and publishing experiences of the creators, disseminators, readers, and critics of Canadian children's illustrated books, it is possible to illuminate the development of Canadian publishing for children as an expression of national identity and cultural consciousness and to locate children's publishing within broader histories of Canadian publishing and cultural production.

The Parameters of the Research

For the purposes of this study, we worked with a definition of what constituted a Canadian children's illustrated book that sought to balance inclusivity and exclusivity. For the period before 1950, we considered literature written by Canadians and literature with a strong Canadian focus by authors living outside Canada, whether published domestically or internationally, for which the intended audience was a child or young adult reader, and in which illustrative material formed a significant element of the final printed book. For the period after 1950, when the range of literature expands, our definition narrowed to focus on material written and illustrated by residents of Canada and published for a Canadian children's audience, primarily by publishers with a Canadian imprint, in which the illustrations formed at least 50 per cent of the content of the work.

In order to identify historical children's illustrated titles about Canada, whether published within Canada or in Britain and the United States, we examined the holdings of Canadian children's books in English at Library and Archives Canada and the Osborne Collection of Early Children's Books in Toronto, the Arkley Collection of Early and Historical Children's Literature and Canadiana Collections in Rare Books and Special Collections at the University of British Columbia Library, and the titles microfilmed as part of the Canadian Institute for Historical Microreproduction (CIHM) Early Canadian Research Collection.

We compiled a comprehensive database of 573 Canadian children's illustrated books by Canadian authors, illustrators, and designers published in Canada between 1947 (the first year that the Canadian Library Association's Book of the Year for Children award was issued) and 2005 (the cut-off year for our study) that have won Canadian juried awards or been shortlisted for awards for their text, art, or design. We located copies of the books, analysed their narrative themes and genres and the illustrative media and techniques used to create the artwork, and traced the contributions of editors, designers, and publishers. We also examined the papers and artwork of Canadian children's writers and illustrators held by the Library and Archives of Canada's Literary Manuscripts Collection in Ottawa, and the papers of individual creators and publishers at McGill University, the Osborne Collection, and the University of British Columbia, which enabled us to further document some of the complexities of the collaboration among author, illustrator, editor, and designer in the production of children's illustrated books.

In order to locate children's illustrated books within the broader histories of print culture in English-speaking Canada and the history of Canadian childhood, we interviewed 136 Canadian authors, illustrators, editors, designers, publishers, booksellers, critics, book reviewers, scholars, librarians, teachers, literacy specialists, and children's literature specialists from Canada, Australia, Germany, Japan, Spain, Sweden, and the United States,. These interviews have been transcribed, edited, and indexed. As required by ethical research protocols and informed-consent requirements of the Social Sciences and Humanities Research Council of Canada, and the Behavioural Research Ethics Board of the University of British Columbia, interviewees were invited to review the final edited transcripts and make any necessary changes.

From Creators to Readers: Methodological Considerations

Through our research project, we have created a documentary record of the literary and artistic approaches and philosophies of Canadian authors and illustrators, placing individual narratives within the history of illustration and book design in Canadian children's books. With the growth of the field in the past two decades, it is not possible in this discussion to mention all significant Canadian illustrated books and their creators. Our intent is not to write a comprehensive survey or prescriptive guide to the literature, but to examine the growth and development of Canadian children's publishing through the lens of illustrated children's books.

Our approach is both chronological and thematic. By focusing on the particular histories of children's publishers and the books they have issued, we hope to trace both changes and continuities, using the books as the primary sources to interrogate the question of cultural identity. Throughout, we have considered the interaction of texts, images, children, and adult creators and mediators in creating communities of readers.

Although we pay close attention to the ideological functions of canon formation, and the role of critics, teachers, librarians, and children's literature specialists in affirming particular forms of literary and artistic production as 'important,' 'significant,' or 'the best,' we are not attempting ourselves to create a canonical list of the best Canadian children's illustrated books, authors, illustrators, or publishers. We have focused in particular on multiple-award-winning authors and illustrators while simultaneously being aware that using peer and professional recognition as criteria for inclusion raises serious issues of representation, marginalization, and exclusion.[54] We have questioned whether awards are legitimate markers of achievement or represent the active working out of hegemonic norms that valorize particular types of dominant cultural production at the expense of minority voices and images.[55]

However, in the end, we considered that the awards lists created by selection committees and juries who evaluate books for the awards given by societies, organizations, and professional associations provide invaluable evidence of a form of reader response. These lists, not only of award winners, but of the longlists and shortlists of candidates, allowed us to trace changes over time in the reception of children's books and to determine not what the 'best books' are, according to an unchangeable and fixed measure of excellence, but to document what children's literature professionals consider to be the most significant and important books at any given time.

This process of limiting our discussion also provided a measure of consistency that shifted the discussion away from directly privileging our own aesthetic tastes and preferences. At the same time, we have also included other titles, authors, illustrators, and publishers whose work raises important questions not addressed by the multiple award winners.

In each time period, we have turned our attention to particular publishers, authors, and illustrators as case studies that can help to elucidate change and continuity over time, and have highlighted the range of children's literary production in Canada. Throughout our research, we have been keenly aware that this is only a partial history, however, as we have limited ourselves to books published in English Canada. With the exception of the Elizabeth Mrazik-Cleaver award for picturebook illustration and the Alcuin Award for Design, children's awards in

Canada are linguistically segregated. Some organizations and associations give awards to both English and French books in separate categories, while others are restricted to one or the other official language. And although we interviewed francophone illustrators who publish with anglophone presses, we are mindful of the problem of speaking for individuals and groups rather than speaking with them. We also believe that the history of francophone children's illustrated books should be told by researchers who have greater access to a wide range of francophone children's publications and the ability to analyse the nuances of cultural preferences in image and text and the particularities of publishing history within Quebec.

The Structure of This Book

This book is arranged chronologically and thematically. We examine the historical context and development and contemporary state of Canadian illustrated books for children, and the simultaneous development of indigenous Canadian publishing for children. We analyse the role of children's illustrated books within the broader histories of print culture in Canada and the history of childhood in Canada. We also consider the material culture of the illustrated book by exploring both aesthetic and commercial trends in the creation and dissemination of Canadian illustrated books for children and consider their role in the reader's awareness of the book as a physical and aesthetic object.

In chapters 2 through 6, we trace the development of children's publishing and children's illustrated books from the nineteenth century through the 1980s and document the institutions and organizations that have supported the creation of indigenous publishing in Canada. In chapters 7 and 8, we examine the recent series of challenges to children's publishing and the strategies and responses of publishers to the changes brought about by globalization.

In the final chapter, history, practice, and theory are drawn together as we explore the role of children's illustrated books in creating, sustaining, and resisting dominant sociocultural themes and images as publishers, authors, illustrators, readers, and critics debate the idea of creating national identities through children's illustrated books.

CHAPTER TWO

Beginnings to the 1890s: Canadian Children's Books in the Imperial Era

When children in centuries past picked up illustrated books with Canadian subject matter, they usually saw a reflection of the country in texts and images created by expatriates, visitors to Canada, and armchair travellers, published in Britain and the United States for middle-class domestic readers fascinated with the exotic and unfamiliar. These publications, written from the metropolitan centre, draw on the literary traditions of travellers' tales, pioneer and emigrant narratives, outdoor adventure and survival sagas, in an imaginative recreation of the colonial space as a romantic and alien wilderness, very different from the urban domesticated social space inhabited by the reader.[1] Narratives of exploration and travel seek equally to entertain and to instruct, and the didactic and moral tone of most early nineteenth-century children's books was partially ameliorated in these Canadian-themed works through the emphasis on adventure and survival and through descriptions of the startling unfamiliarity of the Canadian landscape, Aboriginal peoples, and wildlife.[2] For young readers, the idea of 'Canada' was shaped by narratives that emphasized geographic and cultural Otherness – a place of ice and snow, dark and dangerous wooded forests, infinite prairie expanses, and towering mountains, populated by mysterious, savage, and primitive peoples and dangerous wild animals. The subtexts of these stories and illustrations point to the freedom from the constraints of 'civilized' society, as the fictive characters seek adventure in the untamed and romantic wilderness.[3]

'Penny Plain and Twopence Coloured'

The commercial production of children's illustrated literature as a distinctive genre specifically designed to instruct and amuse children developed in the mid-eighteenth century in England.[4] Thomas Boreman's ten-volume series, the *Gigantick Histories*, tiny volumes illustrated with woodcuts, were issued between 1740 and 1744 in London. John Newbery adapted Boreman's compact format, beginning with *A Little Pretty Pocket-Book* in 1744. The more than four hundred titles for children issued by Newbery and his family were designed to catch the eye of children and parents alike. They were enlivened with many carefully chosen illustrations and bound in Dutch floral paper ornamented with gilt overstamping.[5]

Children also had access to chapbooks, tiny books of folk and street literature,

printed on a single sheet of rough paper and folded into a booklet, and sold cheaply by travelling peddlers. They combined a few crude woodcuts, often only loosely
connected to the narrative with brief texts, usually drawn from romance, folklore,
and ballads. Calendars, alphabets, and counting books and lives of the saints were
also published in chapbook form.[6] By the late eighteenth century, Evangelical moral reformers and educators inspired by the Romantic ideas of childhood purity
and innocence in Rousseau's writings decried the popularity of the chapbook and
promoted a new, rational literature for children designed to educate and improve
young minds. The books that they created for child readers were leavened with
illustrations that furthered the didactic and moral purposes of the texts. Working-class readers were the target of the politically conservative Cheap Repository Tracts, illustrated with woodcuts, and sold for a penny by chapmen or given
away by Sunday schools and religious societies with the goal of instilling loyalty,
gratitude, and deference to the existing social order.[7] Improving verses, illustrated
geographies, and travel narratives rounded out children's literary production.[8]

The quality of illustration in children's books began to improve as new technologies of engraving allowed for greater control and subtlety in the printing of
images. While illustrated books for adults included images engraved on copper
or steel plates, the cost of engraving on metal meant that wood engraving continued to be the dominant technology of reproduction of images in most children's
books.[9] Many titles were issued in two versions, sometimes dubbed 'penny plain
and twopence coloured,' in which a black and white edition would be hand-coloured with watercolours by home workers paid at a piece-rate.[10]

'A Land of Ice': Narratives of Exploration and Settlement

In the early part of the nineteenth century, interest in Britain in the Far North and
Inuit life was stimulated by the accounts of Arctic exploration and the attempts
by Barrow, Parry, and Franklin to locate the Northwest Passage. The unnamed
author of *Northern Regions: or, a Relation of Uncle Richard's Voyages for the Discovery
of a North-West Passage* (1825) presented information from published accounts of
exploration within the structure of a travel narrative, with the didactic aim of con-
vincing young readers 'that courage, resolution, and perseverance, will support
men through toils and dangers, and enable them to act an honourable and useful
part in the service of their country.'[11] While the narrative aspires to present young
readers with factual information, rather than 'an overdrawn picture … calculated
merely for their amusement, and exciting an unhealthy taste for the marvellous
and the fictitious,' the illustrations are far more imaginative in their attempt to
interpret the text.[12] Icebergs look like a rococo wedding cake on a cake stand with
layers of icicles hanging from the rim; a wolf and an explorer mimic each other's
posture; while the walruses, which the text describes as lying 'huddled together
on a piece of ice like pigs,' somewhat disturbingly resemble both sunbathing odal-
isques and seals with dog-like faces and long tusks.[13]

In contrast, the forty hand-coloured engravings in *A Peep at the Esquimaux; or,
Scenes on the Ice* (1825) are based on images published in the accounts of the Parry
and Franklin expeditions. As Judith St John noted, the main source of informa-

2.1 *Northern Regions: or, A Relation of Uncle Richard's Voyages for the Discovery of a North-West Passage, and an Account of the Overland Journies of Other Enterprizing Travellers.*
London: J. Harris, 1825.

Reproduction from the Arkley Collection of Early and Historical Children's Literature, Rare Books and Special Collections, University of British Columbia Library.

tion for the anonymous author was undoubtedly the private journal of Captain George Francis Lyon, the second in command on the second Parry voyage of discovery, which was published in 1824 in London.[14] Twenty verses of rhyming couplets describe the animals of the Arctic, and the dress, diet, and material culture of the Inuit. The British child reader was encouraged by text and images to move between fascination and disgust with the unfamiliar and non-British in this strange world, while learning that the 'Esquimaux' are blameless because they are untaught, Rousseau-like 'savages' living in a state of nature without Euroamerican consciousness and civilized manners, but also without 'crime, vice or angry passion.' The depiction of birds and wolves, tattooed faces, clothing and tools, and the daily activities of life are modelled on the details of Lyon's published images and are among the most realistic of Canadian images in early children's illustrated books. (See colour plate 1.)

The expansion of empire, however, required literature that would support the drive to settle colonial spaces, and so narratives of wilderness adventure competed with stories of courageous immigrants reconstructing their environment into a simulacrum of metropolitan society, an imagined community almost like home. The tension between wilderness and domesticity was only partially resolved in stories like *The Young Emigrants, or Pictures of Canada. Calculated to Amuse and Instruct the Minds of Youth* (1826), by Catharine Parr Traill, written in England and based on letters from a settler family. Traill combined the genres of epistolary novel, conduct literature, and immigrant manual, framing her story in the reversal of fortune suffered by the Clarence family and their determination to emigrate and take up farming, a plan that the father describes as clearing the land 'from the forest-trees that have encumbered it since the earliest ages of the world,' in order to 'bring it into a state of tillage.' The father warns that this task will require great firmness on the part of the family and be highly disagreeable to them, as the wilds of Canada will not provide the luxuries that the family enjoys in England.[15] While the text alternates between the exotic (Aboriginal people, sugaring-off) and the familiar (cozy scenes of the domestic reading of the scriptures), the illustrated frontispiece locates the narrative clearly within the realm of the imagined and exotic – a picturesque chalet farmhouse is set in a romantic alpine landscape. While Traill drew on letters from an immigrant family for her description of life in British North America, the unnamed illustrator felt free to imaginatively reconstruct exotic elements into a scene that existed only in the metropolitan imagination.

'Is It Possible to Grow Up So Ignorant of the History of Our Native Land?'

By mid-century, English publishers met the demand by the growing middle class for children's books for the nursery with illustrated books of varying degrees of sophistication that utilized the new technologies of chromolithography and other colour printing processes. At the same time, the range of the artefacts of popular culture for children expanded to include commercially produced games and toys, peep shows, panoramas and toy theatres, and brightly coloured 'toy books' with a minimum of text and large, attractive pictures.[16] The majority of children in England, the United States, and British North America, who laboured on family farms and in factories, however, had at best a rudimentary introduction to literacy and numeracy, limited access to print, and neither the leisure nor the family resources to participate in the cultural consumption of children's books for pleasure.

The range of available books for children in English-speaking British North America was relatively narrow and utilitarian, consisting of moralizing secular texts, primers, catechisms, and instructional materials. They were brought with settlers, imported in small numbers by booksellers and stationers, and printed locally in Lower Canada, Upper Canada, and the Atlantic Colonies.[17] As well, the various religious and missionary societies imported cheap tracts, pamphlets, and missionary literature from England and the United States, as well as improving children's literature that could be given as Sunday school prizes. The majority of these titles were not illustrated, or included a single cut or a publisher's ornament.[18]

As there were few skilled illustrators and engravers in the colonies, and the technological infrastructure to support the development of a graphic arts industry was lacking until the mid-nineteenth century, very few Canadian-produced titles were illustrated, compared with the contemporary material for children printed in England.[19] Canadian printers usually made use of imported woodblocks and metal cuts, or woodcuts copied directly from European or American sources.[20] The images and texts frequently were unrelated, as was the common practice with broadsides and chapbooks printed elsewhere, and woodblocks would be repeatedly reused, despite wear and consequent loss of crispness in the finished product.[21] Further complicating any attempt to trace the provenance of these illustrations, many of the first Canadian engravers did not sign their work. Printers would also create decorations from whatever stock ornaments and flourishes were at hand, or import stereotype plates from American or British editions, in order to print a 'Canadian' edition with a new title page. *Peggy Hill, or, The Little Orphan* (1834), by Mrs Lovechild, published by Walton and Gaylord in the Eastern Townships, is a typical example of these modest local productions. 'Intended for Sabbath Schools and Families,' the chapbook uses imported woodblocks as well as a variety of different fonts and printer's ornaments to enliven the page and make it attractive to young readers.[22]

In contrast to the generic illustrations of the chapbook and magazine format, the two engraved plates in *Little Grace, or, Scenes in Nova Scotia* (1846), published in Halifax, were drawn and signed by the author, 'Miss Grove,' and are specific to the textual narrative.[23] The author's pedagogical intention is wrapped in a lively family story. As the engagingly curious young heroine, Grace Severn, learns of the particular history, geography, and botany of the colony, she and her reader alike gain an awareness of and sympathy for its diverse population, including Mi'kmaq peoples, Acadian settlers, and African-American slaves and Loyalists, and their role in the settlement of Nova Scotia. The half-title page recreates a scene from a Mi'kmaq camp, with explicit references to Mi'kmaq material culture. A woman wearing a peaked hood, skirt, jacket, and leggings tends a pot suspended over a fire, near a rack of drying fish, while a second woman, sitting in front of a birch-bark covered wigwam, begins to weave a woodsplint basket. A similar attention to detail of place is evident in the frontispiece, a landscape scene with a Mi'kmaq camp on the hill to the right of the image and a lone figure in a canoe in the middle ground to the left. Through these opening images, the reader is oriented to the geographical space in which the story is set and introduced to the particulars of Aboriginal life that so interest the young heroine.

Manuscripts and Magazines

In the colonial environment, where authors faced considerable challenges in publishing and disseminating their work, illustrated manuscripts were created for the amusement and instruction of children and as gifts for friends.[24] A few striking examples that remain in private hands or in research libraries provide evidence of the range of illustrated material for children that circulated in Canada, and of the production of literary works by authors with family connections to literary culture in England.

The best-known Canadian children's manuscript is *An Illustrated Comic Alphabet*, dated 1859, by Amelia Frances Howard-Gibbon, and given as a Christmas gift to Howard-Gibbon's friend Martha Poussette in 1865.[25] For her text, Howard-Gibbon chose 'Tom Thumb's Alphabet,' a traditional nursery rhyme dating back to the early eighteenth century which progresses in rhyming couplets from 'A was an archer, and shot at a frog,' to 'Z was a zany, and looked like a fool.'[26] The manuscript is hand-lettered, with rubricated initials and a title page lettered in black, red, and ochre.[27] Howard-Gibbon was an accomplished artist whose overall design aesthetic was clearly influenced by the work of contemporary British illustrators and their use of framing and hand-lettering.[28] Howard-Gibbon frames each page of illustration with a rustic border of branches and twigs, which focuses the reader's attention on the children who enact the textual narrative. Some of these framing devices are embellished with emblematic references to the text, such as grapes for the Drunkard, folded military flags for the Captain, grasses and flowers for the Farmer, and ship's tackle for the Merchant waiting at a port.

At the time of the creation of her manuscript, Howard-Gibbon was a drawing mistress in Sarnia, Canada West.[29] She had a privileged childhood and an upper-class education, including art lessons in Paris and Stuttgart. Her leather-bound sketchbook is in the possession of descendant Yvonne Watson and includes over fifty drawings by Amelia and her sister Caroline, created between 1838 and 1843.[30] The drawings, of their six siblings in childhood play through various seasons at their different family homes in Surrey and Sussex, England, are very similar in style to that of her adult sketches for the alphabet book. Some of the same activities are common to both volumes, and there is a playful freedom and humour in Howard-Gibbon's depiction of childhood that is retained in her adult work. Howard-Gibbon's artwork for her *Comic Alphabet* clearly includes some reworking of family pictures or is based on the memories of her life as a child in England. She makes specific visual reference to Arundel Castle and its surrounding countryside and townscapes as the background for her child actors, rather than the local scenery of Canada West, perhaps in an attempt to recreate the familiar images of home in the new colonial environment.[31]

Howard-Gibbon was not relying on her literary output to supplement her income, and there is no evidence that she attempted to publish her manuscript.

2.2 Miss Grove. *Little Grace, or, Scenes in Nova Scotia*. Halifax: C. Mackenzie, 1846.

Reproduction from the Arkley Collection of Early and Historical Children's Literature, Rare Books and Special Collections, University of British Columbia Library.

For other women, the limited opportunities for publication in the colonies and the uncertain revenue to be derived from publication would be a continuing source of frustration. *The Snow Drop, or, Juvenile Magazine* (1847–53) was launched in 1847 in Montreal by Harriet Vaughan Cheney and Eliza (or Elizabeth) Lanesford Cushing, sisters who had emigrated from the United States.[32] Their mother was a novelist, and both sisters were published authors who had contributed articles to *The Literary Garland and British North American Magazine* (1838–51), published in Montreal by Lovell and Gibson. The sisters took over the editorship of *The Literary Garland* from John Gibson during its last year of publication, when competition from the American market and declining public interest led to its demise.[33]

   The Snow Drop, also published by Lovell and Gibson, was devoted to the moral education of young readers and reflected both John Gibson's interest in creating a respectable literary culture in British North America and the sisters' liberal Congregationalist Unitarian family background. The articles in *The Snow Drop* focused on the progress and improvement of its young readers through short stories and poems designed to inculcate charitable feelings, instruct children in personal morality, develop citizenship through the study of British and Canadian history, and reinforce appropriate gender and social roles.[34] *The Snow Drop* had a rival in the equally short-lived *The Maple Leaf* (1852–4), published in Montreal by Robert W. Lay, and after his death in 1853 by his widow Eleanor H. Lay.[35] *The Maple Leaf* provided an outlet for work by Canadian women writers, including Catherine Parr Traill's *The Governor's Daughter*, and *The Step-Sister* serially, as well as a poem and a reminiscence by Traill's sister Susanna Moodie.

'Never Let Difficulties Overcome You'

By mid-century, narratives of adventure and survival predominated in children's books with a Canadian setting. Catherine Parr Traill's *Canadian Crusoes: A Tale of the Rice Lake Plains* (1852), written after she emigrated to Canada, exemplifies the outdoor adventure survival saga.[36] Set in the backwoods of Upper Canada, three lost adolescents save a young Mohawk girl, who in turn teaches them the necessary skills for survival in the forest wilderness. As critics have noted, Traill's romance dramatizes interdependence among the French, English, and Aboriginal characters as a metaphor for nation-building, while continuing previous themes of settlement and the continuance of cultural traditions in the new colonial space.[37] While the focus on the text is living in and surviving the wilderness, the illustrations, by British artist William Harvey, who trained under Thomas Bewick, place sentimentalized children in a tamed and domesticated pastoral landscape that makes little or no reference to the forest environment as described by Traill. Harvey's subsequent illustrations for *Lady Mary and Her Nurse* (1856) are far more successful at matching Traill's closely observed descriptions of animals and the natural world, although they fail to make reference to Aboriginal material culture, which forms an important part of the narrative, suggesting that the circulation of Canadian images in the metropole was somewhat limited.

   Survival, settlement, and potential friendships with Aboriginal people also form the narrative themes in Frederick Marryat's *Settlers in Canada; Written for Young Peo-*

ple (1844), which combined the emigrant story and the adventure saga to chronicle one family's life as pioneers in Upper Canada, as they made the difficult voyage to the new country and adjusted to the rigours of the land. The frontispieces for the two volumes are both generic rather than specific character sketches, with a tamed wilderness in comparison with the drama of the text. The frontispiece to volume two shows the older character, Malachi, leaning on a long-bore gun, dressed in ragged clothing, with a powder horn hanging from his belt, surrounded by flowers that form a roundel around his feet. The landscape is welcoming, rather than threatening, and the enclosed forest of the text is transformed by the suggestion of an expansive horizon in the distance.

Domesticity as a powerful tool in taming the wilderness forms the backdrop to Margaret Murray Robertson's *Shenac's Work at Home: A Story of Canadian Life* (1868), in which immigrants leave Scotland for the 'strange new world beyond the sea' to make a 'home for themselves and their children.' The title page includes a medallion vignette of a log cabin and a man with rifle, framed by a border of rifles entwined with axes and scythes and other tools of farm labour. The cover is embossed with iconic Canadian images: snowshoes, a fir tree, and Shenac, the pioneer Canadian girl in her little house in the backwoods, the roof dripping with icicles.

'Far Removed from the Abodes of Civilized Men'

Traill and Marryat explored the tensions between wilderness and settlement and the precariousness of survival in the new environment. A new variant of this isolation genre growing in popularity from the mid- to late nineteenth century was the illustrated boys' adventure story, published in books and magazines directed at young male readers. In England, longer children's stories were illustrated in black and white by artists who also drew on their experience with painting, political cartoons, and illustrations for adult books to create complex images that encouraged children to engage imaginatively with the narrative while furthering the moral and didactic function of the text. The illustrated magazines and adventure stories combined a similar mix of the pedagogic and imaginative, circulating imperial knowledge through narratives and images that simultaneously disseminated middle-class values and promoted patriotism among their metropolitan readers.[38]

By the end of the nineteenth century, Canada had become one of the favoured settings for the illustrated boys' adventure story, in which the youthful male protagonist battles hostile natives and fierce animals in the farthest reaches of the British Empire and demonstrates the pluck, initiative, and self-assurance that mark him as a successful participant in the colonial enterprise.[39] Many of these stories emphasized the author's travels in Canada in order to stress the authenticity of their narratives and images, even when the illustrations were imaginatively reinterpreted by the metropolitan engraver.

Robert Michael Ballantyne, a prolific author-illustrator, traveller, and adventurer, set more than twenty of his titles in Canada, beginning with *Hudson's Bay, or Every-day Life in the Wilds of North America During Six Years' Residence in the Territories of the Honourable Hudson's Bay Company* (1848).[40] Ballantyne had been apprenticed to the HBC at the age of sixteen and served at various posts throughout Rupert's Land.[41] As the preface to *Hudson's Bay* makes explicit, Ballantyne was claiming expert knowledge on the basis of lived experience in his 'minute description of everyday life' and woodcuts created from drawings 'made on the spot by the author.'[42] This claim was reiterated in the preface of his first story for children, *Snowflakes and Sunbeams; or, the Young Fur Traders: A Tale of the Far North* (1856), in which he emphasized his particular geographic knowledge gained during his HBC service, stating that the work was 'an exact copy of the picture which is indelibly stamped on my own memory. I have carefully avoided exaggeration in everything of importance. All the chief, and most of the minor incidents are facts.'[43]

The complex design of the illustrated title page for *Snowflakes and Sunbeams* includes various narrative elements that immediately identify the work's setting as the New World, while challenging any unity of time, place, and circumstance. In the title page vignettes of Aboriginal people in feathers and buckskin hunting in a canoe and on snowshoes, snow-laden evergreen branches, a beaver with its paw caught in a trap, a duck and ducklings swimming before a promontory with tipi and trees, a flock of geese receding in middle horizon, a bison, a calèche, and a toboggan are arranged with more care for their decorative potential than possible geographic proximity. Even the hand-lettered titling, which combines letters dripping with icicles, letters barbed like the flèches of arrows, and letters seemingly arranged from twigs, reinforces the 'Canadian-ness' of the outdoor setting, even as the carefully constructed imagery challenges Ballantyne's claim to be creating an exact copy of his memories.

Ballantyne paid close attention to narrative detail in selecting decorative elements for the elaborate illustrated title pages that featured prominently in the original editions of his adventures. In his instructions on the original artwork, Ballantyne, an accomplished watercolourist, provides clear directions to the engraver regarding colouristic effects and scale, and explains salient points in the narrative. The original artwork for the frontispiece of *Erling the Bold, A Tale of the Norse Sea-Kings* (1869) includes the handwritten notation: 'Follow the design exactly, but let minute details be improved.'[44]

In his 1893 autobiography, *An Author's Adventures, or Personal Reminiscences in Book-Making,* Ballantyne stated, 'I formed the resolution always to visit – when possible – the scenes in which my stories were laid, converse with people who, under modification were to form the dramatis personae of the tales, and to generally, obtain information in each case, as far as lay in my power, from the fountain-head.' His Canadian titles continued to draw on his memories of his time in Rupert's Land, and on his authorial claims to be reproducing what was real and factual.[45]

'He Came of Sturdy, Sensible Stock': Oxley and the Boys' Adventure Story

In the late nineteenth and early twentieth centuries, a steady flow of Sunday school papers, missionary magazines for young readers, annuals like the popular *Boys' Own Paper* (1879–1967) and *Girls' Own Paper* (1880–1956), and children's magazines, including the influential *St Nicholas* (1873–1943), were imported from England and the United States to meet the demand for reading material for Cana-

2.3 R.M. Ballantyne. *Snowflakes and Sunbeams, or, the Young Fur Traders: A Tale of the Far North.*
London, Edinburgh, and New York: T. Nelson, 1856.

Reproduction from the Arkley Collection of Early and Historical Children's Literature,
Rare Books and Special Collections, University of British Columbia Library.

dian children and young adults.[46] As well as the direct imports, British annuals like *Young England: An Illustrated Magazine for Boys throughout the English-Speaking World* (1880–1937), issued by the London Sunday School Union, were republished in a Canadian edition as *Young Canada: An Illustrated Annual for Boys* (1880–1933?), using stereotypes of the British plates, with the addition of a Canadian title page, interspersed with a modicum of additional Canadian material on topics like the Northwest Mounted Police.[47]

The papers and annuals sought to reinforce class-bound norms of appropriate gendered behaviour.[48] The girls' papers mixed stories, advice, and improving literature, focusing inward on the domestic sphere, while the boys' papers promoted muscular Christianity, imperialism, and bravery in the face of improbable danger far removed from the domestic centre.[49]

The tropes of wilderness in the popular papers were familiar territory for the readers of historical fiction with a Canadian setting and outdoor adventure novels, many of which were also published by missionary societies as an alternative to the sensational literature that was thought to coarsen the moral sensibilities of young readers.[50] G.A. Henty's *With Wolfe in Canada, or, The Winning of a Continent* (1887) was one of a series of stories for boys in which historical figures faced conflict with bravery, providing readers with lessons in imperial patriotism, loyalty, and fortitude.[51] The wild is a place of learning the skills necessary for successful warfare and a primitive and dangerous place that must be conquered by the forces of civilization and commerce. For many authors, the Canadian wilderness provided the perfect backdrop against which virile young heroes could demonstrate their nobility of character, toughness, and survival skills, and their chaste heteronormative masculinity.[52]

James Macdonald Oxley, a prolific and successful Nova Scotian writer, penned 321 boys' adventure stories, most focused on early exploration and the fur trade in Canada and adventures in the north and west.[53] The illustrations for *Up among the Ice-Floes* (1890), a tale of a fourteen-year-old Halifax boy who sails on a polar expedition, help to locate the reader spatially and emotionally: they include a map from the fortieth parallel north to the pole, and dramatic incidents from the text, including a ship caught in the ice and a boy fighting a polar bear. This visual theme of a young hero threatened by a wild animal continues in subsequent Oxley novels to signify danger and adventure. In the coloured frontispiece of *Ti-Ti-Pu: A Boy of Red River* (1890), a ferocious bear rears up and attacks a boy and his dogs, who are surrounded by an equally menacing forest, a thrilling scene that has little to do with the text, which recounts the adventures of a Scottish family lost on the prairies. Similarly, the frontispiece of *The Young Woodsman, or, Life in the Forests of Canada* (1895) shows the young hero, wearing high leather boots and snowshoes, lying face down in the snow, as a bear raised up on its hind legs looms over him.[54]

The autobiographical narratives of Egerton Ryerson Young, a Methodist missionary, sought to attract young readers with accounts of his personal bravery and daring during travels in the 'wild north lands.' Images of Aboriginal people seated in front of tipis and paddling birchbark canoes reinforced the idea that Aboriginal people live in a precontact wilderness, while simultaneously reminding the reader of the high moral purpose of Young's goal of preaching the Gospel to unchurched 'savages' in order to civilize them into modernity. Similar themes predominated in his boys' adventure stories, including *Three Boys in the Wild North Land* (1897), illustrated by J.E. Laughlin.[55] As the illustration 'How I Missed My First Bear' from *Stories from Indian Wigwams and Northern Campfires* (1893) makes clear, Young as missionary hero and the boys of his adventure stories are manly and virile, as at home in the woods as in the pulpit, and able to conquer the challenges of the Canadian landscape.

'These Stories Are True': Ernest Thompson Seton and the Wild Animal Biography

At the end of the nineteenth century, Ernest Thompson Seton, Official Naturalist to the Government of Manitoba, developed a new genre of children's literature, the wild animal biography. In his first book, *Wild Animals I Have Known: Being the Personal Histories of Lobo, Silverspot, Raggylug, Bingo, The Springfield Fox, The Pacing Mustang, Wully and Redruff* (1898), Seton's drawings of animals in their natural habitat have a vigour and a respect for the natural world that matches his straight-forward language. Together, the words and pictures present animals with a degree of closely observed realism that had not been evident in children's book illustration since the animal and bird wood engravings of Thomas Bewick in England a century before and found an immediate readership.[56] At the same time, he invests his animal studies with distinctive character traits and an overall romanticism that convey a strong sense of individual personality somewhat at odds with his naturalist's accuracy in the visual depiction of animals. For Seton, his stories were tragic, because they were true.[57]

The design for the book shows Seton's rejection of the modern and the influence of the Arts and Crafts movement in the combination of hand-lettering and a Kelmscott Press–influenced typeface, with hand-lettered initials at the start of each story. Seton, who used a paw print as his personal emblem, included animal tracks among the silhouette drawings and marginal vignettes of animals and their environments, and frontier life. Some of these vignettes are anthropomorphized to some degree in order to provide humorous insight into animal behaviour, in contrast to the dramatic natural presentation of the animals in the plates of illustrations in loose pen and ink with wash.

This respect for the natural world features prominently in *Two Little Savages: Being the Adventures of Two Boys Who Lived as Indians and What They Learned* (1903), a semi-autobiographical account of two boys in Ontario who develop their skills at woodcraft and outdoor activities.[58] Seton's pen and ink line illustrations and marginal sketches recall a naturalist's handbook in their attention to detail. Seton's wife, Grace Gallatin Seton, was responsible for the overall design of the volume, in which the hand-lettered title page and chapter headings, and reproductions of animal tracks and paw marks trailing across the page, create multiple layers of reference to the natural world and echo the textual emphasis on woodcraft.[59]

Seton's work marks the beginning of a shift from the depiction of Canadian wilderness as a place of fear and dread to be tamed by intrepid settlers to a place to be celebrated, embraced, and protected.[60] *Mooswa and Others of the Boundaries* (1900) by W.A. Fraser, and illustrated by Arthur Heming, further 'naturalizes' the Athabascan wilderness as a backdrop to an animal fantasy, in which animals speak in elevated Kiplingesque English and people speak in a comic habitant dialect. Heming, who had studied in New York at the Art Students League, and was a member of Toronto's Arts and Letters Club, specialized in outdoor scenes of the north. His illustrations capture the same combination of naturalism and fantasy as Fraser's text. In the frontispiece image, a group of northern woodlands wildlife are seated in a circular council, listening intently to a black fox, who raises his left paw in a posture somewhat reminiscent of a dog being invited to 'shake hands.'

Charles G.D. Roberts, who had been publishing animal stories since the 1890s, employed a more poetic vision of animal life than Seton in his biographies of wild animals. The international popularity of Seton's *Wild Animals I Have Known* inspired publishers to rush animal stories into print, and Roberts found an enthusiastic readership for *The Kindred of the Wild* (1902), which drew on his memories of a childhood in New Brunswick.[61] Like Seton, Roberts personified his animal subjects as heroes, imbuing animals with character and intelligence. *Red Fox* (1905), Roberts's only full-length animal biography, is a rare example in which the wild animal triumphs over his hunters.[62] *The Kindred of the Wild* and *Red Fox* were both illustrated by Charles Livingston Bull, an American naturalist and painter who brought a sharp trained eye and an understanding of animal anatomy from his work as a taxidermist to his depiction of wildlife.[63]

There was a gradual transition throughout nineteenth-century children's books from textual and visual depictions of Canada as a place of alien otherness, to a theatre in which explorations of manliness and empire-building were played out against a backdrop of the ferocious wilderness, to the wilderness as a welcoming and natural 'home place.' By the end of the century, images and texts in children's books included representations of Canada's peoples, land, and wildlife and their relationship to each other that were domesticated and familiar, rather than alien and exotic. In the coming decades, Canadian creators and publishers would explore the issues of domesticity and familiarity, creating a literature for a community of readers in which national identity would increasingly shift from 'home' being a place from which one was exiled to 'home' being contiguous with one's geographic location.

CHAPTER THREE

The 1890s to the 1950s: 'And Whether We Are Yet a Nation'

By the late nineteenth century, the culture of children's literary production had been transformed in the English-speaking world. In 1871, the majority of Canadians lived in rural areas, and were Canadian-born. Rapid social, economic, and demographic changes brought about by industrialization and urbanization stimulated anxiety about social stability, heightened by concerns about the assimilation of immigrant populations. By 1921, 3.8 million immigrants had arrived in Canada, and almost 10 per cent of the population were foreign-born. Montreal and Toronto each had tripled in size, and almost half of all Canadians lived in urban areas.[1]

Measurements of the degree of literacy in populations, as revealed by census data, were heralded in political discourse as a benchmark of a nation's economic and social progress.[2] In response to the rapidly changing social composition in Canada, both social reformers and social conservatives promoted the role of the public school system to inculcate respect for social hierarchies, integrate immigrant populations into the social fabric of the country, and prepare children for participation in democratic citizenship.[3] Between 1871 and 1917, all the provinces in Canada except Quebec passed compulsory school attendance legislation.[4] The total enrolment in publicly funded schools more than doubled between 1891 and 1923, and the average daily attendance rates steadily increased.[5] Other institutions, including free public libraries, settlement houses, and supervised playgrounds also were charged with countering the negative consequences of city living and furthering the socialization of immigrant and working-class children by teaching and reinforcing democratic values and promoting moral reform.[6] The introduction of compulsory education and child labour legislation, and new social policies and programs for the protection of vulnerable children, all contributed to a reconceptualization of childhood as a distinct and separate stage of life that needed particular forms of nurturance.[7]

Increasing numbers of bourgeois families could afford to supply their children with non-utilitarian printed material specifically created for their amusement and indirect moral betterment.[8] To meet this growing market, the content and form of children's books for middle-class readers were transformed. Publishers in Eng-

land and the United States moved away from wood and metal engraving to pho-
tomechanical reproduction, which made it possible to reproduce images on metal
plates directly, ultimately replacing the engraving process and the engraver. The
development of half-tone printing made possible luxurious gift books for children
with fine bindings and tipped-in coloured plates on glossy paper and more modest, but beautifully printed, books with black and white illustrations that demonstrated the potential of the new technologies to produce appealing books for
children.[9]

However, the domestic market for children's books in Canada remained relatively small in the period before the First World War. The gift book trade was
dominated by imports. The majority of Canadian publishers focused primarily on
issuing directories, almanacs, devotional books, and cheap reprint editions of British and American titles, rather than investing capital in original works by Canadian authors.[10] Indigenous Canadian publishing for the young was largely restricted
to the lucrative authorized school text market.[11] The size of the country, a small
population divided among anglophone, francophone, and allophone communities of readers, the geographical axis of north-south trade, the continuing colonial mentality that saw Canadian literary production as inferior to that produced
in foreign metropoles, and the limitations imposed on Canadian authors by the
Imperial Copyright Act, all helped to limit the growth of a vigorous indigenous
Canadian book publishing industry, particularly for children's books.[12]

Ironically, it was the importation of American and British books through the
agency system, in which Canadian-owned publishers acted as distributors for
books published in the United States and the United Kingdom in exchange for
exclusive distribution rights, which provided Canadian publishers with opportunities for financial consolidation and expansion. The agency system also ensured
protection of foreign copyrights by allowing Canadian publishers to republish
works not previously issued in Canada and copyrighted elsewhere by their foreign partners as an authorized Canadian edition. Canadian agents could import
bound copies of books, finished sheets printed outside for binding in Canada, or
the stereotype plates to print in Canada.[13] As the majority of expense in publishing consists of start-up costs (author payments, editing, typesetting, proofing, and
office overhead) that would not be recoverable should the final product not generate an adequate return, the agency system provided Canadian trade publishers
with a less capital-intensive and potentially more profitable publishing activity,
which, in turn, could finance the considerably more risky publication of original
Canadian works.[14]

As well as the Canadian-owned agencies, between 1896 and 1913, seven major
British and American publishing houses opened branches in Toronto, acting as
the exclusive agent for the distribution of books for both the parent company and
for other foreign publishers as well as publishing original Canadian material.[15]
Although several trade publishers centred in Toronto issued a limited selection
of children's titles, no Canadian publishing firm, whether Canadian or foreign-
owned, had a strong children's trade list of Canadian-authored titles comparable
to the range issued by American and British publishers and distributed widely
in Canada through department store catalogues and booksellers and stationers.[16]

Thus, limited opportunities for publication within the country meant that many Canadian-authored and illustrated books published in Canada had a smaller market and reached a more limited audience than their British and American counterparts, while Canadian authors who sought publication outside Canada faced obstacles in articulating nationalist themes and images.[17] As there were no Canadian mass-circulation juvenile magazines, apart from the denominationally based Sunday school papers, many Canadian authors for children sought publication in American magazines like *St Nicholas* and the *Youth's Companion*, and attempted to place book manuscripts with American publishers.[18] At the same time, the creation of transnational communities of readers sharing common interests allowed the successful circulation of British and American-authored titles among Canadian readers and provided literary models that Canadian authors would attempt to emulate.[19]

Palmer Cox and the Brownies

The career of Palmer Cox, a Canadian writer and illustrator who lived and published in the United States, provides one model of achieving recognition and success in a North American literary marketplace. Cox, who was born in Granby, Quebec, moved to the United States as a young man and eventually retired to Granby. He was received as an American author, publishing for an American readership, which coincidentally also included Canadian readers by virtue of the accessibility of imported material.[20]

In 1883, Cox wrote and illustrated the first of his rhyming couplet Brownie stories, which was published in the influential and widely circulated American children's magazine, *St Nicholas*. Cox's Brownies are anarchic, playful cartoon figures with squat bodies, puckish faces, and long, almost spider-like arms and legs, who travel to new lands and get into various sorts of fairly harmless mischief in a world populated only by peers without any external authority figures or institutions.[21] In all the Brownie books, racialized ethnic caricatures are ubiquitous. The members of Cox's band of Brownies are dressed in the adult fashions of the era and differentiated one from another only by specific recurring ethnocultural types and parodies of various employment groups. Cox, mindful of sales, excluded African-Americans from the band of Brownies, nor were there 'girl Brownies.'[22] Despite their international adventures, the Brownies are urbanized and geographically decontextualized, existing squarely within the world of the modern, exploring new technological innovations and the modern urban world and espousing a sort of socially improving utopian democracy.[23]

A collection of Brownie stories, *The Brownies: Their Book* appeared in 1887 and found an immediate readership, selling over a million copies. Sixteen large-format Brownie collections eventually sold more than twelve million copies.[24] One of the first children's book characters to be mass-marketed as a brand and commercialized as spin-off product, the Brownies were commodified through Brownie figurines, dolls, games, calendars, comic strips, and, most lastingly, the Brownie, the first simple hand-held camera, which was advertised using Cox's drawings.[25]

While there was nothing distinctively Canadian about Cox's characters, *The*

Brownies around the World (1894) begins in Canada and includes visual tropes of culture that tie narrative to geography. The 'Canada' explored by the Brownies is both urban and rural, French and English. Images include a Brownie on snowshoes wearing a capote, sash and toque, a Brownie gazing at a beaver in a glass box, Brownies congregating outside the pillared entrance to the Bank of Montreal on Yonge Street in Toronto, Brownies in boats shooting the Lachine rapids and visiting Nelson's statue in Montreal, Brownies gazing at the old town and fortifications in Quebec, and Brownies snowshoeing through the Canadian wilds.

'Almost Exactly as I Imagined': L.M. Montgomery

Other Canadian authors for children were first published in the United States, with subsequent editions either printed in Canada from American plates or issued as separate Canadian editions. The most successful were Marshall Saunders's *Beautiful Joe* (1894) and Lucy Maud Montgomery's *Anne of Green Gables* (1908), both of which were immediate best-sellers, were translated into multiple languages, and published in multiple editions.[26] The Anne books have had an interesting history as illustrated works. The image of 'Anne' by George Gibbs on the front cover paste down of the 1908 edition first appeared as an illustration in an unrelated magazine and was reused by her publisher.[27] In subsequent editions, Anne changed in the illustrations from a young adult to a much younger child heroine, even though Montgomery was unhappy that her books continued to be marketed as novels for juveniles. Bernard Katz has tracked the changing illustrative materials in various editions of the first Anne books, noting that Montgomery's diaries and letters reveal her interest in the physical design and production of her books and her displeasure when illustrators took creative licence with the characters as described in her texts.[28]

'Hooray! Hooray! Hooray! The Maple Leaf! Dominion Day!'

Cox, Saunders, and Montgomery all represented different strategies by which Canadian authors could find larger communities of readers than existed in Canada. Cox, who moved to the United States, was widely perceived to be American and made no particular reference to his country of origin. At the suggestion of her British publisher, Saunders reworked *Beautiful Joe* (1894), the autobiography of an abused dog, for the English edition, reinserting Canadian references removed from the American edition, and eliminated a chapter that made deprecating references to an 'Englishman.'[29] Montgomery, while explicitly writing about a particular geographic location, framed her discourse in generalities that could be read by the non-Canadian reader as village life anywhere along the northern Atlantic seaboard.

Gender also played a role in their public identities as authors, particularly for Montgomery, whose professional career was always constrained by competing family obligations. For other Canadian authors, finding a community of readers was a challenge. Women who had obtained professional training were excluded from many of the professional networks, clubs, and associations available to men who pursued literary and artistic endeavours in the major cities of central Canada.[30] Children's literature, while a respectable pursuit for women, brought women writers and artists little cultural capital, and the women's organizations that sprang up in the period before World War One could provide social and emotional, but not economic, support. As well, the relatively small size of Canadian publishers and the smaller domestic market, compared with the United States and Britain, meant that some authors found that their works had very limited sales, while others resorted to non-commercial publishers, whose production standards were not competitive.

Some of these determinedly Canadian publications were noticeably amateur in execution. *The Little Manitoban, A Child's Story-Book* (1900), published by the Manitoba Free Press, is a collection of stories by various authors, illustrated with a mixture of stock cuts, photos, and lithographs. The front cover, reminiscent of contemporary immigration promotional literature, shows a baby standing chest deep in a field of wheat scattered with poppies, framed by a border of simplified and stylized maple leaves. Patriotic in spirit, the work is clumsily designed.

M.A. Bonnell's *Mother Goose's Bicycle Tour* (ca 1901), published by William Briggs, presents a tour of familiar nursery rhymes in rhyming couplets, in a melange of English and French, with a glossary and pronouncing guide of the French words, accompanied by black and white line illustrations.[31] The black and white line drawing on the first page, captioned, 'The Departure,' shows Mother Goose in a shawl and a tall conical hat on a quay, waiting to depart in a small sailboat. The accompanying text explains that 'Her fame had spread through many lands, – / A princess came from France to see / The tree that bore the golden pear: / At least such was l'on dit / But years rolled by, the dame grew old, – / Alas, the universal fate! / She found herself almost forgot, / And with her goose left tête à tête.' Also included in the work are several songs with music, the whole designed to provide a humorous way to teach anglophone children a few phrases in French.

Issued at the height of imperial enthusiasm surrounding the sixtieth anniversary of Queen Victoria's accession to the throne, Elizabeth Rollitt Burns's *Little Canadians* (1899), illustrated by Mary M. Phillips, is a paean to the jolly times that the children of the Dominion enjoy.[32] Burns also intersperses French words and phrases throughout her rhymes about seasonal activities in Canada, emphasizing the pleasures of sleigh rides and sugaring-off, in a nod to Québécois culture, before concluding with a rapturous salute to Dominion Day, the Queen, and Empire. The illustrator, Mary M. Phillips, had studied at the Art Students' League in New York. In 1900, she was the president of the Montreal Branch of the Women's Art Association of Canada and principal and founder of the School of Art and Design.[33] Her illustrations for the privately published work alternate between lithographed half-tones of somewhat generic outdoor activities like skating, and lively line drawings of children engaged in everyday pastimes and games. While the production values overall are fairly modest, the small format of the book, the images of children engaged in familiar Canadian pursuits, and the sprightliness of the verse are a deliberate attempt to create a work with direct appeal to children.

For authors and illustrators with a source of funding, private printing of a work provided opportunities for limited circulation beyond the immediate family circle,

especially for those who were connected to the various literary and artistic societies for women. Emma Scott Raff's *Of Queen's Gardens*, illustrated by Stella Evelyn
Grier, originated in 'an address to a class of girl graduates,' during graduation
exercises at Grier's Margaret Eaton School of Literature and Expression in Toronto.[34] Raff offered lectures on Ruskin, and the title of the work, a series of thematically linked, rather slight stories about different gardens and the lessons learned
therein, may have been inspired by one of his essays in *Sesame and Lilies*. The volume is bound in sepia brown paper with a buckram spine, and flat stamped lettering in dull gold, with text printed in sepia ink on deckle-edged paper. Grier, the
daughter of a Canadian portrait painter, had studied at the Art Students' League
in New York, and in London, and worked as a commercial artist in Toronto, Boston, and London. She created delicate pen and wash illustrations of flowers and
gardens that frame the central text block in an Arts and Crafts style consistent with
the overall design aesthetic of the publication.[35]

'Some Rhymes with a Flavor of Canada': C.W. Jefferys and Uncle Jim's Canadian Nursery Rhymes

Even finely illustrated and produced Canadian picturebooks had difficulties in
finding a market. David Boyle's pseudonymously authored *Uncle Jim's Canadian
Nursery Rhymes for Family and Kindergarten Use* (1908), illustrated by the noted artist C.W. Jefferys, was a lively attempt to create new rhymes inspired by the environment and wildlife of Ontario.

Boyle was the curator-archaeologist of the Ontario Provincial Museum and an
educator influenced by the child-centred pedagogy of Johann Pestalozzi.[36] Jefferys
was an experienced artist and graphic designer who had apprenticed with the
Toronto Lithographing Company, studied with the Toronto Art Students' League,
and worked at Grip, Ltd., the influential Toronto printing and publishing company.[37] An admirer of William Morris and Walter Crane, in the 1890s Jefferys had
been one of the instigators of the annual Art League Calendar, which featured
poetry by Canadian authors and Canadian-themed decorative borders and illustrations, which provided him with the opportunity to experiment with drawing
for reproduction.[38] In the years immediately preceding the publication of *Uncle Jim*,
he had illustrated magazine and newspaper articles and three children's books by
Marjorie Pickthall for the Toronto publisher Musson.[39]

In contrast with superficially Canadianized volumes of traditional nursery
rhymes that retained the look of their British antecedents, Boyle's text and Jefferys's pictures together were the first attempt to create authentically and explicitly Canadian textual and visual signs and symbols, in what critic Robert Stacey
has described as the patriation of the 'international idiom of the nursery rhyme.'[40]
The cover art for *Uncle Jim* presents a Canadian version of the Peaceable Kingdom
in which birds and beasts co-exist happily. Jefferys, who was a founding member
of the Canadian Society of Painters in Water Colour, exploits the potential of the
medium, employing subtle shading and delicate washes to model realistic images
of animals and birds arrayed against a stylized foreground screen of maple trees,
through which can be glimpsed a lakeshore and cloud-filled sky.

The interior page design skilfully integrates the hand-lettered poems with the stylized and decorative illustrations, alternating two-colour printing in red and green, or brown and blue, with multi-coloured pages. References to Canadian flora and fauna, royalty and government, people and places, sporting activities and industries are woven into both text and image, creating a work in which the hand-crafted and modern, serious and comic are balanced. (See colour plate 2.)

Sadly, the book was never distributed into Canada due to publishing complications. Most Canadian publishers could not afford colour printing for the tiny Canadian market, and few Canadian printers had experience with four-colour printing.[41] The Toronto publisher, Musson Book Company, chose to use De La More Press in London, known for its fine arts printing, which went into bankruptcy shortly after finishing the press work, negatively affecting the distribution and marketing of the book. Only 830 copies were ever sold according to Jefferys's sole royalty statement, and he felt cheated both by the commercial failure of the publication and by his treatment by his publisher.[42] Although he continued to illustrate Canadian textbooks that showcased his strong draughtsmanship and meticulous historical research, he never worked again on a full-colour trade publication for children.[43]

'Canada Is a Country with a Romantic Past'

In contrast to the failure of *Uncle Jim*, Cyrus Macmillan's two books of Canadian folk and fairy tales, published in England and illustrated by non-Canadians, found wider readership both in Canada and abroad. *Canadian Wonder Tales* was published in 1918 in London and New York by John Lane, and in a Canadian edition by S.B. Gundy. Macmillan, a McGill instructor who served with the Canadian Expeditionary Force during the First World War, noted in his preface that 'the proofs were corrected by the writer in the intervals between other duties on Vimy Ridge, France.'[44]

Drawing on his research into Canadian oral literature, Macmillan explained that he was retelling material from his larger academic study of folk tales and folk songs, collected in order to preserve the 'traditions and tales' of the country's 'romantic past' that were fading from the public memory.[45] Macmillan saw the purpose of the collection as informing Canadian children of 'the traditions of the mysterious past in which their forefathers dwelt and laboured' in the 'early days of exploration and colonization.'[46] Although he was careful to add that Canada's Aboriginal people continued to tell these stories, the elegiac tone of the text makes it clear that Macmillan, like his contemporaries, believed that Aboriginal peoples were a pre-modern remnant of a dying race, whose 'real greatness has long since gone' and who are 'no longer powerful as in the old days.'[47] This view was reiterated in the foreword by the principal of McGill, Sir William Peterson, who described the archetypal quality of oral literature as expressing 'the Indian's elemental ideas of the Universe around him' and placed Macmillan's collection squarely within the tradition of salvage anthropology, an attempt to reconstruct pre-contact Aboriginal culture by stripping away post-contact influences.[48]

The volume was designed in the tradition of luxury editions of children's books

3.1 Cyrus Macmillan. *Canadian Wonder Tales*. Illustrated by George Sheringham.
London: John Lane, The Bodley Head; Toronto: S.B. Gundy 1918.

Reproduction from the Arkley Collection of Early and Historical Children's Literature,
Rare Books and Special Collections, University of British Columbia Library.

intended for Christmas gift-giving, rather than a scholarly compilation. Macmillan's romanticized view of the past was furthered by the illustrations by the British decorative designer George Sheringham, which alternate between full-colour plates that reflect the influence of Klimt and the Viennese Secessionists and the Japonism of Edmund Dulac's illustrations, and highly stylized and graphically sophisticated two-colour plates that echo William Nicholson's revival of coloured woodblock prints.[49] Although Macmillan's stories are drawn from the cultural traditions of the eastern woodlands, Sheringham's depiction of Aboriginal people in the two-colour plates utilizes familiar visual tropes of tipis, feathered headdresses, fringed leggings, and bison.

The second volume, *Canadian Fairy Tales* (1922), continued Macmillan's retelling of Canadian oral literature, with illustrations by Marcia Lane Foster, a young British artist and woodcut illustrator, whose work is more conventional and less mannered than Sheringham's tableaux. Her animal portraits are less realistic, and somewhat anthropomorphized for comic effect, and overall the illustrations are simplified and carefully designed for dramatic intent, with a strong sense of texture. However, what is notable about both volumes is the way that the illustrations remove the stories from any specific cultural context, transforming them into the universalized world of 'once upon a time.'[50]

The retelling of French Canadian folktales and Aboriginal legends was also the focus of Katherine Hale's *Legends of the St Lawrence* (1926), a small luxury volume commissioned by the Canadian Pacific Railway Company to give to children on their shipping line's round-the-world tours.[51] The full-colour illustrations and decorative headpieces by Canadian commercial artist Charles Walter Simpson and the volume's fine binding, patterned board covers, and rubricated first letters show a meticulous attention to aesthetic details of design and art.[52] As in the Macmillan volumes, the Quebec habitant imagery in the CPR picturebook was designed to interpret Canadian cultural traditions for a primarily non-Canadian readership.

'A Land of Vast Natural Resources and Wonderful Opportunities'

If Cyrus Macmillan was intent on teaching Canadian children about the past, *Bob and Bill See Canada: A Travel Story in Rhyme for Boys and Girls* (1919), written by Alfred E. Uren and illustrated by W. Goode with humorous black and white line drawings, introduced children to contemporary Canada as a means of inculcating a sense of patriotism, a 'greater conception of Canada and things Canadian.'[53]

The two protagonists who journey across each province of the Dominion are not the strapping Canadian youth of earlier travelogues and outdoor adventures, but Bob and Bill, a pair of anthropomorphized bunnies stylishly dressed in the fashion of each region that they visit. As they tour each province, their diary tells of its wonders, taking special pleasure in leading industries, and the local colour. In the Maritimes, the bunnies appear dressed as fishermen, with the Bluenose in the background. In Quebec, the rabbits burl logs on the river, dressed in checked pants and flannel shirts with the sleeves rolled up. Bill and Bob don feathered headdresses to become Aboriginal bunnies in a canoe. They even visit the frequently photographed hollow tree of Vancouver's Stanley Park. Bob and Bill end

"Before they left for farther west, they paddled a canoe to test."

3.2 Alfred E. Uren. *Bob and Bill See Canada: A Travel Story in Rhyme for Boys and Girls.*
Illustrated by W. Goode. Toronto: Musson, 1919.
Reproduction from the Arkley Collection of Early and Historical Children's Literature,
Rare Books and Special Collections, Univer-sity of British Columbia Library.

their celebratory travels in Banff, where 'in the midst of the natural grandeur, Government Officials have erected a cozy bungalow for them, to be used as their headquarters.'[54] The *Canadian Bookman* recommended the work as being 'so Canadian and so pleasing' to child readers, who naturally love rabbits, that they would incidentally learn 'a great deal about the Dominion.'[55]

'Before Tea Was Served, It Was Suggested That the Section Be Organized'

In the late nineteenth century, the children's library movement developed in large urban public libraries under the guidance of strong-minded women like Anne Carroll Moore of the New York Public Library and her protégée Lillian Smith, who established the Toronto Public Library's Boys' and Girls' Division in 1912.[56] Children's librarians positioned themselves as both powerful advocates and cultural authorities on children's literature and the specialized, physically segregated children's room as their gendered domain of influence.

Children's librarians saw themselves as conduits and gatekeepers standing between children's publishers and child readers. As agents of social control, librarians could prevent the moral harm that they believed would result from reading series fiction, 'potboilers in juvenile literature,' 'written-to-order information book[s],' and 'atrocious picture book[s] modeled after the comic supplement[s]' with 'hideous daubs of color and caricature of line.'[57] Instead, by carefully guiding reading choices, and rigorously excluding unworthy literature from their collections, librarians could transform the lives of children beyond the walls of their libraries by providing access to the best literature, which in turn would influence 'the ideals, the tastes, the occupations, the amusements, the language, the manners, the home standards, [and] the choice of careers' of their young patrons.[58]

Professional recognition of children's librarians as a distinct specialization within public libraries developed in tandem with the expansion of children's services. In 1911, Patricia Spereman taught a session on children's services as part of the training for librarians offered at the first intensive Ontario Summer Library School.[59] Two years later, Lillian Smith began to teach courses in children's work and storytelling. In 1925, when a one-year course was established, Smith lectured to the general class and offered an elective for students planning to specialize in children's services.[60]

Professional organizations also fostered a sense of collegiality. The 'Round Table of Librarians interested in work among Boys and Girls,' which was established in 1917 as a group within the Ontario Library Association, organized Round Table Conferences at the Association's annual meeting.[61] The OLA's journal, *The Ontario Library Review*, which was distributed to libraries across Canada, regularly published articles by and for children's librarians, lists of recommended books, and news of annual meetings and conferences. In the absence of a national professional organization, children's librarians across Canada joined the American Library Association and participated in the annual conferences.[62] Lillian Smith sat on the Executive Board of the ALA from 1932 to 1936, and twice served as chair of the ALA's Division of Libraries for Children and Young People, first in 1923–4 and again in 1942–3.[63] In 1939, she was instrumental in forming the Canadian Association of Children's Librarians, to further professional recognition of children's services as a distinct specialization, and to encourage the writing and publishing of children's books in Canada.[64] When the Canadian Library Association was formed in 1946, CACL became a section of the new organization.

By the 1920s, public libraries in urban centres across Canada had established separate children's rooms and carefully built up their children's collections.[65] Many offered a variety of programs directed at child readers, including reading clubs and circles, stamp clubs, and puppet shows.[66] Story Hours, in which a librarian told a carefully prepared story from memory, were an important part of children's services and were believed to encourage an interest in 'good literature' and to habituate children to appropriate behaviour in the library.[67] Story cycles drawn from European epic literature and folk literature were particularly popular. By the early 1940s, story hours were broadcast over the radio in Toronto and Saskatoon.[68]

To further the work of educating 'non-English citizens' and to foster patriotism, Lillian Smith and George Locke, the head of the Toronto Public Library, developed a Canadian Story Hour, featuring stories of exploration and settlement.[69] They believed that if immigrant children were introduced to 'the history of Canada and Canadian heroes,' they would be acculturated into the dominant social norms of society and become 'enthusiastic citizens and patriots.'[70] The Canadian stories would encourage all children to develop a sense of Canadian national identity and grow up to be 'intelligent citizens and well informed Canadians.'[71] Smith believed that Canadian boys and girls needed 'books which will give them a knowledge of the traditions and history which produced the great men of Canada,' adding that 'history in the form of stirring and picturesque stories is the kind that "sticks."'[72]

Lists of recommended new trade books for children played an important role in children's library services, although the prominence given to Canadian titles was variable.[73] In an attempt to steer the public towards purchasing the 'best books' for children, rather than the most popular books, the librarians of the Toronto Public Library's Boys' and Girls' Division had established an annual display and list of books suitable for holiday gifts in 1912.[74] Beginning in 1923, the Toronto Public Library compiled an annual catalogue of Canadian titles to be used as a checklist by librarians 'and others particularly interested in Canadiana.' The lists, which included children's titles, were also printed in the widely read *Ontario Library Review*.[75] In 1924, a committee of librarians from the Library, on behalf of the Canadian Authors' Association, selected, assembled, and had shipped a selection of five hundred Canadian publications for the British Empire Exhibition in London, including forty-six children's titles, and issued an annotated catalogue to accompany the display.[76] Canadian librarians who met during the American Library Association annual conference in 1925 called for a graded list of five hundred books for boys and girls for school use and an annotated catalogue of one thousand recommended children's books.[77] Their wish was met in 1927, when the Toronto Public Library published *Books for Boys and Girls*, edited by Lillian Smith, an annotated list of books chosen by the librarians of the Boys and Girls Division as being 'of definite and permanent interest.' One hundred and twenty-four titles by sixty-one Canadian authors, or titles by non-Canadians with a Canadian focus, were listed among the two thousand recommended works.

'I Think You Are a Darling': Creating Canadian Readers

The fall season was the main focus for the marketing of children's trade books in North America. Publishers and booksellers alike advertised children's books suitable for gift-giving.[78] The October and November issues of the trade journal *Canadian Bookman* regularly included notices of new children's books, and department store advertisements and publishers' notices in the weekend edition of newspapers like the *Globe* and the *Vancouver Daily Province* alerted shoppers to the latest children's annuals and gift editions, although few of the featured titles were Canadian-authored or -published.[79] To bring greater public attention to books by Canadian writers, the Canadian Authors' Association established Canadian Book Week in November 1921.[80] The Association sent out press releases for local newspapers to redact in their book sections. Teachers and librarians were encouraged to introduce the work of Canadian authors to readers through book displays and

book talks, and, if possible, arrange for author visits to their schools and libraries.[81] The same year, the first Children's Book Week was celebrated in libraries
in mid-November, an event first held in 1919 in the United States and organized
by American publishers, the American Booksellers' Association, the American
Library Association, and the American Scouting movement.[82]

The promotion of children's trade books was furthered in 1922, when the *Canadian Bookman* urged Canadian booksellers to adopt the Children's Book Week celebrations. To help booksellers create Book Week displays, the *Canadian Bookman*
reprinted a list drawn up by the American Library Association of 'one hundred
select books for a home library for children,' adding only that '[t]o supplement
this list there might well be a special list of Canadian juvenile books,' without
venturing to recommend specific Canadian titles.[83] By the mid-1920s, Children's
Book Week had become an annual celebration at the Boys' and Girls' House of the
Toronto Public Library, generally held at the same time or close to the Canadian
Authors' Association event.[84]

Coordinated institutional support for Canadian children's authors within the
public education system was absent, however. The school library movement in
Canada did not fully develop until the 1950s and 1960s.[85] School libraries in the
interwar period were unevenly distributed across the country depending on
whether there was enabling provincial legislation and on the degree of provincial and local funding in support of school library collections.[86] While in some
locations public and school libraries worked together effectively, budgetary constraints and territoriality could prove barriers to developing cooperative programs
and services.

Children's exposure to, and familiarity with, Canadian literature in public
schools depended largely on the selections made for authorized textbooks by provincial departments of education and school boards, and on the enthusiasm of
individual classroom teachers. In the early 1920s, when Vancouver school teacher Margaret Cowie determined to interest her class in Canadian writers and set
about to create a class library of Canadian titles, the students were responsible
for raising the funds to purchase volumes.[87] To further stimulate interest in the
project, Cowie wrote to a wide cross section of Canadian authors, asking them
for a short biographical sketch and a photograph, and inviting them to visit her
classroom. Many responded with letters, while some arranged with their publishers to have copies of their books sent for the classroom library.[88] The letters reveal
the degree to which Canadian writers were surprised and moved by the interest
shown in their work by Cowie and her pupils. Nellie McClung stated emphati-
cally, 'I think you are a darling, and every writer in Canada owes you something.'[89]
L.M. Montgomery commented, 'I'm glad that you are interesting the young fry in
our Canadian books. Something else that is much needed in our schools today.'[90]
Isabel Eccleston McKay indicated how important she considered Cowie's work in
developing a readership for Canadian literary production: 'You are doing just the
kind of work which is so badly needed if Canada is ever to develop a Canadian
literature. In my own youth, no one ever dreamed of giving me a Canadian book
to read – in fact, I did not realise that there were any. And many Canadian "grown-
ups" have never found out better. But if the children begin to value Canadian

work, the next ten or fifteen years will soon change that. So I think that you may feel that you are doing a pioneer work of real value to the development of our Canadian national spirit.'[91]

'A New Departure in Canadian Publishing'

Throughout the 1920s, demands by children's librarians for quality children's trade books increased. In response, several major publishing houses in the United States appointed specialist children's editors to develop children's trade lists, beginning in 1919 with Louise Seamon Bechtel at Macmillan in New York.[92] The picturebook as a distinct genre gained prominence on trade publishers' children's lists in the interwar period. Talented European artists and designers who emigrated to the United States brought a new artistic sensibility into what had been a conservative book illustration tradition. Their knowledge of modern art trends, experience with graphic design, and familiarity with the folk art of various countries would significantly change the look of the American picturebook and introduce new narrative themes.

In contrast, the Canadian market was more conservative, and publishers lacked the wherewithal to hire specialist editors. In the interwar period, Canadian subsidiaries of English and American publishers and Canadian-owned publishers who acted as agents and distributors for foreign publishers derived the majority of their income through importing foreign-authored and -published works into Canada and through the lucrative educational publishing market. McClelland and Stewart, Musson Book Company, Macmillan Company of Canada, Ryerson Press, Thomas Nelson and Sons, Copp, Clark Company, and W.J. Gage and Company all issued trade books for children, but competition from inexpensive imported reprints and series, and the continued preference of the book-buying market in English Canada for British and American titles available in bookshops, stationers, and by mail through the Eaton's catalogue, meant that relatively few Canadian-authored and illustrated trade books were published, reviewed, or sold.[93] Publishers and booksellers complained that the seasonal pattern of children's book sales further hindered the development of sustained public interest in children's literature and, consequently, of a stable industry.[94] In turn, librarians accused booksellers of pandering to easy sales by stocking the popular series titles rather than cultivating a love of enduring classics in child readers.[95]

Few Canadian children's books were issued with coloured illustrations. Most Canadian-produced titles had simple black and white illustrations, inspired by popular British and American children's imports, with narratives that exploited the precious and whimsical aspects of childhood.[96] Others somewhat uneasily mixed naturalism and fantasy. The text of Carol Cassidy Cole's *Velvet Paws and Shiny Eyes: Adventures of a Little Canadian Boy in Natures* [sic] *Wonderland, among Furry Friends and Feathery* (1922), illustrated by William Dudley Burnett Ward, and the sequel *Downy Wing and Sharp Ears: Adventures of a Little Canadian Boy among Little Wild Friends in Natures* [sic] *Wonderland* (1923), illustrated by Marjory Sankey, both feature identifiably Canadian animal mentors, in stories located in real wilderness places, who teach the young protagonist to be kind to wild animals.

3.3 Carol Cassidy Cole. *Velvet Paws and Shiny Eyes*. Illustrated by Dudley Ward; with toy pictures by Leo L. Stead. London: Hodder and Stoughton, [1933?].

Reproduction from the Beatrice Roslyn Robertson Collection, Rare Books and Special Collections, University of British Columbia Library.

Dudley Ward's black and white pen and ink drawings of the creatures are a similar mix of naturalism and anthropomorphism, in which foxes, Canada geese, weasels, and mink are represented realistically, while the frog and owl characters have exaggerated, cartoon-like eyes. Cole's works were promoted as 'a new departure in Canadian publishing' and praised in the *Canadian Bookman* as 'an ideal thing for the very youngest Canadian readers to start on.'[97]

When in 1933, the British publisher Hodder and Stoughton issued a new edition of *Velvet Paws*, with 'toy pictures,' in pockets pasted onto the pages, Cole's text and a selection of the black and white illustrations by Ward were retained in the enlarged-format volume.[98] The word 'Canadian' was dropped from the subtitle (which appears only on the pocket facing the title page), and all traces of the wilderness were removed from the standup cutouts. In Ward's illustration, the Goose is a Canada Goose with a long dark neck and sleek body. The toy goose is blue, huge-eyed, short necked, and plump. Leo Stead, the artist credited with creating the toy picture animals, domesticated them for the British reader, rendering them mild, friendly, and playful: the cover illustration shows the stand-up cutout shaped animals holding hands/paws with the boy, dancing across the front and back boards.[99]

A well-designed series of small picturebooks with rhyming comic stories by Hugh Heaton of the Heaton Printing and Publishing Company in Toronto, and illustrated by H.E.M. Sellen, were jointly issued by Heaton and McClelland and Stewart. *The Story of Albert the Camel's Son* (1936) and *The Story of Madam Hen and Little Horace* (1936) were praised for the multi-generational humorous appeal, equally suitable as a gift for children, or for an adult 'friend or invalid,' and for the 'deft' and 'delightful' illustrations by an experienced British-born commercial artist, trained in Europe, whose work had appeared in *Maclean's* magazine.[100] The books were unusual for the period in being issued first in a Canadian edition, and then in successive British and American editions over the next decade by Faber and Faber in London and Oxford University Press in New York.

The majority of Canadian children's poets were derivative, inspired by the subject matter and metrical rhythms of influential British titles like Robert Louis Stevenson's *A Child's Garden of Verses* (1885). The success of A.A. Milne's *When We Were Very Young* (1924) and *Now We Are Six* (1927), illustrated by Ernest Shepard, encouraged a host of imitations that varied in quality, usually with minimal Canadian content. Illustrator Elsie Deane directly evokes Shepard's scenes of young children engaged in whimsical activities in her drawings for the revised and expanded edition of Vancouver poet Isabel Ecclestone Mackay's *The Shining Ship and Other Verse* (1929), a theme also taken up in the pen and ink drawings by Elisabeth Kerr for *A Rhyme for a Penny* (1929) by academic and poet Herbert Thomas John Coleman.[101] The Ottawa firm Graphic Publishers, and its imprint Rou-Mi-Lou, issued several children's volumes of poetry during its few years of operation, including Arthur Stanley Bourinot's *Pattering Feet: A Book of Childhood Verses* (1925), illustrated with black and white line drawings by Alan B. Beddoe, and New Brunswick author and illustrator Grace Helen Mowat's *Funny Fables of Fundy and Other Poems for Children* (1928). Other writers and illustrators working in the genre were less skilled. Constance Ward Harper's *The Moon Man and the Fairies*, illustrated by Grace Judge and published by the *Vancouver Sun* newspaper was dismissed by Sheila Egoff as an example of 'the type of rhymed rubbish considered suitable for children at the time.'[102]

'And Whether We are Yet a Nation'

Throughout the interwar period, the few professional designers and illustrators employed by Canadian publishers continued to be influenced by the Arts and Crafts design aesthetic, applying themes and motifs from nature and the handwork tradition.[103] Flattened ornamental surfaces, decorative borders, and the combination of hand lettering and woodblock illustrations were commonly used in Canadian titles issued by the major presses, rather than the modernism of contemporary European graphic design.[104]

McClelland and Stewart and Ryerson Press were committed to fine book design in their adult publications and included decorative endpapers, spot vignettes, and illustrated title pages in many of their volumes.[105] A 1922 edition of Pauline Johnson's *Legends of Vancouver*, designed by Group of Seven artist J.E.H. MacDonald, featured endpapers decorated with a strongly linear arrangement of repetitive motifs in which the upper band of vertical conifers against mountain peaks contrasts with horizontal patterns of undulating waves, salmon, and canoes filled with paddlers.[106]

J.E.H. MacDonald's son, Thoreau MacDonald, adapted this design vocabulary in *A Canadian Child's ABC* (1931), with text by R.K. Gordon. Gordon's verses celebrate moments of Canadian history and geography from a distinctly whiggish anglocentric perspective, in which 'I' stands for Indians, 'still here, but their fierce pride / And wild free life have passed away'; 'K' for the Kicking Horse Pass, 'con-

3.4 R.K. Gordon. *A Canadian Child's ABC*. Illustrated by Thoreau MacDonald.
Toronto and Vancouver: Dent, 1931.
Reprinted with permission of the estate of Thoreau MacDonald.

quered by man's will'; 'M' for Mounties who brought law and order to the west; 'Q' for Quebec, which moved from Aboriginal to French to English occupation; and 'W' for Wolfe, triumphing over Montcalm. Other letters focus on the Chinook wind, Sugaring-off, and Hockey, everyday events in the lives of Canadian children. The sly humour of the verse is enhanced by MacDonald's illustrations, which balance stylized modernism with a close observation of natural and rural imagery. The design of the cover, printed for the cloth edition in green and red on a beige linen background announces the intentional nationalism of the work: images of the conifers and maple leaves of Central Canada are combined with Prairie images (sheaves of wheat, bison, and tipis) within a diamond-shaped grid. The distinctive Canadian imagery carries forward on the hand-lettered title page, which utilizes a framing device of pine boughs and cones, punctuated with Canadian flora and fauna. MacDonald had closely studied the work of calligraphers and typographers like Edward Johnson and Eric Gill, and frequently incorporated beautifully designed calligraphic title pages in his work for Musson, McClelland and Stewart, and Ryerson Press. In *A Canadian Child's ABC*, he employs his distinctive reinterpretation of Roman letter forms for the hand-lettered swash capitals, which interact with and are visually echoed in the images in the vignettes. Throughout the work, he plays with simplified forms and the graphic possibilities of black against white, for example, juxtaposing the white plumes of smoke from the engine of a train, confined to the lower right of the image, against the jagged black mass of the snow-capped Rockies in the image to accompany the letter K. His eye for the small telling detail provides rewards for the observant reader. In the illustration accompanying C for Chinook, a child bundled into a winter coat (a capote?) and toque, holding the rope of a sled in mittened hand, peers at a thermometer mounted on the side of a building, while in the background trees sway in a strong wind and snow recedes in the sudden warmth, and a small bird (a cardinal?) perches on the curve of the C. The politicians in O for Ottawa clearly are working late – the accompanying image shows the centre block of Parliament in silhouette under a night sky spangled with stars, the hands of the clock in the Peace Tower set to 8:00.

The contrast between the natural world and the urban, and between Aboriginal and European values, forms the backdrop to *Sajo and Her Beaver People* (1935). The author, whose birth name was Archibald Stansfeld Belaney, had adopted an Aboriginal identity and the name Grey Owl (or Wa-sha-quon-asin) after immigrating to Canada from England. He was a passionate environmentalist, who brought conservation issues to the attention of the Canadian public through a series of best-selling books and well-publicized speaking tours in North America and Britain in which he recreated his identity as a Métis man and traditionalist interpreter of Aboriginal culture for non-Aboriginal audiences.[107]

Sajo, Grey Owl's sole children's book, illustrated with naive pencil sketches by the author, intertwines closely observed, realistic descriptions of a pair of beaver kits who are raised by a young Ojibwa girl and her brother, with a non-sentimental but intense emotionalism, designed to stir feelings in the reader of empathy for the natural world.[108] In the Preface, he claimed that the 'delineations of animal character' in the story were not 'make-believe' but authentic representations based on 'a lifetime of intimate association with wild life, in its own environment.'[109] Within five years of its initial publication in London and Toronto, the work had been issued in an American edition, and had been translated into French, German, Swedish, Danish, Polish, and Russian.

An interest in the interpretation of Canadian culture informed Hazel Boswell's stylized images in *French Canada: Pictures and Stories* (1938). Boswell, whose maternal grandfather, Henri-Gustave Joly de Lotbinière, served as premier of Quebec and lieutenant governor of British Columbia, had spent summers on the family seigneury of Lotbinière.[110] A trained artist who had studied in Paris before the First World War, Boswell based her illustrations on her childhood experiences and on the folk-art traditions of Quebec. Inspired by the designs for hooked rugs, her highly stylized full-page illustrations are framed by a flat coloured border, while individual objects are reduced to geometrical shapes. For example, in the illustration of 'Christmas Trees,' facing page eighteen, a person wrapped in a scarf sits in a sleigh pulled by a horse, whose mane is a series of black jagged triangles. Trees are represented by green triangles on sticks, while Quebec country architecture is translated into stone-coloured squares with darker lines for doors and windows. The effect is sophisticated and naive at the same time, and suited to the nostalgic tone of the text.

The image of Canada in Canadian-published titles, however, continued to focus primarily on heroic exploits in a romanticized past. J.S. Morrison and Maud Morrison Stone's *This Canada of Ours: A Pictorial History* (1929), which first appeared as

3.5 Hazel Boswell. *French Canada: Pictures and Stories*. New York: Viking Press, 1938.
Reproduction from the Arkley Collection of Early and Historical Children's Literature,
Rare Books and Special Collections, University of British Columbia Library.

a cartoon strip in several Canadian newspapers between 1925 and 1929, featured illustrations in simple black and white line drawings by J.S. Morrison, the majority in a multi-pane format, usually four panes to a page. The copy preserved in the Osborne Collection is encased in a box with marbled paper edges, the top lid illustrated with a pasted-on full-colour image of a boy in a Norfolk jacket, poring over a book, against a background of Cartier landing among Aboriginal people wearing feathers and blankets, with a two-masted ship at anchor in the background. The image is clearly meant to evoke the daydreams of the boy, imagining the heroic actions of the characters described in the history contained within the box. The 1937 edition of the same work was a much less lavish production, smaller in format, with a plain maroon cloth binding stamped in black and no box.

C.W. Jefferys, whose early experience with *Uncle Jim's Canadian Nursery Rhymes* had proved so disappointing, also emphasized the heroic aspects of Canadian history in his work for Ryerson Press. His detailed drawings for *Canada's Past in Pictures* (1934) and *The Picture Gallery of Canadian History* (3 vols, 1942–50), were conceived as 'imaginative pictorial reconstructions of Canadian history' based on meticulous research, which would introduce readers to the material culture of Canada's past.[111] For Lorne Pierce, the editor of Ryerson Press, Jefferys consistently captured 'the supreme dramatic moment' of the historical narrative. At the same time, his finely executed pen and ink drawings were enriched by an absolute fidelity to the fine details of landscape, architecture, costume, and weapons.[112] His artwork for the *Ryerson Canadian History Readers* series and George M. Wrong's *The Story of Canada* (1929) encouraged several generations of Canadian children to visualize Canadian history as a dramatic and romantic epic, in which explorers and settlers inscribed a series of 'firsts' upon an empty landscape: 'Cabot's first sight of North America,' 'the founding of Halifax,' 'Loyalists drawing lots for their land,' 'meeting of the first legislature of Upper Canada, 1792,' 'Alexander Mackenzie reaches the Arctic Ocean,' 'the first furrow' ploughed into prairie soil. These images powerfully encouraged the reader to construct a seamless metanarrative of progress that transformed the wilderness of New France into a civilized settler space.[113]

The near-collapse of Canadian trade publishing for children in the 1930s, when the economic realities of the global Depression sharply reduced the already small domestic market, as well as the labour shortages and restrictions on printing during the Second World War, resulted in further limitations for Canadian authors.[114] At the same time, the relative prosperity resulting from nearly full employment during the war stimulated consumer interest in children's books. Several small Canadian regional publishers attempted to capitalize on the popularity of the American 'Little Golden Books' series by publishing inexpensive children's books and supplementary readers.[115] School Aids and Text Book Publishing of Regina issued a series of stories by the playwright Ray Darby, illustrated by John Phillips, a commercial artist, beginning with *Peter Smith and the Bugs* (1944).[116] Darby and Phillips also collaborated on *Oomah* (1945), a small cartoon-style book about the value of cooperation, published on very cheap pulp paper by Contemporary Publishers of Winnipeg.[117]

In this context of scarcity and restraint, contemporary Canadian images of home, and the particular emotional and geographical space and place of the nation, developed slowly in trade publications. While Mary Graham Bonner's *Canada and Her Story*, published in 1942 in the United States, and 1943 in England and Toronto, assured both child and adult readers that the book was not a 'sugar-coated half-truth, half-fiction account, but a readable, authentic, straightforward story, in which the history, geography, occupations and present-day life are presented simply yet vividly,' the images used to illustrate Bonner's text were all very dull stock photographs from the Canadian National Railway and the Dominion Government.[118] The literary and political question posed by R.K. Gordon's *Canadian Child's ABC*, in which 'the chosen' travel to Ottawa to make laws and discuss the National Policy ('The railway line to Hudson Bay / Taxes and tariff, immigration / The great St Lawrence waterway, and whether we are yet a nation') would be taken up with increasing fervour in the postwar period, as Canadians began to debate 'whether we are yet a nation,' and whether Canada could, in fact, support an indigenous children's publishing industry.

CHAPTER FOUR

The Postwar Period: Creating a Children's Publishing Industry

The financial constraints on publishers and institutional budgets during the 1930s, and paper rationing and labour shortages throughout the Second World War resulted in an overall downturn in publishing in English Canada, despite heightened nationalism during the war years.[1] While Canada's first graphic design firm, Eveleigh-Dair, was established in the 1940s, the few active book designers in the Canadian publishing industry worked in relative isolation from their American and European counterparts, their work further circumscribed by the limitations imposed by printers' restricted range of typefaces and lack of experience with full-colour printing.[2]

It was in this context that the comments by Sheila Egoff, who joined the staff of the Toronto Public Library's Boys and Girls Division in 1942, become particularly illuminating. She remembered that she was asked by Lillian Smith, head of the Division, to review five or six Canadian children's books that had been released in a single year. In her assessment, Egoff explained, 'I clobbered every one of them. And she [Lillian Smith] came downstairs and she said, "Sheila! You can't do this." And I said, "Well, Miss Smith, what do you mean, I can't do it?" I said, "You've always taught us that Canadian children's books had to meet the same standards as good literature from other countries." And she said, "Yes, but I think you can temper criticism with a little mercy." She made me go back and rewrite the whole thing.'[3]

Despite her comments about tempering criticism with mercy, Smith insisted on unwaveringly high standards in the selection and purchase of books for children's collections, based on the evaluative criteria of 'good writing.' Her critical approach shaped a canon of children's literature in which librarians were charged with identifying and valorizing literature of 'enduring quality.'[4] While the Toronto Public Library included 'every usable Canadian book,' in the children's collections, Smith made a distinction between purchasing a single representative copy of a Canadian title for the collection and selecting books that children would be encouraged to read, which were purchased in multiple copies.[5] Her mantra, 'only the best is good enough for children,' adapted from a comment by the poet Walter de la Mare, would provide at best ambivalent institutional support for Canadian children's publishing.[6]

The intersection of economics and institutional practices continued to work against the development of a robust children's book industry in Canada. Estimates of a profitable print run varied. One estimate placed the minimum number of copies needed to be sold for a publisher to meet expenses at four thousand copies of a book in French, three thousand in English.[7] The sales necessary to cover costs would be higher for an illustrated children's book, especially if printed in colour. John Morgan Gray of Macmillan Canada estimated that 15,000 copies of what he called an 'expensive read-aloud type of picture book' would need to be printed at a cost of $20,000 in order to be reasonably priced, adding that even if the title was successful, that number of copies would not sell, even over several years. The resulting expenses to the publisher would mean that other books would go unpublished.[8] Gray's estimation of a profitable print run can be contrasted with that of the Vancouver bookseller Bill Duthie, who noted that Canadian publishers would try to arrange for the publication of new titles in other English-speaking markets in order to attract international publicity and offset costs, adding that when international publication isn't possible, publishers 'will grit their teeth and print the 3,500 or 4,000 copies that the economies of publishing dictate, and hope like hell that they will sell all or most of these, while admitting to themselves that they will be lucky to sell 1,500 copies though there is always at least the possibility that they will sell 10,000.'[9] The difference between the two estimates, of course, is between the size of print run that would lower the unit cost to allow for 'reasonable' pricing, and the average size of the print run. In contrast, in the 1950s, authorized school texts, adopted by provincial departments of education for use in schools, could have print runs of up to 50,000 copies.[10]

Canadian children's books continued to be evaluated and found wanting compared with the well-subsidized, well-marketed, high-quality children's books published in the thousands in England and America, which could be sold relatively cheaply due to the economies of scale in their home country markets, and in Canada, through the well-established agency system.[11] Despite the expense of production, children's books would not sell at prices comparable to literature for adults, resulting in reduced profitability. As a result, very few publishers could afford to focus exclusively on children's trade books, and those general trade publishers with a children's list usually regarded it as a secondary concern, unlikely to improve the cash flow or prestige of the company.

Debates about high culture versus low culture took on a new urgency in the political climate of the postwar period, in which experts generated moral panic about the ability of families to reconstruct their lives after the disruption of wartime.[12] The 1949 amendments to the Criminal Code and the 1952 Senate Special Committee on the Sale and Distribution of Salacious and Indecent Literature suggested that children were fragile creatures at risk of being led away from heteronormativity into social and gender role rebellion. The campaigns focused attention on the perceived ability of crime and horror comic books to morally corrupt Canadian youth and encourage juvenile delinquency.[13] The campaign to ban the comics also brought into focus a nationalist cultural stance in which the Canadian government assumed the role of controlling the infiltration of American mass culture by restricting access to literature that would threaten 'normal' Canadian citizens. The debate over comics expressed a vision of Canadian cultural production

in which national identity was intertwined with moral values and aesthetic preferences, and high culture was represented as authentic and Canadian.[14] Children's
librarians had long argued against the danger to child readers posed by popular
series books.[15] They believed that children's emotions were 'over stimulated by
the unreal sensationalism and lurid thrills' and 'anaesthetized by … saccharine
sentimentalities' in the 'questionable subject matter' of genre fiction, true-story
magazines, serials, and mysteries.[16] In response to the Canadian debates over the
social role of literature to shape morality in the wake of the comic book controversy, many children's librarians redoubled their efforts to maintain collections
from which all potentially contaminating literature had been excluded, to preserve
the innocence of children.[17]

Children's Publishing in the Postwar Period

Circumstances overall for Canadian publishers began to change slowly as Canadian critics, commentators, and politicians began to debate Canadian identity and
its expression in the intellectual and cultural life of the country. In 1951 the Royal
Commission on National Development in the Arts, Letters and Sciences, popularly known as the Massey Commission for its chair, Vincent Massey, issued its
report.[18] Among other recommendations, the Commission called for the creation
of a Canada Council for the Encouragement of the Arts, Letters, Humanities and
Social Sciences, and recommended that a National Library be established without
delay.[19] The submissions to the Commission, which had explicitly linked discourses of Canadian nationalism and anti-Americanism with support for Canadian
publishers, public libraries, and literary production to counter American mass culture were to provide an ideological basis on which support for Canadian cultural
institutions was linked to the strengthening of national identity.

The colonial mentality that saw Canadian literature as an inherently secondary
product of the periphery compared with work published in the metropoles of London and New York was gradually shifting towards a greater interest in Canadian
cultural production. The inception of the New Canadian Library at McClelland
and Stewart in the late 1950s created a body of texts that would introduce students
to Canadian writing and contributed to the formation of a new national canon of
Canadian literature.[20] By the 1960s, the implementation of some key aspects of the
Massey Report, most notably federal funding for the arts, had begun to transform
Canadian cultural production overall.[21] The publication of the *Literary History of
Canada* in 1965, supported by research grants from the Canada Council and the
Humanities Research Council of Canada, marked the transition of Canadian lit-
erature into the realm of academic literary critics and furthered the debate about
the mimetic function of literature to show Canadians their own identity and create
a shared national consciousness.[22]

'Great Men of Canadian History': Picturebooks and Illustrated Series

Despite the rapid increase in the birth rate in the postwar period, and the resulting expansion of the public education system, children's publishing was slow to

respond to the changing demographic and cultural landscape.[23] While Boys and Girls Book Week at the Toronto Public Library and Children's Book Week continued to attract child readers in the interwar and immediate postwar period, through a combination of displays, book-related activities, and presentations by popular children's authors, there was no deliberate Canadian focus.[24] In 1949, the newly formed Canadian Library Association organized 'Young Canada's Book Week / La semaine du livre pour la jeunesse canadienne' under the auspices of the Canadian Association of Children's Librarians to better promote Canadian authors and books, bring wider public attention to the role that books play in a child's life, and stimulate a 'demand for good reading among young Canadians.'[25] In its inaugural year, the YCBW had wide support from a cross section of professional, women's, and children's organizations, including the Girl Guides of Canada, the Canadian Education Association, and the National Council of Women, as well as publishers and booksellers, under the patronage of the wife of the Governor General.[26]

Other measures designed to bring Canadian titles to the attention of the reading public, including awards to children's authors, were only partially successful in creating an awareness of and interest in Canadian children's publishing. In 1947, the Canadian Association of Children's Librarians, as a division of the Canadian Library Association, established its Book of the Year Award for text. The small number of titles that met the award criteria, however, meant that on five occasions in the 1940s and 1950s, and on one occasion in the 1960s, no award was granted due to the lack of suitable publications. Some illustrated works issued for children, like the two volumes of poetry by Desmond Pacey, *The Cow with the Musical Moo, and Other Verses for Children* (1952), and *Hippity Hobo and the Bee, and Other Verses for Children* (1952), issued by Brunswick Press in the Maritimes seem to have had limited circulation, and failed to receive critical attention and a place on the library lists.

The career of Clare Bice typified the range of Canadian illustrated trade books for children in the immediate postwar period. Bice's first book, *Jory's Cove: A Story of Nova Scotia* (1941), reflects his knowledge of the sea and deep affection for fishing life in Nova Scotia villages.[27] The location of the story is introduced by the illustrated map of the community, titled 'This is Jory's Cove, the little fishing village in Nova Scotia where Jamie lives' on the endpapers. Macmillan risked the high costs of printing four full-page coloured illustrations, which alternate with black and white illustrations interspersed throughout the text that introduce the reader to the architecture of the Maritimes, humorous details of village life, and the wharves and dories, rowboats, and schooners of the Cove. In the postwar period, Bice, an accomplished gallery artist, was the curator of the Williams Memorial Art Gallery and Museum in London, Ontario, exhibited widely, and served as the president of the Royal Canadian Academy from 1967 to 1970. He continued to write and publish his own stories, as well as illustrating the work of other authors, including Hilda M. Hooke's *Thunder in the Mountains* (1947) and Catherine Anthony Clark's *The Sun Horse* (1951). Bice's matter-of-fact representational realism in *Across Canada: Stories of Canadian Children* (1957) portrays the external as opposed to the internal world of his protagonists, providing the reader with lessons in human and physical geography, somewhat thinly disguised as story.[28] (See colour plate 3.)

If Bice represented the best in Canadian children's publishing, however limited by the technologies employed to reproduce his artwork, his career also serves as a reminder that most Canadian illustrators, of necessity, were generalists who worked on contract for both trade and academic publishers. Artists like Vernon Mould, who had studied with Franklin Carmichael at the Ontario College of Art, and John Alexander Hall, who also had attended the OCA and studied with the Toronto sculptor Frances Loring, both taught art at Upper Canada College, a private boys' school in Toronto.[29]

In 1920, Lillian Smith had argued that 'the great need in the education of Canadian boys and girls to-day is for books which will give them a knowledge of the traditions and history which produced the great men of Canadian history.'[30] Most trade publishers remained cautious about investing in original works without an obvious curricular link and thus a limited potential for sales. Series titles, which Janet Lunn described as having 'something to teach,' rather than being written 'just for the joy of writing,' dominated the Canadian juvenile lists.[31] Designed primarily for the school and library market, series like Macmillan's thirty-three-volume *Great Stories of Canada,* continued the genres of nineteenth-century children's literature in Canada, in their focus on outdoor life, dramatic incidents from Canadian and British history seen through the eyes of a child protagonist, and heavily romanticized Aboriginal stories.[32] The majority of the most popular Canadian children's authors of the postwar era, including Roderick Haig-Brown, James Houston, Christie Harris, Jean Little, and Farley Mowat, sought first publication outside of Canada.

While the constraints of working in a limited tonal range could inspire some skilled illustrators to exploit the graphic possibilities of the play of black and white, the small budgets of most trade publishers and the high cost of colour reproduction resulted for the most part in publications with a few banal black and white line drawings.[33] In the United States, Margaret Bloy Graham, a Canadian who received her initial training at the Art Gallery of Toronto, before moving to New York in the 1940s for further art education, made brilliant use of her experience as a commercial artist. Working with a limited colour palette dictated by contemporary printing technology, she skilfully exploited the graphic energy of the drawn line. Her illustrations, infused with energy and good humour, brought a sharp modernist sensibility to the series of picturebooks by her husband, the author Gene Zion, about *Harry, the Dirty Dog* (1956), issued by the American publisher Harper and Row.[34]

In contrast, illustrators in Canada were encouraged to strive for accuracy and correctness of detail, rather than decorative effect.[35] As one reviewer of Clarke, Irwin's *Canadian Portraits* series noted tartly, the resulting illustrations were 'flat and undistinguished,' adding that 'perhaps economy – or rather false economy – raised its little head and frightened the publishers.'[36]

William Toye and the Growth of the Illustrated Book

From the 1950s, under the guidance of William Toye, Oxford University Press developed a groundbreaking Canadian children's list modelled on the work of his English editorial colleagues.[37] One of the first great Canadian editors to work with children's titles, Toye was also a self-taught designer who recognized the significance of fine book design and typography. His goal was to produce 'strong-looking books that are not only appropriate but are completely and permanently pleasing to the most critical eye.'[38]

The cost of printing illustrated books, particularly the full-colour printing used in children's books coming from the United States and Britain in the 1950s and 1960s, was still beyond the reach of most Canadian publishers. At first, Oxford Canada produced illustrated books with a few carefully positioned full-page black and white images interspersed throughout the text. Theo Dimson's illustrations for James McNeill's collection of folktales, *The Sunken City, and Other Tales from Round the World* (1959), effectively play the potential of black line against the white space of the page.[39]

As few authors were submitting publishable manuscripts, Toye created new texts by judicious selection and editing of existing works. He also wrote original material in a variety of different genres, varying his narrative voice according to the source and his desire to suit the material to the age of his readers.[40] He recruited experienced illustrators through a network of personal contacts among graphic artists and designers, carefully selected for their ability to work within the restriction of limited highlighting in a second colour, which he believed would 'captivate the eye.'[41] He slowly built up a line of distinctively Canadian books, beginning with two significant collections of stories drawn from Canada's oral literature. *Glooskap's Country and Other Indian Tales* (1955), with stories selected by Toye from Cyrus Macmillan's collections, was illustrated by John Hall, a past president of the Canadian Society of Graphic Arts, with energetic black and white drawings overprinted in red. Hall's well-designed full-page illustrations combine tradition and modernism through the use of a flexible, fluid line with cross-hatched shading reminiscent of woodblock prints.

Michael Hornyansky's retelling of Marius Barbeau's *The Golden Phoenix and Other French-Canadian Fairy Tales* (1958), is enlivened with Arthur Price's highly stylized imagery in black and white line with saturated spot colour in cyan and yellow. Price, who was Barbeau's son-in-law, had previously illustrated many of his works and brought a sympathetic understanding of the shape and rhythm of stories from the oral tradition.

Toye was also interested in making Canadian history accessible to children. He worked with British illustrator Clarke Hutton on *A Picture History of Canada* (1956), part of a series issued by the parent company in England. As Toye explains, 'I did a lot of research for it and I really wrote the text, although I gave my boss, Ivon Owen, top-billing as co-author: he read it, advised, and contributed a few sentences at the end.'[42] Three years later, he followed up with *The St Lawrence* (1959), published to coincide with the opening of the St Lawrence Seaway. Toye's work on *The St Lawrence* was a breakthrough for creative non-fiction for young people and one of Canada's first cross-over books originally produced for youth that became a success in the adult market. He notes, 'I began it because I was interested in history and wanted to let [high school students] see how interesting primary history was. However, the book was taken up by adults. It won the CLA medal – but I got a lot

4.1 Cyrus Macmillan. *Glooskap's Country and Other Indian Tales*. Illustrated by John A. Hall.
Toronto: Oxford University Press, 1955.
Reprinted with permission of the estate of John A. Hall.

of letters from adults.'[43] A consummate work of overall design, the book benefits from Leo Rampen's decorative maps and fine line drawings, which in combination with the judiciously chosen primary source quotations, engage the reader in the history and geography of Canada's primary transportation corridor.[44]

'An Inventive Flair for Evocative Detail'

When Frank Newfeld arrived in Toronto in 1954, most Canadian publishers did not employ art directors or designers as regular staff.[45] Newfeld, who grew up in Czechoslovakia and studied art, stage, and graphic design in England, had worked as a designer in Israel before emigrating to Canada. According to Randall Speller, he 'quickly emerged as a central figure in the post-war history of the Canadian book. Although he is best known today as a children's book illustrator, Newfeld's contribution to design of the Canadian book was far more significant ... [He] transformed the history and development of English-Canadian publishing.'[46]

Newfeld opened his own design studio and worked as a director of art, design, and production for several Canadian publishers, including Oxford, McClelland and Stewart, and Macmillan. William Toye considers Newfeld neither illustrator nor designer, but 'an illustrator-designer, not merely because he often decorates or illustrates the books he designs but because he brings ... an inventive flair for evocative detail, for ingenious yet pleasing and disciplined type patterns, for graceful solutions to fussy textual problems, and these things show both the painter's eye and the designer's taste. In the best of his work designer and artist are balanced and a kind of inspired rightness prevails.'[47] Newfeld's modernist sensibility helped to bring a new design aesthetic to Canadian publishing, in which typeface, paper, binding, and illustration all helped to shape the reader's interaction with the text.

At Oxford, Newfeld illustrated *The Princess of Tomboso: A Fairy-Tale in Pictures* (1960), a comedic French-Canadian tale of a princess with an ever-growing nose, adapted by Toye and Newfeld from a story in *The Golden Phoenix* (1958).[48] Although this collaboration with Toye produced the first Canadian children's picturebook to be co-published in England and other Commonwealth countries, they were forced to alternate coloured illustrations with pages of black and white line drawings to reduce costs. Toye remembers, 'We did it that way because it was cheaper. It meant that the four colours were only on one side of the sheet. It would have been double the cost in those days to have colour on both sides of the sheet.'[49]

A modernist sensibility also prevails in Oxford's 1968 publication, *The Wind Has Wings: Poems from Canada*. To illustrate Mary Alice Downie and Barbara Robertson's selection of poetry, William Toye chose a first-time illustrator, Elizabeth Cleaver, whom he had met at a reception at the Toronto Public Library's Osborne Collection of Early Children's Books, housed at Boys and Girls House. After examining slides of her collage art, Toye immediately commissioned her to illustrate the anthology of seventy-seven poems.[50] Her illustrations are a mix of sharply executed black and white linocuts and bold, vibrant collages created from richly textured paper monoprints, a medium that she believed allowed her to paint without a brush.[51] The creative balance of image and word in Cleaver's imaginative interpretation of the mood of the poems, and the refined aesthetic sensibility of Toye's page design, combined to produce one of the first fully successful integrations of pictures and text in children's book illustration in Canada.

Toye's editorial vision shaped both the text and the illustrations. He supervised every aspect of the book, including the colour corrections while the sheets were on the offset press at T.H. Best of Toronto, so that the colour balance could be corrected immediately. Co-publication arrangements lowered the cost of colour printing. Of the 17,000 copies of the first print run, 5,000 went to the United States for the H.Z. Walck edition, another 5,000 were sent unbound to Britain for the 1969 Oxford UK edition, while 7,000 were retained in Canada. Of the 6,000 copies initially bound in Canada, 4,000 were sold between September and December 1968.[52]

Collections of poetry and verse offered opportunities for creative use of design and illustration. Following on the success of *The Wind Has Wings*, McClelland and Stewart issued *Sally Go Round the Sun: Three Hundred Children's Songs, Rhymes and Games* (1969), a collection of Canadian children's songs and playground rhymes from the folklorist Edith Fowke. Frank Newfeld's innovative book design and joyous, playful illustrations by Carlos Marchiori fully exploit the possibilities of decorative embellishment, repetition, pattern, and bold colour contrasts to create a work with a strongly modernist feel that also draws on folk art traditions.[53] Graphic modernism and decorative embellishment also characterize Alan Suddon's bilingual *Cinderella*, published by Oberon Press in 1969.[54] Suddon, head of the Fine Arts division of the Metropolitan Toronto Reference Library, created collage illustrations from nineteenth-century and contemporary advertising images, scraps of typeface and sheet music, heraldic devices, Victorian marbled endpapers, coloured paper, and pen and ink drawings to accompany his witty and sophisticated parody of Perrault's fairy tale. (See colour plate 4.)

'Room for Us to Have Our Own Traditions': The Toye-Cleaver Collaboration

In the late 1960s, Sheila Egoff mentioned to William Toye that Canada was lagging behind Britain and the United States in the publication of children's literature, adding that Aboriginal creation stories would make good texts for picturebooks.[55] Toye took up her challenge and worked with Elizabeth Cleaver in creating the first true picturebooks published in Canada. Their collaboration began in 1969 with *How Summer Came to Canada* and *The Mountain Goats of Temlaham* and continued into the 1970s with *The Loon's Necklace* (1977) and *The Fire Stealer* (1979). As Egoff commented, the results showed 'that there was room for us to have our own traditions' and changed the attitudes of librarians, teachers, and the general public towards Canadian picturebooks.[56]

Toye's retelling of the stories is minimal, utilizing a spare narrative voice directed to the youngest reader. In the late 1960s, the concept of cultural appropriation of voice was as yet not a consideration in the publishing industry, nor was there recognition of the deep significance of the Temlaham story for the Gitxsan people as an *adaawk*, a precise oral history that articulates the relationship between a Nation and their hereditary land.[57] Toye first looked in the National Archives of Canada for resource materials but decided that Aboriginal narratives were unsatisfacto-

4.2 Alan Suddon. *Cinderella*. French translation by Claude Aubry.
Ottawa: Oberon Press, 1969.
Reprinted with the permission of the publisher, Oberon Press. Reproduction from Rare Books and
Special Collections, University of British Columbia Library.

ry for his purposes. Instead he created his own versions, explaining that '*How Summer Came to Canada* was really based on the Cyrus Macmillan story. *Temlaham* was based on my reading these Native tellings; there were several versions and I turned it into my own version. I did this, too, for *The Loon's Necklace*.'[58]

Cleaver's love of folk art and fascination with indigenous people's art is evident in her illustrations, which also incorporate her extensive research into the material culture of the Aboriginal peoples whose stories she was interpreting. At a time when most children's illustrators in Canada employed a careful and fairly literal naturalism, she brought a graphic design sensibility to her work. She combines linocut prints, collographs printed from collage, and textured and vividly coloured monoprints, cutting, tearing, and layering the printed papers, overprinting them with potato prints, and adding organic materials, including sprays of cedar leaves, birch bark, pine needles, mosses and grasses, to create complex, three-dimensional images.[59] As a keenly self-aware artist, Cleaver was eloquent in articulating the particular attraction that collage held for her, explaining, 'I feel I can achieve more sensitivity and feeling through scissors than with a pencil … I carefully choose my paper for colour, texture to convey a certain feeling. Through collage one learns to simplify and bring out the essence. Collage represents feeling because all the decisions made are based on feeling … The different types of edges of paper torn or cut, have a certain character. It depends on the artist to know when to use which one to express a certain feeling, an idea.'[60] (See colour plate 5.)

'No One Else Had Gotten an Indian into Print': Aboriginal Stories

Toye's choice of Aboriginal stories for the first Canadian picturebooks was not without precedent. In the 1960s, increasing numbers of non-Aboriginal writers had turned their attention to Aboriginal stories, seeing in them a connection to Canada's past, although rarely as part of living, contemporary Aboriginal culture. McClelland and Stewart issued Ella Elizabeth Clark's *Indian Legends of Canada* (1960), a scholarly anthology of stories grouped by theme and genre to reflect Clark's interest in comparative mythology. Macmillan published Robert Ayre's *Sketco the Raven* (1961), a collection of Haida stories about Raven, the trickster, with illustrations by Philip Surrey. In 1963, Oxford published Dorothy Reid's *Tales of Nanabozho*, Ojibwa stories illustrated by Douglas Grant, who makes effective use of positive and negative spaces in his black and white line drawings. McClelland and Stewart issued *Badger, the Mischief Maker* (1965), a collection of Abenaki stories retold by Kay Hill and illustrated by John Hamberger, and Ronald Melzack's *The Day Tuk Became a Hunter* (1967), a retelling of Inuit stories with illustrations by Carol Jones.[61]

In the 1960s, there were only a few Canadian children's books in which the unified vision of an author-illustrator was brought to the creative process. As a boy, James Houston had taken drawing lessons at the Art Gallery of Toronto (now the Art Gallery of Ontario) from the painter Arthur Lismer, a founding member of the Group of Seven. From 1938 to 1940, he trained at the Ontario College of Art. After the war, he studied drawing and engraving in Paris, before moving in the late 1940s to Inukjuak to paint the Inuit people and the Arctic landscape.[62] He began to collect Inuit sculpture, and worked with the Canadian Guild of Crafts in Montreal, the federal government, and the Northern Stores division of the Hudson's Bay Company to develop domestic and international markets for Inuit carvings. In the late 1950s, Houston, who was living at Cape Dorset on Baffin Island, introduced printmaking to the Inuit and formed the West Baffin Eskimo Co-operative to promote and market Inuit graphic arts and sculpture.

In 1962, Houston moved to New York, where a chance meeting with Margaret McElderry, children's editor at Harcourt, Brace and World, led to the publication of his first Inuit stories, *Tikta'liktak: An Eskimo Legend* (1965), and *The White Archer* (1967).[63] Houston's texts, based on Inuit stories and his own lived experience of the Arctic, explore the psychological drama of his characters' moral and spiritual growth, while the roundness and massing of his graphite drawings are directly inspired by Inuit sculpture.[64]

Aboriginal storytellers and artists also began retelling and illustrating their own stories, beginning with *Son of Raven, Son of Deer: Fables of the Tse-shaht People* (1967) by author-illustrator George Clutesi, a member of the Tseshaht First Nation on the west coast of Vancouver Island.[65] Clutesi began to draw while attending the Alberni Indian Residential School. In the 1940s, he met Ira Dilworth, an administrator with the Canadian Broadcasting Corporation in Vancouver, who encouraged him to retell Tseshaht stories for broadcast. Through Dilworth, he also developed friendships with Lawren Harris and Emily Carr, who left him her brushes, oils, and blank canvases in her will.

In the mid-1960s, the British Columbia publisher Gray Campbell heard about Clutesi's storytelling and sought him out to try to persuade him to write down his stories. Clutesi was initially reluctant but eventually produced a collection of twelve teaching stories of the Tseshaht that he illustrated with reinterpretations of traditional Nuu Chah Nulth animal forms. *Son of Raven, Son of Deer* was issued by Gray's Publishing in 1967 as a centennial project, and after the work was adopted by the British Columbia Department of Education, they issued a second print run of 60,000 copies for use in schools. Campbell subsequently noted that 'no one else had gotten an Indian into print and it raised [Gray's Publishing's] prestige.'[66]

About the same time that Gray Campbell was in conversation with George Clutesi, Christie Harris began research on the life of Haida carver Charles Edenshaw. Harris, who had experience writing scripts for CBC Radio broadcasts, obtained an introduction to Florence Davidson, Edenshaw's daughter, through the artist and craftsperson Bill Reid, Edenshaw's great-great-nephew. After Harris travelled to Haida Gwaii to interview Davidson about the 'old days,' she decided to extend the biography of Edenshaw into a multi-generational narrative that she described as 'a tragedy of culture contact.'[67] She consulted with Wilson Duff, Provincial Anthropologist in Victoria, regarding details of the historical context, and at the request of her publisher convinced Reid to illustrate the novel *Raven's Cry* (1966).[68] As Harris later explained, 'My gratitude to Bill Reid knows no bounds … He gave me my first genuine appreciation of what had happened to the aboriginal population along the west coast.'[69] In turn, Reid described Harris's book as 'one of the strongest voices speaking for the people of Haida Gwaii and their neighbours.'[70]

4.3 James Houston. *The White Archer: An Eskimo Legend*. New York: Harcourt Brace and World; Don Mills, ON: Longmans Canada, 1967.

Illustration from *The White Archer*, copyright © 1967 and renewed 1995 by James Houston, reproduced by permission of Houghton Mifflin Harcourt Publishing Company, and the estate of the author.

The illustrations that Reid created for the book demonstrate his increasing confidence in his understanding of the ovoids and u-shapes created by the formline, the basic component of traditional Haida art. Maria Tippett notes that Reid drew inspiration from the woodcuts of Canadian artist Walter J. Phillips, and from his experiments in the 1950s with printing techniques in collaboration with the noted Vancouver book designer Robert Reid, particularly the use of crosshatching to create tonal variations.[71]

Other projects by Aboriginal illustrators were also published in the 1960s. Norval Morrisseau, a noted Ojibwa artist, illustrated H.T. Schwartz's *Windigo and Other Tales of the Ojibway* (1969). Founder of the Woodlands School of painting, Morrisseau in his illustrations captures the spiritual and visionary power of the stories. A collaboration between the children of Kettle Point reserve and the noted type designer Allan Fleming resulted in *The Alphabet Book* (1968), published by the University of Toronto Press. According to critic Jeffrey Canton, the work began as a centennial project. Anne Wyse, a teacher on the reserve, and Alex Wyse, an artist, worked with the children to create definitions for each letter, which the children then illustrated. The children selected the pictures, and Fleming selected the typeface and designed the cover of the book. Canton notes, 'What was fascinating was that some of the kids no longer remembered who had done what picture. So they knew who'd been involved in the project but except for one illustration that actually had a little boy's name on it, who knows [who created] the rest of them?'[72]

Encouraging the Development of a Literature

While a few trade publishers were beginning to develop children's lists in Canada in the 1960s, obtaining information about Canadian titles continued to be a challenge for librarians, teachers, and the general reading public. In 1964, the Children's Recreational Reading Council of Ontario, an organization composed of representatives from librarianship, education, and publishing, commissioned Sheila Egoff, professor at the University of British Columbia's School of Librarianship, and the first tenured faculty member teaching children's literature in a university in Canada, to write a book on Canadian children's literature as a centennial year project.[73] The result was *The Republic of Childhood: A Critical Guide to Canadian Children's Literature in English*, edited by William Toye, and published by Oxford Canada in 1967.[74]

Egoff had maintained the very rigorous critical standards that she had learned at the Toronto Public Library, in which the idea of 'enduring quality' and 'good writing' featured prominently. She believed in cultural mimesis, that the literature of a country 'cannot help but reveal a good deal about that country.'[75] She was rigorously unsentimental in her assessment of the relative strengths and weaknesses of Canadian children's literary production and believed that the state of writing and illustrating in Canada indicated an unwillingness to meet what she called 'the steady gaze of children.'[76] At the same time, she was making cosmopolitan claims about her evaluative criteria. As she stated in the introduction to *The Republic of Childhood*, 'To achieve such objectivity (insofar as this is possible), I have sought to relate the contemporary Canadian books closely to the general body of literature and specifically to the children's books of other countries. If the scope of my book is exclusively national, my standards of judgment are not so.'[77] Egoff's articulation of her critical approach drew directly on Matthew Arnold's critical theory, the 'touchstone' approach that she had adopted from Lillian Smith.[78] It also reflected the debates over high culture and Canadian identity that had informed the Massey Commission Report fifteen years earlier.[79]

The tension between nationalist discourse and evaluative critical norms created certain conceptual and logistical challenges, and the result, she believed, was 'a very unusual book, because I had to deal with very poor Canadian books,' adding that because so many titles were out of print at the time of publication, she did not have enough material from which to choose.[80] Her steely criticism, which she believed would be of value to Canadian writers by encouraging them to improve their standards, while simultaneously rendering 'credit for some achievement' for 'a body of writing that deserves recognition and evaluation, and not merely from Canadians,' suggested that Canadian children's literature was, in fact, distinctly second-rate compared with 'the best modern writing' from Britain and the United States.[81]

Her approach generated a certain amount of resentment from those people in the book trade who believed that the children's book industry needed uncritical and unqualified acceptance until it was on a more secure footing, arguing not unreasonably that children's literary production was unlikely to improve without a marketplace that was willing to support it.[82] Her editor, William Toye, responded to the criticism with the comment, 'We weren't interested in being kind to writers. We wanted to give the straight goods. That was the only thing you could do if you wanted to encourage the development of a literature … I worked with Sheila on that, certainly. I wasn't out to praise people for no reason.'[83]

Egoff was the first scholar to attempt to categorize Canadian children's literature by identifying common themes, genres, and issues, serving as a literary cartographer mapping an unfamiliar terrain. At the same time, reflecting the best contemporary professional practice, *The Republic of Childhood* emphasized the evaluative critical role of the informed adult in selecting books for a library collection serving child readers. The work was issued a year after the publication of the fourth edition of *Books for Boys and Girls: A Standard Work of Reference for Librarians*, edited by Marguerite Bagshaw. *Books for Boys and Girls*, first published in 1927 under the editorial direction of Lillian Smith, emphasized the descriptive and evaluative function of criticism.[84] Bagshaw argued that the listing of 2,000 books in English in the 1966 edition, published in the United States, Canada, and Britain, represented 'books of enduring quality' that would 'remain most desirable in a children's library' because of their 'structure, style and presentation.'[85] The irony was that Egoff and Bagshaw's continued insistence that the evaluative function of criticism served children by shaping library collections based on the criterion of 'only the best is good enough for children' was given wide circulation at the same moment when literary criticism in Canada was, on one hand, disclaiming any evaluative role, and simultaneously enshrining a literary canon from which children's literary production was firmly excluded. Inadvertently, children's literary critics found themselves outside the academic mainstream, further reinscribing the gendering of Canadian canon formation that had characterized the interwar period.[86]

'Irma Was a Guardian Angel': Reviews and Reviewing

Overall, children's book reviewing in Canada had been meagre, exacerbating the difficulties that school and public librarians faced in obtaining information about new Canadian publications, and hindering the expansion of the market. In earlier decades, the displays of new books and bibliographies compiled by the Boys and Girls Division of the Toronto Public Library, and the reviews of Canadian material included in the *Ontario Library Review*, had allowed librarians to add Canadian titles to their collections, but the coverage was uneven, especially for books by regional publishers and works deemed unsuitable for library use. Lillian Smith's influential introduction to the evaluation of children's literature, *The Unreluctant Years* (1953), commissioned by the American Library Association, and the various editions of *Books for Boys and Girls*, included a selection of Canadian titles, but the focus was on the breadth of children's English-language publishing, rather than the promotion of a national literature.

The situation began to change in 1967, when the Provincial Library Service of Ontario established the first library journal to systematically review Canadian children's books, under the editorship of Irma McDonough, the Service's children's specialist. *In Review*, which continued publication until 1982, included important articles, publishing statistics, and profiles of the creators and producers of children's books. Janet Lunn remembers the journal's impact, explaining that 'Irma McDonough's *In Review* … was an invaluable publication. These were clear, brief but thoughtful reviews of current books and the authors of those books were very grateful for them. At a time when there was no other way to get our books in front of teachers and librarians, I think we writers considered Irma a guardian angel.' The importance of *In Review* as a source of information about Canadian children's publishing is also suggested by the 1972 study by Alixe Hambleton of publishing and library selection in five public libraries in the Toronto area. *In Review* was the only reviewing journal cited by all five libraries as a selection tool.[87]

The journal was not without its critics, however. Like Egoff, who refused to praise a book simply because it was Canadian, May Cutler of Tundra Books felt that *In Review* should have been more uncompromising. 'When I told its editor Irma McDonough that children's books in Canada were god awful, she agreed but insisted they were getting better. I didn't see how they would get better if their dismal state was not acknowledged. Saying that things were awful did not make me popular, but I didn't give a damn.'[88] Ironically, McDonough had also argued strongly that Canadian publishers needed to 'recognize and capitalize on the growing demand for good books.' She believed that editors had a critical role to play in 'freeing Canadian publishing from the mediocre book,' and that creative and informed criticism would 'definitely promote the development of good writing.'[89]

For other children's book writers and publishers, however, the standards of the review journals and the librarians' selection standards were overly stringent. They felt excluded from the recognition they believed that they deserved. Just as Egoff's *The Republic of Childhood* had stirred debate about balancing criticism and sympathy, there was ongoing debate in library, reviewing, and writing circles over whether Canadian children's books should be supported in principle or whether they should be subjected to the same evaluation as international titles.[90] Writer Jean Little observes that her books received mostly negative reviews within Canada, and positive reviews in the United States, which she saw as an outcome of the selection standards of children's librarians. As Little remembers it, 'We couldn't find any Canadian children's books at the Toronto Public Library's Boys and Girls House. Canadian children's books were unwelcome and unwanted. Most [librarians] were wedded to the European and British books. The librarians also didn't understand the realistic contemporary children's books. When John Sorfleet [English literature professor and children's literature scholar] asked at Boys and Girls House if he could find my books ... he was told no, but they might be in the branches.'[91]

Nonetheless, as the first reviewing journal, and the only consistent source of reviews of Canadian children's titles, *In Review* played a critical role in connecting the various communities of readers. As well as librarians and teachers who used the journal as an information source and selection aid, children's book writers and the general public valued its window onto the world of publishers and books in Canada. Writer Claire Mackay remarks: 'I own a full set of *In Review* ... I read each issue back to back ... I could count on *In Review* to cover everything; it was a wonderful resource ... There wasn't a lot around. Little reviews in the *Canadian Author and Bookman* ... There wasn't much in the daily newspapers or glossies. Children's books were ignored and Canadian ignored more.'[92]

Janet Lunn recalls what it was like to be a reviewer for newspapers in Kingston and Toronto in the 1950s and 1960s, when there was no serious attention paid to children's books.[93] As she remembers, the children's librarians in Toronto were 'wonderfully kind. They would let me take home arms full of books at least twice a week and I read compulsively.' Lunn believes that her children's book reviews, which appeared in *Quill and Quire, The Toronto Star, The Star Weekly* magazine, and *The Globe and Mail* 'had some impact, although, not all of it positive; I remember going to Eaton's bookshop to ask for a book one day and was told sourly that they were all sold out "because of that woman's review in *The Globe and Mail*."'[94]

By the end of the 1960s, Frank Newfeld and William Toye, with the collaboration of emerging authors and illustrators, had taken children's book design in Canada in a new direction.[95] Strong and innovative design was recognized and welcomed. Their juggling of multiple roles as editors and art designers, writers and illustrators, and senior publishing administrators provided a model for the newcomers to publishing who would specialize in children's books. Sales of Canadian-authored and -published books in Canada had increased, even though the number of children's books published annually was very small compared with the United States and Britain, and the bookstore and library shelves continued to be dominated by foreign imports.[96] In the next decade, small independent and specialist publishing houses would transform children's publishing in Canada, changing the perception that Canadians did not create picturebooks, they imported them.[97] Upheavals in publishing and the book trade paralleled the excitement, change, and political and social unrest of the period. The branch plant publishers such as Oxford under Toye with a commitment to Canadian cultural identity in children's books were to be joined by a new generation of children's book editors, writers, and illustrators whom Roy MacSkimming names 'The Mavericks of Kidlit.'[98] The era of explicit Canadian nationalism in Canadian children's books was just beginning.

CHAPTER FIVE

The 1970s: Developing a Children's Publishing Industry

At the outset of the 1970s, despite the critical acclaim given to the picturebooks and illustrated books published by Oxford University Press and McClelland and Stewart, the majority of Canadian trade publishers who issued children's books were cautious in developing their children's lists. They continued to focus on a few narrow genres with strong curricular links. May Cutler, who ran a bookshop in Montreal in the 1960s, remembers that a sales representative, on hearing that she was interested in publishing children's books commented, '"That's easy. You just bring out a hockey book and an Eskimo or Indian legend each year." That was really all that was being published in Canada.'[1]

Imported books distributed through the agency system continued to dominate the retail and institutional markets, accounting for 65 per cent of book sales in Canada.[2] Canadian titles by Canadian publishers represented a mere 34 per cent of publishers' overall sales, the majority issued by 'young houses with small lists.'[3] The situation was even more imbalanced for children's books.[4] In the early 1970s, thirty to sixty English-language children's books were published annually. By the late 1970s, that number had risen to between sixty and one hundred titles annually.[5] However, compared with the several thousand titles published each year in both England and the United States, original Canadian titles represented a tiny fraction of the range of children's books available to libraries and bookstores, and imported children's books continued to account for more than 90 per cent of sales in Canada.[6]

The high cost of book manufacturing in Canada resulting from short print runs that raised the unit cost per book, and the geographic challenges of distributing, marketing, and promoting books into the various regions from Toronto, exacerbated the problems resulting from competition for attention in a market saturated with foreign imports. As designer and illustrator Frank Newfeld noted, '[T]he majority of our authors have to be content with just the local market. This greatly and negatively affects the selling-price of our books. Our preparatory costs become a punishing factor compared to the constant running costs. Thus, amortization of the former imposed by our shorter press runs usually limited our ambitions.'[7] And, as William Toye warned, while foreign rights sales of Canadian children's titles allowed Canadian publishers to increase the size of a print run and lower the unit cost of production, limited opportunities for domestic sales continued to hinder profitability. He concluded that Canadian publishers were 'probably best advised to stick with children's books of mainly Canadian interest – books whose main sale will be in Canada,' rather than trying to pursue international rights sales in a competitive market unless they were able to issue titles 'whose literary and artistic qualities and universal interest ... will recommend them to a wider market than the Canadian one alone.'[8]

The challenges collectively resulted in what has been described as the vicious circle of children's publishing.[9] Publishers complained that there was not enough support for Canadian children's books from the retail and institutional markets. They argued that they could not find talented writers or illustrators, rarely received publishable unsolicited manuscripts, and had no valuable backlist of Canadian classics to underwrite new ventures.[10] Children's librarians and teacher-librarians were often reluctant to purchase Canadian titles if they did not meet the same selection criteria as imported books. Booksellers did not stock titles because the public did not ask for them; the public did not ask for them because they received little publicity, resulting from the small promotional budgets by cash-strapped publishers whose books did not sell as well as expected.[11] The public's lack of interest in and support for Canadian children's literature discouraged authors and illustrators, who lacked access to trained and specialized children's editors, who were not hired by the publishing companies because the small number and variable quality of indigenous children's titles produced meant poor reception in the market in the face of competition from foreign-produced titles.[12]

The weak domestic market for Canadian-authored and -published titles, and the extent of sales of foreign titles within Canada, worried cultural nationalists. Gérard Pelletier, Secretary of State for Canada and the cabinet minister responsible for cultural issues, clearly articulated the issue, asking, 'Will the place allotted to the Canadian book, the Canadian writer, be proportional to their importance in our cultural development? Will Canadians have to rely solely on Europeans and Americans to interpret the world through foreign thoughts and emotions?'[13] There would need to be a major shift in markets, government support, infrastructure, and a new generation of publishers, writers, and illustrators before a national children's literature, and, in particular, an illustrated children's literature, could fully emerge in Canada.

'A Steady Flow of New Canadian Books by Canadian Authors'

In 1970, the loss of two established Canadian publishers to American interests in a single year – with the sale of Ryerson Press to McGraw-Hill, and the educational publisher W.J. Gage to Scott Foresman – and the threatened sale of McClelland and Stewart, generated a public uproar over the threat to Canadian cultural sovereignty.[14] In response, the Ontario provincial government called a Royal Commission on Book Publishing, charged with examining all aspects of the publishing industry in Ontario and Canada, including issues of cultural production and foreign ownership.[15]

In its recommendations, the commission promoted the idea of a 'moderate cultural naturalism in book publishing,' achieved by 'continuous access to a steady flow of new Canadian books by Canadian authors.'[16] Furthermore, it argued that the indigenous Canadian publishing industry could not survive in a competitive market against large foreign publishers and their branch plants without some form of government subsidies in the form of title grants, assistance to reissue out-of-print Canadian titles, help in marketing Canadian books domestically and internationally, and restrictions on foreign ownership.[17]

The Ontario Royal Commission's promotion of domestic ownership of the publishing industry provided a rationale for new state support of publishing within Canada, in the form of emergency financing, loan guarantees, interest subsidies, and grant programs for Canadian-owned publishers. Once the federal government began to offer support through expanded Canada Council grants and export initiatives, provincial arts councils quickly followed suit. The establishment of the Canadian Book Publishing Development Program in 1979 offered further assistance in stimulating the industry.[18]

'No Tradition of Our Own': The Editors' Experience

The larger trade publishers who issued illustrated children's books in Canada before the 1970s relied on their existing editorial staff to provide textual and visual editing. Children's titles were a minor part of the trade publishers' lists, not issued in sufficient numbers to warrant a separate imprint or division. When Clarke, Irwin appointed Janet Lunn as an editor in 1972, she was the first children's specialist at a Canadian publishing house. As she remembers, there was 'no tradition of our own to work on … We were learning as we went along.'[19] Writer Claire Mackay recalls that in the established publishing houses, 'there were real editors, but we had to develop [children's] editors along with ourselves as writers.'[20]

Lunn also remembers how difficult it was as an editor to find manuscripts, explaining that '[p]ractically nobody was doing picturebooks … all of the little old ladies who'd ever thought they'd write a picturebook were getting them out of the bottom drawer. I used to call them the "Elf under the Mushroom" stories. Annabel [Slaight] said she called them "All the Fluffy Bunny" stories.'[21] On the other hand, there were so few specialized children's editors that the professional marginalization of children's lists and editors that characterized many of the large American and British trade houses seems to have had little direct effect in Canada.[22]

'We Were All Kind of Making It Up as We Went Along': Illustrators and Designers

A lack of formal mentoring characterized the working lives of many illustrators and designers. Although Canadian art schools provided opportunities to study graphic design and commercial art, there were still relatively few Canadians who had specialized training in book design and children's book illustration compared with their peers in the United States and Europe. While the major trade and educational publishers had experienced book designers on staff, they were usually generalists who were responsible for the visual style of a number of different genres from poetry to non-fiction.[23]

Many experienced designers worked on contract for specific projects for a number of publishers, building an informal professional design network in the process. Others learned on the job. Tim Wynne-Jones began his career in publishing in 1974 as a book designer at Peter Martin Associates (PMA) in Toronto. As he later recalled, at the time he was hired he had a degree in Fine Arts but 'didn't know anything about book design … We were all kind of making it up as we went along.'[24] Between 1974 and 1978, he also taught visual arts at the University of Waterloo, and when several of the students expressed an interest in book design, he developed an ad hoc typography course.[25] When Wynne-Jones left PMA in 1976 to travel, he recommended one of his students, Michael Solomon, to fill the position of designer. Solomon subsequently joined with Wynne-Jones as partners in a graphic design firm focusing on book design and magazine work.[26]

While the majority of illustrators were also generalists, working across a number of genres, some who had trained outside Canada had benefited from opportunities to study with experienced children's book illustrators. Author-illustrator Eugenie Fernandes, who attended the School of Visual Art in New York, notes that she took a course on illustrating children's books, taught by the Danish illustrator Erik Blegved, with guest lectures by several noted illustrators, including Maurice Sendak. During the course, students were able to create their own book.[27] No similar opportunity seems to have been available to Canadian students.

Publishing houses who were in the process of developing children's lists had a relatively small talent pool of illustrators from which to draw and had to develop various strategies to compensate. Kathryn Cole began her publishing career in the late 1960s at Scholastic Book Service (later Scholastic Canada) after graduating from the Ontario College of Art. Although she was the art director when the company began a Canadian publishing program, she was asked to illustrate their first books, changing her artistic style with each title 'to make it look like a multifaceted department.'[28] Writer Norma Charles remembers that in the 1970s, 'if a manuscript was illustrated before it was submitted, it had a greater chance of being published because publishers didn't have or couldn't find suitable illustrators.'[29]

The economics of publishing further restricted the number of illustrators who could make a career in children's publishing. Unlike authors, who received royalties on sales, illustrators were paid a flat fee, the rate depending on whether the illustration was black and white or full-colour.[30] The financial incentive was so minimal that only an illustrator desperately wanting to do a children's book would take on a project.[31] Illustrators found it necessary to supplement their income by working as graphic artists and designers, magazine illustrators, and commercial illustrators. Vladyana Krykorka's career path was typical for the period. She had specialized in illustration and design during her studies at the School of Applied Art in Prague, and studied drawing, printmaking, and illustration at the Ontario College of Art after moving to Canada in the late 1960s. After graduation, she worked as an illustrator for educational publishers, and then freelanced as a magazine illustrator and art director at Maclean-Hunter before turning to picturebook illustration.[32]

Others found work in the educational publishing houses. Barbara Reid, who graduated from the Ontario College of Art in 1980, believes that '[i]llustrating textbooks was very good training. You learn the discipline of deadlines, you have to be extremely true to the text, and the restrictions force you to be creative in solving problems. Once you have learned the rules for good textbook or non-fiction illustrating you have a lot of fun bending them and breaking them with the freedom of editorial or picturebook work.'[33]

In addition to the lack of remuneration, illustrators also found it difficult to gain professional respect. Illustrator Ken Nutt (aka Eric Beddows) studied fine art at York University from 1970 to 1972 at a time when narrative art and representational art were out of favour among instructors. He remembers that he and fellow students who admired the work of nineteenth-century illustrators 'used to go and draw pictures that were not realistic but more fantasy-related on the chalkboards as an act of protest.'[34] As author-illustrator Ian Wallace observes, 'the Canada Council didn't recognize illustration as a legitimate art form. Prejudice in the fine art world saw illustrative art as inferior and commercial. Real art was only paintings or sculpture. Illustration was not viewed as having the same credibility. It took years of lobbying before illustrators were eligible for grants and tours.'[35]

The Look of the Books: Design and Production Values in the 1970s

By the early 1970s, American and British picturebook authors and illustrators were experimenting with new subject matter and artistic approaches in response to the tone and mood of increasingly culturally diverse narratives in the wider society. The rapid expansion of school libraries in the United States after the introduction of federal legislation, designated funding, and block grants to public schools, beginning in the late 1950s, had stimulated American children's trade publishing.[36] Technical improvements in offset photolithography meant that it was possible for illustrators to create more complex artwork in a wider range of media with greater tonal range and subtlety.[37] Illustrators were encouraged to create picturebooks with sophisticated images that interacted with and extended the textual narrative, and explored themes once absent from picturebooks: the sometimes troubled worlds of the child's psyche, family, and environment; stories of urban life and poverty; stories of ethnocultural diversity; and the experiences of disadvantage or disability.

In comparison, the majority of Canadian illustrated books for children issued by the major trade publishers in the same period looked conservative and less sophisticated than their American and British counterparts. Limitations in domestic book production restricted design possibilities, and for many publishers, aesthetic decisions had to take second place to economic necessity. Although William Toye had worked in full colour at Oxford University Press since the late 1960s, there were only a few Canadian printers of the period who could produce high-quality colour printing. Many smaller publishers could not afford the cost of colour separations for children's books and resorted to printing in one or two colours. Children's illustrators were required to master the time-consuming process of completing colour pre-separations for books by hand and plan around the design limitations imposed by a colour range that could be extended only by overlay printing.[38] The quality of binding was also problematic until Friesens, the printer in Altona, Manitoba, purchased new machinery that improved the strength of the spine in a thirty-two-page picturebook.[39]

As a result, production values in illustrated books printed in Canada were often quite poor compared with those published in Britain and the United States. As Dave Jenkinson, professor emeritus, the University of Manitoba's Faculty of Education, remembers: 'The two-colour books ... were bought for libraries because they were Canadian and we felt morally obliged to do so. We would think politely, "Well, for a Canadian book, it's pretty good," damning with faint praise.'[40]

Even larger trade publishers who had money for promotion and marketing could find that the cost of producing full-colour picturebooks could not be justified by domestic sales. In 1973, Holt, Rinehart and Winston of Canada published Elizabeth Cleaver's *The Miraculous Hind* in English and French editions.[41] The book received enthusiastic reviews and in 1974 won the Canadian Association of Children's Librarians award for the best Canadian children's book of the year. The publisher mounted a vigorous marketing campaign and received widespread publicity. Despite all of this, the book sold only 891 copies over the fifteen months after its publication.[42]

'The Look of the Word and the Sound of the Illustration'

If *The Miraculous Hind* served as a reminder to the industry that even an award-winning Canadian children's book might not find an immediate market, the overwhelming success of Dennis Lee's *Alligator Pie* (1974) and *Nicholas Knock and Other People* (1974) stimulated new interest among trade publishers in the sales potential of children's literary production. At the time of the simultaneous publication of the two volumes, some critics were surprised that Lee would turn to writing children's books. He was an established poet and fierce Canadian nationalist with extensive editorial experience as co-founder of the House of Anansi Press and a Governor General's Award for poetry.[43]

It was his nationalism, however, that led him to explore poetry for Canadian children. While reading familiar Mother Goose rhymes to his children, he realized how foreign and unfamiliar the cultural references were.[44] They lacked what Margaret Laurence referred to as 'our-ness,' reflecting instead 'another land, a different consciousness from ours.'[45] In *Alligator Pie*, Lee uses Canadian place names and cultural references in combination with metrical rhyme and playground chant to create a distinctly nationalist collection of verse reflecting the lives of contemporary Canadian children.[46] The liveliness and inventiveness of Lee's poetry and the novelty of the national references captured immediate popular and critical attention.

Frank Newfeld used his experience as a designer and his familiarity with the technical challenges of reproduction to exploit the maximum graphic possibility in the interplay of image and text in his illustrations for the two volumes, turning the limitations of colour printing into a deliberate design feature.[47] His use of type ornaments, flat blocks of colour, and a heavy black line to define shape, are strongly reminiscent of his linocut designs for volumes of poetry in the McClelland and Stewart Design for Poetry series.[48] The highly decorative and distinctive repeating motifs used throughout the book give a crisp graphic effect. As he explains, he tried to achieve 'the look of the word, and the sound of the illustration,' giving the child reader imaginative freedom in the interpretation of the images.[49] (See colour plate 6.)

Alligator Pie marked a commercial and aesthetic turning point in Canadian children's publishing. Dennis Lee credits the willingness of Hugh Kane, president of Macmillan of Canada, to go out 'on a limb,' and insist that 'everything be done first-class.'[50] Macmillan printed 10,000 copies of *Alligator Pie* and 7,5000 copies of *Nicholas Knock*, and heavily advertised both titles.[51] They also instigated a cross-country promotional tour, funded in part by the Canada Council.[52] Judy Sarick of the Children's Book Store remembers that in advance of the launch of *Alligator Pie*, which was held at the store, she ordered 250 copies, and a further 250 copies of *Nicholas Knock*. She explains that her decision, based on her experience in ordering for the Metropolitan School Board in Toronto, was 'outrageous, as other bookstores were only ordering two of each.' Her instinct was correct, as the print run sold out immediately, and the Children's Book Store was the only shop with stock.[53]

Alligator Pie was the first children's title published within Canada to achieve overwhelming commercial success, which, in turn, stimulated interest by other trade publishers in the potential market for children's books.[54] As Tim Wynne-Jones remembers, after *Alligator Pie*, 'it became plausible to actually sell children's books in quantity, not as a make-work project but as a viable money making proposition. Prime Minister Trudeau had opened the coffers and said, "Come on kids, invent Canada!" And so we did on a thousand fronts and it turned out that Canadians were thrilled to discover we had this homegrown culture just waiting to happen.'[55]

The success of the title also caused authors and publishers to rethink the look of children's books. *Wiggle to the Laundromat* (1970), Lee's first poetry anthology for children, including most of the material subsequently published in *Alligator Pie*, was issued by New Press, a small alternative publisher. The strong expressionist black and white illustrations by the artist Charles Pachter in combination with the tall, oversize format resembled an art book for adults, rather than a children's picturebook, and failed to find an audience. The popularity of the more mainstream *Alligator Pie* served as a reminder that in order to have broad market appeal, the physical format of a children's book needed to signify its genre on first glance.

The Trade Publishers

At Oxford University Press, William Toye continued to expand the children's trade list with a careful selection of books with strong visual and narrative appeal. He collaborated with the illustrator Laszlo Gal on *Cartier Discovers the St Lawrence* (1970), one of the first full-colour children's picture-storybooks published in Canada. Gal's paintings in gouache and watercolours reflect his experience as a designer for the Canadian Broadcasting Corporation and his interest in theatre.[56] Their stately monumentality evokes the world of the St Lawrence in the early seventeenth century, matching the formality of Toye's prose, which reflects the cadences of Cartier's diaries of his three voyages of exploration.

In 1977, Toye once again collaborated with Elizabeth Cleaver on the third in their quartet of Aboriginal stories. *The Loon's Necklace* (1977) is a retelling of a Tsimshian story of how the loon received its distinctive white markings as a reward after the bird magically restores the sight of a blind man. In preparation, Cleaver investigated textual variants of the story, researched images at the McCord Museum in Montreal, gathered a collection of material relating to Tsimshian material culture, and revisited the notes that she made in 1969 during her trip to the Skeena River in north-western British Columbia.[57] The resulting illustrations synthesize her research with subtlety and sensitivity.[58] She extends her collage technique, combining linocuts with complex layers of deeply saturated monoprinted paper, transforming the two-dimensional page through the careful juxtaposition of compositional elements to suggest texture and depth.[59] Cleaver was keenly interested in the potential of Jungian archetypes to evoke emotional responses in her reader, and the illustrations for *The Loon's Necklace* are carefully balanced between the real world and that of myth and dream, combining visual symbolism and non-natural colour to express the emotional tone of the story.[60]

Other publishers also developed strong children's trade lists. In 1974, McClelland and Stewart appointed Marilyn Fisher as children's book editor.[61] Throughout the 1970s, the firm extended their list of retellings of Aboriginal stories that could be sold in both the educational and trade markets. Christie Harris's *Once More upon a Totem* (1973) and *Mouse Woman and the Mischief-Makers* (1977) were both illustrated in black and white by Douglas Tait, who appropriated Haida art forms for his abstracted images. Ronald Melzack's *Why the Man in the Moon Is Happy and Other Eskimo Creation Stories* (1977), with Laszlo Gal's romantic illustrations, was a companion to Melzack and Gal's previous collaboration, *Raven, Creator of the World: Eskimo Legends* (1970). McClelland and Stewart also published *Up in the Tree* (1977), written, hand-lettered, and illustrated by Margaret Atwood in two colours, as well as a few full-colour picturebooks, including Maria Campbell's *Little Badger and the Fire Spirit* (1977), illustrated by David MacLagan.[62]

The Canadian branch of Methuen published a small range of children's books, including the 'Kids Like Us' series of contemporary multicultural urban stories by Beverley Allinson, illustrated with photographs by Barbara O'Kelly.[63] Brant Cowie's design for Janet Lunn's *The Twelve Dancing Princesses* (1979), in which double pages of text alternate with double-page, full-colour illustrations by Laszlo Gal, gives the picture storybook a cinematic breadth of vision. Gal's gouache and watercolour illustrations set Lunn's retelling of the Grimm fairy tale within a romantic reinterpretation of Renaissance costume and architecture. His experience with theatrical design is apparent in his use of varying points of view, framing, and shallow pictorial space that foregrounds figures.[64]

Despite the costs of production, some of the more commercially oriented smaller presses found a way to publish well-designed children's books in full colour, most notably Oberon Press of Ottawa, a literary house started by Michael Macklem and Anne Hardy in 1966. They issued Mary Alice Downie's *Witch of the North: Folktales of French Canada* (1975), brilliantly illustrated by Elizabeth Cleaver with complex collage images, and Macklem's sly retelling of a Quebec folktale, *Jacques the Woodcutter*, with watercolour illustrations by Ann Blades (1977).[65]

5.1 Christie Harris. *Once More upon a Totem*. Illustrated by Douglas Tait.
Toronto: McClelland and Stewart, 1973.
Reprinted with permission of the illustrator, Douglas Tait.

'Alternative to What?' The New Children's Publishers

The media attention to the publishing crisis in the early 1970s occurred within the context of a broader discussion in Canadian society about nationalism and national identity. Despite Sheila Egoff's background paper on the perilous state of publishing for children, the Royal Commission's report made only brief mention of children's books in the section on book markets and book marketing. The commission's recommendations to increase and diversify government funding, however, resulted in new initiatives and programs that would help to make indigenous Canadian children's publishing viable.[66] A new generation of authors, illustrators, and publishers, determined to expand the national discourse on Canadian cultural, social, and political issues, would transform children's publishing.[67] Many focused on the importance of picturebooks in developing Canadian cultural nationalism as a way of addressing the cultural displacement that occurs when children only have books with words and images that come 'from outside.'[68]

In contrast to the established trade publishers, for whom children's books were only one aspect of their publishing program, the new children's specialist publishers were driven by social conscience and ideology more than commerce. They saw themselves as alternative publishers, although, as Rick Wilks tartly notes, 'one might also pose the question "alternative to what?"' As he remembers, at the time, 'There were Canadian publishers and there were a handful of books being done, but the industry … was governed by the branch plants, which had no real commitment to Canada or Canadian voices and an absolutely minimal commitment to Canadian children's literature.'[69] The new publishers were committed to addressing issues of Canadian identity, multiculturalism, feminism, and children's rights in their publications, the same concerns that had led baby boomers who had come of age in the 1960s to create new social movement organizations.[70] In common with the social movement organizations, most of the new publishers were heavily dependent on state funding in the form of small provincial grants and federal Canada Council, Local Initiatives Program (LIP), and Opportunities for Youth (OFY) grants.[71] All shared a sense that they were doing something innovative in publishing 'stories with an intent for human liberation in Canadian settings.'[72]

'We Wanted to Do Things Differently': Books By Kids / Annick Press

In Toronto in 1975, Rick Wilks and Anne Millyard established Books by Kids with a LIP grant to investigate reading and writing for children in Ontario schools.[73] Millyard had a background in art and psychology, and volunteer experience in an alternative Toronto 'free' school. Wilks, who was a recent university graduate, had worked in a children's bookstore. In his words, he and Millyard shared a concern about the disenfranchisement of children, 'a very deep passion, a kind of visceral response, to the whole issue of kids being marginalized, on the edge, having no voice, having no representation in the literature.'[74] They were determined that Books by Kids would serve as an outlet for the creative writing of local children. Their first book, the anthology *Wordsandwich* (1975), was written and illustrated by children for children. In 1976 they also began issuing books under the name

Annick Press, while continuing to publish Books by Kids until 1979.

Millyard and Wilks wanted to create non-racist and non-sexist books that reflected contemporary children's lives in urban multicultural Canada. They were both nationalists, committed to creating distinctively Canadian children's books. As Millyard explains, 'We wanted to do things differently ... We did not want to publish books that looked like American books, or, for that matter, British books. I found my son in front of the television set when he was four and a half years old, saluting the American flag, pledging allegiance to the United States of America ... It was funny for five seconds and then I got very upset. We really, really wanted to be Canadian.'[75]

'Everyone Would Express an Opinion about a Manuscript': Collectives and Small Presses

Canadian Women's Educational Press (later Women's Press), founded in the spring of 1972 with the support of government grants, was run as a collective non-profit organization with a mandate to publish Canadian material relevant to women's lives, especially on themes and issues for which there was no other outlet.[76] They began publishing children's books to 'counter the present stereotyping of girls and boys into rigid sex roles and pose alternatives to the competitive authoritarian values present in so much of children's literature.'[77]

Women's Press also acted as the Canadian agent for Britain's Virago Press, and for other small Canadian feminist presses, including the Waterloo-based collective Before We Are Six.[78] Established with an OFY grant to investigate children's books in Ontario daycares, Before We Are Six issued a series of picturebooks between 1973 and 1977 that focused on the lives of contemporary children and their issues and concerns, including divorce and disability, among them Tim Wynne-Jones's *Madeline and Ermadello* (1977), illustrated by Lindsey Hallam.[79]

Other small presses developed a children's publishing program almost by accident. The writer Sue Ann Alderson believed that in a conservative picturebook environment, 'there should be more books about single-mother or single-father families.' She deliberately sent the manuscript for *Bonnie McSmithers, You're Driving Me Dithers* (1974) to Tree Frog Press, which had published only a few poetry chapbooks, because she found that established publishers were 'unwelcoming and unfriendly to alternative style and content in writing for children.'[80] The resulting picturebook, illustrated by Alderson's friend Fiona Garrick, was a critical success that transformed the direction of the publishing house.[81]

Kids Can Press was founded as a ten-person collective in Toronto in 1973.[82] Initial funding came from an OFY grant.[83] Members of the collective included artists and writers who wrote, illustrated, and published the press's first handmade books. Early titles were produced for about $1,000 in an edition of 1,000 copies, hand-lettered or typed, Gestetner-printed in monochrome or two colours by another group who had also received OFY grants, and staple bound between construction paper. Author-illustrator Ian Wallace, who joined the collective in 1974, remembers that editorial meetings were structured as conversations about 'Canadian content, multiculturalism, and positive sex identification.' The collective discussed story ideas and manuscripts at their group meetings, during which 'everyone would express an opinion about a manuscript and whether it should be published.' They edited manuscripts communally, a process that Wallace found honest, constructive, and inspiring.[84]

Although the new small presses approached publishing with enthusiasm and commitment, their restricted budgets meant that they did not have access to professional assistance to shape the textual and visual impact of their titles.[85] Production values suffered in comparison with titles issued by the mainstream trade publishing houses. Ian Wallace remembers that Kids Can's books 'looked like pamphlets. [They] weren't beautifully illustrated in full colour nor were they well produced.'[86] Contemporary reviews echoed Wallace's assessment, sharply criticizing Rosemary Allison's *The Travels of Ms Beaver* (1973), illustrated by Ann Powell, for a 'ghastly format (sideways with badly drawn lettering and garish red and blue used to expand pen and ink cartoons),' and dismissing the use of the honorific Ms as 'coy.'[87] Janet Lunn remembers being on a panel with Judy Sarick of the Children's Book Store, who held up 'a handful of picturebooks and said, "This is Canadian children's book blue." It was that swimming-pool blue colour [cyan] that dominated our picture-book shelves in those days. It was cheap to produce.'[88] Virginia Davis, former director of the Canadian Children's Book Centre and children's literature consultant, also remembers the limited colour palette that dominated the books of the period, describing them as 'the symphony of brown, brown and brown pictures.'[89]

While many reviewers at the time dismissed the books produced by the collectives and small presses as flawed by didacticism or amateur production values, the children's book reviewer and critic Jeffrey Canton comments that it is 'the innocence and … the naivety that makes those early books like *The Travels of Ms Beaver* so totally charming.' He adds that Carol Pasternak's and Allan Sutterfield's *Stone Soup* (1974), illustrated by Hedy Campbell, which sets the traditional folk tale in the contemporary ethnoculturally diverse urban milieu of Toronto's Kensington Market, 'just sing[s] despite the fact that it's a stapled book. It has a liveliness to it that is unbelievable.'[90] Ian Wallace remembers that the Kids Can collective believed that they were 'breaking new ground and pushing the boundaries of what publishing for children could be in Canada.'[91] He concludes that 'it was right for this time in Canadian history … Canadian nationalism was everywhere … Canadian baby boomers were coming of age and stepping up to the responsibility of taking Canada and running with it.'[92]

Regional Presses

Small presses, whether collectives or regional houses, all struggled with similar issues of financing, distribution, and promotion. Despite their commitment to bringing diverse voices and stories to the field of children's literature in Canada, they often had difficulty placing their books in bookstores. Regional presses might find a local interest for their books but were generally ignored by the mainstream reviewers in national newspapers and magazines. Breakwater Books, the largest publisher in Atlantic Canada, was established in St John's in 1973 by four profes-

Ferenc decided to stay and help George with the stirring, but Mario and Angelina went with Ms. Rogers. So did Manuel, whose family, from Lisbon, owned a fish store in the market, and Jennifer and Vicky, who were from Jamaica and often went with their mothers to the West Indies shops there. Kam Sau, who had come from Shanghai only last year, lived near the market, and decided to walk along with them to his home.

5.2 Carol Pasternak and Allan Sutterfield. *Stone Soup.* Illustrated and designed by Hedy Campbell. Toronto: Canadian Women's Educational Press, 1974. Reprinted with permission of the illustrator, Hedy Campbell.

sors in Memorial University's English Department.[93] Under Clyde Rose, it developed trade and educational books that would help to preserve the culture of the Atlantic provinces, including Al Pittman's poetry collection *Down by Jim Long's Stage: Rhymes for Children and Young Fish* (1976) and *Borrowed Black: A Labrador Fantasy* (1979), by Ellen Bryan Obed.[94] In Nova Scotia, Nimbus Publishing, established in 1978, focused on books about the Maritimes. Their first picturebook, *From Ben Loman to the Sea* (1979), features the naive, joyful paintings of self-taught artist Maud Lewis, with a poem written by Lance Woolaver to accompany the images.

Margie McMillan, co-owner with Nora Flynn of Granny Bates Children's Books in St John's, Newfoundland, comments on the challenges facing the small Atlantic Canadian publishers, from the lack of funding and limited market to a dearth of knowledge and experience in editing, noting that they 'have not had the money to pay attention to things like editing and design and illustration. That's not where their money has gone. They're cash-strapped as I suppose many of us are in the book industry ... I think by and large people don't realize that and there's not a large enough industry for people to take that into consideration.'[95] Her assessment could be generalized to many of the alternative, regional, and small publishers across the country in the 1970s.[96]

Douglas and McIntyre: A Regional Success Story

In 1972, the British Columbia-based publisher J.J. Douglas issued Jack Richards's *Johann's Gift to Christmas* (1972), illustrated by *Vancouver Sun* cartoonist Len Norris. The picture-storybook was a regional and national success, and encouraged Douglas, in partnership with publisher's representative Scott McIntyre, to develop further picturebooks and illustrated informational books for children, including Lois McConkey's *Sea and Cedar: How the Northwest Coast Indians Lived* (1973), illustrated by Douglas Tait, and Anne Simeon's *The She-Wolf of Tsla-a-wat: Indian Stories for the Young* (1977), also illustrated by Tait.[97]

By 1975, Douglas was ready to withdraw from active involvement in the company, which was renamed Douglas and McIntyre.[98] The house continued to focus on regional books and published its first best-selling children's picturebook in 1978, Betty Waterton's *A Salmon for Simon* (1978), illustrated by Ann Blades, about a child's relationship with his Pacific Northwest environment as he struggles to rescue a salmon trapped on the beach. Waterton remembers that she had sent the manuscript to a number of the major Toronto-based Canadian publishers before someone suggested that she should try a local publisher who might be more interested in the subject matter.[99] Blades believes that her illustrations for *A Salmon for Simon* are her best work, although she subsequently discovered that she had made an error in one of the pictures and had Simon digging a channel to free the salmon in the wrong direction from Waterton's text, which was corrected in subsequent editions by amending the narrative to match the images.[100]

'Canadian Children's Books as Works of Art': Tundra Books

While the majority of small publishers in the 1970s struggled with the physical and conceptual aspects of publishing, May Cutler of Tundra Books pursued her vision of original works of art in beautifully produced books for children. Cutler began her career as a book publisher almost by accident during Expo 67, the World Fair held in Montreal as part of Canada's centennial celebrations. Cutler self-published an autobiographical essay, *The Last Noble Savage* (1967), and a series of bilingual pamphlets on the arts.[101] After her positive experiences with self-publishing, she went on to establish Tundra Books of Canada / Les Livres Toundra, drawing on her background as an art critic to publish 150 illustrated children's books, under the rubric 'Canadian Children's Books as Works of Art.' Tundra quickly developed a distinct aesthetic identity for its picturebooks, often using noted Montreal graphic designer Rolf Harder as a designer. Cutler describes the results as a clean, readable page layout, resulting from Harder's Bauhaus training and preference for International Modernist design and sans serif Helvetica type.[102]

Ensuring printing quality was challenging for most small publishers, and Cutler remembers that she 'hung over the presses,' an editorial practice also favoured by William Toye at Oxford.[103] In the early years, the cost of full-colour reproductions, and Cutler's difficulties in locating sources of funding to offset those costs, repeatedly delayed the publication of new titles.[104] Adding to her frustration, she felt that her goal of excellence in all aspects of book design, including the reproduction of illustrations, was seriously under-appreciated by critics and funding agencies, stating in print that 'Canadian publishing for children is the most backward in the civilized world, and if it wasn't for Tundra Books, it would be virtually non-existent internationally. No purely commercial publisher in this country is interested – or can afford – to make the initial investment we put into our full color books for children. Examine any of them and compare.'[105]

In order to offset some of the initial costs by increasing the size of the print run, Tundra Books actively pursued sales in the American and international markets. Cutler opened Tundra Books of Northern New York in Plattsburgh, New York, in 1971 in order to create American editions of her books. She also pursued opportunities to license her picturebooks to both American and foreign publishers, by attending the Frankfurt Book Fair, beginning in 1976, and the Bologna Children's Book Fair the following year, although she refused to exhibit in the Canadian booth, preferring to display independently.[106] She also contacted publishers directly to enquire about their interest in her titles.[107] As she explains, Tundra did not profit from the first printing of a children's book and was dependent on international co-publications and sales to account for a major portion of its economic success.[108]

Cutler's acquisition methods were unusual. Using her sophisticated critical understanding of visual imagery, she located artists whom she believed were creating original and lasting art, and then encouraged them to write a memoir to accompany their images.[109] As Cutler explains, she chose artists because she believed that 'illustrators tend to follow styles, but a good artist is always a complete original and can't really be imitated.'[110] As editor, Cutler was active in shaping and at times rewriting the texts, explaining that she had discovered that 'artists can write. They can't necessarily make up a fictional story but if you recognize their particular field of interest, they can describe in words as well as they can with pictures.'[111]

In a political climate in Canada in which policies of multiculturalism were being debated, Tundra's memoir series treated cultural diversity as an element of daily life in Canada while sharing a commonality of viewpoint in which the past was reconsidered without nostalgia or sentiment and irony was deployed to protest against the personal and social injustices experienced by the child protagonist. Titles included William Kurelek's *A Prairie Boy's Winter* (1973) and *A Prairie Boy's Summer* (1975); Shizuye Taskashima's *A Child in Prison Camp* (1971); Sing Lim's *West Coast Chinese Boy* (1979); and John Lim's *At Grandmother's House* (1977).

Of these early works, Kurelek's books are perhaps the best known.[112] Cutler had approached Kurelek at one of his gallery shows and asked him to write and paint his memoirs. The results were a form of visual autobiography, an act of consciously and deliberately recreating the past in image and text. Like many of the other early Tundra titles, Kurelek's third-person narratives describe the life of an outsider. The William of the story is an awkward and intense boy on a Manitoba dairy farm during the Depression who fails at sports but acutely observes the natural world around him with a mystic's sense of awe.[113] The extreme unhappiness of Kurelek's childhood, shaped by his tormented relationship with his father, is muted in his picturebook memoirs, which emphasize the happier moments of his character's daily routines.[114]

Kurelek employs a combination of coloured pencil, graphite, acrylic, and watercolour to construct his meticulously detailed artwork for *A Prairie Boy's Winter* and *A Prairie Boy's Summer*. The relationship between a farming community and the land is explored through the seasonal rhythms of work and the world of childhood play, set against vast prairie skies and an endless horizon. The result was a best-seller that won multiple awards, received international recognition, and was translated into six different languages, including Norwegian, Swedish, Dutch, Danish, Finnish, and German, and was issued in Canadian, American, British, and Greenlandic editions.[115]

A Child in Prison Camp, by gallery artist Shizuye Takashima, was the first book for children on the North American internment of Japanese Canadians during the Second World War, preceding other Canadian children's books on this difficult subject by at least twenty years. Cutler extensively edited Takashima's text, reshaping the author's prose poetry into a more structured narrative.[116] In combination with Takashima's floating, translucent watercolours, the lived experience of internment, fear, and disorientation is transformed into a subtle meditation on family loyalty and community strength, loss and dislocation, and the restorative power of nature.[117]

The artist Sing Lim was also an animator for the National Film Board. His *West Coast Chinese Boy* was the first significant picturebook in Canada to consider the Chinese-Canadian experience. His memories of childhood in the racially segregated Vancouver of the 1920s delicately contrast the hostility of the Euro-Canadian citizens with the close ties of his family in Chinatown, lovingly describing the cultural life of his community. Lim used the unusual medium of oil on glass to create vivid, deeply saturated coloured images, alternating with black and white line sketches of daily activities.

5.3 William Kurelek. *A Prairie Boy's Winter*. Montreal: Tundra Books, 1973.

Taken from *A Prairie Boy's Winter* © 1973, written and illustrated by William Kurelek, published by Tundra Books, Toronto.

Mary of Mile 18: *'A Very Interesting Primitive'*

In her quest for originality, May Cutler was willing to read unsolicited manu-scripts and view the portfolios of newly emerging artists. Ann Blades, a self-taught artist, wrote and illustrated her first picturebook *Mary of Mile 18* (1971), about a girl's growing love for a part-wolf cub and the struggle with her father to keep it, during a year of teaching in a remote Mennonite community in north-eastern British Columbia on the Alaska Highway. Blades, who had turned to illustration because of her social isolation, used the inexpensive children's watercolours and rough paper available in her classroom to create a story that reflected the lives of her students and their community. Her dependence on limited materials and lack of formal artistic training shaped her naive artistic style.[118] Cutler, however, imme-diately recognized the originality and universality of the story and the freshness of the images, and worked extensively with Blades to reshape the text.

The publication of *Mary of Mile 18* began Cutler's ongoing quarrel with the Canada Council. In the days before block funding for publishers was established, Cutler sought aid to offset the costs of full-colour printing by applying to the Council for a grant.[119] In her letter of application, she argued that Blades's illus-trations had particular appeal for children because they closely resembled the way that children themselves draw and paint. As she explained, the merit of the work, which had a 'very interesting primitive' aesthetic, was apparent not only to her but to the art critics whom she had consulted. She added that the story was unique in Canadian children's writing in its portrayal of the hard life of con-temporary pioneers.[120]

Cutler was outraged when the Council turned down her request for assistance, and pressed for a reason for the negative decision. As she recalls, the manuscript 'was sent to readers for comment and they said "Isn't it a pity that with so lit-tle coming out of Canada, we can't do better than this."'[121] She then complained loudly and vociferously that publishers were subjected to an unfair, ill-informed, and biased reviewing process that did not apply to other arts sectors. When the book won the 1972 Canadian Library Association's Book of the Year for Chil-dren Award, and the Council turned down a grant to assist Blades to attend the award ceremony in Regina, Cutler launched a boycott of the Council in retali-ation.[122] Over the years, her dislike of the Council was reiterated in a series of media interviews, letters to the Council, speeches to organizations, and letters to the editors of several Canadian newspapers, including the trade paper *Quill and Quire*.[123]

Cutler's fury with the Canada Council's inability to see the quality in Blades's illustrations is even more interesting in the context of her own sharply articulated distinction between innovative artists and imitative illustrators, and her prefer-ence for the former over the latter. In her application, she positioned Blades as an innovative artist. In response, the Council seemed to be upholding a hierarchy of visual production in which fine arts are privileged over illustration and graphic arts, and rejected Blades's work as failing to meet the criteria for fine arts produc-tion. However, it was precisely the 'outsider' quality of the 'primitive' style of Blades's artwork, the very attributes that led the Canada Council to turn down the

5.4 Ann Blades. *Mary of Mile 18*. Montreal: Tundra Books, 1971.

Taken from *Mary of Mile 18* © 1971, written and illustrated by Ann Blades, published by Tundra Books, Toronto.

application for funding, that attracted Cutler to the work, and which has evoked the deepest response from readers, both in Canada and internationally.[124]

Blades went on to write and illustrate a second picturebook for Tundra, *A Boy of Taché* (1973), which was shortlisted for the 1974 Amelia Frances Howard-Gibbon Illustrator's Award. Her subsequent picturebooks for other publishers, including Betty Waterton's *A Salmon for Simon* (1978), which won the Canada Council Children's Literature Prize for Illustration, and the Amelia Frances Howard-Gibbon Illustrator's Award, and *By the Sea: An Alphabet Book* (1985), which won Elizabeth Mrazik-Cleaver Canadian Picture Book Award, confirmed Cutler's initial belief that she was a significant illustrator with a fresh vision and a distinctive voice.

'Canadian Children's Literature Needs Serious Scrutiny': Awards, Criticism, and Reviewing

The contretemps between May Cutler and the Canada Council highlights the importance of awards for children's publishers. The renewed interest in children's literary production in Canada was furthered by the work of Canadian librarians to promote Canadian books. Literary awards and prizes established by government cultural bodies and by library, bookselling, and professional associations recognized the contributions of authors and illustrators to the literature. The Canadian Library Association created the Amelia Frances Howard-Gibbon Illustrator's Award in 1971 to recognize excellence in illustration. In 1975, the Canada Council Children's Literature Prizes were awarded for the first time. The following year, the Canadian Booksellers' Association established the Ruth Schwartz Children's Book Award, administered by the Ontario Arts Council. Award ceremonies and the attendant publicity were designed to raise public awareness of the literature and its place in children's lives, although general media attention and increased institutional and retail sales did not necessarily follow.

In the wake of the Ontario Royal Commission, which raised particularly troubling questions about the educational market and Canadian identity, further research was carried out to explore what Canadian children were reading. Major studies, including John P. Wilkinson's *Canadian Juvenile Fiction and the Library Market*, clearly demonstrated the lack of institutional support for Canadian publications, even award-winning Canadian children's books.[125] For example, while 28, or 82 per cent, of the 34 public libraries surveyed by Wilkinson held a copy of *Mary of Mile 18*, only 22, or 20 per cent, of the 111 school libraries had a copy. The study also inadvertently demonstrated the degree to which Canadian school libraries were 'buying around,' in other words, ordering Canadian titles from an American wholesaler rather than buying from a Canadian source.[126]

It was clear that those responsible for purchasing children's materials for school and public libraries needed better access to reviews and information about new titles, as well as a commitment to developing Canadian collections. As a result, new reviewing and professional journals were developed. The Canadian Library Association published *CM: A Reviewing Journal of Canadian Materials for Young People* from 1971 to 1994. Originally an annual bibliography, it evolved into a journal published six times a year, featuring articles and reviews of direct curricular interest for teacher-librarians and teachers.[127]

In 1973, *Emergency Librarian* was founded as a 'Canadian librarians' underground newsletter,' offering an alternative, feminist-oriented voice in a field in which the majority of professional librarians were women, managed by a small cadre of men.[128] From 1973 to 1979 the newsletter cum journal was edited primarily by Sherrill Cheda and Phyllis Yaffe. Significantly, the first article published was 'Sex-Role Stereotyping in Children's Books: Sources.' The co-editorship and publishing responsibilities were taken up by school library administrators and advocates Ken Haycock and Carol-Ann Haycock in 1979, who shifted the focus of the publication to library services for children and young adults in schools and public libraries, including columns, bibliographies, lists, and reviews of professional reading and print and audio-visual resources for youth.[129]

In 1975, *Canadian Children's Literature / Littérature canadienne pour la jeunesse*, the first scholarly, peer-reviewed journal devoted to Canadian children's literature, was established by the University of Guelph's English Department faculty Mary Rubio, John Sorfleet, Glenys Stow, and Elizabeth Waterston, offering scholars the opportunity to study Canadian culture through the lens of anglophone and francophone children's literature.[130] Authors crossed the boundaries between the scholarly and professional spheres as they discussed the role of children's literature in cultural formation.[131] Rubio remembers that the initial reception was somewhat uneven. 'People laughed at us when we started [the journal], saying there wasn't enough of an industry to write about it. If you write about it and increase people's awareness of it, then that helps create the market and therefore helps the industry, and I think CCL did that.'[132]

Sheila Egoff had been working on revisions to *The Republic of Childhood: A Critical Guide to Canadian Children's Literature in English*, and in 1975, an expanded second edition was published. Although she acknowledged that the field of Canadian writing for children had altered and grown since the first edition was released, she firmly believed that quality was still lacking. She remembered that as she finished work on the manuscript, she put her head down on top of her typewriter and wept, believing that 'there had been no appreciable change in Canadian children's literature since 1967 … I concluded that the problem with Canadian children's books was the banality of the writing and the predictable fictional situations that many Canadian authors created. In the mid-seventies, I saw no future in Canada for literature for young people.'[133] However, some critics also questioned the limitations of her methodology, arguing that a survey of literary genres with annotated checklists had failed to address the need for a critical evaluation and synthesis of Canadian children's literature.[134]

'Meant to be Enjoyed by Children': Reviewing in the Popular Media

The popular media slowly began to expand their coverage of Canadian children's literature. In 1971, *Books in Canada* was established 'to bring every worthwhile Canadian book to the attention of readers wherever there is a library or a bookstore,' stating that 'our own books remain the most accurate record and reflection of what kind of people we really are.'[135] The magazine's commitment to children's literature was less secure. The editors, perhaps imbued with new notions of child empowerment, explained that they believed that reviews written by the intended readers would help children and their parents to choose books that would be enjoyed.[136] So, while books by authors including Alice Munro and Michael Ondaatje were reviewed by Margaret Laurence, Jane Rule, and Margaret Atwood, among others, William Toye and Elizabeth Cleaver's *How Summer Came to Canada* was reviewed by Emma, age nine, who praised the work 'because of the magical and beautiful way in which the author and illustrator put it ... The pictures look really real.'[137] Their decision reinforced the critical distinction that continued to be made between serious literature worthy of serious review, and children's literature, which required no specialized critical skill to appreciate or evaluate.

In an era when parents were being encouraged to take a more active role in their children's education, magazines directed at women readers and daily newspapers publishing in major urban centres also increased their reviewing of children's books. William French, literary editor of the *Globe and Mail* from 1960 to 1990, regularly included information about children's authors, publishers, and publishing in his columns. Janet Lunn's reviews for the *Globe and Mail* were praised for having a sound philosophy of criticism, based on the belief that 'children deserve only the best,' a sentiment familiar to readers of Sheila Egoff's work.[138] Michele Landsberg, who began working at the *Globe and Mail* in 1962, also 'took up the cause of children's books' as literary works, 'every bit as complex and demanding in their execution as adult literature,' and worthy of respect despite having been 'slighted for so many generations as mere trivia.'[139] Landsberg also expanded her reviewing to include other media, including a monthly column on children's books for *Chatelaine* magazine. She notes that she was shocked when she received letters from children's librarians in communities with limited access to books, asking for recommendations.[140]

In 1976, an exhibit of children's book illustration at the Norman Mackenzie Art Gallery in Regina drew attention to the importance of children's illustrated books. The exhibit comprised books and original art lent to the gallery from collections across Canada and the United States, including rare treasures from the Toronto Public Library's Osborne Collection, and original illustrations by two Canadians, James Houston and Frank Newfeld. Unusual for the time, the catalogue prepared for the exhibit called on gallery attendees to attend to book design and the peritext in picturebooks and consider the interaction of image and text on the page in order to become better informed consumers of children's literature.[141]

The National Library of Canada and the Canadian Children's Literature Service

In July 1973, as part of Festival Canada, the National Library of Canada organized an exhibit, *Notable Canadian Children's Books / Un choix de livres canadiens pour la jeunesse,* tracing the history of Canadian children's literature from earliest times to the contemporary period. An annotated catalogue prepared by Sheila Egoff and Alvine Bélisle, former director of the Office of School Libraries of the Quebec Department of Public Instruction, and instructor in children's literature at the

University of Montreal, accompanied the groundbreaking exhibit, and formed the first chronological record of anglophone and francophone Canadian children's literature. Subsequent to the festival in Ottawa, the exhibit was sent on tour in central and eastern Canada.[142]

In the same year, the Canadian Library Association and the Association canadienne des bibliothécaires de langue française presented a brief to the Secretary of State requesting the appointment of a children's librarian/consultant at the National Library.[143] The brief argued that a specialist was needed to organize and administer the existing collection of Canadian children's titles acquired through the copyright deposit program, augment the collection, and raise the profile of Canadian children's literature.[144] As a result, in 1975, Irene Aubrey was appointed as chief of the newly organized Children's Literature Service of the National Library of Canada, with a mandate to implement many of the recommendations of the brief.[145] During her tenure, Aubrey made the new unit a focal point for the study and criticism of Canadian children's literature. She coordinated the unification of the scattered collections of children's books, which allowed her to identify significant early Canadian titles that were missing from the National Library's collection. She encouraged children's authors and illustrators to deposit their papers and original artwork with the Library's Literary Manuscripts collection.[146]

Aubrey also coordinated a range of thematic bibliographies and catalogues of best books that assisted other libraries in developing quality collections of Canadiana, including the bilingual annotated series *Notable Canadian Children's Books / Un choix de livres canadiens pour la jeunesse*, first issued in 1976 as an update of Egoff and Bélisle's 1973 catalogue, and updated annually or biennially until 1993, and the 1976 *Canadian Children's Books: A Treasury of Pictures / Livres canadiens d'enfants: Un trésor d'images*.[147] She instituted a series of displays and events that helped bring together teachers, librarians, children's literature scholars, writers, and publishers, beginning with the exhibits prepared for the Montreal International Book Fair and the Pacific Rim Conference on Children's Literature in 1976. The 1979 exhibit and annotated catalogue *Pictures to Share: Illustration in Canadian Children's Books / Images pour tous: Illustration de livres canadiens pour enfants*, mounted in celebration of the International Year of the Child, brought new attention to historic and contemporary Canadian children's illustrators.[148]

As part of her mandate to promote Canadian children's literature, Irene Aubrey represented Canada's children's writers, illustrators, publishers, and books at the Children's Book Fair at Bologna, Italy, and at the International Children's Youth Library in Munich. In 1980, IBBY-Canada, the Canadian national section of the International Board on Books for Young People, was established to foster knowledge in Canada and abroad of Canadian children's books after years of planning and negotiating by Aubrey, Canada's official liaison to IBBY from 1975 to 1980, and a like-minded group of advocates.[149]

'They're Coming in the Windows': Children's Literature Conferences and Academic Programs

As the study of children's literature developed within the academy and professionals took greater interest in Canadian materials, academic and professional conferences on children's literature acted as forums for the exchange of creative knowledge and publishing information. In 1975, the Eighth International Loughborough Conference on Children's Literature was held at the University of Toronto, followed by the Pacific Rim Conference on Children's Literature at the University of British Columbia in 1976, and the first Kaleidoscope, Canadian Rockies Conference on Literature for Children and Youth in Calgary in 1977.

Sheila Egoff, who organized the Pacific Rim Conference, remarked on the response to the 'Canada Day' portion of the conference, during which the attendance tripled to over 800 people. The event proved to be so popular that she remembers that her student assistants came to her and said, 'Sheila, they're coming in the windows, they're coming in the doors.' She responded by telling them to let everyone in, adding that she realized that 'Canada Day' could have been extended over several days during the conference.[150] Despite the popularity of the event, Egoff felt it necessary to comment in the published conference proceedings that the Canada Day papers 'are not to be thought of as a nationalistic intrusion in an international conference' but 'a comprehensive view of the state of children's literature in Canada within an international context.'[151]

The academy slowly began to acknowledge the value of children's literature as a topic for academic research and study. Courses in children's literature had long been staples in faculties of education and schools of librarianship, but were not taught in English departments, where the modernist canonization of literature had excluded consideration of literature by women or for children.[152] The 1975 thematic issue of *Canadian Children's Literature* on the work of L.M. Montgomery was the first serious academic consideration of her writing in a scholarly journal and represented the beginning of the rethinking of the distinction between 'serious' and 'popular' Canadian literature promoted by professional and academic critics in the interwar period.[153] Kieran Kealy of the University of British Columbia's Department of English, in discussing his institution's reluctance to institute a senior-level credit for a children's literature course, explains that Egoff's *The Republic of Childhood*, which introduced Canadian children's literature to the academic community, was instrumental in persuading his colleagues that the subject had sufficient merit and breadth of scholarship to justify its inclusion in the department's course offerings.[154]

As well as academic study of the literary analysis of children's literature, and courses for the professions in the selection and use of literature in classroom and library settings, courses on the creation of the literature were offered in universities for the first time. In 1980, at the University of British Columbia's Creative Writing Department, children's author Sue Ann Alderson developed the first courses for writing for children offered by a Canadian degree-granting academic program. Many students who had the opportunity to write picturebooks and novels for their BFA and MFA theses found publishers for their work because of the experience they gained in the program. Alderson was the first children's writer and first woman hired by a creative writing department in Canada as a full-time tenure-track member, the first to teach credit courses in writing for children, and the only full professor and Acting Head who taught children's writing and remained active in the children's literature community.[155]

The first Children's Literature Roundtable was established in Edmonton in the fall of 1977 by Ronald Jobe and Annabelle Bourgoin, consultants with the Edmonton Public School Board, and Dianne Woodman, a bookseller, to provide a forum where school and library professionals, researchers and students, and booksellers could discuss children's books and meet the writers and illustrators who created them. When Jobe moved to the University of British Columbia's Department of Language Education in the Faculty of Education in 1978, he shared the idea with his colleagues, and the Vancouver Children's Literature Roundtable was launched.[156] Subsequently, roundtables have been organized across the country and have had a strong influence on building community and spirit among a broad cross-section of people with an interest in children's books.

The Children's Book Store: Leading the Way

Two centres that benefited the Canadian children's literature and publishing communities were established in Toronto a few years apart – the Children's Book Store in 1974 and in 1976 the Children's Book Centre (renamed the Canadian Children's Book Centre in 1987). Both supported the development of Canadian children's books and were significant marketing and promotional forces locally and across Canada.

The Children's Book Store in Toronto, owned by Judy and Hy Sarick, was the largest independent specialist bookstore for the young in North America when it opened in 1974. Judy Sarick, who had worked as a children's librarian in the Toronto Public Library, and as a teacher-librarian and head of School Libraries at the Toronto Board of Education, was determined to create a space where people involved in the children's publishing industry could meet and learn from each other.[157] A range of well-publicized activities from readings to signings welcomed children, teachers, parents, librarians, and the creators and publishers.[158] During school visits to the store, classes were invited to participate in selecting books for purchase for the classroom. Sarick believed these visits taught children 'to be intelligent consumers of books as well as readers ... I always said the bookstore was like a library except that you didn't have to bring the books back.'[159]

Sarick refused to stock formulaic literature, including the popular mass-produced children's mystery series. As she explained, she was adhering to the selection criteria she had learned at the Toronto Public Library, promoting 'only the best in children's literature ... in the store.'[160] She applied her rigorous standards of evaluation to Canadian as well as non-Canadian titles, rejecting books that did not meet her criteria for excellence. As Ian Wallace explains, Sarick 'could make or break books especially from small experimental houses like Kids Can Press. Our books became more professional in part because she demanded quality in her store ... She made us understand that if we wanted to play in the big leagues, we had to do better.'[161] Patsy Aldana of Groundwood Books comments that Sarick was critically engaged in her work, understood what publishers were trying to achieve, and praised her for consistently promoting Canadian children's books on award panels and juries.[162]

In 1978, as a result of the Ontario government's Wintario Half-back Program, in which one could redeem half of a non-winning lottery ticket towards the purchase of a Canadian-authored book, the store moved into wholesaling. As Sarick remembers, 'We had over 70,000 tickets and the government gave us back the money … [The program] made us realize we could actually sell to schools and libraries … That was the best promotion for Canadian children's literature in the history of publishing.'[163] Author Celia Lottridge, who worked at the store during the Wintario program, explains that not only did it stimulate interest in Canadian books, it focused the attention of publishers on the potential market for Canadian children's books.[164]

The Canadian Children's Book Centre: The Glue That Held It All Together

In 1976, after recommendations in briefs and background papers to the Ontario Royal Commission on Publishing, and after many years of lobbying by several groups and organizations, the Children's Book Centre began as a pilot project under the auspices of the Book and Periodical Development Council, with Irma McDonough serving as the interim director.[165] In March 1977, to further the work of the project, a group of librarians, publishers, booksellers, and educators formed a board of directors and applied for Canada Council funding to develop the centre. In May of the same year, Phyllis Yaffe, editor of *Emergency Librarian*, was appointed executive director.[166] Financial support from the Ontario Arts Council and the Canada Council made it possible for the centre to act as a promotional organization and information clearing house, with the mandate of raising public consciousness of Canadian children's books.[167] Through its programs and publications, it serves publishers, booksellers, teachers, and librarians, as well as the general public, and encourages publishers to donate copies of their titles to the centre's library, which acts as a depository collection for researchers.

From 1949 through 1974, the Canadian Library Association organized 'Young Canada's Book Week' under the auspices of the Canadian Association of Children's Librarians.[168] In November 1977, the Children's Book Centre revived the idea as the Children's Book Festival and began to arrange tours for children's book creators, funded by the Canada Council.[169] The tours, and public readings in schools and libraries across the country, funded by the Council and by provincial arts councils, would become a popular way to connect authors and illustrators with communities of readers.

Ian Wallace notes that touring was critical in his early career, when his publisher did not have a budget for promotion. As he explains, 'the Centre had a huge impact getting the word out about Canadian books … [and] promoted the careers of young authors, making us visible to Canadians.'[170] The writer Sandy Frances Duncan adds that 'in the 1970s, we were cultural pioneers. I like to think that one of the reasons the current generation of Canadian children's books is of such high calibre is due to the number of writers criss-crossing the country giving workshops and readings in schools and libraries under the aegis of the Children's Book Centre.'[171]

The wide range of publications from the centre added to the resource base of information on Canadian children's literature, including the *Children's Book News*, the annual *Our Choice* catalogue of recommended books and audio-visual materials, and the many thematic bibliographies and activity guides, including the *Meet the Author* series of biographies.[172] Gillian O'Reilly, freelance writer and current editor of the *Canadian Children's Book News*, notes that the centre has provided invaluable support to children's book creators and publishers. It 'has provided a vehicle for making books, authors and illustrators better known. It has provided a venue for interaction among Canadian publishers and between Canadian publishers and their counterparts in other countries.'[173]

'We Had a Sense That It Was OK to Be a Writer'

Before the mid-1970s, many Canadian authors and illustrators for children were geographically dispersed and had limited contact with other creators. For some, the Canadian Authors Association had provided connection with other writers. Jean Little remembers, 'I felt isolated in my writing in the early years as I didn't know any writers. At a Canadian Authors Association ceremony when I received the Little, Brown award for my first book, *Mine for Keeps*, I was so excited that I was going to meet real writers for the first time. I sat at a table where everyone wrote textbooks and was horribly boring.'[174]

The Writers' Union of Canada, founded in 1973, which lobbies government and cultural agencies for its members' interests and concerns, has provided a social network and community support to some children's authors. Janet Lunn observes, 'I was drawn to the Union because it was organized to get a better deal for writers. I thought I might be able to work on getting better relations between publishers and writers ... And the union had room for all genres. I liked that.'[175] Sandy Frances Duncan remembers, 'Five of us new writers joined in 1977 ... and found a community there. We had a sense that it was OK to be a writer and to be a writer of children's books. I never felt in the Writers' Union that children's writers were treated differently from writers of other forms.'[176]

However, other members note that there were continuing tensions, often based on the perception that writers of adult fiction received a different level of respect, access to grants, and ability to negotiate contracts than did writers for children. As Sue Ann Alderson tartly notes, 'We were beggars, scratching at doors with pleas to publishers to publish our books.'[177] Some children's authors also felt ridicule from those who wrote for adults, particularly in the Writers' Union. Norma Charles remembers that adult writers at Writers' Union meetings used 'terms such as "Kiddy Litter" for children's writing and writers.' While she was bothered by the lack of respect shown to children's writers, she believes that non-fiction writers and poets 'felt that same lack of respect.'[178] Similarly, Claire Mackay observes that among adult writers who had not tried writing for children, 'there was barely concealed contempt. No one had an understanding that fine picturebooks or children's novels take as much creativity and work as adult writing ... Women were more sympathetic than the academic males who wrote fiction and thought we were little old ladies in running shoes ... The attitude was dismissive of us and we felt fragile.'[179] Janet Lunn sees this dismissive attitude as part of the generalized lack of understanding in society as a whole to anything involving attitudes to children's culture, explaining that 'children's writers know the books written for adults, the other writers do not generally know the children's books – even when they are parents ... When it comes to negotiating contracts, writers of books for adults generally get bigger advances – but then, their books don't always stay in print as long as ours do.'[180]

'It Was a Kinship Connection': The Formation of CANSCAIP

In 1977, formation of the Canadian Society of Children's Authors, Illustrators and Performers (CANSCAIP) brought together children's writers with illustrators and performers for children, who were excluded from membership in the Writers' Union. The initial impetus was a Canada Day Conference organized in 1977 by the Port Colborne Public Library, during which some of the participants discussed their need for professional stimulation and collegial support. As Claire Mackay, one of the founders explains, the inclusion of illustrators was important, as they were not represented in other professional organizations. For Mackay, CANSCAIP 'was a kinship connection, and felt like a family ... We were out to claim our rights and find our identity.'[181]

To disseminate information about the work of its members, CANSCAIP publishes a newsletter and compilations of biographical profiles of its members, and organizes programs, workshops, and touring illustration exhibits. The association has also developed links with the children's literature community by instituting an associate member category for aspiring authors and illustrators, teachers, librarians and parents, and others interested in Canadian children's culture.[182]

The Canada Council, Government Funding, and a New Generation of Writers and Illustrators

The expansion and diversification of children's book markets and the growth of opportunities for children's book creators with the emergence of new publishers in the 1970s was a heady experience for writers and illustrators. Janet Lunn remembers that when she first visited schools to talk about her work, 'teachers and librarians would say in very matter-of-fact tones, "Oh, I never read Canadian books."' The situation changed as authors began to tour with the help of the Canada Council and the Children's Book Centre, and developed public profiles.[183] Similarly, Ian Wallace remembers that the period 'was a terribly exciting time, with the publishing world bursting open ... Creators, aficionados, publishers, and teachers felt there was a possibility for a Canadian children's literature to develop that could reflect Canadian children's realities and lives.'[184] Writer Claire Mackay remembers that she 'felt like a pioneer at the birth of a national literature ... There were new publishers, patriotism, money, new confidence and skill among writers [who had] honed their craft in the educational publications ... [and a] sense that we had built something. We were telling our own stories; we had a public voice.'[185]

Book week tours, school visits, public library readings, and activities such as young authors' conferences raised the profile of children's authors and writers, and helped to provide an important source of income for struggling creators.[186] Readings by children's writers built a welcoming audience of adults and children, and helped create a new community of readers, who for the first time saw themselves in the books they were reading. The increase in Canada Council funding and the institution of provincial arts council grants for public readings helped to connect Canadian writers and readers. Children's librarians, teacher-librarians, teachers, booksellers, and parents became more vocal advocates and promoters of a national literature. Growing budgets for school and public library acquisitions also directly helped to sustain the creators through royalties received on institutional sales.[187]

Many authors and illustrators have commented on the profound significance of governmental financial support, not just on their personal incomes but on the Canadian social and cultural community the judicious use of public money has created. Eugenie Fernandes describes how touring has helped to connect non-metropolitan readers with authors. In her encounters with children during author visits, 'the books become real things to them.' She remembers that after one reading, 'a little boy came back into the room after everyone had left, [and] stood there silently looking at me. He touched me and said, "I just wanted to make sure that you were real." Because of the government support, these children find out that, yes, we are indeed real.'[188]

The financial challenges, however, remained. As Norma Charles comments, 'The wave of 1970s writers had a strong emotional drive to create Canadian children's books ... Nonetheless it was still hard to get published, because Canada had fewer markets and fewer books published from each publisher.'[189] And, as Claire Mackay has noted, 'The founding of the Children's Book Centre and CANSCAIP set us all aflame. Unfortunately this also set us up and gave us a number of false expectations for our future. We all thought that with the number of dedicated and enthusiastic children's publishers and sufficient funding from the government, we were set for a life career. But in a few years, by the early 1980s, we realized we might be better off than the Canadian poets, but not much.'[190]

'A Great Feeling of Camaraderie'

Smaller publishers, who had begun their careers in relative isolation, gradually developed professional networks. Initially there was little infrastructure to support children's publishing. New publishers had to learn the business and mechanics of publishing, and work out how to distribute and market their books on their own. According to Rick Wilks, 'there wasn't much community. There was an understanding that we had mutual interests and a lot of commonality in terms of problems to resolve, but we hadn't set out in any kind of cooperative way to deal with those things.'[191] By the end of the decade, as Patsy Aldana remembers, children's publishers had become 'a very close-knit group' and the most effective group within the Association of Canadian Publishers.[192] By the time Ricky Englander joined Valerie Hussey as co-publisher of Kids Can Press in 1981, she found that 'there was a great feeling of camaraderie. We were all speaking to each other and we were all seeing a lot of the same material. We would talk back and forth and freely share information.'[193]

The 1970s had been a period of dramatic transition from the model of Canadian children's publishing within large, foreign-owned, branch plant publishers to an alternative model of viable, independent, Canadian-owned small presses. New writers and illustrators had reason to believe that they could sustain careers in children's literature within Canada. By the end of the decade, the new generation of publishers, writers, and illustrators had matured and were about to have a significant role to play in reshaping the market for children's literature.

CHAPTER SIX

The 1980s: The Flowering of Canadian Children's Illustrated Books

In the 1980s, the Canadian publishing scene for children expanded rapidly. Knowledgeable authors, illustrators, and editors, and a new focus on the design and marketing of children's titles, transformed children's illustrated books. Strong international co-publishing agreements and foreign rights sales increased publishing of Canadian editions of foreign titles, and joint projects between trade and educational publishers expanded the economic potential for growth. Affluent baby-boomer parents who supported specialty children's book stores, widening media coverage, and increasingly popular events like writers' festivals and author tours all helped to bring Canadian children's books to a broadening market, and in the process reshaped the industry.

'A Strong Sense of Excellence': Developing Professionalism

A sustainable market had to develop before writers, illustrators, editors, and publishers could fully develop careers comparable to those of their peers in Britain and the United States. Tim Wynne-Jones points out that the publishers of the 1970s were driven by an approach that was didactic and highly moralistic, based on an ideological commitment 'to look at sexism and racism and any other isms we could root out in children's literature.' A professional approach to editing and design was not the first priority. As he remembers, 'There was not a lot of literary interest or expertise ... But a firm belief in the importance of literature was at the base of the experiment and the belief that our own values and newly expanded consciences had a right to be in print.'[1]

The lack of seasoned professionals in the children's publishing community in Canada meant that editors continued to develop their skills by trial and error on the job. As Valerie Hussey, former publisher of Kids Can Press observes, 'After thirty years we just now have the doyennes and the mentor/protégé relationships so that the next generation is being taught by an experienced group. That experienced group, the mentors, all had to learn on their own. There is that process of passing on when you start to let go and be more comfortable in your own shoes because the ground that you stand on is firm, and that takes time.'[2]

The learning curve for a new editor could be steep. Ricky Englander, former co-publisher with Valerie Hussey of Kids Can Press, was working as a librarian at the Canadian Children's Book Centre when Hussey asked her to join the press. As a result of her training in 'the principles of children's literature,' learned at the Toronto Public Library 'at the hands of the mistresses of children's literature in Canada,' she had developed 'a strong sense of excellence.' She adds wryly, 'It made me a very difficult person to work with, because … I had the sense that what we did had to be better than what anyone else did.' Englander concludes that the discussions that she had with Hussey regarding editorial decisions were critical. Had she been working on her own, she would never have published anything, 'because nothing would ever have been good enough.'[3]

The importance of mentoring is particularly noticeable in the history of Peter Martin Associates (PMA Books), founded by Peter and Carol Martin in 1965 and sold in 1982. PMA published a relatively small number of finely produced children's books, most notably the 1980 Northern Lights series of six Canadian historical picturebooks.[4] Their real influence, however, was in the subsequent careers of the young editors and publishers who learned the essentials of their craft at PMA. Patsy Aldana, who also volunteered at Women's Press, went on to found Groundwood Books. Tim Wynne-Jones, who worked as a designer at PMA, became a children's writer published by Groundwood, the children's book reviewer for the *Globe and Mail*, and the first children's book editor for Red Deer College Press. Michael Solomon, today Groundwood's art director, took over the position of designer at PMA from Wynne-Jones, with whom he subsequently formed a design firm. Peter Carver moved first to the Canadian Children's Book Centre, where he organized their publishing program and coordinated Children's Book Week, and later succeeded Wynne-Jones as children's editor at Red Deer Press, until his retirement in 2007. Shelley Tanaka became the fiction editor at Groundwood Books and an award-winning writer of non-fiction for children. Valerie Wyatt moved first to *Owl* magazine as editor and has written and edited many of the popular science and math titles for Kids Can Press.

Stretching the Boundaries: New Technologies

Throughout the decade, children's book design developed a new level of sophistication. Although the cost of producing illustrated books had been somewhat ameliorated in 1972 with the introduction of Canada Council Block Grant funding to publishers, it was still prohibitively expensive to print in full colour in Canada. Continuing problems with the choice of papers, the availability of printers, antiquated typesetting technologies, and budgetary limitations all restricted design choices.[5] The move in the late 1980s to using offshore companies for colour separations, printing, and binding rapidly changed the look of Canadian picturebooks by expanding the technological possibilities of fully integrated image and text on the page.[6]

At the same time, publishers increasingly redirected their lists from the institutional to the trade book market. North American and British publishers all developed picturebooks designed explicitly for the non-bookstore retail market and stretched the age range of the target audience for illustrated books. Book formats designed for babies and toddlers, including waterproof books for the bath, books printed on cloth 'pages,' sturdy board books with thick cardboard pages, and sim-ple pop-up books and flap books, were marketed equally as toys and as a way to introduce the conventions of book handling at the earliest opportunity to very young children. Increasingly sophisticated movable books designed by 'paper engineers' and assembled by pieceworkers in developing countries, challenged the two-dimensionality of the printed page, added an element of surprise to the picturebook, and blurred the boundaries between the book as an object of aesthetic appreciation and the book as an information container.[7]

Even though there were still technical limitations at the beginning of the dec-ade, Canadian publishers increasingly recognized that design was an important function of book production, particularly as they developed and expanded their children's picturebook lists. Some appointed specialist book designers, while oth-ers contracted freelance designers for specific projects. The disparate fields of com-mercial art, graphic design, and children's book illustration continued to converge. Canadian colleges of art and design were graduating increasing numbers of artists who had design training and were equally competent in children's book illustra-tion, advertising, editorial and commercial art, although the majority required stu-dents to choose between degree programs in the fine arts and degree programs in design. It would be increasingly difficult for a self-educated illustrator to find a publisher willing to take the risk of developing their technical expertise with the specifics of book production.[8]

Selling to the United States and Overseas

Throughout the 1980s, there were vigorous debates about the sustainability of the Canadian publishing industry, the relevance of the agency system, and the abil-ity of the federal government to support Canadian cultural production through grants and subsidies.[9] Canadian publishers increasingly saw the potential of inter-national sales to address the systemic limits of the domestic market.[10] The sale of foreign rights generated needed revenue to support domestic production as well as increased royalties for authors and illustrators. Co-publication of illustrated books, in which publishers share an initial colour print run and then use separate black plates to add the text in the appropriate language, allowed Canadian pub-lishers to lower their initial production costs and extend their print runs beyond the numbers that they could hope to sell in the domestic market.[11]

Facilitated by grants from the Department of External Affairs, Canadian chil-dren's publishers first began to exhibit at the Bologna Children's Book Fair (the Fiera del Libro per Ragazzi) in 1976.[12] Some participants initially complained that government policy regarding the international fairs did not meet their particular economic realities, as partial subsidies for travel limited the ability of small pub-lishers to participate, and the criteria for state support initially made four-colour co-publications unattractive to foreign publishers.[13] The benefits of expansion into international publishing outweighed the structural challenges, however, and by the late 1980s children's publishers were attending Bologna and the International Frankfurt Book Fair (the Frankfurter Buchmesse) in increasing numbers. Some publishers, like May Cutler of Tundra Books, arranged for authors to attend Bologna to garner further attention for books available for co-publication agreements.[14] The opportunities to develop professional contacts and keep track of new trends further convinced children's publishers to persevere at the international rights fairs, although the experience left some feeling like new initiates in a club where everyone knew everyone else.[15]

The international bookfairs, the Salon du livre in Montreal, and the American Booksellers Association Trade Exhibit (now BookExpo America) all became important venues to generate publicity for Canadian titles, pursue sale of foreign and translation rights, and arrange co-publication with international publishers.[16] The burgeoning children's publishing market in the United States, driven by retail expansion and strong institutional support, was equally eager to bid for rights to Canadian titles and arrange for co-publications, sometimes acquiring an entire season's list from a Canadian publisher.[17] Some publishers even anticipated the day when a single print run of an English-language title would be shared among all the publishers participating in that edition, with centralized distribution to the various countries involved.[18]

'Freedom for Creation': Groundwood Books

The rapid expansion of the children's retail market and changes to the school curriculum that decreased the use of authorized textbooks in place of a wider range of trade publications stimulated a new group of Canadian children's publishers to join the existing small collectives and independent houses. Each brought a diversity of viewpoints and approaches and a pragmatic willingness to attend to the business of publishing in pursuit of creating viable children's lists for Canadian readers. The balancing of nationalist commitment with careful business planning is typified by Patsy Aldana's description of the inception of Groundwood Books as 'an act of optimism born from the belief that Canadian children were entitled to find their own lives and experiences in their books.'[19] The history of Groundwood's commitment to quality, commercial viability, and national identity provides a case study for the development of independent children's publishing in Canada in the 1980s.

Aldana was born in Guatemala to a Guatemalan father and an American mother and grew up with an awareness of the complex and subtle dynamics of class discrimination and cultural marginalization. In 1971, she moved to Canada, disillusioned with life in the United States during the Vietnam War. After teaching art history at York University, she found employment as a bookseller at the Toy Shop in Toronto and gained experience in publishing at Women's Press and Peter Martin Associates.[20] In 1978, she established Groundwood Books while simultaneously serving as the president of the Association of Canadian Publishers.[21]

From the outset, Aldana was determined that the children's books she intended to publish would be distinct. The house's first list was issued in the fall of 1978 and consisted of Brian Doyle's first novel, *Hey Dad*, and two picturebooks, Blair Drawson's *Flying Dimitri*, and *Geranimal, Daddy Lion, and Other Stories* by Francesca Vivenza.[22] The new publishing house was launched at the Children's Book Store in Toronto. The party was shared with Vancouver's Douglas and McIntyre, who were celebrating the publication of Betty Waterton and Ann Blades's *A Salmon for Simon*, which Aldana had helped to edit.[23]

In 1979, Aldana took on the position of Toronto manager for Douglas and McIntyre, while serving a second term as ACP president and policy researcher.[24] Douglas and McIntyre served initially as Groundwood's distributor and then as their partner in a complex relationship unique in Canadian publishing. Groundwood became an imprint of Douglas and McIntyre, with Aldana retaining ownership of her company while also serving as their children's publisher.[25] As she notes, the Douglas and McIntyre arrangement was critical for the growth of her company, giving her 'a more secure base from which to negotiate international co-publishing deals for expensive classic picturebooks.'[26]

Aldana served as publisher, editor, and art director, drawing on her knowledge of art history and children's literature to create what she called the 'library list – a list of the highest quality with real voices of illustrators and authors that weren't mainstream, with freedom for creation, with strong editorial standards and good design.'[27] As the press grew, editorial responsibilities were gradually distributed among the small staff. Fiction editor Shelley Tanaka notes that 'virtually all editorial work is handled in-house. We seldom use freelancers. Patsy has always done the acquisition and first edit of all picturebooks. [She] is the driving force behind everything that Groundwood does and stands for.'[28]

Aldana and Michael Solomon share responsibility for the art direction, or what she calls 'the editing of pictures, as opposed to the editing of text.'[29] As art director, Solomon strives for 'clarity, balance, appropriate communication of authorial intent, tone, theme; harmony with the pictures and words.'[30] Titles published by the house have a distinctive look, adapted to the needs of the text, reflecting Aldana's interest in the aesthetics of picturebooks and Solomon's skilled integration of illustration, typeface, and peritextual elements. The ideal result, according to Solomon, is a picturebook in which there is a sympathetic relationship between text and illustrations, a ready communication of theme, mood and period, and surprise and dissonance 'when fruitful and interesting.'[31]

Groundwood pioneered the first sophisticated fantasy picturebooks in Canada with the *Zoom* trilogy, written by Tim Wynne-Jones and illustrated by Ken Nutt (using his illustrator's pseudonym Eric Beddows for the third book). Wynne-Jones, who is inspired by 'the idea that we build the world with our imagination,' creates a series of narratives in which the eponymous cat protagonist and his companion, the enigmatic, gypsyish Maria, explore meticulously realized imaginative worlds, from an endless ocean enclosed within a small room in *Zoom at Sea* (1983), to a voyage to the North Pole to rescue Zoom's Uncle Roy in *Zoom Away* (1985), to the ancient Egyptian world in *Zoom Upstream* (1992).[32]

The subtle wit and mystery of the tales are aptly extended by Ken Nutt's detailed black-and-white graphite drawings in which Zoom's world is fully realized as an internally coherent three-dimensional space that at the same time makes the fantasy of the narrative apparent. Nutt's domestic interiors evoke the 1930s, a deliberate reference to his paternal grandparents. He explains that 'they lived in a modern bungalow, but they'd never thrown out a piece of furniture in their

6.1 Tim Wynne-Jones. *Zoom Away*. Illustrated by Ken Nutt. A Groundwood Book.
Toronto and Vancouver: Douglas and McIntyre, 1985.
Reprinted with the permission of the publisher, Groundwood Books.

very long lives and so going to the basement was like going on an archival dig ...
Because they didn't throw anything out, the house was kind of layered with patterns on patterns, and great floral wallpaper, all of which I thought was so beautiful.'[33] Throughout the series, Zoom remains an abstracted idea of a cat, while the figure of Maria changes over the trilogy from a cartoon figure in the first two titles into a sensuous and sensual goddess by the third book, a transformation that was a deliberate decision on the part of the illustrator to capture the archetypal quality of her character.[34]

In the late 1970s, Ian Wallace was hoping to develop his career beyond the possibilities offered by the Kids Can collective. Wanting the opportunity to write and illustrate 'a full-colour, hardcover, jacketed book that was internationally published' and frustrated by the lack of opportunity in Canada, he decided to travel to New York to try to market his work.[35] At Atheneum, he was asked to leave his portfolio, which included a picturebook manuscript, for noted children's book editor Margaret McElderry to review. Several weeks later, he received from McElderry a detailed critique of the strengths and weaknesses of both text and illustrations. She assured him that if he was willing to rewrite the story, she was willing to reread it.

Her praise of his talent stood out in his memory, because as he later commented, 'No one in Canada had ever done that for me.'[36]

McElderry then suggested to Patsy Aldana that she contact Wallace to help him with the editing. He worked with both editors to develop a story that was 'inspiring, universal and multicultural.' The resulting book, *Chin Chiang and the Dragon's Dance* (1984), was the first picturebook in Canada to have been co-edited, co-produced, and co-published as a joint project by Canadian and American publishers.[37]

Wallace's careful preliminary research shapes his choices of peritextual elements, illustrative style, and artistic medium. *Chin Chiang*, the story of a young Chinese-Canadian boy who learns the steps of the dragon dance from a middle-aged woman, and in the process overcomes his fears, is set in an unnamed, contemporary urban community that combines architectural and geographical elements of both Vancouver and Victoria. While the authenticity of his narrative was questioned by both non-Chinese critics and members of the Chinese community, as women traditionally are not participants in the ceremony, he defended his narrative choice, stating it was a considered decision on his part to include a feminist element.[38]

Wallace employs colour symbolism to highlight the emotional state of the protagonist. The sinuous and intertwining dragon motif for the borders that frame each illustration and unify the page design simultaneously remind the reader of the cultural context of the narrative and the dragon dance that is central to the plot. His complex spatial constructions and unusual perspectives heighten the emotional effect of the text on the reader. As he explains, 'Not only did Chin Chiang have to be shown feeling humbled, but the reader had to experience it too. The only way I could capture those emotions was to perch the reader above him.'[39] (See colour plate 7.)

In 1988, Teddy Jam's *Night Cars* (1988), illustrated by Ken Nutt (using his illustrator's pseudonym, Eric Beddows), brought a new complexity to picturebook illustration in Canada. The text by Jam (the carefully guarded pseudonym of Matt Cohen, the award-winning Canadian novelist and Aldana's husband) has the lilting rhythm of a lullaby designed to soothe a sleepless baby. Nutt's full-colour paintings play with perspective, temporal sequencing, and multiple and simultaneous points of view as the reader looks with the baby through a window onto a snowy city street at night, watching the changes in the passing scene. At the same time, the reader is shown the baby, who appears in a panel at the bottom of each double-page opening as part of the framing device. This doubled picture plane helps create a perfectly realized world that follows its own logic: one view looks down on the world of the street that the baby sees, while the other looks at the baby.[40]

The streetscape of storefronts is a combination of College Street in Toronto, as Matt Cohen imagined the setting for his story, Dundas Street in Nutt's hometown of Woodstock, Ontario, and aspects of Stratford, Ontario, where he was living at the time he created the illustrations. This architectural assemblage creates what he calls a 'pentimento of things being torn down and replaced and plastered over.' The specificity of his lighting and the detail of the illustrations are an expression of his belief that if something is real for the artist, 'it will translate anywhere in the world.'[41]

If *Chin Chiang* introduces children to multicultural themes, and *Zoom* to the world of imagination, Janet Lunn's *Amos's Sweater* (1988), illustrated by Kim LaFave, the story of an aged ram who will not give up his wool, provides readers with a perfect example of the power of the anthropomorphic humour of a curmudgeonly animal protagonist and, by extension, insight into their own feelings. Lunn's rhythmic prose repeats key phrases for comic effect, reflecting the popularity of patterned language picturebooks for literacy instruction in the 1980s. Lunn found the impetus for the story during a visit to a friend in Vermont, who subsequently sent her a shawl made from the wool of one of the sheep on the farm. As Lunn explains, she 'got to thinking about that particular sheep, whose name was Amos. I thought how much he wouldn't like to give away his wool because he was an awfully cantankerous old thing.'[42] For Lunn, LaFave's gently humorous watercolour illustrations captured the emotions that she had imagined, noting that he 'could see very easily that this sheep was angry, hurt, and upset – all the things I would feel if I were Amos.'[43]

Both author and illustrator found their close collaboration and lengthy discussions about the text and images an exciting challenge. LaFave added details that expanded the text, like the image of the shorn Amos, blue with cold and covered in stick-on bandages, while Lunn's questions pushed him to think about the broader context of his illustrations. As he describes the working relationship, 'There would be these scenes in the text and it would be inside the house looking out, and she would want to know what was outside the window. It just made me think in terms of this little contained universe, rather than just the flat edges [of the page]. There was so much more going on than was just said in the text.'[44]

As the list matured, Groundwood developed sophisticated illustrated books for older children. In *Tales from Gold Mountain: Stories of the Chinese in the New World* (1989), the historian and archivist Paul Yee blends historical fact and folklore motifs in a series of short stories that recreate the daily hardships and emotional lives of the nineteenth-century Chinese immigrants to the Pacific coast. Yee wanted to introduce the history of the contribution of Chinese workers to the building of British Columbia from the gold rush to the construction of the Canadian Pacific Railway in a way that would be 'interesting, and alive and full of life ... It is not history in a straightforward way, but it's about people in history,' as well as creating an empathetic understanding of the immigrant experience.[45] For Yee, the history also highlighted the social and cultural constraints experienced by the workers, showing dramatic tension in the conflict between 'the old world and the new world, between freedom and being constrained by racism.'[46] The stylized full-page illustrations by Simon Ng enhance the emotional power of the narratives while simultaneously explicating the nuances of character of the protagonists.[47]

'Children Should Connect to the People Who Created the Book': Annick Press

By 1979, Anne Millyard and Rick Wilks had changed their focus from books by children to books for child readers. Hampered by a lack of experience, they relied initially on the help of their printers, who taught them how to put a book together and calculate their expenses.[48] They also received advice from a neighbour with banking experience, who insisted that their business was not financially viable.

6.2 Janet Lunn. *Amos's Sweater*. Illustrated by Kim LaFave. A Groundwood Book.
Vancouver and Toronto: Douglas and McIntyre, 1988.
Reprinted with the permission of the publisher, Groundwood Books.

Despite his dire prediction, a year later Millyard remembers that the publishing house was doing 'very nicely' and continued to grow by 20 per cent every year for the first few years.[49] Wilks recalls that at the beginning, 'We were the art directors, we were the editors … We had a lot to learn about how to fuse text and art, about compatibility, about design. We had to work within the limits of what now feels like the dinosaur age of technology. The first books we did were laid out on the back of wallpaper … It was whatever we could improvise. Some of the books reflected that, but they still resonated.'[50]

Gradually, the picturebook style of the house evolved. Millyard explains that they believe 'that children should be exposed to a huge variety of art styles, so that ultimately they are able to make judgment of what is right for them.'[51] In consultation with a designer recommended by Annick's printers, they developed a standardized format based on an eight-inch square, with a photograph and mini-biography of the author on the back cover, because they felt that 'children should connect to the people who created the book.'[52] The formatting gave their picture-books a consistent look that made their books stand out in a bookstore display, despite the diversity of artistic styles employed by their illustrators.

They developed a publishing program that reflected their interest in children's voices and the lives of contemporary urban children, beginning with a series of picturebooks by Robert Munsch. Millyard remembers that they received four unsolicited manuscripts from Munsch by mail. They immediately recognized 'that here was an adult who fit right in with what we were hoping to do for the child … [who] wrote so well, who was so much in touch with the world of the child without ever talking down to kids. His work embodied child empowerment.'[53]

The first two Munsch titles, *The Mud Puddle* and *The Dark*, issued in 1979, were illustrated by Sami Suomalainen. A year later, Annick issued Munsch's feminist fairy tale *The Paper Bag Princess* (1980), illustrated by Michael Martchenko, whose comic vision enhances and expands the narrative of a brave and resourceful heroine who tames dragons and copes with crises. *The Paper Bag Princess* eventually sold over a million copies, and Munsch became the first contemporary superstar of Canadian children's literature. He creates and refines the cumulative narratives of his taboo-breaking tall tales through repeated storytelling recitations to groups of children, and incorporates chanted refrains and sound effects in which children can readily join. Martchenko, who continues as Munsch's primary illustrator, shares his enthusiasm for anti-authoritarian chaos trumping authority. His freely sketched, satirical watercolours take the side of rebellious and defiant child protagonists who face bullying and pompous antagonists and resist the societal imposition of propriety and rules.

In 1981, Annick released the first series of three Annikins, ninety-nine-cent reprints of their Robert Munsch stories in miniature format that were designed as impulse purchases in book stores and toy stores and that would, in the words of Rick Wilks, 'promote reading and book ownership at a price that was about one-third of a greeting card.' The following year, a non-Munsch set was issued, followed in 1983 with three more Munsch titles, in Annikin format, and the success of the miniature line was assured.[54]

Throughout the 1980s, Annick published picturebooks for toddlers and pre-

6.3 Robert Munsch. *The Paper Bag Princess*. Illustrated by Michael Martchenko.
Toronto: Annick Press, 1980.
Reprinted with the permission of the publisher, Annick Press.

schoolers that treat the minutiae of domestic life and the world of relationships with humour and insight, with the goal of helping children 'walk in the world.'[55] Subjects included Kathy Stinson's *Red Is Best* (1982), illustrated by Robin Baird Lewis, about a little girl's obsession with the colour red. Lewis's images capture the exuberance and stubbornness of the protagonist, fully exploiting the potential of simple line drawings highlighted with spot colour. Other picturebooks for young children dealt with issues as varied as divorce, children with Down's syndrome, bodies and body parts, toilet training, and food preferences. The success of Annick titles was recognized in 1984 when the press was awarded Publisher of the Year by the Canadian Booksellers Association which also marked the first time that a children's publisher was given the distinction by the Association.[56]

The pragmatic exploration of childhood also led to Annick titles being challenged and censored. A parental challenge to Roger Paré's *The Annick ABC* (1985), in which 'N is a nudist eating noodles in Naples,' resulted in a school librarian making the decision to discard the book, ostensibly because of the physical condition of the library's copy.[57] Wilks comments that the illustration was 'simply a nude person, you couldn't see a whole lot. This was not much of a lesson in anatomy, but nevertheless that's all it took.'[58] Images of nudity affected sales of Kathy Stinson's *The Bare Naked Book* (1986), illustrated by Heather Collins.[59] Stinson describes the response of some school librarians to the book as 'censorship by anticipation,' explaining that the decision not to purchase the book on the basis of book selection guidelines 'might have more to do with fear of controversy than with any professional concerns.'[60] Robert Munsch's *Thomas' Snowsuit* (1985) has been challenged in several Canadian locations for undermining school authority and teaching disrespect, while *The Paper Bag Princess* has been seen as anti-family, because of the princess's refusal to marry Prince Ronald.[61] Clearly, child empowerment had the potential to threaten the status quo.[62]

'Self-Recognition Is the Main Reason for Localizing a Book': Tundra in the 1980s

In the late 1970s, as an extension of their books focusing on the childhood memories and experiences of illustrators, Tundra Books began to publish picturebooks with a strong sense of regional identity. While May Cutler, a fierce opponent of both Canadian and Quebec nationalism, was not deliberately attempting to create a series about Canada's national identity and regional diversity, she believed that stories with an identifiable location should be illustrated by artists from the same locale. As she explains, she did not want 'somebody who grew up in Toronto illustrating a book about the prairies.'[63]

Her first forays into regionalism include Ted Harrison's *Children of the Yukon* (1977) and *A Northern Alphabet* (1982). Harrison had trained at the West Hartlepool School of Art, received a certificate as an art teacher from the University of Durham, and taught in schools in Malaysia and New Zealand.[64] In 1968, while teaching in a school on reserve in Wabasca-Desmarais in northern Alberta, Harrison created *Northland Alphabet* to meet the needs of his Woodlands Cree students. When he moved to the Yukon to teach at first at Carcross and then, beginning in

But I can jump higher in my red stockings.

6.4 Kathy Stinson. *Red Is Best*. Illustrated by Robin Baird Lewis.
Toronto: Annick Press, 1982.

Reprinted with the permission of the publisher, Annick Press.

Hudson Bay   Hay River   Holman Island   Haines   Herschel Island   Harrison Bay   Haakon Fiord   Hantzsch River   Hyde Inlet   Hubbard

Henrietta Maria   High Prairie   Hopedale   Hebron   Hayes River   Haakon Fiord   Hubbard

Healy   Holy Cross   Hooper Bay   Holman Island   Haines   Herschel Island   Harrison Bay

Hh

The **husky**
is watching
the boys play
hockey.

Hall Beach   Healy   Holy Cross   Hooper Bay   Hazelton   Hayes River   Hebron   Hopedale   High Prairie   Henrietta Maria   Hydaburg

6.5 Ted Harrison. *A Northern Alphabet.* Montreal: Tundra Books, 1982.
Taken from *A Northern Alphabet* © 1982, written and illustrated by Ted Harrison,
published by Tundra Books, Toronto.

1970, in Whitehorse, he was inspired to paint the landscape, filtered through his own artistic imagination.[65]

Cutler contacted Harrison to create a book on the children of the Yukon, instructing him to 'keep it simple.'[66] The resulting illustrations and texts introduce readers to contemporary life in the north. Harrison explains his artistic style has been influenced by 'Maori curvilinear designs' and by the realization 'that the land and the sea and the sky, the swirls and the mountains of sea and the mountains of land, are all similar. There is a rhythm to the earth. If you stratify the sea, you would get a look of land in mountainous waves, because they tend to break up.'[67] His abstracted simplification of shape and the expressive intensity of his bright non-naturalistic colour palette accentuate the dynamism and vastness of the landscape.[68]

Place and time also featured prominently in Quebec author Roch Carrier's *The Hockey Sweater* (1984). The picturebook, which has become an anglo-Canadian cultural icon and a metaphor for the tensions between anglophones and francophones, has a complex literary history.[69] The work began in 1970 as a radio broadcast for CBC, in response to the question 'What does Quebec want?'[70] Carrier wrote a sly and ironic tale of hockey-mad children in the late 1940s in the rural village of

St Justine where he grew up, who worship Maurice Richard of the Montreal Cana-diens. When the young Roch outgrows his hockey sweater, to his endless humilia-tion, he is forced to wear the Maple Leafs sweater sent in response to his mother's order to the Eaton's catalogue, lest M. Eaton be personally offended. The story was translated into English by Sheila Fischman, who coached Carrier on English pronunciation before the taping for broadcast on the CBC.[71]

The story then appeared in a volume of Carrier's short stories, *Les enfants du bonhomme dans la lune*, published in Montreal by Stanké in 1979, and published in English the same year by the House of Anansi Press as *The Hockey Sweater and Oth-er Stories*, in a translation by Fischman. It was then turned into an animated short film by Sheldon Cohen for the National Film Board of Canada in 1980. Cutler, who had seen the NFB film, approached Carrier about translating the story into a pic-turebook. After several attempts to find an illustrator, she settled on having Cohen rework some of his illustrations specifically for the book.[72] His intensely coloured humorous paintings convey the tone of Carrier's small-town satire while locating the story within the particular visual milieu of the period.

Other Tundra books with a strong regional presence focused on the urban expe-rience. Stéphane Poulin was a recent art school graduate when Cutler discovered his work. His first book for Tundra was the bilingual *Ah! belle cité!: ABC / A Beau-tiful City: ABC* (1985), which cleverly intertwines visual images of ethnocultural diversity in contemporary Montreal with alphabetic references in both English and French. In the subsequent hide-and-seek series *Have You Seen Josephine?* (1986) and *Can You Catch Josephine?* (1987) a group of children race after Josephine, a runaway white cat, through the streets, alleys, and schools of the working-class district of east end Montreal and pursue her through the Quebec countryside in *Could You Stop Josephine?* (1988). His warm-toned oil paintings employ a variety of cinematic perspectives from close-ups to wide-screen panoramas, while the depiction of his small protagonists as slightly squashed figures with spiky hair and darkly shad-owed eyes humorously contrasts with the meticulously realized streetscapes. Cut-ler described the specificity of Poulin's vision, saying that 'self-recognition is the main reason for localizing a book … You are so strong in your description of the local, and hopefully not the superficial, that it becomes universal.'[73]

A strong sense of place and period is also found in the series of books writ-ten and illustrated by Dayal Kaur Khalsa, set in the Queens, New York, neigh-bourhood of her childhood in the 1950s.[74] Khalsa, who moved to Canada in the 1970s, placed her protagonist May (named after Cutler) at the centre of a linked cycle of stories that explore narrative, biography, and memory. *Tales of a Gambling Grandma* (1986) is a first-person reminiscence of May's loving relationship with her somewhat transgressive grandmother, who warns her granddaughter against invading Cossacks and gypsy kidnappers, and teaches her to play poker. *I Want a Dog* (1987) relates May's struggle to convince her sceptical parents that she is suf-ficiently responsible and mature enough to be granted her dearest wish of a family pet. May also appears in *My Family Vacation* (1988), *Sleepers* (1988), *How Pizza Came to Our Town* (1989), as an adult in *Julian* (1989), and finally in the posthumously published *Cowboy Dreams* (1990).

Khalsa's use of a deliberately naive style, with flat blocks of bright colours and

6.6 Stéphane Poulin. *Can You Catch Josephine?* Montreal: Tundra Books, 1987.
Taken from *Can You Catch Josephine?* © 1987, written and illustrated by Stéphane Poulin,
published by Tundra Books, Toronto.

decorative details and visual allusions to famous paintings, are very different from the more straightforwardly narrative illustrations favoured by Canadian publishers of the era.[75] She builds an entire world in each of her picturebooks through her use of detail, drawing from memory and photographs to anchor scenes in the specificity of contextualized references drawn from popular culture and fine art, building up a vocabulary of visual quotations that were personally meaningful.[76] Khalsa uses these visual quotations, peritextual elements like narrative endpapers, and different narrative voices to explore the themes of memory and the unreliable narrator in the series, expanding the interplay of child and adult perspectives in her narratives, and providing visual humour for the adult reader.[77]

Popular culture also pervades Khalsa's books, the minutiae of mid-twentieth-century childhood and middle-class family life, from Gene Autry movies and saddle shoes through linoleum and chrome kitchens to a visit to FAO Schwartz toy store in New York, providing temporal specificity to her memories. The cycle constitutes a self-referential visual autobiography unique in Canadian children's literature. (See colour plate 8.)

'We Wanted Our Books to Be Child Friendly': Kids Can Press

In 1979, Valerie Hussey, who had worked in large American educational publishing houses, joined Kids Can Press with the intention of transforming the collective into a viable commercial venture. Two years later, she established a partnership with Ricky Englander and in 1986 purchased the assets of the company from the former collective and turned it into a privately held company.[78] Englander remembers their goal was to create child-friendly books with educational value and market appeal, adding that 'we wanted them to sell. We wanted people to buy them. That just wasn't on the minds of the early collective.' At the same time, Englander wanted to maintain the emphasis on quality that she had learned as a children's librarian.[79]

Their complementary knowledge of children's literature, education, libraries, and publishing allowed them to develop a strong publishing identity for their list. Their desire to balance commercial success and adhere to high standards also characterized Kids Can's approach to design. As Englander notes, 'Of course, good design is seamless ... We argued about our covers a lot and we argued about the internal pages. It was a great source of positive tension. We cared a lot about the design.'[80]

The decision to develop a range of non-fiction titles resulted from Englander's frustration with trying to find suitable Canadian material for her children's school assignments and her recognition 'that there were no Canadian books that would fit their needs at every level.'[81] Working with Valerie Wyatt, former editor of *Owl* magazine, Kids Can developed an innovative approach to information books, based on a double-page layout 'designed to give the information a certain coherence, a careful pacing and a sequential logic.'[82] The results are child-centred information books with a strong experiential component that encourages active, hands-on exploration and learning.[83] Titles included *Cat's Cradle, Owl's Eyes: A Book of String Games* (1983), by children's librarian Camilla Gryski, packaged with a nylon cord for playing the games, *Scienceworks: An Ontario Science Centre Book of Experiments* (1984), illustrated by Tina Holdcroft, and *How to Make Pop Ups* (1987) by Joan Irvine.[84] At a time when a print run of 3,000 copies might remain in stock for several years, *Cat's Cradle, Owl's Eyes* sold an unprecedented 5,000 copies in its first eight weeks, giving Kids Can a secure financial base to begin publishing full-colour picturebooks.[85]

Their picturebooks were developed with the same careful balancing of design and marketability, including Maryann Kovalski's *Brenda and Edward* (1984), a canine romance with 1930s-style imagery, and Ann Blades's *By the Sea: An Alphabet Book* (1985), in which two siblings enjoy a day at the beach exploring sand and water.[86] In Monica Hughes's *Little Fingerling: A Japanese Folk Tale* (1989), a retelling of the story *Issun Bōshi*, the text and images work together to provide a lively immersion in the cultural setting of the story. Brenda Clark based her illustrations on extensive research at the Royal Ontario Museum's H.H. Mu Far Eastern Library in Toronto, drawing inspiration from Ukiyo-e woodblock prints for details of clothing and domestic interiors during the Edo period.[87] The Japanese children's literature scholar Hideaki Honda interviewed Professor Asaoka of the National Museum of Japanese History (Kokuritsu Rekishi Minzoku Hakubutsu-kan) about the historical time period of the story before interviewing Clark about her research for the book. Honda concludes that although Clark mixes images from different Japanese time periods, and includes details that are anachronistic, like a child lying on the floor reading a book, her artistic skill and sensitivity allow her to imaginatively and creatively reinterpret an unfamiliar culture for a modern reader, opening up the possibility of intercultural dialogue.[88]

Kids Can also experimented with collections of poetry, including David Booth's anthology *Til All the Stars Have Fallen: Canadian Poems for Children* (1989), with illustrations by Kady MacDonald Denton that skilfully respond to the shifting emotions of the poetry. Denton had studied fine arts at the University of Toronto and illustration at the Chelsea School of Art and brought an interest in the style of great British illustrators like Edward Ardizzone to her use of a thin, flexible line that defines her three-dimensional figures against the background.[89] Single poems issued in picturebook format include Ted Harrison's illustrated editions of *The Cremation of Sam McGee* (1986) and *The Shooting of Dan McGrew* (1988), which introduced Robert Service's colloquial narratives of life in the Yukon during the Klondike gold rush to a new generation of readers.

The press's most successful picturebook series began with Paulette Bourgeois's *Franklin in the Dark* (1986), illustrated by Brenda Clark, about Franklin, the green and endearing turtle Everychild and his animal friends, who model ethnocultural diversity within a multicultural society.[90] As the vulnerable yet brave anthropo-morphized turtle faces the challenges of a typical preschooler with courage and ingenuity, he functions as a bibliotherapeutic counselling service for developmental issues, modelling appropriate responses for his child reader. Ricky Englander describes the careful editorial work that went into crafting *Franklin*, explaining that 'it was a story that worked. It had rhythm, it was touching, it touched the child, it made it easy to read as an adult.' The book's success generated a sequel, which quickly turned into a series. As Englander comments, with each new title in the series, it became increasingly difficult to develop new age-appropriate, child-centred scenarios that sustain the characters, 'not only for twenty-eight pages, but for twenty-eight books.'[91]

By the end of the 1980s, Kids Can Press had evolved in its balance of commercial and non-commercial publications, particularly in picturebooks, and had reduced its dependence on state funding from approximately one-third of its revenue in the early days to approximately 4 per cent of total revenues.[92] According to Valerie Hussey, the press's balance between art and commerce means there is no identifi-able, unique quality or look to the book design and illustration. Instead, Kids Can gives illustrators 'a very strong voice; we permit them to be who they are. I think we have a very strong editorial hand, but we don't look to conform one book to the next to the next.'[93] In 1989, in recognition of the success of the press at creating attractive, marketable books, the Canadian Booksellers Association awarded them Publisher of the Year.[94]

Franklin was a turtle. He was afraid of crawling into his small, dark shell. And so, Franklin the turtle dragged his shell behind him.

6.7 Paulette Bourgeois. *Franklin in the Dark*. Illustrated by Brenda Clark. Toronto: Kids Can Press, 1986.

'There's Always Someone Doing Something in the Background': Scholastic and Barbara Reid

The American publishing firm Scholastic Books expanded into Canada in 1957 to distribute its lines of inexpensive paperback reprint editions sold through Scholastic Book Clubs and Book Fairs in the public schools of Canada. In the early 1970s, under publisher Larry Muller, Scholastic Books instituted a Canadian publishing program of original and reprinted Canadian titles, issued as Scholastic-TAB Publications. They also developed a trade imprint, North Winds Press, named in parallel to the Scholastic U.S. trade imprint Four Winds Press.[95] Art director Kathryn Cole provided guidance for the new trade list, bringing new author-illustrators like Phoebe Gilman, Robin Muller, and Barbara Reid into the fold.

The new North Winds trade list responded to the curricular trend in Canadian schools to incorporate trade books into the classroom to augment or replace authorized textbooks. American author Edith Newlin Chase's *The New Baby Calf* (1984) was an immediate best-seller because of the witty and innovative three-dimensional artwork of Barbara Reid. Reid creates her images from layers of shaped and textured Plasticine, pressed onto illustration board. This layering allows her to create depth and define shape, and to blend gradations of colour to enhance the three dimensionality of her images, with further nuances of shadow and light provided by the photography by Reid's husband, Ian Crysler. Reid explains that the flexibility and three-dimensionality of the medium suit her working style, allowing her to repeatedly change and add to her images. As she describes the medium, '[w]ith Plasticine, it starts out very plain … [t]hen it gets more and more exciting as you add the little details.'[96] It is these little details that she uses to extend the text by adding subplots or moments of humour, such as the duck and pig families in *The New Baby Calf* and the mouse running away from the owl in *Have You Seen Birds?* (1986), written by the American author Joanne Oppenheim. Reid refers to these extra narrative details as 'little jokes,' explaining 'that's how I've always drawn. There's the main subject of the picture, but then there's always someone doing something in the background. It's like making fun in the back of the classroom. I always did that too.'[97]

In *Sing a Song of Mother Goose* (1987), Reid's approach to the illustration of Mother Goose rhymes relies on meticulous overall page design, in which horizontal ivy-entwined, lattice-work friezes at the top and bottom of each page frame small vignette images in which characters from the rhymes act out comic tableaux, breaking the flatness of the two-dimensional page. Like *The New Baby Calf*, *Sing a Song of Mother Goose* was an early example of Scholastic's ability to cross-market trade books during the whole-language trend in curriculum, appearing on the trade list in English and in French translation, as well as in various educational formats, including the Scholastic Big Book format for group reading in primary classes, accompanied by a teaching guide, and as a kit with the big book accompanied by the teaching guide, six little books, and an audiocassette.

'The Feeling of Offering Quality': Oxford University Press

At Oxford University Press, the children's list under William Toye's editorial direc-

Whooooooo!
Have you heard the night birds?
Move-by-moonlight-bright birds,
scaring rabbits into holes,
hunting bats and rats and moles.

Have you heard the haunting *whooo*
of the hunting night-time birds?

6.8 Joanne Oppenheim. *Have You Seen Birds?* Illustrated by Barbara Reid. Richmond Hill, ON: North Winds Press, Scholastic-TAB, 1986.
Reprinted with the permission of the publisher, Scholastic Canada.

tion continued to emphasize fine design and meticulous production values. Elizabeth Cleaver's last published works, while all very different from one another, benefited from technical improvements in the reproduction of colour illustrations and from her willingness to experiment with new illustrative techniques. The 1984 revision of Mary Alice Downie and Barbara Robertson's anthology *The New Wind Has Wings* gave her the opportunity to return to her first illustrated book, revising some of the images and creating illustrations to accompany the new selection of poetry. Cleaver's subtle and profound colour sense and use of texture were much more evident on the printed page than in the 1968 edition. Her *ABC* (1984), influenced by her work with artist's books, is square-shaped and small in size. Her intensely toned paper collages, interlayered with found objects, incorporate clever visual jokes that challenge the two-dimensionality of the page. In contrast, *Enchanted Cariboo* (1985), her final publication before her death, was developed after a visit to an Inuit community, during which she shared shadow puppetry with the children and immersed herself in Inuit art and mythology. A striking contrast to her usual blazing colours, the collage illustrations that accompany the Inuit legend are created by photographing black shadow puppet figures against a white ground, movement suggested by the shifting in and out of focus, accenting the mystical and archetypal nature of the story.

When Kathryn Cole left Scholastic in 1989, she took over the editorship of children's books at Oxford from William Toye.[98] She describes careful attention to design and excellent colour reproduction as the hallmarks of Oxford's picturebooks, adding that they 'had a real pride in that image and that feeling of offering quality and educational value.'[99] The tradition of excellence, established by Toye, would continue as long as the company remained committed to publishing children's books in Canada.

Trade Publishers Expand Their Children's Lists

As library and school budgets grew in the 1980s, some trade publishers expanded their existing children's list while others published books for children and young adults for the first time. At Methuen, Margaret Crawford Maloney's retelling of *Hans Christian Andersen's The Little Mermaid* (1983) provided Laszlo Gal with the opportunity to create lavish full-colour illustrations. A comparison of the printed book with Gal's original artwork, however, demonstrates the limitations of printing technology on the reproduction of images before the introduction of digitized colour separations.[100] In the preparatory sketches, the influence of Alphonse Mucha and Viennese art nouveau are apparent in Gal's compositional devices, his fine, sinuous line, strong patterning, and decorative details. Gal builds up layers of watercolour or ink wash with areas of finely crosshatched chalk or pastel on a heavily gessoed and textured ground. The elegance and luminosity of the original art did not completely survive the printing process, however. The delicacy of Gal's line and the fine details are obscured, and the three-dimensionality, depth of perspective, and sense of progression through space are flattened in the reproduction. (See colour plate 9.)

'Words Dancing on the Page': Stoddart Publishing

In 1984, Stoddart Publishing, newly formed out of the Canadian houses acquired by General Publishing, developed a children's list, beginning with Dennis Lee's *Lizzy's Lion* (1984), an absurdist cautionary poem in which a girl's pet lion, trained as a guard dog, tears a robber limb from limb.[101] The black humour of the text was both moderated and amplified by the clever illustrations by Marie-Louise Gay, a young Quebec illustrator previously unpublished in English Canada. While both text and art were subsequently challenged in censorship struggles, Gay's non-naturalistic style and her use of figure and ground division as characters burst through broken picture frames achieve a subtle spatial distancing that accentuates the fantasy of the text. The violent ending of the robber happens 'off-screen,' in the imagination of the reader. As Gay remembers, 'Parents found it frightening and without any pedagogical value. Children loved it! It touched their funny bone, it expanded their imagination: it was a great story.'[102]

Subsequently, Gay began to write her own texts to illustrate. The artwork for *Rainy Day Magic* (1987), based on her memories of time spent as a child in Vancouver, manipulates the conventions of the picture frame and challenges the logic of fictive three-dimensionality on the two-dimensional page, playing the real against the imaginative, just as her text contrasts the tedium of a wet afternoon with the possibility of a suburban basement being transformed into an ocean playground.[103] Gay is highly conscious of the relationship between art and text in building a world within the picturebook, adding that the words and pictures 'are meant to complete, enhance and expand each other.' For Gay, picturebooks have 'the possibility of so many different levels of meaning. In the text you can have plays on words, alliterations, words dancing on the page, and in the illustrations you can give new meanings to certain words, add details to the story, and even add a whole other story that unravels in parallel to the main action.'[104] (See colour plate 10.)

In addition to their Canadian picturebooks, Stoddart developed 'Stoddart Young Readers,' a series of illustrated informational books on scientific and environmental issues. The first title, *David Suzuki: Looking at Plants* (1985) by David Suzuki with Barbara Hehner, was followed by books by Suzuki on the senses, insects, the body, weather, and the environment, all designed to appeal to children through a mixture of information and hands-on activities. Rounding out the list, Stoddart co-published a careful selection of picturebook titles by British illustrators, and in 1988 acquired the Canadian rights to the first titles in the Eyewitness series of informational books for children by the British packager Dorling Kindersley.[105]

Information for Young Readers

Other publishers also developed new formats for informational books. In 1975, Greey de Pencier Books acquired *The Young Naturalist* magazine. The following year, *Owl*, a completely redesigned publication, was launched with the first issue appearing in January 1976. The new magazine, under the editorship of Annabel

Slaight, attracted readers between the ages of nine and thirteen with an appealing mix of science and nature in an exciting graphic presentation that was designed to stimulate them 'to think beyond the printed page.'[106] The rebranding was so successful that Greey de Pencier developed a line of magazines for different ages of readers, beginning in 1979 with *Chickadee*, for children aged six to nine, and a series of books for children based on the interactive hands-on approach of the magazines. Throughout the 1980s, the line expanded as Owl Books repackaged material from the magazine in titles like *The Winter Fun Book* (1980) and *Owl's Amazing But True* (1983), both edited by Laima Dingwall and Annabel Slaight, and Gordon Penrose's *Dr Zed's Dazzling Book of Science Activities* (1982), designed and illustrated by Linda Bucholtz-Ross, as well as developing full-colour natural history picturebooks like Jan Thornhill's *The Wildlife ABC: A Nature Alphabet* (1988), with intricate illustrations in gouache and ink on scratchboard.

Somerville House Books, founded in 1983 by Jane Somerville, developed a series of innovative children's science and nature titles, as 'Books Plus.' The format of a book plus a three-dimensional manipulative, such as a toy or science object, was exemplified by the 1987 *Bug Book* by Hugh Danks, packaged in a plastic 'bug catcher' container for collecting and observing insects that proved wildly popular with the children's gift market.[107]

'A Good Supply of Kleenex Tissues Will Be Needed': Love You Forever

Firefly Books, founded in 1977, served as the distributor for several smaller specialized publishers, including Black Moss Press, Exile Editions, Porcupine's Quill, Annick Press, and Owl Books. They also published the trade editions of titles by Camden House, including Terence Dickinson's *NightWatch: An Equinox Guide to Viewing the Universe* (1983) and *Exploring the Night Sky: The Equinox Astronomy Guide for Beginners* (1987), which proved equally popular with adults and children.[108]

Firefly's big breakthrough, however, was their publication of Robert Munsch's picturebook *Love You Forever* (1986), illustrated by Sheila McGraw, a freelance commercial artist and illustrator. Munsch explains that the book, a story about the cyclical and enduring nature of parental love, began as a song that he sang to himself after he and his wife experienced two stillbirths.[109] He then transformed the song into a story over successive public retellings to both child and adult audiences at diverse venues, including an author breakfast at the Canadian Booksellers' Association annual convention and several children's literature conferences. When Annick Press declined to publish the manuscript, believing that the sombre tone was not suitable for children, Firefly issued the work as a picturebook.[110] While they retained the square book format employed by Annick, McGraw's mixed-media illustrations, in which she combined contemporary and nostalgic elements to give, as she describes it, a 'timeless' quality, set the book apart visually from the comedic child-centred Munsch-Martchenko series of picturebooks.[111]

The subject matter and emotional tone were also very different from Munsch's previous work, although his hallmark use of patterned language and repetition of phrases remains. While some reviewers at the time the book was published questioned whether the sentimentality of the work made it more suitable for adults than children, and whether the connections in the story between 'lullaby, sleep, death as an eternal sleep, and the renewal of rituals with successive generations' could be understood by preschoolers, the title quickly found a market precisely because of the sentimentality and 'tear-jerking' quality of the story.[112] Munsch, who refers to the story as 'bi-modal,' working at different levels for child and adult audiences, commented shortly after the book's publication that while adults understand it as a 'story about death and loss' and weep, children 'see it as a story about role reversal' and laugh during his public readings.[113]

Love You Forever also continues to stir passionate feelings among its fans and foes and provides a useful case study of reader responses to popular children's literature. Some scholars have questioned the lack of mutuality in the relationship between mother and son, suggesting that the message that one can never escape an omnipotent mother is a 'fantasy more appealing to adults than children,' and that the adult grief-centred themes of the story are 'far removed from the normal developmental concerns of a child audience.'[114] Others embrace the grief-centred theme, seeing the work as having a useful bibliotherapeutic role for adults struggling with the need to care for aging parents, addressing 'issues of responsibility, pressure, stress, and connectedness.'[115]

In a speech delivered to the Society of Children's Book Writers and Illustrators in 2000, the American author Jane Yolen likened the book to a 'kalliope,' a fairground steam organ which can pump out tunes that may make one smile, 'or just hurt your ears,' adding 'You may adore *Love You Forever*, but I hear it as a story about an overbearing and smothering mother who infantilizes her son and can only tell him she loves him when he is fast asleep.'[116] Her acknowledgment that the work is loved by some and loathed by others characterizes the extreme nature of reader responses, which has only grown since the book was published.[117]

The 1988 edition of *Children's Choices of Canadian Books* included reviews by children and their parents that were split between children who appreciated the story and found it funny or appealing, and parents who found it upsetting, or noted their child's puzzlement at the tears generated by a reading of the story.[118] Michael Valpy, in his column for the *Globe and Mail* in 1989, referred to the 'son's powerful love for his mother' as 'just a little bit emasculating.'[119] By 1995, when Jeffrey Garrett tracked the responses among academics, teachers, and librarians who posted messages to the internet discussion group Child_Lit: Children's Literature Criticism and Theory, few were neutral about the book, which he describes as 'igniting controversy' among adults 'who care about children's books.'[120] Subscribers to Child_Lit noted their polarized 'visceral reaction' to the book and heatedly debated the issue of sentimentality and the sentimentalization of childhood, the depiction of emotions in children's picturebooks, literary quality and mass-market 'popular' children's literature, and the validity of evaluating a work for children on the basis of one's own emotional responses as an adult.[121]

A similar pattern of response is evident in the customer reviews posted to online bookstore websites in Canada, the United States, and Europe, which either rate the book very highly or very poorly, with almost no middle ground.[122] Those who love the work praise it as a story of unconditional parental love, value the emotional experience of reading it to children, believe that it gives children a reassuring message about the cycle of life, and argue passionately that the book affirms that love endures from generation to generation. Reviewers consistently mention their own emotional response to the story, and the theme of weeping as the book is read predominates. The book is described as a perfect gift for an expectant or new mother, a view reiterated by Sheila McGraw's website, which sells giclée prints of the illustrations with the note that the image of the mother rocking her infant baby makes a 'perfect focal point for any nursery' and 'an outstanding gift when paired with a copy of *Love You Forever*,' and that the image of the mother creeping into her child's room is 'a loving, caring gesture that speaks of protection and delight in his quiet repose,' and a suitable gift for 'a new mom or for Mother's Day.'[123]

Those who dislike the book cite many of the same themes as negatives, describing the story as creepy, infantilizing, manipulative, sick, slimy, and wrong in its depiction of a co-dependent relationship between parent and child, and a disturbing portrait of the overprotective love of a mother who 'can't let go.' Some customer reviews raise questions about Oedipal overtones to the story, describing the relationship between mother and son as dysfunctional and a cycle of abuse, while others objected to the depiction of what they believed to be multi-generational single-parent families. Still other reviewers describe their child's distress about the possibility that one's parent might die, and their own discomfort at weeping in front of their children while reading the story. Just as the positive reviews recommend the book as a perfect gift, the theme of receiving the book as a gift and then hiding it or throwing it away threads through the negative reviews. While readers consistently respond to the emotional import of the text and debate the depiction of the parent-child relationship, few have directly commented on the semiotic tensions and slippages in the shifting emotional tone of Munsch's narrative and McGraw's realistic, yet static, images.[124]

Despite the divergent reader responses, *Love You Forever* has become an international best-seller with 17 million copies in print by 2001, and continued sales of around 400,000 copies a year in paperback.[125] It has been translated into Braille, Chinese, French, German, Hebrew, Japanese, Korean, and Spanish, and ranked sixth on a National Education Association list of teachers' top 100 books for children in 2007.[126] It has been widely cross-marketed as a book suitable for both children and adults. Lionel Koffler, the president of Firefly, has commented that the typical customer is someone making a purchase in a bookstore for a gift, or to replace their 'own paperback copy with a hardcover.' Word of mouth through parent groups, church groups, and 'psychological awareness groups' have also promoted the title.[127] It was featured prominently in an episode of the popular TV program *Friends* and has been set to music by the distinguished Canadian composer Marjan Mozetich for the chamber group Quartetto Gelato, who gave the world premier performance of the composition at a Stratford Summer Music concert on 5 August 2005.[128] In December 2005, McGraw's original artwork was auctioned at the Loch Gallery in Toronto at a reported asking price of $300,000 for the fifteen images, and purchased by a Winnipeg couple who planned to exhibit the images.[129] Undoubtedly, the academic debate over the merit of the work and sustained criticism by readers and reviewers has not impaired its continued sales, which show no signs of diminishing, nor its status as the best-selling Canadian children's picturebook of all time.

'Really the Only Way Is to Try It Out on Kids': Aboriginal Publishers

Two small Aboriginal-owned publishing houses were established in 1980 that significantly extended the presentation of indigenous themes by Aboriginal writers in children's books.[130] In 1980, Randy Fred, a member of the Nuu-cha-nulth Nation and a nephew of author-illustrator George Clutesi, founded Theytus Books in Nanaimo.[131] In 1982, he sold Theytus to the Okanagan Indian Curriculum Project and the Nicola Valley Indian Administration, who relocated the publishing house to the newly formed En'owkin Centre in Penticton, run by the Okanagan Indian Education Resources Society. According to publishing manager Anita Large, the Theytus mission and vision are exemplified by its name, a 'Coast Salishan word that means "preserving for the sake of handing down."'[132]

Initially run as an educational publisher producing curriculum materials for Okanagan children, Theytus moved into adult fiction, non-fiction, and children's trade books. As the first totally Aboriginal-owned and -operated publisher in Canada, the press focuses on publishing Aboriginal, Métis, and Inuit authors and illustrators. Former publishing manager Greg Young-Ing notes that Theytus has deliberately moved away from stereotypical images of Aboriginal people while maintaining a look that is 'identifiably indigenous to indigenous and non-indigenous peoples,' as exemplified by the 1984 *Okanagan Legend* trilogy illustrated by Barbara Marchand, *How Food Was Given*, *How Names Were Given*, and *How Turtle Set the Animals Free*.[133] Children's books proved to be Theytus's greatest strength, accounting for about a quarter of their publishing program and half of their sales.[134] Reflecting Aboriginal cultural values, authors have considerable editorial input, working closely with the publisher in a more collaborative relationship than is common in larger publishing houses. Theytus also actively seeks the opinion of child readers. As Young-Ing explains, 'I would try books out on my daughter … and different kids around the En'owkin Centre … Really the only way to do it is to try it out on kids.'[135]

Pemmican Publishing was established in Winnipeg in1980 by the Manitoba Métis Federation to promote Métis culture and history.[136] As Diane Ramsay, managing editor at the press explains, as a non-profit organization Pemmican's mandate is to give 'new Métis authors an opportunity to get their work published, and to document the oral traditions, stories before they're forgotten, and the Michif language.'[137] Like Theytus, Pemmican works with non-professional writers whose stories they believe should be published, providing substantial help in the editing process, to ensure that the voices of Métis people are available to readers in the school system, the Métis community, and the general public.

Pemmican has published history, poetry, fiction and non-fiction, actively seeking out Métis, Aboriginal, and Inuit creators, including noted CBC radio journalist Bernelda Wheeler, whose picturebooks *I Can't Have Bannock, but the Beaver Has a Dam* (1984) and *Where Did You Get Your Moccasins?* (1986) have been cited as picturebooks with particular cultural relevance and appeal to Aboriginal children.[138] At the same time, Pemmican, which 'does not support segregation in publishing,' has published non-Aboriginal authors and illustrators whose work has strong Aboriginal content, including Peter Eyvindson's *Kyle's Bath* (1984), illustrated by Wendy Wolsak.[139] Children's books form the majority of their list, reflecting their commitment to the development of Métis children's literacy and identity and recognizing that children gain pride when they see their culture and heritage reflected in books that relate to 'who they are and where they come from.'[140] Former managing editor Audreen Hourie echoes these sentiments, explaining, 'Someone asked me why we publish so many kids' books when there's no money in it ... I told them we do children's books because our children need them.'[141] And like Theytus, Pemmican's authors test out their manuscripts on children before their work goes into print, using the reaction from the children as part of the editing process.[142]

The development of these small Aboriginal publishers closely parallels the experiences of the early alternative publishers of children's books, where non-commercial production values, limited authorial and editorial experience, small multi-tasking staff, and insufficient funds to systematically promote and market their books all proved barriers to wider distribution and critical recognition.[143] However, Aboriginal presses provide important educational and trade materials unavailable anywhere else, give space to otherwise marginalized voices, and meet a cultural mandate that is the primary reason for their publications.

'Gender-Positive, Non-Violent Books': Feminist Publishers

Throughout the 1970s and 1980s, feminist publishers issued children's books as part of their mission to promote gender equality and diversity, and to further women's political education.[144] According to Margie Wolfe, who began volunteering at Women's Press in Toronto in 1976, the collective decided that if they 'wanted women to be aware of themselves and particular things in the world as adults, why not introduce that into children's literature?' They hoped that their 'gender-positive, non-violent books' would introduce issues to children through pictures and text.[145]

The collective fractured several times, in part as a result of interpersonal conflict and then over the broader ideological issues of 'racism, false consciousness, and cultural appropriation' that divided the women's movement in the 1980s.[146] In 1988, Margie Wolfe, Lois Pike, Liz Martin, and Carolyn Wood established Second Story Press in Toronto, after they were locked out of Women's Press in a divisive debate over issues of racism in publishing politics.[147] Four others from Women's Press joined them as supporters, and the new press began to issue fiction and non-fiction for adults, children, and young adults. Their picturebook list began in 1989 with Rachna Gilmore's *Wheniwasalittlegirl*. Emily Hearn's *Franny and the Music Girl* (1989), with illustrations by Mark Thurman, a sequel to the two earlier Women's Press *Franny* titles about a spunky young girl in a wheelchair, carried on the series' modelling of diversity in an urban environment. Under Wolfe, now the sole owner, Second Story Press made children's publishing a priority. As she explains, 'We have developed our little niche, we are interested in books that empower kids, that have a social justice dimension to them … What we try to do as much as possible … is create books that have that kind of content but that kids want to read.'[148]

Organizations, Conferences, Courses, Workshops, and Awards

Throughout the decade, the expansion of writers' and illustrators' organizations and conferences provided opportunities for creators and readers to network and exchange information. As author Sandy Frances Duncan notes, some writers felt that the Canadian Society of Children's Authors, Illustrators and Performers (CANSCAIP) was very Toronto-based and welcomed the founding of the British Columbia branch of the Writers' Union in 1980 and, in 1985, CANSCAIP-West, a Vancouver-based branch of the organization.[149]

Children's literature conferences took on new prominence. The first *Kaleidoscope* conference, organized by the Learning Resources Council of the Alberta Teacher's Association in Calgary in 1977, evolved into a quadrennial multi-day conference showcasing high-profile Canadian and international authors and illustrators. The annual *Serendipity* conference, hosted by the Vancouver Children's Literature Roundtable for the first time in 1982, provides a similar opportunity for the children's literature community to hear Canadian and international authors, illustrators, and publishers speak about their work. Other conferences had an exclusive Canadian focus, most notably the *Canadian Images Canadiennes* conference, sponsored by the Manitoba School Library Association and held in Winnipeg every four years between 1986 and 1998.

For child audiences, school and library tours served a similar purpose, bringing creators together with communities of readers. A teacher's activity guide on using Canadian children's books in the classroom was added to the Children's Book Festival kit in 1982.[150] In 1985, illustrators were added to the festival roster, and in 1987, the inclusion of science writers further expanded the number of creators participating in the tours. In 1988, the event was renamed the 'Children's Book Week,' to better reflect its scope, and by the following year, the Centre referred to it in its publicity as the 'Canadian Children's Book Week.'[151]

As the circle of children's literature enthusiasts widened and publishing opportunities increased, events like CANSCAIP's annual 'Packaging Your Imagination' workshop, inaugurated in 1984, provided opportunities for aspiring writers and illustrators to network with one another and with working professionals.[152] Following the success of workshops in writing for children offered by the University of British Columbia's Creative Writing Program, other colleges and universities developed similar opportunities for aspiring children's authors to draft picturebooks and novels, including two very popular writing courses that Peter Carver offered through George Brown College in Toronto.[153] Writers-in-residence programs at public libraries and academic institutions, beginning with Janet Lunn's tenure as writer-in-residence at the Regina Public Library in 1982–3, provided further opportunities for community engagement with children's book creators. Two exhibits, 'The Secret Self: An Exploration of Canadian Children's Literature / Le moi secret: Une exploration de la littérature de jeunesse canadienne,' at the

National Library of Canada in 1988, and the Vancouver Art Gallery's 1988 'Once Upon a Time,' curated by Ellen Thomas Cartwright, the first major art gallery exhibition focusing on original Canadian picturebook illustration, brought further attention to Canadian illustrators.[154]

The number and type of children's book awards increased throughout the 1980s, further raising the profile of children's literature in the media and with the general public, and bringing into play the political context of award decisions and jury composition. In 1981, IBBY-Canada inaugurated the Claude Aubry Award for distinguished service in children's literature, named in honour of the children's writer, translator, and Ottawa Public Library director. In 1982, the organization established the Frances E. Russell Award for research in Canadian children's literature. The visual and peritextual elements in children's books were recognized for the first time in 1981 with the Vancouver-based Alcuin Society's awards, given for excellence in book design. The Elizabeth Mrazik-Cleaver Canadian Picture Book Award was established by IBBY-Canada in 1985, with funds left for that purpose by Cleaver in her will, to recognize Canadian illustrators of picturebooks published in Canada. In 1987, the Canada Council's Children's Literature Prizes were incorporated into the Governor General's Literary Awards to recognize Canadian authors and illustrators of Canadian books published in English and in French. The same year, the Children's Literature Roundtables of Canada founded the first national children's literature award for excellence in non-fiction, the Information Book Award, and the British Columbia Book Prizes inaugurated the Sheila A. Egoff Children's Literature Prize. Businesses also saw the value of associating their trade name with children's awards. The Mr Christie's Book Award (1989–2004) was sponsored by the biscuit manufacturer Christie Brown and Company and recognized text and illustration in both English and French children's books published in Canada.[155]

'A Bossy Woman Trying to Tell People What to Read': Criticism and Reviewing

One of the most popular forms of children's book reviewing began in the early 1980s, when the CBC's *Morningside* radio program began a children's book panel feature, during which three children's literature experts discussed new books with host Peter Gzowski.[156] Judy Sarick of the Children's Book Store, Virginia Davis, director of the Canadian Children's Book Centre, and journalist and author Michele Landsberg formed the original panel. Sarick and Landsberg both remember Landsberg's initial reluctance to review Canadian materials, because she believed few titles were 'of any worth whatsoever.'[157] Gradually, more Canadian titles were added, until about 80 per cent of the books reviewed were Canadian.[158] Landsberg notes that as the program evolved, it 'became the most popular feature on the *Morningside* show. [The CBC] would get a thousand requests for the booklist.'[159]

Landsberg raises the issue of critics becoming the subject of criticism. She explains that after she published *Michele Landsberg's Guide to Children's Books* in 1986, she was attacked by some reviewers as 'a bossy woman trying to tell people what to read.'[160] As she remembers, opposition to her guide, and to the idea of evaluative standards, 'put a damper on criticism.' Summing up the experience, she concludes that 'there's a danger in trying to make criticism more popularly accessible. People misunderstand your motives or ascribe other motives.'[161]

Another attempt to democratize the reviewing of children's books began in 1976, when a group of parents calling themselves the Citizens' Committee on Children began a project to familiarize Canadians with the range of Canadian children's books. Between 1979 and 1991, the committee published seven volumes of *Children's Choices of Canadian Books*, a series of reviews of Canadian children's books compiled from the responses of a group of child readers, aged four to fourteen. Parents of children in the Ottawa area gathered their children's comments on a selection of Canadian books recommended by librarians and teachers. Each title was read by a number of children, whose responses were then collated by the committee. These collective reviews, which ranked titles into five groups, based on the percentage of readers in the suggested age range who enjoyed them and rated them highly, attempted to identify the titles that children wanted to read and found attractive, and to aid parents selecting books from libraries and bookstores. The publications were also designed to provide teachers, librarians, and publishers with evidence of 'what children really like in books,' the committee believing that 'what children think of books is one of the valid criteria for assessing the value of a children's book.'[162] They warned that some books that were 'highly regarded by adults' but rated poorly on the popularity scale with child readers would require 'considerable effort' by parents and teachers to make them 'acceptable to most children.' For the committee, the differences between children's tastes and adult judgement suggested that 'the enjoyment children will derive from reading on their own and for recreation' could not be predicated on professional evaluative criteria.[163] In turn, the professional reviewing journals were doubtful about the value of the reviews as a selection tool for teachers and librarians, questioning the project's methodology and subjective evaluation criteria, and cautioning that the reviewers were not necessarily representative of the majority of Canadian children.[164]

Comments by the children and their parents included in the reviews, however, provide valuable insight into the response of readers to Canadian books. Repeatedly, in the early years of the publication, parents and children stated that certain books were 'too Canadian' and too 'locality conscious,' that they were 'tired of Indians' and 'the North,' did not want to read any more 'books about the past,' and disliked 'Indian and Eskimo stories' and legends. Twelve years later, comments focused more on the suitability of narrative and illustrations for the age range of the assumed audience, the degree to which particular books sustained the reader's interest, and the acceptability of particular genres. Readers often mentioned covers and images, both positively and negatively. Some children commented that an unattractive or uninteresting cover detracted from the book and that illustrations distracted them from the story, were of no importance, or failed to let one's 'imagination run free.' Other reviewers said that the pictures made them happy, made them feel like they were 'in the book,' helped them to understand and remember the story ('I don't really know the words, and the pictures show what they're doing'), went 'good' with the story, or made them 'think of a movie.'

By the final edition of *Children's Choices* in 1991, the editor noted that when the project began, 'there were few Canadian children's books produced annually and few Canadians were familiar with many of them. Today bookstores regularly stock a wide selection of Canadian books, from publishers large and small. More of the books have high production values, particularly beautiful, colourful artwork. They contain exciting plots, believable child characters, and literate prose … Canadians can be proud of the burgeoning children's publishing industry, for our books rank with the finest in the world.'[165]

'It Truly Was a Heyday': Children's Bookstores

Following the success of Judy Sarick's Children's Book Store, new specialist children's bookstores opened throughout the late 1970s and 1980s, responding to growing demand by parents and teachers for access to a wide range of carefully chosen literature. Fifteen bookstores with at least 50 per cent of children's stock operated in Canada in 1980.[166] By 1985, that number had risen to forty-nine, and by 1991, fifty-five children's bookstores were spread across Canada.[167] Some stores developed a strong regional and national reputation, including Woozles in Halifax, established in 1978 by Ann Connor Brimer and Liz and Brian Crocker, and managed by Trudy Carey; Granny Bates Children's Books in St John's, established in 1986 by Margie McMillan and Nora Flynn; and Vancouver's Kidsbooks, now Canada's largest children's bookstore, established by Phyllis Simon in 1983 and now co-owned by Simon and Kelly McKinnon. Through the 1980s, Toronto-area specialist stores such as Mabel's Fables, established by Eleanor LeFave and Susan McCulloch in 1988, opened in competition with the Children's Book Store.

In the economic boom years of the early to mid-1980s, bookstores were able to draw on the overwhelmingly middle-class, well-educated, and affluent client base that typifies book buyers, developing close relationships with the community, acting as a resource for teachers, librarians, parents, writers, illustrators, and publishers, and promoting Canadian titles.[168] They hosted book launches, author readings, book clubs, storytelling events and workshops, as well as acting as wholesalers for the school and library market. Some independent bookstores were also willing to carry titles from smaller presses when the larger chain stores would not place orders. Toronto's Another Story Bookshop, owned by Sheila Koffman, was established in 1987 with a focus on diversity, equity, and social justice issues, stocking books with anti-racist, anti-classist, anti-sexist, and anti-homophobic themes.[169]

Michele Landsberg remembers the exhilaration of book tours during the 1980s, when the specialist and independent stores were opening across the country, explaining that 'it truly was a heyday. There were these great children's bookstores and they were so pleased to show me their special children's sections … I really felt that we were riding a wave. I didn't know that wave was going to go out with the tide at any moment but it did feel like a tremendous crest of interest and enthusiasm for children's books. There was a dawning understanding in Canada that children's literature could add so much to the lives of children and to their ultimate success in school.'[170]

While institutional sales of Canadian titles to schools and public libraries still formed only a small percentage of their overall purchases, support for Canadian print materials steadily increased.[171] By the end of the 1980s, enthusiasm and optimism permeated the Canadian children's book world.[172] Advocates of Canadian children's literature could claim international recognition and a thriving domestic institutional and retail market. A generation of Canadian children were growing up with children's books created and produced in Canada. Publishers and retailers, who expected that the market would continue to expand, would look back later from the perspective of the economic and publishing downturns of the 1990s and regard the decade with nostalgia as the halcyon days of children's publishing.

CHAPTER SEVEN

The 1990s to the Present Day: Structural Challenges and Changes

The concerns and obstacles facing Canadian children's publishers in the last two decades are generally the common plight of all Canadian publishers in the broader context of increasing globalization. Canadian publishers have had to respond to a rise in production and distribution costs, cutbacks in government subsidies and grants, and ongoing mergers, consolidations, and bankruptcies among publishers, distributors, and retailers.[1] They have also had to deal with issues of particular concern to children's publishers, from the shrinking of childhood populations in Canada, to reductions in funding for school and public libraries, the competition for the attention of young readers from new electronic media, and the potential of the internet to transform the consumption of print.[2]

The international face of publishing has changed as long-established independent, editorially-driven American and British publishing houses have merged, or been sold and resold, and subsumed into vertically integrated international media conglomerates whose management is primarily profit-driven.[3] Many experienced children's book editors have been made redundant by the mergers, and those who have retained their positions have found that commercial success is the new publishing criterion.[4] The shift to market-driven publishing has resulted in increased numbers of titles being issued each season in shorter print runs. If a book does not enjoy immediate sales success and strong reviews, long-term support is withdrawn. As a result, children's publishing increasingly has been commodified as content becomes more homogeneous, and marketability and the possibility for 'synergy,' or the cross-marketing of brands, rather than literary or artistic merit, determine whether a book will be published. Commercial merchandising trends now dominate children's publishing, ranging from the book-plus-toy combinations to multimedia and movie and television tie-ins, and the use of children's book characters to sell toys, clothing, and other products.[5]

Patsy Aldana of Groundwood Books has strong opinions on the destructive effects of the mergers on the editorially driven children's publishing houses, noting that the multinationals who have bought respected children's book companies face intense pressure to generate sales volume to pay staff and service the debt incurred in buying the lists. As she explains, the strength of the children's book market in the 1980s led publishers to believe that they could continue to publish profitably a large number of titles each season. After a merger, companies that might have published twenty-five books a year were required to publish fifty or seventy-five titles to increase the revenue generated by the list. The result is that publishers are 'always looking for best-sellers, and you can be pretty sure you'll have a best-seller if it's a TV tie-in.'[6] She concludes that in a globalized economy, it is increasingly difficult to survive as an independent, publisher-owned company.[7]

Instability in Government Funding of Publishing and Cultural Programs

Canadian publishers were significantly affected by the sharp downturn in the economy in the early 1990s in a climate of political uncertainty after the failure of Meech Lake and Charlottetown accords. Changes to the regulations governing foreign ownership of Canadian publishers (the Baie Comeau agreement), the introduction of the Goods and Services Tax on books, and radical federal and provincial budget cuts resulting from a combination of high interest rates and massive deficits further destabilized the publishing industry.[8] In 1992, the federal government introduced Bill C-93, proposing the merger of the Canada Council with the Social Sciences and Humanities Research Council. The merger was vigorously opposed by the arts and academic communities, and the bill was defeated at the Senate level. However, the combination of a reduction in parliamentary appropriations to the Canada Council and government-mandated reductions in administrative costs resulted in a one-third cut to the Council's staff and restrictions on grants to cultural organizations.[9] As Virginia Davis, former director of the Canadian Children's Book Centre, recalls, the Council 'cut back all of their support for established programs and associations in favour of freeing up more money to support authors and illustrators directly … [putting] tremendous strain on the organizations that depended on their funding.'[10]

The cuts had a serious impact on the Children's Book Centre, which relied on the Council for funds to support its touring programs for authors and illustrators. The Centre was forced into a period of retrenchment at a time when advocacy and support for children's literature from the National Library of Canada was also challenged. In 1993, Irene Aubrey, the founder of the Children's Literature Service at the National Library, retired and was not replaced.[11] The loss of the position, and the resulting diminution of collection development, reference work, promotion, and outreach deeply concerned children's literature specialists.[12] Although the position was reinstated when Josiane Polidori was appointed head of the Canadian Children's Literature Service in 2000, it was unfortunate that during a critical period for Canadian children's books, there was no strong advocate at the National Library.

In the same difficult environment in the early 1990s, government support for publishing was in upheaval. The Canadian Book Publishing Development Program was established by the federal government's Department of Communication in 1979 to provide support for Canadian publishers.[13] The government also funded the Publications Distribution Assistance Program, which made it possible for Canadian-owned houses to compete with foreign publishers. When the two programs were merged and the combined agency's budget was cut by more than 50 per cent in the February 1995 federal budget, the five-year business plans developed by publishers were undermined, resulting in retrenchment, reduction of new initiatives, and a focus on commercially viable projects.[14] Although much of the government's support was restored by 1998, it took great resourcefulness, fortitude, and business acumen on the part of the publishers to continue their commitment to an indigenous publishing program of Canadian writing for children.

The Changing World of Public Libraries

At the same time that Canadian children's publishers faced a barrage of structural challenges resulting from funding cuts, an even more threatening problem developed as the domestic institutional market began to decline precipitously. In 1971, children fourteen years of age and under represented just under 30 per cent of the population of Canada.[15] By 1995, that figure had dropped to 20 per cent, and by 2005 had dropped again to just under 18 per cent.[16] Across Canada, public library systems, provincial ministries of education, and local school boards have had to make funding decisions in light of these changing demographics among preschool and school-aged populations, a financial climate of restraint in public expenditures, and new demands for technology. While school library and public library sales continue to account for 46 per cent of the market in Canada, numerous recent studies have documented the changes in declining institutional support for the purchasing of Canadian children's books.[17]

Many public library systems have experienced reductions in their budgets, resulting from a combination of tightening of civic and provincial fiscal support, shrinking allocations within the budgets for acquisitions, increased prices, particularly in the cost of journal and online database subscriptions, and redistribution of acquisition budgets to accommodate new technologies.[18] Public libraries have responded to budgetary constraints by refocusing the responsibilities of professional staff away from cataloguing and collection development, by centralizing the book selection process, by reducing staffing levels, and by deprofessionalizing or downgrading job descriptions.[19]

Some large systems have re-envisioned children's services, most notably at the Toronto Public Library (TPL) in the mid-1990s, as a result of reductions in provincial allocations for library services, civic budget cuts, and then an amalgamation of library systems in the Metro Toronto area. Staff was redeployed, the number of designated children's positions were reduced, children's librarians were recategorized as generalists, and decisions about acquisitions were centralized, ending the practice of specialist librarians sharing their reviews of books as part of the selection and ordering process.[20] A spirited campaign, led by the 'Friends of Toronto Public Library' and authors Dennis Lee and Michele Landsberg, including a well-publicized 'Read-in' at Toronto City Hall and a presentation before the Library Board, resulted in the reconsideration of some policy decisions, but the long-term consequences were a departure from TPL's tradition of specialist children's services, despite the appointment of Ken Setterington as the first 'Advocate for Children and Youth Services.'[21]

Even as public library systems struggle with budget reductions, they have introduced dedicated programs for teenagers, created and enhanced spaces for children and teens, reached out to families and children from ethnocultural minority groups, and improved online access to library resources.[22] Public libraries have engaged in collaborative outreach programs with a variety of businesses and non-profit agencies to reach children and families outside the walls of the library in pre-schools, daycares, pre-natal classes, and hospitals, and through intergenerational family literacy initiatives, funded in partnership with provincial governments, literacy associations, school boards, and public health programs. Various early literacy programs distribute literacy kits with a selected book or books, a library card, suggested parent-child literacy activities, and information on reading and child development, including British Columbia's Ready Set Learn and Books for Babies kits, and the Vancouver Public Library's Ready to Read program; Ontario's Newborn Literacy Kit, which includes a board book written and illustrated by Barbara Reid; and Nova Scotia's Read to Me! Nova Scotia Family Literacy Program.[23] The TD Summer Reading Club, a program created by the Toronto Public Library in 1994 and expanded across Ontario in 2001, became a joint initiative with Library and Archives Canada in 2004 and is now a fully bilingual program offered in eleven provinces and territories.[24]

The Changing World of Teacher-Librarians

In the last fifteen years, the erosion of school library budgets has resulted in the reduction, replacement, or elimination of teacher-librarian positions, inadequate staffing levels in libraries, and restricted hours of access.[25] For example, in Alberta, between 1980 and 2001, there was a more than 80 per cent reduction in the number of teacher-librarians working at least half-time, from 550 to about 100, while in the same period, more than 200 new schools were constructed.[26] In Nova Scotia, between 1990 and 2002, there was an 87 per cent decline in teacher-librarians, while in Manitoba, provincial funding for school libraries remained static between 1993 and 2003.[27]

Unlike teacher-librarians, who have a degree in education as well as additional coursework for qualification, the library technicians, non-professionals, and volunteers who have replaced teacher-librarians in many school libraries generally lack the extensive training in the evaluation of children's literature and the specialist knowledge of materials that is part of professional education. Many two-year library technician programs at community colleges in Canada offer only a single course in children's library services and do not provide the education to support ongoing collection development.[28] In fact, the need for collection development at all is called into question by some decision makers, who have argued that because the virtual library would soon replace printed sources, school libraries (and teacher-librarians) would soon become entirely obsolete.[29]

The shifting of staff from professionals to paraprofessionals and volunteers comes at the same time that many school boards have moved to decentralized purchasing and provincial ministries of education have reduced or eliminated designated school media specialists, placing increasing demands on school library staff.[30] The Association of Canadian Publishers' (ACP's) *Canadian Books in School Libraries* study found that 60 to 70 per cent of school libraries' purchases are acquired from library wholesalers, who provide pre-selected and pre-catalogued material.[31] The number of schools subscribing to a range of professional resources to aid in the selection process has decreased, especially subscriptions to reviewing journals, which 'tend to be expensive and out of reach of many budgets.' In the absence of the reviewing journals, word of mouth becomes one of the main sources of information about new titles.[32] The erosion of professional status for teacher-librarians, however, has reduced the opportunities to share information about children's books with interested colleagues at conferences and round tables.

The situation for school libraries has become so grave that a new body, the Canadian Coalition for School Libraries (CCSL), was formed in 2002 from a broad cross-section of librarians, teachers, parents, authors, publishers, literacy advocates, and academics to raise awareness of the imperilled state of school libraries and teacher-librarianship.[33] The CCSL held a summit at the 2003 International Forum on Canadian Children's Literature in Ottawa, at which the results of Ken Haycock's 2003 report, *The Crisis in Canada's School Libraries: The Case for Reform and Re-Investment*, were highlighted.[34] Haycock documents the link between student achievement and the presence of well-stocked libraries and professional teacher-librarians in the schools.[35]

Despite various lobbying efforts over the last decade, the situation for school libraries and teacher-librarians continues to erode. A 2005 Statistics Canada study identified a decline in the number of full-time teacher-librarians. The national average was 0.25 FTE, or a quarter-time teacher-librarian, with considerable variation among provinces, from a high of 0.56 in Prince Edward Island to a low of 0.03 in Quebec, while the median expenditure on books and magazines was $2,000 per year.[36]

Children's literature specialists, children's librarians, and teacher-librarians wonder if there will be a new generation of professionals with the same commitment to Canadian children's literature that marked their own careers. Their concerns are not unreasonable. When academics in English, education, creative writing, and information studies retire, their positions are not necessarily filled by children's literature specialists, and the programs and courses that they have taught may be eliminated from the academic calendar.[37] Teacher-librarians have watched the steady erosion of their profession, as courses in teacher-librarianship have shifted to online delivery or have been discontinued.[38]

There are concerns that education programs lack systematic instruction in Canadian literature.[39] Although most professionals believe that it is important that Canadian books are included in library collections, the estimated percentage of Canadian content in school libraries remains between 10 and 30 per cent.[40] The ACP study notes that when respondents to the survey were asked to identify the significant barriers to increasing Canadian content in school libraries, 65 per cent of respondents said lack of awareness of Canadian titles, and 55 per cent said lack of budget.[41] A study by Joyce Bainbridge at the University of Alberta on the inclusion of Canadian children's literature in the classrooms of 170 elementary school teachers determined that while 96 per cent of the interviewees stated that it was important to include Canadian materials, the majority continued 'to rely heavily on American materials, and many found it difficult to list a Canadian children's

Plate 1 A Lady (attributed to Mary Love). *A Peep at the Esquimaux, or, Scenes on the Ice:*
To Which is Annexed, A Polar Pastoral: With Forty Coloured Plates, from Original Designs.
London: H.R. Thomas, 1825.
Reproduction from the Arkley Collection of Early and Historical Children's Literature, Rare Books
and Special Collections, University of British Columbia Library.

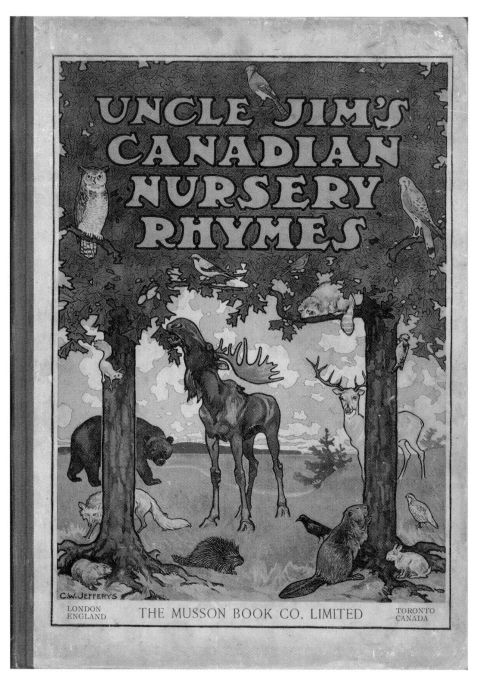

Plate 2 [David Boyle]. *Uncle Jim's Canadian Nursery Rhymes: For Family and Kindergarten Use*. Illustrated by C.W. Jefferys. London and Toronto: Musson, 1908.

Reproduction from the Arkley Collection of Early and Historical Children's Literature, Rare Books and Special Collections, University of British Columbia Library.

Plate 19 Thomas King. *A Coyote Columbus Story*. Illustrated by William Kent Monkman.
A Groundwood Book. Toronto and Vancouver: Douglas and McIntyre, 1992.
Reprinted with the permission of the publisher, Groundwood Books.

Plate 20 Leo Yerxa. *Last Leaf First Snowflake to Fall*. A Groundwood Book. Toronto and
Vancouver: Douglas and McIntyre, 1993.
Reprinted with the permission of the publisher, Groundwood Books.

author by name.'[42] In effect, those purchasing for school libraries increasingly see only a small selection of available literature, do not have consistent access to reviews of Canadian material, and are not necessarily aware of the range of books being published in Canada, a situation all too reminiscent of the findings of studies of school libraries in the early 1970s.[43]

Patsy Aldana is forthright in her bleak assessment of the changes to the publishing industry that have resulted from the decline in institutional sales, believing that Canadian young people are at risk of losing the opportunity to see themselves reflected in the books that they read.[44] Virginia Davis, former executive director of the Canadian Children's Book Centre, observes that changes in the curriculum that focus on skill development have further reduced opportunities for students to experience reading as a pleasurable activity and develop an awareness of what she describes as 'the culture of a country.'[45]

'You Can Never Tell What a Best-seller Is Going to Be': Publishers Respond to the Loss of Institutional Sales

May Cutler, founder of Tundra Books, would only publish books she felt would have at least a ten-year life span, believing that her backlist represented a collection of timeless classics that would continue to generate revenue and international recognition. Cutler's view, that a publisher's list has value and that books have an enduring power to communicate with successive generations of readers, has been challenged in recent years by the changes in publishing, distribution, and sales. Many publishers have shifted their focus in response to the diminution of the Canadian school library market and the vagaries of retail sales, eliminating midlist titles (books that are expected to sell in numbers to justify their publication but are unlikely to be best-sellers), in favour of work by established authors and illustrators with strong sales records, books with immediate 'brand recognition,' and books with the potential for international sales.[46] Publishers, however, find it difficult to predict which books will find immediate sales in a highly competitive market. As Kathy Lowinger, publisher of Tundra Books, comments, 'you can never tell what a best-seller is going to be or what will really touch a child.'[47]

Taking a risk on a midlist title with limited sales potential by a new or emerging author is no longer seen as an economically viable publishing decision. In a tight economic climate, publishers argue that each book on their list must be distinctive and have the potential for strong sales. As Rick Wilks explains, at Annick 'every book has to have a real identity.'[48] Similarly, Patsy Aldana explains that while Groundwood has not cut back its overall list, it has shifted away from midlist titles, and from the standard thirty-two-page picturebooks, to a greater breadth of genres, including 'longer books, books with more text or books in which illustration is essential.'[49]

The relationship between canon formation and backlist is called into question by the relentless move towards the commodification of books. The person shopping in a bookstore increasingly has a limited selection of current books from which to choose, rather than a wide range of new and older titles. New books must find their place in the market immediately or disappear from the publishers' lists, eliminating the possibility of consumers finding reprints of 'old favourites' in their local bookstore or being able to purchase copies of titles more than eighteen months to two years after a title's initial release.[50] At the same time, the rapid growth of online used and out-of-print booksellers, including Advanced Book Exchange and Amazon.ca's used book service, suggests that the idea that books have as short a shelf life as pots of yogurt is more the perception of marketing departments than of consumers.[51]

The current economics of publishing mean that children's publishers no longer believe that they can afford to retain a warehouse of backlisted titles, and bookstores no longer see backlist as a complement to the new season's titles, and capable of generating sufficient revenue to justify shelf space.[52] As Aldana explains, while Groundwood titles in the past were not allowed to go out of print, the loss of school libraries has meant that backlist books that previously would sell several thousand copies a year now only sell several hundred copies. As a result, when stock runs out of a backlist title, publishers look carefully at the decision to reprint while others move quickly to remainder stock. Aldana summarizes the problem by stating, 'We can't really justify a reprint that's not going to sell out for five years … All our cash would be sitting in unsold books that were getting yellow.'[53] Kathy Lowinger also points out that the long-standing practice of reducing unit costs for full-colour picturebooks by printing larger runs in anticipation of sales over several years also increases warehousing costs, takes up inventory space, and ties up money in stock that will not see an immediate return on the investment. As she explains, the decision to reprint backlist is difficult 'in an industry that seems to be moving towards "three months out the door and then it is old news."'[54]

Declining school library sales not only affect the decision to reprint older titles, but contribute to decisions about initial print runs. Some publishers have cut initial runs by one-third to one-half, based on projected institutional sales.[55] Rick Wilks summarizes the changed market and how it has hampered Annick's ability to publish new authors and illustrators, noting that 'the market does not have a big appetite for a large selection of books beyond the best-sellers. Getting shelf space, review attention, and publicity is hard if you're not on the "A" list. Ten years ago, well over half our list would be picturebooks. Now we can't do more than two picturebooks a season, and that's in a list of thirty … This isn't a literary decision. It's a market-driven decision. They're just too hard to sell.'[56] Other publishers argue that while picturebooks today make up a smaller percentage of their overall children's lists than they did in the 1990s, the shift is a result of diversification into a wider range of children's book genres, rather than a deliberate reduction.[57]

'People Would Begrudge Ten Dollars for a Book': Changing Consumer Patterns

In the last decade, there have been significant changes in the book purchasing habits of the general public. The price in Canada of a new hardcover picturebook rose in the early 1990s, resulting from a combination of a weak Canadian dollar, increased production costs, and decreasing sizes of print runs in response to the downturn in institutional sales. As Phyllis Simon of Kidsbooks in Vancouver explains, as a consequence, bookstores saw a significant decline in sales, exacer-

bated by shifting trends in the teaching of reading away from the use of trade picturebooks in the classroom.[58] Despite the independent stores' knowledgeable staff
and ability to match readers with books (known in the trade as 'hand-selling'),
there has been a drop-off in picturebook sales.

The increasing cost of children's titles, and consumer resistance, were also cited
as factors in the changing world of bookselling by Judy Sarick of the Children's
Book Store in Toronto.[59] As she notes, children's retail bookstores face additional
challenges in controlling overhead. While the retail prices of children's books are
lower than adult titles, staffing levels in specialist bookstores have traditionally
been greater to support hand-selling, and the cost of processing orders remains
the same whatever the price of the book, resulting in significantly higher overall
costs for sales. Balancing the need to provide specialized service while ensuring
continued profitability has been a significant factor in the demise of some specialist children's bookstores.

Consumer resistance to the price of books is also cited as a problem by Michele
Landsberg, who notes that independent children's bookstores tried to improve
profitability in the1990s by diversifying their stock to include non-book items with
a higher profit margin. She describes the decision to add games, toys, dolls, and
puzzles to the retail mix as 'a necessary, desperate measure' to survive. As she
remembers, at the time that her guide to children's literature was published in the
mid-1980s, she 'had to address the issue of the cost of children's books, because
people would always say, "Ten dollars. That's so expensive."' She adds that she
was 'shocked that people would begrudge ten dollars for a book of lasting worth
when they would throw it away on any toy, easily.' She concludes that price resistance continues to be an ongoing struggle for children's book retailing.[60]

The Rise of the Mega-Bookstore

The 1990s also saw new pressure on publishers and independent booksellers due
to retail consolidation. The controversial 1995 merger of Coles Book Stores and
SmithBooks, the country's two largest bookstore chains, to form Chapters, Inc.,
further changed the nature of bookselling and publishing in Canada.[61] The new
company moved quickly to expand its locations, announcing that it would open
seventy-five new large-footprint superstores, while closing 150 smaller locations,
mostly in shopping malls.[62] Unlike other retail sectors, bookstores order their stock
from the publisher or wholesaler at retail price, minus a discount that traditionally
ranged from 40 to 45 per cent, with the option to return undamaged books within
a set period of time. With Chapters controlling approximately half of retail sales in
Canada, they used their purchasing power to demand bigger discounts and better
payment policies than those given to independents and charged publishers for
exhibiting books in high-visibility areas of their stores.[63]

Although Chapters and its rival chain Indigo, established in 1996, have been
credited with bringing non-readers into bookstores and books to a wider range of
readers, in what one publisher called 'the democratization of reading,' the advent
of the mega-bookstores in Canada resulted in increasing challenges to Canadian
publishers and independent booksellers, in a pattern already observed by the

American book industry.[64] Chapters moved to centralize purchasing, accelerated a process that had begun in the mid-1990s with the introduction of computerized 'just in time' inventory control, leading to initial orders being reduced by up to 80 per cent in some cases. In other cases, prepublication orders for projected best-sellers were disproportionately high, with the rate of returns soaring to 50 per cent or more of the initial order, well above the industry average of 30 per cent.[65] The combination of demands for higher discounts, mass ordering of titles, slow payment of invoices for books shipped, and the subsequent return of large numbers of unsold books placed many small Canadian publishers in a precarious financial position. Publishers would increase their print runs on the basis of pre-publication orders from Chapters and then face heavy returns at the end of the season, leaving them with unwanted inventory that was unlikely to sell in subsequent seasons.[66]

By the time that the Standing Committee on Canadian Heritage released its report, *The Challenge of Change: A Consideration of the Canadian Book Industry*, in June 2000 the effects of the concentration of power in the hands of a few major retailers were being felt by publishers and booksellers across the country.[67] Chapters was the dominant presence in the Canadian bookselling community, controlling anywhere between 25 and 75 per cent of the retail trade.[68] Its worsening economic situation, caused by rapid expansion and the cost of instituting an online retail presence to compete with Amazon, caused increasing concern among Canadian publishers.[69] When Indigo Books and Music bought Chapters in a hostile takeover in 2001 and became Canada's largest single book retailer, the pressures on both publishers and independent booksellers remained unaddressed, with the new company controlling between 60 and 70 per cent of the market.[70]

'A Core of Highly Knowledgeable Booksellers': The Decline of the Independent Bookstore

Many independent bookstores and small regional chains, including long-established stores in major urban areas, downsized or closed in the wake of the rise of the mega-bookstores, unable to compete on equal terms. Some independents saw their sales drop 15 per cent or more within months of a mega-bookstore opening in their community.[71] The practice of deep discounting selected frontlist and best-selling titles forced independents to respond by offering similar discounts to their customers, while not themselves enjoying the additional discounts offered to the mega-bookstores. Some independents carried out costly renovations to add cafes and reading areas in order to resemble the mega-bookstores.[72] Even children's speciality stores, which had enjoyed significant consumer support in an expanding market throughout the 1980s, were affected. In 1991, there were fifty-five bookstores that devoted at least 50 per cent of their stock to children's literature.[73] By 1997, the number had declined to forty-one, and by 2003, only twenty-four specialist children's bookstores remained in Canada.[74] With the decline in independent bookstores, children's publishers have seen a dramatic shift in their distribution patterns. According to Rick Wilks, some Canadian publishers report that their sales to independent bookstores have dropped over the last decade from 50 to 12 per cent.[75]

Dennis Johnson, former publisher and managing editor of Red Deer Press, expresses his deep concern and frustration with the impact of retail consolidation on North American children's book publishing. As he explains, publishers can no longer count 'on a core of highly knowledgeable, highly experienced independent booksellers to bring the first buzz to a book the way you could in the past ... When they loved a book they made it their mission to get out on the floor of their store and hand-sell it to customers ... [but] there aren't enough of them around any more to create that kind of upward sales momentum for a book.'[76] Judy and Hy Sarick's decision to retire and close the Children's Book Store in Toronto in 2000, after twenty-five years of promoting children's literature in Canada, is emblematic of the loss to the publishing community of passionate, opinionated, and committed advocates who could connect creators, publishers, and readers.[77]

The reduced numbers of titles carried in the inventory of the mega-bookstores and the reduction of backlist have altered publishing patterns. Johnson argues that the independents recognized the cultural value in bookselling and were willing to take risks in ordering, based on their confidence to match readers and authors and their belief that particular titles were important. As marketing values have come to predominate, the taste of the small number of buyers ordering from the head offices of the mega-bookstores for stores across Canada, as well as their ordering patterns, begin to shape what is published. As he explains, 'publishers are beginning to internalize the values that they perceive are held by the category managers and buyers of those major chains. I can't help but believe that what they feel is the ideal expression of a children's picturebook is ultimately going to be internalized by publishers.'[78]

From a different perspective, Judy Sarick observes the difference that the focus on retail marketing has made in children's publishing, noting that 'when children's publishers were publishing for a school and library market, they looked at levels of meaning, depth, and artistic relevance.'[79] With the shift to a retail market, publishers have increasingly favoured eye-catching design and striking graphic presentation as the means to entice customer purchases, sometimes at the expense of content. The lack of expert staff in the children's areas of the mega-bookstores, and the consequent lack of assistance in helping adults select books that are appropriate for the child's age, reading level, and interests, further the trend of publishers relying on immediate visual appeal and 'brand recognition' to sell a book, rather than taking a risk on titles that need hand-selling.[80] As Patsy Aldana has commented, the mega-bookstores are 'not an effective way to sell children's books, except series books based on TV or best-sellers' compared with the independents and specialist children's bookstores.[81]

The overall reduction in backlist, and the aversion to risk-taking that seems to characterize the buying patterns of the mega-bookstores, have adversely affected Canadian children's writers and illustrators, who find that their older titles are no longer stocked unless the writer is well known or the book is a best-seller. Children's writer Celia Lottridge has experienced this shift in the market for her books, noting that the reluctance to carry backlist as well as frontlist books, and the reduction of non-mainstream books in inventory, mean that when she is asked where someone might obtain her books, she frequently tells them to order online, because 'you can't tell them what bookstore to go to.'[82]

The surviving children's bookstores in Canada had to develop strategies to fight the power of the mega-bookstores. Phyllis Simon remembers that 'in Canada we have the privilege, in a way, of observing the situation in the United States. It was a good three or four years before it happened here ... [so] we were able to see what worked and what was lethal in the American climate.'[83] Simon believes that the successful independent children's booksellers who survived the introduction of mega-bookstores have a strong sense of how to run a business while at the same time promoting good literature and reading, making themselves an exciting and important part of their community.[84]

In the face of competition from the mega-bookstores, children's bookstores have moved to emphasize their expertise in connecting children with books. Trudy Carey of Woozles: A Place For and About Children in Halifax found that although customers returned to the independents after being lured away by the deep discounts of the mega-bookstores, the need to compete with 'Costco, Walmart, drug stores, and supermarkets' for the sale of best-sellers has been difficult. Woozles continues to cultivate committed readers by ensuring that their stock appeals to different age groups and by offering an enticing range of programs and events that attract diverse groups of customers.[85]

Distribution Woes

In the period between 1999 and 2002, the difficulties in the book industry identified in the report of the Standing Committee on Canadian Heritage were exacerbated by the financial instability and eventual bankruptcy of Stoddart Publishing and General Distribution Services (GDS), which was owned by Stoddart and served as a warehousing and order fulfilment and distribution service for about 70 per cent of Canadian publishers. Publishers would contract with General to warehouse and ship their stock and to manage the invoicing of retail and institutional accounts. As problems with payments and returns from Chapters accumulated, GDS had difficulty covering its own outstanding bills to publishers and struggled with its own problems of distribution and the timely fulfilment of orders.[86] When the restructuring of GDS failed in 2002, many publishers lost both their current inventory and their backlist that had been warehoused with them, as well as outstanding payments for sales. Some small publishing houses closed, while others experienced cash flow problems and had difficulties meeting salaries and paying royalties to authors and illustrators. Publishers were forced to reduce or curtail their frontlists, cut back on their children's publishing programs, eliminate staff positions, or close altogether.[87] Authors and illustrators were affected by the loss of long-standing working relationships and by the uncertainty about whether their work would continue to remain in print.[88]

'We Act as a U.S. Publisher': Moving into Direct Sales in the American Market

Within the context of international consolidation and merger of publishing houses, and the commercialization of publishing in the 1990s, American publishers were no longer willing to take as many risks with midlist titles and works by authors without 'name recognition.' As a result, their interest in acquiring the rights to Canadian children's books and negotiating co-publications diminished.[89] Valerie Hussey, former president and publisher of Kids Can Press, notes that by the early 1990s, American publishers were reducing their requests for quotes on first print-ings from 15,000 to 25,000 copies to runs of 6,000 or 7,000 copies.[90] Consequently, if a title does not sell through quickly enough, it will no longer be given the time to establish a market through reviews and word of mouth. Instead, the rights revert to the originating publisher, who loses money.[91]

As a consequence, the changes brought by reduced rights and co-publication sales have had a serious impact on Canadian children's publishing at a time when Canadian institutional sales are declining and the retail market is in a state of upheaval. The list of a typical American children's publisher is about 120 titles a year, compared with the five to ten titles for a small publisher, and twenty to forty titles for a large publisher in Canada. Sales are on a similarly different scale.[92] An American frontlist title by a well-known author or illustrator can have domestic sales in excess of 450,000 copies.[93] While Canadian series like Marie-Louise Gay's *Stella* titles can sell 100,000 copies in the United States, and a commercial block-buster like Robert Munsch's *Love You Forever* (1986) has sold more than seventeen million copies worldwide, they are anomalies.[94]

A decade ago, domestic print runs in Canada for a picturebook ranged on aver-age from 3,000 to 10,000 copies in both paperback and hardcover editions, the range reflecting the difference between frontlist titles and midlist titles. Expected sales in Canada for a picturebook by an established author, issued by a well-estab-lished publishing company, were between 3,000 and 5,000 copies, spread over sev-eral years.[95] A best-selling title might sell 5,000 copies on its initial print run and be reprinted quickly if sales proved especially strong.[96] Today, while Scholastic might plan an initial print run of 25,000 copies for a new Robert Munsch title, and Kids Can may print 35,000 copies of a new Franklin picturebook, most Canadian pub-lishers have adjusted their initial print runs downward to between 3,000 and 4,000 copies, with expectations for sales in Canada similarly reduced.[97]

In contrast, foreign rights sales of Canadian titles can result in royalties on print runs of 30,000 copies in foreign-language markets.[98] As a result, direct sales into the United States and rights sales in the international market have become critical to the survival of many children's publishers in Canada.[99] Taking their books direct-ly into the United States, bypassing rights sales to an American publisher, involves risks, including the problems introduced by currency fluctuations, but gives Cana-dian publishers the ability to increase the size of print runs, ensure production qual-ity, directly control publicity and marketing of their lists, and ultimately generate greater sales.[100] In 1997, Kids Can made the decision to enter the American market directly by establishing itself as an American publisher with separate catalogues, pricing, sales and marketing, and, in some cases, a separate U.S. edition of titles.[101] Rick Wilks notes that Annick Press has stopped selling rights to its titles to American publishers, explaining that they need to sell between 2,000 and 2,500 copies in the United States for direct sales to be more lucrative than licensing.[102] For other pub-lishers, like Bob Tyrrell of Orca Book Publishers, direct sales in the United States pro-vide the opportunity to market their full list rather than a few selected highlights.[103]

Patsy Aldana describes Groundwood's move into the U.S. market, explaining that they are an incorporated publishing company in the United States. They send out review copies, promote their books, and submit books for awards as a U.S. publisher. She notes that 70 per cent of their sales are now in the United States, adding that if they were limited to sales in the Canadian market, Groundwood would cease to operate.[104] Her estimates of the percentage of sales outside Canada are typical of an industry-wide trend that sees the majority of Canadian children's book publishers' market outside of Canada, with 63 per cent of sales in the export market in 2000, a 17 per cent increase over a five year period.[105]

The Children's Book Centre Reinvents Itself

In an era in which children's publishing is seen as an increasingly risky venture, Canada's children's literature creators, publishers, and readers have found it helpful to come together to build supportive relationships and renew their sense of community. The cuts in Canada Council funding to the Canadian Children's Book Centre in the early 1990s forced the Centre to reinvent itself. In 1999, the Centre began to move from public to private funding of its activities, establishing partnerships with corporate sponsors to stabilize funding. Charlotte Teeple, the Centre's executive director, explains that they now rely on funding from a variety of different sources including membership fees, sponsorships, grants from various government agencies and private foundations, donations, endowments, fees for services, and sales, a situation that is similar to not-for-profit organizations across Canada.[106]

In 2000, the TD Bank Financial Group became the title sponsor for Book Week, with Pearson Education Canada and the Imperial Oil Charitable Foundation signing on as co-associate sponsors.[107] In 2001, a new project, the TD Grade One Book Giveaway was launched to distribute a children's book to each Grade One student throughout Canada as part of the renamed TD Canadian Children's Book Week.[108] The same year, Communication-Jeunesse joined with the Centre in the first coordinated touring schedule of francophone and anglophone authors and illustrators during Book Week.[109]

The Children's Book News continues to play an important role in disseminating information about Canadian children's books, authors, and illustrators, and promoting the work of the Centre. The publication has undergone physical changes, from black and white on plain paper, to the present full colour, and a change of title in 2003 to The Canadian Children's Book News to emphasize its national focus.[110] The frequency with which it has been issued also changed, as well as the intended audience and scope of coverage. According to current editor Gillian O'Reilly, the expanded publication, which is now available on newsstands, gives readers a greater understanding of and appreciation for Canadian children's books and the children's publishing industry, knowledge that they can use in promoting the books with young readers.[111]

Promoting the Book: Festivals and Tours

Writers' festivals and fairs are an opportunity for Canadian children's writers to interact with readers. The 'Word on the Street' book and magazine fair, a celebration of literacy and print culture that began in Toronto in 1989, is now held in five urban communities across the country and includes a variety of activities designed to bring readers together with the printed word.[112] The Vancouver International Writers Festival, begun in 1988 by founding artistic director Alma Lee, has included children's programs from the outset. The festival's Schools program is the largest literary event for children in Canada, involving more than 6,000 children each year in festival events and outreach programs in schools.[113] Since 1997, the Montreal Blue Metropolis International Literary Festival, and the workshops and educational programs offered by the Blue Metropolis Foundation, help to connect children and literature in English, French, and Spanish as part of its mandate to bring people from different cultures together to share the pleasure of reading and writing.[114] In Toronto, 'ALOUD: A Celebration for Young Readers,' an annual three-day literary festival designed for an audience of children, has been held since 2005 as part of the activities of International Readings at Harbourfront Centre.[115]

Many publishers feel that book fairs and promotional tours have become essential for children's writers and illustrators to ensure a sustained reading audience for their work. Bob Tyrrell, publisher of Orca, notes that economic realities also encourage creators to participate in school tours. As he explains, most children's authors in Canada cannot sustain themselves on royalties alone. Authors with interesting and well-shaped presentations not only directly increase the sales of their books when on tour, but also generate extra income. Tyrrell also identifies the tension between touring and creating, adding that while some writers see the time spent in touring as detracting from their writing, touring has helped to determine whether a children's writer will be successful.[116]

Organizations and Retreats for Writers and Illustrators

When not on tour, authors and illustrators often work in relative isolation. Many welcome the opportunities provided by regional and local professional organizations to network and exchange information. In 1993, the Children's Writers and Illustrators of British Columbia (CWILL) organization grew out of local CAN-SCAIP membership to address the needs of published authors and illustrators.[117] CWILL has organized panels for aspiring writers and illustrators, and is one of the co-sponsors of the Canadian Book Camp held at the Vancouver Public Library.[118] Informal organizations, including the 'Group of Eight' illustrators' group in the Toronto area, and the Island Illustrators' Society, based in Victoria, provide mutual support and opportunities to discuss work with other professionals.[119] Writers' conferences and retreats that include sessions on writing for children include Saskatchewan's Sage Hill Writing Experience and Toronto's Humber School for Writers, established in1992, which began an annual 'Writing for Young Readers Workshop' in the summer of 2005.[120] Writers-in-residence programs at public libraries and universities across Canada have provided another venue for authors to connect with readers through consultations, public readings, school visits, and workshops.

Conferences and Courses

National conferences and symposia have been organized to bring the scholarly and professional communities together to discuss children's literature. The University of Ottawa, in conjunction with the National Library of Canada, held a bilingual Children's Literature Symposium in 1999 to discuss Canadian national literature for children.[121] In 2003, the National Library celebrated its fiftieth anniversary with a bilingual gathering, 'The Fun of Reading: An International Forum on Canadian Children's Literature / Lire me sourit: Forum international sur la littérature canadienne pour la jeunesse,' a four-day conference that attracted an international group of authors, illustrators, educators, librarians, academics, publishers, politicians, administrators, and others interested in children's literature and children's literacy issues.[122] Professional conferences continue to provide a forum for creators of children's books and readers to meet, including the well-established Serendipity and Kaleidoscope conferences and the Newfoundland-based Eastern Horizons conference on Canadian children's literature (2000–3).

Opportunities for the formal study of children's literature and literary production have also expanded over the last decade. In 1999, the University of Alberta began to offer a new online course, 'Canadian Literature for Young People in Schools and Libraries.' In the same year, four departments at the University of British Columbia founded a multidisciplinary Master of Arts in Children's Literature Program, which includes courses on Canadian children's literature across two faculties. In 2005, Mavis Reimer, professor of English at the University of Winnipeg, was named Canada Research Chair in the Culture of Childhood, the only such position in Canada. In 2006, the University of Winnipeg established the Centre for Research in Young People's Texts and Cultures to further research in the field. Canadian scholars and professionals have continued to publish critical guides to the literature from varying disciplinary perspectives, contributing to a greater understanding of the range of Canadian children's literature and the work of key authors and illustrators.[123]

Over the past thirty years, credit courses and specialized programs in illustration, graphic design, communication design, visual design, and publishing have been developed at post-secondary institutions across Canada.[124] Canadian illustrators have been appointed to faculty positions. Harvey Chan has taught illustration at Sheridan College in Oakville. Michèle Lemieux and Marie-Louise Gay have both taught at L'École de Design at the Université de Québec à Montréal. Community colleges also began to offer non-credit illustration courses, such as the course taught by Kathryn Shoemaker at Langara College in Vancouver.

Domestic and International Exhibits and Awards

International literary events and international book trade fairs have focused attention on Canadian children's books and on Canadian illustrated books. The Bologna Children's Book Fair held a major retrospective of Canadian children's book illustration in 1990, 'Canada à Bologne / Canada at Bologna,' curated by designer Michael Solomon.[125] In 1996, the Canadian Society of Children's Authors, Illustrators and Performers' collection of original works of art from Canadian children's books was exhibited at the Guadalajara International Book Fair.[126] In 1997, a travelling exhibit of 300 Canadian children's books, primarily picturebooks, 'Creat-

ing the Mosaic: A Celebration of Canadian Children's Literature,' circulated in
ten cities in Japan, culminating in a one-day symposium in Nagoya on Canadian
children's literature.[127] The Internationale Jugendbibliothek (International Youth
Library) in Munich mounted an exhibit of one hundred Canadian books from
its collection in 2002, accompanied by a catalogue, *Children's Books from Canada:
A Recent Selection*, which included an essay by Josiane Polidori of Library and
Archives Canada on 'Canadian Children's Literature: Multifaceted Landscape.'[128]
The International Board on Books for Young People Canada (IBBY Canada) has
created a travelling exhibition of fifty recent French- and English-language Canadian picturebooks, *Show and Tell: Outstanding Canadian Picture Books, 2000–2003 /
Montre et raconte: Albums illustrés canadiens remarquables 2000–2003*, which toured
domestically and internationally.[129] Canadian illustrators have been included in
international exhibits. Gilles Tibo won Japan's Owl Prize in 1989; Barbara Reid
won the UNICEF-Ezra Jack Keats International Award for Excellence in Children's
Book Illustration in 1988, also awarded to illustrator Jan Thornhill in 1990. Pop-up
book artist Celia King received an honourable mention at the 1992 Bologna Children's Book Fair. Quebec illustrator Pierre Pratt won the 1993 Bratislava Golden
Apple Award for *Follow That Hat!* and was awarded a plaque at the 2005 Biennale
of Illustrations Bratislava. Illustrator Warabé Aska won first prize at the Tehran
International Biennale of Illustration for *Aska's Birds*. Illustrator Michèle Lemieux's
Stormy Night was awarded the Bologna Ragazzi Award at the 1997 Bologna Fair.
Ange Zhang's *Red Land, Yellow River* won the same award in the young adult non-
fiction category in 2005.

Library and Archives Canada continues to showcase children's books by developing innovative exhibits at the Library in Ottawa and online. In 1997, 'The
Art of Illustration: A Celebration of Contemporary Canadian Children's Book
Illustrators / L'art d'illustrer: un éloge des illustrateurs canadiens contemporains
de livres pour enfants' drew on Sheila Egoff and Judith Saltman's discussion of
artistic style in *The New Republic of Childhood* to categorize the work of twenty-nine
illustrators.[130] 'Celebrating Dayal Kaur Khalsa: A Retrospective at the National
Library of Canada' provides a critical examination of her work, based in part on
the original artwork and manuscripts held in the Literary Manuscripts Division.[131]
In 2003, to accompany the Fun of Reading conference, 'Beyond the Letters: A Retrospective of Canadian Alphabet Books,' was curated at the National Library by
the critic Jeffrey Canton.[132] The 2007 'Picture Perfect!' exhibit by the Toronto Public
Library featured artwork by Canadian book illustrators, drawn from the Osborne
Collection of Early Children's Books.[133]

Regional Awards and Children's Choice Awards

The range of awards for children's literature continued to expand within Canada.
Regional awards included the Ann Connor Brimer Award for Children's Literature, established by the Nova Scotia Library Association in 1991 to recognize the
author of an English-language fiction or non-fiction children's book that has made
an outstanding contribution to children's literature in Atlantic Canada. In 2003,
the British Columbia Book Prizes inaugurated the Christie Harris Illustrated Chil-

dren's Literature Prize for excellence in the writing and illustration of picture storybooks and illustrated non-fiction books.

In the past, most winners of awards for children's literature would receive a certificate or a medal presented at an awards ceremony. Only a few awards included a modest cash prize. That situation began to change in the late 1990s, as new awards were established with a mandate to help market children's books. The $10,000 Norma Fleck Award, established in 1999 and administered by the Canadian Children's Book Centre, was created to promote Canadian non-fiction books for young people and includes $5,000 in marketing funds to help to publicize the shortlisted titles. In 2004, the TD Canadian Children's Literature Award was established, which brings with it a $20,000 cash award, administered by the Canadian Children's Book Centre. In 2006, retired TD Bank Financial Group CEO Charles Baillie created the Marilyn Baillie Picture Book Award to celebrate excellence in text, illustration, and design in Canadian English-language illustrated children's books. The award, which initially carried a $10,000 prize, is managed by the Canadian Children's Book Centre.[134]

In the last decade, young readers' choice awards, in which children and young adults read from a selected shortlist and vote for their favourite book, have been instituted across Canada, including the Hackmatack Children's Choice Book Award of the Atlantic provinces; the Ontario Library Association 'Forest of Reading' awards; the Manitoba Young Readers' Choice Award; the Saskatchewan 'Willow Awards'; the Rocky Mountain Book Award of Alberta; and British Columbia's Red Cedar and Stellar Book Awards and Chocolate Lily Young Readers' Choice Awards. These children's choice awards are designed to stimulate interest in reading and books, promote literacy, help children connect with Canadian literature, and develop their critical thinking skills.

In the opinion of some children's literature experts, the young readers' choice awards have a bigger impact on public demand and on sales than the juried awards given by library associations, the book trade, and writers' organizations. According to Virginia Davis, juried awards have some effect on sales only if there is good publicity for the award. In contrast, children's choice awards mean that 'the kids know the books, they know the program, they're champing at the bit to get to the books every year because they've found out how good they are. And of course they're going off and buying them for themselves in addition to the fact that the schools and public libraries are buying them ... the effect on sales has been phenomenal.'[135]

Patsy Aldana is more sceptical about the direct connection between awards and increased sales. She notes that although Groundwood books were well represented initially on the young readers' lists, over time 'they have become less and less well represented, because they're considered to be too difficult ... They're afraid that boys won't read the books, so they're looking for the lowest common denominator, which I think is a terrible shame, because if they're going to read books only once a year, shouldn't they read the best books?'[136]

However, the process of reader participation in the young readers' awards is meant to reach the widest possible range of interests in diverse communities of child readers, not to directly address the marketing needs of publishers. The shortlists usually reflect the varied experiences of the selection committees, who may be public librarians, teachers, teacher-librarians, publishing representatives and writers, and the particular selection criteria of the award. And as teacher-librarian Martha Cameron notes about the Red Cedar awards, while the intention of the award is not to function as a reading recovery program, the diversity of titles on the shortlists ensures that children of differing reading abilities and skill in reading in English can be active and enthusiastic participants. She explains that the social element has been critical in promoting the awards within the school environment, so that children not only take an interest in the awards, but begin to discuss the common list of books that they have read and gain pride in the status conferred by having been a 'Red Cedar voter.'[137] As a way of bringing children and books together, the readers' choice awards, in both schools and public libraries, have been an unqualified success.

Criticism and Reviewing

In a period of retrenchment and regrouping, the proliferation of new journals has slowed, and some of the well-established journals have changed their focus. The bimonthly *Emergency Librarian* turned towards the larger market of the United States, gradually reducing Canadian content. In 1998, the title was changed to *Teacher Librarian: The Journal for School Library Professionals* to more clearly reflect its increasingly school-library focus and, in 2004, was sold by Ken Haycock to the American publisher Scarecrow Press.[138]

The journal *Resource Links: Connecting Classrooms, Libraries and Canadian Learning Resources* was founded by Haycock in 1995 and published by Rockland Press for the Council for Canadian Learning Resources. In 1998, responsibility for the publication was assumed by a restructured Council, made up of members of the executive of the Association for Teacher-Librarianship in Canada, under the editorship of Victoria Pennell. The journal cut back on some columns and features, but retained the original focus of reviewing a broad range of Canadian print, electronic, and audiovisual resources to aid teacher-librarians and public librarians in the selection of material for children and young adults. The focus has also shifted to a greater emphasis on the curricular use of materials in school libraries and classrooms.[139]

A 2004 study of school libraries by the Association of Canadian Publishers listed four publications as the most frequent sources of information about books that influence the purchasing decisions of teachers and teacher-librarians: *Resource Links*, *Teacher Librarian*, *Quill and Quire*, and the *Globe and Mail* books section.[140] Teachers cited lack of awareness of Canadian books as the most significant barrier to having more Canadian titles in school library collections. As budgets come under strain and school libraries and public libraries cut back on the more expensive professional reviewing journals, newspapers and non-professional reviewing sources have become important conduits to disseminate information about new children's publications. *Quill and Quire* continues to run a section, 'Books for Young People,' which features reviews by authors, librarians, teachers, writers, and journalists, as well as a longer, 850-word 'guest review.'

The systematic reviewing of Canadian children's books for the general public in the popular media, however, continues to be problematic. Very few newspapers feature regular reviews of children's books, let alone Canadian children's books, a situation that concerns the creators and critics of children's literature.[141] One study showed that between 1997 and 2002 children's reviewing declined 56 per cent in the *Vancouver Sun*, 50 per cent in the *Montreal Gazette*, and 100 per cent in the *Halifax Chronicle-Herald*, with only 6 per cent of total review space in the newspapers owned by CanWest Global given to children's books.[142] Critic and reviewer Jeffrey Canton argues that the national papers, including the *Globe and Mail* and the *National Post*, and magazines like *Maclean's* should be covering Canadian children's literature. He believes that what is needed is 'an informed press.'[143] Canton's view is reiterated by Michele Landsberg, who makes a direct link between the shrinking amount of space allocated to children's book reviewing and the decline in the number of children's bookstores with the consequent reduction in the number of paid ads. She adds that the papers have the resources to review children's books, but speculates that they have 'a contempt for this genre.'[144] Tundra publisher Kathy Lowinger agrees with Landsberg that reviewing is directly tied to advertising dollars, noting that very few children's publishers have the money to advertise extensively. As she explains, however, a picturebook in a print run of 6,000 selling for $20 will have a budget of $6,000 for all promotional costs. Since 'one ad in the *Globe and Mail* is $4,000, one ad in the *New York Times* is $10,000,' she concludes that newspaper advertisements are not necessarily the most effective use of an advertising budget.[145]

As newspapers across North America scramble for readers in the face of declining subscriptions and the shift to online digital editions and podcasts of news, book sections face further pressures. The *Toronto Star* is somewhat anomalous in continuing to run a weekly column of children's book reviews by Deirdre Baker, a professor of English at the University of Toronto. Changes at the beginning of 2009 to the *Globe and Mail* that resulted in a new integrated 'Globe Focus and Books' section, rather than a separate pull-out section for books, further reduced space for the sustained coverage of Canadian publishing news and reviews, with children's reviews allocated a single column of brief reviews. It remains to be seen whether the December feature section on children's books will continue to be produced.

Small publishers have a particularly difficult time in getting their books reviewed, as their advertising budgets are limited and they often lack the resources to send out review copies of new titles.[146] Reviews can have a significant impact on sales for small publishers, however. Former publishing manager of Theytus Books, Greg Young-Ing, notes that when a new edition of the Kou-skelowh [We Are the People] Series was published in 1999, Elizabeth McCallum of the *Globe and Mail* wrote a very positive review that directly resulted in additional sales of at least 1,000 books.[147] Allison Taylor McBryde, coordinator of children's services, North Vancouver District Library, and former editor of *Resource Links*, reiterates the ability of newspaper reviews to stimulate interest in a title, noting that parents arrive in the library with clippings of recent children's book reviews. In Taylor McBryde's view, 'the newspaper has got to be one of the most powerful tools and it's totally underutilized.'[148]

The overall quality of reviewing in Canadian journals and magazines, however, is questioned by some scholars of children's literature. Many reviewers are print-oriented and more familiar with textual than visual analysis, and thus more effective at assessing narrative than images.[149] The lack of rigour in the reviewing process and the timeliness of reviews in some of the reviewing journals continue to be problematic.[150] The personal connections in the relatively small children's literature community in Canada have also proved challenging for some reviewers. Mary Rubio, co-founder of *Canadian Children's Literature*, notes that 'it is difficult to be a reviewer and not review works of one's personal friends.'[151] Similarly, author and critic Sarah Ellis discovered that a small community with friendships between reviewers and authors and illustrators can inhibit criticism. She remembers Sheila Egoff saying 'I do not want to know any of these people because I can't – then I would have to pull my punches.'[152] However, as Allison Taylor McBryde argues, the reviewing process is 'essential to the dissemination of information and the promotion of the books.'[153] She describes the reviewing process as 'one that's universally hated by publishers, authors, and illustrators. Everybody loves reviews when they are very positive, and everybody hates them when they're not.' She adds that the writing process is gruelling, especially when a review is negative, because the reviewer has an obligation to be conscientious and appreciate both the strengths and weaknesses of a book.[154]

The Online Presence

In the last five years, the importance of the internet as a means of disseminating information about children's books and their creators has grown exponentially. By 2005, 80 per cent of single-family households with unmarried children under the age of eighteen and almost 100 per cent of public elementary and secondary schools in Canada had internet access.[155] According to a recent Statistics Canada survey, almost seven million Canadians placed an order online for goods and services in 2005, with purchases for books, magazines, and online newspapers making up 35 per cent of the orders (the second-highest category after travel arrangements) and 28 per cent of online 'window shopping.'[156]

As a result, online information about Canadian children's literature has become increasingly popular. Library and Archives Canada launched PIKA: Canadian Children's Literature Database, a bilingual search tool that enhances and expands access to children's books in the AMICUS database with annotations from the Canadian Children's Book Centre and Communication-Jeunesse (http://www. collectionscanada.ca/pika/index-e.html). Biographical information about authors and illustrators is featured prominently on the Canadian Children's Book Centre website (www.bookcentre.ca), as well as student and professional resources, including extensive lists of award winners.

Some journals have moved from print to online distribution. *CM: Canadian Review of Materials* (www.umanitoba.ca/cm), the weekly online reviewing journal is the successor to the Canadian Library Association's print journal *CM* and continues the tradition of author profiles and reviews of new books. Electronic journals like *The Looking Glass: New Perspectives on Children's Books* provide wide access to critical writings on Canadian and international children's literature.[157]

Many publishers have also developed strong online profiles to appeal to the educational community and child readers. A well-designed corporate website can be an effective promotional venue to connect authors and readers. Kids Can's website (www.kidscanpress.com) includes a descriptive interactive catalogue of current and backlist titles, a section on authors and illustrators, and 'The Resource Room,' a free members-only section with educational resources for classroom use, including unit and lesson plans, and thematic bibliographies.[158] Scholastic Canada's website (www.scholastic.ca) includes sections for children, parents, teachers, librarians, and booksellers, showcasing Scholastic's authors and illustrators, series books, and bookclubs. High-profile, popular authors like Robert Munsch (www. robertmunsch.com) have their own child-friendly websites that encourage interactivity, including audioclips of author readings, promotional information about class and school visits, upcoming public events, space for children to post their reviews of the books, and children's artwork and stories inspired by the books.

The decline in newspaper and popular media reviewing of children's books by knowledgeable professional critics has occurred at the same time that reviews by non-expert communities of readers posted to online book retailers' websites and blogs, and fan pages on social networking sites like Facebook, have become increasingly popular. Amazon.ca, a subsidiary of Amazon.com, debuted in Canada in 2002 in direct competition to Chapters.Indigo.ca, the successor to Chapters.ca. Both online retailers include information about individual titles, mostly drawn from publishers' catalogue descriptions and reviews written by customers.[159] Amazon.ca also includes reviews from the American Library Association journal *Booklist* for some titles, while Chapters.Indigo.ca includes short author biographies. On both sites, despite the extensive inventory of books compared with a bookstore, including backlist and used copies of books currently out of print, the casual 'window shopping' customer of the Statistics Canada survey would be hard pressed to develop an awareness of the range of children's books being published in Canada. Although Chapters.Indigo.ca includes a variety of lists to aid customers in their purchases, including titles that have won the Governor General's, Ruth Schwartz, and Mr Christie awards, and a 'Kids Need More Canada' list of current titles, there are no markers that identify individual titles as Canadian.

Despite the difficulties that the Canadian children's book industry has experienced since the early 1990s, publishers and booksellers have shown the will to reinvent themselves to meet new challenges. If the optimism that characterized the children's publishing boom in Canada in the 1980s has been tempered by nearly two decades of rapid change in the face of globalization, mergers, and shifting markets, there is a still a willingness among the children's literature community to connect the creators, producers, distributors, and readers of indigenous Canadian books. The interdisciplinary communities concerned with the continued existence of Canadian children's literature and publishing for children have responded to the nearly two decades of upheaval and crisis by joining together in a spectrum of supportive programs, organizations, and ventures. Despite the uncertainty of the future, the tenacity and commitment of the stakeholders to the importance of literary production for children and the inculcation of literacy have not lessened. The question posed by Gérard Pelletier in 1972, whether Canadians would have to rely on foreign interpretations of the world, is still relevant, but Canadian children's illustrated books have found a place allotted to them that could only have been dreamed about in earlier decades.[160]

CHAPTER EIGHT

Children's Illustrated Books, 1990 to the Present Day

From the early 1990s to the present day, the publishing industry has had to adapt to changes brought about by the rapidly shifting globalized market. At the same time, the introduction of computerization at every level of industry from initial creation to layout and design, and changes in the technology of printing, have significantly improved the quality of reproduction of coloured images on the printed page. The combination of flexible printing technologies and the cost savings realized by moving printing offshore to countries with lower wages have brought full-colour printing within the reach of the smallest publishers.

The range of media used by children's book illustrators has expanded with new printing technologies, resulting in a willingness of some publishers to push the boundaries of picturebooks and illustrated books. Digitization allows a greater accuracy in the reproduction of images and the preservation of subtleties of colour and tone than was possible with reproduction based on photographs of the original artwork.[1] Digitization has also encouraged more adventurous book design. In the past, the technical demands of multiple-language print runs meant that Canadian publishers who hoped to arrange co-publications in the international marketplace adopted a fairly conservative book design in which images and text were physically isolated on the page, or completely divided between image pages and text pages. As digital separation and printing have become common, the ability to drop text into a page of illustration ceased to be a significant design and printing issue.

However, new technologies also bring new challenges to the field of book design. In an era of mergers and consolidation, fewer art directors are employed by publishing houses, and editors who are more used to working with text sometimes have to double as designers without having particular training in the subtleties of graphic art. The need to have picturebooks market themselves visually in a bookstore display and the proliferation of highly sophisticated software for page design can result in picturebooks that are visually arresting but harder to decode textually because of the choice of typeface and layout.[2]

Picturebook Design and the Peritextual

There has been a marked shift in recent picturebooks from works designed to appeal directly to children to works that will appeal to the adult sensibility in children, and to the primary adult purchaser.[3] The relatively conservative, realistic illustrations of the traditional picturebook designed for young children employ the mimetic conventions of mutually reinforcing, symmetrical textual and visual narratives.[4] Words and pictures are congruent, and the storytelling process moves in an orderly linear progression from one to the next double-page opening. Text is either confined to the left-hand side of a double-page opening, with a single image on the right-hand side, or text and image are separated into discrete spaces on the page. The passage of time may be indicated by transitions in text or by changes in the images in successive openings. The book as a constructed object is largely invisible to the relatively passive reader/viewer.[5]

Many authors, illustrators, and designers now experiment with multiple narratives, shifting points of view, and self-referential metafictive play, incorporating into picturebooks the temporal progression of juxtaposed sequential panels characteristic of comic books and graphic novels.[6] This new approach emphasizes the book as a literary and visual artefact. The picturebook has become a space that the illustrator can manipulate by deconstructing and reconstructing sequential linear narratives. Images may complement, contradict, subvert, or deviate from the text, reflecting changing semiotic codes and conventions.[7] The separation of text and image on the page, and the successive single moments in time of traditional picturebook images, have been transformed into a dynamic interaction on the page between text and image, sometimes by layering multiple textual narratives onto the page or by adopting the comic book's multiple panels and text placed within the image. The reader/viewer becomes an active participant, interpreting the text, the illustration, and peritext, engaged in the construction of meaning through the act of reading as performance.[8]

New printing technologies have expanded the tradition of black and white line drawings to accompany longer texts in illustrated books for older readers, making full-colour head and tail pieces and spot illustrations a realistic design option. Non-fiction has also become a heavily illustrated genre incorporating the typographic equivalent of hypertextual links and sound bytes with generous use of white space, photorealistic images and photography, and visual conventions drawn from comic books and graphic novels.[9]

The audience of the picturebook and illustrated book has expanded beyond its once firmly set developmental boundaries. While babies, toddlers, and preschoolers remain the main readers of traditional picturebooks, audiences of older school-aged children and even teenagers and adults are attracted by the postmodern picturebook's sophistication, complex interweaving and interplay of image and text, and use of irony and satire.[10] Graphic novels further extend the range of illustrated materials for older readers.[11]

Challenging the Mainstream

Just as the look of books changed over the past several decades, the multiple identities of children's book publishers and communities of readers have changed. By the early 1990s, children's books promoting gender equity were issued by mainstream publishers. Small feminist publishing houses, who in earlier decades had led the way in promoting inclusive children's literature, were forced to redefine their audience in a changed environment. Emerging from the fierce debates about the marginalization of women of colour within the feminist movement, Sister Vision: Black Women and Women of Colour Press was established in 1985 by Makeda Silvera and Stephanie Martin to provide a space for 'Caribbean, Asian, First Nations, African and mixed-race women' to discuss issues of concern.[12] In the early 1990s, Sister Vision issued a series of children's books with an explicit anti-racist standpoint, including Ramabai Espinet's *The Princess of Spadina: A Tale of Toronto* (1992), illustrated by Veronica Sullivan, and Adwoa Badoe's *Crabs for Dinner* (1995), illustrated by Belinda Ageda.

In the past decade, there has been a steady erosion of an ideological commitment to feminist books and institutions, as a younger generation of women increasingly define themselves as post-feminist.[13] At the same time that feminist publishers have had to retrench or ceased publishing entirely, women's bookstores across North America have closed, further reducing the market for small alternative presses.[14] Second Story Press, however, has found a way to reach a broader community of readers while remaining committed to its original vision of inclusiveness and social justice in picturebooks like *Treasure for Lunch* (2000), in which the ethnocultural diversity of a contemporary Canadian urban elementary school is brought to life and made real through Shenaaz Nanji's text and Yvonne Cathcart's illustrations. Unlike Ian Wallace and Angela Wood's *The Sandwich* (1975), in which a child was teased by his schoolmates for bringing a non-conforming 'stinky meat sandwich' in his lunchbox, it is Shaira's worries about being rejected by her classmates that causes her to hide the food that her grandmother has packed for her lunch. When her secret cache is discovered, her classmates are happy to share her 'samoosas' and proclaim them delicious.

Foreign rights for Rachna Gilmore's *Lights for Gita* (1994), illustrated by Alice Priestley, about friendship and change as a young immigrant girl adjusts to a new country, and its sequels *Roses for Gita* (1994) and *A Gift for Gita* (1998), have been sold to Mantra, a multicultural publisher in England, who issued bilingual editions of the stories in English and Arabic, Bengali, Gujarati, Somali, Tamil, Turkish, and Urdu. In 2001, *Lights for Gita* was turned into a film for children as part of the National Film Board's *Talespinners* series, with animation by Gregory Houston.

Second Story Press's greatest commercial and literary success in international children's publishing, however, came with Karen Levine's *Hana's Suitcase*, which has sold a quarter of a million copies in twenty countries, in seventeen languages.[15] The story, which evolved from a CBC radio documentary, weaves together a Jewish girl's life and death in a concentration camp, a Japanese educator's quest for information on her life, and her surviving brother's experience in Canada. As Wolfe explains, the archival and family photographs that illustrate the work play an important role in giving the reader 'a real sense of time and place.'[16] The success of *Hana's Suitcase* has allowed Second Story to expand their publishing program, and has provided new opportunities for marketing and distribution.

'Everybody Is Concerned about Issues of Equity'

Although Margie Wolfe, publisher of Second Story Press, argues that 'everybody is concerned about issues of equity, gender, diversity, non-sexist, non-racist materials,' many of the large trade publishers are often reluctant to publish children's books that explore potentially controversial subject matter.[17] Deirdre Baker, professor of English at the University of Toronto and children's book review columnist for the *Toronto Star*, identifies the connection between the difficulty in writing and publishing what she calls 'real' stories on topical issues of societal concern in picturebook form with an increasingly conservative book-buying public that is seeking not to broaden children's experiences but instil tightly defined normative values and behaviours.[18] The need to reach a broad readership in a highly competitive market influences the willingness of publishers to jeopardize profitability on titles that may generate controversy or raise problematic questions about the management of difference.[19] Censorship challenges to children's books that address social issues and the reluctance of the chains to stock anything overtly controversial encourage publishers and authors to self-censor, restricting the depiction of diversity in the everyday lives of Canadian children.[20] As a result, the majority of picturebooks that deal explicitly with controversial issues continue to be issued mainly by small presses with a non-commercial, social justice mandate.

Censorship challenges to children's books often focus on stories that deal with sexuality, reproduction, sexual orientation, or that include images of nudity. Marie-Francine Hébert's picturebook parable on evolution and birth, *The Amazing Adventure of LittleFish* (1990), was challenged for Darcia Labrosse's illustrations of a naked child on the cover.[21] In 1997, the decision by the Surrey School Board in British Columbia to ban classroom use of three picturebooks about families with same-gendered parents, including Rosamund Elwin and Michele Paulse's *Asha's Mums* (1990), illustrated by Dawn Lee, on the grounds that they promoted homosexuality, was the subject of a lawsuit brought against the board by parents, teachers, and students. The case eventually reached the Supreme Court of Canada, which ruled in 2002 that such books have a place in the secular, diverse, and pluralistic Canadian public school system.[22] They required the board to re-evaluate the books without reference to religious beliefs or parental pressure. The board then reinstated the ban in 2003, citing errors of grammar, clarity, and quality in the picturebooks. Another group of picturebooks that included stories of same-gendered parents was not approved in 2006 by the Surrey District Standing Advisory Committee for Learning Resources for use as learning materials. This included a split decision on the one Canadian picturebook in the group of books, Ken Setterington's *Mom and Mum Are Getting Married!* (2004) illustrated by Alice Priestley, and published by Second Story Press.[23]

Setterington chose to write a simple story focusing on a flower girl at a same-gendered wedding, in which the title would reveal the subject to make it easily identifiable to readers searching for children's books about same-gendered couples, while simultaneously alerting parents about the subject matter. While he expected that the book might raise concerns, he discovered that his identity directly affected the book's reception among some readers.[24] As he explains, he was 'surprised to see it, and me, identified in *REALity*, the on-line newsletter of Real Women of Canada, in the following manner: "The book is written by a Toronto homosexual, Ken Setterington." It immediately brought back my high school years and various taunts. I wondered if the writer had read the book.'[25] The circulation of harsh

8.1 Ken Setterington. *Mom and Mum Are Getting Married!* Illustrated by Alice Priestley. Toronto: Second Story Press, 2004. Published with permission from Second Story Press, Toronto. www.secondstorypress.ca.

critiques of the book on the internet by groups dedicated to the preservation of heteronormative social values and legal structures emphasized that Second Story Press had received government funding for the publication of the book and suggested that the title was one of many books 'teaching' homosexuality. In response, Setterington adds: 'Actually, I don't know of other same-sex marriage books for children in Canada, and I would not have bothered writing one if there really was a plethora.'[26]

Trade Publishers Expand and Contract

While small, alternative publishers struggled in the new publishing and retail environment, the mergers and consolidations in the Canadian publishing industry meant that several trade publishers who had developed strong children's lists in the boom years of the 1980s discovered that the market was supersaturated. Some publishers downsized or marginalized their children's lists in the mid- to late 1990s when publishing children's books became less profitable, particularly in the expensive picturebook category, while others had to rethink the focus for their children's publishing programs once it was no longer possible to find an immediate market for every title issued.

Doubleday Canada, before its merger into Random House Canada in 1999, published several visually innovative, award-winning, editorially driven picturebooks designed to appeal to diverse age groups of readers. The series of poetry books for children by Sheree Fitch, including *Toes in My Nose* (1987), illustrated by noted artist Molly Lamb Bobak, and *There Were Monkeys in My Kitchen!* (1992), with stylish and witty line-and-wash drawings by the Quebec illustrator Marc Mongeau, successfully marry images and texts. Other pairings are more problematic. In one notable example, *Seasons* (1990), the editor John Pierce selected a group of dreamlike surrealist paintings, exquisitely rendered with a fine brush in oil on canvas by Warabé Aska, and then commissioned Alberto Manguel, one of Canada's most respected anthologists and translators, to select complementary poems to accompany the images. Aska, who worked with Manguel to approve the selections, believes that the anthology works as an introduction to art for both children and adults, explaining that 'when you take children to a gallery or museum, you do not say, "This painting is for children. It's not for adults." Painting is for all ages.'[27] The anthology, however, has been criticized by some reviewers, who argue that it is a coffee table book to be looked at, rather than a picturebook or poetry collection to be read aloud to children. Other reviewers questioned whether a picturebook succeeds when it becomes an aesthetic object in which text is subsidiary to existing images, rather than a hybrid form in which text and image are integrally linked. The desire by some critics to maintain a strict demarcation between picturebooks for children and books for adults also raises questions about the editorial decisions that shaped the initial impetus to publish, and the expected market for the volume, despite the care with which the sophisticated, imaginative paintings were matched with the poems.[28]

Other publishers teamed with book packagers, also known as book producers, who combine the roles of editor and designer to create finished titles that can be issued under the imprint of the purchasing house. Madison Press, established in 1979 in Toronto, achieved success in assembling attractive non-fiction titles on popular themes for publishers like Atheneum, Little, Brown, Viking, Random House, and Scholastic Books. *Polar, the Titanic Bear* (1994), a crossover title marketed at both adult and child readers, incorporates an eyewitness account of the sinking of the *Titanic*, written in 1913 by a wealthy American woman, Daisy Corning Stone Spedden for her young son, with additional text by her descendent, Leighton H. Coleman III. The detailed and realistic watercolour illustrations by the Ontario artist Laurie McGaw are augmented with family and archival photographs and realia, including postcards, telegrams, a luggage label from the *Titanic*, and photographs of a Steiff teddy bear similar to the story's protagonist.[29] Madison sold the package to Little, Brown in Canada and the United States, Hodder in Australia, and the rights to translation to German, Spanish, Dutch, and Japanese publishers. Successful cross-marketing to adult teddy bear enthusiasts was furthered by the licensing of Polar to several toy companies.

'Preserving and Passing on Canadian History': Lester Publishing

In the era of mergers, it was sometimes difficult to keep track of the movement of experienced editors and publishers between houses. In 1991, when Lester and Orpen Dennys was sold, Malcolm Lester established a new publishing house in partnership with Key Porter, taking Kathy Lowinger, the children's editor with him. She quickly developed an outstanding children's list, building on the knowledge of authors and illustrators that she had acquired while executive director of the Children's Book Centre. The children's list had an auspicious beginning with Janet Lunn's *The Story of Canada* (1992, rev. ed. 2000) co-authored with historian Christopher Moore, and illustrated by Alan Daniel. An introduction to the social history of Canada from precontact to the present day, Lunn and Moore enlivened and extended their narrative with a mixture of oral histories, folktales, and folksongs to create an illustrated history for readers of all ages. The illustrations incorporated archival photographs, maps and posters, and Daniel's detailed pen and watercolour wash images. Lunn praises Daniel for his meticulous research, explaining that the historical accuracy of the smallest details of costume is important to him, whether or not those details will appear in the final drawings.[30] Daniel himself sees his art as a conscious effort to help 'to preserve and pass on Canadian history.'[31]

The importance of social history also informs Barbara Smucker's *Selina and the Bear Paw Quilt* (1995). The pain of exodus, as Selina's pacifist Mennonite family is forced to leave their family farm in Pennsylvania for Waterloo County in southern Ontario during the American Civil War, is conveyed with subtlety in Smucker's narrative. Selina, who is overwhelmed with sadness at parting from her grandmother, finds solace in a quilt made from fabric scraps, each square a memory of family history.

The illustrations by Janet Wilson combine realistic oil paintings with a framing device of real miniature quilt blocks made in traditional patterns. Like Daniel, Wilson is a careful researcher, who strives for authenticity. She worked with quilter

Lucy Anne Holliday to design the quilt blocks, and purchased fabric from a shop in the Mennonite community of St Jacob's, near Waterloo, in the reds, yellows, and greens of the original quilt that inspired this true story.[32] The relationship between the colours and patterns of the quilts and the colours and qualities of the illustrations they frame help to convey mood and tension. The quilting art symbolizes the heritage of strength and grace across three generations of women, and both art and text subtly convey Mennonite values of tolerance, humility, perseverance, and non-violence. (See colour plate 11.)

As reproduction technologies have increased in sophistication, photography is increasingly used in mixed-media art to illustrate many Canadian informational texts. Linda Granfield's non-fiction titles for Lester Publishing integrate a variety of primary source materials, including archival and personal photographs, found objects, realia, and vintage posters, cards, and postcards.[33] She gathers the visual documentation of her social histories from the ephemera of everyday life for her own research and for her illustrators to incorporate into their finished artwork.[34] This visual archive was helpful to Janet Wilson when she was preparing to illustrate Granfield's *In Flanders Fields: The Story of the Poem by John McCrae* (1995), about the First World War and the life of the Canadian war physician and poet. To better understand the historical context of the poem, Wilson travelled to Flanders to tour the battlefield sites.[35] She also personalized the illustrations by reflecting on her own feelings about war and empathetically intuiting the emotions experienced by the characters in the book, adding that 'the [grieving] mother on the bed – that was me.'[36]

In 1996, plagued with financial problems resulting from the cancellation of the Ontario government's loan guarantee program for publishers, Lester Publishing suspended operations. Stoddart Books acquired Lester's children's list, while Kathy Lowinger moved to McClelland and Stewart, which in turn had recently acquired Tundra Books.[37]

Tundra Books

In the early 1990s under May Cutler's guidance, Tundra continued to develop its distinctive approach to children's publishing, selecting illustrators with strong art training to continue the tradition of 'picture books as works of art.' She worked with the self-taught Mohawk artist C.J. Taylor to develop a series of books exploring Aboriginal creation stories and traditional teaching stories from a variety of cultural traditions, including the quartet *How Two-Feather Was Saved from Loneliness: An Abenaki Legend* (1990); *The Ghost and Lone Warrior: An Arapaho Legend* (1991); *Little Water and the Gift of the Animals: A Seneca Legend* (1992); and *The Secret of the White Buffalo* (1993), all illustrated with Taylor's powerful, expressive acrylic paintings on canvas.

Ludmila Zeman's retelling of the Gilgamesh stories in the trilogy *Gilgamesh the King* (1992), *The Revenge of Ishtar* (1993), and *The Last Quest of Gilgamesh* (1993) evokes the art and landscape of ancient Babylon. Zeman, who has studied puppetry, film, and animation, notes the influence of the work of her father, the Czech film-maker Karel Zeman, and her continued interest in the beautifully illustrated books and fairy tales of her childhood in her own artwork.[38] For the *Gilgamesh* trilogy, Zeman's delicate use of cross-hatching and exploitation of the dramatic possibilities of narrative illustration evoke her admiration of the nineteenth-century French artist and engraver Gustave Doré. Her careful research of Mesopotamian artefacts and interest in cuneiform are incorporated into her meticulous book designs, which make use of framing devices and multi-picture sequences to complement the illustrations, add contextual and cultural references, insert humour, and extend the narrative.[39] Tundra also published Zeman's trilogy of stories about the adventures of Sinbad, retold from the *Arabian Nights* and illustrated with exquisite paintings that invoke Mughal art forms. Both trilogies found an international market, with foreign rights sales for French, Japanese, Brazilian, Portuguese, Danish, and Spanish editions.

The artist's memoir in picturebook form reached a new degree of complexity with *A Little Tiger in the Chinese Night: An Autobiography in Art* (1993), in which Song Nan Zhang locates his narrative of suffering and personal growth in the context of the chaos of the Cultural Revolution and the Tiananmen Square protest, before he began a new life as a refugee in Montreal. Zhang juxtaposes the artificiality of social realist poster art style in which he was trained with a more emotional realism, using page layout and peritext to further the emotional trajectory of his story and show temporal and geographical dislocation. Zhang returned to playing with temporality and the mimetic in his artwork for *From Far and Wide: A Canadian Citizenship Scrapbook* (2000), written by Jo Bannatyne-Cugnet, in which he invokes a three-dimensional scrapbook format on the two-dimensional page, complete with graphic recreations of photographs.[40]

After the 1995 sale of Tundra Books to McClelland and Stewart, the house moved to Toronto in 1996, to be operated as an autonomous imprint, with a staff of seven under the direction of the new publisher Kathy Lowinger.[41] She has extended the children's list to incorporate fiction for young adults, innovative information books, children's Judaica, and a broader range of more traditional, story-driven picturebooks, as well as continuing Tundra's tradition of publishing gallery artists.[42] Geoff Butler's *The Killick: A Newfoundland Story* (1995) expands the genre into an elegiac picture-storybook in three chapters, focusing on an intergenerational relationship in which a grandfather recounts stories within stories to his grandson, in a sharp pungent dialect, interspersed with folksongs and sea shanties. Butler's paintings in alkyd and acrylics and additional small black and white pencil sketches capture details of outport life in fishing villages and the terrible beauty of ice and sea.

In his next book, *The Hangashore* (1998), set at the end of the Second World War, Butler returns to the world of the outports to tell the story of a stiff and pompous magistrate, sent from England, and the lesson he learns about kindliness and respect from the minister's teenage son John, who has Down's syndrome. When resourceful John comes to the rescue in a boating accident, the magistrate's understanding of who is, in fact, the pitiful, hapless 'hangashore' is altered. Butler's narrative, which more closely resembles a short story for adult readers rather than a picturebook text for children, captures the rhythms and rich vocabulary of Newfoundland speech, just as his unsentimental oil on board paintings introduce the

We were in the second row, behind Sophia and Maria. They are twins. They are in kindergarten at Queen Elizabeth. Their parents had to escape from Ethiopia at night, or maybe be killed. The family came to Canada as refugees sponsored by a church.

The man beside me was Mr. Nguyen. Mama said he looked worried because his English was not so good. His wife and two boys became Canadians last year. Mr. Nguyen couldn't because he did not speak enough English or French. Baba told him, "Relax. You already passed the citizenship test. This is like a party." But he still looked worried.

The gym got very crowded once the students and teachers filed in.

8.2 Jo Bannatyne-Cugnet. *From Far and Wide: A Canadian Citizenship Scrapbook.*
Illustrated by Song Nan Zhang. Toronto: Tundra Books, 2000.
Taken from *From Far and Wide: A Canadian Citizenship Scrapbook* © 2000, written by Jo Bannatyne-Cugnet, illustrated by Song Nan Zhang, published by Tundra Books, Toronto.

reader to the social world of a small community. Colour is used to cue the emotional shifts in the story, while shifting cinematic perspectives move the reader through the narrative and firmly establish its temporal and spatial setting.

New genres for Tundra include picturebooks for younger audiences. In Richard Scrimger's trilogy *Bun Bun's Birthday* (2001), *Princess Bun Bun* (2002), and *Eugene's Story* (2003), sibling rivalry and love between members of a squabbling family are affectionately portrayed. In *Eugene's Story*, Gillian Johnson's sharply satirical watercolour cartoons express the dual vision of a child's internal and external life, subtly extending the narrative voice of the text.

Tundra also continues to work with established authors and illustrators. In 2002, May Cutler, who had worked closely with William Kurelek in the creation of his picturebooks in the 1970s, wrote a picturebook biography, *Breaking Free: The Story of William Kurelek.* Cutler explored his painful childhood, his experiences as an immigrant and outsider, his passion for the prairie landscape, and his struggle with depression, creating her text in direct response to his images.[43]

Kathy Lowinger persuaded Roch Carrier to return to children's books with *The*

8.3 Geoff Butler. *The Killick: A Newfoundland Story*. Montreal: Tundra Books, 1995.
Taken from *The Killick* © 1995, written and illustrated by Geoff Butler, published by
Tundra Books, Toronto.

Flying Canoe (2004), a retelling of the Québécois folktale, 'La Chasse-galerie.' In his version, eleven-year-old Baptiste and a group of homesick loggers make a pact with the devil and enter a magic canoe that will transport them home from their logging camp in the Ottawa Valley to Beauce before the stroke of midnight on New Year's Eve, 1847. Carrier found it challenging to reinterpret the story for a contemporary audience that no longer believes in the devil as a real and terrible presence, as he did in his childhood.[44] The strong sense of pacing and movement in Sheldon Cohen's illustrations and his faux naif style extend the gentle satire of the narrator's satirical and affectionate observation of village life, emphasizing the sly humour of the tale.

Kathryn Cole at Oxford Canada and Stoddart Publishing

In her six years at Oxford Canada from 1989 through 1995, Kathryn Cole drew on her experience as an artist and editor to revitalize the picturebook list by seeking out new illustrators who had a strong personal vision. One of her first titles was Tololwa Mollel's *The Orphan Boy* (1990), a story from the Maasai tradition of how the planet Venus, the morning star, came to be known as the orphan boy.[45] The oil on canvas illustrations by Paul Morin evoke the beauty and shimmering, intense heat of the African landscape. Morin uses colour and light to embody the twilight time or dream state between consciousness and unconsciousness, reflecting his interest in Jungian symbolism and the ability of illustration to respond to the mythic and spiritual elements of a narrative.[46] In preparation for the book, he travelled to Africa to meet elders, collect indigenous instruments, and photograph the people and the landscape, as well as making sketches and sound recordings in a visual and aural diary. Once he returned to his studio, he created a soundtrack of original music that directly related to the mood and atmosphere of the story and played it while painting in order to recreate 'sound impressions' on the canvas.[47]

Morin's illustrations combine oil paints with found objects, materials, and modelling pastes used for textural effects and dimensionality. For *The Orphan Boy*, he integrated sand and twigs into the painted matrix of the gesso, which he describes as texture 'plasticized right onto the canvas.'[48] The three-dimensionality is heightened by his use of impasto, thick layers of paint, that builds texture and depth on the two-dimensional surface of the painting, an effect further enhanced by the dramatic raking lighting that he uses in the photographs of the paintings for reproduction.[49] (See colour plate 12.)

In 1995, Kathryn Cole left Oxford University Press for Stoddart Publishing when the new Secretary of the Press in Britain closed all of the international children's trade divisions in Canada, Australia, and New Zealand in order to focus on reference publishing.[50] Stoddart acquired Oxford Canada's children's backlist, except for the Cleaver and Toye picturebook list. Cole set about to extend the children's list at Stoddart by further developing fiction for young adults and a range of illustrated non-fiction and picturebooks, as well as entering into a wide range of co-publication agreements with foreign publishers.[51]

Titles issued under Cole's editorship include *The Shaman's Nephew: A Life in the Far North* (1999), a collaboration between Inuit artist and shaman Simon Tookoome and Winnipeg author and storyteller Sheldon Oberman, who gathered Tookoome's life narratives from an extended series of interviews over a ten-year period and had them translated from Inuktitut. Oberman weaves together Tookoome's memories of the seasonal cycles of life in a nomadic hunting camp in the Kivalliq region of Nunavut with the traditional teaching stories of the Utkusiksalingmiut. Life on the land is contrasted with the painful culture shock that resulted from the community's forced transition in the 1960s to the settled world of Qamani'tuaq (Baker Lake) during a time of severe game shortages that threatened the survival of the Inuit. Tookoome's illustrations in coloured pencil describe everyday life in the hunting camp and the world of his dreams and shamanic trances, in which animals and humans interact with the spirit world.

Fitzhenry and Whiteside

Fitzhenry and Whiteside was founded in 1966 as a distributor for American publishers and as a close affiliate of Harper and Row. For over forty years it published school and college educational materials, moving into children's trade books in the 1980s. The acquisition of Stoddart Publishing's children's list in 2002 and Red Deer Books in 2005 provided a stable of best-selling and award-winning backlist titles, which in combination with new work by emerging and established authors under the direction of the children's publisher, Gail Winskill, has substantially increased their trade children's publishing program.[52]

Linda Granfield returned to the archival material that she had gathered over a ten-year period during her research for *In Flanders Fields* and other works of historical non-fiction published by Lester before its acquisition by Stoddart. Adopting the same format that she pioneered in her previous work, *Where Poppies Grow: A World War I Companion* (2001), designed by Blair Kerrigan/Glyphis, is heavily illustrated with photographs, letters, postcards, advertisements, cigarette cards, maps, and stereoscopic views from her own extensive collection of memorabilia. The result is a social history of the everyday experiences of people in North America whose lives were transformed by war.[53]

We'll All Go Sailing (2001), written by Maggee Spicer and Richard Thompson, and illustrated by Kim LaFave, is the first in a series of picturebooks with an unusual format that includes an extra half-page that unfolds into a panorama view. The title also reflects the changes that technology has brought to both the creation of illustration and the methods of communication between illustrators and publishers. Each digitally created double-page spread is an intensely coloured illustration of children in a boat on a vivid sea, looking down at equally bright sea creatures. LaFave argues that computer art has made it easier to work from his home in rural British Columbia with publishers located in central Canada. He scans his preparatory black and white line drawings and then works with them using the software program Fractal Painter. When the images are completed, they can be sent to the publisher on a CD, and because they have been created digitally, they retain the intended tonal qualities when reproduced. He adds that where he would be hesitant to redo images in the past because of the time investment, the computer has freed him to create multiple iterations of an image to try different colours, a process that he finds very liberating.[54] For LaFave, the only disadvantage of his new method is not having the physical artwork, his 'little babies propped up against the wall and sitting on a shelf.'[55] Of course, digitization has also meant that unless an illustrator deliberately prints out successive stages and revisions of a project, the physical evidence of the creative process involved in the creation of a picturebook is eliminated from the archival record.

Playing with Plasticine: Scholastic Canada and North Winds Press

At Scholastic Canada, the range of children's authors and illustrators reflects the economic clout of a multinational company that through aggressive global expansion and domination of the lucrative school book fair and book club market has become the world's largest publisher of children's books, able to negotiate multibook contracts with high-profile Canadian creators like Robert Munsch.

Scholastic's trade books imprint, North Winds Press, continues to issue picturebooks of artistic complexity. In *Something from Nothing* (1992), Phoebe Gilman retells a traditional Jewish story about a piece of fabric that begins as a baby blan-

8.4 Linda Granfield. *Where Poppies Grow.* Illustrated with archival photographs.
Fitzhenry and Whiteside, 2001.
Reproduced from *The Granfield Collection.*

"Grandpa can fix it," Joseph said.
Joseph's grandfather took the handkerchief and
turned it round and round.

8.5 Phoebe Gilman, *Something from Nothing: Adapted from a Jewish Folktale*.
Richmond Hill, ON: North Winds Press, Scholastic Canada, 1992.
Reprinted with the permission of the publisher, Scholastic Canada.

ket and wears away through time and use until it finally becomes nothing but the memory of its creation preserved in story, the 'something from nothing' of the title. Her egg tempera illustrations recreate an extended family within a bustling, early twentieth-century village. Double-page spreads show domestic household activities, relationships among the family, and religious rituals, and detailed, historically researched exteriors of street, market, and school, reminiscent of Roman Vishniac's photographs of the vanishing world of Orthodox Eastern European Jews. To extend her narrative, she adds the contrapuntal story of a Jewish mouse family in their floorboard world, told only in pictures, which echoes and comments upon the human family's daily round above them, creating a counter-narrative within the framed page. Gilman's page design and use of visual imagery to further the narrative allow the reader to engage simultaneously with the mouse family's domestic narrative, the changing lives of different family members, and the outside world of the Jewish shtetl.

Through the interplay of art and text, Gilman immerses the child reader in the ethos and values of the generation that will be swept away by the Holocaust. She referred to photographs of her family in composing her pictures, which she said called out to her 'to act as their witness. The book took on another dimension. It became a way of remembering and recording the lives of my people.'[56] As Lissa Paul, professor of education at Brock University observes, the blue skies and gold stars on the endpapers are Gilman's cosmological statement of this lost community, in a polysemic text in which 'the pictures tell you something about this story that's completely not available in the text.'[57]

Barbara Reid's continued experimentation with modelling clay as a medium has resulted in artwork of startling originality. She has worked with Diane Kerner, her editor at Scholastic, and Yuksel Hassan, the art director, to develop picturebooks in which text and images are perfectly balanced in a relationship that she likens to the transformation that a great singer brings to the interpretation of music.[58] In *The Party* (1997), set in the 1960s, Reid recreates a summer reunion, told from the point of view of a young girl, as family members gather in the backyard to celebrate her grandmother's ninetieth birthday. The illustrations extend the text, carrying a secondary plot line of the children's separate subculture and the slowly unfolding friendship of two wary teenagers. Reid notes that the narrative required her to develop 'a cast of characters with clothing and personalities and relationships,' before she could design the 'set' or location of the party, adding that 'once that was all established it was a matter of letting them all interact on the stage.'[59] Reid uses unorthodox viewpoints and perspectives to create movement and drama, and reverses the usual directionality of the gaze, making the reader the subject of contemplation by the characters. At other times, the photographs of the plasticine illustrations are deliberately blurred to impart the effect of dizziness experienced by twirling children. All of these effects serve to break the two-dimensional page by pushing figures beyond the frame and bringing the viewer into the picture plane, while simultaneously using surface pattern to provide variation and counterbalance to the three-dimensionality of her characters and medium.[60]

The play of real and fictive in Reid's sculpted illustrations reaches new levels of sophistication in *The Subway Mouse* (2003), in which she integrates found objects and allusions to the work of other artists into her plasticine images to build texture, depth, and a sense of scale. The peritextual elements add temporal and geographical sequencing to the textual narrative. The half-title includes vertical imagery of human movement from the world outside the subway through the escalators carrying people down to the mouse level of the subway tracks. The opening endpapers depict the underground tunnel wall of greys and browns with mouse paw prints, resembling pre-historic cave paintings with imprinted human hands. The closing papers offer the counter spirit of the open skies and clouds – the blues and whites of freedom and light that the mouse hero has journeyed towards.

'Regaining the Balance of Justice': Groundwood Books

While many trade publishers and foreign-owned publishers operating in Canada have responded to shifting markets by downsizing their children's lists or focusing on brand recognition, Groundwood's philosophy of publishing has stretched the parameters of the picturebook. Paul Yee's *Ghost Train* (1996), about a girl's search for her father and the Chinese-Canadian immigrant experience, is a powerful indictment of racism and the exploitation of Chinese workers during the construction of the Canadian Pacific Railway. Awarded the 1996 Governor General's Award for Children's Literature for the text, the 1997 Elizabeth Mrazik-Cleaver Canadian Picture Book Award, and the 1997 Amelia Frances Howard-Gibbon Illustrator's Award, *Ghost Train* is, in Aldana's opinion, 'a perfect marriage of art and text.'[61]

In Yee's story, Choon-yi, a young artist, arrives in North America from China to join her father, only to discover that he has been killed. His ghost asks her to paint the train engine and the souls of the dead Chinese railway labourers. Returning with her painting to China, she burns it in a grief ritual so that the men may be at rest. The girl's courage and fidelity balance the tone of haunting melancholy. As Yee explains, his use of ghosts in his books is about addressing imbalances in relations of power by allowing the disadvantaged to transcend 'the horrible earthbound reality … [and] regain the balance of justice that ought to be in this world.'[62] Harvey Chan's powerful, dark illustrations in umber, sepia, and cadmium red use images symbolically to create emotion, rather than illustrate particular moments in the text.[63] (See colour plate 13.)

The peritextual elements were carefully planned to further extend the narrative. As Chan explains, 'the art is part of the whole design – the paintings, the choice of typography and the way it is laid down.' For *Ghost Train*, he asked Derick Pao to design a special typeface for the book and created drypoint etchings on copper for the front and end pieces that set the narrative in its temporal trajectory, opening with a railway worker in the New World and concluding by returning to a farmer in China. Chan notes that the etchings were particularly appropriate because the sepia tone recalled contemporary photographs of the Canadian Pacific Railway, adding that his choice of drypoint as a medium allowed him to achieve ghostly effects that no other medium would allow and provided a contrast to the paintings.[64]

If Paul Yee and Harvey Chan's dark exploration of the brutal exploitation of

Chinese railway workers represents the willingness of Groundwood to tackle difficult subjects in picturebooks for older readers, Marie-Louise Gay's best-selling Stella and Sam stories reach out to an international audience of preschool readers through the exploration of new life experiences.[65] In the first title of the series, *Stella, Star of the Sea* (1999), the imaginative Stella introduces her apprehensive and younger brother Sam to the seashore for the first time.

Gay describes the role of drawing in her development of the narrative. *Stella, Star of the Sea* began as she sketched 'a small character walking on the beach, exploring, observing, questioning.' As she moved between the text and the preparatory drawings, she was surprised to find that Stella 'wasn't alone: she had a small anxious-looking little brother trailing behind her.' With the addition of Sam, 'a sibling relationship came into being, which wasn't present in the beginning of the story.'[66] Subsequent titles in the series expand on the relationship and, in a parallel set of books, give Sam his own space as the central character.[67]

Gay's artistic style, which seems deceptively simple, is complex and multidimensional. After drawing preliminary pencil and ink sketches, she creates her illustrations using layers of pencil crayons and ink on gessoed paper. In the *Stella* series, she integrates collage with other painterly media to capture different visual and tactile aspects of the natural world.[68] Gay's sense of drama is present in her exploitation of the physical structure of the picturebook. She often uses a cinematic double-page spread and shifting point of view and perspective to engage her reader's attention.[69] The impetuous and determined Stella, always eager for another adventure, represents the untamed nature of all of Gay's child figures. Her flaming, curly, and unruly hair – a characteristic that she shares with other Gay heroines – and her big head and tiny feet reveal a particular aesthetic and a vision of children as awkward, vulnerable and heroic, imperfect and real.

Two British Columbian ecosystems are central to texts of a child's relationship with place and space, family and generational loss, and the cycle of death and rebirth within the natural world. Annette LeBox sets *Wild Bog Tea* (2002) in the Blaney Bog regional park of Maple Ridge, a suburban community in the Greater Vancouver area which has been the focus of conservational efforts to preserve its unique ecosystem. The wilderness of the marshy bog is central to a story that works on multiple levels to tell of a child's discovery of life's changes, the beauty of the natural world, and the pleasure of the senses. Harvey Chan's illustrations, which mix collage with red umber and white chalk pencil, are reminiscent of faded and torn photographs in an old album, conveying layers of time. He observes: 'It's a story about memory. I thought I could introduce collage technique into the story as a piece of memory put back together.'[70] In *Salmon Creek* (2002), Annette LeBox returns to themes of loss and survival and the fragility of the environment as she tells the story of the life cycle of a Pacific salmon in rhythmic prose, rich with alliteration and inner rhyme, creating a picturebook that crosses genres between informational text and poetry. Karen Reczuch's luminous watercolour illustrations use unusual perspectives and compositions to locate the story within its specific west coast setting.

Ange Zhang's artwork in his memoir of adolescence in China of the 1960s, *Red Land, Yellow River: A Story from the Cultural Revolution* (2004), combines computer graphics with archival and family photographs and evocations of revolutionary

A Story from the Cultural Revolution   Red Land   Yellow River

Ange Zhang

8.6 Ange Zhang. *Red Land, Yellow River: A Story from the Cultural Revolution.*
A Groundwood Book. Toronto and Vancouver: Douglas and McIntyre, 2004.
Reprinted with the permission of the publisher, Groundwood Books.

posters. Zhang's illustrations, which both refer to and counterbalance the social realism of Chinese poster art, are a change from his earlier illustrative work in oils. As he explains, when Aldana saw his roughs, created in the computer program Painter, she encouraged him to complete the illustrations using the digital medium that he had previously used as an animator for the filmmaker Nelvana. Zhang believes that the finished images have a simplicity which links them with the art forms produced in China during the Cultural Revolution and a realistic quality that matched the photographs.[71]

This mixing of photographs, historical artefacts, and computer-generated art gives his autobiography a documentary sensibility. Zhang's use of perspective and compression of figures against the bottom of the page convey the period's political and psychological oppression. Throughout, visual references to printed pages and writing allude contrapuntally to both the false ideological words of propaganda and the true words of authentic self. As the adolescent Zhang moves into the countryside, the images of calligraphy and of urban printed word on paper disappear from his life. The final image of Zhang sitting on a rooftop looking out over the city's rooftops, which simultaneously resemble the open pages of a book and birds taking flight, emphasizes the underlying theme of knowledge and creativity as freedom.

New Directions for Groundwood: 'As Much Art in Books as We Can Possibly Get Away With'

In recent years, feminism, pacifism, and global interdependence have all been featured in picturebooks published by Groundwood. They have published Canadian editions of non-European titles, including books from Africa. Beginning in 1998, they developed a Spanish imprint *Libros Tigrillo*, which publishes books by Latino Canadians such as Louis Garay and Elisa Amado's *Cousins* (2003), and issues translations of books from Spanish into English for the North American market and simultaneous Spanish editions of original English-language books for the growing Latino communities in the United States.[72] In the process, Groundwood has introduced child readers to new cultural perspectives and viewpoints of the world beyond Canada, reinforcing the idea of respecting difference.[73]

Aldana believes that 'older children need and like illustration,' adding that Groundwood always tries to have 'as much art in books as we can possibly get away with.'[74] At a time when few Canadian publishers are representing Canadian oral traditions, they have published illustrated collections of northern-focused folklore, including Jan Andrews's *Out of the Everywhere: Tales for a New World* (2000), illustrated by Simon Ng, in which stories from different immigrant communities are adapted by placing them within Canadian environments and settings, while Bob Barton's *The Bear Says North: Tales from the Northern Lands* (2003), illustrated by Jirina Marton, reinvents traditional tales from the circumpolar north. They have also developed new illustrated genres like Kevin Major's verse novel, *Ann and Seamus* (2003), an epic told in two contrapuntal voices: that of seventeen-year-old Ann Harvey and Seamus Ryan, a young Irishman whom she rescues from the Atlantic. Major, who based his poem on a shipwreck that occurred in 1828, highlights the psychological experience of the isolation of living on the Isle aux

Morts off the Newfoundland coast. David Blackwood illustrated the book with spare, sombre monochromatic blue-grey prints that echo the sadness of loss as the lovers are separated.[75]

Intertextuality and the graphic novel influence of Hergé's *Tintin* books are evident in Nicolas Debon's *Four Pictures by Emily Carr* (2003), which explores Carr's struggles against the limitations in her life. Debon combines third-person narrator, balloon dialogue, and first-person monologues in a creative, dynamic, and fluid narrative flow, focusing on four periods of Carr's life and four famous works of art symbolizing those periods to build a portrait of her life. Debon, a realist whose style changes subtly with each work that he illustrates, brings an awareness of the narrative potential of the peritextual design elements to each of his picturebooks. In *Four Pictures by Emily Carr*, the endpapers are reproductions of Carr's sketches and notes, while selections from her paintings introduce each narrative section. He places Carr's paintings within the frames of his own illustrations, the interrelationship of the two serving as a visual meditation on the work of an artist.

Aldana has continued to promote the importance of Canadian cultural identity though her editorial decisions, and through political lobbying in organizations such as the Canadian Coalition for School Libraries and the Association of Canadian Publishers, while retaining a self-critically reflexive stance about the nature of nationalism in a country with a long history of colonialism.[76] While Groundwood is committed to seeking out marginalized voices, Aboriginal writers from North and South America, and those 'whose contribution to our society is not always visible,' she is also a pragmatist who is dedicated to ensuring the economic survival of her publishing house. In 2005, Aldana and Scott McIntyre of Douglas and McIntyre, recognizing the need to ensure the press's continued existence after her retirement, sold Groundwood Books to House of Anansi Press. She retains a seat on the Anansi board and the title of publisher of her imprint.

'Taking More Risks': Annick Press

At Annick Press, the sustained demand for Robert Munsch titles provided a secure financial base to weather the downturn in the 1990s. By the time Munsch moved to Scholastic in 1996, the Munsch list at Annick had grown to twenty-five titles, with more than 20 million books in print.[77] They retained the rights to the backlist titles, and a steady stream of translations, reprinted editions, special anniversary editions, and collections of previously published Munsch stories have continued to generate revenue for the company.

Annick Press has continued to be guided by its original vision of publishing books that empower children and represent their everyday lives, while extending their range by being willing to take risks, 'both in cultural and business terms.'[78] Their interest in multiculturalism has led them to publish authors with a strong connection to oral traditions. Richardo Keens-Douglas's retelling of Caribbean stories like *La Diablesse and the Baby: A Caribbean Folktale* (1994), a variant of the African-American folk tale 'The Hairy Man,' involving a devil figure's attempt to kidnap a baby, reflects his career in theatre as an actor and playwright. Marie Lafrance's richly coloured and patterned illustrations add narrative detail only suggested by the author, depicting La Diablesse as a beautiful, seductive, and terrifying woman

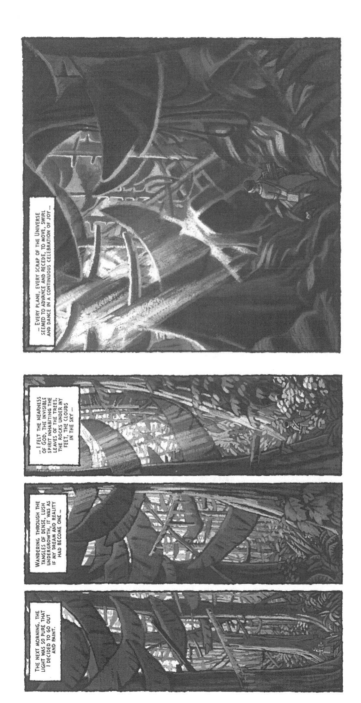

8.7 Nicolas Debon. *Four Pictures by Emily Carr.* A Groundwood Book. Toronto and Vancouver: Douglas and McIntyre, 2003. Reprinted with the permission of the publisher, Groundwood Books.

whose demonic nature is revealed by her one-horned foot. Marie Day's *Edward, the 'Crazy Man'* (2002) introduced young readers to issues of mental illness and homelessness through her story of the friendship that develops between Charlie and Edward, who concocts and wears wildly imaginative costumes confected from the junk that he scavenges and stores in a battered baby carriage. Day's vivid and humorous mixed-media illustrations in pen and ink, pencil crayon, and marker capture the energy and wit of Edward's unique vision and affirm his worth as a person with a 'brain disease called schizophrenia,' whose resourcefulness and creativity contribute to his ability to make fantastic, 'crazy' costumes valued by a 'famous rock star.'

In recent years, Annick has developed illustrated books in different genres for older readers. Priscilla Galloway's *Tales of Ancient Lands* series of ancient Greek myths are novel-length psychological studies and social histories that place new characters and unusual perspectives at the core of the tales. *Atalanta: The Fastest Runner in the World* (1995) and *Aleta and the Queen: A Tale of Ancient Greece* (1995) focus on women's lives, while *Daedalus and the Minotaur* (1997) reshapes the story into an exploration of family secrets, compassion, and choice. Normand Cousineau's ink and gouache drawings in tones of bronze, brown, gold, red, and blue are abstracted interpretations of Greek and Minoan art, recalling the flat colour fields, curvilinear shapes, patterned borders, and strong outlines of statues, murals, and amphorae, augmenting the context that Galloway has represented textually.

While their illustrated books for older readers stretched the genre, Annick has also published some of the most experimental picturebooks in Canada for very young readers. In the *Mole Sisters* series, Roslyn Schwartz depicts the small dramas and adventures of a pair of moles in very few, carefully chosen words and very small, rather abstracted images in muted pencil crayon. Their love of discovery, generous spirit, and sunny temperaments are evident in *The Mole Sisters and the Rainy Day* (1999), in which they transform a wet day into a watery paradise, and in *The Mole Sisters and the Piece of Moss* (1999), in which vegetation is rescued from a life of boredom and ennui. As Deirdre Baker notes, Schwartz's subtly sophisticated illustrations are like cartoons in the *New Yorker*, in which the ideas in image and text diverge through unexpected juxtapositions.[79]

Annick has also moved into the area of illustrated children's information books in which the visual is emphasized through experimentation with typography, layout, and other peritextual elements. The differences between the first edition of Claire Mackay's *The Toronto Story* (1990), illustrated by Johnny Wales, and the second edition, issued in 2002, demonstrate changing tastes in the design of information books. The 1990 edition is a handsome outsized volume, 36 × 28 cm, in which Wales's vignettes are interspersed throughout the text block and margins, visually matching Mackay's textual shifts between broad historical narrative and telling detail in her recounting of key moments in the development of the city. The designer, Helmut W. Weyerstrahs, chose blocks of crisp black text, set ragged right in a classic serif font with small cap sideheads and serif drop cap headers marking each section of text, and wide white margins. Throughout the work, the vignette illustrations move beyond the margins into the space of the text block, which is reshaped around the illustration to give variety to the page. In each chapter, a double-page panoramic illustration of the development of the urban streetscape at the intersection of Church and Front streets is framed in a pale lemon yellow, emphasizing both continuity and change from decade to decade. In combination with the muted colours of the pen and ink and watercolour wash illustrations, the design is pleasantly restrained, open, and highly readable.

In sharp contrast, the 2002 edition, with revised text and illustrations by Mackay and Wales, and design by Irvin Cheung/iCheung Design, is much brighter and busier. The size of the volume has been reduced to a more standard 29 × 21 cm. The new illustrations that Wales created for the revised edition are more painterly and much brighter than those of the first edition. The table of contents introduces the colour-themed layout of the chapters, which move the reader forward through the decades in a rainbow progression from a greyed sage green to deep indigo. Each chapter has an introductory page, white text superimposed on the designated colour, which is repeated in the coloured border that surrounds the double-paged panoramas, 'fun facts' text boxes inserted into the text block, and in the light-toned wide band at the bottom of each page, on which is superimposed the relevant dates of the chapter in white. The single column text has been redeployed into two columns of justified type and the drop caps replaced with coloured display type initial words at the beginning of each chapter, and coloured sideheads and bold initial words in black for sub-sections. Illustrations and coloured text boxes alternate with the text block within the strict column grid. In the 1990 edition, the imagined reader is invited to read the work as a continuous and sustained narrative. In the 2002 edition, while the information about growth and change in Toronto remains unaltered, the lively and crowded design invites the reader to dip into and browse the chapters.

The shift in information book design continued in Tanya Lloyd Kyi's *The Blue Jean Book: The Story behind the Seams* (2005), which won the 2006 BC Book Prizes' Christie Harris Illustrated Children's Literature Prize. The book, in fact, has no illustrator in the sense of a single artist creating specific images to accompany the text. Instead the two book designers, Irvin Cheung and Peter Pimentel, were responsible for the creative assemblage of vintage and contemporary photographs, posters, and photographs of realia that comprise the illustrations.

From the early years of the two co-founders, the staff at Annick Press has grown to eleven. In 1999, as Anne Millyard prepared to retire, Annick opened a west coast office with Colleen MacMillan as associate publisher. Rick Wilks describes what makes Annick Press distinctive in a crowded market, explaining that they publish books that are 'exciting, edgy and compelling alternatives … [and that offer the reader] a fresh, contemporary, dynamic, and creative way of looking at the world. We encourage critical thinking and risk-taking without ever being didactic.' For Wilks, it is the ability to both connect with and challenge their audience that makes their books stand out.[80]

The Little Green Turtle Grows Up: Kids Can Press

Over the decades, the range of genres published by Kids Can Press has continued to expand. They have become adept at selling international rights. Valerie Hussey estimates that about 80 per cent of the Kids Can list is suitable for licensing, and the overwhelming majority of those titles find an international market, whether in the United States, Europe, or Asia.[81]

While cultural diversity has been an important factor in the development of their lists, Kids Can's picturebooks have never been explicitly Canadian in content and imagery and continue to focus on marketability.[82] They have developed a range of well-designed, sophisticated picturebooks, particularly in the areas of folk tales and historical narratives. Aubrey Davis's *Bone Button Borscht* (1995), illustrated with angular watercolour and pencil images by Dusan Petricic, is based on the 'stone soup' motif, in which a trickster creates a dinner from the contributions of unsuspecting bystanders. In Davis's retelling, the dialogue and inner monologues of the beggar who brings the villagers out of isolation, selfishness, and darkness into a renewed communal life of giving and sharing have a Yiddish inflection, recalling the stories of Sholem Aleichem and Isaac Bashevis Singer. Petricic's stylized illustrations, which resemble sepia-toned engravings, add a wry counterpoint to the narrative and locate the story geographically and temporally in a nineteenth-century eastern European shtetl. As golden, radiant light slowly fills the dark pages, the village is moved by charity towards a grand celebration, the symbolism of the colour emphasizing the transformative nature of the story.

In David Booth's *The Dust Bowl* (1996), illustrated by Karen Reczuch, a grandfather tells his grandson about the experience of drought, plagues of grasshoppers, and blowing topsoil during the hard years of the 1930s. The grandfather's storytelling is a healing act that links the family of three men to their own history, inspiring courage and the ability to persevere in the face of current hardships. In planning the illustrations for her many historical picturebooks, Reczuch imagines the visual narrative unfolding like a film and researches the visual details of the period that she is depicting through archival photographs to fill in the gaps in the film. For *The Dust Bowl*, she drew on her own family history of settlement on the prairies and her own family members to portray the three generations trying to farm in a marginal area in the heart of the Palliser Triangle.[83]

Kids Can has also developed non-traditional picturebooks that extend the form for older readers. Michèle Lemieux's *Stormy Night* (1999), first published in German in 1996 as *Gewitternacht*, and the recipient of the 1997 Bologna Ragazzi Award, is a philosophical inquiry into the human condition. A young girl, who is unable to sleep one stormy night, lies awake in bed with her dog beside her and poses a series of open-ended metaphysical and personal questions like 'Can we each see our own soul?' Her musings are accompanied by black and white, pen and ink sketches that resemble the drawings and cartoons of Americans Jules Feiffer, Ben Shahn, and Saul Steinberg, whom she cites as a direct inspiration for her line art.[84] Lemieux, who has taught drawing and illustration in L'École de Design at the Université du Québec à Montréal since 1988, explains that she is not a storyteller but a visual thinker. She wanted 'to talk of life, fate, dreams, anxiety and even death, for death is a part of life.'[85] Language and image inspired each other, as everyday words triggered images that she added to her sketchbook, each question opening 'a universe of pictures and metaphors, which are already a part of the answer.'[86] As she describes it, 'I can [complete] 500 drawings before I even know what I'm going

8.8 David Booth. *The Dust Bowl*. Illustrated by Karen Reczuch. Toronto: Kids Can Press, 1996.
Material from *The Dust Bowl*, written by David Booth, illustrated by Karen Reczuch, is used by
permission of Kids Can Press Ltd., Toronto. Illustrations © 1996 Karen Reczuch.

to do … Then when I see the primary material, I wonder, "Now, what can I do with
that?"'[87] The final picturebook, which she describes as 'an open door between our
childhood world and the world of adults,' represents the process of creation, in
which drawing precedes the construction of narrative.[88] She designed the format
and layout to resemble her sketchbook, and deliberately refrained from reworking
her sketches to retain the 'graphical transcription of thought into pictures.'[89]

The work, which was nominated for the Governor General's Award for children's literature illustration in the French translation, *Nuit d'orages* (1998) has been
translated into a total of thirteen languages. In 2002, Terrapin Puppet Theatre of
Hobart, Tasmania, created a dramatization of *Stormy Night*, and in 2003, Lemieux
translated the work into an animated film for the National Film Board of Canada.

Kids Can's poetry anthologies have continued to present a diversity of voices
and images for different groups of readers. David Booth's collection of nature

8.9 Michèle Lemieux. *Stormy Night*. Toronto: Kids Can Press, 1999.
Material from Michèle Lemieux, *Gewitternacht*, 1996, is used by permission of the publisher, Beltz &
Gelbert, Weinheim, Germany.

poetry, *Voices on the Wind: Poems for All Seasons* (1990), is a fresh selection by classic and contemporary poets for both children and adults. The painterly illustrations by Michèle Lemieux are placed in intriguing relationship to the words on the page, images forming a secondary world that serves as both a backdrop to the poems and an invitation into their world. In contrast, Kady MacDonald Denton's pastel-toned watercolour drawings for her Mother Goose collection, *A Child's Treasury of Nursery Rhymes* (1998), emphasize a tone of gentle comfort and amusement for very young children. Images of babies, toddlers, and school-age children rollick across the pages in a loving depiction of children and families and the odd, quirky characters who inhabit the rhymes.[90]

In preparation for *Doctor Knickerbocker and Other Rhymes: A Canadian Collection* (1993), David Booth, with the help of his son Jay, collected regional Canadian variants of children's street and game lore. The biting and satirical schoolyard rhymes move between the parodies and taunts of contemporary children and those of previous generations. Maryann Kovalski's drawings of children in late Victorian dress reflect the layering of past and present children's voices. The varied page design, which incorporates comic strip speech balloons, and the visual onomatopoeia of differing typefaces, further enliven the printed surface, echoing the individualism and gentle anarchy of the rhymes.

The look of poetry has also featured prominently in the *Visions in Poetry* series, which blends narrative poems with edgy, provocative art in an attempt to entice young adult readers into engaging with the classics. The postscript to each volume provides a brief sketch of the writer's period, the poem's history, and the illustrator's background and visual approach to the particular poem. The handsome bindings with cloth spines and rice paper half-title pages of the series are reminiscent of the gift-book publishing tradition of the early twentieth century, while the illustrations transgress the expected.[91] The first title in the series, Lewis Carroll's *Jabberwocky* (2004), is illustrated by Stéphane Jorisch in a combination of pencil, pen and ink, subdued toned watercolour washes, and Adobe Photoshop computer enhancement, in a style reminiscent of editorial cartoons by Ralph Steadman and Ben Shahn. He sets the poem in a militaristic, Orwellian dystopia in which the Jabberwock, who is depicted on successive pages as a monster, a soldier/dictator, and a hero on a giant television screen, is reduced by the last, wordless page to a small, insignificant being that can be fitted into a box. In his interplay of design, typography, and visual imagery, Jorisch uses a mixture of typefaces to convey the anxiety and instability of the narrative, creating a visual metonym of the sounds of the words in the particular language of Carroll's neologisms. Illustrations play against the text, subverting and extending the text, and reshaping the trajectory of the poem. The result is a fully realized world of existential dread that has its own internal logic but makes no sense, epitomizing Jorisch's observation that 'nonsense is sometimes spoken by those in authority.'[92] (See colour plate 14.)

While beautiful and challenging picturebooks win awards and bring international attention to the house, Kids Can has simultaneously paid close attention to the marketing potential of its titles, ensuring that its picturebooks have a strong visual presence that will effectively translate into the competitive retail market and attract international rights sales. Among the picturebooks designed for the youngest nursery-age child is the Little Mouse series of books by the mother and daughter team of Kim and Eugenie Fernandes, which introduces readers to the tiny, contained domestic world of a little mouse. Kim Fernandes's illustrations, painstakingly created with Fimo modelling substance, are replete with toy-like miniature details, carefully designed to have immediate appeal to both children and adults.[93] Anarchic humour characterizes both text and image in Linda Bailey's *Stanley's Party* (2003), illustrated by Bill Slavin, in which the family dog increasingly breaks the boundaries of acceptable behaviour whenever he is left alone, culminating in a wild party attended by all the neighbourhood dogs.

Bailey and Slavin have also collaborated on the Good Times Travel Agency series, beginning with *Adventures in Ancient Egypt* (2000). The series utilizes a strongly graphic format and a blend of factual information and adventure story to introduce readers to past civilizations. Each page combines a time-travel narrative with historical context. Slavin's illustrations incorporate the sequential art conventions of the European *bande dessinée* tradition, including multiple sequential panels, speech balloons, shifting perspectives, and varied and distinctive typefaces to distinguish between the story, the dialogue of the characters in the story, and factual historical information related to the particular moment in the story.[94] Pictures and words combine in a complex interweaving of narrative and metanarrative. The reader, who is directly addressed through the device of the open pages of a 'personal guide to Ancient Egypt,' at the bottom of each double-page spread, becomes an active participant in decoding the layers of the page by distinguishing the varying elements of the story, conveyed through the repeated design elements and shifting voice.

However, the most significant market-driven development for Kids Can is the phenomenal success of the Franklin books. The strength of the sales of Paulette Bourgeois and Brenda Clark's initial title, *Franklin in the Dark* (1986), and sequels *Hurry Up Franklin* (1989) and *Franklin Fibs* (1991) convinced Kids Can that they had a hit series with significant marketing potential. Valerie Hussey comments on the care that Kids Can took to find the right way to develop Franklin 'with both integrity and fidelity to the character.'[95] They first licensed Franklin in the United States to Scholastic Books, which used the little green turtle as the mascot for the Scholastic Book Clubs program in schools.[96] By 1995, when Nelvana Limited, a Canadian producer of animated television series for children, began to create an animated television and video Franklin series, there were twelve titles in print that had sold more than six million copies in nine languages.[97] A decade later, with aggressive international licensing, more than thirty Franklin titles were in print, which have sold more than sixty million titles in more than thirty languages.[98] A merchandized commodity, Franklin is now a trademark that appears in activity books, videos and DVDs, interactive media, lines of clothes, games, toys, backpacks, and plush puppets. The books developed from the television spin-offs are now written by Sharon Jennings and re-illustrated by animators who have been trained to create narrative illustrations rather than animation stills.[99]

In 1998, Nelvana purchased Kids Can Press for $6.1 million.[100] Ricky Englander retired, and Valerie Hussey stayed on as CEO, president, and publisher. In 2000, another, larger Toronto-based multimedia company, Corus Entertainment, bought Nelvana and, with it, Kids Can Press, and in 2006, Hussey announced her retire-

8.10 Linda Bailey. *Adventures in Ancient Egypt.* Illustrated by Bill Slavin. Toronto: Kids Can Press, 2000.

Material from *Adventures in Ancient Egypt*, written by Linda Bailey, illustrated by Bill Slavin, is used by permission of Kids Can Press Ltd., Toronto. Text © 2000 Linda Bailey. Illustrations © 2000 Bill Slavin.

ment from the day-to-day management of the company. Kids Can has a much larger list than other Canadian publishers for children, with over 575 books in print, encompassing a strong mix of award-winning writers and illustrators and more commercial titles, which Hussey believes has challenged the industry.[101]

'That's How You Get Good Manuscripts': Orca Book Publishers

While the major Canadian children's publishers sought to reinvent themselves in the face of change, some regional publishers expanded their children's lists and new smaller houses emerged. Orca Book Publishers in Victoria was founded in 1984 by Bob Tyrrell to publish non-fiction on topics related to British Columbia.[102] In 1990 Orca moved into Canadian children's publishing. One of their first picture-books was *Waiting for the Whales* (1991), in which Sheryl McFarlane tells the story of a grandfather living by the sea in an unnamed west coast setting, who passes on to his granddaughter his delight in the seasonal cycles of nature and the beauty of his island home. After his death, the child is comforted by the return of the orcas.

The illustrator, Ron Lightburn, was inspired by the artistic styles of N.C. Wyeth and Norman Rockwell.[103] He describes his approach to illustration as cinematic, adding that he likes to 'vary the point of view ... to add interest and drama to scenes.' He compares 'the transition between spreads in a picture book to the editing cuts in a film,' seeing his choice of page breaks as a strong narrative element. For *Waiting for the Whales*, after completing preparatory sketches, he photographed friends and family members in carefully planned sequences to capture body language and facial expressions. He believes that his use of models gives his illustrations 'a verisimilitude [that] helps the reader to suspend disbelief.'[104] The resulting illustrations in coloured pencil crayon on textured paper employ subtle colour symbolism, repeating visual motifs and images, and the use of light as a compositional element that also reflects the emotional trajectory of the narrative. (See colour plate 15.)

The success of *Waiting for the Whales*, which won the Governor General's Award, brought attention to Orca's children's list. Orca began to receive more manuscripts, and they gradually moved to specializing in children's books. As Tyrrell comments, 'That's how you get good manuscripts, by winning awards.'[105] In recent years, the house has moved from a regional focus to publishing Canadian authors and illustrators from across the country and has introduced new subject matter, including folk tales, to expand the range of its picturebooks.

Victor Bosson's illustrations for the Japanese folktales *The Magic Ear* (1995) and *The Fox's Kettle* (1998), both by Laura Langston, are inspired by his life-long interest in Japanese art and design. In *The Magic Ear*, the rectangular border was modelled on 'patterned *washi*, a type of intricately printed and colourful Japanese paper.' The folded corners reminded Bosson of 'the tied paper messages in the Japanese temples' that he had visited on trips to Japan. He describes his art style for the books as 'a western exploration of Japanese *Ukiyo-e* – the popular woodblock print' also known as 'pictures from the floating world.' He was conscious of the details of temporal specificity, setting *The Magic Ear* in the late eighteenth century, while *The Fox's Kettle* takes place in the mid- to late nineteenth century, drawing inspiration from the prints of Yoshitoshi and Kuniyoushi.[106]

The titles also represented a new way of working for Bosson, who has multiple sclerosis. He moved into computer-generated art when his illness began to pose technical challenges. Watercolour is an unforgiving medium that cannot be reworked once dry. The computer allows him the flexibility to work slowly and make multiple changes, while preserving the look of watercolour pigment on paper. He adds that computer illustration enables him to draw and design a book simultaneously.[107]

'Just a Smudge in the Dark': Red Deer Press

Over the last fifteen years, former children's editor Tim Wynne-Jones, who was hired in 1990, and former editor Peter Carver, who replaced Wynne-Jones in 1996, have shaped Red Deer Press's children's list to emphasize literary and artistic excellence, in consultation with designer Blair Kerrigan.[108] Red Deer focuses on titles with broad domestic and foreign appeal while maintaining an emphasis on the prairie west, particularly the rural west environment, and a distinctive regional voice. About one-third of their list is devoted to children's books, with two or three hardcover picturebooks issued each year.[109] The combination of strong editorial input and innovative design has resulted in a list that has won numerous awards for its picturebook creators and designers.

The themes of early twentieth-century prairie immigration and the trials of economic survival weave through Jim McGugan's *Josepha: A Prairie Boy's Story* (1994), a powerful indictment of the process of Othering, of identifying and excluding those who are Other, 'not like us,' different. The narrator remembers the loss of his friend, the immigrant Josepha, who is bullied and excluded due to his language, poverty, age, and size when placed with younger children in a one-room schoolhouse. The narrative of tentative friendship, the humiliation of being a cultural outsider, and the struggle of learning a new language and different cultural ways is enriched by the musical cadences of spoken-language fragments – the chance poetry discovered in the act of learning English. The strength of the friends' non-verbal communication and the power of the prairie environment are visualized through the oil paintings by Murray Kimber, in which strong, hot colours convey the emotional state of the characters, in a style reminiscent of the early twentieth-century American paintings of Edward Hopper, Rockwell Kent, and Thomas Hart Benton. Kimber's non-linear perspective and exaggerations of scale emphasize the emotional and psychological elements of the text. Josepha squeezes into the page and too-small elementary schoolroom desk, uncomfortable, different, but determined. (See colour plate 16.)

In Nan Gregory's *How Smudge Came* (1995), the outsider is Cindy, an adult woman with Down's syndrome who lives in a group home and works in a hospice. When she rescues an abandoned puppy, only to have him taken away by the group home supervisor, her friends in the hospice find a way to reunite Cindy and Smudge. Gregory tells the story from Cindy's point of view, emphasizing her courage and tenderness and her sense of justice. Gregory considers one of the major themes in her writing to be the bravery of the ordinary person, believing that 'everyone has within them a heroic heart.'[110] Ron Lightburn's nuanced coloured-pencil illustrations contrast Cindy's nurturing love with hazy shadows that evoke bars of imprisonment and symbolize the control of her group home. Gregory deliberately created room for the illustrator to extend the text to locate the story in a specific setting.[111] Similarly, Gregory remembers that it was the inspiration of Lightburn and editor Wynne-Jones to depict Cindy as an adult with Down's syndrome, adding that 'people have said to me that they know kids with Down's syndrome, or have friends with Down's syndrome, and that's exactly what they're like. But that's exactly what I'm like inside, that's the best part of me.'[112] Lightburn's images work on different levels with different groups of readers. Shapes are reduced to monumentally simple cones and spheres, adding to the impression of quiet strength of the protagonist Cindy. The blurred softness of the images also reflects the visual deficits of Jan, a patient in the hospice, who gives the puppy a name, calling him '[j]ust a smudge in the dark.' For an adult reader, Lightburn's illustrations also invoke the narrowing world of a young man with AIDS whose sight is destroyed by cytomegalovirus in the days before antiretroviral medications.

Former publisher Dennis Johnson remembers that when the book was first presented to his sales representatives, everyone was silent, before 'one of the braver ones stood and said, "Let me get this straight. This book is not even about a child; it's a retarded girl who gets a puppy amidst death. And this is a kid's book?" And we said, "Well, yes. We believe in it."' While initial orders from bookstores were slow, the title found an audience among diverse groups of readers through word of mouth and the publicity generated by several awards. The rights to the paperback edition in the United States were sold to Walker Books in New York, and then to Scholastic Book Clubs, who were as reluctant initially about the subject matter as the sales representatives and booksellers had been. *How Smudge Came* ended up selling 253,000 copies through Scholastic Book Clubs, and has been translated into four languages. For Johnson, it was his company's initial courage in believing in a book 'that defied a lot of the conventional logic about what kids desire to read and to experience' that ensured its success.[113]

Fears of loss and abandonment are brilliantly explored in Nan Gregory's *Amber Waiting* (2002), a story about a child who suffers anxiety and rage when her neglectful father regularly fails to pick her up on time after kindergarten. Amber imagines herself travelling in the sky around the world, astonishing fathers all over the globe, while her neglectful father is abandoned and alone on the moon, exactly as he has left her waiting. Kady MacDonald Denton's warm pastel images of kindergarten life, drawn in a loose sepia line with gauzy watercolour washes, contrast with the saturated deep blue ink of the dark sky of Amber's fantasy world, in which intricate collages of human figures are layered against an abstract background of moon, sun, and stars. The reader is allowed to enter fully into Amber's complex inner emotional life and to empathize with her independence and the imaginative resolution to her feelings of abandonment. Denton subtly indicates the hurried character of the always-late father, who in each image seems to be leaning forward, his body in a diagonal line, in a rush to get to the next place, in contrast with the precise solidity of his daughter, muffled in her outdoor clothes, sitting under a clock that shows the passage of time.

The diversity and maturity of the Red Deer Press picturebook list benefits from

He swings the door open. "Let's go, sweetie."

Amber trots to keep up.

"Dad," she says, "were you ever on the moon?"

"On the moon?"

She tugs him to a stop. "Waiting for someone. Scared and lonely."

8.11 Nan Gregory. *Amber Waiting*. Illustrated by Kady MacDonald Denton. Northern Lights Books for Children. Calgary: Red Deer Press, 2002.

the willingness of the press to take risks. Unlike many of the other children's houses in Canada, who are increasingly averse to publishing work by new and emerging authors and illustrators, Red Deer continues to leave about 20 per cent of their list available to emerging talent.[114] In 2000, Red Deer Press moved to Calgary, where it affiliated with the University of Calgary. With the advent of new technologies, it has been possible for the press to remain in a smaller urban area outside the Toronto and Vancouver publishing, distribution, and sales centres, while maintaining communication between its editorial staff, and authors and illustrators who live in provinces and territories across Canada.[115] Although the press was acquired by Fitzhenry and Whiteside in 2005 as an independent imprint, and is no longer run as a not-for-profit venture, it remains in Calgary.

Tradewind Books and Simply Read Books

Tradewind Books in Vancouver is an example of an editorially driven house devoted to quality picturebooks and illustrated books in the fine arts tradition. The publisher, Michael Katz, started his press in 1996 while a high school teacher in London, England. From the outset, he was interested in the aesthetics of the books he published, believing that attractive design and presentation directly increase marketability.[116]

While many of the first Tradewind picturebooks were written and illustrated by well-known British creators, the press tries to publish Canadian authors and illustrators while maintaining an international focus and an explicitly multicultural emphasis. As Katz explains, 'I'm not a regional publisher … I will set a book [in British Columbia] … but I don't feel I can target a book just to this market … It doesn't matter if a story is set here or London or Paris or New York or Toronto. I think that if it's a good story, it's a good story [that will] be interesting to everybody.'[117]

In *A Telling Time* (2004), Irene N. Watts weaves a narrative in which a grandmother tells her granddaughter the story from the Hebrew Bible of Esther's rescue of the Jews, framed within the grandmother's memories of her last Purim in prewar Vienna before her family fled from the Nazi occupation. Watts's multi-layered, complex narrative is a testament to the power of storytelling, and to bravery and hope in the face of persecution. Kathryn Shoemaker's illustrations help the reader to decode the temporal interlayering of the story through her use of colour symbolism, typography, and varying artistic style. The story of Esther unfolds as a scroll, in the rich muted colours of an ancient jewelled Persian miniature, while the images of snowy Vienna are framed by oppressive black bars that suggest both the threatening symbol of a swastika and the likely fate of the rabbi facing arrest. Repeating motifs of barbed wire, lost shoes, abandoned suitcases, the mogen david, and the flickering orange of fire remind the reader of the threat of the coming Holocaust. The warmth of the contemporary setting, as the grandmother tells her story, and the clock faces that appear throughout the story symbolize both the need to make decisions (the 'telling time') and the possibility of hope. (See colour plate 17.)

Simply Read Books, established in 2001, is a small, specialized publisher of illustrated books and picturebooks. Publisher Dimiter Savoff was an architect in Bulgaria and Vancouver before he entered publishing and has shaped a children's list in which Canadian and international innovative contemporary design and illustration as fine art are carefully balanced. The first list issued by Simply Read included two classic children's titles illustrated by the Bulgarian artist Iassen Ghiuselev in the tradition of the elaborate gift books of the early twentieth century, a style that Savoff believes has continuing appeal for contemporary readers.[118]

Design is paramount in *Windy* (2002), *Sunny* (2003), and *Snowy & Chinook* (2005), a series of small, square books for toddler-and pre-school aged children. Robin Mitchell and Judith Steedman make conscious use of 1950s pop culture, transforming familiar toys into artwork. They collaborate on creating assemblages from everyday objects that become three-dimensional set designs. Tiny four-inch dolls, interacting in three-dimensional scenes, are integrated with found objects, such as telephone poles made of children's pencils, collage, photographs, and pen and ink line drawings in a childlike style. Collage media include paper, velvet, and felt. The 'sets' are then photographed and manipulated with digital design. Illustrated endpapers add a peritextual design sensibility to the whole with Robin Mitchell's hand-drawn, pen and ink maps, and list of dramatis personae highlighting the dolls' adventures. Even the inside of the book jacket extends the design and narrative, with inserted musical CDs and illustrations and simple activity instructions on making kites, pancakes and hot chocolate, or shoebox guitars, thematically linked to the texts.

A similar fascination with the potential of assemblage and photography as an illustrative medium characterizes Stefan Czernecki's picturebooks, *Ride 'Em, Cowboy* (2004) and *Lilliput 5357* (2006). In *Ride 'Em, Cowboy*, he arranged three-dimensional objects, including wooden cowboy sculptures by Alberta folk artist Martin Schatz, and miniature cowboy paraphernalia into tableaux, which were then photographed. He then rearranged the elements in the photographs, playing with scale and composition until he was satisfied with the ensemble. His reassembled illustrations were then digitized and further digitally modified. The typography was digitally manipulated to visually recreate the sound effects in the text, from rooster crows to clopping hooves and cowboy calls.[119] The resulting illustrations are a witty and affectionate tribute to images of Western life drawn from popular culture and folk art.

Elisa Gutiérrez's *Picturescape* (2005), a wordless picturebook, portrays a boy's imaginative cross-country journey from the west to east coast through famous Canadian landscape paintings. At the Vancouver Art Gallery the boy enters an Emily Carr painting and is carried by a raven through Carr's looming west coast forest, then by tugboat past an E.J. Hughes coastal scene of ferry, beach, and arbutus trees. He sails in a red balloon over the mountains of Lawren Harris's Bylot Island, and across William Kurelek's wheat-filled prairies to rest at Tom Thompson's famous 'Jack Pine,' before racing on the back of Alex Colville's mysterious black horse towards an oncoming train, and finally swimming with the whales in the Atlantic in David Blackwell's painting. Gutiérrez uses elaborate collages of coloured pencil on coloured paper to recreate the landscapes of the famous paintings. Her use of framing, alternating multi-panel pages with double-page spreads of the paintings, varying perspective and point of view, and shifting from a cinematic

8.12 Stefan Czernecki. *Ride 'Em, Cowboy.* Vancouver: Simply Read Books, 2004.
Reprinted with the permission of the publisher, Simply Read Books.

widescreen aerial view to extreme close-up details further play with the idea of the painting or printed page as a window through which one looks. The illustrations form an extended visual metaphor of the dual idea of a picturescape as an escape into pictures and a picturescape as the pictorial quality of regional landscape, captured on a painted surface.

Succession Planning

The publishers who initiated the growth of Canadian children's publishing in the 1970s and 1980s are concerned about succession planning. They are uncertain whether their publishing houses will survive and whether there will be continuity after they retire.[120] In a competitive market with tight profit margins and notoriously low wages, there is little direct incentive to enter the industry. Patsy Aldana laments that 'the passion to publish' is missing and questions 'whether anyone really cares.'[121] Her view is born out by a 2003 survey that noted that 70 per cent of shareholders in eighty-three publishing houses were aged fifty or older. While 49 per cent planned to retire in the next ten years, the majority had not implemented a succession plan.[122] While some publishers have sought partners outside the industry, or discussed the possibility of consolidation or employee purchase, the thin profit margins in trade publishing have made succession planning both urgent and problematic.

Considering the trials that the publishing industry has gone through in the last fifteen years, and the changes that have taken place in the picturebook sector, it is perhaps surprising that there are Canadian children's publishers that are still independently owned and editorially driven. The community of creators of children's books continues to work towards ensuring the Canadian children's publishing industry is sustainable, and Canadian publishers and editors have continued to focus on thoughtful titles that preserve a distinctive authorial voice. It is worth remembering the words of Michele Landsberg, who confirms her faith in the genre of Canadian picturebooks as an enduring signifier of Canadian culture: 'I'd like to say, whatever laments I've made, how far we've come in the past thirty years, what wonderful picturebooks we have, and how ironic that just at the moment of this inflorescence, there comes the destruction of our culture, the globalization of publishing, and perhaps the children's picturebooks will be a little tiny bulwark against that great anonymity. Let's hope so.'[123]

CHAPTER NINE

Canadian Cultural Identity, Canadian Cultural Identities

The question of Canadian cultural identity and literary production has been raised repeatedly by Canadian literary critics and scholars. The idea of a national literature that expresses an identifiable and distinct national character, and reflects a common set of beliefs and values, is embedded in literary criticism. As Sarah Corse notes, traditional definitions of nationalist literature are rooted in the problematic of national exceptionalism, the belief that literature can reflect an essential national character that is identifiable, distinct, and 'unique.' Texts for inclusion into a national canon are evaluated for the degree to which they can be read 'through the lens of national character' and can be differentiated from other national literatures.[1]

The issue of Canadian identity is central to the discussion of the development of indigenous publishing in Canada. In 1967, during Canada's centennial year, when issues of Canadian cultural production were being broadly discussed in the popular and academic press, Sheila Egoff, in the first edition of *The Republic of Childhood*, argued that children's books can show the reader aspects of Canadian identity and Canadian cultural values.[2] Her view is echoed by Elizabeth Waterston, who believes that Canadian children's books can perform the doubled work of acculturating children into a national sense of identity by fixing an enduring image of the country while simultaneously providing insight into the country for international readers.[3] Waterston describes the in-between state of Canadian identity as shaped by the awareness of living in a borderland, in which differences among English, French, and American cultures have sensitized Canadians to marginality, an argument that could be extended to the very nature of children's print culture in Canada.[4] For both authors, Benedict Anderson's idea of nation as an imagined political community created in part through textual production could be extended to the idea of nation as an imagined cultural community, constructed through the complex interactions between authors and readers, mediated by printed texts and images.[5]

Canada has undergone profound societal changes since the 1960s. Government policies on immigration, bilingualism, and multiculturalism have all shaped a new official vision of Canada in which immigrants to Canada are encouraged to retain their heritage languages and ethnocultural traditions, even as they are supported in their engagement with a new local, regional, and national life.[6] The discourse of Canada as a vertical mosaic in which ethnocultural groups collaborate in Cana-

dian society, while simultaneously preserving their distinctive cultural characteristics, has deeply influenced Canadian children's literature.[7]

There is no singular nationalist metanarrative stemming from a homogeneous
culture that would assert a simple answer to the troublesome question of how to
define Canadian identity. The ethnocultural, linguistic, and regional diversity of
contemporary Canadian society, and the inability (and unwillingness) to construct
overarching metanarratives of a synthesized common history from competing
views of English and French colonization and the place of Aboriginal peoples in
state formation, all contribute to the difficulty of defining what are agreed-upon
and identifiable, shared cultural commonplaces.[8] National identity formation in
Canada can be seen as an ongoing discursive project, a set of conversations rather than a finite goal or a common list of attributes. Doubleness, the paradoxical
binary of unity and separation, characterizes the Canadian experience and shapes
identities.[9] Resistance to official, government-sponsored multiculturalism and a
willingness to ascribe multicultural status only to the non-dominant minority,
debates about the value of diversity, nostalgia for a mythical Canadian past in
which all citizens participated in a common set of cultural understandings, and
the powerful role of regionalism further challenge the construction of a unitary
Canadian national identity.[10]

In the place of a stable definition of Canadian identity, many anglophone Canadians have uncritically adopted a set of hegemonic commonplaces or core myths
that help to construct a civic ideology.[11] Jerry Diakiw enumerates one set of these
myths, or commonplaces, of Canadian identity often found in Canadian children's
literature. Canada is a wilderness nation of diverse and distinctive regional identities, an Aboriginal homeland that is also a bilingual, democratic, multi-faith nation
of immigrants, founded on the cultures of France and England, with enormous
resources and rich cultural traditions, a country with a strong sense of social wel-
fare that serves as a peacekeeper for the world.[12] All of these commonplaces may
equally be part of the national identity of other countries, but Diakiw argues that
their particular layering or intersection is distinct to Canada.

On one hand, these hegemonic commonplaces allow the construction of an
inclusive 'community of memory' that transcends regional, cultural and ethnic
identities.[13] On the other hand, questions of racism, exclusion and marginalization may be subsumed under the ideology of Canada as a multicultural mosaic in
which everyone has a valued place in society, and problematic or challenging differences are neutralized or erased by the emphasis on commonalities and the ability to 'tolerate' difference.[14] For some critics, compulsory multiculturalism, because
it naturalizes racialized hegemony, enforces compliance. People of colour are told
that Canada is a mosaic into which they must fit. Any failure to find a place in the
mosaic is personal rather than systemic.[15]

The ascription of a mimetic function in the creation of a national literature takes
on a particularly complex role in the absence of a unitary cultural narrative. If one
of the roles of children's literature in Canada is to show readers aspects of Canadian cultural identity and acculturate readers into that identity, and the criteria
by which the effectiveness of the literature is judged valorizes the mimetic, what
happens when there is no unitary identity to reflect?[16] Picturebooks, because of the

very nature of their dual narrative of image and text, are a particularly rich source for the exploration of national identity formation in which the hegemonic commonplaces and myths about history, ethnocultural identity, landscape and region, and definitions of community are articulated and contested.[17]

'Where Is Here?': Wilderness and the Regional

As in other genres of Canadian children's literature, the rural roots of Canadian society and the imaginative pull of the northern wilderness in Canadian culture have played a role in shaping image and text in Canadian illustrated books for children.[18] The wilderness as the Other of civilization, an uncontrolled and gendered space that shapes masculinity, has long been a trope in Canadian children's adventure stories, a stage on which narratives of survival are acted out.[19] As Margaret Atwood described in *Survival,* her influential and controversial 1972 thematic introduction to Canadian literature, tropes of wilderness as a hostile environment that must be tamed, sometimes extending to the construction of the wilderness as a malevolent, animate entity that can consume the unsuspecting, have helped to shape the Canadian literary imagination.[20] At the same time, Romantic ideas about the unspoiled and innocent nature of childhood, and a persistent strain of agrarian idealism in Canadian political discourse, have intertwined with the idea of wilderness as pastoral, unspoiled, and natural, locating a particularly idealized image of Canadian childhood within an environment from which urban settlement has been erased.[21]

For some critics, wilderness has been extended to become the most appropriate setting for children's stories, shaping a literature in which the Canadian landscape takes on the role of a character within the dramatic narrative.[22] Sheila Egoff argued that meritorious Canadian children's books, by 'concentrating upon the environment as a natural part of our lives,' had rejected the shallow values of the 'personal problem' novels of the 1960s in place of 'larger attitudes of courage and self-reliance.' For Egoff, a true Canadian narrative was one in which the environment was given a central place.[23] Implicit in this view was the responsibility of the author to preserve the innocence of childhood. Narratives that showed children 'visiting a lighthouse, crossing the barrens, discovering a cache of Indian relics' reinforced desired social norms rather than stories located in an urban setting in which children would encounter moral decline in the form of 'drugs, alcohol, homosexuality and racism.'[24] Another critic went so far as to speculate that while it was possible that stories for Canadian children might shift towards city life at some point in the future, this would reduce the specifically Canadian element to a minimum.[25]

Four decades ago, Northrop Frye famously articulated the central question of identity in Canadian literature as 'Where is here?' rather than 'Who am I?'[26] The answer, if one looked at Canadian children's books, would frequently be 'here is the wilderness.' While Frye's framing of discourses of Canadian identity around the notion of a defensive and unsettled colonial garrison mentality has been sharply criticized in recent years for its unexamined Eurocentrism and privileging of representational realism, the idea of the hinterland has continued to shape literary production for children, a genre in which representational realism is also valorized.[27] As John Willinsky notes, Frye's distinction between regional or local identity and the work of national discourses in the promotion of unity is situated within larger issues of the constructs of centre and periphery in the colonial imagination, in which metropole and hinterland refer not only to the urban and regional within Canada, but to the complex intertwining of particular cultures and specific practices of power between the British (or American) metropole and the Canadian hinterland.[28]

And yet, as critic Neil Besner has argued, in a postcolonial context the question of region cannot be limited to a binary opposition of local and national, in which local is subservient to national. Instead the idea of region in literary production needs to be reconceptualized without reference to a centre.[29] Through the particularities of text and image, the reader is able to develop an intuitive understanding of region, in an 'experiential engagement with place' as a ground for imaginative identity.[30] In effect, regions cease to be hinterlands existing only with reference to the urban metropole, but are described by the specificities of place and space, in which communities can inscribe their cultural identities.[31] 'Here,' in Willinsky's words, becomes 'not so much a place as an intersection of lives and imaginations, languages and narratives.'[32]

The diversity of geography and the variety of ethnocultural groups within Canada have worked against the construction of single unifying narratives of national identity. And yet geography plays an important role in shaping cultural identities. The Canadian geographer R. Cole Harris has argued that 'a society and its setting cannot be conceptualized separately.'[33] The regional picturebook that specifically delineates the particularities of place attempts to answer 'where is here' by explicitly linking place and culture as the 'the ground for identity,' to use Besner's term.[34] Each regional picturebook, whether set in a city, village, or small town, on a family farm or in the wilderness, articulates a visual, social, and narrative voice literally grounded in place.

Many children's literature specialists emphasize the role of identifiable regional representation in shaping children's awareness of their own location as Canadians. As Janice Douglas, former director of youth services and programming at the Vancouver Public Library, comments, 'When my generation was growing up, everything seemed to be set in England. The literary world was unattainable.' For her, picturebooks like Sheryl McFarlane's *Waiting for the Whales* (1991) 'help children to connect to their environment and realize "hey, this is about me."' Distinctly Canadian picturebooks, she believes, help to extend our knowledge of the country and provide a sense of place and regional context.[35] The author and critic Kit Pearson also remembers the lack of Canadian literature in her childhood and, like Douglas, stresses the role of picturebooks in introducing children to the world beyond their immediate boundaries, so that their sense of place is 'all of Canada' rather than 'living in one home.'[36] Author and critic Sarah Ellis sees regionalism as playing a role of recognition and discovery in the development of the Canadian child's sense of national identity through the specificity and power of description that allows a reader to 'go to a place and you know it because you've read about it,' arguing that this experience gives the reader a literary familiarity that is essential if Canada is to survive as a country.[37]

In contrast, critic Michele Landsberg points out that Canadian picturebooks reflect myths of childhood and the regional Canadian landscape rather than realities. As she clearly states, 'there's an overwhelmingly rural, pastoral, and northern emphasis in illustration that doesn't reflect my own experience as an urbanite … We displace a lot onto the north – the north has to be our emblem of purity and family life. We think that the country is gentler and kinder than the city, which isn't true, but it is our myth of childhood.'[38]

It is ironic that the wilderness in Canadian picturebooks continues to represent an edenic space for childhood, when the majority of Canadian children today live on the southern borderland in urban, ethnoculturally diverse communities. Children's literature specialist Karen Sands-O'Connor sees the discussion among contemporary Canadian scholars about wilderness themes as the continuance of the privileging of pastoral texts and a deeply embedded Romantic view of childhood.[39] The continuance of wilderness as a space for innocence can also be interpreted not as a construct of the critics but as an artefact of Canadian publishing trends, in which the majority of picturebooks with identifiable Canadian geographical markers continue to depict non-urban settings, even at the same time that geographical markers are increasingly erased to enhance international marketability.

Speaking for the Other or Speaking from the In-Between

Throughout the 1980s and 1990s, the question of the representation of ethnocultural diversity and the right of authors and illustrators to represent the cultural traditions that are not their own was the topic of vigorous, sometimes heated debate. Picturebooks exploring multicultural diversity have been criticized for misappropriation of voice, whatever the level of research of the authors and illustrators, if the creators were not members of the originating cultural community. Authors and illustrators from non-dominant ethnocultural groups in Canada can give voice to the subaltern, articulating the tensions of marginalized and minority groups from within the culture, by speaking from the 'in-between,' which Joyce Bainbridge and Brenda Wolodko define as 'the connected spaces that currently define Canada as a multicultural and inclusive nation.'[40]

At the same time, authors and illustrators who seek to represent cultural norms from outside that culture run the risk of 'speaking for' rather than 'speaking with' the culture they are attempting to represent. The ghettoization of 'ethnic' writing and writers within mainstream publishing was widely discussed throughout the book trade in the late 1980s. In 1989, tensions surfaced over ethnocultural representation in the Writers' Union of Canada.[41] Later the same year, at the PEN World Congress in Toronto, a group of protesters claimed that the organization was 'locking out Canadian writers of colour.'[42] Questions have also been raised about the degree of diversity among those working in the publishing community and the strategies for marketing books by writers from non-dominant ethnocultural communities. Books by writers from ethnocultural minority groups are underrepresented in bookstore orders and sales if booksellers believe that readers will purchase books by writers only if they share the same identity.[43] As Paul Yee notes, he is still considered a 'multicultural' writer rather than a Canadian writer of Chinese heritage.[44]

The issue of cultural appropriation is complex and shifting. A pair of feminist retellings of Aboriginal stories by Anne Cameron, *How the Loon Lost Her Voice* (1985) and *How Raven Freed the Moon* (1985), both illustrated by Tara Miller, followed the pattern that Cameron had set in *Daughters of Copper Woman* (1981), a retelling of Coast Salish and Nuu-chah-nulth stories. Cameron's picturebooks, which gained wide popularity among the educational community for their lively prose, also embroiled her in a debate about the appropriation of voice and whether it was permissible for a non-Aboriginal author to transform traditional narratives by changing the gender of characters.[45]

In the same period, Patsy Aldana stated that Groundwood would no longer publish culturally specific texts if they were created by non-members of the cultural community. A similar position was articulated by Valerie Hussey, who commented in the early 1990s that the staff of Kids Can Press were thinking twice about publishing Aboriginal stories by non-Aboriginal writers, adding: 'The political climate today says, "let's look for a native writer to tell their own story."'[46] Aldana has since commented that her position on the issue of cultural appropriation has changed. Addressing criticism of *Chin Chiang and the Dragon's Dance* and Betty Waterton's *A Salmon for Simon*, in which Ann Blades's illustrations contextualize the setting in the lives of contemporary Aboriginal people while the text makes no reference to any particular cultural group, Aldana explains that she now sees both as fantasies rather than real portraits of people.[47]

And Who Are 'We'? Stories of Ethnocultural Identity and Place

While the daily lives of the majority of Canadian children are shaped by cultural pluralism and the built environment, Canadian trade publishers have been slower to issue picturebooks with images that represent contemporary urban childhood than their British and American counterparts. Even as the Canadian social landscape changed, the major Canadian trade publishers only hesitantly and somewhat self-consciously began to deal with diversity, leaving the work of explicitly anti-racist images and texts to the smaller and often marginalized specialist children's publishers.

Picturebooks can contribute to the discourse of equity through the decentring of power in multicultural relations or, instead, reinscribe relations of power by defining the 'Other,' the 'not We,' as alien and exotic, unlike the socially constructed normative reader.[48] Very few Canadian picturebooks challenge the dominant uncritical and unquestioning acceptance of multiculturalism as an unproblematic social good, a hegemonic construct in which intercultural tensions can be resolved by the majority being tolerant of minority groups without any shifting of relations of power.[49] Critic Perry Nodelman, in assessing a group of contemporary Canadian picturebooks with multicultural themes, finds evidence that a blandly uncritical view of ethnocultural diversity as cause for celebration continues to dominate the literature. At the same time, the frequent reminders that the child reader ought to respect difference suggest that authors and illustrators believe that children, in fact, are intolerant. Nodelman further criticizes the titles for erasing or minimizing difference by universalizing a view of childhood in which there is a profound absence of tension, complexity, or negative experience in the depiction of multi-cultural realities.[50]

In this depiction of cultural diversity favoured by the majority of Canadian trade publishers, children from the dominant culture are encouraged to experience stories of diversity as templates for living a multicultural life.[51] The most conventional books attempt to convince children didactically of the value of multiculturalism by training an optimistic lens on an idealized society filled with food, festivals, and fun. The Other is silent, serving only to reinforce the identity of the not-Other. Canadian picturebooks like Jo Ellen Bogart's *Daniel's Dog* (1990), illustrated by Janet Wilson, and Chieri Uegaki's *Suki's Kimono* (2003), illustrated by Stéphane Jorisch, in which ethnocultural diversity is part of the taken-for-granted contemporary urban cultural milieu in which the characters are situated, continue to remain less common, perhaps because of the reluctance of publishers to limit the potential for international sales by too closely representing the particularities of contemporary Canadian society.

'Boutique Multiculturalism'

Professor Lissa Paul works with pre-service teachers in her children's literature courses in Brock University's Faculty of Education to address issues of multiculturalism and anti-racism, so that they begin to recognize 'how to tell the difference between boutique or fake multiculturalism and real multiculturalism.'[52] She argues that adults often are in naive denial, seeing Canada as a perfectly multicultural country that does not need to engage in discourse on racism with children in the schools. In her view, an uncritical and unnuanced 'we're all friends here together' approach to multiculturalism is 'a discourse that gets repeated in the schools.' Students 'don't understand how they construct those ideas, and that's why the discussions on ideology are very important to figure out how they come to acquire these ideological assumptions.'[53]

For Paul, picturebooks and illustrated books that make visible intercultural tensions serve an important role. She cites the example of Joseph Kertes's *The Gift* (1995), illustrated by Peter Perko. Set in Toronto in 1959, the story focuses on the experiences of Jacob, a Jewish Hungarian immigrant child who wants to fit into the majority culture but instead experiences alienation from both the dominant British-Canadian culture and from the Christian Christmas celebrations of his Polish, Ukrainian, and German neighbours. Paul notes the regional and cultural authenticity and complexity of *The Gift*, explaining that 'the tension is there between longing to be one of the majority and dealing with what it's like to be an outsider.'[54]

It is through stories such as *The Gift*, Jim McGugan's *Josepha* (1994), and Paul Yee's *Ghost Train* (1996), which actively interrogate the tensions between acceptance and intolerance, racism, and respect, by focusing on the personal and moral journeys of children and adults negotiating the complexities of ethnocultural identity, that boutique multiculturalism can give way to a more authentic understanding of the challenges of diversity.

The strangeness of the experience of immigration forms the background to

Adwoa Badoe's *Nana's Cold Days* (2002), illustrated in collage by Bushra Junaid. A grandmother who arrives from Africa for a visit with her family is unsettled by the physical strangeness of the harsh Canadian winter, finding it 'too cold for living things.' When she retreats to her bed, her family struggles to rouse her from the deep sleep of shock and rejection. She engages with her surroundings only when she comes to realize that the cold air is 'good for some things.' Badoe's text and Junaid's images remind readers of the unfamiliarity of the culture of 'home' for immigrant children. The grandchildren are as unappreciative of the grandmother's favourite African hi-life music and supper of plantains with palaver sauce as she is of the cold winter air.

Other authors introduce readers to the dislocation of losing 'home' beyond the borders of Canada, and the meaning of being different.[55] Rukhsana Khan's *The Roses in My Carpets* (1998), illustrated by the American artist Ronald Himler, which deals with the ongoing trauma for child refugees from war-torn Afghanistan, introduces readers to themes of death and loss through the narrative of a young carpet weaver living with his mother and sister in a camp in Pakistan, who dreams of a 'space, the size of a carpet, where the bombs cannot touch us.'

In these stories, which locate the experiences of immigrants and refugees within narratives of loss and acculturation, the challenges and trials of reconstructing life, family, and self in a new place are seen through the lens of social history. The stories provide a powerful example of the need to address the issue of difference within a heterogeneous culture by directly challenging the reader's ideas about inclusion, marginalization, exclusion, and devaluation.[56]

Erasing Indigeneity: Misrepresentation and Cultural Appropriation

Misrepresentation of culture is an ongoing stumbling block in picturebooks and illustrated books that attempt to represent ethnocultural identity and diversity in Canadian society. One of the earliest debates over the depictions of ethnocultural identity in children's books focused on the presentation of Aboriginal cultures for the non-Aboriginal reader. Adapting and retelling narratives from oral cultures is a complex and potentially controversial undertaking when an author attempts to interpret unfamiliar cultural values articulated in the narrative for readers unfamiliar with those cultural norms.[57] The same applies to illustration as well as retelling. How authentic is the visual interpretation to the culture retold? What level of research is required? How can the oral voice be captured visually? What licence does the illustrator have to alter place, character, sensibility, and cultural values?

Doris Seale, the founder and president of Oyate, an American community-based Aboriginal organization dedicated to evaluating textual and resource material about Aboriginal peoples, describes the problem of appropriation of Aboriginal voice by non-Aboriginal authors. On one hand non-Aboriginal authors and illustrators turn to Aboriginal literatures, lives, and histories as sources on which to base their own retellings and adaptations. Their books win awards and gain public recognition for their beauty, sensitivity, and ecological awareness by reviewers 'who do not know enough to know that the works in question are inaccurate, inauthentic, patronizing, full of lies, and altogether a huge insult to the people out of whose lives so much money is being made.' On the other hand, Aboriginal creators find themselves marginalized and excluded from mainstream publishers, an ongoing legacy of the histories of colonization.[58]

The illustrated collections of Aboriginal stories retold by non-Aboriginal writers for a non-Aboriginal readership published before the 1970s were shaped by underlying assumptions about the place of Aboriginal peoples within the modern Canadian state. The oral traditions of Canada's indigenous peoples were usually seen through the lens of salvage anthropology as a pre-modern remnant, a flawed record of pre-contact life that had been irrevocably spoiled by contact.[59] The primitiveness and unproductiveness of Aboriginal people's economies was emphasized to justify their dispossession from the land in favour of settler society.[60] Similarly, the role of Aboriginal people in nineteenth-century children's literature as 'masters of woodcraft and as guides for the white men in the forest,' continued in a slightly different guise in the stories of wilderness survival that dominated juvenile fiction in Canada in the postwar period, in which the non-Aboriginal protagonist/hero was aided by the 'traditional' knowledge of his Aboriginal friend.[61] For some critics, the wilderness and Aboriginal people were interchangeable, oral literatures forming a subset of nature stories.[62]

The degree to which Aboriginal people and their stories were seen as divorced both from their own particular cultural traditions and from modernity led to the assumption that collections of stories from different regions of Canada or from different nations could be culled from the anthropological record, reworked, and presented as evidence of pre-contact life without any reference to the contemporary Aboriginal communities in which the stories were collected.[63] Approaches to folklore that emphasized the commonalities of stories across cultures erased the particular contextual and cultural meaning of stories from the oral tradition.[64] The majority of children's literature experts at the time argued that Aboriginal stories were incomprehensible to the 'average' child reader without significant intervention by the reteller because of their 'intrinsic deficiencies of artistry' and unacceptable cruelty and eroticism.[65]

For librarians, teachers, and scholars, the lack of recognizable narrative structure in Aboriginal stories (recognizable at least to the non-Aboriginal reader) required intervention on the part of the reteller to impose order and familiarity. In 1964, the influential American critic May Hill Arbuthnot dismissed Aboriginal oral literature as being insufficiently dramatic to capture a [non-Aboriginal] child's attention.[66] In order to succeed as literary works, the reteller was obliged to impose the narrative structures, character development, and high moral tone assumed to be inherent in the European canon, conveniently eliding authorial intervention in the shaping of *contes* and *hausmärchen* by Perrault and the Brothers Grimm.[67]

This need to impose narrative structure was reiterated by children's authors and critics throughout the 1960s and 1970s in discussing the process of translating orality into textuality. As James Houston explained, 'most Inuit legends will not translate directly into the kind of stories that our children and adults would find acceptable. Few of their stories have the meaningful kinds of endings that we have grown to expect.'[68] Muriel Whitaker argued that when reinterpreting Aboriginal stories, the reteller needed to provide structure and embellishment to stories that seemed 'rambling and inconsequential,' by imposing 'cause and effect, identifiable characters and a cultural context.'[69] Kathleen Hill, in discussing her stories of Glooscap the transformer, drawn from Mi'kmaq and Abenaki tradition, asked herself if she was exploiting Aboriginal peoples in retelling the stories from her own viewpoint, before concluding that the stories, as represented in the anthropological literature on which she was drawing, were not 'stories at all' but disconnected incidents that required her authorial voice to 'add here, subtract there, combine when I could, delineate characters and invent dialogue – above all, give them a beginning, a middle and an end.'[70] Australian scholar Clare Bradford, drawing parallels with Edward Said's concept of Orientalism, describes this process as Aboriginalism, in which knowledgeable, sympathetic non-Aboriginal experts speak as an intermediary for Aboriginal people, who are assumed to be incapable of speaking for themselves.[71]

By the 1980s, a decade after the White Paper on Indian Affairs had generated widespread awareness of the issue of internal colonization, the Aboriginalist approach of 'speaking-for' was sharply criticized by scholars who were increasingly concerned about the appropriation and reworking of Aboriginal stories for non-Aboriginal readers. As Robin McGrath argued, a lack of understanding about the original purposes of the stories and the failure to distinguish between literature about Aboriginal people and by Aboriginal people resulted in editors twisting and mutilating oral narratives, 'under the guise of "adapting" and "improving" the material to make it more palatable to young people,' so that the stories 'often more closely resemble European fairy tales than aboriginal creation tales.'[72] Christie Harris, whose retelling of Aboriginal stories from the Pacific Northwest involved close research in an attempt to enter into the specifics of cultural context, argued that the efforts of salvage anthropologists and ethnographers to reduce oral narratives to paper with the aid of an interpreter resulted in stories that lacked the detail that a 'knowledgeable and responsive audience' would have provided in the original setting in which the stories would have been told.[73] Her goal was to create a narrative structure that would satisfy modern readers 'while still remaining true to [the story's] origins.'[74] She also argued that authors and illustrators needed the lived experience of familiarity with contemporary Aboriginal communities to 'round out the research they can do in archives' in order to depict cultural nuances authentically.[75] In effect, although Harris was an early proponent of speaking with, rather than speaking for, Aboriginal peoples, her use of Aboriginal oral material collected and transcribed by anthropologists was doubly filtered through the cultural lenses of her sources and her own passionate concern for environmental issues.[76] The majority of her Aboriginal stories were set in a mythic past, rather than the present. Writers, editors, and publishers had not recognized that Aboriginal peoples needed to be able to speak for themselves in the textual and visual spaces of children's literature.

Not surprisingly, the images created by non-Aboriginal artists for these collections raised questions of the representation of culture for readers unfamiliar with the context of the stories. The illustrations inevitably situated the stories in a pre-contact world, often with a pan-Indian emphasis on buckskin and feathers, whatever the geographic location of the culture being depicted. When illustrators attempted to locate the stories within their specific cultural context, indigenous imagery was often added to illustrations as decorative elements, without an understanding of the meaning of the images that were being appropriated.

The insistence on the need to recast Aboriginal stories in the mould of European folk tales and legends with which the non-Aboriginal child reader was assumed to have greater familiarity constructed a colonial duality in which the reader shared in a common cultural and literary heritage from which indigeneity had been erased.[77] At the same time the collections were intended to appeal to a distinctly Canadian readership for whom the Aboriginal stories would become part of a common Canadian heritage through their availability in public libraries and through use as an adjunct to the school curriculum.[78] Thus the Aboriginal Other was simultaneously included and excluded from a common Canadian heritage but was never the implied author or reader of the text. Aboriginal children, in this construct, were not Canadian children.[79]

'Nobody Was Writing the Stories I Wanted to Read': Aboriginal Voices

It is only within the last two decades that stories about and by Canada's Aboriginal peoples have begun to move beyond the past to show contemporary Aboriginal families living in the modern world. It was the advent of the first Aboriginal-owned and -operated publishing houses in the 1980s such as Pemmican Publications and Theytus Books that provided the initial space for Aboriginal people to disrupt the romanticized and sentimentalized narratives of a dying culture in circulation in children's books issued by the trade and educational publishers.

The Métis author Joseph McLellan has created a series of picturebooks about Nanabozho, the shape-shifting trickster hero/teacher and protector of the Anishinaabe people. In *Nanabosho Steals Fire* (1990), illustrated by the Cree artist Don Monkman, McLellan frames the traditional story within the contemporary world of northern Canada, as their Nokomis tells the story to her grandchildren as they gather by the stove during a winter camping trip. In a clever reversal of usual visual tropes, Monkman distinguishes between the world of the storyteller and the story in his coloured pencil illustrations by drawing the present in black and white and the world of the story in sepias, browns, blues, greens, and yellows. Similarly, the specific details of life in a modern bush camp, with Ski-doo parked beside the tent, and a grandfather preparing to skin a pair of rabbits caught on a trapline, are carefully paralleled within the traditional world of the Nanabosho story. A canvas tent becomes a wigwam, the zippered hooded jackets of the children become the beaded fur and skin clothing of the old medicine man and his daughters who guard the fire, the milk containers and bag of bread on the table in the tent become a cooking pot hung over the fire. The Nokomis of the present wears glasses, trousers, and beaded moccasins; the Nokomis of the past sits on a reed mat, stitching a birch bark basket; but both have similar facial features and expressions, visually reinforcing and amplifying the idea of the continuity between past and present.

By the early 1990s, specialist children's publishers also began to publish books by Aboriginal writers and illustrators. Within a decade, the larger and better-funded mainstream publishers also began publishing increasing numbers of picturebooks

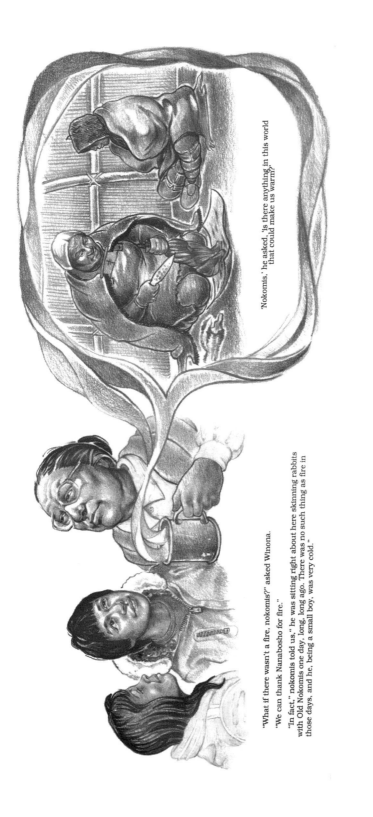

"What if there wasn't a fire, nokomis?" asked Winona.

"We can thank Nanabosho for fire."

"In fact," nokomis told us," he was sitting right about here skinning rabbits with Old Nokomis one day, long, long ago. There was no such thing as fire in those days, and he, being a small boy, was very cold."

'Nokomis,' he asked, 'is there anything in this world that could make us warm?'

9.1 Joseph McLellan. *Nanabosho Steals Fire*. Illustrated by Don Monkman. Winnipeg: Pemmican Publications, 1990. Reprinted with the permission of the publisher, Pemmican Publications.

by Aboriginal authors and illustrators, and Aboriginal peoples began to find their personal and community history reflected in picturebooks for both Aboriginal and non-Aboriginal readers for the first time.[80] As the author Richard Van Camp, a member of the Dogrib Nation and author of *What's the Most Beautiful Thing You Know about Horses?* (1998), explains it, 'Why I became an author is very interesting and simple: nobody was writing the stories that I wanted to read. Nobody was writing the stories about my life and my experience, what I saw, what I felt, what I heard, what I sensed.'[81] His exploration of his family's cultural traditions is illustrated with brilliantly coloured, highly decorative and witty paintings by George Littlechild. Image and text play with the differences between Van Camp, who belongs to 'Dog People,' and Littlechild, who belongs to the horses of the Plains tradition, within the context of a contemporary Aboriginal family's daily life. (See colour plate 18.)

The experience of not seeing oneself and one's culture depicted in text and image has been a powerful motivator for authors and illustrators. Van Camp was inspired to write by the first published author he met, Inuit author and storyteller Michael Kusugak.[82] In turn, Kusugak claims that he became a writer after meeting Robert Munsch in the mid-1980s when Munsch stayed with Kusugak's family in Kangiqiniq (Rankin Inlet) in Nunavut during a reading tour of northern communities. Although Munsch had encouraged him to write down the stories that they had shared during a hunting and fishing trip, it was at the urging of his sons that Kusugak wrote down one of the stories that he began to tell them at bedtime in place of the culturally irrelevant Dr Seuss.[83] The manuscript, which drew on both Inuit oral tradition and his own childhood experiences, became the first draft of *A Promise Is a Promise* (1988), which Annick Press was unwilling to publish until Munsch and Kusugak rewrote it together. The success of the title ensured that Annick was more willing to issue subsequent stories without the intervention of a non-Aboriginal author with mainstream name recognition. With each new title, Kusugak has explored incidents from modern Inuit life, including the pain of residential school and the sense that experiences have been 'ripped from memory,' and the cultural misunderstandings that occur in a colonial context. In *Northern Lights: The Soccer Trails* (1993), his story of the death of a child's mother and her grieving allows him to comment indirectly on the problem of suicide by young people in northern communities.[84]

The illustrations for the picturebooks reflect Kusugak's close collaboration with the non-Inuit artist Vladyana Krykorka, who has increasingly shifted her focus from a somewhat sentimentalized depiction of Inuit children to closely observed details of contemporary indigenous northern life, based on her multiple trips to the region.[85] In *Arctic Stories* (1998), Krykorka's depiction of the loving relationship between Agatha and her parents sharply but subtly delineates the differences between life in the community of Naujat (Repulse Bay) in 1958, and the visually and emotionally restricted world of the boarding school, where 'the nuns did not make very good mothers and the priests, who were called fathers, did not make very good fathers.'[86] The cultural tension between the verbal and visual, Aboriginal and non-Aboriginal, in his picturebooks is unproblematic for Kusugak, as he believes that 'the mark of a good storyteller is the way he can put pictures in your mind without the illustrations. Illustrations for me are just extra.'[87]

9.2 Michael Kusugak. *Arctic Stories*. Illustrated and designed by Vladyana Langer
Krykorka. Toronto: Annick Press, 1998.
Reprinted with the permission of the publisher, Annick Press.

The experiences of cultural dislocation and trauma resulting from the coercive and repressive policies of the Indian Act and its regulation of Aboriginal peoples' lives, economies, education, and culture increasingly have been the subject of picturebooks by Aboriginal authors. In *As Long as the Rivers Flow* (2002), the Alberta Cree author Larry Loyie has written of the experience of being sent away from one's home and community to face forced assimilation in residential school. Loyie and his partner, the writer Constance Brissenden, teamed for a second book with illustrator Heather D. Holmlund. *The Gathering Tree* (2005), issued by Theytus Books, describes the contemporary challenge of a young man returning to his rural Aboriginal family with the news that he is HIV-positive. The work, which is designed to educate young readers about HIV/AIDS, is also a meditation on cultural loss and cultural retention, and the connection between past and present, as Robert moves between the city and his home community.

The theme of waiting to be sent away, with the certain knowledge of the loss of culture, is also taken up by the Interior Salish and Métis author Nicola I. Campbell in *Shi-shi-etko* (2005), with lyrical illustrations by Kim LaFave that emphasize the importance of place for the identity of Shi-shi-etko. Cultural loss and cultural renewal are also the themes of Andrea Spalding and Alfred Scow's *Secret of the Dance* (2006), illustrated by the Coast Salish artist Darlene Gait. Scow, a Kwakwaka'wakw elder, distinguished judge, and member of the Order of Canada, describes the importance of dancing and the role of masks as a means of transmitting stories and culture, in a story set during the years when the potlatch was banned by the federal government.

The challenge to the conventional in stories by Aboriginal authors has not always been well received, however. Some critics have been particularly harsh with Thomas King's sardonic *A Coyote Columbus Story* (1992), with illustrations by Cree artist William Kent Monkman that emphasize the transgressive nature of the narrative.[88] King draws on creation stories and ideas about the exchange of power in the contact zone to reconstruct the story of first contact between Aboriginal people and newcomers through the ironic gaze of Coyote, an unreliable trickster figure. According to King, Coyote was tired of playing ball by herself and danced and sung until others came to join her in her games. They grew tired of her always winning and Coyote becomes dangerously bored. When three ships arrive with a group of newcomers, she tries to engage them in a friendly game, to disastrous effect. King's distinctive, ironic narrative voice, and Monkman's vibrant, neon-hued illustrations, combine ferocity and sly humour, challenging and destabilizing relations of power in a colonial setting.[89] In this encounter, Coyote is a gender-ambiguous figure in shorts and sneakers and the Europeans are devious, manipulative, and greedy, their malign ferocity only partially disguised by their oddly comical appearance. Coyote, who is responsible for putting things right, is unable to fix her mistakes and make the newcomers go away.

One U.S. publisher called the book 'hateful,' while another said: 'American kids have enough depressing news. We need to lighten up!' while the publisher of the British firm Jonathan Cape described it as the most horrible book that he had ever seen.[90] Publisher Patsy Aldana describes the work as 'much more political and aggressive' and 'not easy, palatable, or pretty,' adding that the press was accused of being racist for publishing it.[91] She is frustrated by what she calls the 'disinterest in other people's experiences … on the part of people who buy books in Canada – whether they're librarians or parents – [who] are still essentially looking for a reflection of the world that they consider to be their own, and that they're comfortable with.'[92] (See colour plate 19.)

In contrast, Ojibwa author-illustrator Leo Yerxa's beautifully designed and visually sophisticated layering of collage in *Last Leaf First Snowflake to Fall* (1993), a lyric meditation on the changing seasons and the transmission of culture from one generation to the next, won both the 1994 Elizabeth Mrazik-Cleaver Canadian Picture Book Award and the 1994 Amelia Frances Howard-Gibbon Illustrator's Award. The playwright Tomson Highway's bilingual Songs of the North Wind trilogy, with texts in English and Cree syllabics also received a far more positive reception. Highway's stories, *Caribou Song / Atihko nikamon* (2001), *Dragonfly Kites / Pimi-hákanisa* (2002), and *Fox on the Ice / Mahkesís mískwamíhk e-cípatapít* (2003) are illustrated with luminous, atmospheric oil paintings by Brian Deines that evoke the sense of the mythic and spiritual in the natural world. As the scholar Clare Bradford notes, the incorporation of ancient transformation stories into the narratives of contemporary Aboriginal peoples' lives emphasizes the continuity of Cree traditions by connecting past and present.[93] At the same time, Highway's narratives remind the reader of the relationship between contemporary Aboriginal people's economies and their relationship to the land as they move throughout the seasonal cycle of resource procurement.[94] (See colour plate 20.)

The critical acclaim given to Yerxa and Highway's books in comparison to King's more troubling challenging of colonial myths raises questions about the privileging of certain types of narratives by non-Aboriginal readers of Aboriginality in children's books by Aboriginal authors and illustrators as a form of 'nostalgia for the environmentally friendly Indian' who lives in perfect spiritual harmony with the natural world.[95] Perry Nodelman argues that the popularity of intergenerational Aboriginal narratives, in which the elders pass on their traditions and teach the younger generations about the 'power of nature and meaning of life' reflect a Eurocentric understanding of Aboriginal cultural values, shaped 'to accord with the conventional assumptions of the contemporary marketplace for children's books.'[96]

As well as the question of dominance by non-Aboriginal publishers and majority culture images and themes, the issue of appropriation of culture and voice has continued to polarize members of the writing and publishing community, with strong convictions held on both sides. Some writers and publishers believe that only members of a specific ethnic or cultural group have the aesthetic and moral right to give voice to that group's experiences and beliefs. Others adamantly declare that with appropriate research, sensitivity, and imagination, it is possible to create authentic stories and characters, even if they are not part of the writer's personal life experience.

The careful and respectful collaboration between Tsimshian carver Victor Reece and the non-Aboriginal author Andrea Spalding and non-Aboriginal illustrator Janet Wilson in the artwork for *Solomon's Tree* (2002), the story of an extended First Nations family and the centrality of the environment and cultural traditions to

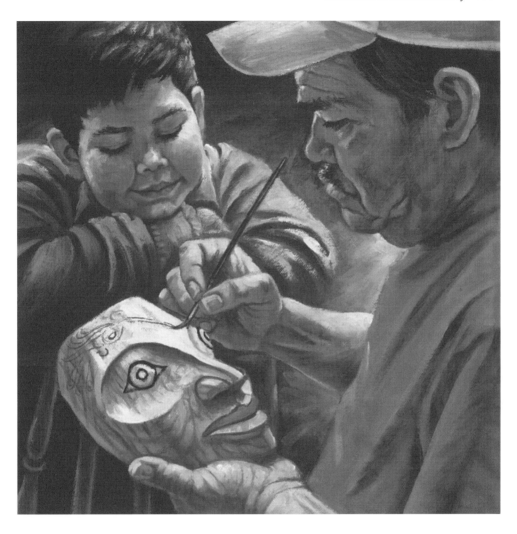

9.3 Andrea Spalding. *Solomon's Tree*. Illustrated by Janet Wilson and Victor Reece.
Victoria: Orca Book Publishers, 2002.

Reprinted with the permission of the publisher, Orca Book Publishers.

their lives, raises interesting questions about the complexities of cultural representation. Wilson's strongly realistic oil paintings are modelled on photographs of Reece's family that she took during a visit to Pender Island, where both Reece and Spalding live. Reece carved the mask that is the fulcrum of the narrative and created original designs of Raven, the trickster of Tsimshian tradition, which became the framing device that Wilson incorporated into her page designs. She explains that she honoured Reece's belief that 'anybody who does that kind of artwork without being from that culture is stealing' and was careful not to create 'any Tsimshian art.'[97] It is surprising, therefore, that Aboriginal protocols of acknowledging one's presence on the land of another nation were not given similar prominence in the text. While the back flap of the book makes the Pender Island setting of the illustrations clear, there is no similar acknowledgment that the Tsimshian cultural artefacts are being depicted in Hul'qumi'num territory and are not indigenous to the environment being carefully recreated in the illustrations.

'I'm Going to Pass on Our Teachings'

Greg Young-Ing, former publishing manager of Theytus Books, approaches the question of authenticity of narrative voice, arguing that the major difference between Aboriginal and non-Aboriginal publishers is their commitment to honouring cultural protocols. As he explains, Theytus 'tried to counter all the books that were out there that appropriated the indigenous voice ... and tried to show an example of how to publish indigenous stories without appropriating and according to protocols.'[98]

The invitation to share stories through print provides a contact zone where Aboriginal and non-Aboriginal writers, illustrators, and readers can meet, and non-Aboriginal readers can hear indigenous voices.[99] At the same time, both Pemmican and Theytus have grappled with the challenge of translating material from the oral tradition into print, addressing the needs of children in cultures in which orality and print literacy are both important for the transmission of knowledge.[100] Theytus has developed specific editorial protocols that respect the particularities of the oral tradition, the cadences of Aboriginal speech, and the importance of consulting the Elders on matters related to sacred cultural material.[101] For Anita Large, the house's current publishing manager, the role of orality is critical in Aboriginal communities; she explains that while she was never read to as a child, she was told stories.[102] The author Jan Bourdeau Waboose explains that Aboriginal people write from their own experience and from the experience of others as taught to them in the stories passed down by the elders.[103]

The value of textuality for the preservation of culture and the transmission of oral narratives across time and space as witness to the place of Aboriginal people in contemporary society remains a powerful motivator for Indigenous creators of children's literature. Cree writer and illustrator George Littlechild describes his work as reflecting 'the themes of First Nations experience: that culturally we have survived; that we have risen above our historical experiences; that society has a lot to learn from First Nations culture and people; and that what we have to give to society is important.'[104] For Littlechild, his images pass down stories from generation to generation.[105] And as Dogrib writer Richard Van Camp explains, his writing for children is an invitation to 'listen to my mother's stories, my grandfather's stories, my grandmother's stories, my brother's story. I'm going to be cheeky, I'm going to tell you off, I'm going to make you laugh, I'm going to honour you, but ultimately I'm going to pass on our teachings.'[106]

'Everyone in Canada Loves Hockey': Reading Canadian Culture

How do readers respond to issues of national identity, multiculturalism, and regionalism in Canadian children's illustrated books? Many of Jerry Diakiw's hegemonic 'taken for granted' ideas about Canadian cultural identity were identified in a 1997 survey for the journal *Canadian Children's Literature / Littérature canadienne pour la jeunesse*, which asked Canadian writers, educators, librarians, booksellers, academics, publishers, and critics to define 'What's Canadian about Canadian children's literature.' When Perry Nodelman first put out a paper call on this topic, he was surprised at the passionate responses, which ranged from excitement to objections that the question was irrelevant, old-fashioned, promoted one particular view of Canadian identity over others, and had dangerous political ramifications.[107] The forty-four responses ranged broadly, but the largest groupings commented on Canadian geography, landscape, and regionalism, framed within a discussion of Canadian experiences, cultural diversity, and Canadian history.[108]

Sylvia Pantaleo, professor in the University of Victoria's Department of Curriculum and Instruction, has studied the response by children in two grades in a school in eastern Ontario to the question of national identity and markers of 'Canadianness.'[109] After reading eleven Canadian children's picturebooks which explicitly communicated Canadian settings, a significant number of the grade three class mentioned geography, weather, provinces, and the experiences of the characters in connection with the setting of the story as clues that marked a book as Canadian. Only a small number, however, identified Canada's cultural diversity or historical references as depictions of life in Canada. Pantaleo remarks that 'it seemed that many of the Canadian clues they identified were somewhat stereotypical aspects of Canadian life that many non-Canadians would associate with Canada.'[110] The grade five students' responses were similar to those of the younger children. They identified geography, weather, open space, water, vegetation, regionalism, and experiences of characters and activities such as hockey as salient characteristics of Canada. As in the responses of the younger children, cultural diversity and history were only rarely mentioned by the grade five students. Pantaleo notes that the school's homogeneous cultural composition may have some relevance in the lack of multicultural awareness, inadvertently highlighting the idea that multiculturalism is the preserve of ethnocultural minorities. In both grades, the vast majority of children concurred that it is important for students to read books written by Canadians.[111]

Looking In from the Outside: Non-Canadian Perceptions of Canadian Identity

Do non-Canadians, as outsiders to the debate on the shifting concept of Canadian identity, have a different perspective on elements of Canadian national identity present in Canadian picturebooks? A group of non-Canadian children's literature specialists from Australia, Spain, Sweden, Germany, and Japan with research interests in Canadian children's literature were asked to comment on what they perceive as indicators of Canadian identity in Canadian picturebooks. Judith Thistleton-Martin, a professor in Children's Literature and Literacy Education at the University of Western Sydney, Australia, introduced twenty-five Canadian picturebooks to a grade four class in Western Sydney in order to assess the children's perceptions of Canadian identity as visualized through the picturebooks.[112] Before the study, the students knew very little about Canada. After two weeks, they were interviewed about their newly acquired Canadian cultural knowledge. They concluded from their reading that everyone in Canada loves hockey and skiing and cold temperatures, and that Canadians are very proud of their country.[113]

Thistleton-Martin speculates that none of the students mentioned the Aboriginal books that they had read during the study because they were already familiar with Aboriginal Australians. She believes that they unquestioningly accepted the presence of Aboriginality in Canadian picturebooks on the basis of their own cultural experiences.[114] She notes the Canadian emphasis on multiculturalism and regionalism in picturebooks, adding that Australians could learn from Canadians about the representation of diversity and the inclusion of Aboriginal authors on the lists of trade children's publishers.[115]

Diversity is also one of the cultural identifiers that Isabel Pascua, professor of translation at the University of Las Palmas, Grand Caneria, Spain, feels is most central to Canadian picturebooks. She believes that the implicit diversity in Canadian multicultural picturebooks reflects 'Canadian values of tolerance and respect.' She also notes the willingness of authors and publishers to discuss difficult issues in Canada's past, citing the specific example of Paul Yee's *Ghost Train* as a work that explores issues of racism and multiculturalism, themes that are not often represented in Spanish picturebooks.[116] As a result, she has translated Canadian picturebooks into Spanish for use in schools to sensitize students to new immigrants to the Canary Islands. Pascua explains that as a translator, she has to determine whether references in the original text are important to the particular cultural identity of the narrative and need to be retained, or can be substituted for equivalents that will be more familiar to the reader of the translated text. She comments that in Canadian picturebooks, diversity is the cultural identity, which she finds both fascinating and challenging.[117]

The issues of cultural diversity and identity in Canadian picturebooks are also noted by Swedish academic Björn Sundmark, a professor in the School of Education at the University of Malmö, and by Sumiko Shirai, a professor in the Department of Children's Literature and Culture at Shirayuri College, Tokyo, who has developed and taught a course in Canadian children's literature.[118] Shirai comments that because Japan is an '"almost" homogenous society,' multiculturalism is not a major theme in Japanese publishing. She contrasts the Canadianness of mimetic images of nature and wildlife in Canadian picturebooks with the Japanese preference for picturebooks that are more imagination-oriented.[119] Similar themes are noted by Sundmark, who explains that in Canadian picturebooks 'cultural diversity – or maybe rather the whole issue of national identity – is more pronounced than in Scandinavian picturebooks.'[120]

Martina Seifert, the German Academic Exchange Lecturer at Queen's University Belfast's School of Languages, Literatures and Arts, has studied the translation of Canadian children's literature into German and Canadian images in German-language children's literature from the nineteenth century to the present day. For Seifert, cultural markers that signify national identity to Canadian readers are constructed through images of nature, geographic region, and ethnic diversity.[121] In contrast, German images of Canada are homogeneous, making no distinction between regions and different cultural groups. As she explains, for German readers, their image of Canada is the 'Western Canada / Rocky Mountains area, with many wild animals and almost no people, let alone different ethnic groups – except for Native Peoples.'[122]

'Do American Librarians Like This Kind of Book?' Canadian Identity and American Sales

In one sense, in Canadian publishing, nothing ever changes. The challenges that have faced Canadian publishers have remained a constant theme from the earliest stages of indigenous publishing. Publishers today wrestle with demographics, linguistic fragmentation of the market, geography, and competition from imported titles, just as they did in previous decades. On the other hand, in response to globalization, changing retail and institutional markets and the rise of multimedia conglomerates, many Canadian children's publishers have decided to alter their publishing arrangements by bypassing co-publication and licensing arrangements in order to venture into direct sales in the American market.[123]

The shift has resulted in increased sales for Canadian publishers but comes at a potential cost to maintaining cultural autonomy. There is a long history of Canadian nationalist unease about the influence of the United States, which is often articulated within the publishing industry as the fear that increased trade will bring about the de-Canadianization of Canadian cultural production.[124] Most publishers have adopted American spelling for their texts published in Canada to avoid separate Canadian and American print runs, while others ask authors to rewrite texts to avoid problematic words like 'neighbour' and 'favourite.'[125] Canadian authors have been asked to make changes in spelling, place names, and Canadianisms for the U.S. edition of a title.[126] Betty Waterton discovered, after the American edition of *Pettranella* (1980) was published, that the editor had changed the regional location of the last line of the story from 'Pettranella's flowers bloom each year beside a county road in Manitoba' to Minnesota, adding 'It never is OK when an editor makes changes like that, but I went along with it.'[127] Similarly, Sue Ann Alderson was questioned by the American editor of *Ida and the Wool Smugglers* (1987) about her use of the term 'mountain lion,' rather than the more familiar American term 'cougar,' and whether it should be another species of big cat entirely.[128] Kevin Major remembers one American publisher 'taking exception to the use of "chesterfield" instead of "sofa,"' adding firmly, 'it stayed "chesterfield."'[129]

Other publishers give their writers a choice to publish with Canadian place names and restrict sales to the domestic market, or publish with generic place names and have larger sales in both the domestic and American markets.[130] However, this strategy does not always work. Author-illustrator Kady MacDonald Denton remembers that not only was the text of her first story, *The Picnic* (1988), 'translated into American' for the U.S. edition, but the ending was rewritten, changing the final sentence from 'But for a while Alison kept her Mum rather small' to 'But Alison's mother decided to stay small a little while longer,' which changed the entire narrative trajectory of the story. Denton comments: 'I was happy when British and Canadian sales (with my original story) sold well and the American edition did poorly.'[131]

Differing cultural norms pose difficulties for picturebook creators and disseminators in the North American market, just as the variations in what is acceptable in a children's book shape the sale of rights in the international market.[132] Janet Lunn's *Amos's Sweater* (1988) ran into difficulties when an American editor would not buy rights for an American edition because she found the elderly ram's plaint, 'Amos was old and Amos was cold, and Amos was tired of giving away all his wool' to be ageist.[133] Janet Wilson had to change her illustrations for Patricia Quinlan's *Tiger Flowers* (1994), about a man with AIDS, when the American editor argued that the reference to darkness in the text, and Wilson's accompanying illustration of a silhouetted tree could be interpreted as a 'racial problem.' Wilson adds that the replacement picture 'wasn't nearly as effective as a dark burgundy silhouetted tree against the sunrise.'[134]

Author-illustrator Michèle Lemieux explains that *Stormy Night* (1999) was not published in the United States because 'the publishers wouldn't agree to anything that had to do with nudity, including skeletons … [The image of skeletons opening cupboards] was to be censored, because it is unacceptable for the American market.'[135] Similarly, to meet the requirements of the American publisher of the Franklin the turtle series, witches could not be portrayed in a story about a Halloween party.[136] Illustrator Stefan Czernecki had an editor remove an image of a character dressed as a devil, wearing a papier-mâché devil mask from a Mexican Day of the Dead cemetery scene in *The Hummingbird's Gift* (1994) in order to ensure that the book was marketable in Texas and California. The editor insisted that in those states 'you can't print the image of the devil.'[137]

There is a disagreement, however, as to whether specific Canadian cultural content is a liability in the more conservative American market. Some Canadian publishers admit that they are less likely to take risks in their choices of authors, illustrators, and subject matter once they begin to target American sales. As Patsy Aldana, publisher at Groundwood laments, 'it is alarming that we have almost unconsciously begun to shape our lists to the new imperatives – the need for profit and the need to make ourselves palatable to the U.S. market. Will this book sell in the U.S.? Do American librarians like this kind of book? Is it just too weird, or different, or too shocking for them? … When will disguising Canadian content simply become too bothersome?'[138] Rick Wilks of Annick Press also expresses the ambiguity of maintaining cultural content. He argues that preserving a 'Canadian voice' becomes more difficult as the commitment to Canadian authors and illustrators is balanced against the need to maintain export levels, ultimately resulting in a reduction of diversity in the Canadian publishing industry.[139]

The pressure to tailor books to the demands of an international market has been experienced by former Red Deer Press publisher Dennis Johnson. He argues that because of the cost of production, picturebooks either have to be so Canadian that there will be a strong demand from within Canada or else universal in appeal and able to compete in the international marketplace. The image of a Union Jack flying above the schoolhouse in one of the illustrations for *Josepha: A Prairie Boy's Story* (1994) caused particular difficulties for the American publisher, who argued that they could not hope to sell the book unless the flag was changed to the Stars and Stripes. In the end, while no change was made for the American edition, Johnson still wonders how the tiny image of a flag would alter 'the meaning of the prairie immigrant experience at the turn of the century' for the reader.[140]

However, some publishers and authors claim that despite the pressures to sell internationally, there has been no alteration in the way that manuscripts are handled; nor has there been a lessening of Canadian content. Valerie Hussey argues that specificity of place is important to some texts and not to others, just as a character's name may be integral to the plot, or extrinsic and interchangeable. She believes that for narratives in which specificity is not required, a universal name is appropriate, adding that if a place name 'truly informs a work, there's absolutely no discussion.'[141] Similarly, Sheryl McFarlane, author of *Waiting for the Whales* (1991) argues that it is more important to her to explore the relationships between characters and place than to include specific and identifiable place names in the text. She explains that in a picturebook 'it isn't the name you're after so much as really having people feel what you feel. You know, saying "Victoria" to a kid in Minnesota is meaningless. But saying, "Taste the misty morning fog" is very concrete and useful.'[142] On the other hand, she actively resisted attempts on the part of her American publisher to anthropomorphize the relationship between humans and whales in *Waiting for the Whales*, noting that 'they wanted the whales to be friendlier, but these are wild animals.' She also insisted that salal, a plant native to British Columbia be named as such, because it was integral to the story.[143]

Erasing Identity

The widely held belief by many publishers that distinctive regional and national markers in children's books will lessen the possibility of international sales is arguably changing children's publishing. The erasing of cultural markers in Canadian picturebooks in response to globalization has been documented by Ronald Jobe, professor emeritus in the Department of Language and Literacy Education of the University of British Columbia. He examined a selection of realistic picturebooks for evidence of Canadian textual and visual markers.[144] He found that only ten of the realistic picturebooks, about 10 per cent of the titles in his study, showed any specific markers of Canadian cultural identity in the form of place names, specific details, and Canadian references. He concludes that the editing out of identifiable visual and textual markers of Canadian setting means that 'Canadian children are not able to see themselves reflected in the realistic picturebooks available.'[145]

In a study that builds on Jobe's research, children's literature specialist Marilynne Black examined 124 historically themed Canadian picturebooks for Canadian markers.[146] She found that 84 per cent of the depictions of the regional setting of the narrative were rural rather than urban, and that regionality was often depicted through landscape, without necessarily showing specific cultural markers.[147] She also found that cultural markers and depictions of Canadian geography in picturebooks decreased by publication date, with a greater number of specific markers found in books issued between 1970 and 1989, and fewer in those published after 1990.[148]

Jobe and Black both question whether Canadian children will have a sense of their own distinctiveness and cultural identity if picturebooks are generic in location, arguing that cultural markers and identifiable, geographically specific landscapes are critical to a sense of belonging to that landscape.[149] For critics who give primacy to the mimetic function of picturebooks to show Canadian children location and cultural identities through specific cultural markers, picturebooks become an agent of acculturation into the values and geographies of citizenship. As Bob Tyrrell, president and editorial director of Orca Book Publishers, argues, it should matter that Orca continues to contribute to 'the cultural education of our children' by publishing books 'written and illustrated by Canadian authors and illustrators … [and] set in Canadian cities and towns.'[150]

Given the erasure of cultural markers, the question of whether American and international readers are even aware that some of the books that they read originated in Canada is raised by a number of children's literature specialists. Ken Setterington argues that the success of Canadian books that are seen domestically as multicultural are not necessarily seen as Canadian in the international marketplace, as they 'reflect cultures that have nothing to do with Canada.' As he explains, unless a reader knows that a particular author 'has chosen Canada as his or her home,' they are unlikely to be able to identify what makes the book Canadian.'[151] Similarly, author and critic Kit Pearson draws a distinction between familiarity with Canadian books among international publishers and children's literature specialists, and the general reader, who might recognize 'Anne of Green Gables and the picturebooks of Robert Munsch' without knowing particularly that they are Canadian.[152] Her view is reiterated by Annette Goldsmith, who has worked as a children's literature specialist in public libraries in Canada and the United States. She explains that while picturebooks by Barbara Reid and other noted Canadian authors and illustrators are widely available in American public libraries, there is little perception that they are, in fact, books by Canadians. She adds that 'having worked in Canadian publishing, where nationality (and nationalism) was a fact of life, it was quite a rude awakening to find that nobody cares about this once you leave the country. There isn't a great hunger on the part of Americans for books from other countries.'[153] This view is echoed by Patsy Aldana, who notes that 'overt Canadian content does not seem to interest the majority of Americans.'[154]

'Everybody Likes Dinosaurs': Canadian Picturebooks in the International Marketplace

Once Canadian publishers began to move aggressively into the global marketplace, they needed to develop a highly nuanced understanding of differing cultural norms about what constitutes appropriate content in a children's book within the broadest possible international context. May Cutler, one of the first Canadian publishers to move into international rights sales, raises the issue of differing cultural views on the acceptability of sexual imagery and violence in children's books, asking if it is 'anything more than strangeness that makes us conscious of the violent and erotic in other cultures while we do not notice it at all in our own.'[155] She remembers turning down the opportunity to publish a picturebook from Hungary, in which a baby's relatives all gathered around and compared the newborn to various family members. As Cutler describes it, she tried to explain to the publisher that selling rights in North America would be difficult, because 'it is not a question that you ask. The baby may have no genetic connection with anyone in the family and it would be tactless to make such remarks.'[156] Similarly, a Spanish publisher turned down a Tundra picturebook because the interior scenes depicted in the book did not resemble familiar cultural norms of domestic life, particularly the lack of distinction shown between formal and informal spaces in a family home.[157]

In the early 1990s, Kathy Lowinger, at that time the executive editor of Lester Publishing, discovered that she was unable to sell the rights to *The Huron Carol*, illustrated by Frances Tyrrell, to German publishers because, as she was told, 'Germans are not interested in anyone else's celebrations of Christmas.' She also found that Danish publishers reject illustrations of animals wearing human clothing.[158] Ted Harrison remembers a German publisher turning down *Children of the Yukon* because, as he explained it, 'We do not publish any book without a face.' Harrison adds that in his experience, 'children don't mind the faces not being in' and accept his reminder that they can use their imagination to 'put your friend's face in if you want, or your mother's or your father's.'[159] Jane Somerville notes that while southern European and British publishers were interested in bidding on rights to Somerville House's popular book, *Bones*, which was packaged with a small plastic human skeleton, the same package was turned down by northern European publishers. Dinosaurs, on the other hand, are universally liked.[160]

Different publishers, librarians, and critics have different perceptions about the economic success and literary and artistic recognition that Canadian children's books receive internationally. Speaking from the perspective of both French- and English-language publishing in Canada, Josiane Polidori, head of the Canadian Children's Literature Service at Library and Archives Canada, reflects on her experiences at international book fairs. She believes that Canadian writers can be more creative because they are less constrained by an overarching editorial point of view, and are free to construct authentic children's voices, rather than adhering to formulaic stereotypes. It is this creativity and originality that is appreciated by foreign readers.[161] For Polidori, picturebooks that depict the north particularly appeal to some foreign publishers, because 'our Canadian wilderness is so much loved in Europe.'[162]

Regarding the ability of picturebooks to travel, Rick Wilks notes that sales of Annick Press titles have been particularly strong in Scandinavia and northern Europe, and speculates that 'we're all cold climate people, and our tastes seem to be fairly similar; we appreciate one another's art, there's a common sense of satire.'[163] In contrast, Tundra Books publisher Kathy Lowinger states that illustrations and art are not a universal language, because 'taste is very culturally determined.'[164] For Lowinger, the most successful picturebooks have had very elaborate illustrations, like Ludmila Zeman's *Gilgamesh* series. Although Tundra has had little success in selling rights to regional books and information books into the international market, some regional books sell well in the United States. As she explains, '*The Prairie Alphabet* … applies to Kansas as much as it does to Saskatchewan. Certainly, the Kurelek books sell marvellously in the United States.'[165] This view is also articulated by Patsy Aldana, who believes that fiction translates in the international market more easily than picturebooks. In her experience, rights to 'the really "Canadian" books' do not sell, because 'the illustration is too foreign for Europeans. Illustration does not travel very well.' She notes that the realist art of English-Canadian picturebooks does not hold a strong aesthetic appeal for European publishers.[166]

Martina Seifert provides insight into some of the factors that can shape the reception of Canadian books in the international marketplace. Cultural preferences play a significant role in the reception of Canadian children's books in Germany. She argues that the titles selected for translation 'bear almost no cultural markers.' As a result, Canadian books are not 'perceived in a Canadian context – they are neither marketed as Canadian, nor do the reviews ever mention their Canadian origin.'[167] These marketing decisions have changed over time. In the 1950s through the 1970s, 'literary imports were still … selected as carriers of ethno-cultural information,' and titles by Ann Blades and William Kurelek were published in German editions. Today, 'social realities … are taboo topics in German picture books; there is almost a fear of realistic imagery. In the vast majority of picturebooks published in Germany, the harmless still reigns, the protective.'[168] The reluctance to engage with the unfamiliar and the controversial means that stories about contemporary Canadian children's lives, and stories with themes of immigration and multiculturalism, are not likely to be picked up by German publishers.

Seifert describes cross-cultural differences in aesthetic preference in artistic style, identifying realistic imagery and cartoon-like art as two styles of illustration frequently employed in Canadian picturebooks but not marketable in Germany. As a result, many imported children's fiction and picturebooks will be re-illustrated by a German artist to erase any cultural signifiers that mark the book as foreign.[169] For example, some of Robert Munsch's titles, like *Jonathan Cleaned Up, Then He Heard a Sound* (1981; *Endstation! Alles Aussteigen!* 1983) have been published with their original Michael Martchenko illustrations, while others, like *The Paperbag Princess* (1980; *Die Tütenprinzessin*, 1987, illustrated by Helge Nyncke) have been re-illustrated to better meet German market demands. *Love You Forever* (1986) has been issued by the same German publisher, Lappan, in two different translations, first in 2000 as *Ich werde dich immer lieben*, with illustrations by the editorial cartoonist Steffen Butz, and then re-translated in 2006 as *Ich lieb dich für immer*, with new soft-pastel-toned illustrations by Jürgen Rieckhoff. Robert Munsch himself has argued that his method of developing stories through repeated storytelling to child audiences pares away the 'nonessentials' of the narrative so that what is left is a 'good oral fairy tale with no specific ties to place or culture.' His belief that it is the lack of specificity that makes his picturebooks 'saleable internationally' also raises the question of whether creators themselves are necessarily aware of the ways in which their own particular cultural understandings shape their work and their interpretations of the cultures of childhood.[170] As the social historian Gillian Avery reminds us, fashions in the child heroes presented in children's literature change and 'show the qualities that elders have considered desirable, attractive, or interesting in the young' in any given time period and culture.[171]

The Two Solitudes: Anglophone and Francophone Illustrators

There are noticeable differences in the artistic styles employed by illustrators working in English Canada and Quebec. Francophone illustrators have developed what has been called 'the Montreal style,' defined by the confluence of cultural and aesthetic preferences.[172] The illustrator and author Marie-Louise Gay describes the shaping of the distinctive voice of Montreal artists as a paradox. She notes that while Quebec is 'set apart from the entire continent,' and has seemed from the outside to be a closed society intent on protecting its cultural traditions, Québécois illustrators are keen observers of trends from 'faraway places' and have been influenced primarily by European rather than North American styles of illustration.[173] In contrast, the illustrator Pierre Pratt argues that it is the lack of a distinctive tradition of children's book illustration within the province that has given francophone illustrators the freedom to develop their own style.[174]

The willingness of francophone illustrators to create images that are witty, playful, sophisticated, and avant-garde is cited by many critics as a key component of the 'Montreal style.' As Josiane Polidori explains, they are willing to 'go to the edge' and work in a conceptual style of illustration.[175] This experimentation is also noted by Toronto Public Library children's librarian and storyteller Mariella Bertelli, who believes that Québécois illustrators employ a more abstracted, graphic, and less realistic style in which the imagination predominates.[176] For publisher Rick Wilks, the work of Québécois illustrators is characterized by their technical strength, their willingness to take risks, and their use of a 'bolder, wider palette.'[177]

The approach to the communication of narrative through images in picturebooks and the relationship between text and image are shaped by the cultural context, reader expectations and preferences, and editorial preferences of the cultural community in which the artwork is created. Critic Jeffrey Canton identifies realism as the main difference between anglophone and francophone illustrators. He believes that the experimentation with non-realistic imagery among Québécois illustrators can present 'a problem for the English-language market ... [more used to an] old-style British type of picturebook illustration.'[178] Critic and author Sarah Ellis believes that francophone illustrators 'don't expect the child to understand the book at every point,' while anglophone illustrators 'expect that every word, every moment in the plot [should] be comprehensible to the child.'[179] For designer Michael Solomon, Québécois illustrators frequently favour 'an energetic, expressive line ... and meaning conveyed by graphic effects,' while in English Canada, the preference is for the amplification of a straightforward text with images that respond meticulously to the words.[180]

Mireille Levert's illustrations for Sharon Jennings's *Jeremiah and Mrs Ming* series published by Annick Press received numerous awards, including *Sleep Tight, Mrs Ming* (1993), which won the Governor General's Award for English-language illustration in 1993. Levert's absurdist sensibility of surreal metaphorical play is evident in *An Island in the Soup* (2001), first issued in an English-language translation by Douglas and McIntyre, and then in a French-language edition as *Une île dans la soupe* by Les 400 Coups in 2002. The gentle domestic narrative of a little boy whose mother encourages him to eat his dinner is imagined as mock-chivalric epic, in which the brave hero does battle with the ingredients of the soup, including a deluge of flying carrots and peas. The absurdist tone of the story is perfectly matched by Levert's images, described by one critic as a form of temporal hybridity, in which the young protagonist wears a colander as a medieval helmet and brandishes a wooden toy sword.[181] Even though the book won the Governor General's Award for English-language illustration, reviews were mixed. While most anglophone and francophone reviews praised Levert's creativity, use of visual metaphors, and valorization of imagination, one prominent anglophone reviewing journal dismissed the work as overly wordy, and 'a lot of melodrama over a bowl of soup.'[182]

One should be cautious, however, of falling into the familiar Canadian dualist trope of Quebec versus the rest of anglophone Canada. The sentimental realism of popular American illustrators like Norman Rockwell has been cited by at least one Québécois illustrator as a factor in helping to form his aesthetic preference for representational imagery in children's book illustration.[183] Lobster Press of Montreal, a bilingual publisher, has deliberately played on the perception of aesthetic differences, pairing anglophone authors with francophone illustrators, in the belief that the combination will make their books stand out, particularly in the crowded anglophone children's book market in Canada.[184]

On the other hand, perceived differences in the publishing cultures of anglophone and francophone Canada can negatively shape publishing decisions. Kathy Lowinger notes that Tundra Books' established practice of publishing bilingual and simultaneous editions in French and English has become increasingly difficult to sustain because of the differing aesthetic and narrative preferences within the two linguistic communities. She notes that, in her experience, francophone picturebooks, while 'gorgeous to look at,' sometimes position the child as the 'innocent viewer' rather than as a protagonist with power to act. She adds that this narrative strategy would receive little attention in the anglophone market, which prefers an active child protagonist. She emphasizes that both approaches are valid and appeal to children, but are difficult to market cross-culturally.[185]

English-Canadian publishers are reluctant to translate and publish French-Canadian picturebooks if they believe the subject matter will be censored or will fail to find a market, especially in the United States, because of differences in cultural mores. Perhaps this is why *Petit Zizi* (1997), the award-winning picturebook by the French author Thierry Lenain and illustrated by the Québécois artist Stéphane Poulin, about a young boy's uncertainty about his ability to attract the

9.4 Mireille Levert. *Island in the Soup*. A Groundwood Book.
Toronto: Douglas and McIntyre, 2001.
Reprinted with the permission of the publisher, Groundwood Books.

attention of Anaïs, the girl whom he likes, after the class bully teases him about the size of his penis, appeared in Danish, Spanish, and Korean editions before being issued in English as *Little Zizi* by a small American publisher, Cinco Puntos Press, in 2008.[186] Poulin explains that English-language publishers 'told us that there was simply no way a book with that title that involved penises was going to launch in North America.' The topic 'would not be discussed, not in books aimed at kids under about twelve.'[187]

It is ironic that English-language publishers who bemoan the American market's discomfort with 'foreignness' in their books respond in the same way to picturebooks published in Quebec. Critic Jeffery Canton raises the point that French-Canadian illustrators also may be perceived as too risk-taking by some English-language children's book reviewers. There have been incidents where the reviewer misconstrued the intent of the artist and the approach to illustration. He cites the example of a review of *Sassy Gracie* (1998), a retelling of the Grimm story 'Clever Gretel,' by British author James Sage. The reviewer responded negatively to the award-winning Québécois illustrator Pierre Pratt's images, because, in Canton's view, they made the person 'really uncomfortable.' Canton explains that Pratt's illustrations present Sassy Gracie as a diminutive adult, rather than a child, which he believes was a political statement by the artist 'to show the place of servants in the greater world.' The reviewer misread the intention of the narrative and the image of Sassy Gracie and was troubled by the story. Canton concludes that 'Québécois illustrators … [are willing to] take real chances.'[188]

Canton's observations are echoed by Annick's publisher Rick Wilks, who also cites differences in aesthetic taste and preferred styles of illustration between the two linguistic markets, and intra-national differences in cultural sensibilities as factors affecting marketability. He explains that some Quebec titles 'that did cross, more or less successfully, into English Canada, bombed in the United States. That helped us make a distinction between English-Canadian sensibilities and American sensibilities. As an example, Pierre Pratt's early books were really embraced by anglo-Canada and rejected, by and large, by the Americans. It was just too far out for them. Cultural sensitivities do emerge through this kind of response.'[189]

Despite instances of resistance in the English-speaking market to titles by Québécois illustrators, however, the success of individual francophone illustrators suggests that the differing aesthetic preferences within the two linguistic communities are not an insurmountable barrier to critical acclaim. After an initial hesitant reception in the United States and in anglophone Canada, Pierre Pratt is now regularly commissioned by American publishers like Dial, Atheneum, and Farrar Straus and Giroux, and the British publisher Candlewick Press to illustrate picturebooks, as well as continuing to illustrate books by Quebec authors for Dominique et Compagnie, and Les 400 Coups. In 2004, he won the Elizabeth Mrazik-Cleaver Canadian Picture Book Award for *Where's Pup?* (2003), and in 2008, he was a finalist for the international Hans Christian Andersen prize. Marie-Louise Gay, arguably the best known of the francophone illustrators, has won eight awards for children's books, been nominated twenty-two times as author, illustrator, and designer of fourteen English-language titles, and in 1984 was the first illustrator to receive the Canada Council Children's Literature Prize for French and English publications in the same year for her artwork for the four small volumes issued collectively as *Drôle d'école* (1984) and for Dennis Lee's *Lizzy's Lion* (1984).

'A Lack of Communication between French and English': The Problem of Translation in Canada

Just as economics and aesthetics intertwine in the dissemination and reception of illustrators, both cultural and economic issues play a significant factor in the frequency with which children's books in Canada are translated from one official language to the other.[190] Although the Canada Council Translation Grants, established in 1972, assist in funding the translation of longer texts, the amount of the grant is based on the word count. Short picturebook texts cannot meet the minimum number of words needed to meet the minimum dollar figure to be eligible for grants.[191]

Many children's literature advocates have noted that relatively few Canadian children's books are translated from one official language to the other, despite the obvious benefits of introducing children to the diversity of national literatures in an officially bilingual country. The author Roch Carrier, former head of the Canada Council and former National Librarian, argues that despite government support for translation, the lack of funding is one of the main barriers to increased publication of translated works.[192] Cultural preferences in subject matter, illustrative style and design, and the difficulty of finding translators who can work with the implied meanings of illustrations in picturebooks and the culture-specific signifiers in both art and text further inhibit the publication of translated editions.[193]

Dave Jenkinson, editor of *CM: Canadian Review of Materials*, describes the differences in the approach to publishing for children in Quebec and anglophone Canada, noting that francophone authors treat their young readers more respectfully and 'trust them more compared to the prudery in English Canada.' He believes that as a result, the French-language titles chosen for translation are those with the broadest and most general appeal because publishers are afraid that translations will not be commercially successful.[194] The small domestic market and the costs of production reduce the willingness of publishers to take risks with unilingual authors and illustrators whose work is unknown outside their own linguistic market and who cannot promote their books through tours, interviews, and book signings. To minimize the costs and the stigma of translation, some publishers and editors translate texts themselves or disguise the fact of translation by not including the name of the translator in the colophon or on the cover to lessen marketing resistance.[195]

Josiane Polidori states bluntly that the library's translation statistics, the Canada Council translation grants, and books submitted for the Children's Literature Translation Award administered by the Children's Literature Service of Library and Archives Canada all provide strong evidence that the translation of picturebooks and children's novels in Canada is decreasing. She believes that there is a pressing need for more publishers to issue translated books so that children are familiar with the literature of 'the other linguistic community.'[196] Placing the issue within the broader economic context, she asks, 'If Canadian publishers can sell abroad, why don't we sell to each other?' She notes, however, that economies of scale make it more profitable for a publisher to sell foreign rights outside the country than to a publisher in the other linguistic community within Canada.[197] Her view is echoed by Alison Fripp, publisher and president of Lobster Press in Montreal, who explains that when she contacts francophone publishers in her city to discuss translation and rights sales, she is often told 'Well, let's meet in Frankfurt or let's meet in Bologna.' As she observes, even though the other publisher is 'just down the road … there's this barrier that we can't quite get across' that continues to divide anglophone and francophone publishers in Quebec.[198]

The situation for bilingual books and titles issued simultaneously in both official languages is even more complex. May Cutler explains that 'if the books were by a francophone, [Tundra] either did two separate editions (one in French and one in English, like the *Simon* series by Gilles Tibo) or a bilingual edition,' adding that 'the Canada Council hated bilingual books. They didn't know what to do with them.'[199] When in 1986 Cutler believed that the Council had mishandled the selection process for the Governor General's Award by placing Stéphane Poulin's *Ah! belle cité!: ABC / A Beautiful City: ABC* (1985) with the English-language translation jury, even though the text was a mere twenty-six words, she took her complaints to anyone who would listen. She argued strenuously that the politics of language in Quebec militated against recognition for bilingual books.[200] Cutler was passionate in her belief that the Council should put the bilingual books in a separate category, arguing that 'if children are not going to read the same books, how are they going to share a culture or similar background of knowledge and experience?'[201]

Beginning in the late 1980s, Annick Press published some of its picturebooks simultaneously in French and English and translated some books from the Quebec publisher La Courte Échelle, which also translated some Annick titles from English into French. Anne Millyard, co-founder of Annick, explains that the decision to publish both French and English editions helped to provide Québécois illustrators who had been contracted to illustrate books by anglophone authors with 'a chance at better sales in their own market.' While sales were moderately strong, it was difficult to identify suitable titles each year, and Annick eventually stopped the program in 1997, choosing instead to sell the rights to titles illustrated by Quebec artists to Les 400 Coups, the publisher connected to Annick's distribution house in Quebec.[202] Annick publisher Rick Wilks adds that, with the exception of some of Robert Munsch's titles, their English-language picturebooks translated into French did not have strong sales in Quebec unless there was a francophone connection.[203]

Quebec publishers have similar difficulties in marketing their books within English Canada. Between 1999 and 2001, Dominique et Compagnie, a subsidiary of the Quebec publisher Les Éditions Heritage, issued picturebooks in simultaneous French and English editions under the imprint Dominique and Friends. The short-lived experiment resulted in the publication of sixty-three children's titles before the company shifted back to selling rights to English-language children's publishers.[204]

Despite the strong growth in children's publishing in both French and English Canada in the last two decades, and tentative initiatives between publishers, the reality today is similar to what it was in 1987, when André Gagnon published the first study of translated Canadian children's books. His words then are still entirely relevant today: 'There is a lack of communication between English and French publishers which needs to be remedied … Children's books published in Canada should be available in both official languages. Canada has excellent authors and illustrators as well as translators. We should begin recognizing national talent through more mutual translations.'[205]

Canada Goes Global

At the turn of the twentieth century, many Canadian authors and illustrators found it necessary to move to the United States in order to expand their professional careers. In the present era of globalization in publishing, Canadian illustrators once again augment their incomes and heighten their profiles by working outside Canada, and Canadian publishers have begun to match Canadian authors and illustrators with non-Canadians. The trend began in the 1980s and 1990s. Laszlo Gal was regularly employed by American publishers to illustrate literary fairy tales by American authors, including *Iduna and the Magic Apples* (1988) with a text by the noted American author Marianna Mayer for Macmillan of New York, and *Pome & Peel: A Venetian Tale* (1990) by Amy Ehrlich for Dial. The poetry of Dennis Lee, an outspoken Canadian nationalist, has been illustrated by non-Canadian illustrators for books issued by Canadian publishers, from *Jelly Belly* (1983), with watercolours by the award-winning British artist Juan Wijngaard, to two collections with artwork by the noted American illustrator David McPhail, *The Ice Cream Store* (1991) and *Bubblegum Delicious* (2000). Tundra Books has published titles by the Canadian author Barbara Nichol with illustrations by the award-winning American illustrator Barry Moser, including *Dippers* (1997) and *One Small Garden* (2001), and British Carnegie winner Jan Mark's Canadian-themed short novel, *Mr Dickens Hits Town* (1999) with Canadian Regolo Ricci's artwork.

Some illustrators continue to live in Canada but work extensively with non-Canadian publishers. Ken Nutt, using his pseudonym Eric Beddows, has illustrated a number of books by the American Paul Fleischman for New York's Harper and Row, including the Newbery-award-winning *Joyful Noise: Poems for Two Voices* (1988), and *Shadow Play* (1990). Michèle Lemieux, whose first full-colour picturebooks were issued by a German publishing house, continues to publish in Europe as well as Canada. Other illustrators, like Ian Wallace and Nicolas Debon, continue to publish in Canada but have relocated outside the country for personal and professional reasons.[206] Canadian author and illustrator Marthe Jocelyn and her husband, respected American printmaker Tom Slaughter, who live in New York and spend summers in Stratford, Ontario, have collaborated on a series of board books for Tundra. *One Some Many* (2004), the trilingual *ABC X 3* (2005) with text in English, French, and Spanish, and *Over Under* (2005), concept books for very young children, are all illustrated with brilliant cut-paper collages.

In other cases, Canadian illustrators whose books are sold into the American market by Canadian publishers, either directly or through co-publication or the sale of rights, gain critical recognition for their work, which in turn leads to further contracts by American publishers. Paul Morin, whose work was initially published by Oxford University Press in Canada, and by Houghton Mifflin and Putnam in the United States, was subsequently contracted for the illustrations for *The Mud Family* (1994) by the American author Betsy James by Putnam. Putnam then sold the rights to Oxford for the Canadian edition. As Kathryn Cole, then editor at Oxford remembers, 'Sometimes you develop partnerships rather than lose someone totally. It was easy to woo Paul away and I thought if I wanted to be named the Canadian publisher of note I had better join in.'[207] For Morin, the migration to publishing in the United States was an economic decision, driven by the need 'to make a living' through the more generous contract terms and larger advances offered by American publishers. As he explains, 'I'm really, really proud of being a Canadian. I've travelled all over the world, and this is the place that I would choose to live. I think it's important, because we're smaller and undervalued. I would never think of living in the States. I'm very proud to reside in Canada. I can't always make it work economically. I'm hoping to find ways that can work.'[208]

Is This Book Canadian? Does It Matter?

In his 2001 study, *Hip and Trivial: Youth Culture, Book Publishing, and the Greying of Canadian Nationalism*, Robert Wright explored the reading habits of young adults and the severing of links between youth, reading, and citizenship, arguing that the powerful discourses of cultural nationalism that shaped the attitudes of the generation that came of age in the 1960s are no longer seen as relevant in a globalized economy.[209] For Wright, the nationalism of the baby boom generation was distinctly literary, linking the ideas of print consumption with identity formation. It was this belief that shaped the formation of the independent children's publishers in the 1970s and 1980s and sustained the struggle of creators, publishers, critics, and readers to create a distinctly Canadian children's literary culture. He emphasizes that readers in their twenties, despite their early exposure to the children's books issued by the independent nationalist publishers, are cosmopolitan and internationalist, and read 'without reference to an expressly nationalistic cultural or political agenda.'[210] He dismisses the old school of literary nationalism as dull and brave and simple, focused on rural and domestic themes, embodying Frye's garrison mentality, in contrast to the new internationalist interest in urban literary themes and innovative literary style and technique. Wright concludes that 'Canadian cultural nationalism is the literary equivalent of Sunday school.'[211]

The current accelerated pace of the globalization of publishing – as mergers and buyouts have increasingly concentrated literary production into the hands of a few, vertically integrated multinational corporations whose primary goal is the maximization of profit for shareholders – suggests that for the next generation, the question of whether Canadian children see themselves in the illustrated books that they read may become a quaint historical conundrum. Joyce Bainbridge and Judith Thistleton-Martin conclude their comparative study of what they call the 'commonplaces of national identity' in Canadian and Australian picturebooks by questioning whether literacy should be 'about helping people to become sophisticated global citizens or sophisticated consumers.' They add that large multinational companies intent on marketing, licensing, and synergy are 'unlikely to produce culturally specific material,' seeking instead to 'develop a global market for culturally non-specific products.'[212] The various solutions to the problems of succession planning among the remaining independent publishing companies, and the need to sell into the international marketplace to ensure continued survival, have significantly altered the face of Canadian children's publishing in the last decade and will undoubtedly continue to shape what is published, and by whom.

The mimetic function of literature, the ability of a text to act as a mirror reflecting reality, is hotly contested by contemporary literary critics, who are sceptical about any claim for a unitary national identity and even more dismissive of the idea that literature can shape political engagement.[213] Novels for young adult and adult readers may be specific in their geographical and cultural references, or generically located, and still engage the reader. Some authors argue that their books are Canadian because they themselves as creators are Canadian, and no other qualifier needs to be added.[214]

However, the textual and visual intertwining of the picturebook means that the genre has an inescapable mimetic role. Unless completely abstract images are employed, they necessarily show the reader something of the world as envisioned by the illustrator. The streetscape created by Ken Nutt for Teddy Jam's *Night Cars* (1988) combines aspects of different Ontario communities, but is distinctly and recognizably regional and could not be mistaken for a streetscape in British Columbia. Harvey Chan's illustrations for Paul Yee's *Roses Sing on New Snow* (1991) locate the story in time and space in an architectural setting and environment that place the story for the alert reader who is able to interpret the visual traces of history in one of the Chinatowns in British Columbia after the completion of the Canadian Pacific Railway and before the overthrow of the Qing dynasty in China in 1911. For the child reader, the consistency and specificity of the world created in the images literally ground the story and add a lightness and sense of humour to the narrative. Kevin Major's *Eh? To Zed: A Canadian Abecedarium* (2000) incorporates a wide range of references to Canadian regions, flora and fauna, history, and cultural icons. Major wanted to write a book 'that was a basic jumping-off point for learning more about this country of ours' and that gave 'a sense of the vastness of this country, both physically and culturally.' As he explains, his intended dual audience of adults and children allowed illustrator Alan Daniel to create tableaux for each group of four words, rooted in the illustrator's knowledge of Canada, which at the same time explored folk art forms.[215] No one other than a Canadian could assemble a page in which the letter M stands for 'maple, moose, McClung and Mountie,' but also, through Daniel's illustrations, Mi'kmaq and maple sugar and multiculturalism (the Sikh Mountie in red serge and turban). Only a Canadian reader could appreciate the cultural nuances that make the interplay of simple text and complex images so satisfying. For the next generation looking into Canadian illustrated books for children, one can only hope that the answer that they find in the text and images to Northrop Frye's question, 'Where is here,' is not 'no place in particular.'

Maple, moose, McClung, Mountie

9.5 Kevin Major, *Eh? to Zed: A Canadian Abecedarium*. Illustrated by Alan Daniel.
Red Deer: Red Deer Press, 2000.

Notes

Abbreviations

Articles in the following publications do not appear in the Bibliography. A full citation is
    included in the notes.
Books in Canada (BC)
Canadian Bookman / Canadian Bookseller (CB)
Children's Book News; Canadian Children's Book News (CBN/CCBN)
Globe (to 1936); Globe and Mail (G&M)
Ontario Library Review (OLR)
Publishers Weekly (PW)
Quill and Quire (Q&Q)

1: Introduction

1 Hearne, 'Margaret K. McElderry,' 756.
2 Stewig, *Looking at Picture Books*, 7.
3 Marantz, 'Picture Book as Art Object,' 148.
4 Ibid.
5 Nikolajeva, 'Picturebook Characterisation,' 39.
6 Sipe, *Storytime*, 16. For an extended discussion of the semiotics of the picturebook, see
    also Kress and Van Leeuwen, *Reading Images*; Moebius, 'Introduction to Picturebook
    Codes'; Nodelman, *Words about Pictures*.
7 Ibid., 37.
8 Meek, *On Being Literate*, 116.
9 Genette, *Paratexts*, (originally published as *Seuils* [or Thresholds]); Genette, *Palimpsests*.
10 Sipe, *Storytime*, 14, 23.
11 Marantz, 'Picture Book as Art Object,' 149.
12 Brenner, 'Graphic Novels 101'; Rudiger, 'Reading Lessons'; McCloud, *Understanding
    Comics*.
13 Hollindale, 'Meanings and Valuations of Children's Literature,' 23–43.
14 Darton, *Children's Books in England*, 1.
15 Townsend, *A Sense of Story*, 9.
16 McGillis, *The Nimble Reader*, viii–ix.

17 Hunt, *Criticism, Theory, and Children's Literature*, 61–2.
18 Gerson, 'Women and Children First?' 6–13. See also Egoff, 'Introduction,' in *One Ocean Touching*, vi–vii, who noted that 'the difference between literature for children and that for adults was the nature of the audience, not the character or quality of the literature,' adding that authors at the First Pacific Rim Conference rejected 'any notion that to write for children is any less an art or of lesser importance than to write for adults.'
19 Leslie McGrath, interview.
20 Townsend, 'Standards of Criticism for Children's Literature.' Lesnik-Oberstein, *Children's Literature*, 102–3, reconceptualizes 'book people' as 'pluralists' who emphasize the teaching of individuality, and 'child people' as 'educationalists' who emphasize the mass teaching of morality and values through literature.
21 Bader, *American Picturebooks*, 1.
22 Nodelman, *Words about Pictures*, 222.
23 Sipe, *Storytime*, 18–21, provides a helpful overview of picturebook criticism based on visual aesthetic theory.
24 Solomon, 'Publishing Children's Picture Books,' 192.
25 Nikolajeva and Scott, *How Picturebooks Work*, chapter 6, 'Mimesis and Modality,' provides a helpful analysis of mimetic and symbolic representation.
26 Lesnik-Oberstein, *Children's Literature*, 108–11, argues that many of the underlying liberal humanist assumptions about the functional role of literature in childhood language acquisition remain unexplored within the prevailing psychological theories of 'educationalists,' posited on particular ideas about recognizing the 'self in the other' through the medium of text.
27 Snow and Ninio, 'The Contracts of Literacy,' 116–38.
28 Celia Barker Lottridge, interview.
29 David Jenkinson, interview.
30 Deirdre Baker, interview.
31 Nodelman and Reimer, *Pleasures of Children's Literature*, 75–7. See also Kress and van Leeuwen, *Reading Images*, 32.
32 See, for example, Bromley, 'Spying on Picture Books,' 101–11, and Arnold, 'Penny Plain, Tuppence Coloured,' 164–77.
33 Meek, *On Being Literate*, 122.
34 Aitken, 'Myth, Legend, and Fairy Tale,' 39–40.
35 Arizpe and Styles, *Children Reading Pictures*, 20–1, draw attention to Wolfgang Iser's theory of aesthetic response and Louise Rosenblatt's transactional theory of literary work. They argue that the asymmetry between reader and text is particularly important in the reading and interpretation of picturebooks.
36 Michele Landsberg, interview.
37 Arizpe and Styles, *Children Reading Pictures*, 22.
38 Mallan, 'Uncanny Encounters,' 17–31, discusses ideas of 'home,' the Other, and nationhood.
39 Bainbridge and Wolodko, 'Canadian Picture Books,' 21.
40 Canton, 'What Is Canadian Children's Literature?' 1.
41 Meek, 'Preface,' *Children's Literature and National Identity*, vii–x.
42 Diakiw, 'Children's Literature and Canadian National Identity,' 44.

43 Karr, 'Addicted to Reading,' 20, notes that historians are insufficiently attentive to literary criticism and semiotics, while literary scholars are insufficiently attentive to archival evidence, context, and chronology, adding that both groups of scholars are not fully engaged with the materiality of print culture, the book as object.

44 Slemon and Wallace, 'Into the Heart of Darkness?' 19–20, provide the helpful reminder that attending to children's texts can make visible the ways in which the historical child reader and the figure of the child are actively and consciously constructed and that an exploration of the social and cultural constructions of childhood can bring into sharper focus discourses of nationality and ethnicity. See also Meek, 'Symbolic Outlining,' 97–115.

45 Bradford, *Reading Race*, 5. Rose, *Case of Peter Pan*, argues that adult creators and critics privilege their own constructions of childhood and mediate the interaction between children and texts for particular social goals.

46 Mallan, 'Uncanny Encounters,' 19, warns that 'children and picture books do not exist in an ahistorical, apolitical realm.'

47 Sheahan-Bright, 'To Market To Market,' chapter 1, 'Going to Market.'

48 Ibid., 9–10. Miller, *Reluctant Capitalists*, 6–12, discusses the tensions between culture and commerce, arguing that by joining together economic and cultural analysis, a more nuanced understanding of the culture of retailing and consumption of print is possible. See also Fisher, 'Boundary Work,' for a helpful consideration of the relations between power and knowledge in the distinction between economic and cultural production.

49 Lundin, 'Introduction,' xiv, notes the agency of texts as material artefacts and conveyers of meaning mediated by creators, disseminators, and institutions in what she calls 'the traffic of texts.'

50 Davis, *Art and Work*.

51 Donnelly, 'Locating Graphic Design History in Canada,' 292–3.

52 Darnton, 'What Is the History of Books'; and Adams and Barker, 'A New Model for the Study of the Book.'

53 Davidson, 'Towards a History of Books and Readers,' 2, discusses the interaction of social, political, and material processes in the cultural production of literature.

54 Corse, *Nationalism and Literature*, 11, 15–17.

55 Gangi, 'Inclusive Aesthetics and Social Justice,' 243–64.

2: Beginnings to the 1890s: Canadian Children's Books in the Imperial Era

Sources of quotations used in headings:
'Penny Plain and Twopence Coloured,' from Robert Louis Stevenson, *Memories and Portraits*.
'A Land of Ice,' from *Northern Regions: or, A Relation of Uncle Richard's Voyages for the Discovery of a North-West Passage*.
'Is It Possible to Grow Up So Ignorant of the History of Our Native Land?' from Miss Grove, *Little Grace, or, Scenes in Nova-Scotia*.
'Never Let Difficulties Overcome You,' from Catharine Parr Traill, *Canadian Crusoes*.
'Far Removed from the Abodes of Civilized Men,' from R.M. Ballantyne, *Snowflakes and Sunbeams, or, the Young Fur Traders*.

'He Came of Sturdy, Sensible Stock,' from James Macdonald Oxley, *The Young Woodsman*.
'These Stories Are True,' from Ernest Thompson Seton, *Wild Animals I Have Known*.

1 For the distinction between metropole and hinterland see Williams, *Country and the City*; and Stoler and Cooper, 'Between Metropole and Colony.' Bradford, 'Saved By the Word,' suggests that colonial texts seek to colonize their readers, who are, in turn, constructed as potential colonists.
2 Egoff and Saltman, *New Republic of Childhood*, 4. The intertwining of discovery and ideology is discussed by Kröller, 'Exploration and Travel.'
3 Whitaker, 'Child in the Wilderness,' 23–30.
4 Whalley and Chester, *History of Children's Book Illustration*, 21–4; Townsend, *John Newbery*. For the influence of John Locke's *Some Thoughts Concerning Education* (1693) on the development of 'easy pleasant books' that would aid in the teaching of reading by entertaining and encouraging the beginning reader, see Pickering, *John Locke and Children's Books*.
5 Schiller, 'Artistic Awareness,' 180–1.
6 Neuburg, *Penny Histories*; O'Malley, *Making of the Modern Child*.
7 Pederson, 'Hannah More'; Jackson, *Engines of Instruction*; Myers, 'Reading Children.'
8 MacLeod, 'From Rational to Romantic'; MacLeod, *American Childhood*, 87–113; Butts, 'How Children's Literature Changed'; O'Malley, 'The Coach and Six.'
9 Sillars, *Visualisation in Popular Fiction*, 16, notes that wood engravings remained the dominant mode of the reproduction of illustrations through the 1860s, used in print runs of up to 100,000 copies.
10 Stevenson, 'Penny Plain,' used the term to describe the sheets of characters for toy theatres that could be bought plain for the purchaser to paint, or coloured. For hand colouring, see Whalley and Chester, *History of Children's Book Illustration*, 99–100; and 'Colour in Children's Books,' in Carpenter and Prichard, *Oxford Companion to Children's Literature*, 124–5.
11 *Northern Regions*, iii. St John, 'Early Canadiana,' 9–10, notes the ongoing interest in William Edward Parry's journal of his 1821 voyage, and its influence on children's books about Arctic exploration.
12 *Northern Regions*, iv.
13 Ibid., 5, and illustration facing p. 4.
14 St John, 'Peep at the Esquimaux,' 43. See also George Francis Lyon, *The Private Journal of Captain G.F. Lyon of H.M.S. Hecla during the Recent Voyage of Discovery under Captain Parry* (London, 1824), and John Franklin, *Narrative of a Journey to the Shores of the Polar Sea in the Years 1819, 20, 21 and 22* (London, 1823). Images from both works are available at http://ve.tpl.toronto.on.ca/frozen_ocean/fo_intro.htm.
15 Traill, *Young Emigrants*, 4–7.
16 Lewis, 'Pop-Ups and Fingle-Fangles.'
17 Amtmann, *Early Canadian Children's Books*; Egoff and Bélisle, *Notable Canadian Children's Books*; and McGrath, 'Print for Young Readers,' 252–6. A similar pattern existed for French-language publications. Lamonde, *La librairie et l'édition*, 24–5, notes that most frequent genres of works printed in Montreal were religious publications, calendars and almanacs, and textbooks.
18 Catalogues published by the various missionary societies provide evidence of the range of material circulating in Canada. See Friskney, 'Christian Faith in Print.'

19 Davis, *Art and Work*, 36–54.

20 Winearls, 'Illustrations for Books and Periodicals.'

21 Ibid., 104–5.

22 'Cheap Repository Tracts,' in Carpenter and Prichard, *Oxford Companion to Children's Literature*, 109–10. Mrs Lovechild's work follows the model established by Hannah More for her Cheap Repository Tracts, improving literature meant to compete with the sensational content of chapbooks, utilizing the same cheap paper and crude woodcuts, and given away or sold at nominal cost.

23 The author may have been Anne Grove, who emigrated to Nova Scotia in the 1830s from England, via Philadelphia, and opened a school for girls in Halifax in 1840. See 'Anne Grove 15 Aug 1813–12 Feb 1899,' Grove Family Tree, http://grove.accesseon .ca/anne.html. Gerson, 'Women and Children First?' 9, identifies the author as 'Miss Elizabeth P. Grove … the proprietor of a girls' school in Halifax,' and Anne's sister.

24 On the circulation of manuscripts, see Parker, 'Local and International Markets'; and Gerson, 'Women and Print Culture.'

25 St John, 'About Miss Howard-Gibbon,' in Howard-Gibbon, *Illustrated Comic Alphabet*, unpaged.

26 The modern facsimile edition was the first time that the manuscript had a wider public audience and resulted in Howard-Gibbon being acclaimed as the first creator of a Canadian picturebook.

27 Toronto Public Libraries, *Osborne Collection*, 682.

28 See, for example, John Ruskin, *The King of the Golden River, or, The Black Brothers: A Legend of Stiria*, ill. by Richard Doyle (London: Smith, Elder, 1851); and Charles Dickens, *The Battle of Life: A Love Story*, ill. by Daniel Maclise, Richard Doyle, Clarkson Stanfield, and John Leech (London: Bradbury and Evans, 1846). Whalley and Chester, *History of Children's Book Illustration*, 68, note the popularity of rustic details and lettering in mid-century illustration.

29 Margo Beggs, 'L Was a Lady.' Howard-Gibbon's father, Edward, was the natural son of Charles Howard, eleventh Duke of Norfolk, and served as his secretary.

30 Yvonne Watson, interview.

31 Beggs, 'L Was a Lady.'

32 From 1852 to 1853 the magazine was published by Robert W. Lay and printed by John Lovell.

33 George L. Parker, 'John Lovell,' *Dictionary of Canadian Biography Online*, vol. 12; Susan Mann Trofimenkoff, 'Eliza Lanesford (Cushing) Foster,' *Dictionary of Canadian Biography Online*, vol. 11, both at http://www.biographi.ca; and Cambron and Gerson, 'Literary Authorship,' 127.

34 Gerson, 'Snow Drop'; Gerson, 'Women and Children First?' 6–13; and Mary Lu MacDonald, 'Foster, Hannah, Elizabeth, Harriet,' Unitarian Universalist Women's Heritage Society, http://www.uuwhs.org/foster.php.

35 Egoff and Bélisle, *Notable Canadian Children's Books*, 24. The title varied, also appearing as *The Illustrated Maple Leaf*. For volumes 1 and 2, the subtitle was 'A Juvenile Monthly Magazine,' while volumes 3 and 4 were subtitled 'A Canadian Monthly Magazine.'

36 On the role of wilderness in nascent Canadian identity, see Turner and Freedman, 'Nature As a Theme'; and Kaufmann, 'Naturalizing the Nation.'

37 See, for example, Fleming, 'Supplementing Self'; Gerson, 'Nobler Savages'; and Murphy, 'Marriage Metaphor.'

38 MacKenzie, *Propaganda and Empire*, 204–5. Sillars, *Visualisation in Popular Fiction*, 73–4, discusses the popularity of illustrated, self-contained short stories in mass-circulation magazines in the late nineteenth century in England.

39 For tropes of empire and colony in Victorian children's literature see Jacobson, *Dickens and the Children of Empire*; Kitzan, *Victorian Writers and the Image of Empire*; Kutzer, *Empire's Children*; Phillips, *Mapping Men and Empire*; and Thacker, 'Victorianism, Empire and the Paternal Voice.' On the role of boys' stories in articulating an image of Canada for the metropolitan reader, see Moyles, '"Boy's Own" View.'

40 For Ballantyne's experiences as an HBC clerk and the genesis of Hudson's Bay, see Bruce Peel, 'Robert Michael Ballantyne,' *Dictionary of Canadian Biography*, vol. 12, http://www.biographi.ca; and Atherton, 'Escape to the Arctic.' For Ballantyne and masculinity, see Phillips, *Mapping Men and Empire*, 45–67; and Phillips, 'Space for Boy-ish.'

41 Story, *Oxford Companion to Canadian History and Literature*, 48–9.

42 Ballantyne, *Hudson's Bay*, [ix]–x.

43 Ballantyne, *Snowflakes and Sunbeams*, Preface.

44 Robert Ballantyne, original artwork, Osborne Collection, Toronto Public Library.

45 Ballantyne, *Author's Adventures*, 15.

46 The *Boys' Own Paper* and the *Girls' Own Paper* were published by the Religious Tract Society from 1879 until 1939 and circulated as yearly bound compilations as the *Boys' Own Annual* and the *Girls' Own Annual*. See Drotner, *English Children and Their Magazines*; Dunae, 'Boys' Literature and the Idea of Empire'; and Reynolds, *Girls Only?*

47 Egoff, *Canadian Children's Books*, no. 367.

48 Galbraith, *Reading Lives*, 9–24, includes a helpful discussion of the intersection of social class and gender and the diversity of childhood experiences.

49 Hunt and Sands, 'The View from the Centre,' suggest that the narratives of empire produced and consumed in the metropole valorized the importance of home and the centre while intertwining ideas about racial superiority with prescriptive definitions of gender roles.

50 Boyd, *Manliness and the Boys' Story Paper*, 49, notes that one of the central themes in the boys' adventure stories was the development of character as preparation for participation in the imperial project. See also Devereaux, 'Perhaps Nobody Has Told You Why'; MacDonald, 'Reproducing the Middle-Class Boy'; and MacKenzie, *Propaganda and Empire*, particularly 198–226, on the entwining of imperialism and masculinity in boys' fiction, and Knowles, 'Empire and School,' for a very helpful analysis of vocabulary and ideology, and the work of binary descriptions in the definition of hegemonic masculinity and Whiteness.

51 Clark, 'Imperial Stereotypes.'

52 Karr, *Authors and Audiences*, 37, notes the shift from taming the wilderness to taming the character in the wilderness through an emphasis on moral character development as characters struggled against forces of nature. See also Dunae, 'Making Good'; and Hugill, 'Imperialism and Manliness.' Bradford, *Reading Race*, 97–101, discusses masculinity and colonial discourse in boys' stories.

53 For a discussion of the role of historical narratives in creating Canadian nationalist sentiment, see Galway, 'Fact, Fiction.'

54 Bradford, *Reading Race*, 101, notes the eroticization of masculinity in boys' adventure stories through their discursive focus on bodies and an insistent praise of physicality.

55 'New Books Reviewed,' *Canadian Bookseller and Stationer* 13, no. 2 (1897): 10, praised the work as 'thoroughly Canadian in spirit and material, and a readable, proper book for boys,' with 'vivid and artistic' illustrations.

56 The first printing of 2,000 copies of *Wild Animals I Have Known* sold out in three weeks. By 1904, the book had sold 100,000 copies. See Mount, *When Canadian Literature Moved*, 103–4.

57 Seton, *Wild Animals I Have Known*, 5, 'The fact that these stories are true is the reason why all are tragic. The life of a wild animal always has a tragic end'; and 9: 'Although I have left the strict line of historical truth in many places, the animals in this book were all real characters. They lived the lives I have depicted, and showed the stamp of heroism and personality more strongly by far than it has been in the power of my pen to tell.' The wild animal story and Seton's use of personality are discussed by Auerbach, 'Congested Mails,' 54–5, and in Mount, *When Canadian Literature Moved*, 104, who argues that Seton drew on the heroic literary model of Carlyle's 'great man.' Whitaker, 'Tales of the Wilderness,' surveys the development of the realistic animal story as a distinctively Canadian literary genre, beginning with Roberts and Seton. See also Sandlos, 'From within Fur and Feathers.'

58 For Seton's biography, see Anderson, *Chief*; for Seton's children's books, see Egoff and Saltman, *New Republic of Childhood*, 22–3. For Seton, his Woodcraft movement, and the development of the Boy Scouts, see Morris, 'Ernest Thompson Seton,' and Rosenthal, *Character Factory*. For Arthur Heming, see 'Arthur Heming Collection Finding Aid,' National Gallery of Canada Library and Archives, http://national.gallery.ca/english/library/biblio/ngc024.html.

59 Egoff, *Canadian Children's Books*, no. 436.

60 Recent work on changing notions of wilderness include Colpitts, *Game in the Garden*; Jasen, *Wild Things*; and Loo, *States of Nature*.

61 Mount, *When Canadian Literature Moved*, 134.

62 Egoff, *Canadian Children's Books*, no. 463; Egoff, *Republic of Childhood*, 115–16.

63 Egoff, *Canadian Children's Books*, Index of Illustrators and Engravers.

3: The 1890s to the 1950s: 'And Whether We Are Yet a Nation'

Sources of quotations used in headings:

'Almost Exactly as I Imagined,' from L.M. Montgomery, *The Green Gables Letters*.

'Hooray! Hooray! Hooray! The Maple Leaf! Dominion Day!' from Elizabeth Rollit Burns, *Little Canadians*.

'Some Rhymes with a Flavor of Canada,' from [David Boyle], *Uncle Jim's Canadian Nursery Rhymes*.

'Canada Is a Country with a Romantic Past,' from Cyrus Macmillan, *Canadian Wonder Tales*.

'A Land of Vast Natural Resources and Wonderful Opportunities,' from Alfred E. Uren, *Bob and Bill See Canada*.

'Before Tea Was Served, It Was Suggested That the Section Be Organized,' from *The Ontario Library Review*.

'I Think You Are a Darling,' from a letter by Nellie McClung to Vancouver schoolteacher Margaret Cowie.

'A New Departure in Canadian Publishing,' from a review of *Velvet Paws and Shiny Eyes*.

'And Whether We Are Yet a Nation,' from R.K. Gordon, *A Canadian Child's ABC*.

1 Whitaker, *Canadian Immigration Policy Since Confederation*, Table 1. [Ottawa]: Canadian Historical Association, 1991.

2 Vincent, 'Progress of Literacy,' 405. Curtis, 'On Distributed Literacy,' 236, raises the problem of interpreting literacy measurements, noting that 'there is a range of capacities running from the complete inability to decipher text to the capacity to read all texts and texts in more than one language and to produce them for others.' Houston and Prentice, *Schooling and Scholars*, 190, note that census records suggest that most parents in Canada West in the mid-nineteenth century had attained at least basic levels of literacy. *Year Book and Almanac of Canada for 1875* (Ottawa: MacLean, Roger, [1875]), 120, reporting on the 1871 Canadian census results, indicates that 8.6 per cent of adults over the age of 20 in the four provinces of the Dominion were unable to read and 11.82 per cent were unable to write, suggesting a basic literacy level among adults of 79.6 per cent. No figures on literacy levels are available for the 1881 census. *Statistical Yearbook of Canada for 1905* (Ottawa: S.E. Dawson, King's Printer, 1905), 54, Table XII, Education of the people, indicates that according to the 1891 census data, 75 per cent of the population 5 years of age and older could read and write, increasing to 82.8 per cent in 1901 census. The drop between 1871 and 1891 may indicate both changes in the reporting methodology and the shifting nature of Canadian society in a period of increased immigration. By 1921, fully 90 per cent of the population 5 years of age and over could read and write, based on the census data compiled by *Canada Year Book 1924* (Ottawa: F.A. Acland, Kings Printer, 1925), 128, Table 36, Illiteracy among the Population. Regional disparity, which in 1901 varied from 92.99 per cent literacy in Ontario to 63.88 per cent in Saskatchewan, had largely disappeared by 1921, except for the Yukon and the Northwest Territories.

3 Axelrod, *Promise of Schooling*, 123–4.

4 Ibid., 35–6. Newfoundland, which did not enact compulsory school legislation until 1942, was not a province of Canada until 1949. See also Statistics Canada, *Canadian Compulsory School Laws*, 7–12.

5 Sutherland, *Children in English-Canadian Society*, 164.

6 For the role of instructional and recreational programs in settlement houses as a means of fostering the goals of citizenship and cooperation, see James, 'Reforming Reform.' See also Comacchio, *Nations Are Built of Babies*, 20.

7 Sutherland, *Children in English-Canadian Society*, 3–12.

8 MacLeod, 'From Rational to Romantic'; Sánchez-Eppler, *Dependent States*; Wadsworth, *Company of Books*, 22–31.

9 Lundin, 'Little Pilgrims' Progress,' 141, discusses the increased interest in the commodification of children's literature and the aesthetics of the book in this period.

10 Gray, 'Trade Publishing in Canada,' 6; Karr, *Authors and Audiences*, chapter 2; Parker, 'Evolution of Publishing in Canada.'

11 For school textbook production and distribution, see Houston and Prentice, *Schooling and Scholars*, 312–15; Clark, 'Publishing of School Books,' 335–40.

12 Canadian authors only received protection from piracy within the Empire under the British Copyright Act of 1842 if their work was first published in London or Edinburgh. However, the Foreign Reprints Act also allowed colonies to import pirated

reprints if duties were levied, thus ensuring that Canadian authors had no recourse if American or British pirated editions of their works were imported into Canada. See Parker, 'English-Canadian Publishers.'

13 Curry, 'US Manufacturing Provisions'; Sharp, 'Some Copyright Concerns'; and Broten and Birdsall, *Paper Phoenix*, 58–9. In agency books that were simply importations of a finished product produced elsewhere, the name of the Canadian distributor appeared on the copyright page, unlike Canadian editions of foreign books, whether printed in Canada or by the foreign publisher, in which the Canadian publisher/distributor was listed on the title page and binding, and the original publisher's name on the copyright page.

14 Audley, 'Book Publishing,' 100; Parker, 'Evolution of Publishing,' 30–2; Parker, 'Trade and Regional Publishing.' See also the discussion in Hagler, 'Selection and Acquisition of Books,' 32–5.

15 In the 1920s, although Macmillan of Canada developed a strong Canadian list under president Hugh Eayrs, they were slower to issue children's titles, the first being Marian Osborne's *Flight Commander Stork and Other Verses* (1925), illustrated by E.A. Kerr. Ironically, Parker, 'Evolution of Publishing,' 31, cites a 1910 letter from Sir Frederick Macmillan, head of the English firm, to the Canadian president, Frank Wise, in which Macmillan argued that the only original material that should be published in Canada was 'the production of school books authorized by one or other of the Provincial governments.'

16 McGrath, 'Print for Young Readers,' 407, notes sixty-three children's book series listed in the 1911 Eaton's *Our Books* catalogue. The advertisements and notices in *Canadian Bookman* suggest a similar range of access to series books and annuals issued in Britain and the United States.

17 For an overview of the development of Canadian authorship and the publishing scene, see Cambron and Gerson, 'Literary Authorship'; and Parker, 'Evolution of Publishing.'

18 Mount, *When Canadian Literature Moved*, 24, notes that the only equivalent Canadian juvenile magazine was *Pleasant Hours* (Toronto: William Briggs, 1881–1929), a Methodist Sunday school paper with a circulation necessarily limited by denominational association. For information on *Pleasant Hours*, see Pierce, *Chronicle of a Century*, 119. For the range of Canadian-authored periodical materials, including serialized novels, short stories, and poetry see Moyles, 'Young Canada.'

19 Brodhead, *Cultures of Letters*, provides a helpful understanding of how social settings shape the literary practices of the authors situated within them. Mount, 31, notes that while Canadian writers struggled to find a common national literary culture, they were surrounded by transnational literary cultures represented in imported books and magazines.

20 Mount, 13, argues that American authors and publications provided literary models for Canadian writers and that the decision of Canadian writers to move to American cities was a strategic decision to move 'from the margins to the centres of a continental literary culture.'

21 Sorby, *Schoolroom Poets*, 90–1.

22 Leslie McGrath, interview, describes a letter from Cox in the Osborne Collection in Toronto, in which he discusses race and marketing in his artistic decisions. Cox's choices in his depiction of ethnocultural identity are also noted in Kunzle, 'Review of *Humorous but Wholesome*.'

23 Kunzle, 'Review,' 455; Mount, 62–3. See also Avery, *Behold the Child*, 143–4.
24 'Cox, Palmer,' in Carpenter and Prichard, *Oxford Companion to Children's Literature*, 132.
25 Sorby, *Schoolroom Poets*, chapter 3, discusses Palmer Cox and the role of St Nicholas in promoting the mass culture of childhood in antebellum America, a point also taken up by Mount, 64–5.
26 Waterston, 'Margaret Marshall Saunders'; Davies, 'Publishing Abroad.' *Beautiful Joe* eventually sold over a million copies in fourteen languages. *Anne* sold in excess of 19,000 copies in the first five months, and has been translated into at least sixteen different languages.
27 Donna Jane Campbell, speech at the 2004 L.M. Montgomery Institute, cited by Rubio, email interview, 15 July 2004. See also Gammell, *Looking for Anne*, 231–2.
28 Bernard Katz, 'Cover Art and Illustrations in Some of L.M. Montgomery's Earliest Books,' unpublished paper. See, in particular, Montgomery, *Green Gables Letters*, 73. Epperly, *Through Lover's Lane*, explores Montgomery's use of photography.
29 Waterston, 'Margaret Marshall Saunders,' 148.
30 On the exclusion of women from the nationalist and modernist Canadian canon, see Gerson, 'Canon between the Wars.' She notes that the attempt by modernist critics to define a Canadian canon characterized by 'virile attributes' led them to disregard women writers, whom they believed were incapable of the 'strong, concrete writing' that they valorized.
31 Egoff, *Canadian Children's Books*, no. 404, notes, 'The recto of the front flyleaf bears, "Written and adapted by M.A. Bonnell." The verso bears an acrostic poem to Queen Alexandra dated July 3, 1901.' 'Books and Periodicals,' *Bookseller and Stationer* 6, no. 11 (1900): 5, identifies the author as 'Mrs. M.A. Bonnell of Bobcaygeon.' The author was probably Mary Arabella Boyd Bonnell (1849–1932) of a prominent Bobcaygeon family. See the Boyd family fonds, Trent University, http://www.trentu.ca/admin/library/archives/88-011.htm, and 'The Boyd Family,' The Boyd Family Museum http://www.theboydmuseum.com/boyd_family.htm.
32 Burns was also the author and composer of 'God Save the Dominion,' a song published in 1900 in Montreal which was 'Dedicated to the boys and girls of Canada.'
33 Dowsett, 'Women's Art Association,' 37–8. McLeod, *In Good Hands*, 24–36, discusses the career of Mary M. Phillips. For the role of literary societies and women's participation in literary culture, see Murray, 'Literary Societies,' and Tippett, *Making Culture*.
34 The Margaret Eaton School, which moved into grand purpose-built quarters on Bloor Street in Toronto in 1906, had the financial support of Margaret Eaton, wife of Timothy Eaton, and the encouragement of Nathanial Burwash, principal of Victoria College at the University of Toronto, who served as first president of the school. See Murray, 'Making the Modern'; 'The Margaret Eaton School of Literature and Expression,' http://www.uoguelph.ca/shakespeare/essays/margareteaton.cfm.
35 For short biographies of Grier, see Stella Evelyn Grier, Artists in Canada database, http://daryl.chin.gc.ca:8015/Webtop/Searchapp/ws/aich/user/wwwe/SearchForm; and 'Official Portraits of the University of Calgary: A Preliminary Listing,' University of Calgary Libraries Special Division, Occasional Paper no. 10, http://www.ucalgary.ca/lib-old/SpecColl/OccPaper/occ10.htm.
36 Killan, *David Boyle*, 24–7.
37 For biographical details, see Colgate, *C.W. Jefferys*; Stacey, *Charles William Jefferys*; and Stacey, *C.W. Jefferys*.

38 Colgate, *C.W. Jefferys*, 8, 10, notes that the 'resolutely Canadian' calendars included quotations from the poetry of Wilfred Campbell, Isabella Valancy Crawford, Charles G.D. Roberts, Archibald Lampman, and Bliss Carman. See also Stacey, *C.W. Jefferys*, 13–18; Robert Stacey, 'Illustration, Art,' *Canadian Encyclopedia*, http:www.thecanadianencyclopedia.com, and Stacey, '*Under Some Malignant Star*,' 53.

39 The three books by Pickthall had been published originally as serials in *East and West*, a journal for young people issued by the Presbyterian Church in Canada. See *Dick's Desertion: A Boy's Adventures in Canadian Forests, a Tale of the Early Settlement of Ontario* (Toronto: Musson, [1905]); *The Straight Road* (Toronto: Musson, [1906]); and *Billy's Hero, or, The Valley of Gold* (Toronto: Musson, [1908]). Although he was credited as the illustrator only for *Billy's Hero*, Jefferys completed the illustration for all three titles. See Colgate, *C.W. Jefferys*, 18; Pantazzi, 'Book Illustration and Design'; and Stacey, '*Under Some Malignant Star*,' 38–9.

40 Stacey, '*Under Some Malignant Star*,' 13. Stacey, a nephew of Jefferys, drew on family papers in reconstructing the book's history.

41 Ibid., 42.

42 Ibid., 53.

43 Egoff, *Republic of Childhood*, 213, in lamenting the total absence of Canadian picture-books, appeared unfamiliar with the title. For Jefferys's textbook illustrations, see Walker, 'C.W. Jefferys,' and Osborne, 'Kindling Touch.' Campbell, 'Romantic History to Communication Theory,' discusses Jefferys's textbook illustrations in the context of Canadian nationalism.

44 Macmillan, *Canadian Wonder Tales*, xi.

45 It would seem that anglophone Canada had no folk traditions, according to Macmillan. Although his 1907 Harvard Ph.D. thesis was titled 'The Folk Songs of Canada,' only francophone songs were included. See Brassard, 'French Canadian Folk Music Studies.'

46 Macmillan, *Canadian Wonder Tales*, xi.

47 Ibid., 53.

48 Ibid., ix.

49 Sheringham, who trained at the Slade School from 1899 through 1901, and in Paris from 1904 through 1906, was noted for his costume and theatre design. In 1918, he also illustrated an edition of Max Beerbohm's *The Happy Hypocrite* for John Lane. See the brief biography at The Tate Art Gallery 'Collection Tate,' Tate Online, http://www.tate.org.uk.

50 Egoff, *Republic of Childhood*: 'This was the veritable stuff of fairy tales – magic coats and wands, ogres, giants, and mermaids – put somewhat into a Canadian setting.'

51 Iain Stevenson, interview. Hale was the pen name of Amelia Beers Warnock Garvin, Canadian journalist and poet, whose husband John Garvin was a prominent critic and editor.

52 Simpson also illustrated William Smith's *Evolution of Government in Canada* (Montreal: Gazette Printing, 1928), issued for the sixtieth anniversary of Canadian Confederation. Library and Archives Canada holds the original paintings for the Smith volume. Simpson's skill at historical recreation is comparable to Jefferys's later work for Ryerson Press.

53 Uren, *Bob and Bill See Canada*, unpaged. *Bob and Bill* was reissued by Musson in a 'popular edition' in 1926 and advertised by Eaton's department store in a list of rec-

ommended books for children: *G&M*, 14 November 1927. Uren also self-published a sequel, *Bob and Bill Go Farming: A Story in Rhyme for Boys and Girls* (Toronto: Bob and Bill Publications, [1935]).

54 Uren, *Bob and Bill See Canada*, unpaged.

55 'The Canadian Bunnies,' *CB* 1, no. 4 (1919): 60.

56 McKechnie, 'Patricia Spereman,' 135–6, notes that Spereman established the first children's reading room in Ontario at the Sarnia Public Library in 1904.

57 Hunt, 'Values in Library Work,' 137–8.

58 Ibid., 137. See also Johnston, 'Lillian H. Smith'; Lundin, 'Anne Carroll Moore'; Lundin, *Constructing the Canon*; McGrath, 'Service to Children'; and Vandergrift, 'Female Advocacy and Harmonious Voices.' For the role of Anne Carroll Moore in the development of children's publishing in the United States, see McElderry, 'Remarkable Women,' and Bader, 'Only the Best.' For a case study of evaluative standards and censorship in public libraries, see Martin, 'Edward Ardizzone Revisited.'

59 McKechnie, 'Patricia Spereman,' 142. See also Hanson, 'Early Canadian Library Education,' 64–6.

60 See, for example 'Ontario Library School,' *OLR* 11, no. 3 (1927): 76–7; and Johnston, 'Lillian H. Smith,' 8–9. See also Lillian Smith, 'Teaching of Children's Literature.'

61 McKechnie, 'Patricia Spereman,' 142. The name of the group and its organizational structure changed repeatedly over the years. 'Work with Boys and Girls,' *OLR* 15, no. 4 (May 1931): 160, noted that during the annual Round Table, 'Before tea was served, it was suggested that the section be organized. Thereupon Miss Milne of Hamilton was nominated as chairman, Miss Loveless of London as secretary. Both Miss Milne and Miss Loveless were elected by acclamation.' *OLR* 20, no. 3 (August 1936): 105, refers to the Boys and Girls Section of the OLA. Two years later, 'Work with Boys and Girls,' *OLR* 22, no. 3 (August 1938): 203, refers to the Children's Section of the OLA. 'Proceedings of the Children's Librarians' Section,' *OLR* 34, no. 2 (May 1940): 135, includes the news that the Children's Librarians Section was formally organized and adopted a constitution at the OLA annual conference.

62 For example, between 1929 and 1932, American Library Association, Children's Library Yearbook lists Canadian members in Toronto (Boys and Girls House, and branches), Calgary, Fort William, Hamilton, Kingston, New Westminster, Ottawa, St Thomas, St Catharine's, Vancouver, Victoria, Windsor, and Winnipeg.

63 Vandergrift, 'Female Advocacy,' 699.

64 'Children's Librarians' Section,' *OLR* 33, no. 3 (1939): 296, notes that at a joint meeting of the Ontario Library Association and the Quebec Library Association in Montreal in April 1939, at which librarians from the Maritimes also attended, children's librarians who belonged to the OLA discussed the possibility of forming a regional group of children's librarians. Trotter, 'Story-Telling in Canada,' 305–6, notes that the newly formed Canadian Children's Library Association hoped to include 'children's librarians from all the western provinces.' *OLR* 26, no. 1 (1942): 19, includes a joint luncheon of the Children's Librarians' Section of the OLA and the Canadian Association of Children's Librarians on the agenda of the OLA annual conference. There is some confusion about the inaugural date of CACL. Ontario Library Association, *Second Quarter Century*, 7, lists a founding date of 1932, an error that is repeated in several sources. For the 1939 date, see Egoff, *Once Upon a Time*, 33, and Fasick, 'Smith, Lillian H.,' 227.

65 Emery, *Library, School and Child*, 85–96, describes the state of children's services in Canada in 1917, including public libraries in Toronto, Hamilton, London, Brantford, Kitchener, Sarnia, Fort William, Ottawa, Niagara Falls, Guelph, Chatham, Stratford, Collingwood, Sault Ste Marie, Windsor, Peterborough, Brockville, Galt, Whitby, Victoria, Calgary, Regina, Winnipeg, Westmount, and St John. While most children's services were provided by taxpayer-supported free public libraries, in Montreal, the Montreal Children's Library was established by the local Council of Women.

66 See Lyons, 'Children Who Read,' 601. On the role of library clubs and reading clubs, see Hewins, 'Reading Clubs'; Milliken, 'Library Clubs'; Sayers, *Children's Library*; and Tyler, 'Library Reading Clubs.' For playground libraries, see Andrus, 'Library Work in Summer Playgrounds.' For the role of instructional and recreational programs in settlement houses as a means of fostering the goals of citizenship and cooperation, see James, "Reforming Reform.'

67 Whiteman, 'Storytelling as a Method,' 32, argues that the children's story hour in a library 'furnishes the opportunity for the librarian to come into personal touch with many children through one effort,' and 'frequently is the first step in the development of a taste for good reading, and an introduction to the possibilities of the library.' Emery, *Library, School and Child*, 62, describes the purpose of the story hour as making 'good readers rather than good listeners.' See also Hardy, *Public Library*, 69.

68 Trotter, 'Story-Telling in Canada.'

69 Emery, *Library, School and Child*, 63, describes the Canadian Story Hours as being 'of peculiar value to an audience of children, many of whom are of foreign parentage.' The 'heroes' included Laura Secord, Samuel de Champlain, Jacques Cartier, Henry Hudson, Madeleine de Verchères, James Wolfe, and Isaac Brock.

70 Lillian Smith, 'Children's Division,' Toronto Public Library, *Thirty-Seventh Annual Report for the Year 1920* (Toronto: Federal Printing Company, 1920), 17–19.

71 George Locke, 'Report of the Chief Librarian,' Toronto Public Library, *Thirty-First Annual Report for the Year 1914* (Toronto: The Armac Press, [1914]), 9, and Lillian Smith, 'The Children's Department,' Ibid., 14.

72 Lillian H. Smith, 'Children's Bookshelf,' *CB* 2, no. 1 (January 1920): 20.

73 'Introduction to the Young People's Number,' *OLR* 7, no. 3 (February, 1923): 66, argues that 'careful selection' in building a children's collection for a public library 'is essential. The work should be conducted methodically, and only approved books should be admitted to the shelves. Model lists made by specialists are the best source from which to select; boards and librarians should avoid slipshod methods and selections from works urged upon them by dealers as they would shun a plague. The highest standard and the highest only should govern in selection.' See also Vandergrift, 'Female Advocacy,' 691, who notes that reading lists were seen as an important tool for children's librarians to promote good reading.

74 See, for example, Lillian H. Smith, 'Children's Division,' *Toronto Public Library, Thirty Seventh Annual Report for the Year 1920* (Toronto: Federal Printing Company, 1920): 17–19, which notes that 'a shelf of books labelled "a girl's own library"' attracted 'the greatest interest from visitors' during the 'annual exhibit of gift books for Christmas held in the art room of the Library.' Lillian H. Smith, 'Children's Division,' *Toronto Public Library, Thirty Eighth Annual Report for the Year 1921* (Toronto: Federal Printing Company, 1921): 18–19, notes that '"Children's Book Week" was celebrated in conjunction with our own

annual Christmas Exhibit of gift-books for children. The Christmas Exhibit was never more successful, and special displays of book-shelves made by the boys were on view in several children's rooms. The children's librarians were also invited to talk to school classes about books during "Book Week," resulting in a great deal of interest in the books mentioned.' See also McGrath, 'Service to Children,' 363.

75 'Editorial Notes and Comments,' *OLR* 7, no. 4 (May 1923): 98.

76 *Catalogue of Canadian Books* (English Section), 2nd and revised ed., British Empire Exhibition, Wembley Park, 1925 (Toronto: Public Library of Toronto, 1925). The Exhibition ran from 1924 through 1925, and the first edition of the catalogue was printed in London in 1924.

77 Beatrice W. Welling, 'Canadian Librarians Meet at the American Library Association,' *OLR* 10, no. 1 (1925): 11–12.

78 The pattern of holiday sales was so entrenched that in 1921, Marion Humble of the [American] National Association of Book Publishers developed a 'Year Round Bookselling Program' to encourage sales outside the September to December period. See 'Year Round Bookselling Program,' *PW* 99, no. 1 (1921): 20–21; Marion Humble, 'Books and the Consumer,' *New York Times*, 8 Nov. 1925; and 'What is Behind the Juvenile Stone-Wall that Prevents Sales?' *Q&Q* 2 (April 1937): 43.

79 See, for example, an ad by Eaton's department store for 'Gift Books for Everybody,' *G&M*, 4 December 1920, and the ads for The Musson Company, McClelland and Stewart, and other publishers in the special supplement, 'In the Realm of Bookdom,' *Vancouver Daily World*, 11 December 1920. The supplement appeared in seven daily papers across western Canada. See W.T. Allison, 21 Dec. 1920, letter to Margaret Cowie, Margaret Cowie fonds, Rare Books and Special Collections, University of British Columbia Library, file 1-1.

80 'Canadian Authors Week,' *CB* 4, no. 1 (1921): 5–6; 'Another Book Week,' *CB* 4, no. 6 (1922): 155–6.

81 'Canadian Book Week,' *G&M*, 8 October 1927.

82 Rees, *Libraries for Children*, 75. For the American program, see the Children's Book Council, 'History,' http://www.cbcbooks.org/about/history.aspx; and Children's Book Week, 'History,' http://www.bookweekonline.com.

83 'For Children's Book Week,' *CB* 4, no. 11 (1922): 295. See also 'Children's Book Week,' *CB* 4, no. 12 (1922): 327: 'Children's Book Week was observed with greater enthusiasm than ever in Canada this year and a notable feature of it was the increased representation of children's books of special Canadian interest, this being an important development from the growth of Children's Book Week in Canada ... The increased activity of Canadian publishers in providing Canadian books for children, essays to supply a need which, however, still falls far short of what ought to be provided.'

84 'Children's Book Week,' *G&M*, 14 November 1929; 'Art and Artists,' *G&M*, 18 November 1930; 'Among Ourselves: Boys' and Girls' Book Week,' *G&M*, 21 November 1932.

85 For an overview of the history of school libraries across Canada, see Emery, *Library, School and Child*; and Mustard and Fennell, 'Libraries in Canadian Schools.'

86 For example, Ontario had a well-developed system of school libraries, dating back to the Common Schools Act of 1850 in Canada West. British Columbia authorized provincial grants for the purchase of school libraries in 1919, if school districts were willing to match the amount. Nova Scotia established a regional distribution system in 1929

but had no coordinated provincial school library service. Alberta had no coordinated school library legislation until the 1980s. In contrast, the American Library Association formed a School Libraries Section in 1915, and school libraries received support from other professional associations of educators. See Cole, 'Origin and Development of School Libraries.'

87 'Canadian Children and Canadian Writers,' *CB* 4, no. 5 (1922): 122.

88 Margaret Cowie fonds, Rare Books and Special Collections, University of British Columbia Library, includes 141 letters by eighty-three Canadian authors.

89 Ibid. Nellie McClung, letter to Margaret Cowie, n.d., file 1-13.

90 Ibid. L.M. Montgomery, letter dated 17 February 1922, file 1-13.

91 Ibid. Isabel Eccleston McKay, letter dated 26 May 1921, file 1-13.

92 Leonard S. Marcus, 'Mother Goose to Multiculturalism,' *PW* 244, no. 31 (1997): 62–70; Clark, *Kiddie Lit*, 72.

93 Egoff, 'Writing and Publishing,' 250, notes that 'only five children's novels were published in 1921–2, five in 1923, and none at all in 1935.'

94 'What is Behind the Juvenile Stone-Wall That Prevents Sales,' *Q&Q* 2 (April 1937): 43; 'Confessions of a Bookseller,' *Q&Q* 2 (April 1937): 18–19; F.D. Knapp, 'Musing on Juveniles,' *Q&Q* 3 (April 1938): 26–7.

95 Lillian H. Smith, 'Catch Them Young,' *Q&Q* 2 (April 1937): 30–1, 33. Smith and her children's colleagues were particularly dismissive of series books, objecting to what they believed to be a combination of questionable subject matter and poor literary values.

96 Leslie McGrath, interview.

97 Review by 'Candide' of *Velvet Paws and Shiny Eyes*, quoted in 'Highlights for Young Canadians,' *CB* 5, no. 11 (1923): 312. A second review of the title in *CB* 5, no. 11 (1923): 314, praised the title as an 'excellent epitome of Canadian geography which might well serve as a text book to many English enquirers regarding our climate and natural environment.' *Velvet Paws* and *Downy Wing* were reissued by Musson in the 1940s in the 'Books for Little Listeners' series. See 'What's What in Native Juveniles,' *Q&Q* 10 (October 1944): 41.

98 Theo Gielen, 'Books with (Re-)Movable Illustrations,' *Movable Stationery* 10, no. 3 (2002): 3, 14–16, notes that more than a century separates the 1933 toy edition from predecessors in the same format, published in the 1830s in Paris, and that it is the only known modern example of a book with removable illustrations that are intended 'to be taken out of the book and placed on the desk whilst reading the text.'

99 Ward illustrated at least one book for Musson and originated the popular 'Dingbats' calendars, issued between 1915 and 1996 by the pharmaceutical company Charles Elliot Frosst. Sankey also illustrated *Jimmy Gold-Coast* by Marshall Saunders (Philadelphia: David McKay, 1924) and volumes of poems issued by Ryerson Press and Musson. The Britishness of Canadian fantasies in the 1920s is discussed by Waterston, *Children's Literature in Canada*, 66–7.

100 'Homemaker,' *G&M*, 20 June 1936, and 18 Nov. 1936. For Sellen, see the Canadian Artist Documentation Files, E.P. Taylor Research Library and Archives, Art Gallery of Ontario.

101 Kerr also illustrated Marian Osborne's *Flight Commander Stork and Other Verses* (Toronto: Macmillan Company of Canada, 1925). Deane, whose work was included in

the 1928 Canadian Society of Graphic Art exhibition, also illustrated Grant Balfour's *On Golden Wings through Wonderland* (Toronto: McClelland and Stewart, 1927); Emma Lorne Duff's *A Cargo of Stories for Children* (Toronto: McClelland and Stewart, 1929); Martha Maud Watterworth and Mary Wenonah Castle's *Our Little Reader: A Preprimer* (Toronto: W.J. Gage, 1932); Frances L. Ormond, comp. and ed., *Canadian Treasury Readers, Book Two*, ill. by Deane and Maud and Miska Petersham (Toronto: The Ryerson Press; Macmillans in Canada, 1932); and Florence Bertha Steiner's *Toy Balloons: Verses for Children* (Toronto: Ryerson Press, [1934]). Her illustrations were also published in the Canadian magazines *Chatelaine* and *Mayfair* in the 1930s. See Meaghan Emily Clarke, '(Re)constructing the Feminine,' 26.

102   Egoff, *Canadian Children's Books*, no. 782.

103   Saltman and Edwards, 'Towards a History of Design.'

104   Novosedlik, 'Our Modernist Heritage, Part I,' 31.

105   Spadoni and Donnelly, *Bibliography of McClelland and Stewart Imprints*, 30; and Stillman, 'Book Illustration.'

106   Saltman and Edwards, 'Towards a History of Design,' 16.

107   For the life of Grey Owl, see Braz, 'Modern Hiawatha'; Chapin, 'Gender and Masquerade'; and Smith, *From the Land of Shadows*.

108   Whitaker, 'Perceiving Prairie Landscapes,' 32, argues that *Sajo* reverses the 'romantic quest motif' of encounters with the wilderness by sending the children away from the wilderness to the city.

109   Grey Owl, *Sajo*, xii.

110   Egoff, *Canadian Children's Books*, no. 835; McDonough, 'Profile: Hazel Boswell.'

111   Jefferys, 'Introduction,' *Picture Gallery*, vol. 1, vi.

112   Pierce, 'C.W. Jefferys,' xiv.

113   Campbell, 'From Romantic History,' argues that Jefferys's illustrations perform the ideological work of constructing a nationalist and unifying 'consensus history' among readers, in which difference is subsumed.

114   Waterston, *Children's Literature in Canada*, 50, notes that weekly newspapers like *The Family Herald and Weekly Star* were one of the few venues in which new Canadian writers for children could find an audience in the 1930s and 1940s. Elliott, *Publishing in Wartime*, 5–9, discusses the shortages of paper, binding cloth and binding materials, and skilled labour, all contributing to manufacturing problems for Canadian publishers. The destruction of publishing houses, printing firms, and warehouses in England, and the interruption of shipping that curtailed the importation of British books, further limited the range of books available in Canada during the Second World War.

115   'Among Bookmen,' *Q&Q* 10 (October 1944): 28, 48–50, identifies an increase in the birth rate, exposure to 'fascinating and colourful school readers,' wartime prosperity, and the availability of inexpensive American series like the 'Little Golden Books' and manipulable books like Dorothy Kunhardt's *Pat the Bunny* (Racine, WI: Golden Books, 1940) as the stimulus for new consumer interest in children's books.

116   'What's What in Native Juveniles,' *Q&Q* 10 (October 1944): 40–1, 51. Phillips had worked at Brigden's in Winnipeg, the graphic art firm that illustrated Eaton's catalogues. See Louise Duguay, 'Pauline Boutal.'

117   Contemporary Publishers was established during the war by the illustrator and cartoonist Harry Gutkin to issue works on social subjects from a labour/socialist

perspective. In the postwar period, Phillips-Gutkin and Associates (PGA) became a leading animation studio. See 'Harry Gutkin, 1916–2004,' Manitoba Historical Society, http://www.mhs.mb.ca/docs/people/gutkin_h.shtml; Walz, 'PGA Connection'; and Mazukewich, 'Animation Cels Products.'

118 Bonner, *Canada and Her Story*, inside front flap, dust jacket of the Harrap edition.

4: The Postwar Period: Creating a Children's Publishing Industry

Sources of quotations used in headings:
'Great Men of Canadian History,' from Lillian H. Smith, 'Children's Bookshelf,' 1920.
'An Inventive Flair for Evocative Detail,' from William Toye, 'Frank Newfeld, Book Designer.'
'Room for Us to Have Our Own Traditions,' from an interview with Sheila Egoff.
'No One Else Had Gotten an Indian into Print,' from an interview by *BC Bookworld* with Gray Campbell.
'Irma Was a Guardian Angel,' from a telephone interview with Janet Lunn.

1 Gray, 'Canadian Books': 'In our circumstances, the emergence of a cadre of professional writers, and of a publishing trade equipped to serve them, was bound to be slow. There are some who believe that it hasn't happened yet' (25); Aubry, 'Author in Canada'; and Lepage, Saltman, and Edwards, 'Children's Authors and Their Markets.' In contrast, francophone publishing increased significantly during the war as importation of books from France ceased. See Michon, 'Book Publishing in Quebec.'

2 Novosedlik, 'Our Modernist Heritage, Part I,' 33–4. See also Speller, 'Book Design in English Canada.'

3 Sheila Egoff, interview. Egoff, *Once Upon a Time*, 37–8, has a slightly different version of the story. See also Library and Archives Canada, Canadian Library Association fonds, MG28 I197, vol. 14, Book of the Year for Children Medal 1947–1952, letter from Alethea Johnston, Kitchener Public Library, to Amy Hutcheson, New Westminster Public Library, 22 January 1951 [both were on the executive of the Canadian Association of Children's Librarians]: 'I am enclosing a copy I made of the book reviews which Sheila Egoff wrote for our bulletin. I asked Miss Smith to have members of her staff do this, since they do get books in proof-sheets, and usually know them before any of the rest of us, and have them reviewed at staff meetings. I feel like a heel now I know that Sheila apparently had to do them all herself, and hated doing it. I wonder, too, whether anyone will say that we are trying to influence the vote [for the Book of the Year award]?' The file also includes letters from librarians at the Vancouver Public Library, the Calgary Public Library, and the London, Ontario, Public Library who protested the sharply critical tone of the reviews, which were published in the March 1951 issue of the *News Letter* of the Canadian Association of Children's Librarians, and the decision of the CACL awards committee, chaired by Lillian Smith, not to confer the prize in 1951 on any of the eligible titles.

4 Smith, *Unreluctant Years*, chapter 3, 'An Approach to Criticism'; Knight, 'Encouraging Children to Read.' Johnson, 'Lillian H. Smith,' 9, describes staff meetings at Boys and Girls House, during which 'older titles and the classics were analyzed and reassessed,' which lead to 'penetrating discussions about universal and lasting literary values.'

5 Egoff, 'Lillian H. Smith as Critic.'
6 De la Mare, *Bells and Grass*, 11. 'Only the rarest kind of best in anything can be good enough for the young,' was quoted in Smith, *Unreluctant Years*, 14. The use of the quotation as a selection guideline has been variously associated with Lillian Smith and Sheila Egoff in Canada, in the United States with Anne Carroll Moore and Frances Clarke Sayers of the New York Public Library, and in Britain with Grace Hogarth of Constable Young Books and Eleanor Graham of Puffin Books. See Reynolds, 'Publishing Practices,' 41fn32.
7 Canada, Royal Commission on National Development in the Arts, Letters and Sciences, *Report* [The Massey Report], ch. 15, 'Book Publishing in Canada,' 228–30.
8 Gray, 'Canadian Books,' 35–6.
9 Duthie, 'Other Side of the Cash Register,' 40.
10 Clark, 'Rise and Fall of Textbook Publishing.'
11 Graham, 'Picture Books,' notes the slow development of colour printing in the immediate postwar period in Britain through the early 1960s.
12 Gleason, *Normalizing the Ideal*; and Korinek, 'It's a Tough Time.'
13 Branigan, 'Mystification of the Innocents'; Adams, *Trouble with Normal*; Gleason, 'They Have a Bad Effect'; Kuffert, *Great Duty*, 143–6; and Beaty, *Frederic Wertham*.
14 Beaty, 'High Treason,' 95.
15 Coughlan, 'Guardians of the Young,' provides an overview of the history of intellectual freedom for children and the desire of adults to shape children's reading for didactic purposes.
16 Lillian H. Smith, 'Catch Them Young,' *Q&Q* 2 (April 1937): 30; Ruth Milne, 'Children Know What They Want When They Want It!' *Q&Q* 6 (September 1940): 16.
17 McGrath, 'Services to Children,' 102–3, 118–23, for a discussion of censorship, selection policies, and the exclusion of series books at Boys and Girls House.
18 Litt, *Muses, the Masses*; and Kuffert, *Great Duty*, 146–53.
19 Canada, Royal Commission on National Development in the Arts, Letters and Sciences, *Report*, Part 2, chapter 20, 'Federal Libraries,' 327–34, and chapter 25, 'A Council for the Arts, Letters, Humanities and Social Sciences,' 370–82.
20 Lecker, *Making It Real*; Friskney, 'Many Aspects of a General Editorship.'
21 New, *History of Canadian Literature*, 203–4, notes the role of state funding through the Canada Council in the new public profile of Canadian writers.
22 Klinck, *Literary History of Canada*.
23 Sutherland, *Childhood in English Canada*, 186–219, describes the regime of formalist education followed by most school boards throughout the 1950s. For the role of authorized textbooks in the curriculum, see Clark, 'The Rise and Fall of Textbook Publishing,' 227.
24 'Boys and Girls Book Week,' *Q&Q* 14 (May 1948): 16–17, describes a wide range of activities with only minimal Canadian content. Minkler, *Voluntary Reading Interests*, reports on a 1948 study of young people's reading preferences based on surveys distributed to children, teachers, and librarians across Canada. Appendix C, 92-4, lists the titles of the books that librarians indicated were the most popular with children. Of the 44 titles, 6 were by Canadian authors or had a Canadian setting: Montgomery, *Anne of Green Gables*, Denison, *Susannah and the Mounties*; Meader, *Trap-Lines North*; O'Brien, *Silver Chief*; Pinkerton, *Adventure North*; Seton, *Animal Heroes*; and Seton, *Two Little Savages*.

25 Elizabeth Morton, 'Pleasant Books of Childhood,' *Q&Q* 16 (August 1950): 14–16, 39; Margaret Turnbull, 'Young Canada's Book Week,' *Q&Q* 29 (November / December 1963): 13, 16.

26 Morton, 'Pleasant Books of Childhood,' 14–16, 39. See also 'Promotion for Young Canada's Book Week,' *Q&Q* 19 (October 1953): 7–8; 'Kids Learn about Books as Libraries Press YCBW to Hilt,' *Q&Q* 20 (November 1954): 25–6.

27 Eleanore Donnelly, 'Profile: Clare Bice'; Megan Bice, 'How a Book Is Made.' The original artwork for *Jory's Cove* is held in the Clare Bice fonds, LMS-0070, Literary Archives, Library and Archives Canada.

28 Egoff, *Republic of Childhood*, 228, criticized Bice's illustration as 'conventional pictures of Canada' and classified them as 'realistic in a narrow sense.' In contrast, Donnelly, 'Profile: Clare Bice,' 21, quotes Paddy O'Brien, curator of the Williams Memorial Art Gallery and Museum in London, Ontario, who praised Bice's work for 'the vigour of his brushwork, his happy choice of colour, his fine draughtsmanship, and the general sensation of energy and freshness that percolates through all his compositions.'

29 For Mould, see 'Exhibition by Vernon and Dorothy Mould,' *Lampsletter: The Newsletter of the Arts and Letters Club of Toronto* 65, no. 1 (2006): 7. http://www.artsandlettersclub .ca/lampsletter/lampsletter-200601.pdf. For Hall, see 'Hall, John Alexander,' Artists in Canada database, http://daryl.chin.gc.ca:8015/Webtop/Searchapp/ws/aich/user/ wwwe/SearchForm; and 'Biography: John Hall,' Canadian Painting in the Thirties, National Gallery of Art Cybermuse. http://cybermuse.gallery.ca/cybermuse/ enthusiast/thirties/artist_e.jsp?iartistid=2275.

30 Lillian H. Smith, 'Children's Bookshelf,' *CB* 2, no. 1 (1920): 21.

31 Janet Lunn, 'Canadian Children's Books,' *Q&Q* 29 (November/December 1963): 12.

32 The continuation of traditional genres was noted by McDowell, 'Children's Books,' 627; and Egoff, 'Writing and Publishing,' 251.

33 Lunn, 'Canadian Children's Books,' 12.

34 See 'Margaret Bloy Graham,' in *More Junior Authors*, ed. Muriel Fuller (New York: H.W. Wilson, 1963), 102–3.

35 Jeanneret, 'Text Book Illustration in Canada.'

36 Read, 'Eyes of Children,' 90. The 'Canadian Portraits' series comprised eleven collective biographies issued by Clarke, Irwin between 1956 and 1965.

37 William Toye, interview. See also Money, 'Profile: William Toye.' Tucker, 'Setting the Scene,' provides a clear overview of the development of children's publishing in Britain in the postwar period, including Oxford University Press.

38 Toye, 'Book Design in Canada,' 61.

39 *The Sunken City* was included on the 1962 IBBY Honour List, issued by the International Board on Books for Young People. Bamberger, Binder, and Hurliman, *20 Years of IBBY*, 226, the 1962 'Honour List.'

40 William Toye, interview.

41 Ibid.

42 Ibid.

43 Ibid.

44 Woodcock, 'Face of a River,' 90, describes the work as 'one of the most attractively produced books I have seen for a long time from a Canadian publisher, and for this also Mr Toye, who is a book designer as well as a writer, must get the credit.' Newfeld,

'Whose Book?' 46, credits Toye, as author and designer who acted as his own art director, as an example of a successful close collaboration with the illustrator, resulting in a work in which the illustrations are 'informative as well as being decorative.'

45 Speller, 'Book Design in English Canada,' 382–3, notes that the arrival of European book designers, including Newfeld and Leslie Smart, transformed the industry, aided by the creation in 1956 of the Society of Typographical Designers of Canada, which provided a meeting ground for the exchange of ideas. See also Toye, 'Book Design in Canada,' 52–63; Smart, 'Book Design in Canada'; Donnelly, 'At Forty'; and Donnelly, 'Picturing Words, Writing Images.'

46 Speller, 'Frank Newfeld.'

47 Toye, 'Frank Newfeld, Book Designer,' *Q&Q* 27, no.1 (1961): 18.

48 *The Princess of Tomboso* was on the runner-up list for honourable mention in the 1962 Hans Christian Andersen award, given by IBBY, the International Board on Books for Young People. See Bamberger, Binder, and Hurliman, *20 Years of IBBY*, 226, the 1962 'Runner-Up List'; and Smiley, 'Profile: Frank Newfeld,' 15.

49 William Toye, interview. On the co-publication, see Frank Newfeld, correspondence.

50 Munro, 'Wind Has Wings'; Foy, 'Profile: Elizabeth Cleaver.'

51 Saltman and Edwards, 'Elizabeth Cleaver, William Toye,' 40.

52 Munro, 'Wind Has Wings,' 8.

53 'Children's Book Withdrawn from School,' *Q&Q* 39 (January 1973): 8, notes that *Sally Go Round the Sun* was removed from a school in Hamilton following a complaint by a mother that some of the verses were 'not suitable for her eight year old daughter.' Fowke responded by noting that 'it would be a misrepresentation of children's lore to (omit) any of the slightly naughty verses in which children take delight.'

54 Kennedy, 'Prince Charming and Glooscap.'

55 Sheila Egoff, interview.

56 Ibid.

57 Sterritt, et al., *Tribal Boundaries*, ch. 1, 'Adaawk Record and Tribal Boundaries in the Nass Watershed'; and McDonald, 'Key Events in Gitxsan History: A Gitxsan Time Line.'

58 William Toye, interview.

59 Thompson, 'Transformation and Puppetry,' 72; Elizabeth Cleaver, original art for 'How Summer Came to Canada', Box 1985-12-2-11; Box 1085-12-2-14; Box 1985-12-2-4, Cleaver fonds, Literary Archives, Library and Archives Canada; Saltman and Edwards, 'Elizabeth Cleaver, William Toye,' 35.

60 Elizabeth Cleaver to Gloria Smedmore, n.d., Box 1, File 5, 'How Summer Came to Canada' correspondence, Cleaver fonds. Parts of the letter reappeared in Cleaver, 'Visual Artist.'

61 Smart, 'Book Design in Canada,' includes a list of 124 Canadian books included in the exhibit Impressions 58/68, organized by the Society of Graphic Designers of Canada and sponsored by the Canada Council. *Indian Legends of Canada*, designed by Frank Newfeld and Keith Scott; *Tales of Nanabozho*, designed by William Toye; and *The Day Tuck Became a Hunter*, designed by Frank Newfeld, were included in the exhibition. For a sustained and thoughtful criticism of the problematic of Melzack's appropriation of Inuit stories, see Faye, 'Revealing the Storyteller,' 160–3.

62 Stott, 'Interview with John [*sic*; should be James] Houston'; Houston, 'Vision of That Mask'; Harker, 'Interview with James Houston.'

63 'James Houston,' Art of Illustration, Library and Archives Canada, http://epe.lac-bac
    .gc.ca/100/200/301/lac-bac/art_of_illustration-ef/www.lac-bac.gc.ca/3/10/t10-705-e.
    html.

64 Stott, 'Form, Content,' 221, notes that throughout *Tikta'liktak*, Houston speaks to his
    non-Inuit reader from a non-Inuit perspective; Grace, *Canada and the Idea of North*,
    184–96, discusses the gendering of wilderness as anachronistic space in narratives of
    North.

65 Temple, 'Profile: George Clutesi'; Bennett McCardle, 'Clutesi, George Charles,' Cana-
    dian Encyclopedia, http://www.thecanadianencyclopedia.com; and 'George Clutesi,'
    Tseshaht First Nation website, http://www.tseshaht.com/tradition_history/figures/
    george_clutesi.php. For Clutesi's artwork and resistance to assimilation, see Hawker,
    Tales of Ghosts, 122–5.

66 Gray Cambell, 'Interview,' *BC Bookworld* (1991), http://www.abcbookworld.com/
    ?state=view_author&author_id=2548.

67 Harris, 'Caught in the Current.'

68 Christie Harris, 'Raven's Cry,' *BC Bookworld* (Summer 1989), http://www
    .abcbookworld.com/ [under Harris, Christie].

69 Charles Lillard, 'Lillard History Column, 1993, issue 2,' *BC Bookworld* (1993), http://
    www.abcbookworld.com/?state=view_author&author_id=7478.

70 Harris, 'Raven's Cry.'

71 Tippett, *Bill Reid*, 142–3.

72 Jeffrey Canton, interview; Egoff and Saltman, *New Republic of Childhood*, 168.

73 William Toye, interview.

74 Egoff, *Once Upon a Time*, 58, notes 'I was fortunate to have an editor and publisher
    already in place, since William Toye was a member of the committee.'

75 Egoff, *Republic of Childhood*, 3.

76 Ibid., 261.

77 Ibid., 5.

78 Egoff, 'Lillian H. Smith,' 132, quoting Matthew Arnold, 'The Function of Criticism at
    the Present Time' (1865).

79 Galway, 'From Nursery Rhymes to Nationhood,' 8–9, suggests that the debate about
    when a distinct national literature emerged in Canada is, in part, a subjective debate
    about the emergence of national literature of quality.

80 Sheila Egoff, interview.

81 Egoff, *Republic of Childhood*, 4–5.

82 Egoff, *Once Upon a Time*, 68. She also noted that the children's librarians that she inter-
    viewed in preparation for the book held a double standard of evaluation in order to
    support the Canadian book trade, respond to curricular demands, and 'counteract the
    number of books pouring into Canada from the United States.' See also Egoff, *Republic
    of Childhood*, 11.

83 William Toye, interview.

84 Bagshaw, *Books for Boys and Girls*; Toronto Public Libraries, *Books for Boys and Girls*
    (1927).

85 Bagshaw, *Books for Boys and Girls*, Preface; Knight, 'Encouraging Children to Read.'

86 Gerson, 'Canon between the Wars.' Frye, 'Conclusion,' *Literary History of Canada*, 822,
    dismissed evaluation as the guiding principle for the Literary History, adding that had

evaluation been the goal, the result would have left 'Canadian literature a poor naked alouette plucked of every feather of decency and dignity.'

87 Janet Lunn, telephone interview; Wilkinson, *Canadian Juvenile Fiction*, 8.

88 May Cutler, interview.

89 Irma McDonough, 'Away with the Mediocre,' *Q&Q* 33, no. 10 (1967): 24–5.

90 Egoff's submission to the Ontario Royal Commission was, in part, a response to critics of *The Republic of Childhood*. See Egoff, 'Writing and Publishing,' especially 245–8.

91 Jean Little, telephone interview.

92 Claire Mackay, telephone interview.

93 'Promotion for Young Canada's Book Week,' *Q&Q* 19 (October 1953): 7–8, recommended that public interest in children's books could be stimulated by incorporating reviews of books by local children into the popular 'children's club' page that many newspapers ran as a regular feature, with guidance from librarians and teachers in the choice of books to be reviewed.

94 Janet Lunn, telephone interview. See also Williams, 'Profile: Janet Lunn.' Janet Lunn, 'Narrow Professionalism Frustrates the Child,' *Q&Q* 30 (September–October 1964): 16, 18, 20, describes the competing goals of librarians, booksellers, publishers, and teachers in determining what a child wants to read, and what they as adults want children to read.

95 Annabel Slaight, 'Art for Children's Books,' *Q&Q* 39, no. 10 (1973): 4, lists titles praised by the noted Canadian graphic designer Allan Fleming. These include Theo Dimson's illustrations for James McNeill's *The Sunken City* (Oxford, 1959), Elizabeth Cleaver's illustrations for Mary Alice Downie and Barbara Robertson's *The Wind Has Wings* (Oxford, 1968), Allan Suddon's *Cinderella* (Oberon, 1969), and Carlos Marchiori's illustrations for Edith Fowke's *Sally Go Round the Sun* (McClelland and Stewart, 1969).

96 Janet Lunn, 'Canadian Children's Books,' *Q&Q* 29 (November–December 1963): 10, noted that approximately 50 children's titles were published in 1962, compared with 2,126 new titles in Britain, and 2,584 titles in the United States. According to Gray, 'Canadian Books,' 27, the situation changed sufficiently in the decade from 1957 to 1967 that his earlier assessment that Canadian publishers could not make a net profit from Canadian publishing had changed to the possibility of profit.

97 Egoff, 'Children's Books in English,' 32.

98 MacSkimming, *Perilous Trade*, 273.

5: The 1970s: Developing a Children's Publishing Industry

Sources of quotations used in headings:

'A Steady Flow of New Canadian Books by Canadian Authors,' recommendation by the Ontario Royal Commission on Book Publishing.

'No Tradition of Our Own,' from a telephone interview with Janet Lunn.

'We Were All Kind of Making It Up as We Went Along,' from an autobiographical sketch by Tim Wynne-Jones.

'The Look of the Word and the Sound of the Illustration,' from correspondence by Frank Newfeld with the authors.

'Alternative to What?' from an interview with Rick Wilks.

'We Wanted to Do Things Differently,' from an interview with Anne Millyard.

'Everyone Would Express an Opinion about a Manuscript,' from a telephone interview with Ian Wallace.

'Canadian Children's Books as Works of Art,' the Tundra Books of Canada / Les Livres Toundra rubric.

'A Very Interesting Primitive,' from a letter by May Cutler to the Canada Council.

'Canadian Children's Literature Needs Serious Scrutiny,' a paraphrase from Mary H. Rubio, 'The History of CCL/LCJ from 1975–2005.'

'Meant to be Enjoyed by Children,' from an editorial, 'To Begin With,' in *Books in Canada*.

'They're Coming in the Windows,' from an interview with Sheila Egoff.

'We Had a Sense That It Was OK to Be a Writer,' from a telephone interview with Sandy Frances Duncan.

'It Was a Kinship Connection,' from a telephone interview with Claire Mackay.

'A Great Feeling of Camaraderie,' from an interview with Ricky Englander.

1 May Cutler, interview.

2 Canada, Department of Industry, Trade and Commerce, *Book Publishing and Manufacturing Industry*, 27.

3 Ibid., 28; Gray, 'Trade Publishing in Canada,' 7.

4 Egoff, 'Writing and Publishing,' 260–2, provides an overview of the economics of Canadian children's publishing in the 1970s. See also Irma McDonough, 'The Outlook for Children's Books,' *Q&Q* 38, no. 10 (1972): 1, 5; Irma McDonough, 'New Support for Children's Literature,' *Q&Q* 42, no. 5 (1976): 14–15; and William French, 'Four Children's Books Provide Optimism for the Industry,' *G&M*, 26 September 1978.

5 Canada, Department of the Secretary of State, Arts and Culture Branch, *Publishing Industry in Canada*, 83–6, table 3.6a, indicates that between 1972 and 1974, 106 children's titles were published by Canadian-controlled English-language publishers, and 58 children's titles by foreign-controlled English-language publishers. The Association of Canadian Publishers, *Children's Book Publishing in Canada*, 2–3, stated that fewer than 100 original English-language children's books had been published each year in the period 1975–7, with an average print run of 5,000 to 7,500 copies. In comparison, between 1975 and 1980, 130 French-language titles in total were published in Quebec for young people. See L'Association pour l'avencement des sciences et des techniques de la documentation, *Les tendances actuelles*, 11.

6 McDonough, 'Modern Canadian,' 7.

7 Frank Newfeld, correspondence.

8 William Toye, 'Publishers Answer.'

9 Paule Daveluy, founder and first president of Communication-Jeunesse, cited in Daveluy and Boulizon, *Création culturelle*, 121–2.

10 William French, 'Alligator Pie Is the Librarians' Choice But Children May Not Agree,' *G&M*, 5 July 1977, notes that the first survey of Canadian children's librarians by the review publication *The World of Children's Books*, to determine the five best Canadian children's books ever written, did not include any 'classics' with the exception of *Anne of Green Gables*.

11 Margaret Tyson, 'Where Are the Books for Canadian Children?' *Q&Q* 37, no. 11 (1971): 8, commented on the scarcity of books for preschool children and the general lack of

information about Canadian books. Tyson's article was based on her presentation to the Ontario Royal Commission on Book Publishing.

12 Lepage, Paule Daveluy, 182, drawing on a presentation by Suzanne Martel and Monique Corriveau, 'La ronde du marché du livre,' at the Rencontre de Communication-Jeunesse in 1972. See Daveluy and Boulizon, *Création culturelle*, 59–67; and Martel, 'Ring-around-a-Roses.'

13 Pelletier, 'Books and Libraries,' 1–2. See also 'Stimulate Writing … Or Big Mistake?' *Q&Q* 38, no. 7 (1972): 2.

14 Parker, 'Sale of Ryerson Press'; MacSkimming, *Perilous Trade*, 147.

15 Order in Council OC-3991/70, cited in Ontario, Royal Commission on Book Publishing, *Canadian Publishers and Canadian Publishing*, [unnumbered pages following title page].

16 Ibid., 76.

17 Ibid., 256–78.

18 MacSkimming, 'Crisis and Renewal,' 16–18.

19 Janet Lunn, telephone interview.

20 Claire Mackay, telephone interview.

21 Janet Lunn, interview.

22 Reynolds, 'Publishing Practices.'

23 See, for example, Speller, 'Frank Newfeld and McClelland and Stewart'; Shaw, 'Rear-View Mirror.'

24 Tim Wynne-Jones, 'An Autobiographical Sketch,' http://www.timwynne-jones.com/pages/autobio.html.

25 Tim Wynne-Jones, email interview, 14 February 2005.

26 Ibid.; Tim Wynne-Jones, 'A Handful of Dates,' http://www.timwynne-jones.com/index.html; Jenkinson, 'Tim Wynne-Jones.'

27 Eugenie Fernandes, interview.

28 Kathryn Cole, interview.

29 Norma Charles, telephone interview.

30 Kathryn Cole, interview. See also Laurie Bildfell, 'Keeping the Wolf From the Door: The Financial Drawbacks of Illustrating Children's Books,' *Q&Q* 50, no. 11 (1984): 8–9.

31 See Ghan, 'Interview with Frank Newfeld.'

32 Vladyana Krykorka, interview.

33 Barbara Reid, interview. See also Reid, 'Colouring the Road': 'Being a beginner, I did much of my work for school textbooks. To my surprise I enjoyed the challenges of making fun, exciting pictures within the strict restrictions imposed by textbooks' (48).

34 Ken Nutt, interview.

35 Ian Wallace, telephone interview.

36 National Center for Education Statistics, *America's Public School Libraries*, for the development of school libraries in the United States.

37 Lewis, *Reading Contemporary Picturebooks*, 62.

38 Shulevitz, *Writing with Pictures*, 214–41, describes the process of preparing overlays in detail.

39 Virginia Davis, interview. The problems of printing and binding were noted by Doug Gibson, book editor at Doubleday, 'It's Hard to Publish Children's Books,' *Q&Q* 38, no. 10 (1972): 'If the contents of an adult book are enthralling it can be shoddily printed in

discoloured paper without the sale being disastrously affected. A children's book, however, has to look attractive and cheap materials don't produce an attractive book. For obvious reasons sturdy binding is often important' (4). See also Dyck, 'Growing Pains': '[T]here are only two printers in Canada who can bind mechanically a 32-page hardback picture book. Such binding is more expensive than comparable foreign binding and is neither equal in quality nor as acceptable to librarians' (20).

40 Dave Jenkinson, interview.

41 Cleaver, 'An Artist's Approach,' documents her research into the visual and cultural components that she incorporated into her work. She drew on her own Hungarian cultural traditions in preparing the illustrations for *The Miraculous Hind*, a story from the Hungarian oral tradition. The work was first produced by the National Film Board as a filmstrip and then turned into a book with the help of William Toye and Irene Aubrey, who translated the text into French.

42 Wilkinson, *Canadian Juvenile Fiction*, 67. See also McDonough, 'Wilkinson Survey.'

43 MacSkimming, *Making Literary History*, discusses Lee's role as editor and co-founder of Anansi. See also Lee, 'Cadence, Country, Silence,' for his views on Canadian nationalism and the influence of George Grant; and MacDonald, 'Lee's *Civil Elegies*.'

44 Charles Taylor, 'A Heavyweight Poet Becomes Children's Troubadour,' *G&M*, 28 September 1974.

45 Margaret Laurence, 'You Can Almost Hear the Skipping Rope Slapping,' *G&M*, 5 October 1974, in a review of *Alligator Pie* and *Nicholas Knock*.

46 Rogers, 'Saurian Saga,' 104, praised Lee for creating a work that could be placed 'on the nursery shelf beside Grimm and Carroll and Milne,' adding that concern over the lack of Canadian poetry for children was significant, because 'children learn by looking in mirrors and hearing the sounds and rhythms of their own world in words. It is not nationalism, but a desire for self-knowledge that creates the need for good Canadian books for children.' See also Demers, 'Dennis Lee's Poetry'; and Parsons, 'Like a Muscle.'

47 Speller, 'Frank Newfeld and McClelland and Stewart,' 24, notes that 'Newfeld's reputation in the trade was that he knew more about reproducing illustrations than any other illustrator in Toronto.' See also Newfeld, 'Book Design and Production'; and Stott, 'The Marriage of Pictures and Text.'

48 Speller, 'Frank Newfeld and McClelland and Stewart,' particularly 6–16.

49 Frank Newfeld, correspondence; Terry Kelly, 'Escape Artist,' *BC* 6, no. 9 (1977): 10; Judith Finlayson, 'Writing Children's Books of Our Own,' *Q&Q* 43, no. 11 (1977): 8, quotes Newfeld as saying 'I don't want to do anything that's too slick, too perfectly complete. I want to start something in the child, not finish it forever,' adding that 'precise illustration inhibits the child and saps his imagination.'

50 Finlayson, 'Writing Children's Books,' 8.

51 Taylor, 'A Heavyweight Poet,' 27.

52 Finlayson, 'Writing Children's Books,' 8.

53 Judy Sarick, interview.

54 Judith Finlayson, 'Canadian Juvenile Publishing Comes of Age,' *Q&Q* 43, no. 11 (1977): 6–7, 9, reported that *Nicholas Knock* and *Alligator Pie* had sold over 90,000 copies in three years.

55 Tim Wynne-Jones, email interview, 5 June 2006.

56 Jenkinson, 'Laszlo Gal.'
57 Cleaver, 'Idea to Image.'
58 Finlayson, 'Canadian Juvenile Publishing,' 7, notes that *The Loon's Necklace* had an initial print run of 10,000 copies.
59 Saltman and Edwards, 'Elizabeth Cleaver,' 46–8; and Elizabeth Cleaver, original art for 'The Loon's Necklace,' box 1985-12-11, Cleaver fonds, Literary Archives, Library and Archives Canada.
60 Cleaver's approach was sharply criticized by Nodelman, 'Non-Native Primitive Art,' who took particular exception to her use of figurative art traditions in the illustration of the oral literature of cultures with a tradition of non-figurative visual forms.
61 Irma McDonough, 'Foreword,' *IR* 8, no. 2 (Spring 1974): 4, for the appointment of Fisher.
62 Beckmann, 'Margaret Atwood'; Ross and Davies, 'Interview with Margaret Atwood'; Stott, 'Conversation with Maria Campbell.'
63 Sakthi Murthy, 'Face to Face,' *Asianadian* 2, no. 2 (Fall 1979), http://faculty.washington.edu/chanant/asianadian/volumes/two/issue2/.
64 Jenkinson, 'Laszlo Gal,' 65, cites Gal as saying that his illustration style was not realistic, but 'more like a theatrical stage where the people are being manipulated.' Van Vliet, 'Profile: Laszlo Gal,' notes that Gal spent two years working on *The Twelve Dancing Princesses*, exhaustively researching Renaissance architecture and costume design before he began to block out the preparatory sketches. See also Gal, 'Illustrating the Text.'
65 Kit Pearson, interview, described the problems resulting from changes to the text from the version of the story in *The Golden Phoenix*, on which Blades had based her illustrations. When the reworked story, created independently of the illustrations, was placed against Blades's work, there were discrepancies between image and text. In 1990, Groundwood Books asked Pearson to create a new text to better match Blades's pictures, which was published as *The Singing Basket*.
66 Egoff, 'Writing and Publishing.'
67 For a brief description of the cultural context of anti-war protest and Canadian publishing, see MacSkimming, *Making Literary History*. For a fuller account, see MacSkimming, *Perilous Trade*, chapter 8, 'Printed in Canada by Mindless Acid Freaks,' 167–98. Mark Witten, 'Bound for Glory,' *BC* 7, no. 2 (1978): 3, provides a helpful overview of what he describes as a 'book-publishing revolution,' publishers dedicated to addressing the failure of the Canadian publishing community to bring Canadian writing to public attention and providing 'alternative channels to the sluggish mainstream of Canadian culture.'
68 Patsy Aldana, interview.
69 Rick Wilks, interview.
70 Dominique Clement, 'Anachronism Failing to Function,' notes that social movement organizations proliferated in the 1960s and 1970s, in part, because of funding from Local Initiatives Program and Opportunities for Youth grants. See also Carstairs, 'Roots Nationalism,' on differing strategies in the promotion of Canadian culture between the 1950s through the 1970s and the 1980s; Edwardson, 'Kicking Uncle Sam,' on the 'new nationalism' and the production and consumption of Canadian culture; and Gault, 'Grooving the Nation,' who argues that identity politics in the period between 1965

and 1980 was shaped by two dominant social movements, Canadian nationalism and second-wave feminism, which in turn shaped the literature of the period.

71 See Clarke, 'CYC, OFY, LIP,' 29; and Blake, 'LIP and Partisanship,' for a discussion of the goals of the grant programs. For a helpful overview of their impact on publishing, see Lorimer, 'Book Publishing in English Canada.'

72 Nancy Naglin, 'Consciousness Raising for Kids,' *Q&Q* 39, no. 12 (1973): 5.

73 'Books by Kids,' *Q&Q* 41, no. 10 (1975): 10. See also Diane Pullan, 'This Is the House That Kids Built,' *Q&Q* 45, no. 2 (1979): 11; Gillian O'Reilly, 'Anne Millyard Retires,' *CBN* 23, no. 3 (1999): 12–13; and Wyatt, 'Publishers in Profile: Annick Press.'

74 Rick Wilks, interview.

75 Anne Millyard, interview.

76 For the importance of collectives for feminist publishers and bookstores, see Onosaka, *Feminist Revolution in Literacy*, 41.

77 Naglin, 'Consciousness Raising,' 5. This overt, didactic intent to raise awareness of sexism was dismissed by Egoff, *Republic of Childhood*, 2nd ed., 2, as an attempt by 'pressure groups such as feminists to propagate or stifle certain kinds of children's books.'

78 Katherine Govier, 'Coach House and Women's Press: Staying Small and Thriving,' *Q&Q* 45, no. 8 (1979): 16. See also Stuewe, 'Rumblings on the Left'; and McDonough, 'Publishers in Profile: Women's Press.'

79 Jenkinson, 'Tim Wynne-Jones,' notes that Wynne-Jones was one of the OFY grant applicants, representing the 'creative side.'

80 Sue Ann Alderson, interviews, 2003 and 2004.

81 Heritage Community Foundation, Alberta's Arts Heritage, 'Tree Frog Press,' *Alberta Online Encyclopedia*, http://www.abheritage.ca/abarts/literary_arts/literary_treefrog.htm.

82 Smiley, 'Publishers in Profile: Kids Can Press,' notes that Frieda Forman, Coordinator of the Women's Research and Resource Centre at the Ontario Institute for Studies in Education, was the instigator of the collective.

83 Naglin, 'Consciousness Raising,' 5. Smiley, 'Publishers in Profile: Kids Can,' 20–1, notes that other funding was provided by Local Initiative Program grants and support from The Canada Council, the Ontario Arts Council, and the Federal Government Multilingual Program.

84 Ian Wallace, telephone interview.

85 William Rueter, 'The Grand Designs Behind the Look of the Book,' *Q&Q* 51, no. 4 (1985): 48, notes the effect of private press and small literary press design on trade book development. There seems to have been little overlap, however, between the handpress and design community and the new children's presses.

86 Ian Wallace, telephone interview.

87 McLean, 'Bookmaking by Grants,' 10. The assessment of the Kids Can titles by Catherine Benko in the same article was somewhat more positive but argued that 'the illustrations are stiff and add nothing to enhance the themes of the stories.' Professional reviewing journals remained unconvinced that titles issued by the small feminist and alternative presses met the 'high literary standards' that would merit including them in library collections. See Abernethy and Kubjas, 'Look at Non-Sexist'; and Yaffe, 'Another Look,' who responded with a sharp criticism of the 'gold seal committee of the High Literary Standards Association.'

88 Janet Lunn, telephone interview.

89 Virginia Davis, interview.

90 Jeffrey Canton, interview.

91 Ian Wallace, telephone interview.

92 Ian Wallace, interview.

93 Smiley, 'Publishers in Profile: Breakwater Books.'

94 Thompson, 'Topophilia.'

95 Margie McMillan, interview.

96 For regional presses in Alberta, Saskatchewan and Manitoba, see Lorne Daniel, 'Prairie Publishing.'

97 Zola, 'Publishers in Profile: Douglas and McIntyre.'

98 MacSkimming, *Perilous Trade*, 224–9.

99 Betty Waterton, telephone interview.

100 Ann Blades, interview.

101 Adrian Waller, 'The Quest for the Best,' *Q&Q* 40, no. 11 (1974): 17–18.

102 May Cutler, interview. Harder was born in Germany and studied at the Hamburg Academy of Fine Arts. In 1959, he opened Rolf Harder Design in Montreal, followed by a graphic design firm, Design Collaborative with three other partners, which published *Pitseolak: Pictures Out of My Life* (1971). Harder also worked as a contract designer for McClelland and Stewart and Clarke, Irwin, as well as Tundra, designing *A Child in Prison Camp, Mary of Mile 18*, and *Thomasina and the Trout Tree* for Tundra. In 1972, with Ernst Roch, he founded Signum Press, which published Anna Smodlibowska's *The Farmer's Year* (1973) and Roch's *Paper Zoo* (1974), among other titles. See Sarah E. McCutcheon, 'Emphasis Is on Design,' *Q&Q* 40, no. 1 (1974): 8.

103 May Cutler, interview.

104 May Cutler, 'Ah, Publishing!' 220, provides a tantalizing glimpse of a project offered to her by Gilles Vigneault, John Glassco, and Elizabeth Cleaver, in which Cleaver would illustrate a Vigneault lullaby, with an English translation of the text by Glassco. As Tundra did not offer advances to authors or illustrators, Cleaver applied to the Canada Council for a small grant to help in the preparation of the illustrations. The Council turned her down, effectively ending the collaboration before it had begun.

105 May Cutler, 'Tundra Books,' [letter to the editor], *G&M*, 22 September 1977.

106 May Cutler, interview: 'In those early years, I took my own stand and stayed away from the Canadian stand, which I didn't want to be associated with. As Canadian books got better in the late 80s and 90s, Tundra joined the Canadian stands. But I never geared my publishing in any way to an international market just as I never did marketing studies of any kind. If I had, many Tundra books would never have been published.' See also Fiona Mee, 'Canadian Publishers Stepping Out,' *Q&Q* 42, no. 7 (1976): 2.

107 For Cutler's correspondence with foreign publishers, see McGill University Library, Special Collections, Tundra Collection, box 2, file 2, May Cutler and Ann Blades correspondence, and box 2, file 5, Promo and Publicity Correspondence, 'Boy of Tache' and 'Mary of Mile 18,' which includes correspondence between Cutler and publishers in the United States, England, Sweden, Germany, Switzerland, Japan, Denmark, Norway, Austria, Hungary, Russia, Yugoslavia, and Czechoslovakia regarding Tundra picturebook titles. Annabel Slaight, 'Art for Children's Books: Is It Good Enough?'

Q&Q 39, no. 10 (1973): 5, notes that Cutler had sold the film and radio dramatization rights for Takashima's *A Child in Prison Camp*, as well as syndication rights in daily newspapers in Canada and Japanese translation rights, and was negotiating with Morrow for a U.S. edition.

108 Finlayson, 'Canadian Juvenile Publishing,' 7, notes that the Norwegian Book Club signed an agreement to print 70,000 copies of the two Kurelek titles, and Cutler expected that co-publication agreements with Sweden, Denmark, France, and Germany could boost the initial print run to 100,000 copies.

109 May Cutler, interview.

110 Maruszeczka, 'Publishing Picture Books,' 43.

111 Beverley Mitchell, 'We Don't Need More Books, We Need More Good Books,' *Montreal Scene*, 6 March 1976.

112 Carpenter, 'William Kurelek'; Morley, 'Good Life, Prairie Style'; and Sybesma-Ironside, 'Through a Glass Darkly.' While Cutler complained that the Prairie Boy books were 'money losers,' a decade after publication, *A Prairie Boy's Winter* had sold 300,000 copies. May Cutler, 'Tundra Books,' [letter to the editor], *G&M*, 22 September 1977; and Matthew Fraser, 'May Cutler Is One for the Book,' *G&M*, 14 January 1988.

113 Sybesma-Ironside, 'Through a Glass Darkly.'

114 Jones and Stott, 'William Kurelek,' in *Canadian Children's Books*, 238–9.

115 Carpenter, 'William Kurelek,' 261; and information printed on the verso of the title page in the 1982 fourth printing of the Canadian edition.

116 Correspondence between May Cutler and Shizuye Takashima, file 2, box 5, Tundra Collection.

117 Kay Kirtzwiser, 'Colorful Recall in an Artist's Book,' *G&M*, 11 September 1971.

118 Ann Blades, interview; Davies, 'Conversation with Ann Blades,' 21–2.

119 'Best Children's Book,' *Q&Q* 38 (July 1972): 2, indicates that it would have cost Cutler in the range of $10,000 to publish the book with all twenty of the illustrations. Eighteen months after being turned down by the Canada Council, she had raised $2,000 for the colour separations and convinced the printer to extend her credit to cover the rest of the cost.

120 Letter from May Cutler to Naim Kattan, Canada Council, 5 March 1970, file 8, box 1, Tundra Books Collection.

121 May Cutler, 'Ah, Publishing!' 213; the comment is also quoted in Maruszeczka, 'Publishing Picture Books,' 43.

122 William French, 'Alligator Pie Is the Librarians' Choice but Children May Not Agree,' *G&M*, 5 July 1977, which briefly noted Cutler's 'personal boycott of the Council – an unprecedented move for a publisher,' instigated a series of angry exchanges between Cutler and Mario Lavoie, the Canada Council's Chief of Information Services, conducted in the Letters to the Editor section of the *G&M*. See Mario Lavoie, 'Tundra Books,' *G&M*, 4 August 1977; May Cutler, 'Tundra Books,' *G&M*, 22 August 1977, in which she explained her boycott was a protest against the need to submit manuscripts as a condition for receiving a grant before the block grant process was instituted; Beryl Rowland, 'Book Publishers,' *G&M*, 26 August 1977; Mario Lavoie, 'Tundra Books,' *G&M*, 8 September 1977; May Cutler, 'Tundra Books,' *G&M*, 19 September 1977; and May Cutler, 'Tundra Books,' *G&M*, 22 September 1977.

123 William French, 'Tundra Back in the Book Wars,' *G&M*, 21 July 1981, notes that in

1980, Tundra suspended publication for a year in order to restructure in the face of inflation and high interest rates. However, French notes that Cutler had also announced that her decision to cease to publish children's books was a consequence of the cost of production, which was not covered by Canada Council grants. See also May Cutler, 'Book Publishing,' [letter to the editor], *G&M*, 19 March 1979; May Cutler, 'Publisher Insists Cuts Made,' [letter to the editor], *G&M*, 7 April 1979; and 'Tundra Drops Children's Books,' *G&M*, 5 December 1979.

124 Davies, 'Conversation with Ann Blades,' 24.
125 Wilkinson, *Canadian Juvenile Fiction*, and Toronto Board of Education, *Canadian Books*. Other studies include Hurtig, *Never Heard of Them …*; Haycock, *Canadian Learning Resources*; Hodgetts, *What Culture?*; Robinson, *Where Our Survival Lies*; Hambleton and Jobe, 'Teacher Awareness'; Stuart-Stubbs, *Canadian Books*; and Halpenny, *Canadian Collections in Public Libraries*.
126 Wilkinson, *Canadian Juvenile Fiction*, 76–7, includes a list of titles ordered by an elementary school, March 1974. The three Canadian titles on the list of twenty-eight titles were being ordered in their American editions: James Houston, *Ghost Paddle* (Harcourt Brace 1972), William Kurelek, *A Prairie Boy's Winter* (Houghton Mifflin 1973), and Shizuye Takashima, *A Child in Prison Camp* (Morrow 1974).
127 *CM* was later renamed in 1980 and expanded its mandate to include the reviewing needs of public librarians. In 1994 it was sold to the Manitoba Library Association and is now published weekly as an electronic journal under the title *CM: Canadian Review of Materials*. See 'A View of Our Past: CM Turns 20 with a Retrospective on Kids' Books,' *CM* 19, no. 6 (1991), http://www.umanitoba.ca/outreach/cm/cmarchive/vol19no6/aviewofourpast.html.
128 Haycock and Haycock, 'Introduction' in *Kids and Libraries*, 11.
129 Ibid.
130 Mary Henley Rubio, 'The History of CCL/LCJ from 1975–2005,' http://ccl.freeculture.ca/index.php/ccl-lcj/about/editorialPolicies#custom0.
131 Elizabeth Waterston, email interview.
132 Mary Rubio, email interview. Other early critics, while noting that it was 'difficult to footnote non-existent materials,' found the critical approach lacking in rigour and encouraged the journal to develop 'philosophical musings as well as analytical pieces' on children's literature genres. See Broderick, review of *CCL*.
133 Egoff, *Once Upon a Time*, 82.
134 McDonough, review of *The Republic of Childhood*, 2nd ed., 15.
135 Val Clery, 'Editorial,' *BC*, introductory edition [1, no. 1] (May 1971): 5.
136 'To Begin With,' *BC*, 1, no. 4 (November 1971): 16–17.
137 'To Begin With,' *BC* 1, no. 5 (December 1971): 22. The approach, however, was appreciated by some readers at the time. See Jim Saunders, 'By Their Dawn's Early Light,' *BC* 1, no. 8 (February 1972): 4–5, who argued that the preponderance of American and British picturebooks in school libraries led children to be impressed by 'a Star Spangled Union Jack' and to yearn avidly for experiences 'involving congressional castles.'
138 See also Williams, 'Profile: Janet Lunn.'
139 Michele Landsberg, interview.
140 Ibid.
141 Phillips, *Illustration of Books*, 6, 10.

142 National Library of Canada, *Annual Report of the National Librarian 1973/74*, 8.
143 'Brief Submitted in May to the Canadian Association of Children's Librarians on the Need for a Children's Librarian/Consultant in the National Library,' 1970, and Canadian Library Association and L'Association Canadienne des Bibliothécaires de Langue Française, 'Brief to the Secretary of State on a Need for a Children's Librarian/Consultant in the National Library,' Ottawa, 1 March 1973, Canadian Library Association archives. See also National Library of Canada, *Annual Report of the National Librarian 1975/76*, 30; and Aubrey, 'Children's Services.' According to Egoff, 'National Treasure,' 45, the idea of a children's literature consultant was first proposed in 1969 by Elinor Kelly, Chair of the Canadian Association of Children's Librarians.
144 Egoff, 'National Treasure,' 45, notes that W. Kaye Lamb, the first National Librarian, found the idea of a children's collection within a National Library dedicated to 'essential and scholarly work' puzzling. See also Egoff, *Once Upon a Time*, 51, in which she comments that Lamb had asked her, 'What does the National Library have to do with children's books?'
145 Aubrey, 'National Library of Canada'; and Polidori, 'Irene Aubrey.' Irene Aubrey, telephone interview, remembers that when she first arrived at the National Library to take up the position, 'there was no welcoming committee, no office, no chair, no budget for salary or service. Management hoped I would go away. I was told that I would last a couple of months ... I stayed eighteen years. I had a fierce determination. It was a lot of hard work.'
146 Aubrey, 'Children's Services,' 13–14. The identification of children's materials within the National Library was first reported in 1977. See National Library of Canada, *Annual Report of the National Librarian 1976/77*, 35–6. By 1979, the consolidation of the collections was completed and researchers were able to consult the material. See National Library of Canada, *Annual Report of the National Librarian 1978/79*, 19.
147 The National Library received hundreds of requests for *Notable Canadian Children's Books* in its first year of publication. See National Library of Canada, *Annual Report of the National Librarian 1977/78*, 36. In 1990 the Library began publication of *Read Up On It / Lisez sur le sujet*, an annual thematic subject kit, with bibliographies, bookmarks, poster, and activities information. *Notable Canadian Children's Books* was discontinued in 1993.
148 National Library of Canada, *Annual Report of the National Librarian 1978/79*, 19. See also Aubrey, *Pictures to Share*, the annotated catalogue prepared to accompany the exhibition.
149 'IBBY-Canada 20th Anniversary Retrospective,' *IBBY Canada Newsletter* 20, no. 1 (2000): 10. In 1973, the Canadian Association of Children's Librarians voted to support a Canadian section of IBBY at a time when it appeared that the Canadian Library Association could no longer coordinate the affiliation with the international organization. Aubrey, Irma McDonough Milnes, and Ruth Osler formed the committee to draft the goals and objectives of IBBY Canada.
150 Sheila Egoff, interview.
151 Sheila Egoff, 'Introduction,' in *One Ocean Touching*, viii.
152 Clark, *Kiddie Lit*, traces the exclusion of children's literature from serious consideration by influential American writers and critics like Henry James, and its reclamation

by feminist scholars, beginning in the late 1970s. See also Paul, 'Enigma Variations';
Gerson, 'Canon between the Wars'; Thacker, 'Disdain or Ignorance?'; Lundin, *Constructing the Canon*; and Nodelman, 'Preface.'

153 Lefebvre, 'Editorial,' 6, notes that Elizabeth Waterston's essay, 'Lucy Maud Montgomery, 1874–1942,' was the first scholarly assessment of Montgomery. Lefebvre also
notes that some Montgomery scholars still claim her work as serious literature by
devaluing her as a writer for children. See also Gerson, 'Anne of Green Gables'; and
Mary Henley Rubio and Elizabeth Hillman Waterston, 'Introduction,' in Montgomery,
Selected Journals of L.M. Montgomery, xvii–xviii, for a discussion of the distinction
between high culture and popular culture promoted by the influential critic William
A. Deacon.

154 Kealy, 'Ever-Present Inspiration.'

155 Sue Ann Alderson, interview, 2003.

156 'About VCLR,' The Vancouver Children's Literature Roundtable, http://www
.library.ubc.ca/edlib/table/history/history.htm. See also Jobe, 'West Coast Children's
Literature Roundtable.'

157 Judy Sarick, interview.

158 Ibid.

159 Ibid.

160 Ibid.

161 Ian Wallace, telephone interview.

162 Patsy Aldana, interview.

163 Judy Sarick, interview.

164 Celia Lottridge, interview.

165 Irma McDonough, 'The Outlook for Children's Books,' *Q&Q* 38 (October 1972): 1, 5,
described a proposed mandate for a Centre for Canadian Children's Books as promotion, documentation, research, coordination of needs and responses, and contact with
related centres, drawn from the brief presented to the Ontario Royal Commission
on Publishing; McDonough, 'Professional Reading,' included another version of the
prospectus. 'Canadian Books for Children Project,' *IR* 10, no. 3 (Summer 1976): 27
announced the project 'to focus public and professional attention on Canadian books
for children.' For the history of the Centre, see O'Reilly, '"Everything Was Possible":
Looking Back as the Centre Turns 25.' *CBN* 24, no. 3 (2001): 5–7. The Centre's French
Canadian counterpart, Communication-Jeunesse, had been founded in 1971. See
Virginia Davis, 'Children's Book Centre'; and Lepage, *Paule Daveluy*, 182–95.

166 Yaffe, 'Children's Book Centre,' 5.

167 Finlayson, 'Canadian Juvenile Publishing,' 7, notes that the Canada Council provided
a $60,000 grant to the Centre.

168 Library and Archives Canada, Literary Archives, 'Young Canada's Book Week Fonds,'
LMS-1099, description at http://www.collectionscanada.ca/literaryarchives/
027011-200.147-e.html; and Library and Archives Canada, Canadian Library Association fonds, vol. 15, Young Canada Book Week. See also 'Values in Children's Literature,' *Q&Q* 39, no. 7 (1973): 8, in which Adele Ashby of the Brampton Public Library
is quoted as saying 'it is incredible that we are running a national celebration in a
purely amateurish way. Either YCBW should be handled by a professional publicist
or it should be dropped.' Ashby added that 'Council is looking into the feasibility of
changing the emphasis to a national celebration of the book.'

169 For an account of the first year's activities, including the 1977 Book Week, see Yaffe, 'Children's Book Centre.' See also William French, 'It's Great Timing for a Kid's Book Week,' *G&M*, 15 November 1977.
170 Ian Wallace, telephone interview.
171 Sandy Frances Duncan, telephone interview.
172 *Children's Book News* (1978–2002), renamed *Canadian Children's Book News* (2002–present); *Our Choice* (1977–2008), and renamed *Best Books for Kids and Teens* in 2008. *Meet the Author Kit*, nos 1–4 (Toronto: Children's Book Centre, [1979–1983]), included biographical information, a bibliography, and a poster-sized photograph of each of the six profiled authors. Subsequent kits, published by Mead School Services in Toronto, included a filmstrip and a sound cassette, packaged with a teacher's guide, or in later years, a videocassette and teacher's guide.
173 Gillian O'Reilly, email interview.
174 Jean Little, telephone interview.
175 Janet Lunn, telephone interview.
176 Sandy Frances Duncan, telephone interview.
177 Sue Ann Alderson, interview, 2004.
178 Norma Charles, telephone interview.
179 Claire Mackay, telephone interview.
180 Janet Lunn, telephone interview.
181 Claire Mackay, telephone interview. See also 'What Is CANSCAIP'S History?' CANSCAIP website, http://www.canscaip.org/faq.html.
182 'Join Us,' CANSCAIP website, http://www.canscaip.org/joining.html.
183 Janet Lunn, telephone interview.
184 Ian Wallace, telephone interview.
185 Claire Mackay, telephone interview.
186 Ann Blades, telephone interview.
187 Jean Little, telephone interview.
188 Eugenie Fernandes, interview.
189 Norma Charles, telephone interview.
190 Claire Mackay, telephone interview.
191 Rick Wilks, interview.
192 Patsy Aldana, interview.
193 Ricky Englander, interview.

6: The 1980s: The Flowering of Canadian Children's Illustrated Books

Sources of quotations used in headings:
'A Strong Sense of Excellence,' from an interview with Ricky Englander.
'Freedom for Creation,' from an interview with Patsy Aldana.
'Children Should Connect to the People Who Created the Book,' from an interview with Anne Millyard.
'Self-Recognition Is the Main Reason for Localizing a Book,' from an interview with May Cutler.
'We Wanted Our Books to Be Child Friendly,' from an interview with Ricky Englander.
'There's Always Someone Doing Something in the Background,' from an interview by Susan Gaitskell with Barbara Reid.

'The Feeling of Offering Quality,' from an interview with Kathryn Cole.

'Words Dancing on the Page,' from an interview with Marie-Louise Gay.

'A Good Supply of Kleenex Tissues Will Be Needed,' from a review by André Gagnon of *Love You Forever*.

'Really the Only Way Is to Try It Out on Kids,' from an interview with Greg Young-Ing.

'Gender-Positive, Non-Violent Books,' from an interview with Margie Wolfe.

'A Bossy Woman Trying to Tell People What to Read,' from an interview with Michele Landsberg.

'It Truly Was a Heyday,' from an interview with Michele Landsberg.

 1 Tim Wynne-Jones, email interview, 5 June 2006.
 2 Valerie Hussey, interview.
 3 Ricky Englander, interview.
 4 Saltman and Edwards, 'Towards a History of Design,' 34. See also Wyatt, 'Publishers in Profile: PMA Books.'
 5 Robert MacDonald, 'A Designer's Dilemma,' *Q&Q* 48, no. 11 (1982): 5–6.
 6 Michael Solomon, correspondence; William R. Forbes, 'Over There: Publishers Weigh Offshore Printing Savings against Canadian Convenience,' *Q&Q* 56, no. 11 (1990): 16, 18, notes that publishers saw an average 30 per cent reduction in costs by sending printing, colour separation work, and binding work to printers in Asia. See also Feather, *History of British Publishing*, 212–15, for the impact of offset lithography on book design.
 7 Doreen Carvajal, 'Boing! Pop-Up Books Are Growing Up; Flaps, Foldouts and Complexities Attract Adult Eyes,' *New York Times*, 27 November 2000, describes the process as a 'cottage industry' in which movable books are 'painstakingly printed and cut in Cali Colombia, and assembled and glued by dozens of Andean piece workers in Ibarra, Ecuador.'
 8 Saltman and Edwards, 'Towards a History of Design,' 34–5.
 9 Gillespie, 'Books and Cultural Sovereignty.'
10 Association of Canadian Publishers, *Children's Book Publishing*, 8.
11 Jobe, 'International Children's Book Industry,' 9–10. Wilks, 'Economics of Canadian Children's Book Publishing,' provides a sample cost analysis for a full-colour picture-book, printed in a run of 5,000 copies, at a retail price of $10.95. Wilks concludes that a publisher would incur a loss of $1.36 for each copy sold. He adds that a first run of 15,000 copies would be necessary to achieve full cost recovery.
12 Irma McDonough, 'New Support for Children's Literature,' *Q&Q* 42 (May 1976): 14–15.
13 Association of Canadian Publishers, *Children's Book Publishing*, 10, notes that 'no publisher outside of Canada will participate in a co-edition at the unit costs which are quoted by Canadian printers. This may mean that in order to arrange a co-edition it is necessary for a Canadian publisher to print a book outside of Canada'; Dyck, 'Growing Pains,' 20.
14 Ted Harrison, interview, remembers that he and Cutler had 'great adventures' at Bologna, adding that he found her 'a woman of rare character' and an icebreaker who 'sailed through the ice and got people to do things, even politicians.'
15 See comments by Rick Wilks of Annick Press, in Carolyn Dodds, 'A Child's Garden of Publishers: Canadian Kid Lit Comes of Age,' *Financial Post Magazine* (1 August 1984), 29–35.

16 Frieda Wishinsky, 'A New Era in Canadian Children's Books,' *PW* 231, no. 11 (20 March 1987): 36, notes that forty-seven Canadian publishers exhibited at Bologna.

17 Leonard S. Marcus, 'Mother Goose to Multiculturalism,' *PW* 244, no. 31 (1997): 62–70.

18 Fiona Mee, 'Canadian Publishers Stepping Out,' *Q&Q* 42, no. 7 (1976): 1–3. MacDonald, 'A Designer's Dilemma,' 5–6, also discussed the idea of international co-production and co-editions. May Cutler, interview, noted that some European publishers wanted 'illustrated books that had no specifically recognizable locale, so they could be sold (with other languages stripped in) anywhere in Europe,' what Cutler called 'the common denominator factor.'

19 Patsy Aldana, [Preface], Groundwood Books catalogue, Fall 2003, 1.

20 Patsy Aldana, interview.

21 Joyce Wayne, 'Building Groundwood from the Ground Up,' *Q&Q* 47, no. 7 (1981): 36.

22 The uncredited designer for the first list was Michael Solomon. See Solomon, 'Publishing Children's Picture Books,' 194.

23 William French, 'Four Children's Books Provide Optimism for the Industry,' *G&M*, 26 September 1978, noted that Douglas and McIntyre and Groundwood, 'a new Toronto company founded specifically to publish children's books,' had 'pooled their production and marketing resources and worked with Hunter Rose Ltd, the Toronto printing company, to get highest quality for lowest cost' on four books by Canadian authors and illustrators.

24 Wayne, 'Building Groundwood from the Ground Up,' 36.

25 Ibid.; Sandra Martin, 'Telling Rewards of Nationalism,' *G&M*, 20 April 1985.

26 Martin, 'Telling Rewards of Nationalism.'

27 Patsy Aldana, interview.

28 Shelley Tanaka, email interview.

29 Patsy Aldana, interview. Margo Beggs, 'Book Making,' *Q&Q* 60, no. 10 (1994): 1, traces the collaboration between Aldana, Solomon, and illustrator Harvey Chan in the creation of a picturebook.

30 Michael Solomon, correspondence.

31 Michael Solomon, correspondence. See also Margo Beggs, 'Solomon's Judgement Forms Deft Design,' *Q&Q* 55, no. 3 (1990): 19; and Solomon, 'Publishing Children's Picture Books,' 191–200.

32 Tim Wynne-Jones, interview; and Wynne-Jones, 'Adult Writing for Children,' 101–3.

33 Ken Nutt, interview; Jenkinson, 'Eric Beddows,' 68.

34 Ken Nutt, interview.

35 Ian Wallace, interview; Stott, 'Profile: Ian Wallace.'

36 Ian Wallace, interview.

37 Ian Wallace, telephone interview. Sandra Martin, 'Dancing the Tail of the Dragon,' *G&M*, 4 August 1984, notes that *Chin Chiang* was also co-published by Methuen Children's Books of the UK, which she credited as accounting 'for its firesale price. A hardcover, full-color children's book for $10.95 is virtually unknown in this country.' While Frank Newfeld's *The Princess of Tomboso* (Toronto: Oxford University Press, 1960) appears to have been the first Canadian children's book co-published with a British publisher, the editing was done entirely by William Toye in Canada.

38 Ian Wallace, interview; Elizabeth MacCallum, 'Following the Twisted Trial of a Book Unfairly Maligned,' *G&M*, 13 July 1991, discusses the title and self-censorship in public

schools as a result of concerns about the book in Toronto schools in 1991. See also Bennett, 'Top Shelf: Censorship,' 24–5; and Edwards and Saltman, 'Looking at Ourselves.'

39 Ian Wallace, interview.

40 Ken Nutt, interview.

41 Ibid.

42 Janet Lunn, interview.

43 Ibid.

44 Kim LaFave, interview.

45 Paul Yee, interview.

46 Ibid.

47 Ibid.

48 Anne Millyard, interview.

49 Ibid.

50 Rick Wilks, interview.

51 Anne Millyard, interview.

52 Ibid.

53 Ibid.

54 Rick Wilks, email interview. The first series (1981) included *The Paper Bag Princess*, *Jonathan Cleaned Up*, and *Mud Puddle*. The second series (1982) consisted of Blair Drawson, *The Special Birthday Book* (a new edition of *Do Something Special on Your Birthday*, published by Gage in 1977), Wendy St Pierre, *Henry Finds a Home*, ill. by Barbara Eidlitz (originally published by Annick under their Books By Kids imprint, 1980), and Janosch *The Mole and the Cricket* (a translation of *Die Grille und der Maulwurf*, published by Beltz and Gelberg in 1979). The third series (1983), all original Munsch titles appearing for the first time in the Annikin format, included *Mortimer*, *Fire Station*, and *Angela's Airplane*.

55 Anne Millyard, interview.

56 'Publisher of the Year,' *CB* 6, no. 5 (1984): 16.

57 Jenkinson, 'Good Libraries Don't,' 52–4.

58 Rick Wilks, interview; Montpetit, 'Book Banning,' 10–11.

59 Rick Wilks, interview.

60 Stinson, 'From Kathy Stinson,' 136.

61 Jenkinson, 'Good Libraries Don't,' 43–4; Rick Wilks, interview.

62 See chapters 8 and 9, for other instances of the censoring of text and images.

63 May Cutler, interview; and May Ebbitt Cutler, 'Some Background Information on Tundra Books, prepared for McGill University Rare Books Collection, November 1997,' 9–10 (private collection), in which she strenuously opposed the Canadian nationalism espoused by George Grant in *Lament for a Nation* (Toronto: McClelland and Stewart, 1965), as 'waspy, smug, Niagara peninsula insularism.' See also Matthew Fraser, 'May Cutler Is One for the Book,' *G&M*, 14 January 1988.

64 Harrison, 'Images of the North'; Ted Harrison biography at http://www.tedharrison .ca/about.html; and Ross, 'A Pint of Mild and Bitter.'

65 Ted Harrison, interview.

66 Ibid.

67 Ibid.

68 Paul, 'The Lay of the Land.'

69 Hébert, 'Roch Carrier au Canada anglais'; Hayward and Lamontagne, 'Le Canada anglais,' discuss the reception of Carrier among anglophone readers.

70 Roch Carrier, speech. See also Tarasoff, 'Roch Carrier and "The Hockey Sweater."'

71 Roch Carrier, speech. See also Canadian Broadcasting Corporation, CBC Archives, 'The Hockey Sweater,' http://archives.cbc.ca/IDC-1-41-1546-10372/sports/ spirit_of_hockey/clip1 for a sound file of a 1984 broadcast of Carrier reading his story on Peter Gzowski's radio program, *Morningside*.

72 Roch Carrier, speech.

73 May Cutler, interview.

74 Lyons, 'Dayal Kaur Khalsa'; Cutler, 'Dayal Kaur Khalsa.'

75 Sybesma, 'Illustrated Children's Books as Art.'

76 May Cutler, email interview.

77 Edwards, 'Dayal Kaur Khalsa.' In *Tales of a Gambling Grandma*, Paul Cézanne's *The Card Players* hangs over the dining room table where Grandma teaches May to play cards, while Grandma's bedroom draws direct inspiration from Van Gogh's *Vincent's Bedroom at Arles*. In *I Want a Dog* (1987), the cover is a parody of George Seurat's *Un dimanche après-midi à l'Île de la Grand Jatte*, the living room includes Edward Hopper's *Early Sunday Morning*, while Van Gogh's *The Bridge at Arles*, Gilbert Stuart's *Portrait of George Washington*, and Kasushika Huokusai's *The Great Wave off Kanagawa* appear on the panelled walls of the basement.

78 MacSimming, *Perilous Trade*, 292–3.

79 Ricky Englander, interview.

80 Ibid.

81 Ibid.

82 Valerie Hussey, interview.

83 Ibid.

84 Beggs, 'Solomon's Judgement Forms Deft Design,' 19, quotes Valerie Wyatt, who credits Michael Solomon with 'launching the whole Kids Can non-fiction list' with his design for *Scienceworks*.

85 Ricky Englander, quoted in Isabel Vincent, 'Small Fry Mean Big Sales for Kids' Publisher,' *G&M*, 6 March 1990, A17. By 1990, 60,000 copies were in print in Canadian and foreign editions.

86 Maryann Kovalski, 'Kids Can Press: Publisher of the Year,' *CB* 11, no. 5 (1989): 30, describes her first meeting with Hussey and Englander. See also Jenkinson, 'Maryann Kovalski.'

87 Jones and Stott, *Canadian Children's Books*, 73. However, Brenda Yamakami, 'Little Fingerling: An Analysis of a Picture Book Illustration' (paper for LIBR 522E, Children's Illustrated Books, School of Library, Archival and Information Studies, University of British Columbia, December 2006), comments on the multiple inaccuracies in the depiction of Japanese norms of behaviour.

88 Honda, 'Multiculturalism and Canadian Picture Books.'

89 Kady MacDonald Denton, email interview; Jenkinson, 'Kady MacDonald Denton'; Annette Goldsmith, 'Denton's Dictum: Paint Like a Child,' *Q&Q* 55, no. 2 (1990): 13.

90 Jenkinson, 'Paulette Bourgeois'; Wilde, 'Franklin.'

91 Ricky Englander, interview.

92 Isabel Vincent, 'Small Fry Mean Big Sales for Kids' Publisher,' *G&M*, 6 March 1990.

Isabel Vincent, 'The Fight for a Truly National Literature,' *G&M*, 8 July 1991, quotes Valerie Hussey as saying that 'ninety-eight per cent of publishing is about business,' adding that the marketability of a text is everything.

93 Valerie Hussey, interview.

94 Andrew H. Malcolm, 'The Media Business: Publisher for Children, A Canada Success Story,' *New York Times*, 3 April 1990.

95 Kathryn Cole, interview.

96 Gaitskell, 'An Interview with Barbara Reid,' 8–9.

97 Ibid., 11–12.

98 MacPhee, 'Kathryn Cole.'

99 Kathryn Cole, interview.

100 Laszlo Gal, original art for 'Hans Christian Andersen's The Little Mermaid,' box 1986-3-2-14; box 1986-3-2-3, Gal fonds, Literary Archives, Library and Archives Canada.

101 For the development of Stoddart, see MacSkimming, *Perilous Trade*, 348–9.

102 Marie-Louise Gay, interview; Marie-Louise Gay, 'Marie-Louise Gay,' *Q&Q* 51, no. 10 (1985): 6.

103 Sandra Martin, 'Inventive Illustrator Works Magic with a Rainy Day,' *G&M*, 4 July 1987; Mary Collis, 'Art of Illustration.'

104 Marie-Louise Gay, interview; Davis, 'Un penchant pour la diagonale.'

105 The first six titles in the series published by Stoddart included titles on arms and armour, birds, ponds and rivers, rocks and minerals, skeletons, sports, and trees.

106 Wyatt, 'Publishers in Profile: Greey de Pencier Books,' 12.

107 As one reviewer astutely noted, the format of Somerville's *Bug Book* was designed for the retail market. Libraries found it difficult to catalogue and shelve the plastic bug catcher. See Winham, '1987 Notable Canadian Non-Fiction for Children.'

108 MacSkimming, *Perilous Trade*, 283–6.

109 'Love You Forever,' Official Robert Munsch Website, www.robertmunsch.com/books .cfm?bookid=40.

110 Liam Lacey, 'The World According to Munsch,' *G&M*, 24 January 1987, E01.

111 Sheila McGraw, 'The Interview: Sheila McGraw Talks About Love You Forever,' Loch Gallery, http://www.lochgallery.com/content/view/67/50/.

112 Richmond, 'Children and Death'; André Gagnon, 'Review of "Love You Forever,"' *CM* 15, no. 2 (1987), http://umanitoba.ca/cm/cmarchive/vl15no2/loveyouforever .html.

113 Lacey, 'World According to Munsch.'

114 Rollin and West, *Psychoanalytic Responses to Children's Literature*, 108; Fraustino, 'Apple of Her Eye,' 66.

115 English, 'Children's Literature for Adults,' 18.

116 Jane Yolen, 'The Alphabetics of Story,' speech given at the Society of Children's Book Writers and Illustrators, New York, 2000, http://www.janeyolen.com/auxiliary/ scbwi2000.html.

117 Hurley, 'Affective Stylistics and Children's Literature,' discusses the complex critical response to the book. See also Nodelman, 'Illustrators of Munsch.'

118 *Children's Choices of Canadian Books* 6, no. 1 (1988): 41.

119 Michael Valpy, 'Fathers Fare Poorly in Children's Books,' *G&M*, 11 October 1989, A8.

120 Garrett, 'Guilty as Accused,' 26.

121 An extended discussion of the title on the Child_Lit listserv is archived at http://www.fairrosa.info/disc/loveyouforever.html.
122 Of the more than 1,100 reviews posted to amazon.ca and amazon.com, almost 70 per cent rated the title as 'five star,' the highest rating, while 20 per cent rated the title as 'one star,' the lowest rating. Reviews posted to chapters.indigo.ca and barnesandnoble.com show a similar pattern, although the positive and negative reviews are not quantified on the website. Ninety-two per cent of reviewers on amazon.co.uk gave it a five-star rating. Reviewers on the German amazon.de site rated the German translation highly, while the Munsch/McGraw edition was split (120 reviews, 84 per cent 5 star, 8 per cent 1 star).
123 http://sheilamcgrawfineart.com/giclees.htm.
124 Sipe, 'Picturebooks as Aesthetic Objects,' 31, suggests that style and subject are mismatched, the naturalistic illustrations not adding to the meaning of the text, which he describes as a 'dream-like reverie.' Rollin and West, *Psychoanalytic Responses*, 107, argue that the text, which resembles 'an orally-transmitted folktale,' would be more effective without the illustrations.
125 Firefly Books advertisement, *Q&Q* 67, no. 5 (2001), back cover; *PW* 253, no. 17 (24 April 2006): 8; *PW* 255, no. 12 (24 March 2008): 41.
126 'Teacher's Top 100 Books for Children,' National Education Association, www.nea.org/grants/13154.htm. It also appeared on the 1999 list and was chosen one of the 'Top 50 Kids Books Ever,' and one of the top 25 picturebooks in surveys of teachers' favourites conducted by Scholastic Publishing's *Instructor* magazine. For the international reception of the illustrations, see below, chapter 9.
127 Sally Lodge, 'Books on Parental Love Prove an Easy Sell,' *PW* 245, no. 16 (1998): 25–6.
128 *The Sunlife Guide to Stratford Summer Music, 2005*, 27, http://www.stratfordsummermusic.ca/archived_guides/guide05.pdf.
129 'Winnipeg Couple Buys "Love You Forever" Art,' CBC Arts news story, 2 December 2005, http://www.cbc.ca/arts/story/2005/12/02/loveyouforever-art-051202.html.
130 Sue Sutton, 'First Nations' New Shoots,' *Q&Q* 60 (December 1995): 10–11. See also Canada, *Report of the Royal Commission on Aboriginal Peoples*.
131 Alan Twigg, 'Fred, Randy,' BC Bookworld, Author Bank, http://www.abcbookworld.com/?state=view_author&author_id=7372; 'Theytus Books,' *CM* 12, no. 6 (1984), http://umanitoba.ca/outreach/cm/cmarchive/vol12no6/theytusbooks.html.
132 Anita Large, interview.
133 Greg Young-Ing, interview.
134 Ibid.
135 Ibid.
136 Culleton, 'Images of Native People'; Loewen, 'Pemmican Press'; Horning, 'Contributions of Alternative Press Publishers'; Collene Ferguson, 'Pemmican Publications Fills a Need,' *CBN* 26, no. 3 (2003): 12.
137 Diane Ramsay, interview.
138 Lesley Kruger, 'The Inuktitut Munsch: Why Aboriginal Translations of Popular Canadian Books Rarely Work in Native Schools,' *Q&Q* 63, no. 6 (1997): 66.
139 Ferguson, 'Pemmican Publications,' 12.
140 Diane Ramsay, interview.
141 Ferguson, 'Pemmican Publications,' 12.

142 Diane Ramsay, interview.
143 Greg Young-Ing, interview, compared Aboriginal presses to women's presses, gay and lesbian presses, and other cultural presses as philosophical or cultural publishers, for whom economics are a secondary reason for publishing.
144 Katherine Govier, 'Coach House and Women's Press: Staying Small and Thriving,' Q&Q 45, no. 8 (1979): 15–16.
145 Margie Wolfe, interview.
146 Patsy Aldana, interview.
147 Lisa Rochon, 'Race Issue Splits Women's Press,' G&M, 9 August 1988; H.J. Kirchhoff, 'Second Story Publishes Fiction That Caused Friction,' G&M, 31 July 1989; Cynthia Hayhurst, 'Second Story Press Launches First List,' Q&Q 55, no. 9 (1989): 9; White, 'New Perspectives on Feminist Publishing'; and Gillian O'Reilly, 'Inside Second Story Press.' CCBN 27, no. 3 (2004): 15, 35.
148 Margie Wolfe, interview.
149 Sandy Frances Duncan, telephone interview.
150 Carol-Ann Hoyte, 'Book Week Past and Present,' CCBN 30, no. 3 (2007): 20–1, notes that the activity guide was created in response to a survey by Ronald Jobe of UBC and Alixe Hambleton of the University of Regina, which determined that teachers were unfamiliar with most of the titles in the Our Choice catalogue and used even fewer in their classrooms. See also Hambleton and Jobe, 'Teachers' Awareness.'
151 'Festival Renamed Children's Book Week,' CBN 11, no. 1 (Summer 1988): 1; 'Touring Program for 1989 Book Week,' CBN 11, no. 4 (Spring 1989): 1.
152 'Packaging Your Imagination,' CANSCAIP website, http://www.canscaip.org/pyi.html.
153 Tim Wynne-Jones, email interview; and 'Writing for Children Class Spawns Published Authors,' What's New, Continuing Education, George Brown College (21 September 2004), available at http://www.coned.georgebrown.ca/info/article-040921.html.
154 National Library of Canada, Secret Self. Expanded edition of the catalogue available online at http://epe.lac-bac.gc.ca/100/206/301/lac-bac/secret-ef/secret/index-e.html; Cartwright and Creighton, Once Upon a Time.
155 The Alcuin Society, 'About the Book Design Awards,' http://www.alcuinsociety.com/awards/index.html; IBBY Canada, 'The Elizabeth Mrazik-Cleaver Award,' http://www.ibby-canada.org/cleaver.html; Canada Council for the Arts, 'The Governor General's Literary Awards,' http://www.canadacouncil.ca/prizes/ggla/; Vancouver Children's Literature Roundtable, 'Information Book Award,' http://www.library.ubc.ca/edlib/table/awards/information.htm; Canadian Children's Book Centre, 'Canadian Awards Index,' http://www.bookcentre.ca/awards/sheila_a_egoff_childrens_literature_prize; Canadian Children's Book Centre, 'Mr Christie's Book Award,' http://www.bookcentre.ca/awards/mr_christies_book_award.
156 The children's book panel continued as a feature on CBC Radio One's Sounds Like Canada program and generated increased sales for titles mentioned on the broadcasts. See 'Bookbuyers Go for Titles Mentioned on Canadian TV, Radio,' CBC news release, 29 June 2007, http://www.cbc.ca/news/story/2007/06/29/book-sales.html.
157 Michele Landsberg, interview.

158 Judy Sarick, interview.
159 Michele Landsberg, interview. Hambleton, 'Use of Canadian Materials,' 122, cites
     reference made to the *Morningside* program by many of the librarians in the 120
     school and public libraries surveyed as playing a positive role in promoting Canadian
     resources to parents and the general public.
160 Michele Landsberg, interview. The book was published in the United States as *Read-
     ing for the Love of It*. See Lesnik-Oberstein, *Children's Literature*, 100–1, for a discussion
     of Landsberg and her critics.
161 Michele Landsberg, interview.
162 *Children's Choices of Canadian Books* 7, no. 2 (1991): 69, note from the editor, Jane Charl-
     ton.
163 *Children's Choices of Canadian Books* 4, no. 1 (1985): v, preface by the editor, Jane Charl-
     ton.
164 See, for example, reviews in *CLJ* 37, no. 4 (1980): 284; *CM* 8, no. 2 (1980): 67–8; *CLJ* 39,
     no. 2 (1982): 108; *CM* 14, no. 4 (1986): 164.
165 *Children's Choices of Canadian Books* 7, no. 2 (1991): 69.
166 Filomena Simora, comp. and ed., *Bowker Annual of Library and Book Trade Information*,
     26th ed. (New York and London: R.R. Bowker, 1981), 354.
167 Filomena Simora, comp. and ed., *Bowker Annual of Library and Book Trade Information*,
     31st ed. (New York and London: R.R. Bowker, 1986), 439; Catherine Barr, ed., *Bowker
     Annual Library and Book Trade Almanac*, 37th ed. (New Providence, NJ: R.R. Bowker,
     1992), 516.
168 Feather, *History of British Publishing*, 208–9; Greco, Rodriguez, and Wharton, *Culture
     and Commerce of Publishing*, 171–7.
169 Jeffrey Canton, email interview.
170 Michele Landsberg, interview.
171 Hambleton, 'Use of Canadian Materials,' found that the majority of the sixty school
     libraries surveyed included between 50 and 75 per cent of a checklist of sixty-seven
     Canadian children's titles, while 75 per cent of the sixty public libraries held at least
     75 per cent of the titles. Canadian materials accounted for between 15 and 20 per
     cent of book budget expenditures in public libraries. Use of Canadian titles in pro-
     gramming activities was stronger in school libraries than public libraries. Overall
     she notes that despite continuing concerns about the quality of Canadian books,
     there was 'growing awareness and support for Canadian materials among librar-
     ians.'
172 Margo Beggs, 'Children's Publishing: An '80s Success Story,' *Q&Q* 55, no. 12 (1989):
     13–14.

7: The 1990s to the Present Day: Structural Challenges and Changes

Sources of quotations used in headings:
'You Can Never Tell What a Best-Seller Is Going to Be,' from an interview with Kathy
     Lowinger.
'People Would Begrudge Ten Dollars for a Book,' from an interview with Michele Lands-
     berg.

'A Core of Highly Knowledgeable Booksellers,' from an interview with Dennis Johnson. 'We Act as a U.S. Publisher,' from an interview with Patsy Aldana.

  1 Lorimer and O'Donnell, 'Global Restructuring in Publishing'; and MacSkimming, 'Crisis and Renewal.'
  2 Marie Campbell, 'Beyond Books: Fiction Put Up a Fight, But It Was CD-Roms and Novelties That Held the Field at the 94 Bologna Book Fair,' *Q&Q* 60, no. 6 (1994): 7; Derek Weiler, 'Toy Story: In the Lucrative Licensing Business, Canadian Publishers are Mostly Stuck on the Sidelines,' *Q&Q* 65, no. 10 (1999): 10; Scott Anderson, 'They Might Be Giants: The Canadian Book Industry Goes Global,' *Q&Q* 66, no. 1 (2000): 18; John Neale et al., 'The Future of Canadian Publishing,' *Q&Q* 66, no. 4 (2000): 19.
  3 Crandall, 'UK Children's Book Business.' Miller, *Reluctant Capitalists*, 132–9.
  4 Taxel, 'Children's Literature'; Zipes, *Sticks and Stones*, 51; Reynolds and Tucker, 'Preface,' *Children's Book Publishing in Britain*, xi–xiv.
  5 Hade, 'Curious George Gets Branded'; Hade, 'Storyselling'; Hade and Edmondson, 'Children's Book Publishing.' Nodelman, 'As Canadian As,' 97, lists the pressures facing American children's publishers, including the marketing of books as merchandise, the focus by multinationals on the bottom line, demands for profitability, the unwillingness to take risks on 'innovative or even mildly unusual books,' leading to the focus on tie-ins, series, 'imitations of previous bestsellers,' and the necessity of books meeting curricular demands. For an overall exploration of culture and globalization, see Grant and Wood, *Blockbusters and Trade Wars*.
  6 Patsy Aldana, interview.
  7 Ibid.
  8 See, for example, Yaffe, 'Double Jeopardy'; Lorimer, 'Book Publishing in English Canada'; Martin, 'Writing Off Canadian Publishing'; Roy MacSkimming, 'HarperCollins and the Feds,' *Q&Q* 59, no. 2 (1992): 6; and John Lorinc, 'Nothing for Granted,' *Q&Q* 58, no. 12 (1992): 1, 10–11.
  9 Canada Council, 'A Brief History of the Canada Council for the Arts,' http://www.canadacouncil.ca/aboutus/Background/kd127729037949843750.htm. See also Lori McDougall, 'ACP Goes Pro,' *Q&Q* 59, no. 5 (1993): 4.
 10 Virginia Davis, interview.
 11 Polidori, 'Irene Aubrey'; Jane Aspinall, 'The National: The National Library of Canada Juggles Massive Mandate and Cutbacks,' *Q&Q* 61, no. 6 (1995): 30.
 12 Anne M. Galler, President, Canadian School Library Association, to Dr John English, [commissioner, Review of the Role of the National Archives and the National Library for Heritage Canada,] 'Brief Concerning the Role of the National Library of Canada,' 10 July 1998. The final report, which is archived at http://www.collectionscanada.gc.ca/webarchives/20071115092821/http://www.pch.gc.ca/pc-ch/pubs/johnenglish/english.html, makes no reference to children's services or collections.
 13 Lorimer, *Book Publishing in British Columbia*, 59–60; Association of Canadian Publishers, *Book Publishing and Canadian Culture*, 11–13; and Canada, Canadian Heritage, Planning and Corporate Affairs, Corporate Review Branch, *Final Report*, 2.0, Program profile, 2.1, Origins and historical overview of BPIDP.
 14 Bert Archer, 'Meaner, Leaner Times,' *Q&Q* 61, no. 4 (1995): 4. The BPIDP received a 33.5 per cent cut, and the PDAP received a 71 per cent cut. The Canada Council lost 2.6 per

cent of its funding, and the Department of Heritage was scheduled to receive 20 to 25 per cent less funding in 1996, as well as having funding withdrawn from arts service organizations not directly contributing to the creation, production, and distribution of art. See also Scott Anderson, 'ACP Shifts Shape as Funding Climate Worsens,' *Q&Q* 61, no. 5 (1995): 12–13; John Lorinc, 'Paper Cuts,' *Q&Q* 61, no. 7 (1995): 25; MacSkimming, 'Crisis and Renewal,' 19–20.

15 Statistics Canada, Historical Statistics of Canada, 11-516-XIE, Series A78-93, Population, by age and sex, census dates, 1851 to 1976, http://www.statcan.gc.ca/pub/11-516-x/sectiona/4147436-eng.htm.

16 Statistics Canada, CANSIM, Table 051-0001, Estimates of population, by age group and sex, Canada, provinces and territories, annual. These figures do not represent differences within provinces, which range from a low of 15 per cent in Newfoundland to a high of just under 19 per cent in Manitoba and Saskatchewan, nor do they reflect the burgeoning population of children under 15 in Aboriginal communities. According to the 2006 census, 29.7 per cent of the population reporting an Aboriginal identity were fourteen years of age or younger. See Statistics Canada, Population reporting an Aboriginal Identity, by age group, by province, and territory (2006 Census), http://www40.statcan.gc.ca/l01/cst01/demo40a-eng.htm.

17 Association of Canadian Publishers, *Canadian Children's Book Market*; Association of Canadian Publishers, *Canadian Books in School Libraries*; Cavill and Bodnar, *Transition*; Cavill, Gopaul, and Harkness, *Collections*. Haycock, *Crisis in Canada's School Libraries*.

18 Cavill, Gopaul, and Harkness, *Collections*, 2–3; Harris and Marshall, 'Reorganizing Canadian Libraries.'

19 Harris and Marshall, 'Reorganizing Canadian Libraries'; Frieda Ling, 'Selection Natural,' *Q&Q* 61, no. 10 (1995): 17; McKechnie, 'Children's Access to Services in Canadian Public Libraries,' 51.

20 Jane Aspinall, 'Tradition vs Technology: "Reorganization" of Children's Services,' *Q&Q* 61, no. 11 (1995): 5; Theo Heras, 'Browsing the Shelves: The Lillian H. Smith Children's Literature Resource Collection,' *CANCSAIP News* 25, no. 1 (2003): 23–4; email correspondence with Toronto Public Library staff.

21 Michele Landsberg, 'Why Kill Acclaimed Library Service for Children,' *Toronto Star*, 2 September 1995; Landsberg, 'Speak Up about Destructive Cuts to Libraries,' *Toronto Star*, 23 September 1995; Landsberg, '"Friends" Enter the Fray Over Cuts at Library,' *Toronto Star*, 11 November 1995; Donna Jean MacKinnon, 'Read-in Protests Cuts in Library Kids' Programs,' *Toronto Star*, 21 November 1995; Landsberg, 'Library Friends Score a Victory for Children,' *Toronto Star*, 9 December 1995; Susan Walker, 'Danger Ahead for Free-Library Legacy?' *Toronto Star*, 10 February 1996; Devin Crawley, 'TPL Appoints Advocate for Youth Services,' *Q&Q* 65, no. 8 (1999): 8; Krista Foss, 'Libraries Aren't Closing the Book on Reading,' *G&M*, 19 March 2001.

22 Information from the 2000–7 annual reports of public library systems in Calgary, Edmonton, Greater Victoria, Halifax, Ottawa, Regina, Saskatoon, Toronto, Vancouver, and Winnipeg.

23 Interviews with Janice Douglas, Celia Lottridge, Carol McDougall, Barbara Reid, and Allison Taylor McBryde. See also 'Nova Scotia Report,' *CCBN* 26, no. 2 (2003): 31.

24 Harris/Decima, '2008 TD Summer Reading Club: Final Report of Program Statistics for Library and Archives Canada,' http://www.collectionscanada.gc.ca/obj/009003/

f2/009003-142-e.pdf. In 2008, 752 public library systems participated, distributing 272,300 themed reading kits to 269,112 participants.

25 Association of Canadian Publishers, *Canadian Children's Book Market*, 8–9; Haycock, *Crisis in Canada's School Libraries*, 11.

26 Bainbridge, Carbonaro, and Wolodko, 'Teacher Professional Development'; and 'Canadian Books in Canadian Schools: How Are We Doing,' *CCBN* 26, no. 2 (2003): 8–9.

27 Gillian O'Reilly, 'School Libraries: A Call to Action,' *CCBN* 26, no. 3 (2003): 2.

28 Canadian Association for School Libraries, 'Students' Information Literacy Needs in the 21st Century: Competencies for Teacher-Librarians,' 1.5, states that as part of their professional competency, teacher-librarians have 'expert knowledge in evaluating learning resources in different formats and media, both on-site and remote, to support the instructional program.' http://www.cla.ca/casl/literacyneeds.html. In contrast, Canadian Library Association, *Guidelines for the Education of Library Technicians*, 2nd ed. ([Ottawa: The Association], 1991), 9, lists under minimum competencies, 'Selection: Contribute to collection development policies, Assist with selection of materials for collection.' See also Tilley and Callison, 'Preparing School Library Media Specialists.'

29 Cavill and Bodnar, *Transition*, 3, 38–40, 52, 65; Mary Land, 'Saving Grades: Budget Cutters See Teacher-Librarians as Expendable,' *Q&Q* 62, no. 4 (1996): 8; Mary Land, 'Symposium to Address Danger of School Library "Collapse,"' *Q&Q* 63, no. 2 (1997): 13.

30 Association of Canadian Publishers, *Canadian Books in School Libraries*, 2.

31 Association of Canadian Publishers, *Canadian Children's Book Market*, 45.

32 Association of Canadian Publishers, *Canadian Books in School Libraries*, 25; Russ McMath, email interview.

33 John Lorinc, 'The Crisis in School Libraries: How Did We Fall So Far So Fast?' *Q&Q* 68, no. 2 (2002): 18–20, 27.

34 'School Library Coalition Pushes for New Funding, Awareness,' *CBN* 25, no. 3 (2002): 5; Canadian Coalition for School Libraries, 'Viewpoints Panel Discussion,' School Library Summit, the National Library of Canada, Ottawa, 26 June 2003.

35 Haycock, *Crisis in Canada's School Libraries*, 11.

36 Statistics Canada, *Canadian School Libraries*; and Statistics Canada, *The Daily*, 'School Libraries and Teacher-Librarians,' 4 May 2005, http://www.statcan.gc.ca/daily-quotidien/050504/dq050504a-eng.htm. See also Derek Weiler, 'Small Steps for School Libraries,' *Q&Q* 71, no. 5 (2005): 25.

37 Dave Jenkinson, interview; Saltman, 'Twice Told Tale.' In 2008, a wide range of courses in youth services and children's literature is offered in Library and Information Science graduate programs at the University of Alberta and the University of British Columbia, with more limited course scheduling at Dalhousie, University of Toronto, and Western. No courses in youth services are listed in the calendar at McGill and Université de Montréal.

38 Haycock, *Crisis in Canada's School Libraries*, 37; Bainbridge, Carbonaro, and Wolodko, 'Teacher Professional Development'; Tilley and Callison, 'Preparing School Library Media Specialists.' In 2008, courses in aspects of teacher-librarianship (including online courses) were offered at the University of British Columbia, the University of Alberta, the Ontario Institute for the Study of Education, Brock University, Queen's University, and the University of Prince Edward Island.

39 Association of Canadian Publishers, *Canadian Books in School Libraries*, 9; Canada Coun-
    cil for the Arts, 'English-Language Canadian Literature in High Schools.' Commis-
    sioned by the Council and prepared by The Writers' Trust of Canada (2002), http://
    www.canadacouncil.ca/publications_e/research/aud_access/di127234254927656250
    .htm#2.
40 Association of Canadian Publishers, *Canadian Books in School Libraries*, 3.
41 Ibid., 4.
42 'Canadian Books in Canadian Schools: How Are We Doing,' *CCBN* 26, no. 2 (2003): 9.
43 Dave Jenkinson, interview; Devin Crawley, 'Fortress Scholastic: High Discounts Are
    Keeping Canadian Titles Out of the Company's Book Clubs, Publishers Say,' *Q&Q* 68,
    no. 2 (2002): 22–3. See also 'Canadian Books in Canadian Schools: How Are We Doing,'
    CCBN 26, no. 2 (2003): 8–9. The lack of awareness of Canadian titles is sadly reminis-
    cent of the findings from the 1976 John Wilkinson study.
44 Patsy Aldana, interview.
45 Virginia Davis, interview.
46 Greco, *Book Publishing Industry*, 221, documents a similar pattern in the United States,
    in which the expansion of the retail market in the 1980s and the decline in institutional
    budgets have resulted in a major shift away from libraries and institutions dominat-
    ing the juvenile market towards a market 'dependent on the latest trends (and often
    whims.)' See also Schiffrin, *Business of Books*, 103–28, for a general discussion of market
    censorship and the decline of the midlist; and Tara Walker, 'The Checklist: Getting a
    Picture Book Published in a Bunny-Eat-Bunny World,' *CCBN* 31, no. 1 (2008): 6–7.
47 Kathy Lowinger, interview.
48 John F. Barker and Nathalie Atkinson, 'The World Needs More Canada,' *PW* 251, no. 20
    (17 May 2004), S2–S20.
49 Patsy Aldana, interview.
50 Wright, *Hip and Trivial*, 47, quotes Morgan Entrekin of the American publisher Grove/
    Atlantic Press on the labelling of authors whose first and second books fail to sell in
    sufficient quantities as 'damaged goods.'
51 Craig Riggs, 'The New Used,' *Saturday Night* (September 2005): 17.
52 Reynolds, 'Publishing Practices and the Practicalities of Publishing,' 26, discusses the
    same trend in Britain.
53 Patsy Aldana, interview.
54 Kathy Lowinger, interview.
55 Dennis Johnson, interview.
56 Rick Wilks, interview.
57 Gillian O'Reilly, 'Tough Times: New Challenges for Picture Books,' *CCBN* 31, no. 1
    (2008): 8.
58 Laurie Bildfell, 'Bloom Is Off the Boom,' *Q&Q* 58, no. 10 (1993): 1, 13–16; Phyllis Simon,
    interview.
59 Judy Sarick, interview.
60 Michele Landsberg, interview.
61 John Lorinc, 'One Big Bookseller: 434-Store Strong Smith-Coles Colossus Faces Com-
    petition Review,' *Q&Q* 60, no. 4 (1994): 4. MacSkimming, *Perilous Trade*, 360–1. Smith-
    books was itself a merger in 1985 between the Canadian-owned Classic Books chain
    and Smithbooks, formerly W.H. Smith of Canada.

62 John Lorinc, 'Rollout Picks Up Speed: With $40m Stock Sales, 15 New Superstore Leases, Chapters Aims to Outflank Now,' *Q&Q* 62, no. 12 (1996): 1; Scott Anderson, 'The Size of the Prize,' *Q&Q* 65, no. 12 (1999): 16; Canada, *Challenge of Change*, chap. 3, 'Distribution: Wholesale and Retail,' section B, Relevant Legislation, i. Market Share. Jones and Doucet, 'Big Box,' 497, indicate that in 1999, Chapters had fourteen outlets in the Greater Toronto area, with a total floor area of 73,000 square metres, while Indigo, with seven outlets, had a further 19,000 square metres.

63 John Kennedy, 'Chapters Sets Placement Fees,' *Q&Q* 62, no. 5 (1996): 4.

64 Leah Eichler, 'Canadian Publishing: Adapting to Change,' *PW* 247, no. 20 (2000): 52–62, quoting Cynthia Good, president of Penguin Canada on 'the democratization of reading,' which Good described as an attempt to attract new readers, especially those who might previously have been uncomfortable in a bookstore.

65 'SmithBooks Tightens Up Inventory,' *Q&Q* 60, no. 12 (1994): 4; John Lorinc, 'Returns Rising: Books Are Being Sent Back at an Alarming Rate and Everyone's Got a Theory as to Why,' *Q&Q* 63, no. 2 (1997): 1; John Lorinc, 'Murphy's Law: Chapters Enters New Era, New Retail CEO Plans Sweeping Changes to Buying and Merchandising Strategy,' *Q&Q* 66, no. 7 (2000): 4; Devin Crawley, 'Industry Divided on Returns Issue,' *Q&Q* 66, no. 9 (2000): 4; Devin Crawley, 'The Fate of the Fall Season: Chapters' Shift in Retail Strategy Has Publishers Guessing,' *Q&Q* 66, no. 10 (2000): 6.

66 MacSkimming, *Perilous Trade*, 362–5; John Lorinc, 'The Pegasus Effect: How the New National Wholesaler Will Change the Face of the Trade,' *Q&Q* 65, no. 7 (1999): 8; Derek Weiler, 'Pegasus in Standoff with Publishers over Terms,' *Q&Q* 65, no. 10 (1999): 5; Anita Lahey, 'See Nothing, Hear Nothing, Say Nothing: Publishers' Vague Comments about Chapters Offer Heritage Standing Committee Little to Go On,' *Q&Q* 66, no. 4 (2000): 17. For another perspective, see comments by Dennis Zook, Pegasus's president, quoted in Leah Eichler, 'Canadian Publishing: Adapting to Change,' *PW* 247, no. 20 (2000): 52–62. Problems were exacerbated in 1999, when Chapters established Pegasus, a warehouse designed to fulfil shipments to stores in the Chapters chain, as well as offering wholesale services to institutions and independent bookstores, and demanded discounts in excess of 50 per cent.

67 Canada, *Challenge of Change*.

68 The exact percentage of Chapters' market share was a subject of debate. The wide variation in percentages resulted from differing methods of measuring sales, a disagreement over whether non-book sales should be included in the estimates and whether sales by non-traditional retailers should be counted. See Canada, *Challenge of Change*, chap. 3, 'Distribution: Wholesale and Retail,' Relevant Legislation, 1, I, Market Share. See also Lahey, 'See Nothing, Hear Nothing,' 17.

69 Canada, *Challenge of Change*, chap. 3, 'Distribution: Wholesale and Retail,' section A, Recent Trends in Book Distribution, 2, Changing Dynamics in Book Distribution and Retail, and section B, Relevant Legislation, i, Market Share. There were 4,298 independent bookstores in Canada, 70 Chapters superstores, 261 other Chapters stores, 14 Indigo superstores, and 25 stores in a Quebec chain, as well as the troubled Pegasus book wholesaler and distributor. Oda and Sanislo, *Book Publishing USA*, 65–6, notes how the poor performance of Chapters Online placed further pressure on the company, which lost $24.3 million on sales of $25.6 million in 1999.

70 John F. Baker and Leah Eichler, 'In Canada, Higher Hopes After a Rough Year,' *PW*

248, no. 17 (2002): S2–S12, under 'ACP: Focusing on Supply Chain,' notes that Indigo represented 60–70 per cent of the market in Canada. John Lorinc, 'Troubleshooting,' *Q&Q* 67, no. 9 (2002): 17, noted that publishers had been informed by the new Chapters/Indigo officials that any title selling less than thirty-five copies a year would be dropped from the master inventory list, and that the number of titles being carried would be reduced overall.

71 Derek Weiler, 'What Next? Big Box Competition Has Independents Wondering about Their Future,' *Q&Q* 65, no. 6 (1999): 27; Carol Toller and Shirley Hewitt, 'Vancouver Hit by Wave of Store Closures: Five Independents Have Shut Down since December,' *Q&Q* 66, no. 4 (2000): 5. Jones and Doucet, 'The Big Box,' 501, note that a number of long-established independent bookstores in Toronto closed after new book superstores had opened in the area, and cite one instance in which an existing bookstore was forced to leave its mall location when the mall was expanded to include a new Chapters and the lease conditions forbade competition.

72 Karen Moffat, 'Small Bookstores Go Big,' *Financial Post Magazine*, August 1999, 13; Marjo Johne, 'Children's Room: Creating a Kid-Friendly Environment Will Cultivate Young Customers and Keep Their Parents Coming Back to Buy,' *CB*, 24, no. 6 (2002): 26.

73 Catherine Barr, ed., *Bowker Annual Library and Book Trade Almanac*, 37th ed. (New Providence, NJ: R.R. Bowker, 1992), 516.

74 Dave Bogart, ed., *Bowker Annual Library and Book Trade Almanac*, 50th ed. (Medford, NJ: Information Today, 2005), 546.

75 Rick Wilks, 'Publishing Today: An Independent Publisher's Perspective,' *CCBN* 29, no. 4 (2006): 2–4. Trachtenbery, 'Book Chains,' 35, notes that according to the American Booksellers Association, independents in the United States made up about 18 per cent of the market share of retail sales.

76 Dennis Johnson, interview.

77 John Lorinc, 'Children's Book Store Closes after 25 Years,' *Q&Q* 66, no. 2 (2000): 4; Derek Weiler, 'Pegasus Buys Children's Wholesaler,' *Q&Q* 66, no. 2 (2000): 5.

78 Dennis Johnson, interview. See also 'Open Borders,' *Q&Q* 71, no. 10 (2005): 4.

79 Judy Sarick, interview.

80 Karen Hammond, 'Goodbye Hockey Sweater, Hello Casey at the Bat,' *Q&Q* 66, no. 10 (2000): 24. Leah Eichler, 'Canadian Publishing: Adapting to Change,' *PW* 247, no. 20 (2000): 60, quotes Valerie Hussey's suggestion that publishers could help to educate buyers and their staff on educating the 'big boxes' as a way of replacing the knowledgeable hand-selling of independents.

81 John F. Barker and Nathalie Atkinson, 'The World Needs More Canada,' *PW* 251, no. 20 (17 May 2004): S19.

82 Celia Lottridge, interview.

83 Phyllis Simon, interview.

84 Ibid.

85 Trudy Carey, email interview.

86 Carol Toller, 'GDS Distribution Woes Prompt Publisher Outcry,' *Q&Q* 66, no. 5 (2000): 5.

87 Scott Anderson, 'Heritage May Help GDS Clients through Cash Crunch,' *Q&Q* 67, no. 4 (2001): 4; Coté, 'Cultural Industries,' 200; Paul Spendlove, 'Unfinished Business: GDS Clients Still Standing, but Effects of the Collapse Linger,' *Q&Q* 69, no. 5 (2003): 5.

88 Kathryn Cole, interview.

89 Sally Lodge, 'Canadian Children's Offerings Finding a Wider U.S. Market,' *PW* 245, no. 21 (25 May 1998), 53, notes that 'with the past decade's slew of mergers and acquisitions, the number of children's imprints seeking to buy foreign rights has been markedly reduced.' See also Marcus, 'International Children's Books Rights,' 51–6.

90 Valerie Hussey, interview.

91 Ibid.

92 Josh Kerbel, 'Dos and Don'ts of Selling in Canada,' *PW* 253, no. 42 (23 October 2006): 19, notes that the Canadian market for English-language books is 7 to 8 per cent the size of the U.S. market.

93 Diane Roback, 'Potter Leads the Pack,' *PW* 253, no. 13 (27 March 2006): 37–48. In 2005, Laura Numeroff, *If You Give a Pig a Party*, illus. by Felicia Bond (New York: Harper Collins / Laura Geringer Books, 2005), is reported to have sold 479,589 copies, while Eric Carle, *10 Little Rubber Ducks* (New York: HarperCollins, 2005), sold 373,862. The best-selling hardcover backlist title, Chris Van Allsburg, *The Polar Express* (Boston: Houghton Mifflin, 1985), has sold 898,187 copies.

94 For sales of the Stella titles, see Patsy Aldana, interview. For sales of *Love You Forever*, see Firefly Books advertisement, *Q&Q* 67, no. 5 (2001), back cover. Diane Roback and Jason Britton, 'All-Time Bestselling Children's Books,' *PW* 248, no. 51 (17 December 2001): 24–32, reports sales of 6,970,000 in the United States for the paperback edition of *Love You Forever*. '50 Years of Children's Books,' *New York Times*, 16 November 1997, included *Love You Forever* on its list of fifty new and enduring children's books. The title was number one on a 1994 *New York Times* list of 'Children's Best Sellers' in the picturebook category. See 'Children's Best Sellers,' *New York Times*, 22 May 1994, and Eden Ross Lipson, 'Children's Books: What the Children Are Reading,' *New York Times*, 22 May 1994.

95 Susan Lawrence, 'The Turtle Turns Fifteen: Just One More Reason to Celebrate Spring Children's Titles,' *Q&Q* 67, no. 1 (2001): 20.

96 On the economics of Canadian publishing see Thring, 'This Little Book.'

97 These figures are compiled by information provided in interviews with representatives at the major children's publishing companies in Canada, including Annick, Tundra, Orca, Red Deer, Groundwood, and Kids Can. Lawrence, 'The Turtle Turns Fifteen,' 20, notes that Scholastic planned an initial print run of 25,000 for a new Robert Munsch title, *Up, Up, Down* (2001), while Kids Can Press announced that they were printing 30,000 copies of Paulette Bourgeois's *Franklin and Harriet* (2001) in softcover and 5,000 in hardcover.

98 Wilks, 'Economics of Canadian Children's Book Publishing.'

99 Anita Elash, 'Outward Bound,' *Q&Q* 61, no. 4 (1996): 18–19.

100 Josh Kerbel. 'Canadian Publishing,' *PW* 255, no. 21 (2008): S1–S16, discusses the Canadian Copyright Act, book pricing, currency fluctuations, and the impact on Canadian publishers, distributors, and retailers.

101 Valerie Hussey, interview.

102 Rick Wilks, interview.

103 John Burns, 'Western Presses Diversifying: Sales in U.S. Offer Greatest Potential, Publishers Say,' *Q&Q* 63, no. 3 (1997): 10; Paul Spendlove, 'Southern Exposure: Marketing to the U.S. Can Be Tricky,' *Q&Q* 69, no. 4 (2003): 5–6.

104 Patsy Aldana, interview.

105 Association of Canadian Publishers, *Canadian Children's Book Market*, 6.

106 Charlotte Teeple, email interview.

107 'AGM 2000,' *CBN* 23, no. 3 (2000): 15; 'Score Big with Books,' *CBN* 23, no. 2 (2000): 7.

108 'Uncover a Mystery, Discover the Fun,' *CBN* 24, no. 3 (2001): 1, 12; 'Far Reaching Book Giveaway Delights Grade Ones,' *CBN* 26, no. 1 (2003): 9, notes distribution of 450,000 books printed for the giveaway; 'First Franklin for Grade 1 Readers,' *CCBN* 29, no. 3 (2006): 21, notes that nearly 500,000 copies of the chosen title are distributed each year.

109 '20 French Authors Tour for Book Week,' *CCBN* 24, no. 3 (2001): 30; Tim Johnson, 'A Most Unusual Book Tour,' *Q&Q* 72, no. 9 (2006): 12.

110 Gillian O'Reilly, 'From the Editor,' *CCBN* 26, no. 2 (2003): 1.

111 Gillian O'Reilly, email interview.

112 The Word on the Street, http://www.thewordonthestreet.ca/.

113 Vancouver International Writers Festival, 'Spreading the Word,' http://www.writers-fest.bc.ca/schools.

114 Blue Metropolis, Educational Programs, http://bluemetropolis.org.

115 International Readings at Harbourfront, http://www.readings.org.

116 Bob Tyrrell, interview.

117 Claire Mackay, telephone interview.

118 Norma Charles, 'CWILL BC, A Bit of History,' 25 August 2005, updated by James McCann, 16 November 2006 [unpublished document].

119 On the Toronto 'Group of Eight,' see Vladyana Krykorka, interview. The eight illustrators are Veronica Charles, Brenda Clark, Heather Collins, Linda Hendry, Vladyana Krykorka, Loris Lesynski, Barbara Reid, and Andrea Von Konigslow. On the Victoria group, see Victor Bosson, interview.

120 Gillian O'Reilly, 'Write Thinking: Workshops and Courses on Writing for Children,' *CBN* 23, no. 2 (2000): 24.

121 For the edited papers from the Symposium, see Hudson and Cooper, *Windows and Words*.

122 'Fun of Reading to Celebrate Canadian Kidlit,' *Q&Q* 69, no. 2 (2003): 19; Trevor Clayton, 'The Fun of Reading,' *Bulletin* (National Library of Canada) 35, no. 6 (November-December 2003), http://epe.lac-bac.gc.ca/100/202/301/bulletin_nlc/2003/no6/p2-0603-04-e.html.

123 Titles include Baker and Setterington, *Guide to Canadian Children's Books*; Egoff, *Canadian Children's Books*; Egoff and Saltman, *New Republic of Childhood*; Jobe and Hart, *Canadian Connections*; Jones and Stott, *Canadian Children's Books*; Saltman, *Modern Canadian Children's Books*; Reimer, *Home Words*; and Waterston, *Children's Literature in Canada*.

124 Gillian O'Reilly, 'Teaching Children's Book Illustration,' *CCBN* 27, no. 1 (2004): 6–7, 27.

125 *IBBY Canada Newsletter* 20, no. 2 (Fall 2000): 4; 'The Coming of Age of Children's Literature in Canada: A Chronology,' in National Library of Canada, *The Art of Illustration*.

126 CANSCAIP, 'The CANSCAIP Collection,' http://www.canscaip.org/collection.html; 'Canadians in Mexico: The Guadalajara Book Fair,' *IBBY Canada Newsletter* 19, no. 1 (1997): 10–11.

127 Copithorne, 'Creating the Mosaic.'
128 Marie-Louise Gay, 'Canadian Children's Books in Munich,' *IBBY Canada Newsletter* 22, no. 2 (2002): 6.
129 IBBY Canada, *Show and Tell.*
130 National Library of Canada, *The Art of Illustration,* http://epe.lac-bac.gc.ca/100/200/301/lac-bac/art_of_illustration-ef/www.lac-bac.gc.ca/3/10/index-e.html.
131 http://epe.lac-bac.gc.ca/100/206/301/lac-bac/celebrating_dk_khalsa-ef/3/7/index-e.html.
132 National Library of Canada and National Archives of Canada, *Beyond the Letters,* http://epe.lac-bac.gc.ca/100/206/301/lac-bac/beyond_letters-ef/abc/index-e.html.
133 See the 'Picture Perfect' virtual exhibit at http://ve.tpl.toronto.on.ca/PicturePerfect/more.html.
134 'News Roundup,' *CCBN* 32, no. 1 (2009): 4, notes that the value of the TD Canadian Children's Literature Award is being increased to $25,000 and the Marilyn Baillie Picture Book Award is being increased to $20,000.
135 Virginia Davis, interview; Gillian O'Reilly, 'The Kids Are (All) Right,' *CCBN* 29, no. 3 (2006): 2, notes that 'awards do matter. In the increasingly tight markets of institutional sales and bookstore shelves, awards help to create a buzz and attract attention.'
136 Patsy Aldana, interview.
137 Martha Cameron, telephone interview. Cameron, a teacher-librarian in the Surrey school district in Metro Vancouver, was on the non-fiction selection committee of the Red Cedar awards in 2005.
138 Ontario Library Association, 'Headlines and News Archives,' 20 October 2004, http://www.accessola.com/ola/bins/content_page.asp?cid=2-301-347-356.
139 Victoria Pennell, email interview; Allison Haupt, 'Editor's Notebook,' *RL* 1, no.1 (1995): 5; and Ken Haycock, 'Introducing Resource Links,' *RL* 1, no. 1 (1995): 6. In 2007, the Council for Canadian Learning Resources was renamed the Society for Canadian Educational Resources.
140 Carol Toller, 'Media Blackout: Why Does the Press Ignore Children's Books,' *Q&Q* 61, no. 1 (1995): 14; Gillian Stewart, 'When Little Guys Don't Count Anymore: New Patterns in Book Buying and Book Reviewing Could Spell Bad News for Some Authors,' *Media* 5, no. 3 (1998): 24; Derek Weiler, 'The Battle of the Book Sections,' *Q&Q* 65, no. 11 (1999): 22; Peter Carver, 'Looking into the Abyss: Children's Book Reviewing in the Popular Media,' *CBN* 23, no. 1 (2000): 2, 17; Devin Crawley, 'The Shrinking Book Review Section,' *Q&Q* 66, no. 1 (2002): 8.
141 Association of Canadian Publishers, *Highlights from Canadian Books in School Libraries,* 27, 32.
142 Charles Mandel, 'The State of Book Reviewing,' *Q&Q* 69, no. 3 (2003): 14–15; Peter Carver, 'Looking into the Abyss,' 2–3.
143 Jeffrey Canton, interview.
144 Michele Landsberg, interview.
145 Kathy Lowinger, interview.
146 Dave Jenkinson, interview.
147 Greg Young-Ing, interview.
148 Allison Taylor McBryde, interview.
149 Mary Rubio, email interview; Jeffrey Canton, interview; Dave Jenkinson, interview.

150 Jeffrey Canton, interview; Carmine Starnino, 'In Praise of the Sharp Word: Carmine Starnino on Why Negative Reviews Are Necessary,' *Q&Q* 70, no. 9 (2004): 13; Aislinn Hunter, 'A Few Good Critics: Why Book Reviewing Should Be Left to the Experts,' *Q&Q* 71, no. 3 (2005): 9.

151 Mary Rubio, email interview.

152 Sarah Ellis, interview. The smallness of the Canadian children's book community and the issue of reviewing was also discussed by Annette Goldsmith, email interview.

153 Allison Taylor McBryde, interview.

154 Ibid.

155 Canada, Statistics Canada, *Connectivity and ICT Integration*; Statistics Canada, 'Canada Internet Use Survey, 2005,' *The Daily*, Tuesday, 15 August 2006, http://www.statcan .gc.ca/daily-quotidien/060815/dq060815b-eng.htm.

156 Canada, Statistics Canada, 'E-Commerce,' *The Daily*, Wednesday, 1 November 2006, http://www.statcan.gc.ca/daily-quotidien/061101/dq061101a-eng.htm.

157 'About the Looking Glass,' *The Looking Glass*, http://www.lib.latrobe.edu.au/ojs/ index.php/tlgaboutus.html.

158 Bruce Gillespie, 'How to Reach a Teacher-Librarian,' *Q&Q* 72, no. 1 (2006): 53–4.

159 David and Pinch, 'Six Degrees of Reputation,' discusses online review systems, cultural commerce, and the problem of plagiarized reviews.

160 Pelletier, 'Books and Libraries.'

8: Children's Illustrated Books, 1990 to the Present Day

Sources of quotations used in headings:
'Everybody Is Concerned about Issues of Equity,' from an interview with Margie Wolfe.
'Preserving and Passing on Canadian History,' from an interview with Alan Daniel.
'Regaining the Balance of Justice,' from an interview with Paul Yee.
'As Much Art in Books as We Can Possibly Get Away With,' from an interview with Patsy Aldana.
'Taking More Risks,' from an interview with Rick Wilks.
'That's How You Get Good Manuscripts,' from an interview with Bob Tyrrell.
'Just a Smudge in the Dark,' from Nan Gregory, *How Smudge Came*.

1 Jeffrey Canton, interview.

2 Dean Allen, 'Saving Face: Typography Is a Vital, But Often Neglected, Part of Kids' Book Design,' *Q&Q* 65, no. 2 (1999): 20–1; Dean Allen, 'Function Meets Beauty: Canadian Book Design Comes of Age,' *Q&Q* 66, no. 4 (2000): 34–5; John Pressick, 'Production Can Get It Done,' *Q&Q* 70, no. 3 (2004): 13.

3 Hearne, 'Perennial Picture Books,' 26–33.

4 Nikolajeva and Scott, *How Picturebooks Work*, 6–7.

5 Lewis, 'Constructedness of Texts,' 132.

6 Bader, 'American Picture Books,' 145; McCloud, *Understanding Comics*, 7–9.

7 Goldstone, 'Brave New Worlds'; and Anstey, 'Postmodern Picture Books.'

8 Wyile, 'Metafictive Picturebooks,' 176–96.

9 Sarah Ellis, 'What Makes Kids' Non-Fiction Great,' *Q&Q* 70, no. 2 (2004): 24; Gillian O'Reilly, 'Beyond Projects: Publishing Non-Fiction,' *CCBN* 27, no. 4 (2004): 13–15.

10 Cianciolo, *Picture Books for Children*, 70.
11 Susan Catto, 'The Manga Revolution,' *Q&Q* 72, no. 9 (2006): 18–19; Naseem Hrab, 'How I Learned to Love the Graphic Novel,' *CCBN* 30, no. 1 (2007): 8–9; Scott MacDonald, 'Graphica: The Next Generation,' *Q&Q* 74, no. 6 (2008): 20–3.
12 'Women in the Canadian Book Trade: Sister Vision Press,' Library and Archives Canada (2000), http://www.collectionscanada.gc.ca/women/002026-291-e.html; Cooper, 'Founders of Sister Vision Press.'
13 'Out of Print,' *Q&Q* 71, no. 11 (2005): 5, notes that with the closure of Women in Print bookstore in September 2005, all five women's bookstores in Vancouver had ceased operations.
14 'Keep Women in Print: Writing What Is Wrong,' http://www.uah.edu/english/wip/, notes that in 1997, according to statistics compiled by the Feminist Bookstore Network, there were 107 women's bookstores in Canada and the United States. By 2005, this number had fallen to 74. For a list of women's bookstores in operation as of 2009, see 'Women's Bookstores,' Women's Institute for the Freedom of the Press, http://www.wifp.org/DWM/Bookstores.html.
15 Margie Wolfe, interview; Paul Lungen, 'Hana's Story One of Tragedy, Hopefulness,' *Canadian Jewish News* 32, no. 19 (9 May 2002): 18; Mark Pupo, 'Hana and Her Suitcase,' *Q&Q* 68, no. 6 (2002): 20. See also Carpenter, Hillel, and van der Walt, 'Same But Different,' 189, which notes that the book 'is of particular significance because it embodies so many things Canadians cherish' and 'reaches beyond the local through its subject matter.'
16 Margie Wolfe, interview.
17 Ibid.
18 Deirdre Baker, interview.
19 Karen Sands-O'Connor, 'Why Are People Different,' discusses various strategies used in picturebooks to address difference. See also Jiménez, 'Review of *Mom and Mum*,' for an analysis of the depiction of LGBT families in children's picturebooks.
20 Ken Setterington, interview; Esther Vincent, 'The Money-Go-Round,' *Q&Q* 68, no. 9 (2002): 19, notes the unwillingness of bookstores to take risks on stocking titles from small publishers.
21 Montpetit, 'Book Banning,' 6–7, points out that 'strangely enough, nobody complained about the inside illustrations, which are much more explicit.'
22 Chamberlain v. Surrey District School Board No. 36, [2002] 4 S.C.R. 710, 2002 SCC 86.
23 Collins, 'Culture, Religion and Curriculum'; Schneiderman, 'Supreme Court Addresses Gay-Positive Readers'; Schrader and Wells, 'Queer Perspectives on Social Responsibility'; Freedom to Read website, Censorship in Canada, Challenged Books, Challenged Books List, http://www.freedomtoread.ca/docs/challenged_books.pdf; Paula Carlson, 'Struggle Over Books Continues in Surrey, B.C. School Board,' *Surrey Leader*, 12 May 2006.
24 Reviewers have also approached the depiction of gender roles from different perspectives. Jiménez, 'Review of *Mom and Mum*,' 97, praises Priestley's illustrations for including images of non-conforming gender expression, liberating Mum from 'compulsory dress-wearing,' while Cumming, 'Queer Childhoods,' 170, criticizes the depiction of the women as maintaining stereotypes of a butch-femme relationship, asking, 'Why can

they not both wear dresses or pants to the cottage wedding?' Similarly, Jiménez suggests that Setterington has imagined a world in which social justice has been realized and a wedding between same-gendered partners is not an area of controversy, while Cumming argues that the picturebook fails to embrace queer sexualities and reinforces heteronormative values by focusing on the 'conventional trappings of weddings.'

25 Ken Setterington, 'Waiting to Be Banned,' Freedom to Read 2006, http://www .freedomtoread.ca/docs/2006/kit2006.pdf, 20.
26 Ibid.
27 Warabé Aska, interview.
28 Lissa Paul, interview.
29 Signe Ball, 'Curl Up with the Voyages of a Bear and His Boy,' *In the Hills* (Fall 1994), http://www.lauriemcgaw.com/a_bear_and_his_boy.htm. See also Polar, the Titanic Bear, Press, http://www.polarthetitanicbear.com/presspage.html.
30 Janet Lunn, interview.
31 Alan and Lea Daniel, email interview.
32 Janet Wilson, interview; Janet Wilson, 'Janet Wilson Accepts Cleaver Award,' *IBBY Canada Newsletter* 19, no. 1 (1997): 2–4.
33 Linda Granfield, interview; Linda Granfield, 'Just the Facts,' *Q&Q* 61, no. 10 (1995): 16.
34 Linda Granfield, interview.
35 Janet Wilson, interview.
36 Ibid.
37 Scott Anderson, 'Stoddart Picks Up Lester's Kids' List,' *Q&Q* 62, no. 4 (1996): 6.
38 Ludmila Zeman, interview; and Gillian O'Reilly, 'Four Czech Chicks,' *BC* 30, no. 2 (August 2001): 27–9.
39 Ludmila Zeman, interview.
40 Gillian O'Reilly, 'Song Nan Zhang: An Artist's Journey,' *CCBN* 26, no. 2 (2003): 16–17.
41 Scott Anderson, 'M&S Buys Tundra, Sells College,' *Q&Q* 62, no. 2 (1996): 4; John Lorinc, 'No Way Out?' *Q&Q* 62, no. 3 (1996): 9.
42 Kathy Lowinger, interview.
43 May Cutler, interview.
44 Roch Carrier, speech on writing for children.
45 Tololwa M. Mollel, 'Feasting on Words.'
46 Paul Morin, interview.
47 Ibid.
48 Ibid.
49 Ibid.
50 Kathryn Cole, interview.
51 Ibid.
52 John Lorinc, 'Taking Flight: Fitzhenry and Whiteside Aspires to New Heights,' *Q&Q* 68, no. 10 (2002): 16–17, 41; 'Stoddart Kids Line Goes to Fitzhenry,' *CBN* 25, no. 3 (2002): 4.
53 Linda Granfield, interview.
54 Kim LaFave, interview.
55 Ibid.
56 Phoebe Gilman, 'Something from Nothing,' 289.

57 Lissa Paul, interview.
58 Barbara Reid, interview.
59 Ibid.
60 Margo Beggs, 'Art for Art's Sake,' notes that Reid names Toulouse-Lautrec as one of her influences. Beggs draws a parallel between the cover art of *The Party* and Toulouse-Lautrec's painting *Training of the New Girls by Valentin at the Moulin Rouge* (1889–90).
61 Patsy Aldana, interview.
62 Paul Yee, interview.
63 Harvey Chan, interview.
64 Ibid.
65 The Stella series has been translated into seven languages and published in American, Australian, and British editions.
66 Marie-Louise Gay, interview; Marie-Louise Gay, 'Si une image.'
67 'In the Works,' *Q&Q* 72, no. 1 (2006): 14, notes that Radical Sheep, a Toronto-based production company, was in negotiation to turn the Stella and Sam books into an animated children's television series. According to the Radical Sheep website, the project is now in development. See http://www.radsheep.com/stellasam.html.
68 Marie-Louise Gay, interview.
69 Solomon, 'Publishing Children's Picture Books,' 197, discusses his choice of Futura as typeface for the Stella books, to match Gay's original 'careful and unfussy' layout.
70 Harvey Chan, interview.
71 Ange Zhang, interview.
72 Sally Lodge, 'Canadian Children's Offerings Finding a Wider U.S. Market,' *PW* 245, no. 21 (25 May 1998): 53.
73 Galway, 'Windows on the World,' 125, argues that these works created 'a sense of a universal, shared experience of childhood' that reinforces the ideological work of teaching tolerance.
74 Patsy Aldana, interview.
75 In June 2006, a chamber opera by Stephen Hatfield, based on Major's book, premiered at the Reid Theatre of Memorial University's St John's campus in Newfoundland. See 'Shallaway Presents Ann and Seamus, A Chamber Opera,' http://www.annandseamus.com.
76 H.J. Kirchhoff, 'Kidlit Stars Celebrate 10 Years of Success,' *G&M*, 5 November 1988, quotes Aldana as saying 'I'm a bit more dubious about nationalism now, at least Canadian nationalism, which seems to me anti-American in all the wrong ways. I'm anti-American because it's an imperial power. Anti-Americanism in Canada tends to be nostalgia for British power. It's a bit racist, too.'
77 'Kindergarten Superstar: Profile of Robert Munsch,' *Report on Business Magazine* (December 1989): 94; Carol Toller, 'Munsch Heads to Scholastic,' *Q&Q* 62, no. 5 (1996): 7; 'Scholastic Signs Munsch to Multi-Book Deal,' *PW* 244 (27 January 1997): 33. According to Toller, Munsch moved to a multi-book contract with Scholastic because the company 'offered better distribution for his titles, particularly in international markets.' Titles by Munsch whose rights remained at Annick have been translated into at least nine languages, including French, Armenian, Chinese, Hebrew, Japanese, Korean, Spanish, Swedish, and Welsh. Other Munsch titles published by Scholastic have been

translated into Arabic, Dutch, Icelandic, Inuktitut, Mohawk, and Ojibwa.

78 Bridget Donald, 'Annick Charts a Fresh Course: The Longtime Picture Book Publisher Reinvents Itself Post-Munsch,' *Q&Q* 66, no. 2 (2000): 24–5.

79 Deirdre Baker, interview.

80 Rick Wilks, interview.

81 Valerie Hussey, interview.

82 Ibid.

83 Karen Reczuch, email interview.

84 Michèle Lemieux, interview.

85 Quoted in Jeffrey Canton, 'Review of "Stormy Night,"' *Books in Canada* (September 1999), http://www.booksincanada.com/article_view.asp?id=1237. Sarrasin, *Double espace*, 18, notes that for Lemieux, death is not a dramatic act but an everyday occurrence that stimulates profound reflections on existence.

86 Quoted in Canton, 'Review.'

87 Lemieux, interview.

88 Daniel St-Hilaire, 'Drawing Life … or Inner Enchantment: An Interview with Michèle Lemieux,' A Symphony of Words, Canadian Children's Books with Musical Themes, Read Up On It 2000 kit, http://www.collectionscanada.gc.ca/lisez-sur-le-sujet/015020-2017-e.html.

89 Jeffrey Canton, 'Michèle Lemieux Wins Cleaver Award,' *IBBY Canada Newsletter* 20, no. 2 (2000): 4–5.

90 Beggs, 'Art for Art's Sake,' notes that Denton pays homage in her illustration of the verse 'Lavender's Blue, Dilly, Dilly' to the Mother Goose collection by Kathleen Lines, *Lavender's Blue: A Book of Nursery Rhymes*, illustrated by Harold Jones (London: Oxford University Press, 1954), adding that 'Denton doesn't tell us what a debt of gratitude she feels she owes to Jones and Lines – she shows us.'

91 Alicia Cox, 'Kids Can Aims High with Poetry: But Will the New Series Fly over Children's Heads,' *Q&Q* 70, no. 9 (2004): 11.

92 Ibid.

93 Eugenie Fernandes and Kim Fernandes, interview.

94 Gillian O'Reilly, 'Bill Slavin Tells Stories in Pictures,' *CCBN* 31, no. 2 (2008): 18–19, quotes Slavin as naming Alberto Uderzo, the illustrator of Asterix, and 'early Mad Magazine artists' as early influences on his work.

95 Valerie Hussey, interview.

96 Kate Jaimet, 'Under Valerie Hussey's Leadership, Kids Can Went from a Small Press …' *CanWest News*, 26 September 2006.

97 Diane Turbide, 'Franklin: Million Dollar Turtle,' *Maclean's*, 11 December 1995, 50–1.

98 Jaimet, 'Under Valerie Hussey's Leadership,' 1, and Kristin Rushowy, 'Franklin Celebrates 20 Years: Shy Turtle Is a Worldwide Phenomenon,' *Canadian Press News Wire*, 13 November 2006. Franklin titles have been published in Arabic, Braille, Bulgarian, Catalan, Complex Chinese, Croatian, Czech, Danish, Dutch, Estonian, Finnish, Flemish, French, German, Greek, Hebrew, Hungarian, Icelandic, Indonesian, Italian, Japanese, Korean, Latvian, Norwegian, Polish, Portuguese, Simplified Chinese, Slovenian, Slovak, Spanish, Swedish, and Turkish.

99 Valerie Hussey, interview. See also Wild, 'Franklin.'

100 Jaimet, 'Under Valerie Hussey's Leadership'; Sandy Fife, 'Kids' Lit Goes Commer-
     cial,' *Financial Post Magazine*, November 1998, 22; Derek Weiler, 'Hussey's Kids Can
     Legacy,' *Q&Q* 72, no. 9 (2006): 10–11.
101 Kids Can Press website, http://www.kidscanpress.com.
102 Carol-Ann Hoyte, 'Orca: From Pub Guides to Prizewinners,' *CCBN* 27, no. 2 (2004):
     17.
103 Ron Lightburn, email interview; Collins, 'Ron Lightburn'; Jenkinson, 'Profiles: Ron
     Lightburn.'
104 Ron Lightburn, email interview.
105 Bob Tyrrell, interview.
106 Victor Bosson, interview.
107 Ibid.
108 Maureen Garvie, 'Peter Carver Covers All Bases,' *Q&Q* 63, no. 5 (1997): 39.
109 Dennis Johnson, interview; Peter Carver, email interview.
110 Nan Gregory, interview.
111 Ibid.
112 Ibid.
113 Dennis Johnson, interview; Maureen Garvie, 'Not Just for Children Anymore: Litera-
     ture for the Young Is Reaching a Growing Audience of Adult Readers,' *Q&Q* 64, no.
     10 (1998): 1, notes that the crossover appeal of *How Smudge Came* to adult readers had
     resulted in strong sales.
114 Dennis Johnson, interview.
115 Ibid.
116 Michael Katz, interview.
117 Ibid.
118 Dimiter Savoff, interview.
119 Stefan Czernecki, interview; Stefan Czernecki, telephone interview.
120 John Lorinc, 'A Certain Age,' *Q&Q* 60, no. 1 (1994): 1; Zsuzsi Gartner, 'Coast with
     the Most,' *Q&Q* 60, no. 8 (1994): 10; Devin Crawley, 'Buyers Wanted,' *Q&Q* 66, no. 4
     (2000): 33; Paul Spendlove, 'Looking For a Way Out: Heritage Committee Mulls Suc-
     cession Issue,' *Q&Q* 69, no. 6 (2003): 10; Paul Spendlove, 'The Next Generation: Who
     Will Take the Reins at Canadian Presses,' *Q&Q* 70, no. 1 (2004): 13–17; Eddie Paul, 'In
     Search of an Exit,' *Q&Q* 70, no. 8 (2004): 11; Hildebrandt, 'Planned Departure,' 16.
121 Patsy Aldana, interview.
122 Spendlove, 'Looking For a Way Out,' 10.
123 Michele Landsberg, interview.

9: Canadian Cultural Identity, Canadian Cultural Identities

Sources of quotations used in headings:
'Where Is Here?' from Northrop Frye, 'Conclusion,' *Literary History of Canada*.
'Boutique Multiculturalism,' from an interview with Lissa Paul.
'Nobody Was Writing the Stories I Wanted to Read,' from an interview with Richard Van
    Camp.
'I'm Going to Pass on Our Teachings,' from an interview with Richard Van Camp.
'Everyone in Canada Loves Hockey,' from an interview with Judith Thistleton-Martin.

'Do American Librarians Like This Kind of Book?' from Patsy Aldana, 'Crossing the Money Boundary.'

'Everybody Likes Dinosaurs,' from Val Ross, 'Book Learning.'

'A Lack of Communication between French and English,' paraphrased from André Gagnon, 'Translation of Children's Books in Canada.'

1 Corse, *Nationalism and Literature*, 1–9.

2 Egoff, *Republic of Childhood*; Nora Story's *Oxford Companion to Canadian History and Literature* (Toronto: Oxford University Press, 1967), like *The Republic of Childhood*, was also published under the editorial direction of William Toye. New, *History of Canadian Literature*, 203, 211, notes that the centennial celebrations had a strong symbolic function, in which economic nationalism buttressed cultural nationalism. See also New, 'Read Canadian.'

3 Waterston, *Children's Literature in Canada*, 11.

4 Ibid., 3.

5 Anderson, *Imagined Communities*, 12.

6 For differing perspectives on the development of multiculturalism and the Canadian mosaic ideology, see Kallen, *Ethnicity and Human Rights*, 168–77; Day, *Multiculturalism*, 177–208; and Mackey, *House of Difference*, 50–70.

7 Young, 'Multiculturalism Policy and Canadian Literature'; Carpenter, 'Enlisting Children's Literature.'

8 Nodelman and Reimer, 'Teaching Canadian Children's Literature,' discuss resistance by a group of pre-service teachers to exploring Canadian cultural identity in the classroom. See also Johnston, Bainbridge, Mangat, and Skogen, 'National Identity,' who also found that some education students resisted challenges to their own identities when the idea of 'whiteness' as the Canadian norm was interrogated.

9 McGillis, 'Where Is Here?' 8–9.

10 Manning, *Ephemeral Territories*, xvi–xvii, argues that the language of the nation and the image of home necessarily exclude and oppress by defining categories of belonging, furthered by 'the myth of Canadians as a harmless, open, and generous people.' Critics have employed postcolonial theory in the debate over authenticity, hybridity, polyculturalism, and métissage in children's literature as a way to challenge the unproblematized tropes of multiculturalism. See, for example, Bradford, *Unsettling Narratives*, particularly 64–9; Dudek, 'Approaching the Other,' who draws on the work of Vijay Prashad; Mo and Shen, 'Rexamining the Issue of Authenticity'; Sorin, 'Métissage culturel'; and Thaler, 'Métissage et acculturation.'

11 Francis, *National Dreams*, 10–12.

12 Diakiw, 'Children's Literature and Canadian National Identity,' 42–3.

13 Ibid., 43.

14 Xie, 'Discourse of Difference, 3–4.

15 Saldanha, 'Canadian Multiculturalism and Children's Literature,' 165–6.

16 Lecker, *Making It Real*, 32–3, discusses the role of mimesis in relationship to Canadian national consciousness and literary history.

17 Corse, *Nationalism and Literature*, 9, argues that 'national literatures are both the product and partial creator of the nation and our collective sense of national identity. National literatures are not passive reflections of naturally occurring phenomena, but

integral components in the process of national development, consciously constructed pieces of the national culture, and creators of the world in which we live.'

18 For the broader historiography of the ways that the North and Wilderness have been constructed and contested, see Berger, 'True North'; Grace, *Canada and the Idea of North*; Harris, 'Myth of the Land'; and Kaufmann, 'Naturalizing the Nation.'

19 Mackey, *House of Difference*, 40–9, discusses northern wilderness and settler identities. Brymer, 'Canadian, Eh?' 120, notes that in her study, region was generally portrayed but rarely exact in detail, relying on a generic depiction of 'a forest setting' or 'the North.'

20 Atwood, *Survival*.

21 Lundin, *Constructing the Canon*, 9–13, discusses the intersection of Romanticism and constructions of childhood as an innocent paradise. See also Carpenter, 'In Our Own Image'; Higonnet, *Pictures of Innocence*; Jones, 'Tomboy Tales'; Jones, 'Childhood, the Urban and Romanticism.'

22 McDowell, 'Children's Books,' 627.

23 Egoff, 'Children's Literature to 1960,' 136.

24 Egoff and Bélisle, *Notable Canadian Children's Books*, 14, 16. The negative grouping of health issues with issues of sexual and ethnocultural identity is characteristic of Egoff's dislike of the inclusion of what she called 'sociology' or 'harsh interpretation of reality' in 'problem novels' for young readers. See, for example, Egoff, *Republic of Childhood*, 2nd ed., 3, on the 'modern trend' of 'facile, simplistic, sterile novels with sociological "meaning"' that she believed dominated the American children's lists.

25 McDowell, 'Children's Books,' 627. In contrast, Muller, 'Writing for Children,' 23, commented that judging from Canadian children's books, 'one would almost think there were no cities in Canada,' and added, 'Let us have children's stories that reflect our lives, not our landscape.' At the time, Muller was the manager of the promotional and editorial department of Scholastic Publications.

26 Frye, 'Conclusion,' *Literary History of Canada*, 826; and Frye, *Bush Garden*.

27 Henderson, 'Critical Canadiana'; Lecker, *Making It Real*, 32; Fiamengo, 'Regionalism and Urbanism.'

28 Willinsky, 'Frye among (Postcolonial) Schoolchildren,' 9.

29 Besner, 'Canadian Children's Regional Literature,' 18–19. See also Harker, 'Canadian Literature in Canadian Schools,' who discusses the role of regional identification in national identity formation.

30 Besner, 'Canadian Children's Regional Literature,' 18–19.

31 Lutz, 'Space in Canadian Prairie Fiction.'

32 Willinsky, 'Frye among (Postcolonial) Schoolchildren,' 18.

33 Harris, 'Power, Modernity, and Historical Geography,' 680.

34 Besner, 'Canadian Children's Regional Literature,' 18–19.

35 Janice Douglas, interview.

36 Kit Pearson, interview.

37 Sarah Ellis, interview.

38 Michele Landsberg, interview.

39 Sands-O'Connor, 'Canada, Children's Literature.'

40 Bainbridge and Wolodko, 'Canadian Picture Books,' 22, 25.

41 H.J. Kirchhoff, 'Writers Reject Bid to Study Plight of Minorities in Publishing,' *G&M*,

30 May 1989. At the annual meeting of the Writers' Union, a motion proposed by writer Judith Merrill to establish a task force to examine 'the relationship between the publishing industry and cultural minorities in Canada,' was rejected following a hotly debated panel discussion on racism in writing and publishing. Kirchhoff also noted a constant stream of jokes playing off the 'women of colour' movement in feminism. See also Scott Anderson, 'Bread and Races: Writers' Union, Divided over Writing Thru Race Conference, Tries to Get Down to Business,' Q&Q 60, no. 7 (1994): 21; Brian Fawcett, 'Notes from the Inner Circle,' BC 18, no. 6 (1989): 2–3; Philip, 'Gut Issues in Babylon'; Philip, 'Disappearing Debate'; Scheier, 'Writing Authentic Voices.'

42 Isabel Vincent, 'The Fight for a Truly National Literature,' G&M, 8 July 1990. Vincent also discusses the situation of George Elliott Clarke, who had to apply for a multiculturalism grant to finish a poetry project about exile and the Black Loyalist community in Nova Scotia after being turned down by the Canada Council. For the PEN conference, see Bronwyn Drainie, 'Minorities Go Toe to Toe with Majority,' G&M, 30 September 1989. See also Crean, 'Culture in the Crunch,' for a discussion of cultural equity programs and the critique of multiculturalism by arts groups.

43 Anita Lahey, 'Where Is Everyone? Minorities in Publishing,' Q&Q 66, no. 5 (2000): 16; Donna Nurse, 'Writing through Race: Black Writers on Being Edited, Published and Reviewed in Canada,' Q&Q 66, no. 5 (2000): 18–19; May Lui, 'Racism in Canadian Publishing Does Exist,' Q&Q 66, no. 6 (2000): 13. For the contemporary American debate, see Aronson, Beyond the Pale.

44 Paul Yee, interview.

45 Atleo, 'This Is about Raven,' and 'Reviews: Books about Raven.'

46 Isabel Vincent, 'The Fight for a Truly National Literature,' G&M, 8 July 1991.

47 Patsy Aldana, interview. The simultaneous specificity and erasure of identity were noted by Whitaker and Sybesma-Ironside, 'On Reviewing Picture Books,' 61. DePasquale and Wolf, 'Select Bibliography,' 149, cite A Salmon for Simon as an example of the dominance of non-Aboriginal voices in the Canadian publishing industry.

48 Bertanees and Thornley, 'Reading Cultural Representations,' explore the critique of colonial texts as a way to disrupt notions of the stability of the colonial subject and beliefs about culture.

49 Mackey, House of Difference, 5, both drawing on and critiquing Homi Bhaba's theories of the dominant seeking to obliterate difference, notes that in Canada 'liberal "tolerance" is mobilized to manage populations and also to create identities,' drawing attention to construction of difference through liberal policies of pluralism, diversity and tolerance.

50 Nodelman, 'What Children Are,' 146.

51 Bainbridge, Pantaleo, and Ellis, 'Multicultural Picture Books'; Bainbridge and Fayjean, 'Seeing Oneself in a Book.'

52 Lissa Paul, interview.

53 Ibid. See also Wollman-Bonilla, 'Outrageous Viewpoints,' for pre-service teachers' attitudes towards children's literature that challenges dominant understandings of society.

54 Ibid.

55 Tabassum Siddiqui, 'Tales of Diversity,' Q&Q 74, no. 7 (2008): 8.

56 Edwards and Saltman, 'Looking at Ourselves.'

57 Waterston, Children's Literature in Canada, 29.

58 Seale, 'Introduction,' *A Broken Flute*, 4.
59 See, for example, the preface to George H. Griffin, *Legends of the Evergreen Coast*, illus. W. H. Probus Pleming (Vancouver: Clarke and Stuart, 1934); and Hugh Weatherby, *Tales the Totems Tell*, illus. Hugh Weatherby (Toronto: Macmillan Company of Canada, 1944). Weatherby's collection was still in print and recommended in the first edition of *The Republic of Childhood*.
60 Bradford, 'Saved by the Word,' 90, discusses the same tropes in colonial Australian children's texts.
61 Egoff, 'Writing and Publishing of Canadian Children's Books': 'Their Indian characters were not just primitive warriors; they were often shown in their natural and contemporary role as masters of woodcraft and as guides for white men in the forest. Their personal characters and characteristics were indistinguishable from those of the white man' (350).
62 Lucas, 'Nature Writers and the Animal Story,' 378.
63 Jenness, *Corn Goddess*.
64 Hearne, 'Cite the Source,' 23.
65 Hawthorn, 'Myths and Sources,' was critical of Clark's undifferentiated pan-Indian approach. See also Frazer, 'Legends Old and New,' and Egoff, *Republic of Childhood*, 20.
66 Grant, 'Canadian Fairy Tale,' 29.
67 Michael Kusugak, interview: 'When I write, I make up things, but when I tell a story, I tell a traditional story … If I told some of these stories the way they were told traditionally, I would be kicked out of the schools all the time, because they are like the original Grimm tales where there is so much gore and blood.'
68 Houston, 'Vision of That Mask,' 13.
69 Whitaker, 'Raven Cycle,' 47. See also Whitaker, 'Monsters from Native Canadian Mythologies.'
70 Hill, 'Journeying with Glooscap.'
71 Bradford, *Reading Race*, 109–10, citing Bob Hodge and Vijay Mishra, *Dark Side of the Dream: Australian Literature and the Postcolonial Mind* (Sydney: Allen and Unwin, 1991) on the idea of Aboriginalism.
72 McGrath, 'Genuine Eskimo Literature,' 23, 24.
73 Harris and Kealy, 'Caught in the Current,' 10.
74 Harris, 'Shift from Feasthouse to Book,' 9–11.
75 Harris, *Once More Upon a Totem*, 192–5.
76 Grattan, 'Vitality … Waiting in the Wilderness.'
77 Egoff, *Republic of Childhood*: 'Tom Thumb and Robin Hood are part of the Canadian child's heritage and are effortlessly absorbed into his consciousness. Na-pe and Wisakedjak become known only by purposeful discovery' (20).
78 Bradford, *Reading Race*, 9, points out that in colonial classrooms Aboriginal children would also have come into contact with the same texts that constructed them as the Other. See also Culleton, 'Images of Native People.'
79 Egoff, *Republic of Childhood*: 'Indigenous though they are to Canada, the Indian legend is culturally "imported" and no more native to Canadian children than an Eskimo lullaby' (20). Money, 'Profile: William Toye': 'Indian legends are not easy to retell in modern English, partly because of their long oral ancestry and partly because the Indian point of view is so different from the Caucasian' (22).

80 Sue Sutton, 'First Nations' New Shoots,' *Q&Q* 61, no. 12 (1995): 10; Lesley Krueger, 'The Inuktitut Munsch: Why Aboriginal Translations of Popular Canadian Books Rarely Work in Native Schools,' *Q&Q* 63, no. 6 (1997): 66.

81 Richard Van Camp, interview.

82 Ibid.

83 Michael Kusugak, interview.

84 Ibid.

85 Gillian O'Reilly, 'Four Czech Chicks,' *BC* 30, no. 2 (August 2001): 27–9, discusses the particular blue that Krykorka uses for her illustrations.

86 Kusugak, *Arctic Stories*, 30.

87 Michael Kusugak, interview.

88 Davis, 'Tom King'; Davis, 'Kent Monkman'; Truchan-Tataryn and Gingell, 'Dances with Coyote'; Mendoza, 'Goodbye, Columbus: Take Two.'

89 McGillis, 'Knowingness, Postcolonialism, Children's Literature'; Bradford, *Reading Race*, 242–5; Mallan and McGillis, 'Camp Aesthetics and Children's Culture.' Monkman has continued to explore issues of the intersection of colonialism with sexuality and gender, mischief and transgression in Aboriginal-European encounters in his paintings, and through a drag persona, Miss Chief Eagle Testickle in his films and installation pieces. See Monkman's webpage at http://www.urbannation.com/kent.htm, and 'Meet the Artist,' http://cybermuse.gallery.ca/cybermuse/showcases/meet/artist_e.jsp?artistid=26919.

90 Val Ross, 'Book Learning,' *G&M*, 18 April 1992; Patsy Aldana, interview.

91 Patsy Aldana, interview.

92 Ibid.

93 Bradford, *Unsettling Narratives*, 56.

94 Wolf and DePasquale, 'Home and Native Land,' 99.

95 Lissa Paul, interview. Bradford, *Reading Race*, 48–9, discusses encounters with the 'Aboriginal sacred,' and argues that Aboriginality in children's books is presented as a locus of spiritual desire that is seen to offer deep historic traditions and the possibility of transcendence and an encounter with the numinous. Grattan, 'Vitality … Waiting in the Wilderness,' 106–7, discussing the work of Christie Harris, argues that her emphasis on Aboriginal spirituality and connection to nature objectifies Aboriginal people as an extension of the landscape, a 'symbolic, environmental construction,' rooted in the past, rather than the contemporary world.

96 Nodelman, 'What Children Are,' 153.

97 Janet Wilson, interview.

98 Greg Young-Ing, interview.

99 Pratt, *Imperial Eyes*, 6, describes the 'contact zone' as the space of colonial encounters where ongoing relations are established between people who have been geographically and historically separate.

100 Anita Lahey, 'The Unique Challenge of Theytus Books: Aboriginal House Combines Oral and Printed Traditions,' *Q&Q* 66, no. 5 (2000): 18; Collene Ferguson, 'Pemmican Publications Fills a Need,' *CCBN* 26, no. 3 (2003): 12–13.

101 Bradford, *Unsettling Narratives*, 52.

102 Anita Large, interview.

103 Gillian O'Reilly, 'Writing with Pride,' *CCBN* 26, no. 3 (2003): 10–11.

104 George Littlechild, telephone interview.

105 Marke Andrews, 'A Story of Pain behind the Paintings,' *Vancouver Sun*, 31 December 1993; Methot, 'George Littlechild'; Ryan, *Trickster Shift*, 204.

106 Richard Van Camp, interview.

107 Nodelman, 'What's Canadian.'

108 Ibid.

109 Pantaleo, 'What's Canadian,' 42.

110 Ibid., 46. Nodelman, 'As Canadian as Apple Pie,' 96, describes self-consciously Canadian picturebooks that represent the country through a nostalgic 'filter of maple-syrup goo, as a touristy paradise of primeval wilds and idyllic forests and charmingly rustic farmyards.'

111 Pantaleo, 'Exploring Canadian Identity.'

112 Thistleton-Martin, 'How Can Illustrations Introduce "Canadianness."'

113 Judith Thistleton-Martin, interview.

114 Ibid.

115 Ibid.

116 Isabel Pascua, interview; Pascua, 'Translation and Intercultural Education.'

117 Isabel Pascua, interview.

118 Björn Sundmark, email interview; Sundmark, 'Hockey Fictions'; Sumiko Shirai, email interview.

119 Sumiko Shirai, email interview.

120 Björn Sundmark, email interview.

121 Martina Seifert, email interview.

122 Ibid.

123 Nodelman, 'As Canadian as Apple Pie,' 96, notes that of seventy-nine titles published in 2002 that are listed in his review article, 'almost all of these books, produced in Canada by primarily Canadian publishers, announced themselves on the verso of their title pages as being published or distributed both in Canada and the US, and that almost all provide an American address as well as a Canadian one.'

124 Galway, *From Nursery Rhymes to Nationhood*, 23–32, discusses the positive and negative views of the interaction between Canada and the United States in the realm of literature, starting in the late nineteenth century.

125 Michael Katz, interview; Karen Hammond, 'Goodbye Hockey Sweater, Hello Casey at the Bat,' *Q&Q* 66, no. 10 (2000): 24, cites Colleen MacMillan, associate publisher of Annick Press, regarding their decision to alter their editorial style to American spelling. Andrew H. Malcolm, 'The Media Business: Publisher for Children, a Canadian Success Story,' *New York Times*, 3 April 1990, notes that 70 per cent of Kids Can books have the potential for foreign sales, adding that 'the others have more Canadian themes, like "Pay Cheques" and "Let's Celebrate Canada's Special Days."' Presumably it was the spelling of 'cheque' that rendered the title unsuitable for sale in the United States. Marina Strauss, 'U.S. Demands Trample Canadian Kids' Lit,' *G&M*, 1 June 2001, notes that an Annick Press book was rejected by an American publisher for the spelling of the word colour in the title.

126 For the broader issues of translating and renaming in children's books, see Oittinen, 'Translating Picture Books'; O'Sullivan, 'Narratology Meets Translation Studies';

Tabbert, 'Translation of Children's Literature'; Yamazaki, 'Why Change Names?'; and Whitehead, 'Americanization of British Children's Books.'

127 Betty Waterton, telephone interview. See also McDonough, 'Creative National Literature': 'But if (the American) Vanguard publishers decided that an American destination would be more palatable to American book buyers then what are they doing about "international bridges to peace and understanding among nations?" … Surely that beautiful picture book which two talented Canadians conceived has the right to retain its original text' (9).

128 Sue Ann Alderson, interview.

129 Kevin Major, email interview.

130 Barbara Reid, interview, notes that she considered setting *The Subway Mouse* (2003) in Toronto, but 'the consensus was to make it more generic to improve the chances for foreign sales.' Reid adds that the details were specific enough that she did not feel the need to fight over greater specificity of references to place.

131 Kady MacDonald Denton, email interview.

132 Biamonte, 'Crossing Culture.'

133 Janet Lunn, interview.

134 Janet Wilson, interview.

135 Michèle Lemieux, interview.

136 Wild, 'Franklin,' 42.

137 Stefan Czernecki, interview. Cooper, 'Only the Rarest Kind,' discusses her encounter in Australia with authors and illustrators who expressed the same concerns about pressures to sanitize their manuscripts to make them 'safe and marketable' internationally.

138 Aldana, 'Crossing the Money Boundary,' 677; see also Marina Strauss, 'U.S. Demands Trample Canadian Kids' Lit,' *G&M*, 1 June 2001, who quotes Aldana as saying that Groundwood feels a 'huge' pressure to 'de-Canadianize' books, and that 'Americans have no interest in Canadian content.' Galway, 'From Nursery Rhymes to Nationhood,' 62–3, quotes Strauss's article before arguing that fears about de-Canadianization have been part of the world of Canadian children's books since the nineteenth century.

139 Rick Wilks, interview.

140 Dennis Johnson, interview.

141 Valerie Hussey, interview.

142 Sheryl McFarlane, interview.

143 Ibid.

144 Jobe, 'Cultural Identity through Picturebooks,' discusses his examination of 104 realistic picturebooks out of the 181 picturebooks published between 1998 and 2000 and recommended in 1998–2001 issues of the Canadian Children's Book Centre's *Our Choice* catalogues.

145 Ibid., 81, 85.

146 Black, 'Canadian Historical Picture Books,' 38.

147 Ibid., 103.

148 Black and Jobe, 'Telling Our Story?' 13–15.

149 Black and Jobe, 'Gaining a Sense of Place.'

150 Tyrrell, 'School Library Market,' 27–8.
151 Setterington, 'Anne of Green Gables.'
152 Kit Pearson, interview.
153 Annette Goldsmith, email interview.
154 Aldana, 'Crossing the Money Boundary,' 677.
155 William French, 'Magook, Aurora and a Sensitive Question About Goldilocks,' *G&M*, 30 August 1977. The quotation from Cutler was from a speech given at a Children's Book International Symposium at the Boston Public Library.
156 May Cutler, interview.
157 Ibid.
158 Val Ross, 'Book Learning,' *G&M*, 18 April 1992; Kathy Lowinger, interview: 'I remember showing a very charming book called *The Hippo's Wedding* years ago to a Dane and the person slammed the book shut and said, "We do not dress our animals in Denmark."'
159 Ted Harrison, interview.
160 Val Ross, 'Book Learning,' *G&M*, 18 April 1992.
161 Josiane Polidori, interview.
162 Ibid.
163 Rick Wilks, quoted in Carolyn Dodds, 'A Child's Garden of Publishers: Canadian Kid Lit Comes of Age,' *Financial Post Magazine*, 1 August 1984, 29–35.
164 Kathy Lowinger, interview.
165 Ibid.
166 Patsy Aldana, interview.
167 Martina Seifert, email interview.
168 Ibid. See also Martina Seifert, 'Image Trap,' 236.
169 See also Seifert, 'Selective Canadiana.'
170 Robert Munsch, quoted in Dodds, 'A Child's Garden of Publishers.'
171 Avery, 'Children's Books and Social History,' 23–4.
172 Matthew Hays, 'Magic from Montreal,' *Q&Q*, 69, no. 10 (2003): 16–17.
173 Ibid., 16.
174 Ibid., 17.
175 Josiane Polidori, interview.
176 Mariella Bertelli, email interview.
177 Rick Wilks, interview.
178 Jeffrey Canton, interview. Kress and van Leeuwen, *Reading Images*, 159–80, discuss the concept of modality, the means by which visual images persuade readers of their naturalized realism by markers like colour saturation, depth, illumination, and brightness, pointing out that these markers are culturally embedded.
179 Sarah Ellis, interview.
180 Solomon, 'Canada at Bologna 1990,' 3–4.
181 Lepage, 'Le métissage,' xiii, refers to *Une île dans la soupe* as a 'forme de métissage temporel.'
182 Maryann H. Owen, 'Review of "An Island in the Soup,"' *School Library Journal* 47, no. 6 (2001): 122; see also Suzanne Teasdale, 'Review of "Une île dans la soup,"' *Lurelu* 25, no. 3 (2003): 34; Livres ouverts, Éducation, Loisir et Sport Québec, http:// www.livresouverts.qc.ca/rechDetaillee_V3.php?lo=17350.

183 Ray Conlogue, 'Telltale Picture Books: Spirited and Iconoclastic, Quebec Illustrators Are Capturing Children's Fancies and Fantasies around the World,' *G&M*, 11 April 1992, quoting Stéphane Poulin.

184 Alison Fripp, telephone interview.

185 Kathy Lowinger, interview.

186 On the American publisher's decision to issue the book, see http://cincopuntospress. blogspot.com/2008/02/little-boy-is-worried-about-size-of-his.html.

187 Hays, 'Magic from Montreal,' 17.

188 Jeffrey Canton, interview. Alison Mews, in a review of *Sassy Gracie* that appeared in *CM* 6, no. 3 (1999), http://umanitoba.ca/outreach/cm/vol6/no3/sassie.html, objected to the work on moral grounds: 'Sassy Gracie is a very unusual and disturbing story. Gracie, who at first glance appears to be a child, but is actually hired help, cooks two chickens for the Master in Cook's absence, but she unintentionally eats them … There are no creative solutions by which Gracie redeems herself … There is no evidence of any remorse nor any hint by the author that she will have to confess to her deceptions and bear the consequences … I think Sassy Gracie has gone beyond mischievous and is unacceptably deceitful. Not recommended.' In contrast, Erinn Banting, 'Review of *Sassy Gracie*,' *BC* 28, no. 4 (1999): 42, reads the figure of Sassy Gracie as a feisty little girl and praises Pratt's 'stunning visual accompaniment' to 'jovial dialogue.' The review in *PW* 245, no. 25 (1998): 90, criticized the picturebook's 'clamorous presentation,' arguing that Pratt's 'chaotic perspectives and highly saturated colours induce a feeling of frenzy.'

189 Rick Wilks, interview.

190 Gagnon, 'Translation of Children's Books in Canada,' remains the only comprehensive published study in English. Cobban, 'Bridging the Two Solitudes,' provides a comprehensive overview of the historical and contemporary context of the translation of children's books from French into English in Canada. The earliest translated titles specifically published for child readers in Cobban's comprehensive bibliography are Albert Bolduc, *The Koax Family*, trans. R.J. Clark, illus. Henri Beaulac, BB Chapbooks, no. 1 (Montreal: Fides, 1944), also published in French by Fides in 1944 as *La famille grenouille*; and Marius Barbeau's *The Golden Phoenix* (1958), published by Oxford University Press. For the history of the Bolduc title, see Melançon, 'L'Édition d'enfance … chez Fides,' 57–9. She notes that despite the overall quality and exceptional Canadianness of the work, the skilled illustrations by Beaulac, who had studied at the Pratt Institute in New York, and the high quality of the printing, Fides was unable to find a market for an expensive picturebook published on consignment. Thus *The Golden Phoenix* was the first widely marketed Canadian title translated from French into English.

191 For 2007 grants, the rate was $0.14 a word for text. Applications for grants under $100 are not considered. This means that a picturebook text would have to have a minimum of 725 words in order to be eligible for a translation grant, effectively eliminating picturebooks from grant applications. The Canada Council for the Arts, 'Book Publishing Support: Translation Grants,' http://www.canadacouncil.ca/grants/ writing/ex127227344686875000.htm.

192 Roch Carrier, telephone interview.

193 Shaun Smith, 'Stuck at the Border,' *Q&Q* 74, no. 3 (2008): 19–20, discusses the chal-

lenges of funding the translation of international works in Canada, stating that 'there is no support for Canadian publishers wishing to hire Canadians to translate foreign works.'

194 Dave Jenkinson, interview.

195 Gillian O'Reilly, 'Lots in Translation: A Canadian Story,' *CCBN* 31, no. 4 (2008): 10–12.

196 Josiane Polidori, interview.

197 Ibid.

198 Alison Fripp, telephone interview.

199 May Cutler, interview.

200 Ibid.

201 Maruszeczka, 'Publishing Picture Books,' 43.

202 Anne Millyard, interview.

203 Rick Wilks, interview. Madore, 'L'Édition québécoise,' 21, discusses the success of La Courte Échelle at marketing its titles internationally, without any mention of the joint publication arrangement with Annick for the Canadian anglophone market.

204 Cobban, 'Bridging the Two Solitudes,' 46.

205 Gagnon, 'Translation of Children's Books in Canada,' 23.

206 'Interview with Ian Wallace,' Groundwood Books, https://www.anansi.ca/gw_wallace_interview.cfm; 'Author Spotlight: Nicolas Debon,' Tundra Books, http://www.mcclelland.com/author/results.pperl?authorid=81229.

207 Kathryn Cole, interview.

208 Paul Morin, interview.

209 Wright, *Hip and Trivial*, 9–10.

210 Ibid., 147.

211 Ibid., 156. For a response to Wright by a noted Canadian nationalist, see Lorimer, 'Hip and Trivial.'

212 Bainbridge and Thistleton-Martin, 'Children's Literature,' conclude by asking 'should literacy be about helping people to become sophisticated global citizens or sophisticated consumers?'

213 Redekop, 'Canadian Literary Criticism,' provides a clear introduction to the current debates over the construction of nationalist identities.

214 Bainbridge, 'Children's Literature in National Identity Formation,' describes the discussion among the group of elementary and middle-years teachers about their definitions of what constitutes a 'Canadian book' and a 'Canadian author.'

215 Kevin Major, email interview; 'Eh? to Zed,' *CCBN* 24, no. 1 (2001): 21–2.

Bibliography

Primary Sources

Archival Sources

Ballantyne, Robert. Original artwork. Osborne Collection of Early Children's Books. Toronto Public Library.

Beddows, Eric. Eric Beddows fonds [pseudonym of Ken Nutt]. Literary Archives. Library and Archives Canada.

Blades, Ann. Ann Blades fonds. Literary Archives. Library and Archives Canada.

Blades, Ann. Ann Blades fonds. Rare Books and Special Collections. University of British Columbia Library.

Canadian Library Association. Archives. Canadian Library Association Office.

Canadian Library Association. Canadian Library Association fonds. Library and Archives Canada.

Children's Book Store. Children's Book Store fonds. Osborne Collection of Early Children's Books. Toronto Public Library.

Cleaver, Elizabeth. Elizabeth Cleaver fonds. Literary Archives. Library and Archives Canada.

Cowie, Margaret. Margaret Cowie fonds. Rare Books and Special Collections. University of British Columbia Library.

Gal, Laszlo. Laszlo Gal fonds. Literary Archives. Library and Archives Canada.

Gay, Marie-Louise. Mary-Louise Gay fonds. Literary Archives. Library and Archives Canada.

Jefferys, Charles Williams. Original artwork. Osborne Collection of Early Children's Books. Toronto Public Library.

Khalsa, Dayal Kaur. Dayal Kaur Khalsa fonds. Literary Archives. Library and Archives Canada.

Lightburn, Ron. Ron Lightburn fonds. Literary Archives. Library and Archives Canada.

Poulin, Stéphane. Stéphane Poulin fonds. Literary Archives. Library and Archives Canada.

Reid, Barbara. Barbara Reid fonds. Literary Archives. Library and Archives Canada.

Tundra Books. Tundra Collection. Special Collections. McGill University Library.

Young Canada's Book Week. Young Canada's Book Week fonds. Literary Archives. Library and Archives Canada.

Interviews (title and institution current at time of interview)

Aldana, Patsy. Publisher, Groundwood Books. Interview by Judith Saltman. Toronto, 18 June 2003.

Alderson, Sue Ann. Author and Faculty, University of British Columbia. Interview by Judith Saltman. Vancouver, 18 May 2003.

Alderson, Sue Ann. Interview by Judith Saltman. Vancouver, 17 April 2004.

Andrews, Jan. Author and storyteller. Email interview by Judith Saltman. Received 12 September 2003.

Andrews, Jan. Email interview by Judith Saltman. Received 21 September 2003.

Andrews, Jan. Email interview by Judith Saltman. Received 22 August 2006.

Aska, Warabé. Author and illustrator. Interview by Judith Saltman. Toronto, 15 June 2003.

Asselin, Marlene. Faculty, University of British Columbia. Email interview by Judith Saltman. Received 28 October 2004.

Aubrey, Irene. Former Chief, Children's Literature Service, National Library of Canada. Telephone interview by Judith Saltman. 11 December 2006.

Aubrey, Irene. Correspondence with Judith Saltman. Received 2 January 2007.

Bailey, Linda. Author. Interview by Judith Saltman. Vancouver, 12 May 2003.

Bainbridge, Joyce. Faculty, University of Alberta. Interview by Judith Saltman. Ottawa, 29 June 2003.

Baker, Deirdre. Faculty, University of Toronto. Interview by Judith Saltman. Toronto, 22 June 2003.

Bertelli, Mariella. Librarian, Toronto Public Library. Email interview by Judith Saltman. Received 21 October 2003.

Blades, Ann. Author and illustrator. Interview by Gail Edwards, Judi Saltman, and Kathryn Shoemaker. Vancouver, 28 September 2002.

Blades, Ann. Telephone interview by Judith Saltman. 18 April 2004.

Bosson, Victor. Illustrator. Interview by Judith Saltman. Victoria, 6 May 2003.

Bouchard, David. Author and educator. Interview by Judith Saltman. Toronto, 22 June 2003.

Brinklow, Laurie. Publisher, The Acorn Press. Email interview by Kathryn Shoemaker. Received 20 March 2006.

Butler, Geoff. Author and illustrator. Email interview by Judith Saltman. Received 8 September 2003.

Cameron, Martha. Teacher-librarian, Surrey School District, BC. Telephone interview by Gail Edwards. 18 November 2006.

Campbell, Donna Jane. Independent scholar. Email interview by Judith Saltman. Received 19 July 2004.

Campbell, Donna Jane. Email interview by Judith Saltman. Received 12 September 2004.

Campbell, Donna Jane. Email interview by Judith Saltman. Received 12 August 2005.

Canton, Jeffrey. Critic and Faculty, York University. Interview by Judith Saltman. Toronto, 19 June 2003.

Carey, Trudy. Manager, Woozles bookstore. Email interview by Judith Saltman. Received 18 November 2003.

Carrier, Roch. Author and former National Librarian, National Library of Canada. Telephone interview by Judith Saltman. 28 March 2005.

Carroll, Michael. Former Publisher, Beach Holme Publishers, and Editorial Director, the Dundurn Group. Telephone interview by Kathryn Shoemaker. 18 April 2006.

Carver, Peter. Editor, Red Deer Press. Email interview by Judith Saltman. Received 9 July 2003.

Chan, Harvey. Illustrator. Interview by Judith Saltman. Toronto, 20 June 2003.

Charles, Norma. Author. Telephone interview by Judith Saltman. 17 April 2004.

Clark, Karin. Publisher, Raven Publishing. Email interview by Kathryn Shoemaker. Received 3 April 2006.

Cole, Kathryn. Former Editor, Stoddart Publishing. Interview by Judith Saltman. Toronto, 14 June 2003.

Cole, Kathryn. Email interview by Judith Saltman. 25 November 2006.

Copithorne, Tama. Director, Japanese Culture and Communication, Simon Fraser University. Email interview by Judith Saltman. Received 18 July 2004.

Cree, Mary Ann. Junior School librarian, Bishop Strachan School, Toronto. Email interview by Judith Saltman. Received 12 October 2004.

Cutler, May. Former Publisher, Tundra Books. Interview by Gail Edwards. Montreal, 24 April 2003.

Cutler, May. Email interview by Judith Saltman. Received 18 October 2004.

Czernecki, Stefan. Author and illustrator. Interview by Judith Saltman. Vancouver, 24 April 2003.

Czernecki, Stefan. Telephone interview by Judith Saltman. 23 September 2006.

Daniel, Alan. Illustrator. (Interviewed jointly with Lea Daniel.) Email interview by Judith Saltman. Received 3 September 2004.

Daniel, Lea. Illustrator. (Interviewed jointly with Alan Daniel.) Email interview by Judith Saltman. Received 3 September 2004.

Davis, Virginia. Children's literature consultant and former Executive Director, Canadian Children's Book Centre. Interview by Judith Saltman. Toronto, 14 June 2003.

Davis, Virginia. Email interview by Judith Saltman. Received 29 December 2005.

Denton, Kady MacDonald. Author and illustrator. Email interview by Judith Saltman. Received 6 September 2003.

Douglas, Janice. Director, Youth Services and Programming, Vancouver Public Library. Interview by Judith Saltman. Vancouver, 12 May 2003.

Duncan, Sandy Frances. Author. Telephone interview by Judith Saltman. 17 April 2004.

Edwards, Catherine. Director, Pacific Educational Press. Telephone interview by Kathryn Shoemaker. 16 May 2006.

Egoff, Sheila. Professor emerita, University of British Columbia. Interview by Judith Saltman and Kathryn Shoemaker. Vancouver, 24 September 2001.

Ellis, Sarah. Author, critic, and librarian, North Vancouver District Public Library. Interview by Judith Saltman. Vancouver, 13 May 2003.

Englander, Ricky. Former Publisher, Kids Can Press. Interview by Judith Saltman. Toronto, 22 June 2003.

Fernandes, Eugenie. Author and illustrator. (Interviewed jointly with Kim Fernandes.) Interview by Judith Saltman. Toronto, 21 June 2003.

Fernandes, Kim. Author and illustrator. (Interviewed jointly with Eugenie Fernandes.) Interview by Judith Saltman. Toronto, 21 June 2003.

Filipenko, Margot. Faculty, University of British Columbia. Email interview by Judith Salt-
    man. Received 24 June 2004.
Fitch, Sheree. Author. Email interview by Judith Saltman. Received 8 December 2003.
Fripp, Alison. Publisher, Lobster Press. Telephone interview by Kathryn Shoemaker. 13
    April 2006.
Gay, Marie-Louise. Author and illustrator. Interview by Kathryn Shoemaker. Toronto, 2
    March 2003.
Gill, April. Teacher-librarian, West Vancouver School District, BC, and National Chair,
    Information Book Award Committee, Children's Literature Roundtables of Canada.
    Interview by Judith Saltman. West Vancouver, 22 August 2003.
Goldsmith, Annette. Former Editor, *The Looking Glass*, and Information Professional,
    LeRoy Collins Leon County Public Library, Tallahassee, FL. Email interview by Judith
    Saltman. Received 11 November 2003.
Granfield, Linda. Author. Interview by Judith Saltman. Toronto, 21 June 2003.
Gregory, Nan. Author and storyteller. Interview by Judith Saltman. Vancouver, 30 July
    2003.
Harrison, Ted. Illustrator. Interview by Judith Saltman. Victoria, 8 May 2003.
Hatch, Ronald. Publisher, Ronsdale Press. Interview by Kathryn Shoemaker. Vancouver,
    20 March 2006.
Hussey, Valerie. Publisher, Kids Can Press. Interview by Judith Saltman. Toronto, 24 June
    2003.
Jenkinson, Dave. Faculty, University of Manitoba, and Editor, *CM: Canadian Review of
    Materials*. Interview by Judith Saltman. Ottawa, 25 June 2003.
Jobe, Ronald. Faculty, University of British Columbia. Interview by Judith Saltman. Van-
    couver, 16 May 2003.
Johnson, Dennis. Publisher, Red Deer Press. Interview by Cherie Givens. Calgary, 16 June
    2005.
Katz, Bernard. Former Head, Special Collections, McLaughlin Library, University of
    Guelph. Email interview by Judith Saltman. Received 30 November 2004.
Katz, Michael. Publisher, Tradewind Books. Interview by Judith Saltman. Vancouver, 18
    April 2003.
Krykorka, Vladyana. Illustrator. Interview by Kathryn Shoemaker. Toronto, 27 February
    2003.
Kusugak, Michael. Author and storyteller. Interview by Judith Saltman. Vancouver, 26
    May 2003.
LaFave, Kim. Illustrator. Interview by Judith Saltman. Vancouver, 14 May 2003.
Landsberg, Michele. Critic. Interview by Judith Saltman. Toronto, 18 June 2003.
Large, Anita. Publishing Manager, Theytus Books. Interview by Camille Callison. Pentic-
    ton, BC, 29 April 2005.
Lawson, Julie. Author. Email interview by Judith Saltman. Received 29 September 2003.
Lemieux, Michèle. Author and illustrator, and Faculty, L'École de design, Université du
    Québec à Montréal. Interview by Gail Edwards. Montreal, 22 April 2003.
Lightburn, Ron. Illustrator. Email interview by Judith Saltman. Received 20 September
    2003.
Little, Jean. Author. Telephone interview by Judith Saltman. 20 April 2004.

Littlechild, George. Author and illustrator. Telephone interview by Judith Saltman. 20 December 2003.

Lottridge, Celia. Author and storyteller. Interview by Judith Saltman. Toronto, 18 June 2003.

Lowinger, Kathy. Publisher, Tundra Books. Interview by Judith Saltman. Ottawa, 29 June 2003.

Lunn, Janet. Author. Interview by Judith Saltman. Ottawa, 27 June 2003.

Lunn, Janet. Telephone interview by Judith Saltman. 20 April 2004.

Lunn, Janet. Email interview by Judith Saltman. Received 18 June 2006.

Mackay, Claire. Author. Telephone interview by Judith Saltman. 20 April 2004.

MacMath, Russ. Teacher, Richmond School District, BC. Email interview by Judith Saltman. Received 24 November 2003.

Major, Kevin. Author. Email interview by Judith Saltman. Received September 1, 2003.

McDougall, Carol. Director, Read to Me! Nova Scotia Family Literacy Program. Interview by Judith Saltman. Ottawa, 28 June 2003.

McFarlane, Sheryl. Author. Interview by Judith Saltman. Victoria, 6 May 2003.

McGrath, Leslie. Head, Osborne Collection of Early Children's Books, Toronto Public Library. Interview by Gail Edwards and Judith Saltman. Toronto, 13 June 2003.

McMillan, Margie. Co-owner, Granny Bates Children's Books. Interview by Judith Saltman. St John's, 18 October 2003.

Millyard, Anne. Former Publisher, Annick Press. (Interviewed jointly with Rick Wilks.) Interview by Judith Saltman. Toronto, 17 June 2003.

Morin, Paul. Author and illustrator. Interview by Judith Saltman. Toronto, 17 June 2003.

Newfeld, Frank. Book designer and illustrator. Correspondence with Judith Saltman. Received 24 September 2002.

Nodelman, Perry. Faculty, University of Winnipeg. Email interview by Judith Saltman. Received 20 September 2003.

Nutt, Ken (aka Eric Beddows). Illustrator. Interview by Judith Saltman. Toronto, 20 June 2003.

Oberman, Sheldon. Author and storyteller. Email interview by Judith Saltman. Received posthumously 3 May 2004.

O'Reilly, Gillian. Editor, *Canadian Children's Book News*. Email interview by Judith Saltman. Received 20 December 2005.

Pascua, Isabel. Translator and Faculty, the University of Las Palmas, Grand Canaria, Spain. Interview by Judith Saltman. Vancouver, 15 September 2003.

Paul, Lissa. Faculty, University of New Brunswick. Interview by Gail Edwards and Judith Saltman. Toronto, 14 June 2003.

Pearson, Kit. Author and critic. Interview by Judith Saltman. Vancouver, 3 August 2003.

Pennell, Victoria. Editor, *Resource Links*, and former teacher-librarian. Email interview by Judith Saltman. Received 25 November 2003.

Polidori, Josiane. Head, Children's Literature Service, National Library of Canada. Interview by Judith Saltman. Ottawa, 4 July 2003.

Ramsay, Diane. Managing Editor, Pemmican Publications. Interview by Camille Callison. Winnipeg, 7 June 2005.

Reczuch, Karen. Illustrator. Email interview by Judith Saltman. Received 20 July 2004.

Reid, Barbara. Author and illustrator. Interview by Kathryn Shoemaker. Toronto, 26 February 2003.

Reid, Barbara. Email interview by Judith Saltman. Received 15 November 2004.

Rose, Clyde. Publisher, Breakwater Books. Telephone interview by Kathryn Shoemaker. 20 June 2006.

Ross, Julian. Former Publisher, Polestar Press. Telephone interview by Kathryn Shoemaker. 16 March 2006.

Rubio, Mary. Faculty, University of Guelph, and Editor, *CCL: Canadian Children's Literature.* Email interview by Judith Saltman. Received 4 September 2003.

Rubio, Mary. Email interview by Judith Saltman. Received 15 July 2004.

Sapergia, Barbara. Editor, Coteau Books. (Interviewed jointly with Geoffrey Ursell.) Email Interview by Kathryn Shoemaker. Received 20 June 2006.

Sarick, Judy. Former co-owner, The Children's Book Store. Interview by Judith Saltman. Toronto, 24 June 2003.

Savoff, Dimiter. Publisher, Simply Read Books. Interview by Judith Saltman. Vancouver, 8 April 2005.

Seifert, Martina. Researcher, University of Liepzig, Germany. Email interview by Judith Saltman. Received 20 October 2003.

Setterington, Ken. Author, critic, storyteller, and Children's and Youth Advocate, Toronto Public Library. Interview by Gail Edwards and Judith Saltman. Toronto, 15 June 2003.

Shapiro, Jon. Faculty, University of British Columbia. Email interview by Judith Saltman. Received 21 November 2003.

Shilliday, Greg. Publisher, Great Plains Publications. Telephone interview by Kathryn Shoemaker. 31 March 2006.

Shirai, Sumiko. Faculty, Shirayuri College, Tokyo, Japan. Email interview by Judith Saltman. Received 24 April 2004.

Shoemaker, Kathryn. Illustrator. Email interview by Judith Saltman. Received 4 December 2004.

Shoemaker, Kathryn. Email interview by Judith Saltman. Received 9 September 2006.

Shute, Allan. Publisher, Tree Frog Press. Telephone interview by Kathryn Shoemaker. 21 March 2006.

Shute, Katherine. Former Managing Editor, Tree Frog Press, and Executive Director, Book Publishers Association of Alberta. Telephone interview by Kathryn Shoemaker. 3 April 2006.

Simon, Phyllis. Co-owner, Vancouver Kidsbooks. Interview by Judith Saltman. Vancouver, 24 April 2003.

Skrypuch, Marsha Forchuk. Author. Interview by Judith Saltman. Ottawa, 29 June 2003.

Slavin, Bill. Author and illustrator. Email interview by Judith Saltman. Received 31 August 2003.

Smiley, Norene. Children's book specialist and former Atlantic officer, Canadian Children's Book Centre. Interview by Judith Saltman. St John's, 18 October 2003.

Solomon, Michael. Art Director, Groundwood Books. Correspondence with Judith Saltman. Received 11 October 2002.

Stevenson, Iain. Faculty, City University London, England. Interview by Judith Saltman. Hamilton, 28 June 2004.

Sundmark, Björn. Faculty, Malmö University, Sweden. Email interview by Judith Saltman. Received 15 November 2003.

Sutton, Wendy. Professor emerita, University of British Columbia. Interview by Judith Saltman. Vancouver, 9 June 2003.

Tanaka, Shelley. Author and Editor, Groundwood Books. Email interview by Judith Saltman. Received 3 June 2004.

Taylor McBryde, Allison. Coordinator of Children's and Young Adult Services, North Vancouver District Public Library. Interview by Judith Saltman. North Vancouver, 23 July 2003.

Teeple, Charlotte. Executive Director, Canadian Children's Book Centre. Email interview by Judith Saltman. Received 9 January 2006.

Thistleton-Martin, Judith. Faculty, University of Western Sydney, Australia. Interview by Judith Saltman. Vancouver, 31 August 2003.

Toye, William. Author and former Editorial Director, Oxford University Press. Interview by Judith Saltman. Toronto, 17 June 2003.

Tregebov, Rhea. Author and Faculty, University of British Columbia. Email interview by Judith Saltman. Received 21 August 2006.

Tyrrell, Bob. Publisher, Orca Book Publishers. Interview by Judith Saltman. Vancouver, 26 April 2003.

Ursell, Geoffrey. Publisher, Coteau Books. (Interviewed jointly with Barbara Sapergia.) Email interview by Kathryn Shoemaker. Received 20 June 2006.

Van Camp, Richard. Author and Faculty, University of British Columbia. Interview by Judith Saltman. Vancouver, 29 September 2003.

Wallace, Ian. Author and illustrator. Interview by Judith Saltman. Toronto, 19 June 2003.

Wallace, Ian. Telephone interview by Judith Saltman. 20 April 2004.

Waterston, Elizabeth. Professor emerita, University of Guelph, and former Editor, *CCL: Canadian Children's Literature*. Email interview by Judith Saltman. Received 28 October 2003.

Waterston, Elizabeth. Email interview by Judith Saltman. Received 22 July 2004.

Waterton, Betty. Author. Telephone interview by Judith Saltman. 28 April 2004.

Watson, Yvonne. Independent scholar. Interview by Judith Saltman. Victoria, 6 May 2003.

Wilks, Rick. Publisher, Annick Press. (Interviewed jointly with Anne Millyard.) Interview by Judith Saltman. Toronto, 17 June 2003.

Wilks, Rick. Email interview by Judith Saltman. Received 13 November 2006.

Wilson, Janet. Illustrator. Interview by Judith Saltman. Toronto, 23 June 2003.

Wolfe, Margie. Publisher, Second Story Press. Interview by Judith Saltman. Toronto, 23 June 2003.

Wynne-Jones, Tim. Author and Editor, Red Deer Press. Interview by Judith Saltman. Ottawa, 29 June 2003.

Wynne-Jones, Tim. Email interview by Judith Saltman. Received 8 June 2004.

Wynne-Jones, Tim. Email interview by Judith Saltman. Received 14 February 2005.

Wynne-Jones, Tim. Email interview by Judith Saltman. Received 5 June 2006.

Yee, Paul. Author. Interview by Judith Saltman. Toronto, 20 June 2003.

Young-Ing, Greg. Former Publishing Manager, Theytus Books. Interview by Camille Callison. Vancouver, 3 May 2005.

Zeman, Ludmila. Author and illustrator. Interview by Gail Edwards. Montreal, 25 April 2003.

Zhang, Ange. Author and illustrator. Interview by Judith Saltman. Scarborough, ON, 23 June 2003.

Children's Magazines, Nineteenth-Century, Mentioned in the Text

The Boys' Own Paper. London: Leisure Hour Office, Religious Tract Society, 1879–1939; London: Lutterworth Press, 1939–67.
   Frequency: Weekly, 1879–1913; Monthly, 1914–67
   Also issued as a bound annual volume, *The Boys' Own Annual*, v. 1, 1879–v. 38, 1941

The Girl's Own Paper. London: Leisure Hour Office, Religious Tract Society, 1880–1902; London: Girls' Own Paper Office, 1902–39; London: Lutterworth Press, 1939–56; Toronto: Warwick Brothers and Rutter, [1880–1907].
   Title varies
   Frequency: Weekly, 1880–1908; Monthly, 1908–56
   Also issued as a bound annual volume, *The Girl's Own Annual*, v.1, 1880–v. 70, 1950
   Also issued as a bound annual volume, reprinted in Toronto from the British edition, 1880–1907

The Maple Leaf. Montreal: Printed for E.H. Lay, [1852–4].
   Frequency: Monthly. v. 1, no. 1 (July 1852)–v. 4, no. 12 (December 1854)
   Subtitle varies. v. 1–v. 2, 'A Juvenile Monthly magazine'; v. 3–v. 4, 'A Canadian monthly magazine'
   CIHM microfiche series, no. P04716

The Snow Drop; or, Juvenile Magazine. Montreal: Lovell and Gibson; Toronto: Scobie and Balfour, 1847–[1850]; Montreal: R.W. Lay, 1850–3.
   Frequency: Monthly. v. 1, no. 1 (April 1847)–v. 3, no. 12 (March 1850)
   Frequency: Monthly. v. 1, no. 1 (July 1850)–v. 5, no. 6 (June 1853)
   Microfilm. Montreal: Bibliothèque national du Québec, 1977

St Nicholas: An Illustrated Magazine for Young Folk. New York: Century Company, 1873–1943.
   Frequency: Monthly

Young Canada: An Illustrated Magazine for the Young. Toronto: William Bryce, 1880–1922; Toronto: William Briggs, 1922–9; Toronto: The Ryerson Press, 1929–33?
   Frequency: Annual
   Subtitle changes with v. 23, 'An Illustrated Annual for Boys'
   Reprinted material from *Young England*.

Young England: An Illustrated Magazine for Boys throughout the English-Speaking World. London: Sunday School Union, 1880–1937.
   Frequency: Weekly, 1880–4; Monthly, 1885–1937

Youth's Companion. Boston: N. Willis, 1836–1929.
   Frequency: Weekly, 1827–1927; Monthly, 1927–9

Children's Magazines, Twentieth-Century, Mentioned in the Text

Chickadee. Toronto: Young Naturalist Foundation, 1979–97; Toronto: Bayard Canada, 1997–.
   Frequency: ten times a year

Owl. Toronto: Young Naturalist Foundation, 1976–97; Toronto: Bayard Canada, 1997–.
Frequency: ten times a year
The Young Naturalist. Don Mills: Young Naturalists Club, 1959–75.

Children's Books Mentioned in the Text

Bibliographic information includes designer, typeface, and medium used to create the illustration wherever information is available. Awards received by individual titles indicated.

Alderson, Sue-Ann. *Bonnie McSmithers, You're Driving Me Dithers*. Illustrated by Fiona Gar-
rick. Edmonton: Tree Frog Press, 1974. Medium: line drawing.
– *Ida and the Wool Smugglers*. Illustrated by Ann Blades. Designed by Michael Solo-
mon. Vancouver: Douglas and McIntyre, 1987. Medium: watercolour. Amelia Frances
Howard-Gibbon Illustrator's Award Shortlist, 1988.
Allison, Rosemary. *The Travels of Ms Beaver*. Illustrated by Ann Powell. Toronto: Women's
Press, 1973.
Andrews, Jan. *Out of the Everywhere: Tales for a New World*. Illustrated by Simon Ng. A
Groundwood Book. Toronto: Douglas and McIntyre, 2000.
Aska, Warabé. *Seasons*. With poetry selected by Alberto Manguel. Designed by Ross Mah
Design Associates. Toronto: Doubleday, 1990. Medium: oil on canvas. Governor Gen-
eral's Award for Children's Literature Shortlist, 1990; Mr Christie's Book Award Silver
Seal, English-language illustration, 1990.
Atwood, Margaret. *Up in the Tree*. Illustrated by Margaret Atwood. Toronto: McClelland
and Stewart, 1977. Medium: line drawing with duotone colour.
Ayre, Robert. *Sketco: The Raven*. Illustrated by Philip Surrey. Toronto: Macmillan, 1961.
Badoe, Adwoa. *Crabs for Dinner*. Edited by Robert Munsch. Illustrated by Belinda Ageda.
Designed by Stephanie Martin. Toronto: Sister Vision, 1995.
– *Nana's Cold Days*. Illustrated by Bushra Junaid. Designed by Michael Solomon. A
Groundwood Book. Toronto: Douglas and McIntyre, 2002. Medium: collage of painted
and printed paper.
Bailey, Linda. *Adventures in Ancient Egypt*. Illustrated by Bill Slavin. Toronto: Kids Can
Press, 2000.
– *Stanley's Party*. Illustrated by Bill Slavin. Designed by Julia Naimska. Toronto: Kids Can
Press, 2003. Medium: acrylics on gessoed paper. Typeface: Leawood Medium. Amelia
Frances Howard-Gibbon Illustrator's Award, 2004; Christie Harris Illustrated Children's
Literature Prize, 2004.
Ballantyne, R.M. *An Author's Adventures, or Personal Reminiscences in Book-Making*. London:
James Nisbet, 1893.
– *Erling the Bold, a Tale of the Norse Sea-Kings*. London: J. Nisbet, 1869.
– *Hudson's Bay, or, Every-day Life in the Wilds of North America during Six Years' Residence in
the Territories of the Honourable Hudson's Bay Company*. Edinburgh: W. Blackwood, 1848.
– *Snowflakes and Sunbeams, or, the Young Fur Traders: A Tale of the Far North*. London, Edin-
burgh, and New York: T. Nelson, 1856.
Bannatyne-Cugnet, Jo. *From Far and Wide: A Canadian Citizenship Scrapbook*. Illustrated by
Song Nan Zhang. Designed by Ingrid Paulson. Toronto: Tundra Books, 2000. Medium:
graphite pencil and watercolour. Information Book Award Shortlist, 2001.
– *A Prairie Alphabet, ABC*. Illustrated by Yvette Moore. Designed by Dan O'Leary. Mon-

treal: Tundra Books, 1992. Medium: acrylic on canvas. Mr Christie's Book Award Gold
Seal, English-language illustration, 1992.

Barbeau, Marius. *The Golden Phoenix and Other French-Canadian Fairy Tales*. Retold by
Michael Hornyansky. Illustrated by Arthur Price. Toronto: Oxford University Press,
1958.

Barton, Bob. *The Bear Says North: Tales from the Northern Lands*. Illustrated by Jirina Marton.
A Groundwood Book. Toronto: Douglas and McIntyre, 2003. Medium: oil pastel.

Bice, Clare. *Across Canada: Stories of Canadian Children*. Toronto: Macmillan, 1949.

– *Jory's Cove: A Story of Nova Scotia*. New York: Macmillan, 1941.

Blades, Ann. *A Boy of Taché*. Montreal: Tundra Books, 1973. The Amelia Frances Howard-
Gibbon Illustrator's Award Shortlist, 1974.

– *By the Sea: An Alphabet Book*. Designed by Wycliffe Smith. Toronto: Kids Can Press, 1985.
Medium: watercolour. Amelia Frances Howard-Gibbon Illustrator's Award Shortlist,
1986; Elizabeth Mrazik-Cleaver Canadian Picture Book Award, 1986.

– *Mary of Mile 18*. Designed by Rolf Harder. Montreal: Tundra Books, 1971. Medium:
watercolour. Amelia Frances Howard-Gibbon Illustrator's Award Shortlist, 1972; Canadian Library Association Book of the Year for Children Award, 1972.

Bogart, Jo Ellen. *Daniel's Dog*. Illustrated by Janet Wilson. Richmond Hill, ON: North
Winds Press, 1990. Medium: mixed media.

Bonner, Mary Graham. *Canada and Her Story*. New York: A.A. Knopf, 1942; London and
Toronto: George G. Harrap and Co., 1943.

Booth, David. *The Dust Bowl*. Illustrated by Karen Reczuch. Designed by Karen Pow-
ers. Toronto: Kids Can Press, 1996. Medium: Graphite pencil and watercolour on
Lanaquarelle paper. Canadian Library Association Book of the Year for Children Award
Shortlist, 1997; IODE Book Award, Municipal Chapter of Toronto, 1996.

– ed. *Doctor Knickerbocker and Other Rhymes: A Canadian Collection*. Illustrated by Maryann
Kovalski. Designed by N.R. Jackson. Toronto: Kids Can Press, 1993. Medium: woodcuts
and pen and ink drawings on Arches medium tooth paper. Typeface: Veljovic type;
handlettering by Maryann Kovalski.

– ed. *Til All the Stars Have Fallen: Canadian Poems for Children*. Illustrated by Kady Mac-
Donald Denton. Designed by Michael Solomon. Toronto: Kids Can Press, 1989. Medium:
pen and ink, watercolour. Mr Christie's Book Award Silver Seal, English-language
illustration, 1989; Alcuin Society Award for Excellence in Book Design, Honourable
Mention, 1989; Amelia Frances Howard-Gibbon Illustrator's Award, 1990.

– ed. *Voices on the Wind: Poems for All Seasons*. Illustrated by Michèle Lemieux. Toronto:
Kids Can Press, 1990. Amelia Frances Howard-Gibbon Illustrator's Award Shortlist,
1991; IODE Book Award, Municipal Chapter of Toronto, 1990.

Boswell, Hazel. *French Canada: Pictures and Stories*. New York: Viking Press, 1938.

Bourgeois, Paulette. *Franklin Fibs*. Illustrated by Brenda Clark. Toronto: Kids Can Press,
1991. Medium: watercolour.

– *Franklin in the Dark*. Illustrated by Brenda Clark. Toronto: Kids Can Press, 1986. Medium: watercolour.

– *Hurry Up, Franklin*. Illustrated by Brenda Clark. Toronto: Kids Can Press, 1989. Medium:
watercolour.

Bourinot, Arthur Stanley. *Pattering Feet: A Book of Childhood Verses*. Illustrated by Alan B.
Beddoe. Ottawa: Graphic Publishers, 1925.

[Boyle, David]. *Uncle Jim's Canadian Nursery Rhymes: For Family and Kindergarten Use.* Illustrated by C.W. Jefferys. London and Toronto: Musson, 1908.

Brébeuf, Jean de. *The Huron Carol.* Translated by J.E. Middleton. Illustrated by Frances Tyrrell. Designed by Nightlight Graphics. Toronto: Lester and Orpen Dennys, 1990. Typeface: ITC Cheltenham Light. Governor General's Award for Children's Literature Shortlist, 1990; IODE Book Award, Municipal Chapter of Toronto Shortlist, 1990.

Burns, Elizabeth Rollit. *Little Canadians.* Illustrated by Mary M. Phillips. [Montreal]: Desbarats, 1899.

Butler, Geoff. *The Hangashore.* Toronto: Tundra Books, 1998.

Butler, Geoff. *The Killick: A Newfoundland Story.* Montreal: Tundra Books, 1995. Amelia Frances Howard-Gibbon Illustrator's Award Shortlist, 1996; Ann Connor Brimer Award Shortlist, 1996; Governor General's Award for Children's Literature Shortlist, 1996.

Cameron, Anne. *Daughters of Copper Woman.* Vancouver: Press Gang, 1981.

– *How Raven Freed the Moon.* Illustrated by Tara Miller. Designed by Gaye Hammond. Madeira Park, BC: Harbour Publishing, 1985. Medium: line art.

– *How the Loon Lost Her Voice.* Illustrated by Tara Miller. Designed by Gaye Hammond. Madeira Park, BC: Harbour Publishing, 1985. Medium: line art.

Campbell, Maria. *Little Badger and the Fire Spirit.* Illustrated by David MacLagan. Toronto: McClelland and Stewart, 1977.

Campbell, Nicola I. *Shi-shi-etko.* Illustrated by Kim LaFave. A Groundwood Book. Toronto: House of Anansi Press, 2005.

Carrier, Roch. *Les enfants du bonhomme dans la lune: Contes.* Montreal: Stanké, 1979. [Includes the story 'Une abominable feuille d'érable sur la glace.']

– *The Flying Canoe.* Translated by Sheila Fischman. Illustrated by Sheldon Cohen. Toronto: Tundra Books, 2004. Medium: pencil with digital colouring. IBBY Honour List, for illustration, 2006.

– *The Hockey Sweater.* Translated by Sheila Fischman. Illustrated by Sheldon Cohen. Designed by May Cutler and Sheldon Cohen. Montreal: Tundra Books, 1984. Medium: acrylic on masonite. Alcuin Society Award for Excellence in Book Design, Honourable Mention, 1984.

– *The Hockey Sweater and Other Stories.* Translated by Sheila Fischman. Anansi fiction series, AF 40. Toronto: House of Anansi Press, 1979.

Carroll, Lewis. *Jabberwocky.* Illustrated by Stéphane Jorisch. Designed by Karen Powers. Visions in Poetry. Toronto: Kids Can Press, 2004. Medium: pencil, ink, watercolour, and Adobe Photoshop. Typeface: Celeste and DaddyO Hip. Alcuin Society Award for Excellence in Book Design, First Prize, 2004; Governor General's Award for Children's Literature, English-language illustration, 2004.

Chase, Edith Newlin. *The New Baby Calf.* Illustrated by Barbara Reid. Toronto: Scholastic Book Services, 1984. Medium: Plasticine.

Clark, Catherine Anthony. *The Sun Horse.* Illustrated by Clare Bice. Toronto: Macmillan, 1951.

Cleaver, Elizabeth. *ABC.* Toronto: Oxford University Press, 1984. Medium: paper collage and realia.

– *The Enchanted Caribou.* Toronto: Oxford University Press, 1985. Medium: paper cutouts.

– *The Miraculous Hind.* Toronto: Holt, Rinehart and Winston, 1973. Medium: collage, mixed media. Canadian Library Association Book of the Year for Children Award, 1974.

Clutesi, George. *Son of Raven, Son of Deer: Fables of the Tse-Shaht People.* Sidney, BC: Gray's Publishing, 1967.

Cole, Carol Cassidy. *Downy Wing and Sharp Ears: Adventures of a Little Canadian Boy among Little Wild Friends in Natures* [sic] *Wonderland.* Illustrated by M. Sankey. Toronto: Hodder and Stoughton, 1923.

– *Velvet Paws and Shiny Eyes: Adventures of a Little Canadian Boy in Natures* [sic] *Wonderland, among Furry Friends and Feathery.* Illustrated by William Dudley Burnett Ward. Toronto: Hodder and Stoughton, 1922. Reissued Toronto: The Musson Book Company, 1943, in the series Books for Little Listeners.

– *Velvet Paws and Shiny Eyes.* Illustrated by Dudley Ward. Illustrated by Dudley Ward and with Toy Pictures by Leo L. Stead. London: Hodder and Stoughton, [1933?].

Coleman, Herbert Thomas John. *A Rhyme for a Penny.* Illustrated by Elisabeth Kerr. Toronto: Macmillan Company of Canada, 1930; Vancouver: The Clarke and Stuart Company, 1934.

Cox, Palmer. *The Brownies around the World.* New York: Century, 1894.

– *The Brownies: Their Book.* New York: Century, 1887.

Cutler, May Ebbitt. *Breaking Free: The Story of William Kurelek.* Illustrated by William Kurelek. Toronto: Tundra Books, 2002. Medium: mixed media.

– *I Once Knew an Indian Woman.* Illustrated by Bruce Johnson. Montreal: Tundra Books, 1975. Originally published as *The Last Noble Savage: A Laurentian Idyll* (Montreal: Tundra Books, 1967).

Czernecki, Stefan. *Lilliput 5357.* Vancouver: Simply Read Books, 2006. Medium: photographs of vintage tin toys.

– *Ride 'Em, Cowboy.* Vancouver: Simply Read Books, 2004. Medium: photographs of wooden folk art.

Czernecki, Stefan, and Timothy Rhodes. *The Hummingbird's Gift.* Illustrated by Stefan Czernecki. Straw weavings by Juliana Reyes de Silva and Juan Hilario Silva. Winnipeg: Hyperion Press, 1994. Medium: gouache.

Danks, Hugh. *The Bug Book.* Illustrated by Joe Weissmann. Toronto: Somerville House, 1987. [In plastic insect collecting box 14 × 14 × 7 cm, labelled The Bug Bottle].

Darby, Ray. *Oomah.* Illustrated by John Phillips. Winnipeg: Contemporary Publishers, 1945.

– *Peter Smith and the Bugs.* Illustrated by John Phillips. Regina: School Aids and Text Book Publishing, 1944.

Davis, Aubrey. *Bone, Button, Borscht.* Illustrated by Dusan Petricic. Designed by Dusan Petricic and Marie Bartholomew. Toronto: Kids Can Press, 1995. Medium: watercolour and pencil on 140 lb Bockingford watercolour paper. Typeface: Bembo. Alcuin Society Award for Excellence in Book Design, First Prize, 1995; Canadian Library Association Book of the Year for Children Award Shortlist, 1996; IBBY Honour List, illustration, 1998.

Day, Marie. *Edward, the 'Crazy Man.'* Designed by Sheryl Shapiro. Toronto: Annick Press, 2002. Medium: mixed media. Typeface: Cochin Roman.

Debon, Nicolas. *Four Pictures by Emily Carr.* A Groundwood Book. Toronto and Vancouver: Douglas and McIntyre, 2003. Medium: gouache and India ink on Arches cold-pressed watercolour paper. Governor General's Award for Children's Literature Shortlist, 2003; Norma Fleck Award for Children's Non-Fiction Shortlist, 2004.

De la Mare, Walter. *Bells and Grass: A Book of Rhymes.* London: Faber and Faber, 1941.

Denton, Kady MacDonald. *A Child's Treasury of Nursery Rhymes.* Designed by Rebecca Elgar. Toronto: Kids Can Press, 1998. Medium: Pen and ink and watercolour. Governor General's Award for Children's Literature, English-language illustration, 1998; Amelia Frances Howard-Gibbon Illustrator's Award, 1999; Elizabeth Mrazik-Cleaver Canadian Picture Book Award, 1999.

Dickinson, Terence. *Exploring the Night Sky: The Equinox Astronomy Guide for Beginners.* Illustrated by John Bianchi. Designed by Ulrike Bender. Camden East, ON: Camden House, 1987. Governor General's Award for Children's Literature Shortlist, 1987; Information Book Award Honour Book, 1988.

– *NightWatch: An Equinox Guide to Viewing the Universe.* Illustrated by Victor Costanzo and Adolf Schaller. Camden East, ON: Camden House, 1983.

Dingwall, Laima, and Annabel Slaight, eds. *Owl's Amazing But True: By the Editors of Owl Magazine.* Toronto: Greey de Pencier Books, 1983.

Dingwall, Laima, and Annabel Slaight, eds. *The Winter Fun Book.* Toronto: OWL Magazine, 1980.

Dodds, Dayle Ann. *Where's Pup.* Illustrated by Pierre Pratt. Toronto: Tundra Books, 2003. Elizabeth Mrazik-Cleaver Canadian Picture Book Award, 2004.

Downie, Mary Alice. *The Witch of the North: Folk Tales of French Canada.* Illustrated by Elizabeth Cleaver. Designed by Michael Macklem. Ottawa: Oberon Press, 1975. Medium: collage. Amelia Frances Howard-Gibbon Illustrator's Award Shortlist, 1976.

Downie, Mary Alice, and Barbara Robertson, comps. *The New Wind Has Wings: Poems from Canada.* Illustrated by Elizabeth Cleaver. Toronto: Oxford University Press, 1984. Medium: collage, monoprints, linocut prints.

– comps. *The Wind Has Wings: Poems from Canada.* Illustrated by Elizabeth Cleaver. Toronto: Oxford University Press, 1968. Medium: collage, mixed media. Amelia Frances Howard-Gibbon Illustrator's Award, 1971.

Drawson, Blair. *Flying Dimitri.* Toronto: Groundwood Books, 1978.

Ehrlich, Amy. *Pome and Peel: A Venetian Tale.* Illustrated by Laszlo Gal. New York: Dial Books for Young Readers, 1990.

Elwin, Rosamund, and Michele Paulse. *Asha's Mums.* Illustrated by Dawn Lee. Toronto: Women's Press, 1990. Medium: watercolour.

Espinet, Ramabai. *The Princess of Spadina: A Tale of Toronto.* Illustrated by Veronica Sullivan. Toronto: Sister Vision, 1992.

Eyvindson, Peter. *Kyle's Bath.* Illustrated by Wendy Wolsak. Winnipeg: Pemmican Publications, 1984. Medium: charcoal.

Fitch, Sheree. *There Were Monkeys in My Kitchen!* Illustrated by Marc Mongeau. Designed by Tania Craan. Toronto: Doubleday, 1992. Mr Christie's Book Award Gold Seal, English-language text for 8 years and under, 1992.

– *Toes in My Nose.* Illustrated by Molly Lamb Bobak. Designed by Nancy Ruth Jackson. Toronto: Doubleday, 1987. Ann Connor Brimer Award Shortlist, 1991.

Fleischman, Paul. *Joyful Noise: Poems for Two Voices.* Illustrated by Eric Beddows. New York: Harper and Row, 1988.

– *Shadow Play.* Illustrated by Eric Beddows. New York: Harper and Row, 1990.

Fowke, Edith, ed. *Sally Go Round the Sun: 300 Children's Songs, Rhymes, and Games of Canadian Children.* Illustrated by Carlos Marchiori. Designed by Frank Newfeld and Don

Fernley. Toronto: McClelland and Stewart, 1969. Typeface: Palatino. Canadian Library Association Book of the Year for Children Award, 1970; Amelia Frances Howard-Gibbon Illustrator's Award Shortlist, 1971.

Fraser, W.A. *Mooswa and Others of the Boundaries*. Illustrated by Arthur Heming. Toronto: William Briggs, 1900.

Galloway, Priscilla. *Aleta and the Queen: A Tale of Ancient Greece*. Illustrated by Normand Cousineau. Toronto: Annick Press, 1995. Medium: gouache and ink.

– *Atalanta: The Fastest Runner in the World*. Illustrated by Normand Cousineau. Toronto: Annick Press, 1995. Medium: gouache and ink.

– *Daedalus and the Minotaur*. Illustrated by Normand Cousineau. Toronto: Annick Press, 1997. Medium: gouache and ink.

Gay, Marie-Louise. *Drôle d'école*. 4 vols. Sillery: Ovale, 1984. Canada Council Children's Literature Prizes, illustrator, 1984.

– *Rainy Day Magic*. Toronto: Stoddart, 1987. Medium: watercolour and Ecoline ink. Governor General's Award for Children's Literature, English-language illustration, 1987; Amelia Frances Howard-Gibbon Illustrator's Award, 1988.

– *Stella, Star of the Sea*. A Groundwood Book. Toronto and Vancouver: Douglas and McIntyre, 1999. Medium: mixed media, including watercolour, acrylic, collage. Amelia Frances Howard-Gibbon Illustrator's Award Shortlist, 2000; IBBY Honour List, for translation from French to English, 2000.

Gilman, Phoebe. *Something from Nothing: Adapted from a Jewish Folktale*. Richmond Hill, ON: North Winds Press, Scholastic Canada, 1992. Medium: oil and egg tempera on gessoed Arches satin finish watercolour paper. Mr Christie's Book Award Silver Seal, for English-language illustration, 1992.

Gilmore, Rachna. *A Gift for Gita*. Illustrated by Alice Priestley. Toronto: Second Story Press, 1998. Bilingual English and Arabic, and English and Bengali editions published by London: MantraLingua, 1998.

– *Lights for Gita*. Edited by Charis Wahl. Illustrated by Alice Priestley. Toronto: Second Story Press, 1994. Bilingual English and Bengali, Gujarati, Punjabi, Somali, Tamil, Turkish, and Urdu editions published by London: MantraLingua, 1994.

– *Roses for Gita*. Illustrated by Alice Priestley. Toronto: Second Story Press, 1996. Bilingual English and Chinese, Gujarati, Somali, Turkish, and Urdu editions published by London: MantraLingua, 1996.

– *Wheniwasalittlegirl*. Illustrated by Sally J.K. Davies. Toronto: Second Story Press, 1989. Medium: line drawings and wash.

Goose, Mary Susan. (M.S.G.) [Bonnell, M.A.] *Mother Goose's Bicycle Tour*. Toronto: W. Briggs, [1900].

Gordon, R.K. *A Canadian Child's ABC*. Illustrated by Thoreau MacDonald. Toronto and Vancouver: Dent, 1931.

Granfield, Linda. *In Flanders Fields: The Story of the Poem by John McCrae*. Illustrated by Janet Wilson. Designed by Annabelle Stanley. Toronto: Lester Publishing, 1995. Medium: oil on canvas. IODE Book Award, Municipal Chapter of Toronto, 1995; Canadian Library Association Book of the Year for Children Award Shortlist, 1996; Information Book Award, 1996.

– *Where Poppies Grow: A World War I Companion*. Toronto: Stoddart Kids, 2001.

Gregory, Nan. *Amber Waiting*. Illustrated by Kady MacDonald Denton. Designed by Blair

Kerrigan / Glyphics. Northern Lights Books for Children. Calgary: Red Deer Press, 2002. Medium: watercolour. Christie Harris Illustrated Children's Literature Prize, Finalist, 2003.

– *How Smudge Came*. Illustrated by Ron Lightburn. Designed by Limner Imaging Ltd and Kunz + Associates. Northern Lights Books for Children. Red Deer: Red Deer College Press, 1995. Medium: Derwent coloured pencils on Canson paper. Canadian Library Association Book of the Year for Children Award Shortlist, 1995; Elizabeth Mrazik-Cleaver Canadian Picture Book Award Shortlist, 1995; Mr Christie's Book Award Gold Seal, English-language text and illustrations for 7 years and under, 1995; Sheila A. Egoff Children's Book Prize, 1996.

Grey Owl. *Sajo and Her Beaver People*. London: Lovat Dickson and Thompson; Toronto: Macmillan Company of Canada, 1935. Published as *Sajo and the Beaver People*, New York: Scribner, 1936.

Griffin, George H. *Legends of the Evergreen Coast*. Illustrated by W.H. Probus Pleming. Vancouver: Clarke and Stuart Company, 1934.

Grove, Miss. *Little Grace, or, Scenes in Nova-Scotia*. Halifax: C. Mackenzie, 1846.

Gryski, Camilla. *Cat's Cradle, Owl's Eyes: A Book of String Games*. Illustrated by Tom Sankey. Toronto: Kids Can Press, 1983. Medium: line drawings.

Gutiérrez, Elisa. *Picturescape*. Designed by Elisa Gutiérrez. Vancouver: Simply Read Books, 2005. Medium: coloured paper collage and pencil crayon. Alcuin Society Award for Excellence in Book Design, Honourable Mention, 2005; Christie Harris Illustrated Children's Literature Prize Finalist, 2006.

Hale, Katherine, reteller. *Legends of the St Lawrence*. Illustrated by Charles Walter Simpson. [Montreal: Canadian Pacific Railway, 1926.]

Harper, Constance Ward. *The Moon Man and the Fairies*. Illustrated by Grace Judge. Vancouver: Sun Publishing Company, [1931].

Harris, Christie. *Mouse Woman and the Mischief-Makers*. Illustrated by Douglas Tait. Designed by Mary M. Ahern. Toronto: McClelland and Stewart, 1977. Medium: pen and ink.

– *Once More Upon a Totem*. Illustrated by Douglas Tait. Toronto: McClelland and Stewart, 1973. Medium: pen and ink.

– *Raven's Cry*. Illustrated by Bill Reid. Toronto: McClelland and Stewart, 1966.

Harrison, Ted. *Children of the Yukon*. Montreal: Tundra Books of Montreal, 1977. Medium: acrylic on illustration board.

– *A Northern Alphabet*. Montreal: Tundra Books, 1982. Amelia Frances Howard-Gibbon Illustrator's Award Shortlist, 1983. Medium: acrylic on illustration board.

– *Northland Alphabet*. Written and illustrated by Edward H. Harrison; with the collaboration of William. D. Knill. Edmonton: s.n., 1968. Medium: line drawings. Typeface: handlettered.

Hearn, Emily. *Franny and the Music Girl*. Illustrated by Mark Thurman. Toronto: Second Story Feminist Press, 1989.

Heaton, Hugh. *The Story of Albert the Camel's Son*. Illustrated by H.E.M. Sellen. Toronto: Heaton Publishing Company, and McClelland and Stewart, 1936; London: Faber and Faber, 1948.

– *The Story of Madam Hen and Little Horace*. Illustrated by H.E.M. Sellen. Toronto: Heaton Publishing Company, and McClelland and Stewart, 1936; London: Faber and Faber, 1940; New York: Oxford University Press, 1948.

Hébert, Marie-Francine. *The Amazing Adventure of LittleFish*. Translated by Sarah Cummins. Illustrated by Darcia Labrosse. Toronto: Second Story Press, 1990. Originally published as *Le voyage de la vie* (Montreal: La Courte Échelle, 1984).

Henty, G.A. *With Wolfe in Canada, or, The Winning of a Continent*. Illustrated by Gordon Browne. London: Blackie and Son, 1887. Canadian edition from British plates, Toronto: William Briggs, 1896.

Highway, Tomson. *Caribou Song / Atihko nikamon*. Illustrated by Brian Deines. Toronto: HarperCollins, 2001. Medium: oil on canvas.

– *Dragonfly Kites / Pimihákanisa*. Illustrated by Brian Deines. Toronto: HarperCollins Canada, 2002. Medium: oil on canvas. Typeface: Albertus and FF Quadraat. Governor General's Award for Children's Literature Shortlist, English-language illustration, 2002.

– *Fox on the Ice / Mahkesís mískwamíhk e-cípatapít*. Illustrated by Brian Deines. Toronto: HarperCollins, 2003. Medium: oil on canvas.

Hill, Kay. *Badger, the Mischief Maker*. Illustrated by John Hamberger. Toronto: McClelland and Stewart, 1965.

Hooke, Hilda M. *Thunder in the Mountains: Legends of Canada*. Illustrated by Claire Bice. Toronto: Oxford University Press, [1947].

Houston, James. *Tikta'liktak: An Eskimo Legend*. New York: Harcourt Brace and World; Don Mills, ON: Longmans Canada, 1965. Canadian Library Association Book of the Year for Children Award, 1966.

– *The White Archer: An Eskimo Legend*. New York: Harcourt Brace and World; Don Mills, ON: Longmans Canada, 1967.

Howard-Gibbon, Amelia Frances. *An Illustrated Comic Alphabet*. New York: H.Z. Walck; Toronto: Oxford University Press, 1967.

Hughes, Monica. *Little Fingerling: A Japanese Folk Tale*. Illustrated by Brenda Clark. Toronto: Kids Can Press, 1989. Medium: watercolour. Amelia Frances Howard-Gibbon Illustrator's Award Shortlist, 1989; Mr Christie's Book Award Silver Seal, English-language illustration, 1989; IODE Book Award, Municipal Chapter of Toronto, 1989.

Irvine, Joan. *How to Make Pop Ups*. Illustrated by Barbara Reid. Toronto: Kids Can Press, 1987.

Jam, Teddy. *Night Cars*. Illustrated by Eric Beddows. Designed by Michael Solomon. A Groundwood Book. Toronto and Vancouver: Douglas and McIntyre, 1988. Medium: Graphite paper with overlaid coloured glazes of alkyd. IODE Book Award, Municipal Chapter of Toronto, 1988; Amelia Frances Howard-Gibbon Illustrator's Award Shortlist, 1989; Elizabeth Mrazik-Cleaver Canadian Picture Book Award, 1989.

James, Betsy. *The Mud Family*. Illustrated by Paul Morin. New York, Putnam's, 1994.

Jefferys, C.W. *Canada's Past in Pictures*. Toronto: Ryerson Press, 1934.

– *The Picture Gallery of Canadian History*. 3 vols. Toronto: Ryerson Press, 1942–50.

Jennings, Sharon. *Sleep Tight, Mrs Ming*. Illustrated by Mireille Levert. Toronto: Annick Press, 1993.

Jocelyn, Marthe. *ABC × 3*. Illustrated by Tom Slaughter. Toronto: Tundra Books, 2004.

– *One Some Many*. Illustrated by Tom Slaughter. Toronto: Tundra Books, 2004.

– *Over Under*. Illustrated by Tom Slaughter. Toronto: Tundra Books, 2004.

Johnson, E. Pauline. *Legends of Vancouver*. Illustrated by J.E.H. MacDonald. Toronto: McClelland and Stewart, 1922. (Original edition: Vancouver: Privately printed, 1911).

Keens-Douglas, Richardo. *La Diablesse and the Baby: A Caribbean Folktale*. Illustrated by
    Marie Lafrance. Designed by Lizabeth Laroche. Toronto: Annick Press, 1994. Medium:
    acrylics. Typeface: Americana. Alcuin Society Award for Excellence in Book Design
    Third Prize, 1994; Governor General's Award for Children's Literature Shortlist,
    English-language illustration, 1994.
Kertes, Joseph. *The Gift*. Illustrated by Peter Perko. Designed by Michael Solomon. A
    Groundwood Book. Toronto: Douglas and McIntyre, 1995.
Kettle Point School. *Alphabet Book*. Prepared at Kettle Point School, Ontario. A school
    project, prepared by children five to eight years of age under the guidance of Anne
    Wyse. Designed by Allan Fleming. Toronto: University of Toronto Press, 1968.
Khalsa, Dayal Kaur. *Cowboy Dreams*. Montreal: Tundra Books, 1990. Medium: gouache.
    Amelia Frances Howard-Gibbon Illustrator's Award Shortlist, 1990.
– *How Pizza Came to Our Town*. Montreal: Tundra Books, 1989. Medium: gouache. Amelia
    Frances Howard-Gibbon Illustrator's Award Shortlist, 1990.
– *I Want a Dog*. Montreal: Tundra Books, 1987. Medium: Pencil crayon and gouache. Ame-
    lia Frances Howard-Gibbon Illustrator's Award Shortlist, 1988.
– *Julian*. Montreal: Tundra Books, 1989. Medium: gouache.
– *My Family Vacation*. Montreal: Tundra Books, 1988. Medium: Gouache on Saunders
    watercolour paper.
– *Sleepers*. Montreal: Tundra Books, 1988. Medium: gouache. Governor General's Award
    for Children's Literature Shortlist, 1988.
– *Tales of a Gambling Grandma*. Montreal: Tundra Books, 1986. Medium: Pencil crayon and
    gouache.
Khan, Rukhsana. *The Roses in My Carpets*. Illustrated by Ronald Himler. Toronto: Stoddart
    Kids, 1998.
King, Thomas. *A Coyote Columbus Story*. Illustrated by William Kent Monkman. Designed
    by Michael Solomon. A Groundwood Book. Toronto and Vancouver: Douglas and
    McIntyre, 1992. Governor General's Award for Children's Literature Shortlist, English-
    language text, 1992.
Kovalski, Maryann. *Brenda and Edward*. Designed by Wycliffe Smith. Toronto: Kids Can
    Press, 1984. Medium: watercolour. Alcuin Society Award for Excellence in Book Design,
    Honourable Mention, 1984.
Kurelek, William. *A Prairie Boy's Summer*. Montreal: Tundra Books, 1975. Medium: mixed
    media on masonite. Typeface: Garamond. Canadian Library Association Book of the Year
    for Children Award Shortlist, 1976; Amelia Frances Howard-Gibbon Illustrator's Award,
    1976.
– *A Prairie Boy's Winter*. Montreal: Tundra Books, 1973. Medium: mixed media on
    masonite. Amelia Frances Howard-Gibbon Illustrator's Award, 1974; Canadian Library
    Association Book of the Year for Children Award Shortlist, 1974; IODE Book Award,
    Municipal Chapter of Toronto, 1975.
Kusugak, Michael. *Arctic Stories*. Illustrated by Vladyana Langer Krykorka. Decorative
    borders by Rhoda Karetak of Rankin Inlet. Designed by Vladyana Langer Krykorka.
    Toronto: Annick Press, 1998. Medium: Watercolour and coloured pencil. Typeface:
    Trumpet Lite.
– *Northern Lights: The Soccer Trails*. Illustrated by Vladyana Krykorka. Designed by Vla-
    dyana Krykorka. Toronto: Annick Press, 1993. Medium: Watercolour, coloured pencil,

and ink. Amelia Frances Howard-Gibbon Illustrator's Award Shortlist, 1994.

Kyi, Tanya Lloyd. *The Blue Jean Book: The Story Behind the Seams*. Designed by Irvin Cheung, Peter Pimentel, and iCheung Design. Toronto: Annick Press, 2005. Medium: contemporary and archival photographs, posters, advertisements, newspapers. Typeface: Celeste, Info, and GoldenGate. Christie Harris Illustrated Children's Literature Prize, 2006.

A Lady (attributed to Mary Love). *A Peep at the Esquimaux; or, Scenes on the Ice: To which is Annexed, A Polar Pastoral: With Forty Coloured Plates, from Original Designs*. London: H.R. Thomas, 1825.

Langston, Laura. *The Fox's Kettle*. Illustrated by Victor Bosson. Designed by Victor Bosson. Victoria: Orca Book Publishers, 1998. Medium: computer graphics. Alcuin Society Award for Excellence in Book Design, Third Prize, 1998; Governor General's Award for Children's Literature Shortlist, English-language illustration, 1998.

– *The Magic Ear*. Illustrated by Victor Bosson. Designed by Victor Bosson. Victoria: Orca Book Publishers, 1995. Medium: watercolour and pencil crayon. Alcuin Society Award for Excellence in Book Design, Third Prize, 1995.

LeBox, Annette. *Salmon Creek*. Illustrated by Karen Reczuch. Designed by Michael Solomon. A Groundwood Book. Toronto and Vancouver: Douglas and McIntyre, 2002. Medium: watercolour. Amelia Frances Howard-Gibbon Illustrator's Award Shortlist, 2003; Information Book Award, 2003; Christie Harris Illustrated Children's Literature Prize, 2003.

– *Wild Bog Tea*. Illustrated by Harvey Chan. Designed by Michael Solomon. A Groundwood Book. Toronto and Vancouver: Douglas and McIntyre, 2001. Medium: pencil and chalk pastel. Governor General's Award for Children's Literature Shortlist, English-language illustration, 2001; Amelia Frances Howard-Gibbon Illustrator's Award Shortlist, 2002.

Lee, Dennis. *Alligator Pie*. Illustrated by Frank Newfeld. Designed by Frank Newfeld. Toronto: Macmillan, 1974. IODE Book Award, Municipal Chapter of Toronto, 1974; Canadian Library Association Book of the Year for Children Award, 1975.

– *Bubblegum Delicious*. Illustrated by David McPhail. Toronto: Key Porter Books, 2000.

– *Garbage Delight*. Illustrated by Frank Newfeld. Designed by Frank Newfeld. Toronto: Macmillan, 1977. Amelia Frances Howard-Gibbon Illustrator's Award Shortlist, 1978; Canadian Library Association Book of the Year for Children Award, 1978.

– *The Ice Cream Store*. Illustrated by David McPhail. Toronto: HarperCollins Publishers, 1991.

– *Jelly Belly*. Illustrated by Juan Wijngaard. Toronto: Macmillan of Canada, 1983.

– *Lizzy's Lion*. Illustrated by Marie-Louise Gay. Designed by Marie-Louise Gay. Toronto: Stoddart, 1984. Medium: watercolour and gesso mix, coloured pencil, and Ecoline ink. Alcuin Society Award for Excellence in Book Design, Second Prize, 1984; Canada Council Children's Literature Prizes, illustrator, 1984.

– *Nicholas Knock and Other People: Poems*. Illustrated by Frank Newfeld. Designed by Frank Newfeld. Toronto: Macmillan of Canada, 1974.

– *Wiggle to the Laundromat*. Illustrated by Charles Pachter. Toronto: New Press, 1970. Medium: lithographs, drawing, and collage. Typeface: handset and printed by the artist.

Lemieux, Michèle. *Stormy Night*. Toronto: Kids Can Press, 1999. French translation as *Nuit d'orage*. Paris: Seuil jeunesse, 1999. First published in German as *Gewittnach*. Weinheim, Germany: Beltz and Gelberg, 1996. Medium: line drawings.

Lenain, Thierry. *Petit Zizi*. Illustrated by Stéphane Poulin. Laval: Les 400 Coups, 1997.

Governor General's Award for Children's Literature shortlist, French language illustration, 1998.

Levert, Mireille. *An Island in the Soup*. A Groundwood Book. Toronto and Vancouver: Douglas and McIntyre, 2001. Governor General's Award for Children's Literature, English-language illustration, 2001. *Une île dans la soupe*. Montreal: Les 400 Coups, 2002.

Levine, Karen. *Hana's Suitcase*. Designed by Stephanie Martin. Toronto: Second Story Press, 2002. Medium: archival photographs.

Lim, John. *At Grandmother's House*. Montreal: Tundra Books, 1977.

– *Merchants of the Mysterious East*. Designed by Michael M. Cutler. Montreal: Tundra Books, 1981. Amelia Frances Howard-Gibbon Illustrator's Award Shortlist, 1982.

Lim, Sing. *West Coast Chinese Boy*. Designed by Rolf Harder and Associates. Montreal: Tundra Books, 1979. Medium: pen and ink and full-colour monotypes painted on glass.

The Little Manitoban, A Child's Story-Book, Issued Under the Distinguished Patronage of Her Excellency the Countess of Minto For the Benefit of the Children's Aid Society of Manitoba. Winnipeg: Printed and Published for the Society by the Manitoba Free Press Company, 1900.

Lottridge, Celia Barker. *The Name of the Tree: A Bantu Tale*. Illustrated by Ian Wallace. Designed by Michael Solomon. A Groundwood Book. Toronto and Vancouver: Douglas and McIntyre, 1989. Medium: Coloured drawing pencil on Strathmore paper. Typeface: Berthold Van Dijck Display. Mr Christie's Book Award Gold Seal, English-language illustration, 1989; Amelia Frances Howard-Gibbon Illustrator's Award Shortlist, 1990; Elizabeth Mrazik-Cleaver Canadian Picture Book Award, 1990.

Lovechild, Mrs. *Peggy Hill, or, The Little Orphan*. Stanstead: Walton and Gaylord, 1834.

Loyie, Larry. *As Long as the Rivers Flow*. With Constance Brissenden. Illustrated by Heather D. Holmlund. Designed by Michael Solomon. A Groundwood Book. Toronto and Vancouver: Douglas and McIntyre, 2002. Medium: mixed media, watercolour, and archival photographs. Norma Fleck Award for Children's Non-Fiction, 2003.

– *The Gathering Tree*. With Constance Brissenden. Illustrated by Heather D. Holmlund. Designed by Suzanne Bates. Penticton, BC: Theytus Books, 2005.

Lunn, Janet. *Amos's Sweater*. Illustrated by Kim LaFave. Designed by Michael Solomon. A Groundwood Book. Vancouver and Toronto: Douglas and McIntyre, 1988. Medium: watercolour. Amelia Frances Howard-Gibbon Illustrator's Award, 1989; Governor General's Award for Children's Literature, English-language illustration, 1988.

– *The Twelve Dancing Princesses: A Fairy Story*. Illustrated by Laszlo Gal. Designed by Brant Cowie and Art Plus. Toronto: Methuen, 1979. Canada Council Children's Literature Prizes, illustration, 1979; IODE Book Award, Municipal Chapter of Toronto, 1979; Amelia Frances Howard-Gibbon Illustrator's Award, 1980.

Lunn, Janet, and Christopher Moore. *The Story of Canada*. Illustrated by Alan Daniel. Designed by Scott Richardson. Toronto: Key Porter Books, 1992. Medium: mixed media, including oils, watercolour, archival photographs. Typeface: Stone Serif. IODE Book Award, Municipal Chapter of Toronto, 1992; Mr Christie's Book Award Gold Seal, English-language text for 9–14 years, 1992; Information Book Award, 1993.

Mackay, Claire. *The Toronto Story*. Illustrated by Johnny Wales. Edited by Carol J. Martin. Designed by Helmut W. Weyerstrahs. Toronto: Annick Press, 1990.

– *The Toronto Story*. Revised ed. Illustrated by Johnny Wales. Designed by Irvin Cheung / iCheung Design. Toronto and New York: Annick Press, 2002. Medium: watercolour. Typeface: Times New Roman, Memphis, and Interstate.

Mackay, Isabel Ecclestone. *The Shining Ship, and Other Verse for Children*. Illustrated by Thelma Cudlipp. Toronto: McClelland, Goodchild and Stewart; New York: George H. Doran, 1918.

– *The Shining Ship, and Other Verse*. Illustrated by Elsie Dean. Toronto: McClelland and Stewart, 1929.

Macklem, Michael. *Jacques the Woodcutter*. Illustrated by Ann Blades. Ottawa: Oberon Press, 1977. Medium: watercolour.

Macmillan, Cyrus. *Canadian Fairy Tales*. Illustrated by Marcia Lane Foster. London: John Lane, The Bodley Head, 1922.

– *Canadian Wonder Tales*. Illustrated by George Sheringham. London: John Lane, The Bodley Head; Toronto: S.B. Gundy 1918.

– *Glooskap's Country and Other Indian Tales*. Illustrated by John A. Hall. Toronto: Oxford University Press, 1955.

Major, Kevin. *Ann and Seamus*. Illustrated by David Blackwood. A Groundwood Book. Toronto: Douglas and McIntyre, 2003. Governor General's Award Shortlist, English-language text, 2003; Ann Connor Brimer Award shortlist, 2004; IODE Violet Downey Book Award Shortlist, National Chapter of Canada, 2004; Mr Christie's Book Award Silver Seal, 2004.

– *Eh? to Zed: A Canadian Abecedarium*. Illustrated by Alan Daniel. Designed by Blair Kerrigan / Glyphics. Northern Lights Books for Children. Red Deer: Red Deer Press, 2000. Mr Christie's Book Award Silver Seal, English-language text and illustration for 8–11 years, 2000; Amelia Frances Howard-Gibbon Illustrator's Award Shortlist, 2001, Ann Connor Brimer Award Shortlist, 2001.

Maloney, Margaret Crawford. *Hans Christian Andersen's The Little Mermaid*. Illustrated by Laszlo Gal. Toronto: Methuen, 1983. Medium: mixed medium, including watercolour, inks, pastels on gessoed illustration board. Canada Council Children's Literature Prizes, illustration, 1983; Amelia Frances Howard-Gibbon Illustrator's Award Shortlist, 1984.

Mark, Jan. *Mr Dickens Hits Town*. Illustrated by Regolo Ricci. Toronto: Tundra Books, 1999.

Marryat, Captain Frederick. *The Settlers in Canada; Written for Young People*. London: Longman, Brown, Green and Longmans, 1844.

Mayer, Marianna. *Iduna and the Magic Apples*. Illustrated by Laszlo Gal. New York: Macmillan; London: Collier Macmillan, 1988.

McConkey, Lois. *Sea and Cedar: How the Northwest Coast Indians Lived*. Illustrated by Douglas Tait. Designed by Jim Rimmer. Vancouver: J.J. Douglas, 1973. Medium: pen and ink.

McFarlane, Sheryl. *Waiting for the Whales*. Illustrated by Ron Lightburn. Designed by Christine Toller and Ron Lightburn. Victoria: Orca Book Publishers, 1991. Medium: coloured pencil drawings. Alcuin Society Award for Excellence in Book Design Shortlist, 1991; Mr Christie's Book Award Silver Seal, English-language illustration, 1991; Amelia Frances Howard-Gibbon Illustrator's Award, 1992; IODE Violet Downey Book Award, National Chapter of Canada, 1992; Elizabeth Mrazik-Cleaver Canadian Picture Book Award, 1992; Governor General's Award for Children's Literature, English-language illustration, 1992.

McGugan, Jim. *Josepha: A Prairie Boy's Story*. Illustrated by Murray Kimber. Designed by Kunz + Associates. Northern Lights Books for Children. Red Deer: Red Deer College Press, 1994. Medium: oils. Governor General's Award for Children's Literature Shortlist, English-language text, 1994; Mr Christie's Book Award Silver Seal, English-language text and illustrations for 7 years and under, 1994; Alcuin Society Award for Excellence in Book Design, First Prize, 1994; Governor General's Award for Children's Literature, English-language illustration, 1994; Amelia Frances Howard-Gibbon Illustrator's Award Shortlist, 1995; Elizabeth Mrazik-Cleaver Canadian Picture Book Award, 1995.

McLellan, Joseph. *Nanabosho Steals Fire*. Illustrated by Don Monkman. Winnipeg: Pemmican Publications, 1990.

McNeill, James. *The Sunken City, and Other Tales from Round the World*. Illustrated by Theo Dimson. Toronto: Oxford University Press, 1959.

Melzack, Ronald, reteller. *The Day Tuk Became a Hunter, and Other Eskimo Stories*. Illustrated by Carol Jones. Toronto: McClelland and Stewart, 1967.

– reteller. *Raven, Creator of the World: Eskimo Legends*. Illustrated by Laszlo Gal. Toronto: McClelland and Stewart, 1970.

– reteller. [listed on title page as Ronald Melzak]. *Why the Man in the Moon Is Happy and Other Eskimo Creation Stories*. Illustrated by Laszlo Gal. Toronto: McClelland and Stewart, 1977. IODE Book Award, Municipal Chapter of Toronto, 1978.

Mitchell, Robin, and Judith Steedman. *Snowy and Chinook*. Photographed by Mia Cunningham. Designed by Robin Mitchell and Judith Steedman. Vancouver: Simply Read Books, 2005. Medium: photographs of mixed-media dioramas.

– *Sunny*. Photographed by Mia Cunningham. Designed by Robin Mitchell and Judith Steedman. Vancouver: Simply Read Books, 2003. Medium: photographs of mixed media dioramas. Alcuin Society Award for Excellence in Book Design, Honourable Mention, 2003; Christie Harris Illustrated Children's Literature Prize, Finalist, 2004.

– *Windy*. Photographed by Mia Cunningham. Designed by Robin Mitchell and Judith Steedman. Vancouver: Simply Read Books, 2002. Medium: photographs of mixed media dioramas. Alcuin Society Award for Excellence in Book Design, Honourable Mention, 2002.

Mollel, Tololwa Marti. *The Orphan Boy*. Illustrated by Paul Morin. Designed by Kathryn Cole. Toronto: Oxford University Press, 1990. Medium: oil on canvas. Alcuin Society Award for Excellence in Book Design, Honourable Mention, 1990; Governor General's Award for Children's Literature Shortlist, English-language illustration, 1990; Mr Christie's Book Award Silver Seal, English-language illustration, 1991; Amelia Frances Howard-Gibbon Illustrator's Award, 1991; Elizabeth Mrazik-Cleaver Canadian Picture Book Award, 1991; IBBY Honour List, illustration, 1992.

Montgomery, Lucy Maud. *Anne of Green Gables*. Boston: L.C. Page, 1908.

Morrison, J. S., and Maud Morrison Stone. *This Canada of Ours: A Pictorial History*. Toronto: The Musson Book Company, 1929.

Mowat, Grace Helen. *Funny Fables of Fundy: and Other Poems for Children*. Ottawa: Ru-Mi-Lou Books, 1928.

Munsch, Robert. *The Dark*. Illustrated by Sami Suomalainen. Toronto: Annick Press, 1979.

– *Jonathan Cleaned Up, Then He Heard a Sound, or Blackberry Subway Jam*. Illustrated by Michael Martchenko. Designed by Helmut W. Weyerstrahs. Toronto: Annick Press, 1981. Medium: watercolour.

– *Love You Forever*. Illustrated by Sheila McGraw. Designed by Klaus Uhlig Designgroup. Scarborough, ON: Firefly Books, 1986. Medium: mixed media on paper, including pastel, crayon, pencil crayon, and marker.

– *The Mud Puddle*. Illustrated by Sami Suomalainen. Toronto: Annick Press, 1979.
– *The Paper Bag Princess*. Illustrated by Michael Martchenko. Toronto: Annick Press, 1980. Medium: watercolour.
– *Thomas' Snowsuit*. Illustrated by Michael Martchenko. Munsch for Kids. Toronto: Annick Press, 1985. Medium: watercolour.
Munsch, Robert, and Michael Kusugak. *A Promise Is a Promise*. Illustrated by Vladyana Krykorka. Toronto: Annick Press, 1988. Medium: watercolour and ink.
Nanji, Shenaaz. *Treasure for Lunch*. Illustrated by Yvonne Cathcart. Toronto: Second Story Press, 2000.
Newfeld, Frank. *The Princess of Tomboso: A Fairy Tale in Pictures by Frank Newfeld, Based on the Story Collected by Marius Barbeau and Retold by Michael Hornyansky in the Golden Phoenix*. Toronto: Oxford University Press, 1960.
Nichol, Barbara. *Dippers*. Illustrated by Barry Moser. Toronto: Tundra Books, 1997.
– *One Small Garden*. Illustrated by Barry Moser. Toronto: Tundra Books, 2001.
Northern Regions, or, A Relation of Uncle Richard's Voyages for the Discovery of a North-West Passage, and an Account of the Overland Journies of Other Enterprizing Travellers. London: J. Harris, 1825.
Obed, Ellen Bryan. *Borrowed Black: A Labrador Fantasy*. Illustrated by Hope Yandell. St John's, NF: Breakwater Books, 1979. Reissued with new illustrations by Jan Mogensen, 1988. Alcuin Society Award for Excellence in Book Design, Third Prize, 1988 [for new edition].
Okanagan Tribal Council. Okanagan Indian Curriculum Project. *How Food Was Given: An Okanagan Legend*. Illustrated by Kenneth Lee Edwards. Cover design by Doris Williams. Penticton: Theytus Books, 1984. Medium: line drawings. Re-illustrated by Barbara Marchand, and issued as part of Kou-skelowh / We Are the People: A Trilogy of Okanagan Legends. Designed by Robert MacDonald, MediaClone. Penticton: Theytus Books, 1991. Medium: pen and ink and watercolour wash.
– Okanagan Indian Curriculum Project. *How Names Were Given: An Okanagan Legend*. Illustrated by Kenneth Lee Edwards. Cover design by Doris Williams. Penticton: Theytus Books, 1984. Medium: line drawings. Re-illustrated by Barbara Marchand, and issued as part of Kou-skelowh / We Are the People: A Trilogy of Okanagan Legends. Designed by Robert MacDonald, MediaClone. Penticton: Theytus Books, 1991. Medium: pen and ink and watercolour wash.
– Okanagan Indian Curriculum Project. *How Turtle Set the Animals Free: An Okanagan Legend*. Illustrated by Kenneth Lee Edwards. Cover design by Doris Williams. Penticton: Theytus Books, 1984. Medium: line drawings. Re-illustrated by Barbara Marchand, and issued as part of Kou-skelowh / We Are the People: A Trilogy of Okanagan Legends. Designed by Robert MacDonald, MediaClone. Penticton: Theytus Books, 1991. Medium: pen and ink and watercolour wash.
Ontario Science Centre. *Scienceworks: An Ontario Science Centre Book of Experiments*. Illustrated by Tina Holdcroft. Toronto: Kids Can Press, 1984. Medium: line drawings.
Oppenheim, Joanne. *Have You Seen Birds?* Illustrated by Barbara Reid. Richmond Hill, ON: North Winds Press, Scholastic-TAB, 1986. Medium: Plasticine. Amelia Frances Howard-Gibbon Illustrator's Award Shortlist, 1986; Canada Council Children's Literature Prizes, Illustration, 1986; IODE Book Award, Municipal Chapter of Toronto, 1986; Elizabeth Mrazik-Cleaver Canadian Picture Book Award, 1987.

– *Have You Seen Bugs?* Illustrated by Ron Broda. Richmond Hill, ON: North Winds Press, Scholastic Canada, 1996. Medium: paper sculpture and watercolour. Amelia Frances Howard-Gibbon Illustrator's Award Shortlist, 1997.

[Owen, Ivon, and William Toye]. *A Picture History of Canada*. Illustrated by Clarke Hutton. London: Oxford University Press, 1956.

Oxley, James Macdonald. *Ti-Ti-Pu: A Boy of Red River*. London: Religious Tract Society; Toronto: Musson, [1896?].

– *Up among the Ice-Floes*. Philadelphia: American Baptist Publication Society, 1890.

– *The Young Woodsman, or, Life in the Forests of Canada*. London: Thomas Nelson, 1895.

Pacey, Desmond. *The Cow with the Musical Moo and Other Verses for Children*. Illustrated by Milada Horejs and Karel Rohlicek. Fredericton, NB: Brunswick Press, 1952.

– *Hippity Hobo and the Bee: And Other Verses for Children*. Illustrated by Milada Horejs and Karel Rohlicek. Beaver Books. Fredericton, NB: Brunswick Press, 1952.

Paré, Roger. *The Annick ABC*. Designed by Derome et Pilotte. Toronto: Annick Press, 1985. Originally published as *L'Alphabet* (Montreal: La Courte Échelle, 1985). The book is part of *The Annick ABC Activity Set*, which includes two puzzles, one book, and one game. All translated from French.

Pasternak, Carol, and Allan Sutterfield. *Stone Soup*. Illustrated by Hedy Campbell. Designed by Hedy Campbell. Toronto: Canadian Women's Educational Press, 1974. Medium: line drawings and wash.

Penrose, Gordon. *Dr Zed's Dazzling Book of Science Activities*. [Illustrated by Linda Bucholtz-Ross]. Toronto: Greey de Pencier Publications, 1982. Medium: line drawings.

Pittman, Al. *Down by Jim Long's Stage: Rhymes for Children and Young Fish*. Illustrated by Pam Hall. Portugal Cove, NF: Breakwater Books, 1976. Amelia Frances Howard-Gibbon Illustrator's Award, 1976.

Poulin, Stéphane. *Ah, belle cité!: ABC / A Beautiful City: ABC*. Montreal: Livres Toundra / Tundra Books, 1985. Medium: oil on canvas.

– *Can You Catch Josephine?* Designed by Stéphane Poulin. Montreal: Tundra Books, 1987. Translation of *Peux-tu attraper Joséphine?* (Montreal: Livres Toundra, 1987). Medium: oil on canvas. Alcuin Society Award for Excellence in Book Design, Honourable Mention, 1987; Amelia Frances Howard-Gibbon Illustrator's Award Shortlist, 1988; Elizabeth Mrazik-Cleaver Canadian Picture Book Award, 1988.

– *Could You Stop Josephine?* Designed by Stéphane Poulin. Montreal: Tundra Books, 1988. Translation of *Pourrais-tu arrêter Joséphine?* (Montreal: Livres Toundra, 1988). Medium: oil on canvas. IBBY Honour List, illustration, 1990.

– *Have You Seen Josephine?* Montreal: Tundra Books, 1986. Translation of *As-tu vu Joséphine.* (Montreal : Livres Toundra, 1986). Medium: oil on canvas.

Quinlan, Patricia, *Tiger Flowers*. Illustrated by Janet Wilson. Toronto: Lester Publishing, 1994.

Raff, Emma Scott. *Of Queen's Gardens*. Introduction by Nathanial Burwash. Illustrated by Stella Evelyn Grier. [Toronto: Privately printed, ca 1909].

Reid, Barbara. *The Party*. Richmond Hill, ON: North Winds Press, Scholastic Canada, 1997. Medium: Plasticine shaped and pressed onto illustration board; acrylic paint and other materials are used for special effects. Typeface: 18 pt Bookman Medium. Governor General's Award for Children's Literature, English-language illustration, 1997; Amelia Frances Howard-Gibbon Illustrator's Award, 1998.

– *Sing a Song of Mother Goose*. Richmond Hill, ON: North Winds Press, Scholastic-TAB, 1987. Medium: Plasticine. Amelia Frances Howard-Gibbon Illustrator's Award Shortlist, 1988.

– *The Subway Mouse*. Toronto: North Winds Press, Scholastic Canada, 2003. Medium: Plasticine on illustration board, with found objects and acrylic paint. Typeface: 16 point Garamond Medium. Governor General's Award for Children's Literature, English-language illustration, 2003; Amelia Frances Howard-Gibbon Illustrator's Award Shortlist, 2004.

Reid, Dorothy M. *Tales of Nanabozho*. Illustrated by Donald Grant. Toronto: Oxford University Press, 1963.

Richards, Jack. *Johann's Gift to Christmas*. Illustrated by Len Norris. Vancouver: J.J. Douglas, 1972. Medium: pen and ink, watercolour.

Roberts, Charles G.D. *The Kindred of the Wild: A Book of Animal Life*. Illustrated by Charles Livingston Bull. Boston: L.C. Page; Toronto: Copp Clark, 1902.

– *Red Fox: The Story of His Adventurous Career in the Ringwaak Wilds and of His Final Triumph over the Enemies of His Kind*. Illustrated by Charles Livingston Bull. Boston: L.C. Page; Toronto: Copp, Clark, 1905.

Robertson, Margaret Murray. *Shenac's Work at Home: A Story of Canadian Life*. London: Religious Tract Society, 1868.

Sage, James. *Sassy Gracie*. Illustrated by Pierre Pratt. London: Macmillan Children's Books, 1998. Medium: acrylic and oil pastel.

Saunders, Marshall. *Beautiful Joe: An Autobiography*. With an Introduction by Hezekiah Butterworth. Philadelphia: American Baptist Publications Society; C.H. Baines, 1894. Published in Canada as *Beautiful Joe: An Autobiography*. With Introductory Note by the Countess of Aberdeen, and an Introduction by Hezekiah Butterworth. Toronto: Baptist Book Room, 1894.

Schwartz, Herbert T. *Windigo and Other Tales of the Ojibway*. Illustrated by Norval Morrisseau. Toronto: McClelland and Stewart, 1969.

Schwartz, Roslyn. *The Mole Sisters and the Piece of Moss*. Toronto: Annick Press, 1999. Medium: coloured pencil.

– *The Mole Sisters and the Rainy Day*. Toronto: Annick Press, 1999. Medium: coloured pencil.

Scrimger, Richard. *Bun Bun's Birthday*. Illustrated by Gillian Johnson. Toronto: Tundra Books, 2001. Medium: watercolour.

– *Eugene's Story*. Illustrated by Gillian Johnson. Toronto: Tundra Books, 2003. Medium: watercolour.

– *Princess Bun Bun*. Illustrated by Gillian Johnson. Toronto: Tundra Books, 2002. Medium: watercolour.

Service, Robert W. *The Cremation of Sam McGee*. Introduction by Pierre Berton. Illustrated by Ted Harrison. Designed by Peter Durham Dodd. Toronto: Kids Can Press, 1986. Medium: acrylic on illustration board. Typeface: Palacio Roman and Palacio Italics.

– *The Shooting of Dan McGrew*. Illustrated by Ted Harrison. Designed by Michael Solomon. Toronto: Kids Can Press, 1988. Medium: acrylic on illustration board. Typeface: Caslon 540.

Seton, Ernest Thompson. *Two Little Savages: Being the Adventures of Two Boys Who Lived as Indians and What They Learned*. New York: Doubleday, Page, 1903.

– *Wild Animals I Have Known and 200 Drawings: Being the Personal Histories of Lobo, Silvers-
    pot, Raggylug, Bingo, The Springfield Fox, The Pacing Mustang, Wully and Redruff*. New
    York: Scribner; Toronto: G.N. Morang, 1898.

Setterington, Ken. *Mom and Mum Are Getting Married!* Illustrated by Alice Priestley.
    Designed by Laura McCurdy. Toronto: Second Story Press, 2004.

Simeon, Anne. *The She-Wolf of Tsla-a-wat: Indian Stories for the Young*. Illustrated by Douglas
    Tait. Vancouver: J.J. Douglas, 1977. Medium: graphite pencil.

Smucker, Barbara. *Selina and the Bear Paw Quilt*. Illustrated by Janet Wilson. Toronto: Lester
    Publishing, 1995. Medium: oil paints, fabric. Amelia Frances Howard-Gibbon Illustra-
    tor's Award Shortlist, 1996; Elizabeth Mrazik-Cleaver Canadian Picture Book Award,
    1996.

Spalding, Andrea. *Solomon's Tree*. Illustrated by Janet Wilson and Victor Reece. Designed
    by Christine Toller. Victoria: Orca Book Publishers, 2002. Medium: oils on canvas and
    wood. Tsimshian mask made from alder wood and carved with handmade tools. Alcuin
    Society Award for Excellence in Book Design, Honourable Mention, 2002; Amelia
    Frances Howard-Gibbon Illustrator's Award Shortlist, 2003; Christie Harris Illustrated
    Children's Literature Prize Shortlist, 2003.

Spalding, Andrea, and Alfred Scow. *Secret of the Dance*. Illustrated by Darlene Gait. Victo-
    ria: Orca Book Publishers, 2006.

Spedden, Daisy Corning. *Polar, the Titanic Bear*. Illustrated by Laurie McGaw. Introduction
    by Leighton H. Coleman III. A Madison Press Book. Toronto: Little Brown and Com-
    pany, Canada, 1999.

Spicer, Maggee, and Richard Thompson. *We'll All Go Sailing*. Illustrated by Kim LaFave.
    Designed by Wycliffe Smith and Wycliffe Smith Design. Markham: Fitzhenry and
    Whiteside, 2001. Medium: Fractal Painter computer-generated images. Governor Gen-
    eral's Award for Children's Literature Shortlist, 2001; Mr Christie's Book Award Silver
    Seal, English-language text and illustrations for 7 years and under, 2001.

Stinson, Kathy. *The Bare Naked Book*. Illustrated by Heather Collins. Annick Toddler Series.
    Toronto: Annick Press, 1986. Medium: watercolour.

– *Red Is Best*. Illustrated by Robin Baird Lewis. Toronto: Annick Press, 1982. Medium: line
    drawings with spot colour. IODE Book Award, Municipal Chapter of Toronto, 1982.

Stone, Maud Morrison. *This Canada of Ours*. Illustrated by J. Stuart Morrison. Toronto:
    Musson Book Company, 1937.

Suddon, Alan. *Cinderella*. With a French translation by Claude Aubry. Designed by
    Michael Macklem. Ottawa: Oberon Press, 1969. Medium: collage. Amelia Frances
    Howard-Gibbon Illustrator's Award Shortlist, 1971.

Suzuki, David. *David Suzuki: Looking at Plants*. With Barbara Hehner. Toronto: Stoddart,
    1985.

Takashima, Shizuye. *A Child in Prison Camp*. Montreal: Tundra Books, 1971. Medium:
    watercolour. Amelia Frances Howard-Gibbon Illustrator's Award, 1972.

Taylor, C.J. *The Ghost and Lone Warrior: An Arapaho Legend*. Montreal: Tundra Books, 1991.
    Medium: acrylic on canvas.

– *How Two-Feather Was Saved from Loneliness: An Abenaki Legend*. Montreal: Tundra Books,
    1990. Medium: acrylic on canvas.

– *Little Water and the Gift of the Animals: A Seneca Legend*. Montreal: Tundra Books, 1992.
    Medium: acrylic on canvas.

– *The Secret of the White Buffalo.* Montreal: Tundra Books, 1993. Medium: acrylic on canvas.

Thornhill, Jan. *The Wildlife ABC: A Nature Alphabet.* Designed by Wycliffe Smith. Toronto: Greey de Pencier, 1988. Medium: gouache and ink on scratchboard. Governor General's Award for Children's Literature Shortlist, English-language illustration, 1988; Alcuin Society Award for Excellence in Book Design, First Prize, 1988.

Tookoome, Simon. *The Shaman's Nephew: A Life in the Far North.* With Sheldon Oberman. Toronto: Stoddart Kids, 1999. Medium: coloured pencil. Norma Fleck Award for Children's Non-Fiction, 2000; Governor General's Award for Children's Literature Shortlist, 2000.

Toye, William. *Cartier Discovers the St Lawrence.* Illustrated by Laszlo Gal. Toronto: Oxford University Press, 1970. Amelia Frances Howard-Gibbon Illustrator's Award Shortlist, 1971.

– *The Fire Stealer.* Illustrated by Elizabeth Cleaver. Toronto: Oxford University Press, 1979. Medium: collage, linocut, mixed media.

– *How Summer Came to Canada.* Illustrated by Elizabeth Cleaver. Toronto: Oxford University Press, 1969. Medium: collage, linocut, mixed media.

– *The Loon's Necklace.* Illustrated by Elizabeth Cleaver. Toronto: Oxford University Press, 1977. Medium: collage, linocut, mixed media. IODE Book Award, Municipal Chapter of Toronto, 1977; Amelia Frances Howard-Gibbon Illustrator's Award, 1978.

– *The Mountain Goats of Temlaham.* Illustrated by Elizabeth Cleaver. Toronto: Oxford University Press, 1969. Medium: collage, linocut, mixed media. Amelia Frances Howard-Gibbon Illustrator's Award Shortlist, 1971.

– *The St Lawrence.* Illustrated by Leo Rampen. Toronto: Oxford University Press, 1959.

Traill, Catharine Parr. *Canadian Crusoes: A Tale of the Rice Lake Plains.* London: Arthur Hall, Virtue, 1852.

– *Lady Mary and Her Nurse; or, a Peep into the Canadian Forest.* Illustrated by William Harvey. London: Arthur Hall, Virtue, 1856.

– *The Young Emigrants; or Pictures of Canada. Calculated to Amuse and Instruct the Minds of Youth.* London: Harvey and Darton, 1826.

Uegaki, Chieri. *Suki's Kimono.* Illustrated by Stéphane Jorisch. Designed by Karen Powers. Toronto: Kids Can Press, 2003. Medium: watercolour. Typeface: Bembo. Mr Christie's Book Award Shortlist Shortlist – English – 7 years and under – Silver Seal, 2003; Amelia Frances Howard-Gibbon Illustrator's Award Shortlist, 2004; Christie Harris Illustrated Children's Literature Prize Shortlist, 2004.

Uren, Alfred E. *Bob and Bill Go Farming: A Story in Rhyme for Boys and Girls.* Toronto: Bob and Bill Publications, [1935].

– *Bob and Bill See Canada: A Travel Story in Rhyme for Boys and Girls.* Illustrated by W. Goode. Toronto: The Musson Book Company, 1919.

Van Camp, Richard. *What's the Most Beautiful Thing You Know about Horses?* Illustrated by George Littlechild. San Francisco: Children's Book Press, 1998. Medium: mixed media.

Vivenza, Francesca. *Geranimal, Daddy Lion, and Other Stories.* Toronto: Groundwood Books, 1978. Medium: coloured pencil.

Wallace, Ian. *Chin Chiang and the Dragon's Dance.* A Groundwood Book. Vancouver and Toronto: Douglas and McIntyre, 1984. Medium: watercolour. IODE Book Award, Municipal Chapter of Toronto, 1984. Amelia Frances Howard-Gibbon Illustrator's Award, 1985; IBBY Honour List, illustration, 1986.

Wallace, Ian, and Angela Wood. *The Sandwich*. Toronto: Kids Can Press, 1975.

Waterton, Betty. *Pettranella*. Illustrated by Ann Blades. Vancouver: Douglas and McIntyre, 1980. Medium: watercolour.

– *A Salmon for Simon*. Illustrated by Ann Blades. Designed by Marion Llewellyn. Vancouver: Douglas and McIntyre, 1978. Medium: watercolour. Canada Council Children's Literature Prizes, illustration, 1978; Canadian Library Association Book of the Year for Children Award Shortlist, 1979; Amelia Frances Howard-Gibbon Illustrator's Award, 1979.

Watts, Irene N. *A Telling Time*. Illustrated by Kathryn Shoemaker. Designed by Elisa Gutiérrez. Vancouver: Tradewind Books, 2004. Medium: gouache.

Weatherby, Hugh. *Tales the Totems Tell*. Toronto: The Macmillan Company of Canada, 1944.

Wheeler, Bernelda. *I Can't Have Bannock, but the Beaver Has a Dam*. Illustrated by Herman Bekkering. Winnipeg: Pemmican Publications, 1984. Medium: charcoal on paper.

– *Where Did You Get Your Moccasins?* Illustrated by Herman Bekkering. Winnipeg: Pemmican Publications, 1986. Medium: charcoal on paper.

Woolaver, Lance. *From Ben Loman to the Sea*. Illustrated by Maud Lewis. Halifax: Nimbus Publishing, 1979. Medium: oils.

Wordsandwich: Stories by Kids for Kids. Willowdale, ON: Books by Kids, 1975.

Wrong, George M., Chester Martin, and Walter N. Sage. *The Story of Canada*. Illustrated by C. W. Jefferys. Toronto: Ryerson Press, [1929].

Wynne-Jones, Tim. *Madeline and Ermadello*. Illustrated by Lindsey Hallam. Hawkesville, ON: Before We Are Six, 1977. Medium: line drawings.

– *Zoom at Sea*. Illustrated by Ken Nutt. Designed by Michael Solomon. A Groundwood Book. Toronto and Vancouver: Douglas and McIntyre, 1983. Medium: graphite pencil on textured paper. Alcuin Society Award for Excellence in Book Design, Honourable Mention, 1983; IODE Book Award, Municipal Chapter of Toronto, 1983; Amelia Frances Howard-Gibbon Illustrator's Award, 1984.

– *Zoom Away*. Illustrated by Ken Nutt. Designed by Michael Solomon. A Groundwood Book. Toronto and Vancouver: Douglas and McIntyre, 1985. Medium: graphite pencil on textured paper. Amelia Frances Howard-Gibbon Illustrator's Award, 1986.

– *Zoom Upstream*. Illustrated by Eric Beddows [pseud. of Ken Nutt]. Designed by Michael Solomon. A Groundwood Book. Toronto and Vancouver: Douglas and McIntyre, 1992. Medium: graphite pencil on textured paper. Governor General's Award for Children's Literature Shortlist, English-language illustration, 1992; Mr Christie's Book Award, Silver Seal, English-language illustration, 1992.

Yee, Paul. *Ghost Train*. Illustrated by Harvey Chan. Designed by Michael Solomon. A Groundwood Book. Vancouver and Toronto: Douglas and McIntyre, 1996. Medium: oil; front and end pieces are drypoint etchings on copper. Typeface: Berthold Caslon Book. IODE Book Award, Municipal Chapter of Toronto Shortlist, 1996; Governor General's Award for Children's Literature, English-language text, 1997; Amelia Frances Howard-Gibbon Illustrator's Award, 1997; Elizabeth Mrazik-Cleaver Canadian Picture Book Award, 1997.

– *Roses Sing on New Snow: A Delicious Tale*. Illustrated by Harvey Chan. Designed by Michael Solomon and Harvey Chan. A Groundwood Book. Toronto and Vancouver: Douglas and McIntyre, 1991. Medium: watercolour. Amelia Frances Howard-Gibbon Illustrator's Award Shortlist, 1992.

– *Tales from Gold Mountain: Stories of the Chinese in the New World*. Illustrated by Simon Ng. Designed by Michael Solomon. A Groundwood Book. Toronto and Vancouver: Douglas and McIntyre, 1989. Typeface: Berthold Caslon Book. Canadian Library Association Book of the Year for Children Award Shortlist, 1990; IODE Violet Downey Book Award, National Chapter of Canada, 1990; Sheila A. Egoff Children's Book Prize, 1990.

Yerxa, Leo. *Last Leaf First Snowflake to Fall*. Designed by Leo Yerxa. A Groundwood Book. Toronto and Vancouver: Douglas and McIntyre, 1993. Medium: collage of tissue paper dyed with acrylic, ink, and watercolour. Small accent illustrations in watercolour. Typeface: Alphatype Perpetua. Alcuin Society Award for Excellence in Book Design, Second Prize, 1993; Governor General's Award for Children's Literature Shortlist, 1993; Mr Christie's Book Award, Gold Seal co-winner, English-language text and illustrations for 8–11 years, 1993; Amelia Frances Howard-Gibbon Illustrator's Award, 1994; Elizabeth Mrazik-Cleaver Canadian Picture Book Award, 1994.

Young, Egerton Ryerson. *Stories from Indian Wigwams and Northern Camp-Fires*. New York: Eaton and Mains; Toronto: William Briggs, 1892.

– *Three Boys in the Wild North Land*. Illustrated by J.E. Laughlin. London: Ward and Downey; Toronto, William Briggs, 1897.

Zeman, Ludmila. *Gilgamesh the King*. Designed by Dan O'Leary. Montreal: Tundra Books, 1992. Medium: pencil, coloured pencil, and watercolour on paper. Alcuin Society Award for Excellence in Book Design, Second Prize, 1992.

– *The Last Quest of Gilgamesh*. Designed by Dan O'Leary. Montreal: Tundra Books, 1995. Medium: pencil, coloured pencil, and watercolour on paper. Governor General's Award for Children's Literature, English-language illustration, 1995; Amelia Frances Howard-Gibbon Illustrator's Award Shortlist, 1996.

– *The Revenge of Ishtar*. Designed by Dan O'Leary. Montreal: Tundra Books, 1993. Medium: pencil, coloured pencil, and watercolour on paper.

– *Sindbad: From the Tales of the Thousand and One Nights*. Designed by Sari Ginsberg. Toronto: Tundra Books, 1999. Medium: pencil, coloured pencil, and watercolour on paper. Governor General's Award for Children's Literature Shortlist, 1999; IBBY Honour List, illustration, 2002.

– *Sindbad in the Land of Giants*. Designed by Sari Naworynski. Toronto: Tundra Books, 2001. Medium: pencil, coloured pencil and watercolour on paper. Amelia Frances Howard-Gibbon Illustrator's Award Shortlist, 2002.

– *Sindbad's Secret: From the Tales of the Thousand and One Nights*. Toronto: Tundra Books, 2003. Medium: pencil, coloured pencil, and watercolour on paper. Governor General's Award for Children's Literature, English-language illustration, 2003.

Zhang, Ange. *Red Land, Yellow River: A Story from the Cultural Revolution*. Designed by Michael Solomon. A Groundwood Book. Toronto and Vancouver: Douglas and McIntyre, 2004. Medium: mixed media; digital illustrations. Governor General's Award for Children's Literature Shortlist, English-language text, 2004; Canadian Library Association Book of the Year for Children Award Shortlist, 2005; Information Book Award Honour Book, 2005; TD Canadian Children's Literature Award Shortlist, 2005; Norma Fleck Award for Children's Non-Fiction Shortlist, 2005.

Zhang, Song Nan. *A Little Tiger in the Chinese Night: An Autobiography in Art*. Designed by Dan O'Leary. Montreal: Tundra Books, 1993. Medium: Watercolour and graphite pencil.

Mr Christie's Book Award, Gold Seal Co-Winner, English-language text and illustration for 8–11 years.

Zion, Gene. *Harry, the Dirty Dog*. Illustrated by Margaret Bloy Graham. New York: Harper and Row, [1956].

Secondary Sources

Professional and Scholarly Journals, Magazines, and Newspapers Mentioned in the Text

Canadian Children's Book News. Toronto: Canadian Children's Book Centre, 2003–.
  Frequency: quarterly
  Continues *Children's Book News*
Canadian Children's Literature / Littérature canadienne pour la jeunesse. Guelph: Canadian Children's Press, 1975–2004; Winnipeg: University of Winnipeg, 2005–8.
  Title varies: issue 1, 1975 to issue 29, 1983: *Canadian Children's Literature: A Journal of Criticism and Review;* issue 30, 1983 to present, parallel title in French, *Littérature canadienne pour la jeunesse* also included. Subtitle dropped from cover after v. 25, no. 2, issue 94, 1999
  Whole-issue numbering discontinued with 31, no. 1, 2005
  Frequency: varies; three times a year, 1975–85; quarterly, 1986–2004; semi-annual from 31, no. 1 (2005)
  Jeunesse: Young People, Texts, Cultures, 2009–.
Canadian Materials. Ottawa: Canadian Library Association, 1971–94.
  Title change: *CM: Canadian Materials for Schools and Libraries* 1980–94.
  Subtitle varies. 1971, 1972, 'an awareness list for school resource centres of print and non-print materials'; 1991–4: 'A Reviewing Journal of Canadian Materials for Young People'
  Frequency: varies: annual, 1971, 1972; semi-annual, 1975; three times a year, 1976–7; quarterly, 1978–82; bimonthly, 1983–94.
  Continued by: *CM: Canadian Review of Materials, 1995–.*
Children's Book News. Toronto: Children's Book Centre, 1978–2002.
  Later issues published by the Canadian Children's Book Centre
  Title varies. Some issues have title *Book News*
  Frequency: quarterly
  Continued by *Canadian Children's Book News*, 2003–.
Children's Choices of Canadian Books. Ottawa: Citizens' Committee on Children, 1979–91.
  Frequency: semi-annual
CM: Canadian Review of Materials. electronic journal. Winnipeg: Manitoba Library Association, 1995–. http://www.umanitoba.ca/cm.
  Frequency: weekly
  Continues *CM: Canadian Materials for Schools and Libraries*
Emergency Librarian. Vancouver, Seattle: Rockland Press, 1973–98.
  Frequency: bimonthly
  Continued by *Teacher Librarian*
In Review: Canadian Books for Young People. Toronto: Libraries and Community Information Branch, Provincial Library Service, 1967–82.
  Frequency varies. Quarterly 1967–Feb. 1979; Bimonthly, April 1979–April 1982

Our Choice. Toronto: Children's Book Centre, 1977–2008.
   Later issues published by the Canadian Children's Book Centre
   Frequency: annual
   Title varies: *Our Choice, Your Choice*, 1985–9. Subtitle varies
   Continued by: *Best Books for Kids and Teens*, 2008–.
Quill and Quire. Toronto, 1935–.
   Frequency: monthly
   Publisher varies
Resource Links. Vancouver: Rockland Press, for the Council for Canadian Learning
   Resources; 1995–8; Pouch Cove, NF: The Council for Canadian Learning Resources;
   1998–2007; Pouch Cove, NF: The Society for Canadian Educational Resources, 2007–.
   Frequency: five times a year

Monographs, Collections of Essays, and Journal Articles

Abbreviations for journal titles in bibliography:
Canadian Children's Literature (CCL)
Canadian Library Journal (CLJ)
Canadian Literature (CL)
Children's Literature Association Quarterly (CLAQ)
Children's Literature in Education (CLE)
CM: Canadian Materials (CM)
Emergency Librarian (EL)
Horn Book Magazine (HB)
In Review (IR)
Journal of Youth Services in Libraries (JYS)
Lion and the Unicorn (LU)
Resource Links (RL)
School Libraries in Canada (SLiC)

(All URLs cited are current as of September 2009)

Abernethy, Janet, and Tiiu Kubjas. 'A Look at Non-Sexist Canadian Children's Books.' *IR*
   9, no. 1 (Winter 1975): 5–9.
Adams, Mary Louise. *The Trouble with Normal: Postwar Youth and the Making of Heterosexual-
   ity*. Toronto: University of Toronto Press, 1997.
Adams, Thomas R., and Nicholas Barker. 'A New Model for the Study of the Book.' In *A
   Potencie of Life: Books in Society*, ed. Nicholas Barker, 5–43. The Clark Lectures, 1986–7.
   London: The British Library, 1993.
Adorno, Theodor W. *The Culture Industry: Selected Essays on Mass Culture*, ed. J.M. Bern-
   stein. London and New York: Routledge, 1990.
Aitken, Johan Lyall. 'Myth, Legend, and Fairy Tale: "Serious Statements about Our Exist-
   ence."' In Paul, *Growing with Books*, Book 1, 'Literature and Education,' 22–44.
Aldana, Patsy. 'Crossing the Money Boundary.' *HB* 77, no. 6 (2001): 675–81.
Alderson, Brian. *Looking at Picture Books, 1973*. London: National Book League, 1973.
American Library Association. Committee on Library Work with Children. *Children's
   Library Yearbook*. Chicago: American Library Association, 1929–32.

Amtmann, Bernard. *A Bibliography of Canadian Children's Books and Books for Young People, 1841–1867 / Livres de l'enfance et livres de la jeunesse au Canada, 1841–1867.* Montreal: B. Amtmann, 1977.

– *Early Canadian Children's Books, 1763–1840: A Bibliographic Investigation into the Nature and Extent of Early Canadian Children's Books and Books for Young People / Livres de l'enfance et livres de la jeunesse au Canada, 1763–1840: Étude bibliographique.* Montreal: B. Amtmann, 1976.

Anderson, Benedict. *Imagined Communities: Reflections on the Origin and Spread of Nationalism.* London: Verso, 1983.

Anderson, H. Allen. *The Chief: Ernest Thompson Seton and the Changing West.* College Station: Texas A and M University Press, 1986.

Andrus, Gertrude Elizabeth. 'Library Work in Summer Playgrounds.' In Hazeltine, *Library Work with Children,* 325–9. [Originally published in the American Library Association *Proceedings,* 1911.]

Anstey, Michèle. '"It's Not All Black and White": Postmodern Picture Books and New Literacies.' *Journal of Adolescent and Adult Literacy* 45, no. 6 (2002): 444–57.

Anstey, Michèle, and Geoff Bull. *Reading the Visual: Written and Illustrated Children's Literature.* Sydney: Harcourt Australia, 2000.

Arizpe, Evelyn, and Morag Styles. *Children Reading Pictures: Interpreting Visual Texts.* London and New York: Routledge Falmer, 2003.

Arnold, Helen. 'Penny Plain, Tuppence Coloured: Reading Words and Pictures.' In Watson and Styles, eds, *Talking Pictures,* 164–77.

Aronson, Marc. *Beyond the Pale: New Essays for a New Era.* Lantham, MD, and Oxford: Scarecrow Press, 2003.

Association of Canadian Publishers. *Book Publishing and Canadian Culture: A National Strategy for the 1990s.* [Toronto]: The Association, 1991.

– *Canadian Books in School Libraries: Raising the Profile.* Toronto: The Association, 2004.

– *The Canadian Children's Book Market: Final Report.* Prepared for the Association of Canadian Publishers by Evans and Company. [Toronto: The Association, 2001].

– *Children's Book Publishing in Canada: A Brief.* [Prepared by Patricia Aldana]. Toronto: The Association. [1978].

– *Highlights from Canadian Books in School Libraries: Raising the Profile.* Toronto: The Association, 2004.

L'Association pour l'avencement des sciences et des techniques de la documentation (ASTED). *Les tendances actuelles de la littérature de jeunesse en langue française.* Collection à propos, no. 4. Montreal: L'ASTED, 1980.

Atherton, Stan. 'Escape to the Arctic: R.M. Ballantyne's Canadian Stories.' *CCL,* no. 1 (1975): 29–34.

Atkins, Laura. 'A Publisher's Dilemma: The Place of the Child in the Publication of Children's Books.' In Chapleau, ed., *New Voices in Children's Literature Criticism,* 47–54.

Atleo, Marlene R. / ?eh ?eh naa tuu kwiss. 'This is About Raven.' and 'Reviews: Books About Raven.' In Seale and Slapin, eds, *A Broken Flute,* 189–95.

Atwood, Margaret. *Survival: A Thematic Guide to Canadian Literature.* Toronto: House of Anansi Press, 1972.

Aubrey, Irene, comp. *Canadian Children's Books: A Treasury of Pictures / Livres canadiens d'enfants: Un trésor d'images.* Ottawa: National Library of Canada, 1976.

– 'Children's Services at the National Library.' *IR* 11, no. 4 (1977): 12–14.
– 'National Library of Canada: Children's Literature Service.' *CCL*, no. 38 (1985): 6–8.
– ed. *Notable Canadian Children's Books / Un Choix des livres canadiens pour la jeunesse*. Ottawa: National Library of Canada, 1977–93. [Supplements in English and French, with separate French edition, 1977–9; English and French tête-bêche, 1980–93. Supplements issued 1977, 1979, 1980–2, 1984, 1986, 1989, 1990–3; Cumulative editions issued 1985, for 1975–9 titles; and 1989 for 1980–4 titles. Succeeds Egoff and Bélisle, *Notable Canadian Children's Books / Choix de livres canadiens pour la jeunesse*, 1973.]
– *Pictures to Share: Illustration in Canadian Children's Books; Annotated Catalogue / Images pour tous: Illustration de livres canadiens pour enfants; catalogue annoté*. Prepared by Irene E. Aubrey to celebrate the International Year of the Child, 1979. Ottawa: National Library of Canada, 1979.
– *Pictures to Share: Illustration in Canadian Children's Books / Images pour tous: Illustration de livres canadiens pour enfants; catalogue annoté*. Ottawa: National Library of Canada, 1987.
Aubry, Claude. 'The Author in Canada.' *CCL*, no. 4 (1976): 14–19.
Audley, Paul. 'Book Publishing.' In *Canada's Cultural Industries: Broadcasting, Publishing, Records and Film*, 85–136. Toronto: James Lorimer, in association with the Canadian Institute for Economic Policy, 1983.
Auerbach, Jonathan. 'Congested Mails: Buck and Jack's "Call."' *American Literature* 67, no. 1 (1995): 51–76.
Avery, Gillian. *Behold the Child: American Children and Their Books 1621–1922*. London: The Bodley Head, 1994.
– 'Children's Books and Social History.' In *Research about Nineteenth-Century Children's Literature*, ed. Selma K. Richardson, 23–40. Urbana-Champaign: University of Illinois Graduate School of Library Science, 1980.
Axelrod, Paul. *The Promise of Schooling: Education in Canada 1800–1914*. Themes in Canadian Social History. Toronto: University of Toronto Press, 1997.
Bader, Barbara. 'American Picture Books: From Max's Metaphorical Monsters to Lilly's Purple Plastic Purse.' *HB* 74, no. 2 (1998): 141–56.
– *American Picture Books from Noah's Ark to the Beast Within*. New York: Macmillan, 1976.
– 'Only the Best: The Hits and Misses of Anne Carroll Moore.' *HB* 73, no. 5 (1997): 520–9.
Bagshaw, Marguerite, ed. *Books for Boys and Girls: A Standard Work of Reference for Librarians*. 4th ed. Toronto: Ryerson Press, 1966.
Bainbridge, Joyce M. 'The Role of Canadian Children's Literature in National Identity Formation.' *English Quarterly* 34, nos. 3–4 (2002): 66–74.
Bainbridge, Joyce M., and Janet Fayjean. 'Seeing Oneself in a Book: The Changing Face of Canadian Children's Literature.' *English Quarterly* 32, nos. 1–2 (2000): 55–62.
Bainbridge, Joyce, and Judith Thistleton-Martin. 'Children's Literature: Vehicle for the Transmission of National Culture and Identity or the Victim of Massmarket Globalisation.' Paper presented at the Annual Meeting of the Australian Association for Research in Education, Fremantle, Australia, 2–6 December, 2001. http://www.aare.edu.au/01pap/thi01323.htm.
Bainbridge, Joyce M., and Brenda Wolodko. 'Canadian Picture Books: Shaping and Reflecting National Identity.' *Bookbird: A Journal of International Children's Literature* 40, no. 2 (April 2002): 22–5.
Bainbridge, Joyce M., Mike Carbonaro, and Brenda Wolodko. 'Teacher Professional Devel-

opment and the Role of the Teacher Librarian.' *International Electronic Journal for Leadership in Learning* 6 (2002). http://www.ucalgary.ca/iejll/bainbridge_carbonaro_wolodko.

Bainbridge, Joyce M., Sylvia Pantaleo, and Monica Ellis. 'Multicultural Picture Books: Perspectives from Canada.' *Social Studies* 90, no. 4 (1999): 183–8.

Baker, Deirdre, and Ken Setterington. *Guide to Canadian Children's Books in English.* Toronto: McClelland and Stewart, 2003.

Bamberger, Richard, Lucia Binder, and Bettina Hurliman. *20 Years of IBBY.* Prague: Czechoslovak Section of IBBY, 1973. http://www.literature.at/webinterface/library/ALO-BOOK_V01?objid=14797.

Bang, Molly. *Picture This*: *How Pictures Work.* San Francisco: SeaStar Books, 2000.

– *Picture This*: *Perception and Composition.* Foreword by Rudolf Arnheim. A Bulfinch Press Book. Boston: Little, Brown, 1991.

Beaty, Bart. *Frederic Wertham and the Critique of Mass Culture: A Re-examination of the Critic Whose Congressional Testimony Sparked the Comics Code.* Jackson: University Press of Mississippi, 2005.

– 'High Treason: Canadian Nationalism and the Regulation of American Crime Comic Books.' *Essays on Canadian Writing*, no. 62 (1997): 85–107.

Beckmann, Susan. 'Margaret Atwood: Can. Lit. to Kid Lit.' *CCL*, no. 12 (1978): 78–81.

Beggs, Margo. 'Art for Art's Sake.' *Looking Glass* 4, no. 1 (2 April 2000). http://tlg.ninthwonder.com/rabbit/4.1/picture.html.

– '"L Was a Lady": Amelia Frances Howard-Gibbon and "A Comic Alphabet."' *Looking Glass* 3, no. 2 (2 August 1999). http://tlg.ninthwonder.com/rabbit/3.2/picture.html.

Bell, Bill. 'Victorian Paratexts.' *Victorian Literature and Culture* 27, no. 1 (1999): 327–35.

Bennett, Hugh. 'The Top Shelf: The Censorship of Canadian Children's and Young Adult Literature in the Schools.' *CCL*, no. 68 (1992): 17–26.

Berger, Carl. 'The True North Strong and Free.' In Russell, ed., *Nationalism in Canada*, 3–26.

Berridge, Celia. 'Illustrators, Books and Children: An Illustrator's Viewpoint.' *CLE* n.s. 11, no. 1 (1980): 21–30.

– 'Taking a Good Look at Picture Books.' *Signal* 36 (1981): 152–8.

Bertanees, Cherry, and Christina Thornley. 'Reading Cultural Representations: The Limitations of Critical Literacy.' *Pedagogy, Culture and Society* 13, no. 1 (2005): 75–86.

Besner, Neil. 'Canadian Children's Regional Literature: Fictions First.' *CCL*, no. 86 (1997): 17–26.

Biamonte, Christina. 'Crossing Culture in Children's Book Publishing.' *Publishing Research Quarterly* 18, no. 3 (2002): 26–42.

Bice, Megan. 'How a Book Is Made: Jory's Cove.' *IR* 11, no. 3 (Summer 1977): 11.

Black, Marilynne V. 'Canadian Historical Picture Books as Purveyors of Canadian History and National Identity.' Master's thesis, University of British Columbia, 2005.

Black, Marilynne V., and Ronald Jobe. 'Are Children Gaining a Sense of Place from Canadian Historical Picture Books?' *Looking Glass* 9, no. 3 (2 September 2005). http://www.lib.latrobe.edu.au/ojs/index.php/tlg/article/view/35/40.

– 'Are Our Picture Books Telling Our Story?' *CCBN* 29, no. 2 (2006): 13–15.

Blake, Donald E. 'LIP and Partisanship: An Analysis of the Local Initiatives Program.' *Canadian Public Policy* 2, no. 1 (1976): 17–32.

Bodmer, George R. 'The Post-Modern Alphabet: Extending the Limits of the Contemporary Alphabet Book, From Seuss to Gorey.' *CLAQ* 14, no. 3 (1989): 115–17.

Booth, David, ed. *Writers on Writing: A Guide to Writing and Illustrating Children's Books*. Toronto: Overlea House, 198Bourdieu, Pierre. *The Field of Cultural Production: Essays on Art and Literature*, ed. Randal Johnson. Cambridge: Polity Press, 1993.

Boyd, Kelly. *Manliness and the Boys' Story Paper in Britain: A Cultural History. 1855–1940*. Houndsmill, Hants., UK and New York: Palgrave Macmillan, 2003.

Bradford, Clare. *Reading Race: Aboriginality in Australian Children's Literature*. Melbourne: Melbourne University Press, 2001.

– 'Saved by the Word: Textuality and Colonization in Nineteenth Century Australian Texts for Children.' In McGillis, ed., *Voices of the Other*, 89–109.

– *Unsettling Narratives: Postcolonial Readings of Children's Literature*. [Waterloo]: Wilfrid Laurier University Press, 2007.

Branigan, Augustine. 'Mystification of the Innocents: Crime Comics and Delinquency in Canada, 1931–1949.' *Criminal Justice History* 7 (1986): 111–44.

Brassard, François. 'French Canadian Folk Music Studies: A Survey.' *Ethnomusicology* 16, no. 3 (1972): 351–9.

Braz, Albert. 'The Modern Hiawatha: Grey Owl's Construction of His Aboriginal Self.' In *Auto/biography in Canada: Critical Directions*, ed. Julie Rak, 53–68. Waterloo: Wilfrid Laurier University Press, 2005.

Brenner, Robin. 'Graphic Novels 101: FAQ.' *HB* 82, no. 2 (2006): 123–5.

British Columbia. Department of Education. *Catalogue of Books Suitable for Pupils of Grades I–IX: Reference Books for School Library*. Victoria: William Cullin. King's Printer, 1923. Transcription at http://www.mala.bc.ca/history/homeroom/Content/Topics/Programs/libcat.htm.

Broderick, Dorothy M. Review of 'Canadian Children's Literature.' *IR* 10, no. 2 (Spring 1976): 18.

Brodhead, Richard H. *Cultures of Letters: Scenes of Reading and Writing in Nineteenth-Century America*. Chicago: University of Chicago Press, 1993.

Bromley, Helen. 'Spying on Picture Books: Exploring Intertextuality with Young Children.' In Watson and Styles, eds, *Talking Pictures*, 101–11.

Broten, Delores, and Peter Birdsall. *Paper Phoenix: A History of Book Publishing in Canada*. Victoria: CANLIT, 1980.

Brymer, Lois. 'Canadian, Eh? A Content Analysis of Illustrations in Canadian Children's Fiction 1799–1939.' Master's thesis, University of British Columbia, 2005.

Busbin, O. Mell, and Susan Steinfirst. 'Criticism of Artworks in Children's Picture Books: A Content Analysis.' *JYS* 2, no. 3 (1989): 256–66.

Butts, Dennis. 'How Children's Literature Changed: What Happened in the 1840s.' *LU* 21, no. 2 (1997): 153–62.

Cambron, Micheline, and Carole Gerson. 'Literary Authorship.' In Lamonde, Fleming, and Black, eds, *HBIC*, vol. 2, 119–34.

Campbell, Sandra. 'From Romantic History to Communication Theory: Lorne Pierce as Publisher of C.W. Jefferys and Harold Innis.' *Journal of Canadian Studies* 30, no. 3 (1995): 91–126.

Canada at Bologna: An Exhibition of Canadian Children's Book Illustrations. [Toronto]: Canada at Bologna Steering Committee, 1990.

Canada. Canadian Heritage. Planning and Corporate Affairs. Corporate Review Branch. *Final Report: Summative Evaluation of the Book Publishing Industry Development Program*

(BPIDP). Ottawa: Canadian Heritage, 2004. Archived copy of report at http://www. collectionscanada.gc.ca/webarchives/20060129105245/http://www.pch.gc.ca/progs/ em-cr/eval/2004/2004_09/tdm_e.cfm.

– Department of Industry, Trade and Commerce. *The Book Publishing and Manufacturing Industry in Canada: A Statistical and Economic Analysis*. Prepared by Ernst and Ernst Management Consulting Services. Montreal. Canada. Ottawa: Government of Canada, 1970.

– Department of the Secretary of State. Arts and Culture Branch. *The Publishing Industry in Canada*. A Report prepared by the Bureau of Management Consulting. Ottawa: Minister of Supply and Services Canada, 1977.

– Parliament. House of Commons. Standing Committee on Canadian Heritage. *The Challenge of Change: A Consideration of the Canadian Book Industry*. Ottawa: The Committee, 2000. Archived copy of the report at http://www.collectionscanada.gc.ca/webarchives/20061113132512/http://cmte.parl.gc.ca/Content/HOC/committee/362/heri/reports/rp1031737/heri01/04-toc-e.html.

– Royal Commission on Aboriginal Peoples. *Report of the Royal Commission on Aboriginal Peoples*. Vol. 3, *Gathering Strength*. Ottawa: The Commission, 1996. http://www.collectionscanada.gc.ca/webarchives/20071124060708/http://www.ainc-inac.gc.ca/ch/rcap/sg/si1_e.html.

– Royal Commission on National Development in the Arts, Letters and Sciences. *Report*. Ottawa: King's Printer, 1951. http://www.collectionscanada.gc.ca/massey/h5-400-e. html.

– Statistics Canada. Culture, Tourism and the Centre of Education Statistics Division. *Canadian School Libraries and Teacher-Librarians: Results from the 2003/04 Information and Communications Technologies in Schools Survey*, by David Coish. Culture, Tourism and the Centre for Education Statistics Research Papers, no. 028. Ottawa: Minister of Industry for Statistics Canada, 2005. (Catalogue no. 81-595-MIE – No. 028). http://www.statcan. gc.ca/pub/81-595-m/81-595-m2005028-eng.pdf.

– Statistics Canada. Culture, Tourism and the Centre of Education Statistics Division. *Connectivity and ICT Integration in Canadian Elementary and Secondary Schools: First Results from the Information and Communications Technologies in Schools Survey, 2003–2004*, by Johanne Plante and David Beattie. Education. Skills and Learning Research Papers. Ottawa: Statistics Canada, 2004. (Catalogue no. 81-595-MIE, no. 017). http://www. statcan.gc.ca/pub/81-595-m/81-595-m2004017-eng.pdf.

– Statistics Canada. Family and Labour Studies Division. *Canadian Compulsory School Laws and Their Impact on Educational Attainment and Future Earnings*, by Philip Oreopoloulos. Analystical Studies Branch Research Paper Series. Ottawa: Statistics Canada, 2005. (Catalogue no. 11F0019MIE, no. 251). http://www.statcan.gc.ca/pub/11f0019m/11f0019m2005251-eng.pdf.

Canadian Children's Book Centre. *The Canadian Children's Book Centre Art Auction*. Toronto: The Centre, [1995].

– *The Storymakers: Illustrating Children's Books, 72 Artists and Illustrators Talk about Their Work*. Markham: Pembroke Publishers, 1999.

– *Treasures: Canadian Children's Book Illustration*. Toronto: The Centre, [1986].

– *Writing Stories, Making Pictures: Biographies of 150 Canadian Children's Authors and Illustrators*. Toronto: The Centre, 1994.

Canadian Institute for Historical Microreproduction. *Children's Literature: A Feast of Titles /*

Délices de la littérature enfantine. A bibliography published in celebration of the National Library of Canada's 50th anniversary. Ottawa: CIHM, 2003. Also available online at http://www.canadiana.org/pdf/catalog25an.pdf.

Canton, Jeffrey. 'What Is Canadian Children's Literature?' *SLiC* 21, no. 1 (2001): 1.

Carpenter, Carole Henderson. 'Enlisting Children's Literature in the Goals of Multiculturalism.' *Mosaic* 29, no. 3 (1996): 53–73.

– 'In Our Own Image: The Child, Canadian Culture and Our Future,' The Ninth Annual Robarts Lecture, York University, Toronto, 29 March 1995. http://www.yorku.ca/robarts/projects/lectures/pdf/rl_carpenter.pdf.

– 'William Kurelek: Teller of Tales.' *LU* 24, no. 2 (2000): 260–78.

Carpenter, Carole Henderson, Margot Hillel, and Thomas van der Walt. 'The Same But Different: The Dynamics of Local and Global in Australian, Canadian and South African Children's Literature.' In O'Sullivan, Reynolds, and Romøren, eds, *Children's Literature Global and Local*, 173–99.

Carpenter, Humphrey, and Mari Prichard. *The Oxford Companion to Children's Literature.* Oxford: Oxford University Press, 1984.

Carrier, Roch. Speech on writing for children, Serendipity Conference, University of British Columbia, 26 February 2005. Transcription by Judith Saltman.

Carstairs, Catherine. 'Roots Nationalism: Branding English Canada Cool in the 1980s and 1990s.' *Histoire Sociale / Social History* 39, no. 77 (2006): 235–55.

Cartwright, Ellen Thomas, and Heidi Ann Creighton. *Once Upon a Time: Catalogue of an Exhibition Held May 20, July 11, 1988.* Vancouver: Vancouver Art Gallery, 1988.

Cavill, Patricia M., and Mark Bodnar. *Transition: Changes in the Public and School Library Market.* Toronto: Association of Canadian Publishers, 1997.

Cavill, Patricia M., Renée Gopaul, and Malcolm Harkness. *Collections: How and Why Public Libraries Select and Buy Their Canadian Books.* Prepared for the Association of Canadian Publishers. Calgary: Pat Cavill Consulting, 1998.

Chapin, David. 'Gender and Indian Masquerade in the Life of Grey Owl.' *American Indian Quarterly* 24, no. 1 (2000): 91–109.

Chapleau, Sebastien, ed. *New Voices in Children's Literature Criticism.* Shenstone, Lichfield, Staff., UK: Pied Piper Publishing, 2004.

Cianciolo, Patricia. *Illustrations in Children's Books,* 2nd ed. Dubuque, IA: William Brown, 1976.

– *Picture Books for Children.* 4th ed. Chicago: American Library Association, 1997.

Clark, Beverly Lyon. *Kiddie Lit: The Cultural Construction of Children's Literature in America.* Baltimore and London: The Johns Hopkins University Press, 2003.

Clark, Beverly Lyon, and Margaret R. Higgonet, eds. *Girls, Boys, Books, Toys: Gender in Children's Literature and Culture.* Baltimore: The Johns Hopkins University Press, 1999.

Clark, Gail S. 'Imperial Stereotypes: G.A. Henty and the Boys' Own Empire.' *Journal of Popular Culture* 18, no. 4 (2004): 43–51.

Clark, Penney. 'The Publishing of School Books in English.' In Lamonde, Fleming, and Black, eds, *HBIC*, vol. 2, 335–40.

– 'The Rise and Fall of Textbook Publishing in English Canada.' In Gerson and Michon, eds, *HBIC*, vol. 3, 226–32.

Clarke, Alan. 'CYC, OFY, LIP, et al.' *JAE: Journal of Architectural Education* 29, no. 3 (1976): 29.

Clarke, Meaghan Emily. '(Re)constructing the Feminine in Art Writing: The Canadian Magazine "Mayfair" in the 1950s.' Master's thesis, Carleton University, 1996.

Clayton, Trevor. 'The Fun of Reading.' *Bulletin* (National Library of Canada) 35, no. 6 (November-December 2003). http://epe.lac-bac.gc.ca/100/202/301/bulletin_nlc/2003/no6/p2-0603-04-e.html.

Cleaver, Elizabeth. 'An Artist's Approach to Picture Books.' *IR* 8, no. 1 (Winter 1974): 5–8.

– 'Fantasy and Transformation in Shadow Puppetry.' *CCL*, nos. 15–16 (1980): 67–79.

– 'Idea to Image: The Journey of a Picture Book.' *LU* 7–8 (1983–4): 156–70.

– 'The Visual Artist and the Creative Process in Picture Books.' *CCL*, no. 4 (1976): 71–9.

Clement, Dominique. '"An Anachronism Failing to Function Properly": How the Baby Boom Generation Transformed Social Movements in Canada.' Paper presented at the Canadian Historical Association annual conference, Saskatoon, Saskatchewan, 30 May 2007.

Cobban, Michelle. 'Bridging the Two Solitudes: Translated French-Canadian Children's Literature from 1900 to 2004.' Master's thesis, University of British Columbia, 2006.

Cole, Tom J. 'The Origin and Development of School Libraries.' *Peabody Journal of Education* 37, no. 2 (1959): 87–92.

Colgate, William. *C.W. Jefferys*. Canadian Art Series. Toronto: The Ryerson Press, [1944].

Collins, Damian. 'Culture, Religion and Curriculum: Lessons from the "Three Books" Controversy in Surrey, BC.' *Canadian Geographer* 50, no. 3 (2006): 342–57.

Collins, Janet. 'Ron Lightburn: Meet the Man Behind the Pictures.' *CM* 22, no. 4 (1994). http://www.umanitoba.ca/outreach/cm/cmarchive/vol22no4/ronlightburn.html.

Collis, Mary. 'The Art of Illustration: Cartoon Art.' *National Library News* 29, no. 11 (1997): 13–15. http://epe.lac-bac.gc.ca/100/202/301/nlnews/nlnews-h/1997/9711e/e09.htm.

Colpitts, George. *Game in the Garden: A Human History of Wildlife in Western Canada to 1940*. Vancouver: UBC Press, 2002.

Comacchio, Cynthia R. *Nations Are Built of Babies: Serving Ontario's Mothers and Children, 1900–1940*. Montreal and Kingston: McGill-Queen's University Press, 2003.

Cook, Ramsay. *Canada, Quebec and the Uses of Nationalism*. 2nd ed. Toronto: McClelland and Stewart, 1995.

Cooper, Afua. '"Out of a Cardboard Box beside Our Bed Like a Baby": The Founders of Sister Vision Press.' In *Great Dames*, ed. Elspeth Cameron and Janice Dickin, 291–306. Toronto: University of Toronto Press, 1997.

Cooper, Susan. 'Only the Rarest Kind of Best: One View of Literary Criticism.' *Children and Libraries* 3, no. 2 (2005): 14–17.

Copithorne, Tama. 'Creating the Mosaic: A Celebration of Canadian Children's Culture.' In *Yearbook of Exemplary Practice 1998 / Livre annuel du professionnalisme 1998*, 31–8. Ottawa: Canadian Association for University Continuing Education / Association pour éducation permanente dans les universités du Canada, 1998.

Corse, Sarah M. *Nationalism and Literature: The Politics of Culture in Canada and the United States*. Cambridge: Cambridge University Press, 1997.

Côté, Marc. 'Cultural Industries.' *CL*, no. 177 (2003): 200.

Coughlan, Margaret N. 'Guardians of the Young.' In *Reader in Children's Librarianship*, ed. John Foster, 142–54. Englewood, CO: Information Handling Services, 1978.

Crago, Hugh. 'Who Does Snow-White Look At?' *Signal* 45 (1984): 129–45.

Crandall, Nadia. 'The UK Children's Book Business 1995–2004: A Strategic Analysis.' *New Review of Children's Literature and Librarianship* 12, no. 1 (2006): 1–18.

Crean, Susan. 'Culture in the Crunch.' *Canadian Forum* 72, no. 821 (1993): 12–17.

Creating the Mosaic: A Celebration of Canadian Children's Literature. Vancouver: Japanese Culture and Communications Program of the David See-Chai Lam Centre for International Communication, Simon Fraser University at Harbour Centre, 1997.

Culleton, Beatrice. 'Images of Native People and Their Effects.' *SLiC* 7, no. 3 (1987): 47–52.

Cumming, Peter E. 'Queer (and Not-So-Queer) Childhoods.' *CCL* 32, no. 2 (2006): 165–83.

Curry, W.E. 'The Impact of the US Manufacturing Provisions.' In Ontario, Royal Commission on Book Publishing, *Background Papers*, 143–53.

Curtis, Bruce. 'On Distributed Literacy: Textually Mediated Politics in Colonial Canada.' *Pedagogica Historica* 44, no. 1 (2008): 233–44.

Cutler, May. 'Ah, Publishing!' In Egoff, ed., *One Ocean Touching*, 212–20.

– 'Dayal Kaur Khalsa (1943–1989): A Publisher's Tribute.' *CM* 17, no. 6 (1989). http://www.umanitoba.ca/outreach/cm/cmarchive/vol17no6/dayalkaurkhalsa.html.

Daniel, Lorne. 'Prairie Publishing: A Community Grows.' *Canadian Forum* 58, no. 685 (1978): 31–2.

Darnton, Robert. 'What Is the History of Books?' In Davidson, ed., *Reading in America*, 27–52.

Darton, F.J. Harvey. *Children's Books in England: Five Centuries of Social Life.* Cambridge: Cambridge University Press, 1932.

Daveluy, Paule, and Guy Boulizon. *Création culturelle pour la jeunesse et identité québécoise.* Montreal: Lemeac, [1973].

David, Shay, and Trevor Pinch. 'Six Degrees of Reputation: The Use and Abuse of Online Review and Recommendation Systems.' S&T Working Paper. Science and Technology Studies, Cornell University. http://papers.ssrn.com/sol3/papers.cfm?abstract_id=857505.

Davidson, Cathy N., ed. *Reading in America: Literature and Social History.* Baltimore and London: Johns Hopkins University Press, 1989.

– 'Towards a History of Books and Readers.' In Davidson, ed., *Reading in America*, 1–26.

Davies, Cory. 'A Conversation with Ann Blades.' *CCL*, nos. 39–40 (1985): 21–32.

Davies, Gwendolyn. 'Publishing Abroad.' In Lamonde, Fleming, and Black, eds, *HBIC*, vol. 2, 139–46.

Davis, Angela E. *Art and Work: A Social History of Labour in the Canadian Graphic Arts Industry to the 1940s.* Montreal and Kingston: McGill-Queen's University Press, 1995.

Davis, Marie C. '"It's Time for Something Different": Kent Monkman on Illustrative Dissent.' *CCL*, no. 84 (Winter 1996): 65–70.

– 'Parable, Parody, or "Blip in the Canadian Literary Landscape": Tom King on "A Coyote Columbus Story."' *CCL*, no. 84 (Winter 1996): 47–64.

– '"Un penchant pour la diagonale": An Interview with Marie-Louise Gay.' *CCL*, no. 60 (1990): 52–73.

Davis, Virginia. 'The Children's Book Centre and Communication-Jeunesse: Their Origins as Agencies to Promote Canadian Children's Literature.' *CM* 14, no. 6 (1986). http://www.umanitoba.ca/outreach/cm/cmarchive/vol14no6/childrensbookcentrejeuness.html.

Day, Richard J.F. *Multiculturalism and the History of Canadian Diversity.* Toronto: University of Toronto Press, 2000.

Demers, Patricia. 'Dennis Lee's Poetry for Children.' *CLAQ* 9, no. 3 (1984): 129–30.

DePasquale, Paul, and Doris Wolf. 'A Select Bibliography of Canadian Picture Books for Children by Aboriginal Authors.' *CCL*, nos.115–116 (2004): 144–55.

Devereaux, Cecily. '"Perhaps Nobody Has Told You Why the English Are Called Sahibs in India": Sarah Jeanette Duncan's Imperialism for Children.' *CCL*, no. 102 (2001): 6–19.

Diakiw, Jerry. 'Children's Literature and Canadian National Identity: A Revisionist Perspective.' *CCL*, no. 87 (1997): 42–3.

Dodds, Carolyn. 'A Child's Garden of Publishers: Canadian Kid Lit Comes of Age.' *Financial Post Magazine*, 1 August 1984, 29–35.

Donnelly, Brian. 'At Forty: Canadian Graphic Design Comes of Age.' *Applied Arts* 11, no. 4 (1996): 68–71.

– 'Locating Graphic Design History in Canada.' *Journal of Design History* 19, no. 4 (2006): 283–94.

– 'Picturing Words, Writing Images: Design, Contingent Meaning,' PhD diss., Queen's University, 2005.

Donnelly, Eleanore. 'Profile: Clare Bice.' *IR* 1, no. 1 (Winter 1967): 20–1.

Donovan, John. 'Children's Book Publishing on the Ascent.' *Publishing Research Quarterly* 7, no. 3 (1991): 7–14.

Dooley, Patricia. 'The Window in the Book: Conventions in the Illustration of Children's Books.' *Wilson Library Bulletin* 55 (October 1980): 108–12.

Doonan, Jane. 'The Idle Bear and the Active Reader.' *Signal*, no. 55 (1988): 33–47.

– *Looking at Pictures in Picture Books*. South Woodchester, Stroud, Glos., UK: Thimble Press, 1993.

Doonan, Jane, and David Lewis. 'Reading New Books.' *Signal*, no. 65 (1991): 129–42.

Dowsett, Kathleen. 'The Women's Art Association of Canada and its Designs on Canadian Handcraft, 1898.' Master's thesis, Queen's University, 1998.

Dresang, Eliza T. *Radical Change: Books for Youth in a Digital Age*. New York: H.W. Wilson, 1999.

Dressel, Janice. 'Abstraction in Illustration.' *CLE* 15, no. 2 (1984): 102–12.

Drotner, Kirsten. *English Children and Their Magazines, 1751–1945*. New Haven: Yale University Press, 1988.

Dudek, Debra. 'Approaching the Other in Twelve Canadian Picture Books.' *CCL* 33, no. 1 (2007): 107–23.

Duguay, Louise. 'Pauline Boutal: Eaton's Catalogue Fashion Illustrator, 1918–1941.' 'From Order to Delivery,' *Before E-Commerce: A History of Canadian Mail Order Catalogues*, Canadian Museum of Civilization. http://www.civilization.ca/cmc/exhibitions/cpm/catalog/cat2503e.shtml.

Dunae, Patrick A. 'Boys' Literature and the Idea of Empire.' *Victorian Studies* 24 (1980–1): 105–21.

– '"Making Good": The Canadian West in British Boys' Literature.' *Prairie Forum* 4, no. 2 (1979): 165–81.

Duthie, W.J. 'The Other Side of the Cash Register: A Bookseller's View.' *CL*, no. 33 (1967): 37–43.

Dyck, Betty. 'Growing Pains: A Look at Children's Book Publishing in Canada.' *Canadian Author and Bookman* 54, no. 2 (1979): 20–1.

Edison, Margaret. *Thoreau MacDonald: A Catalogue of Design and Illustration*. Toronto: University of Toronto Press, 1973.

Edwards, Gail. 'Dayal Kaur Khalsa: The Art of Remembering.' *CCL*, no. 70 (1993): 48–62.
– 'Talking Pics: Evaluating the Artistic Side of Picture Books.' *CM* 21, no. 2 (1993): 44–52.
Edwards, Gail, and Judith Saltman. 'Looking at Ourselves, Looking at Others: Multi-culturalism in Canadian Children's Picturebooks in English.' Paper presented to the History of the Book in Canada's Open Conference for Volume III, Vancouver, November 2001. http://www.hbic.library.utoronto.ca/vol3edwardssaltman_en.htm.
Edwardson, Ryan. '"Kicking Uncle Sam Out of the Peaceable Kingdom": English-Canadian "New Nationalism" and Americanization.' *Journal of Canadian Studies* 37, no. 4 (2002–3): 131–50.
Egoff, Sheila, comp. *Canadian Children's Books, 1799–1939*. Vancouver: The University of British Columbia Library, 1992.
– 'Children's Books in English.' In *Supplement to the Oxford Companion to Canadian History and Literature*, ed. William Toye, 29–39. Toronto: Oxford University Press, 1973.
– 'Children's Literature to 1960.' In *Literary History of Canada: Canadian Literature in English*. 2nd ed., ed. Carl F. Klinck. Vol. 2, 134–42. Toronto: University of Toronto Press, 1976.
– 'Introduction.' In Egoff, ed., *One Ocean Touching*, v–viii.
– 'Lillian H. Smith as Critic.' In Fasick, Johnston, and Osler, eds, *Lands of Pleasure*, 130–40.
– 'A National Treasure: Some Thoughts on the Accomplishments of Irene Elizabeth Aubrey.' *CCL*, no. 86 (1997): 43–9.
– *Once Upon a Time: My Life with Children's Books*. With Wendy K. Sutton. Victoria: Orca Book Publishers, 2005.
– ed. *One Ocean Touching; Papers from the First Pacific Rim Conference on Children's Literature*. Metuchen. NJ: Scarecrow Press, 1979.
– *The Republic of Childhood: A Critical Guide to Canadian Children's Literature in English*. Toronto: Oxford University Press, 1967. [2nd ed. Toronto: Oxford University Press, 1975].
– 'The Writing and Publishing of Canadian Children's Books in English.' In Ontario, Royal Commission on Book Publishing. *Background Papers*, 245–69.
Egoff, Sheila, and Alvine Bélisle. *Notable Canadian Children's Books / Un choix de livres canadiens pour la jeunesse*. Ottawa: National Library of Canada, 1973. [Supplement. Ottawa: National Library of Canada, 1975; Rev. and updated ed., ed. Irene Aubrey. Ottawa: National Library of Canada, 1976.]
Egoff, Sheila, and Judith Saltman. *The New Republic of Childhood: A Critical Guide to Canadian Children's Literature in English*. Toronto: Oxford University Press, 1990.
Elliott, Ellen. *Publishing in Wartime*. An Address delivered to the Twentieth Anniversary Convention of the Canadian Authors' Association on Friday, August 22nd, 1941. [Toronto]: Privately Printed by The Macmillans in Canada. [1941].
Emery, J.W. *The Library, The School and the Child*. Toronto: Macmillan Company of Canada, 1917.
English, Leona M. 'Children's Literature for Adults: A Meaningful Paradox.' *PAACE Journal of Lifelong Learning* 9 (2000): 13–23.
Epperly, Elizabeth Rollins. *Through Lover's Lane: L.M. Montgomery's Photography and Visual Imagination*. Toronto: University of Toronto Press, 2007.
Evans, Dilys. 'An Extraordinary Vision: Picture Books of the Nineties.' *HB* 68, no. 6 (1991): 759–63.

Evans, Janet, ed. *What's in the Picture?: Responding to Illustrations in Picture Books.* London: Paul Chapman Publishing, 1998.

Fasick, Adele M. 'Relations between Children's Libraries and Children's Publishers.' *EL* 18, no. 5 (1991): 14–21.

– 'Smith, Lillian H.' In *Pioneers and Leaders in Library Services to Youth: A Biographical Dictionary*, ed. Marilyn L. Miller, 226–8. Westport, CT: Libraries Unlimited, 2003.

Fasick, Adele M., André Gagnon, Lynne Howarth, and Ken Settrington. *Opening Doors to Children: Reading, Media and Public Library Use by Children in Six Canadian Cities.* Regina: Regina Public Library, 2005.

Fasick, Adele M., Margaret Johnston, and Ruth Osler, eds. *Lands of Pleasure: Essays on Lillian H. Smith and the Development of Children's Libraries.* Metuchen, NJ, and London: Scarecrow Press, 1990.

Faye, Jefferson. 'Revealing the Storyteller: The Ethical Publication of Inuit Stories.' *American Review of Canadian Studies* 31, nos. 1–2 (2001): 159–70.

Feather, John. *A History of British Publishing.* 2nd ed. London and New York: Routledge, 2006.

Fiamengo, Janice. 'Regionalism and Urbanism.' In Kröller, ed., *Cambridge Companion to Canadian Literature*, 241–62.

Fisher, Donald. 'Boundary Work.' *Science Communication* 10, no. 2 (1988): 156–76.

Fleming, Patricia Lockhart, Gilles Gallichan, and Yvan Lamonde, eds. *History of the Book in Canada*, vol. 1, *Beginnings to 1840.* Toronto: University of Toronto Press, 2004.

Fleming, R. 'Supplementing Self: A Postcolonial Quest(ion) for (of) National Essence and Indigenous Form in Catherine Parr Traill's "Canadian Crusoes."' *Essays on Canadian Writing*, no. 56 (1995): 198–223.

Fox, Geoff, and Graham Hammond, eds. *Responses to Children's Literature: Proceedings of the Fourth Symposium of the International Research Society for Children's Literature at the University of Exeter, September 9–12, 1978.* New York: K.G. Saur.

Foy, Kathleen M. 'Profile: Elizabeth Cleaver.' *IR* 6, no. 1 (Winter 1972): 15–17.

Francis, Daniel. *National Dreams: Myth, Memory, and Canadian History.* Vancouver: Arsenal Pulp Press, 1997.

Fraustino, Lisa Rowe. 'The Apple of Her Eye: The Mothering Ideology Fed by Best-Selling Trade Picture Books.' In *Critical Approaches to Food in Children's Literature*, ed. Karla K. Keeling and Scott T. Pollard, 57–73. New York: Routledge, 2009.

Frayne, June, Jennifer Laidley, and Henry Hadeed. *Print for Young Canadians: A Bibliographical Catalogue of Canadian Fiction for Children from 1825–1920.* Toronto: [s.n.], 1975.

Frazer, F. M. 'Legends Old and New.' *CL*, no. 22 (1964): 69–71.

Friesen, Gerald. *Citizens and Nation: An Essay on History, Communication, and Canada.* Toronto: University of Toronto Press, 2000.

Friskney, Janet B. 'Christian Faith in Print.' In Fleming, Gallichan, and Lamonde, eds, *HBIC*, vol. 1, 138–44.

Friskney, Janet B. 'The Many Aspects of a General Editorship: Malcolm Ross and the NCL.' *Canadian Poetry*, no. 52 (2003): 26–53.

Frye, Northrop. *The Bush Garden: Essays on the Canadian Imagination.* Toronto: House of Anansi Press, 1971.

– 'Conclusion.' In Klinck, ed., *Literary History of Canada*, 821–49.

Gagnon, André. 'French Canadian Picture Books in Translation.' *CLAQ* 15, no. 4 (1990): 212–17.

– 'Translation of Children's Books in Canada.' *CCL*, no. 45 (1987): 14–53.

Gagnon, André, and Ann Gagnon, eds. *Canadian Books for Young People / Livres canadiens pour la jeunesse*. 4th ed. Toronto: University of Toronto Press, 1988.

Gaitskell, Susan. 'An Interview with Barbara Reid.' *CCL*, no. 56 (1989): 6–14.

Gal, Laszlo. 'Illustrating the Text.' In Booth, ed., *Writers on Writing*, 12–15.

Galbraith, Gretchen R. *Reading Lives: Reconstructing Childhood, Books, and Schools in Britain, 1870–1920*. New York: St Martin's Press, 1997.

Galler, Anne M., President, Canadian School Library Association, to Dr. John English, [commissioner, Review of the Role of the National Archives and the National Library for Heritage Canada,] 'Brief Concerning the Role of the National Library of Canada,' 10 July 1998.

Galway, Elizabeth. 'Fact, Fiction, and the Tradition of Historical Narratives in Nineteenth-Century Children's Literature.' *CCL*, no. 102 (2001): 20–32.

– *From Nursery Rhymes to Nationhood: Children's Literature and the Construction of Canadian Identity*. New York and London: Routledge, 2008.

– 'From Nursery Rhymes to Nationhood: Constructing Canadian National Identity through Children's Literature, 1867–1911.' PhD diss., University of Exeter, England, 2003.

– 'Windows on the World: Canadian Publishers Offer Global Perspectives on Childhood.' *CCL* 33, no. 1 (2007): 123–43.

Gammel, Irene. *Looking for Anne: How Lucy Maud Montgomery Dreamed Up a Literary Classic*. Toronto: Key Porter Books, 2008.

Gangi, Jane M. 'Inclusive Aesthetics and Social Justice: The Vanguard of Small, Multicultural Presses.' *CLAQ* 30, no. 3 (2005): 243–64.

Garrett, Jeffrey. 'Guilty as Accused? The Case of Munsch's "Love You Forever."' *Bookbird* 33, nos. 3–4 (1995–96): 25–30.

Gault, Cinda. 'Grooving the Nation: 1965–1980 as a Literary Era in Canada.' *American Review of Canadian Studies* 38, no. 3 (2008): 361–79.

Gay, Marie-Louise. 'Si une image vaut mille mots, un mot peut-il évoquer mille images? / If a Picture Is Worth a Thousand Words, Can a Word Conjure Up a Thousand Images?' trans. David Homel. In *Show and Tell: Outstanding Canadian Picture Books 2000–2003 / Montre et raconte: Albums illustrés canadiens remarquables 2000–2003*, 12–15. [Toronto]: IBBY Canada, [2004].

Genette, Gérard. *Palimpsests: Literature in the Second Degree*. Translated by Channa Newman and Claude Doubinsky. Lincoln: University of Nebraska Press, 1997. Originally published as *Palimpsestes: La littérature au second degré* (Paris: Seuil, 1982).

– *Paratexts: Thresholds of Interpretation*. Translated by Jane E. Lewin. Cambridge and New York: Cambridge University Press, 1997. Originally published as *Seuils* (Paris: Seuil, 1987).

Gerson, Carole. '"Anne of Green Gables" Goes to University: L.M. Montgomery and Academic Culture.' In *Making Avonlea: L.M. Montgomery and Popular Culture*, ed. Irene Gammel, 17–31. Toronto: University of Toronto Press, 2002.

– 'The Canon between the Wars: Field-Notes of a Feminist Literary Archaeologist.' In *Canadian Canons: Essays in Literary Value*, ed. Robert Lecker, 46–56. Toronto: University of Toronto Press, 1991.

– 'Nobler Savages: Representations of Native Women in the Writings of Susanna Moodie and Catherine Parr Traill.' *Journal of Canadian Studies* 32, no. 2 (1997): 22–47.

– 'The Snow Drop and the Maple Leaf: Canada's First Periodicals for Children.' *CCL*, nos. 18–19 (1980): 10–23.

– 'Women and Children First?: Some Observations from the Field.' *CCL*, no. 62 (1991): 6–13.

– 'Women and Print Culture.' In Fleming, Gallichan, and Lamonde, eds, *HBIC*, vol. 1, 354–60.

Gerson, Carole, and Jacques Michon, eds. *History of the Book in Canada*, vol. 3, *1918–1980*. Toronto: University of Toronto Press, 2007.

Gertridge, Allison. *Meet Canadian Authors and Illustrators: Fifty Creators of Children's Books*. Richmond Hill, ON: Scholastic Canada, 1994.

– *Meet Canadian Authors and Illustrators: Sixty Creators of Children's Books*. Rev. ed. Richmond Hill, ON: Scholastic Canada, 2002.

Ghan, Linda. 'Interview with Frank Newfeld.' *CCL*, no. 17 (1980): 13–19.

Gillespie, Jim. 'Books and Cultural Sovereignty.' *CLJ* 42, no. 3 (1985): 121–8.

Gilman, Phoebe. 'The Creation of Something from Nothing: Developing Jewish Themes in Children's Literature.' In *From Memory to Transformation: Jewish Women's Voices*, ed. Sarah Silberstein Swartz and Margie Wolfe, 287–90. Toronto: Second Story Press, 1998.

Gleason, Mona. *Normalizing the Ideal: Psychology, Schooling and the Family in Postwar Canada*. Toronto: University of Toronto Press, 1999.

– '"They Have a Bad Effect": Crime Comics, Parliament, and the Hegemony of the Middle Class in Postwar Canada.' In *Pulp Demons: International Dimensions of the Postwar Anti-Comics Campaign*, ed. John Lent, 129–54. Madison: Fairleigh Dickinson University Press, 1999.

Golden, Joanne M., and Annyce Gerber. 'A Semiotic Perspective of Text: The Picture Book Story Event.' *Journal of Reading Behavior* 22, no. 3 (1990): 203–19.

Goldenberg, Carol. 'The Design and Typography of Children's Books.' *HB* 69, no. 5 (1993): 559–67.

Goldstone, Bette P. 'Brave New Worlds: The Changing Image of the Picture Book.' *New Advocate* 12, no. 4 (Fall 1999): 331–43.

Goodman, Kenneth, Lisa Maras, and Debbie Birdseye. 'Look! Look! Who Stole the Pictures from the Picture Book: The Basalization of Picture Books.' *New Advocate* 7, no. 1 (1994): 1–24.

Grace, Sherrill E. *Canada and the Idea of North*. Montreal and Kingston: McGill-Queen's University Press, 2001.

Graham, Judith. 'Picture Books.' In Reynolds and Tucker, eds, *Children's Book Publishing in Britain*, 60–85.

– *Pictures on the Page*. Sheffield, UK: National Association for the Teaching of English, 1990.

Grant, Agnes. 'A Canadian Fairy Tale: What Is It?' *CCL*, no. 22 (1981): 27–35.

Grant, George. *Lament for a Nation*. Toronto: McClelland and Stewart, 1965.

Grant, Peter S., and Chris Wood. *Blockbusters and Trade Wars: Popular Culture in a Globalized World*. Vancouver: Douglas and McIntyre, 2004.

Gratton, Tricia. '"Vitality … Waiting in the Wilderness': The Construction of the Environmental Native in Christie Harris's Art and Archive.' *CCL* 33, no 2 (2007): 93–111.

Gray, John Morgan. 'Canadian Books: A Publisher's View.' *CL*, no. 33 (1967): 24–36.

– 'Trade Publishing in Canada.' In *Publishing in Canada: Proceedings of the Institute on Publishing in Canada. June 27–30, 1971*, ed. G. Pomahac and M. Richeson, 5–13. Edmonton: The School of Library Science, The University of Alberta, 1972.

Greco, Albert N. *The Book Publishing Industry*. 2nd ed. Mahwah, NJ: Lawrence Erlbaum Associates, 2005.

Greco, Albert N., Clara E. Rodriguez, and Robert M. Wharton. *The Culture and Commerce of Publishing in the 21st Century*. Stanford, CA: Stanford Business Books, Stanford University Press, 2007.

Greenwood, Barbara, ed. *Behind the Story: The Creators of Our Best Children's Books and How They Do It*. Markham, ON: Pembroke Publishers, 1995.

– ed. *The CANSCAIP Companion: A Biographical Record of Canadian Children's Authors, Illustrators and Performers*. Markham, ON: Pembroke Publishers, 1991. 2nd ed. Markham, ON: Pembroke Publishers, 1994.

– ed. *Presenting Children's Authors, Illustrators, and Performers*. Markham, ON: Pembroke Publishers, 1990.

Hade, Daniel. 'Curious George Gets Branded: Reading as Consuming.' *Theory into Practice* 40, no. 3 (Summer 2001): 509–17.

– 'Storyselling: Are Publishers Changing the Way Children Read.' *HB* 78, no. 5 (2002): 509–18.

Hade, Daniel, and Jacqueline Edmondson. 'Children's Book Publishing in Neoliberal Times.' *Language Arts* 81, no. 2 (2003): 135–43.

Hagler, Ronald. 'The Selection and Acquisition of Books in Six Ontario Public Libraries in Relation to the Canadian Publishing System.' PhD diss., University of Michigan, 1961.

Halpenny, Francess G. *Canadian Collections in Public Libraries*. Toronto: Canadian Book and Periodical Council, 1985.

Hambleton, Alixe E. 'The Use of Canadian Materials in the Publicity and Programming Activities of School and Public Libraries,' [Research paper for the Canadian Studies Division of the Department of the Secretary of State.] Regina: Faculty of Education, University of Regina, [1986].

Hambleton, Alixe, and Ronald Jobe. 'Teachers' Awareness of Canadian Children's Literature.' *EL* 9, no. 3 (1982): 6–9.

Hanson, Elizabeth. 'Early Canadian Library Education: The McGill and Ontario Experience, 1904–1927.' In *Readings in Canadian Library History 2*, ed. Peter F. McNally, 57–89. Ottawa: Canadian Library Association, 1996.

Hardy, E.A. *The Public Library: Its Place in Our Educational System*. Toronto: William Briggs, 1912.

Harker, Mary. 'An Interview with James Houston.' *CCL*, no. 61 (1991): 19–28.

Harker, W. John. 'Canadian Literature in Canadian Schools: From the Old to the New Internationalism.' *Canadian Journal of Education* 12, no. 3 (1987): 417–27.

Harms, Jeanne McLain, and Lucille Lettow. 'Book Design: Extending Verbal and Visual Literacy.' *JYS* 2, no. 2 (1989): 126–42.

Harris, Christie. 'People Who Saved the Old Stories for the New Storytellers.' In *Once More Upon a Totem*, 192–5. Toronto: McClelland and Stewart, 1973.

– 'The Shift from Feasthouse to Book.' *CCL*, nos. 31–32 (1983): 9–11.

Harris, Christie, and J. Kieran Kealy. 'Caught in the Current.' *CCL*, no. 74 (1994): 5–15.

Harris, R. Cole. 'The Myth of the Land in Canadian Nationalism.' In Russell, ed., *Nationalism in Canada*, 27–46.
– 'Power, Modernity, and Historical Geography.' *Annals of the Association of American Geographers* 81, no. 4 (1991): 671–83.
Harris, Roma M., and Victoria Marshall. 'Reorganizing Canadian Libraries: A Giant Step Back from the Front.' *Library Trends* 46, no. 3 (1998): 564–80.
Harrison, Ted. 'Images of the North.' In Booth, ed., *Writers on Writing*, 16–19.
Hawker, Ronald W. *Tales of Ghosts: First Nations Art in British Columbia, 1922–61.* Vancouver: UBC Press, 2003.
Hawthorn, Audrey. 'Myths and Sources.' Review of *Indian Legends of Canada*, by Ella Elizabeth Clark. *CL, no.* 8 (1961): 72–3.
Haycock, Ken. *Canadian Learning Resources: A Brief Summary of Recent Developments in School Resource Centres.* Vancouver: Library Services Department, Vancouver School Board, 1977.
– *The Crisis in Canada's School Libraries: The Case for Reform and Re-investment.* Toronto: Association of Canadian Publishers, 2003.
Haycock, Ken, and Carol-Ann Haycock, eds. *Kids and Libraries: Selections from Emergency Librarian.* Vancouver: Dyad Services, 1984.
Hayward, Annette, and André Lamontagne. 'Le Canada anglais: Une invention québécoise?' *Voix et Images* 24, no. 3 (1999): 460–79.
Hazeltine, Alice E., ed. *Library Work with Children: Reprints of Papers and Addresses.* White Plains, NY: H.W. Wilson, 1917.
Heard, Ruth, moderator. "The Picture Link: A Panel of Three Illustrators [Maryann Kovalski, Ken Nutt, and Ian Wallace]." *CCL*, no. 48 (1987): 55–61.
Hearne, Betsy. 'Cite the Source: Reducing Cultural Chaos in Picture Books, Part One.' *School Library Journal* 39, no. 7 (1993): 22–7.
– 'Margaret K. McElderry and the Professional Matriarchy of Children's Books.' *Library Trends* 44, no. 4 (1996): 755–75.
– 'Perennial Picture Books: Seeded by the Oral Tradition.' *JYS* 12, no. 1 (Fall 1998): 26–33.
– 'Respect the Source: Reducing Cultural Chaos in Picture Books, Part Two.' *School Library Journal* 39, no. 8 (1993): 33–7.
Hearne, Betsy, and Roger Sutton, eds. *Evaluating Children's Books, A Critical Look: Aesthetic, Social, and Political Aspects of Analyzing and Using Children's Books.* Urbana-Champaign: University of Illinois, Graduate School of Library and Information Science, 1993.
Hébert, Pierre. 'Roch Carrier au Canada anglais.' *Oeuvres et critiques* 14, no. 1 (1989): 101–13.
Henderson, Jennifer. 'Critical Canadiana.' *American Literary History* 13, no. 4 (2001): 789–813.
Hewins, Caroline Maria. 'Reading Clubs for Older Boys and Girls.' In Hazeltine, ed., *Library Work with Children*, 325–9.
Higonnet, Anne. *Pictures of Innocence: The History and Crisis of Ideal Childhood.* London: Thames and Hudson, 1998.
Higonnet, Margaret. 'The Playground of the Peritext.' *CLAQ* 15, no. 2 (1990): 47–9.
Hildebrandt, Gloria. 'Planned Departure: Five Publishers Share the Secrets of Their Succession.' *The Canadian Bookseller* 27, no. 5 (2005): 16.

Hill, Kathleen. 'Journeying with Glooscap.' In Egoff, ed., *One Ocean Touching*, 186–8.

Hodge, Bob, and Vijay Mishra. *Dark Side of the Dream: Australian Literature and the Postcolonial Mind.* Sydney: Allen and Unwin, 1991.

Hodges, Gabrielle Cliff, Mary Jane Drummond, and Morag Styles, eds. *Tales, Tellers and Texts.* London: Cassell, 2000.

Hodgetts, A.B. *What Culture? What Heritage?* OISE Curriculum Series, no. 5. Toronto: Ontario Institute of Studies in Education, 1968.

Hollindale, Peter. 'Meanings and Valuations of Children's Literature.' In *Signs of Childness in Children's Books*, 23–43. Stroud, Glos., UK: Thimble Press, 1997.

Honda, Hideaki. 'Multiculturalism and Canadian Picture Books.' *Sagami Eibei Bungaku* 16 (1998): 1–19. [Translated for this research project by Toshiyuki Tosa, and Yukiko Tosa, Vancouver, August 2008.]

Hornberg, Brian. 'Beyond the Word / Image Dialectic: A Visual Grammar for Contemporary Picturebooks.' Master's thesis, University of British Columbia, 2004.

Hornberg, Brian. 'Transcending Boundaries in David Wiesner's *The Three Pigs*: Taking an Askew View of Words and Images in Picturebooks.' *Looking Glass* 9, no. 1 (2 January 2005). http://tlg.ninthwonder.com/rabbit/v9i1/picture.html.

Horning, Kathleen T. 'The Contributions of Alternative Press Publishers to Multicultural Literature for Children.' *Library Trends* 41, no. 3 (1993): 524–40.

Houston, James. 'The Vision of That Mask.' *CCL*, nos. 31–2 (1983): 12–14.

Houston, Susan E., and Alison Prentice. *Schooling and Scholars in Nineteenth-Century Ontario.* The Ontario Historical Studies Series. Toronto: University of Toronto Press, for the Government of Ontario, 1988.

Howells, Richard. *Visual Culture.* Cambridge: Polity Press; Malden, MA: Blackwell Publishers, 2003.

Hudson, Aïda, and Susan-Ann Cooper, eds. *Windows and Words: A Look at Canadian Children's Literature in English.* Reappraisals: Canadian Writers, no. 25. Ottawa: University of Ottawa Press, 2003.

Hugill, Peter J. 'Imperialism and Manliness in Edwardian Boys' Novels.' *Cultural Geographies* 6, no. 3 (1999): 318–40.

Hunt, Clara. 'Values in Library Work with Children.' In Hazeltine, ed., *Library Work with Children*, 135–46. [Originally published in *American Library Association Proceedings*, 1913.]

Hunt, Peter. *Criticism, Theory and Children's Literature.* Oxford: Basil Blackwell, 1991.

Hunt, Peter, and Karen Sands. 'The View from the Centre: British Empire and Post-Empire Children's Literature.' In McGillis, ed., *Voices of the Other*, 39–53.

Hurley, Robert. 'Affective Stylistics and Children's Literature: Spirituality and Transcendence in Robert Munsch's "Love You Forever."' *CCL* 31, no. 2 (Fall 2005): 83–107.

Hurtig, Mel. *Never Heard of Them ... They Must Be Canadian.* A Report of the Results of a Canadian Student Awareness Survey. Toronto: Canada Books, 1975.

IBBY Canada. *The IBBY Honour List 1980–2000: A Legacy of Outstanding Canadian Children's Literature.* [Toronto: IBBY Canada, 2000.]

– *Show and Tell: Outstanding Canadian Picture Books 2000–2003 / Montre et raconte: Albums illustrés canadiens remarquables 2000–2003* ([Toronto]: IBBY Canada. [2004].)

The Illustration of Books for Children: An Historical Sampling. Norman Mackenzie Art Gallery, 3 December 1976 to 10 January 1977. Regina: The University of Regina [1976].

Internationale Jugendbibliothek [International Youth Library]. *Children's Books from Cana-*

da: *A Recent Selection / Kinderbucher aus Kanada: Eine Aktuelle Auswahl / Livres de jeunesse du Canada: Une selection actuelle.* Munich: Internationale Jugendbibliothek, 2002.

Jackson, Mary V. *Engines of Instruction: Mischief and Magic: Children's Literature in England from Its Beginnings to 1839.* Lincoln: University of Nebraska Press, 1989.

Jacobson, Wendy S. *Dickens and the Children of Empire.* New York: Palgrave, 2000.

James, Cathy. 'Reforming Reform: Toronto's Settlement House Movement, 1900–20.' *Canadian Historical Review* 82, no. 1 (2001): 55–90.

Jankunis, Myrtice, and Winona Anderson. 'Art, Literature and the Caldecott Books.' *SLiC* 10, no. 2 (1989): 11–13.

Janovicek, Nancy, and Joy Parr, eds. *Histories of Canadian Children and Youth.* Don Mills, ON: Oxford, 2003.

Jasen, Patricia. *Wild Things: Nature, Culture, and Tourism in Ontario. 1790–1914.* Toronto: University of Toronto Press, 1993.

Jeanneret, Marsh. 'Text Book Illustration in Canada.' *Canadian Art* 7, no. 4 (1945): 166–9.

Jenkinson, Dave. 'C.J. Taylor.' (1998). *CM.* http://www.umanitoba.ca/cm/profiles/taylor .html.

– 'Eric Beddows: Award Winning Children's Illustrator.' *EL* 20 (May 1993): 68.

– 'Good Libraries Don't: The Censorship of Canadian Picture Books.' *CCL*, no. 71 (1993): 42–56.

– 'Kady MacDonald Denton: Watercolorist Extraordinaire.' *EL* 21, no. 5 (1994): 61–4.

– 'Laszlo Gal: Award Winning Illustrator.' *EL* 19, no. 4 (1992): 65–9.

– 'Marie-Louise Gay.' *EL* 19, no. 5 (1992): 65–9.

– 'Maryann Kovalski: An Illustrator and Author.' *EL* 18, no. 5 (1991): 64–8.

– 'Paulette Bourgeois: The "Amazing" Creator of Franklin.' *EL* 18, no. 4 (1991): 66–71.

– 'Profiles: Ron Lightburn.' *RL* 1, no. 5 (1996): 200–3.

– 'Tim Wynne-Jones.' *EL* 15, no. 3 (1988): 56–62.

Jenness, Diamond. *The Corn Goddess and Other Tales from Indian Canada.* 2nd ed. Illustrated by Winnifred K. Bentley. Bulletin no. 141. Anthropological Series, no. 39. Ottawa: National Museum of Canada, 1960.

Jiménez, Karleen Pendleton. Review of *Mom and Mum are Getting Married! Journal of the Canadian Association for Curriculum Studies* 2, no. 2 (2004): 95–8.

Jobe, Ronald. 'The Effect of the International Children's Book Industry on Canadian Publishing Endeavours for Children and Young People.' *CCL*, no. 47 (1987): 7–11.

– 'Establishing Cultural Identity through Picturebooks.' In Styles and Bearne, eds, *Art, Narrative and Childhood*, 79–86.

– 'West Coast Children's Literature Roundtable.' *IR* 14, no. 4 (August 1980): 26.

Jobe, Ronald, and Paula Hart. *Canadian Connections: Experiencing Literature with Children.* Markham, ON: Pembroke Publishers, 1991.

Johnson, Paul. 'Children's Books as Architecture.' *CLE* 23, no. 3 (1992): 131–42.

Johnston, Ingrid, Joyce Bainbridge, Jyoti Mangat, and Rochelle Skogen. 'National Identity and the Ideology of Canadian Multicultural Picture Books: Pre-Service Teachers Encountering Representations of Difference.' *CCL* 32, no. 2 (2006): 76–96.

Johnston, Margaret. 'Lillian H. Smith.' In Fasick, Johnston, and Osler, eds, *Lands of Pleasure*, 3–12.

Jones, Kenneth G., and Michael J. Doucet. 'The Big Box, the Flagship, and Beyond: Impacts and Trends in the Greater Toronto Area.' *Canadian Geographer* 45, no. 4 (2001): 494–513.

Jones, Owain. 'Naturally Not!: Childhood, the Urban, and Romanticism.' *Human Ecology Review* 9, no. 2 (2002): 17–30.

– 'Tomboy Tales: The Rural, Nature and the Gender of Childhood.' *Gender, Place and Culture* 6, no. 2 (1999): 117–36.

Jones, Raymond E., and Jon C. Stott. *Canadian Children's Books: A Critical Guide to Authors and Illustrators*. Don Mills, ON: Oxford University Press, 2000.

Judson, Bay Hallowell. 'What Is in a Picture?' *CLE* 20, no. 1 (1989): 59–68.

Kallen, Evelyn. *Ethnicity and Human Rights in Canada*. 2nd ed. Toronto: Oxford University Press, 1995.

Karr, Clarence. 'Addicted to Reading: L.M. Montgomery and the Value of Reading.' *CCL*, nos. 113–14 (2004): 17–33.

– *Authors and Audiences: Popular Canadian Fiction in the Early Twentieth Century*. Montreal and Kingston: McGill-Queen's University Press, 2000.

Kaufmann, Eric. '"Naturalizing the Nation": The Rise of Naturalistic Nationalism in the United States and Canada.' *Comparative Studies in Society and History* 40, no. 4 (1998): 666–95.

Kealy, J. Kieran. 'Bibliography of British Columbian Children's Literature.' *CCL*, no. 74 (1994): 39–62.

– 'An Ever-Present Inspiration.' In *Once Upon a Time: My Life with Children's Books*, by Sheila Egoff, with Wendy Sutton, 149–50. Vancouver: Orca Book Publishers, 2005.

Kelly, Terry. 'Escape Artist.' *Books in Canada* 6, no. 9 (1977): 9–11.

Kennedy, Joyce Deveau. 'Prince Charming and Glooscap: The Children's Picture Book Quest for Canadian Mythology.' *CCL*, nos. 39–40 (1985): 80–90.

Kiefer, Barbara. 'Picture Books as Contexts for Literary, Aesthetic and Real World Understandings.' *Language Arts* 65, no. 3 (1988): 260–71.

– *The Potential of Picturebooks: From Visual Literacy to Aesthetic Understanding*. Englewood Cliffs, NJ: Merrill, 1995.

Killan, Gerald. *David Boyle: From Artisan to Archaeologist*. Toronto: University of Toronto Press, 1983.

Kitzan, Laurence. *Victorian Writers and the Image of Empire: 'The Rose Colored Vision.'* Westport, CT: Greenwood Press, 2001.

Klemin, Diana. *The Illustrated Book: Its Art and Craft*. New York: Clarkson Potter, 1970.

Klinck, Carl F., ed. *Literary History of Canada: Canadian Literature in English*. Toronto: University of Toronto, 1965.

Knight, Lorna. 'Encouraging Children to Read.' In Gerson and Michon, eds, *HBIC*, vol. 3, 484–490.

Knowles, Murray. 'Empire and School: Nineteenth-Century Boys' Books and What Is in Them.' *New Review of Children's Literature and Librarianship* 12, no. 1 (2006): 67–82.

Korinek, Valerie J. '"It's a Tough Time to Be in Love": The Darker Side of "Chatelaine" during the Cold War.' In *Love, Hate, and Fear in Canada's Cold War*, ed. Richard Cavell, 159–82. Toronto: University of Toronto Press, 2004.

Kovalski, Maryann. 'Beginning, Middle and End.' *SLiC* 11, no. 3 (1991): 39–40.

Kress, Gunther, and Theo van Leeuwen. *Reading Images: The Grammar of Visual Design*. London and New York: Routledge, 1996.

Kröller, Eva-Marie, ed. *The Cambridge Companion to Canadian Literature*. Cambridge: Cambridge University Press, 2004.

– 'Exploration and Travel.' In Kröller, ed., *Cambridge Companion to Canadian Literature*, 70–93.

Kuffert, L.B. *A Great Duty: Canadian Responses to Modern Life and Mass Culture, 1939–1967*. Montreal and Kingston: McGill-Queen's University Press, 2003.

Kunzle, David. Review of *Humorous But Wholesome: A History of Palmer Cox and the Brownies*, by Roger W. Cummins. *Art Bulletin* 57, no. 3 (1975): 454–6.

Kutzer, M. Daphne. *Empire's Children: Empire and Imperialism in Classic British Children's Books*. New York: Garland Publishing, 2000.

Lacy, Lyn Ellen. *Art and Design in Children's Picture Books*. Chicago: American Library Association, 1986.

Lamonde, Yvan. *La librairie et l'édition à Montréal 1776–1920*. Quebec: Bibliothèque nationale du Québec, 1991.

Lamonde, Yvan, Patricia Lockhart Fleming, and Fiona A. Black, eds. *History of the Book in Canada*, vol. 2, *1840–1918*. Toronto: University of Toronto Press, 2005.

Landsberg, Michele. *Michele Landsberg's Guide to Children's Books: With a Treasury of More Than 350 Great Children's Books*. Markham, ON: Penguin Canada, 1986.

– *Reading for the Love of It: Best Books for Young Readers*. New York: Prentice-Hall, 1987.

Lecker, Robert. *Making It Real: The Canonization of English Canadian Literature*. Toronto: House of Anansi Press, 1995.

Lee, Dennis. 'Cadence, Country, Silence: Writing in Colonial Space.' *Boundary 2* 3, no. 1 (Autumn 1974): 151–68.

Lefebvre, Benjamin. 'Editorial: Assessments and Reassessments.' *CCL*, nos. 113–14 (2004): 6–13.

Lepage, Françoise. 'Le métissage, une dynamique en perpétuel mouvement.' In Sorin, ed., *Imaginaires métissés en littérature pour la jeunesse*, 7–13.

– *Paule Daveluy, ou, la passion des mots*. Saint-Laurent: Éditions Pierre Tisseyre, 2003.

Lepage, Françoise, Judith Saltman, and Gail Edwards. 'Children's Authors and Their Markets.' In Gerson and Michon, eds, *HBIC*, vol. 3, 145–52.

Lesnik-Oberstein, Karin. *Children's Literature: Criticism and the Fictional Child*. Oxford: Clarendon Press, 1994.

Lewis, David. 'The Constructedness of Texts: Picture Books and the Metafictive.' *Signal* 62 (May 1990): 131–46.

– 'Pop-Ups and Fingle-Fangles: The History of the Picture Book.' In Watson and Styles, eds, *Talking Pictures*, 5–22.

– *Reading Contemporary Picturebooks: Picturing Text*. London and New York: Routledge Falmer, 2001.

Lindauer, Shelley L. Knudsen. 'Wordless Books: An Approach to Visual Literacy.' *CLE* 19, no. 3 (1988): 136–42.

Litt, Paul. *The Muses, the Masses, and the Massey Commission*. Toronto: University of Toronto Press, 1999.

Loewen, Iris. 'Pemmican Press.' *CCL*, no. 49 (1988): 22–6.

Loo, Tina. *States of Nature: Conserving Canada's Wildlife in the Twentieth Century*. Vancouver: UBC Press, 2006.

Lorimer, Rowland. *Book Publishing in British Columbia 1989*. [Vancouver]: Canadian Centre for Studies in Publishing. Simon Fraser University, 1989.

– 'Book Publishing in English Canada in the Context of Free Trade.' *Canadian Journal of Communication* 16 (1991): 58–72.

– 'Hip and Trivial.' *Labour / Le Travail*, no 52 (2003): 275.

Lorimer, Rowland, and Eleanor O'Donnell. 'Global Restructuring in Publishing: Issues for Canada.' In *Global Restructuring: Canada in the 1990s*, ed. Gladys L. Symons, John A. Dickinson, and Hans-Joseph Niederehe, 129–44. Proceedings of the Fifth International Canadian Studies Conference. Kingston. 2–4 June 1991. *Canadian Issues*, vol. 14. Montreal: Association for Canadian Studies, 1992.

Lucas, Alec. 'Nature Writers and the Animal Story.' In Klinck, ed., *Literary History of Canada*, 264–88.

Lundin, Anne. 'Anne Carroll Moore (1871–1961): "I Have Spun Out a Long Thread."' In *Reclaiming the American Library Past: Writing the Women In*, ed. Suzanne Hildenbrand, 187–204. Norwood, NJ: Ablex Press, 1996.

– *Constructing the Canon of Children's Literature: Beyond Library Walls and Ivory Towers*. New York and London: Routledge, 2004.

– 'Introduction.' In *Defining Print Culture for Youth: The Cultural Work of Children's Literature*, ed. Anne Lundin and Wayne A. Wiegand, xi–xxii. Westport, CT: Libraries Unlimited, 2003.

– 'Little Pilgrims' Progress: Literary Horizons for Children's Literature.' *Libraries and Culture* 41, no. 1 (2006): 133–52.

Lutz, Hartmut. 'Race or Place? The Palimpsest of Space in Canadian Prairie Fiction, from Salverson to Cariou.' *Textual Studies in Canada* 17 (2004): 171–85.

Lyons, Chris. '"Children Who Read Good Books Usually Behave Better, and Have Good Manners": The Founding of the Notre Dame de Grace Library for Boys and Girls, Montreal, 1943.' *Library Trends* 55, no. 3 (2007): 597–608.

Lyons, Terri L. 'Dayal Kaur Khalsa.' *CCL*, no. 59 (1990): 70–4.

MacDonald, R.D. 'Lee's *Civil Elegies* in Relation to Grant's "Lament for a Nation."' *CL*, no. 98 (1983): 10–30.

MacDonald, Robert H. 'Reproducing the Middle-Class Boy: From Purity to Patriotism in the Boys' Magazines. 1892–1914.' *Journal of Contemporary History* 24, no. 3. (1989): 519–39.

MacKenzie, John M. *Propaganda and Empire: The Manipulation of British Public Opinion. 1880–1960*. Manchester: Manchester University Press, 1984.

Mackey, Eva. *The House of Difference: Cultural Politics and National Identity in Canada*. Toronto: University of Toronto Press, 2002.

MacLaren, Eli. '"Against All Invasion": The Archival Story of Kipling, Copyright, and the Macmillan Expansion in Canada, 1900–1920.' *Journal of Canadian Studies* 40, no. 2 (2006): 139–63.

MacLeod, Anne Scott. *American Childhood: Essays in Children's Literature of the Nineteenth and Twentieth Centuries*. Athens: University of Georgia Press, 1994.

– 'From Rational to Romantic: The Children of Children's Literature in the Nineteenth Century.' *Poetics Today* 13, no. 1 (1992): 141–53.

Macmillan Company of Canada. *A Canadian Publishing House*. Toronto: The Macmillan Company of Canada, [1923].

MacPhee, Joyce. 'Kathryn Cole: A Life in Children's Publishing.' *CM* 22, no. 5 (1994): 163–7.

MacSkimming, Roy. 'Crisis and Renewal in English-Canadian Book Publishing, 1970–2004.' *Papers of the Bibliographical Society of Canada* 42, no. 2 (2004): 15–24.

– *Making Literary History: House of Anansi Press 1967–1997*. Toronto: Anansi, 1997.
– *The Perilous Trade: Book Publishing in Canada 1946–2006*. Updated ed. Toronto: McClelland and Stewart, 2007.
Madore, Edith. 'L'Édition québécoise pour la jeunesse de nos jours.' *SLiC* 11, no. 3 (1991): 17–21.
Mallan, Kerry. *In the Picture: Perspectives on Picture Book Art and Artists*. Literature and Literacy for Young People: An Australian Series, 3. Wagga Wagga, NSW: Centre for Information Studies, Charles Sturt University, 1999.
– 'Uncanny Encounters: Home and Belonging in Canadian Picture Books,' *CCL*, nos. 115–16 (2004): 17–31.
Mallan, Kerry, and Roderick McGillis. 'Between a Frock and a Hard Place: Camp Aesthetics and Children's Culture.' *Canadian Review of American Studies* 35, no. 1 (2005): 1–19.
Manning, Erin. *Ephemeral Territories: Representing Nation, Home, and Identity in Canada*. Minneapolis and London: University of Minnesota Press, 2003.
Marantz, Kenneth. 'The Picture Book as Art Object: A Call for Balanced Reviewing.' *Wilson Library Bulletin* 52 (1977): 148–51.
Marantz, Sylvia S. *Picture Books for Looking and Learning: Awaking Visual Perceptions through the Art of Children's Books*. Phoenix: Oryx Press, 1992.
Marantz, Sylvia, and Kenneth Marantz. *The Art of Children's Picture Books: A Selective Reference Guide*. New York: Garland, 1988.
Marcus, Kendra. 'Buying and Selling International Children's Books Rights: A Literary Agent's Perspective.' *Publishing Research Quarterly* 19, no. 2 (2003): 51–6.
Martel, Suzanne. 'Ring-around-a-Roses of French-Canadian Book Marketing.' In Egoff, ed., *One Ocean Touching*, 202–11.
Martin, Carol. 'Writing Off Canadian Publishing.' *Canadian Forum* 70, no. 807 (1992): 18–21.
Martin, Rebecca. 'Edward Ardizzone Revisited: Lucy Brown and the Moral Editing of Art.' *CLE* 31, no. 4 (2000): 241–57.
Maruszeczka, Greg. 'Publishing Picture Books, The View from Tundra: May Cutler.' *CM* 21, no. 2 (1993): 42–3.
Massironi, Manfredo. *The Psychology of Graphic Images: Seeing, Drawing, Communicating*. Mahwah, NJ: L. Erlbaum, 2002.
Maxwell, Richard. *The Victorian Illustrated Book*. Charlottesville: University Press of Virginia, 2002.
May, Jill P. *Children's Literature and Critical Theory: Reading and Writing for Understanding*. New York: Oxford University Press, 1995.
May, Jill P. 'Exploring Book Illustration as a Work of Art.' *Children's Literature Assembly Bulletin* 17, no. 2 (1991): 2–4.
Mazukewich, Karen. 'Animation Cels Products: Commercials in Canada.' *Take One*, no. 24 (Summer 1999): 36–7.
McCloud, Scott. *Understanding Comics*. New York: HarperPerennial, 1994.
McDonald, James, with Jennifer Joseph. 'Key Events in Gitxsan History: A Gitxsan Time Line.' In *Potlatch at Gitsegukla: William Benyon's 1945 Field Notebooks*, ed. Margaret Anderson and Marjorie Halpin, 193–216. Vancouver: UBC Press, 2000.
McDonough, D.M. 'Publishers in Profile: The Women's Press.' *IR* 13, no. 4 (August 1979): 14–16.
McDonough, Irma, ed. *Canadian Books for Children / Livres canadiens pour enfants*. Toronto:

University of Toronto Press for the Provincial Library Service Branch, Ministry of Culture and Recreation, 1976.

– ed. *Canadian Books for Young People / Livres canadiens pour la jeunesse*. Toronto: University of Toronto Press, 1978; 3rd rev. ed. Toronto: University of Toronto Press, 1980.

– 'A Creative National Literature for Children.' *IR* 16, no. 2 (April 1982): 5–13.

– 'The Modern Canadian Child's World of Books.' *IR* 15, no. 1 (February 1981): 7–9.

– 'Professional Reading.' Review of the Ontario Royal Commission on Book Publishing, *Background Papers*. *IR* 6, no. 4 (Autumn 1972): 16–19.

– 'Profile: Hazel Boswell.' *IR* 3, no. 3 (Summer 1969): 5–6.

– ed. *Profiles*. Ottawa: Canadian Library Association, 1971; rev. ed. Ottawa: Canadian Library Association, 1975.

– ed. *Profiles Two: Authors and Illustrators, Children's Literature in Canada*. Ottawa: Canadian Library Association, 1982.

– Review of *The Republic of Childhood*, 2nd ed., by Sheila Egoff. *IR* 9, no. 3 (Summer 1975): 15.

– 'The Wilkinson Survey, Canadian Juvenile Fiction: The Publisher–Library Interface 1975.' *IR* 9, no. 3 (Autumn 1975): 10–13.

McDowell, Marjorie. 'Children's Books.' In Klinck, ed., *Literary History of Canada*, 624–32.

McElderry, Margaret K. 'Remarkable Women.' *School Library Journal* 38, no. 3 (1992): 156–62.

McGee, Ted. 'ABCs of ABCs: Two Canadian Exemplars.' *CCL*, no. 71 (1993): 26–32.

McGillis, Roderick. '"And the Celt Knew the Indian": Knowingness, Postcolonialism, Children's Literature.' In McGillis, ed., *Voices of the Other*, 223–35.

– *The Nimble Reader: Literary Theory and Children's Literature*. New York: Twayne Publishers, 1996.

– ed. *Voices of the Other: Children's Literature and the Postcolonial Context*. Children's Literature and Culture, no. 10. New York and London: Garland Publishing, 1999.

– 'Where Is Here?: Canadian Children's Literature.' *CCL*, no. 52 (1988): 6–13.

McGrath, Leslie. 'Print for Young Readers.' In Fleming, Gallichan, and Lamonde, eds, *HBIC*, vol. 1, 252–6.

– 'Print For Young Readers.' In Lamonde, Fleming, and Black, eds, *HBIC*, vol. 2, 401–8.

McGrath, Leslie Anne. 'Service to Children in the Toronto Public Library: A Case Study, 1912–1949.' PhD diss., University of Toronto, 2005.

McGrath, Robin. 'Genuine Eskimo Literature: Accept No Substitutes.' *CCL*, nos. 31–2 (1983): 23–9.

McKechnie, Lynne E.F. 'Children's Access to Services in Canadian Public Libraries.' *Canadian Journal of Information and Library Science* 26, no. 4 (2001): 37–55.

– 'Patricia Spereman and the Beginning of Canadian Public Library Work with Children.' *Libraries and Culture* 34, no. 2 (1999): 135–50.

McLean, Judith. 'Bookmaking by Grants.' *IR* 8, no. 3 (Summer 1974): 10–11.

McLeod, Ellen Easton. *In Good Hands: The Women of the Canadian Handicrafts Guild*. Montreal and Kingston: Published for Carleton University by McGill-Queen's University Press, 1999.

McQuarrie, Jane, and Diane Dubois, comps. and eds. *Canadian Picture Books / Livres d'images canadiens*. Toronto: Reference Press, 1986.

Meek, Margaret, ed. *Children's Literature and National Identity*. Stoke on Trent, UK and Sterling, VA: Trentham Books, 2001.

– *On Being Literate*. Portsmouth, NH: Heinemann, 1991.
– 'Symbolic Outlining: The Academic Study of Children's Literature.' *Signal*, no. 53 (1987): 97–115.
Melançon, Louise. 'L'Édition d'enfance et de jeunesse de la décennie quarante chez Fides: Un programme de lecture pour la jeunesse canadienne-française.' Master's thesis, Université de Sherbrooke, 1998.
Ménard, Marc. *Les chiffres des mots: Portrait économique du livre au Québec*. Montreal: Société de Développement des Entreprises Culturelles du Québec, 2001.
Mendoza, Jean Paine. 'Goodbye, Columbus: Take Two.' In Seale and Slapin, eds, *A Broken Flute*, 196–200.
Messaris, Paul. *Visual 'Literacy': Image, Mind, and Reality*. Boulder, CO: Westview Press, 1994.
Methot, Suzanne. 'George Littlechild: Transformation and Reclamation.' *Aboriginal Voices* 5, no. 2 (1998): 37–40.
Michon, Jacques. 'Book Publishing in French.' In Gerson and Michon, eds, *HBIC*, vol. 3, 198–205.
Miller, Laura J. *Reluctant Capitalists: Bookselling and the Culture of Consumption*. Chicago and London: The University of Chicago Press, 2006.
Milliken, Marie Hammond. 'Library Clubs for Boys and Girls.' In Hazeltine, ed., *Library Work with Children*, 325–9. [Originally published in the *Library Journal*, 1911.]
Minkler, Frederick. *Voluntary Reading Interests in Canadian Elementary Schools*. Toronto: MacMillan Company of Canada, and Ryerson Press, 1948.
Mo, Weimin, and Wenju Shen. 'Reexamining the Issue of Authenticity in Picture Books.' *Children's Literature in Education* 28, no. 2 (1997): 85–93.
Moebius, William. 'Introduction to Picturebook Codes.' *Word and Image* 2, no. 2 (1986): 141–58.
Mollel, Tololwa M. 'Feasting on Words: How I Became a Writer for Children.' *McGill Journal of Education* 36, no. 3 (2001): 251–60.
Money, Darlene. 'Profile: William Toye.' *IR* 14, no. 4 (August 1980): 19–23.
Montgomery, L.M. *The Green Gables Letters from L.M. Montgomery to Ephraim Weber, 1905–1909*, ed. Wilfrid Eggleston. Toronto: Ryerson 1960.
– *The Selected Journals of L. M. Montgomery*, vol. 5, *1935–1942*, ed. Mary Rubio and Elizabeth Waterston. Toronto: Oxford University Press, 2004.
Montpetit, Charles. 'Book Banning: A How-to Guide for Beginners.' *CCL*, no. 68 (1992): 6–13.
Morley, Patricia. 'The Good Life, Prairie Style: The Art and Artistry of William Kurelek.' *Children's Literature*, no. 6 (1977): 141–9.
Morris, Brian. 'Ernest Thompson Seton and the Origins of the Woodcraft Movement.' *Journal of Contemporary History* 5, no. 2 (1970): 183–94.
Mount, Nick. *When Canadian Literature Moved to New York*. Toronto: University of Toronto Press, 2005.
Moyles, R.G. 'A "Boy's Own" View of Canada.' *CCL*, no. 34 (1984): 41–56.
– 'Young Canada: An Index to Canadian Materials in Major British and American Juvenile Periodicals 1870–1950.' *CCL*, no. 78 (1995): 7–63.
Muir, Marcie. *A History of Australian Children's Book Illustration*. Melbourne and New York: Oxford University Press, 1982.

Muller, Larry. 'The Dangerous Art: Writing for Children.' *Canadian Author and Bookman* 49, no. 1 (1973): 2–4, 23.

Munro, June E. 'The Wind Has Wings: The Creative Production.' *IR* 3, no. 3 (Autumn 1969): 5–9.

Murphy, Carl. 'The Marriage Metaphor in Nineteenth-Century English Canadian Fiction.' *Studies in Canadian Literature* 13, no. 1 (1988): 1–19.

Murray, Gail Schmunk. *American Children's Literature and the Construction of Childhood*. New York: Twayne, 1998.

Murray, Heather. 'Literary Societies.' In Lamonde, Fleming, and Black, eds, *HBIC*, vol. 2, 473–8.

– 'Making the Modern: Twenty Five Years of the Margaret Eaton School of Literature and Expression.' *Essays in Theatre* 10 (1991): 39–57.

Mustard, Mary I., and Doris P. Fennell. 'Libraries in Canadian Schools.' In *Librarianship in Canada, 1946 to 1967: Essays in Honour of Elizabeth Homer Morton*, ed. Bruce Peel, 122–39. Victoria: Printed for the Canadian Library Association by the Morriss Printing Company, 1968.

Myers, Mitzi. 'Reading Children and Homeopathic Romanticism: Paradigm Lost, Revisionary Gleam, or Plus ça change, plus c'est la même chose?' In *Literature and the Child: Romantic Continuations, Postmodern Contestations*, ed. James Hold McGavran, 44–84. Iowa City: University of Iowa Press, 1999.

National Center for Education Statistics. *America's Public School Libraries: 1953–2000*. Washington, DC: National Center for Education Statistics, Institute of Education Sciences, U.S. Department of Education, 2005.

National Library of Canada. *Annual Report of the National Librarian*. Ottawa: The National Library, 1974–1979.

– *The Art of Illustration: A Celebration of Contemporary Canadian Children's Book Illustrators*. Ottawa: National Library of Canada, 1997. http://epe.lac-bac.gc.ca/100/200/301/lac-bac/art_of_illustration-ef/www.lac-bac.gc.ca/3/10/index-e.html.

– *The Secret Self: An Exploration of Canadian Children's Literature / Le moi secret: Une exploration de la littérature de jeunesse canadienne*. Exhibition held in Ottawa from 26 October 1988 to 23 April 1989. Ottawa: National Library of Canada, 1988. http://epe.lac-bac.gc.ca/100/206/301/lac-bac/secret-ef/secret/index-e.html.

National Library of Canada and National Archives of Canada. *Beyond the Letters: Retrospective of Canadian Alphabet Books*. By Jeffrey Canton. Ottawa: National Library of Canada, 2003.

Nelson, Claudia. 'Writing the Reader: The Literary Child In and Beyond the Book,' *CLAQ* 31, no. 3 (2006): 222–36.

Neuburg, Victor E. *The Penny Histories: A Study of Chapbooks for Young Readers over Two Centuries*. London: Oxford University Press, 1968.

New, W.H. *A History of Canadian Literature*. 2nd ed. Montreal and Kingston: McGill-Queen's University Press, 2003.

New, W.H. 'Read Canadian.' In Gerson and Michon, eds, *HBIC*, vol. 3, 480–4.

Newfeld, Frank. 'Book Design and Production.' In *Publishing in Canada: Proceedings of the Institute on Publishing in Canada. June 27–30, 1971*, ed. G. Pomahac and M. Richeson, 26–35. Edmonton: The School of Library Science. The University of Alberta, 1972.

Newfeld, Frank. 'Whose Book?' *Canadian Art* 22, no. 2 (1965): 46.

Nikolajeva, Maria. *Children's Literature Comes of Age: Toward a New Aesthetic.* Children's Literature and Culture, 1. New York and London: Garland Publishing, 1996.

– *From Mythic to Linear: Time in Children's Literature.* Lantham, MD: Children's Literature Association and Scarecrow Press, 2000.

– 'Picturebook Characterisation: Word/Image Interaction.' In Styles and Bearne, eds, *Art, Narrative and Childhood*, 37–50.

Nikolajeva, Maria, and Carole Scott. *How Picturebooks Work.* New York and London: Garland, 2001.

Nikola-Lisa, W. 'Play, Panache, Pastiche: Postmodern Impulses in Contemporary Picture Books.' *CLAQ* 19, no. 1 (1994): 35–9.

Nilson, Lenore, comp. *The Best of Children's Choices: An Annotated Selection of Six Hundred Favourite Canadian Children's Books Chosen by Children. Based on the Critically Acclaimed Children's Choices of Canadian Books.* Edited by Jane Charlton. Ottawa: Citizens' Committee on Children, 1988.

Nodelman, Perry. 'Art Theory and Children's Picture Books.' *CLAQ* 9 (1984): 15–33.

– 'As Canadian as Apple Pie and Old Glory.' *CCL*, nos. 111–12 (2003): 91–128.

– 'The Eye and the I: Identification and First Person Narratives in Picture Books.' *Children's Literature* 19 (1991): 1–30.

– 'The Illustrators of Munsch.' *CCL*, no. 71 (1993): 5–25.

– 'Non-Native Primitive Art: Elizabeth Cleaver's Indian Legends.' *CCL*, nos. 31–2 (1983): 69–79.

– 'Preface: There's Like No Books about Anything.' In Chapleau, ed., *New Voices in Children's Literature Criticism*, 3–9.

– 'What Children Are or Should Be.' *CCL*, nos. 113–14 (2004): 140–65.

– 'What's Canadian about Canadian Children's Literature?: A Compendium of Answers to the Question.' *CCL*, no. 87 (1997): 15–35.

– *Words about Pictures.* Athens, GA: The University of Georgia Press, 1988.

Nodelman, Perry, and Mavis Reimer. *The Pleasures of Children's Literature.* 3rd ed. Boston: Allyn and Bacon, 2003.

– 'Teaching Canadian Children's Literature: Learning to Know More.' *CCL*, no. 98 (2000): 15–35.

Novosedlik, Will. 'Our Modernist Heritage. Part I.' *Applied Arts Magazine* 11, no. 1 (1996): 30–5.

Nygaard, Liv. 'Picture Books in Northern Schools.' *CCL*, nos. 39–40 (1985): 66–71.

Oberg, Dianne, and James Henri. 'Changing Concerns in Distance Education for Teacher-Librarianship.' *Education for Information* 17, no. 1 (1999): 21–33.

O'Brien, Leacy. 'An Interview with Marie-Louise Gay.' *CM* 17, no. 2 (1989): 54–5.

Oda, Stephanie, and Glenn Sanislo. *Book Publishing USA; Facts, Figure, Trends: Factors Shaping the US Book Industry 2000–2001.* London and Frankfurt: Holger Ehling Publishing, 2001.

Oittinen, Riitta. 'Where the Wild Things Are: Translating Picture Books.' *Meta* 48, nos. 1–2 (2003): 128–41.

Olson, David R. *The World on Paper: The Conceptual and Cognitive Implications of Writing and Reading.* Cambridge: Cambridge University Press, 1994.

O'Malley, Andrew. 'The Coach and Six: Chapbook Residue in Late Eighteenth-Century Children's Literature.' *LU* 24, no. 1 (2000): 18–44.

– *The Making of the Modern Child: Children's Literature and Childhood in the Late Eighteenth Century.* New York: Routledge, 2003.

Onosaka, Junko R. *Feminist Revolution in Literacy: Women's Bookstores in the United States.* New York and London: Routledge, 2006.

Ontario. Royal Commission on Book Publishing. *Background Papers.* Toronto: Queen's Printer and Publisher, 1972.

– Royal Commission on Book Publishing. *Canadian Publishers and Canadian Publishing.* Toronto: Queen's Printer and Publisher, 1973.

Ontario Library Association. *The Ontario Library Association: An Historical Sketch, 1900– 1925.* Toronto: The University of Toronto Press, 1926.

– *The Second Quarter Century, 1926–1951.* Toronto: [The Association], 1952. Cover title: "Issue of *Ontario Library Review*, May 1952, part 2."

Osborne, Brian S. '"The Kindling Touch of Imagination": Charles William Jefferys and Canadian Identity.' In *A Few Acres of Snow: Literary and Artistic Images of Canada,* ed. Paul Simpson-Housley and Glen Norcliffe, 28–47. Toronto and Oxford: Dundurn Press, 1992.

O'Sullivan, Emer. 'Narratology Meets Translation Studies, or, the Voice of the Translator in Children's Literature.' *Meta* 48, nos. 1–2 (2003): 197–207.

O'Sullivan, Emer, Kimberley Reynolds, and Rolf Romøren, eds. *Children's Literature Global and Local: Social and Aesthetic Perspectives.* Prepared under the auspices of the International Research Society for Children's Literature. Oslo: Novus Press, 2005.

Paley, Nicholas. 'Postmodernist Impulses and the Contemporary Picture Book: Are There Any Stories to These Meanings?' *JYS* 5, no. 2 (1992): 151–62.

Panofsky, Ruth. 'Barometers of Change: Presidents Hugh Eayrs and John Gray of the Macmillan Company of Canada.' *Journal of Canadian Studies* 37, no. 4 (2003): 92–111.

Pantaleo, Sylvia. 'Exploring Canadian Identity through Canadian Children's Literature.' *Reading Online* 5, no. 2 (2001). http://www.readingonline.org/international/inter_ index.asp?HREF=/international/pantaleo/index.html.

– 'Grade 3 Students Explore the Question. "What's Canadian about Canadian Children's Literature?"' *English Quarterly* 32, nos. 3–4 (2000): 42.

Pantazzi, Sybille. 'Book Illustration and Design by Canadian Artists 1890–1940, with a List of Books Illustrated by Members of the Group of Seven.' *National Gallery of Canada Bulletin* 4, no. 1 (1966): 6–24. http://www.national.gallery.ca/bulletin/num7/pantazzi1.html.

Paré, François. 'L'illustration en littérature pour la jeunesse.' *CCL,* nos. 39–40 (1985): 4–5.

Parker, George L. 'Courting Local and International Markets.' In Fleming, Gallichan, and Lamonde, eds, *HBIC,* vol. 1, 339–51.

– 'English-Canadian Publishers and the Struggle for Copyright.' In Lamonde, Fleming, and Black, eds, *HBIC,* vol. 2, 148–59.

– 'The Evolution of Publishing in Canada.' In Gerson and Michon, eds, *HBIC,* vol. 3, 17–32.

– 'The Sale of Ryerson Press: The End of the Old Agency System and Conflicts over Domestic and Foreign Ownership in the Canadian Publishing Industry, 1970–1986.' *Papers of the Bibliographic Society of Canada* 40, no. 2 (2002): 7–56.

– 'Trade and Regional Publishing in Central Canada.' In Gerson and Michon, eds, *HBIC,* vol. 3, 17–32.

Parsons, Marnie. '"Like a Muscle That Sings in the Dark": Semiotics and Nonsense in Dennis Lee's Poetry for Children.' *CCL,* no. 63 (1991): 61–71.

Pascua, Isabel. 'Translation and Intercultural Education.' *Meta* 48, nos. 1–2 (2003): 276–84.

Paul, Lissa. 'Enigma Variations: What Feminist Theory Knows about Children's Literature.' *Signal*, no. 54 (1987): 186–202.

– content ed. *Growing With Books: Children's Literature in the Formative Years and Beyond; Resource Guide 1988.* [Toronto]: Ontario Ministry of Education, 1988. [6 volumes in a slipcase.]

– 'The Lay of the Land: Turbulent Flow and Ted Harrison.' *CCL*, no. 70 (1993): 63–71.

Pederson, Susan. 'Hannah More Meets Simple Simon: Tracts, Chapbooks, and Popular Culture in Late Eighteenth-Century England.' *Journal of British Studies* 25, no. 1 (1986): 84–113.

Pelletier, Gérard. 'Books and Libraries in Canada.' In *Books in Canada 1972*, ed. Basil Stuart-Stubbs, 1–2. Papers presented at a Symposium on the Canadian Book at the Canadian Library Association Conference, Regina, 13–14 June 1972. Ottawa: Canadian Library Association, 1972.

Philip, Marlene Nourbese. 'Disappearing Debate, or, How the Discussion of Racism Has Been Taken Over by the Censorship Issue.' *This Magazine* 23, no. 2 (1989): 19–24.

– 'Gut Issues in Babylon: Racism and Anti-Racism in the Arts.' *Fuse Magazine* 12, no. 5 (1989): 13–26.

Phillips, Carol, comp. *The Illustration of Books for Children: A Historical Sampling.* Essays by Carol Phillips and Alixe Hambleton. [Regina: Norman Mackenzie Art Gallery, 1976.]

Phillips, Richard. *Mapping Men and Empire: A Geography of Adventure.* New York: Routledge, 1997.

– 'Space for Boyish Men and Manly Boys: The Canadian Northwest in Robert Ballantyne's Adventure Stories.' *Essays in Canadian Writing*, no. 59 (1996): 46–64.

Pickering, Samuel F., Jr. *John Locke and Children's Books in Eighteenth-Century England.* Knoxville: University of Tennessee Press, 1981.

Pierce, Lorne, ed. *The Chronicle of a Century 1829–1929.* Toronto: The United Church Publishing House, The Ryerson Press, [1929].

– 'C.W. Jefferys, O.S.A., R.C.A., LL.D.: A Biographical Introduction.' In *The Picture Gallery of Canadian History*, by C.W. Jefferys, vol. 3, 1830 to 1900, ix–xiv. Toronto: Ryerson Press, 1950.

– *New History for Old: Discussions on Aims and Methods in Writing and Teaching History.* Toronto: Ryerson Press, 1931.

Polidori, Josiane. 'Irene Aubrey: A Tribute.' *Bulletin* (National Library of Canada) 33, no. 4 (July-August 2001). http://epe.lac-bac.gc.ca/100/202/301/bulletin_nlc/2001/no4/p2-0107-06-e.html.

Pratt, Mary Louise. *Imperial Eyes: Travel Writing and Transculturation.* London and New York: Routledge, 1992.

Pullman, Philip. 'Invisible Pictures.' *Signal* 60 (1988): 160–86.

Read, S.E. 'For the Eyes of Children.' *CL*, no. 1 (1959): 87–90.

Redekop, Magdalene. 'Canadian Literary Criticism and the Idea of a National Literature.' In Kröller, ed., *Cambridge Companion to Canadian Literature*, 263–75.

Rees, Gwendolen. *Libraries for Children: A History and a Bibliography.* London: Grafton, 1924.

Reid, Barbara. 'Colouring the Road to Oz.' *CCL*, no. 54 (1989): 46–9.

Reimer, Mavis, ed. *Home Words: Discourses of Children's Literature in Canada.* Studies in Childhood and Family in Canada. Waterloo, ON: Wilfrid Laurier University Press, 2008.

Reimer, Mavis, and Clare Bradford. 'Home, Homelessness, and Liminal Spaces: The Uses of Postcolonial Theory for Reading (National) Children's Literatures.' In O'Sullivan, Reynolds, and Romøren, eds, *Children's Literature Global and Local*, 200–17.

Reynolds, Kimberley. *Girls Only?: Gender and Popular Fiction in Britain. 1880–1910*. New York: Harvester Wheatsheaf. Simon and Schuster, 1990.

– 'Publishing Practices and the Practicalities of Publishing.' In Reynolds and Tucker, eds, *Children's Book Publishing in Britain*, 20–41.

Reynolds, Kimberley, and Nicholas Tucker, eds. *Children's Book Publishing in Britain Since 1945*. Aldershot, Hants, UK: Scolar Press, 1998.

Richard, Olga. 'The Visual Language of the Picture Book.' *Wilson Library Bulletin* 44 (1969): 435–47.

Richmond, Sheldon. 'Children and the Thought of Death.' *CCL*, no. 55 (1989): 77–81.

Robinson, Paul. *Where Our Survival Lies: Students and Textbooks in Atlantic Canada*. Halifax: Atlantic Institute of Education and Dalhousie School of Library Service, 1979.

Rogers, Linda. 'Saurian Saga on Bloor Street.' *CL*, no. 63 (1975): 104–5.

Rollin, Lucy, and Mark I. West. *Psychoanalytic Responses to Children's Literature*. Jefferson, NC: McFarland, 1999.

Rose, Gillian. *Visual Methodologies: An Introduction to the Interpretation of Visual Materials*. London and Thousand Oaks, CA: Sage Publications, 2001.

Rose, Jacqueline. *The Case of Peter Pan, or the Impossibility of Children's Fiction.* Rev. ed. London: Macmillan, 1992.

Rosenthal, Michael. *The Character Factory: Baden-Powell and the Origins of the Boy Scout Movement*. New York: Pantheon, 1984.

Ross, Catherine Sheldrick, and Cory Bieman Davies. 'An Interview with Margaret Atwood.' *CCL*, no. 42 (1986): 9–16.

Ross, Paul. 'A Pint of Mild And Bitter: A Conversation with Ted Harrison.' *Aurora Online*, issue 1990 (1990). http://aurora.icaap.org/index.php/aurora/article/view/54/67.

Roxburgh, Stephen. 'A Picture Equals How Many Words? Narrative Theory and Picture Books for Children.' *LU* 7–8 (1983–4): 20–33.

Rudiger, Hollis Margaret. 'Reading Lessons: Graphic Novels 101.' *HB* 82, no. 2 (2006): 126–35.

Russell, Peter, ed. *Nationalism in Canada.* Toronto: McGraw Hill, 1966.

Ryan, Allan J. *The Trickster Shift: Humour and Irony in Contemporary Native Art*. Vancouver: UBC Press, 1999.

Saldanha, Louise. 'Bedtime Stories: Canadian Multiculturalism and Children's Literature.' In McGillis, ed., *Voices of the Other*, 165–76.

Saltman, Judith. *Modern Canadian Children's Books*. Toronto: Oxford University Press, 1987.

– 'Once Upon a Time: Canadian Children's Picture Book Illustration.' *CCL*, no. 51 (1988): 51–65.

– 'A Twice Told Tale: The Legacy of Youth Services Education at UBC's School of Library, Archival and Information Studies,' *YAACING: The Newsletter of the Young Adult and Children's Services Section of the BCLA*, Fall 2006, 28–37. [A condensed version of the article appeared in *BCLA Reporter* 50, no. 7 (2006): 1–4.]

Saltman, Judith, and Gail Edwards. 'Elizabeth Cleaver, William Toye, and Oxford University Press: Creating the Canadian Picturebook.' *Papers of the Bibliographical Society of Canada* 42, no. 1 (2004): 31–64.

– 'Towards a History of Design in Canadian Children's Illustrated Books.' *CCL*, no. 107 (2002): 10–18.

Sánchez-Eppler, Karen. *Dependent States: The Child's Part in Nineteenth-Century American Culture*. Chicago: University of Chicago Press, 2005.

Sandis, Dominique. 'Proposing a Methodology for the Study of Nation(ality) in Children's Literature.' In Chapleau, ed., *New Voices in Children's Literature Criticism*, 105–18.

Sandlos, John. 'From within Fur and Feathers: Animals in Canadian Literature.' *Topia*, no. 4 (2000): 73–92.

Sands-O'Connor, Karen. 'Trailing Crowds of Gables: Canada, Children's Literature, and the Meaning of Culture.' *American Review of Canadian Studies* 35, no. 1 (2005): 149–55.

– 'Why are People Different: Multiracial Families in Picture Books and the Dialogue of Difference.' *LU* 25 (2001): 401–26.

Sarrasin, Francine. *Double espace*. Images, no. 11. Laval: Les 400 Coups, 1997.

Saunders, Jim. 'By Their Dawn's Early Light.' *Books in Canada* 1, no. 8 (February 1972): 4–5.

Sayers, W.C. Berwick. *The Children's Library: A Practical Manual for Public, School, and Home Libraries*. London: George Routledge and Sons, [1912].

Scheier, Libby. 'Writing Authentic Voices: The Writers' Union and Anti-Racism.' *Fuse Magazine* 14, nos. 1–2 (1990): 14–15.

Schiffrin, André. *The Business of Books: How International Conglomerates Took Over Publishing and Changed the Way We Read*. London and New York: Verso, 2000.

Schiller, Justin G. 'Artistic Awareness in Early Children's Books.' *Children's Literature* 3 (1974): 177–85.

Schneiderman, David. 'Canada: Supreme Court Addresses Gay-Positive Readers in Public Schools.' *International Journal of Constitutional Law* 3, no. 1 (2005): 77–85.

Schrader, Alvin M., and Kristopher Wells. 'Queer Perspectives on Social Responsibility in Canadian Schools and Libraries: Analysis and Resources.' *SLiC Online* 24, no. 4 (2005). http://www.clatoolbox.ca/casl/slic/244queerperspectives.html.

Schwarcz, Joseph. 'The Textless Contemporary Picture Book: A Minor Art Form.' *Phaedrus* 9 (1982): 45–50.

– *Ways of the Illustrator: Visual Communication in Children's Literature*. Chicago: American Library Association, 1982.

Schwarcz, Joseph, and Chava Schwarcz. *The Picture Book Comes of Age: Looking at Children through the Art of Illustration*. Chicago: American Library Association, 1991.

Scieszka, John. 'Design Matters.' *HB* 74, no. 2 (1998): 196–208.

Seale, Doris. 'Introduction.' In Seale and Slapin, eds, *A Broken Flute*, 4–5.

Seale, Doris, and Beverley Slapin, eds. *A Broken Flute: The Native Experience in Books for Children*. Walnut Creek, CA: Alta Mira Press; Berkeley: Oyate, 2005.

Seifert, Martina. 'The Image Trap: The Translation of English-Canadian Children's Literature into German.' In O'Sullivan, Reynolds, and Romøren, eds, *Children's Literature Global and Local*, 227–39.

– 'Selective Canadiana: A Translation History of English-Language Canadian Children's Literature into German.' In *Translating Canada: Charting the Institutions and Influences of Cultural Transfer, Canadian Writing in German/y*, ed. Luise von Flotow and Reingard Nischik, 219–42. Ottawa : University of Ottawa Press, 2007.

Setterington, Ken. 'Anne of Green Gables to Love You Forever: The Flowering of Canadian Children's Publishing.' *Logos* 7, no. 2 (1996): 154–8.

Sharp, Roy C. 'Some Copyright Concerns of Canadian Authors and Publishers.' In Ontario, Royal Commission on Book Publishing, *Background Papers*, 110–34.

Shaw, David John. 'Rear-View Mirror: A Designer's Memories of McClelland and Stewart, 1969–1981.' *DA: A Journal of the Printing Arts*, no. 58 (2006): 3–35.

Sheahan-Bright, Robyn. 'To Market to Market: The Development of the Australian Children's Publishing Industry.' PhD diss., Griffith University, 2004.

Shefrin, Jill. *Box of Delights: 600 Years of Children's Books at the Osborne Collection of Early Children's Books.* Toronto: Toronto Public Library, 1995.

Shefrin, Jill, and Dana Tenny. *Legacy of an Indomitable Spirit: Seventy-Five Years of Children's Services in the Toronto Public Library.* Toronto: The Osborne and Lillian H. Smith Collections, Toronto Public Library, 1987.

Shklanka, Diane. 'Oriental Stereotypes in Canadian Picture Books.' *CCL*, no. 60 (1990): 81–96.

Shulevitz, Uri. *Writing with Pictures: How To Write and Illustrate Children's Books.* New York: Watson-Guptill, 1985.

Sillars, Stuart. *Visualisation in Popular Fiction 1860–1960: Graphic Narratives, Fictional Images.* London and New York: Routledge, 1995.

Sipe, Lawrence R. 'How Picturebooks Work: A Semiotically Framed Theory of Text–Picture Relationships.' *CLE* 29 (1998): 97–108.

– 'Picturebooks as Aesthetic Objects.' *Literacy Teaching and Learning* 6, no. 1 (2001): 23–42.

– *Storytime: Young Children's Literary Understanding in the Classroom.* Foreword by P. David Pearson. New York and London: Teachers College Press, 2008.

Sipe, Lawrence R., and Caroline E. McGuire. 'Picturebook Endpapers: Resources for Literacy and Aesthetic Interpretation.' *CLE* 37 (2006): 291–304.

Sipe, Lawrence R., and Sylvia Pantaleo. *Postmodern Picturebooks: Play, Parody, and Self-Referentiality.* Routledge Research in Education, 16. New York and London, Routledge, 2008.

Slemon, Stephen, and Jo-Ann Wallace. 'Into the Heart of Darkness? Teaching Children's Literature as a Problem in Theory.' *CCL*, no. 63 (1991): 6–23.

Smart, Leslie. 'Book Design in Canada.' *IR* 3, no.1 (Winter 1969): 5–14.

Smiley, Barbara, comp. *Illustrators of Canadian Books for Young People.* [Toronto]: Provincial Library Service, Ontario Ministry of Culture and Recreation, 1979.

– 'Profile: Frank Newfeld.' *IR* 9, no. 1 (Winter 1975): 15–16.

– 'Publishers in Profile: Breakwater Books.' *IR* 12, no. 4 (Autumn 1978): 11–12.

– 'Publishers in Profile: Kids Can Press.' *IR* 13, no. 3 (June 1979): 20–1.

Smith, Allan. *Canada: An American Nation?: Essays on Continentalism, Identity, and the Canadian Frame of Mind.* Montreal and Kingston: McGill-Queen's University Press, 1994.

Smith, Donald B. *From the Land of Shadows: The Making of Grey Owl.* Saskatoon: Western Producer Prairie Books, 1990.

Smith, Karen Patricia. 'Introduction.' *Library Trends* 44, no. 4 (1996): 679–82.

Smith, Lillian H. 'The Teaching of Children's Literature.' In American Library Association. Committee on Library Work with Children, *Children's Library Yearbook*, no. 4, 73–80. Chicago: American Library Association, 1932.

– *The Unreluctant Years: A Critical Approach to Children's Literature.* New York: American Library Association, 1953; New York: Viking Press, 1967.

Snow, Catherine E., and Anat Ninio. 'The Contracts of Literacy: What Children Learn from Learning to Read Books.' In *Emergent Literacy*, ed. William H. Teale and Elizabeth Sulzby, 116–38. Norwood, NJ: Ablex Publishing, 1986.

Solomon, Michael. 'Canada at Bologna 1990: Celebrating a Decade of Canadian Children's Book Illustration.' In *Canada à Bologne / Canada at Bologna*, 3–4. [Toronto]: Canada at Bologna Steering Committee, 1990.

– 'Publishing Children's Picture Books: The Role of Design and Art Direction.' In *Windows and Words: A Look at Canadian Children's Literature in English*, ed. Aïda Hudson and Susan-Ann Cooper, 191–200. Reappraisals: Canadian Writers, no. 25. Ottawa: University of Ottawa Press, 2003.

Sorby, Angela. *Schoolroom Poets: Childhood, Performance, and the Place of American Poetry, 1865–1917*. Durham: University of New Hampshire Press, 2005.

Sorin, Noëlle, ed. *Imaginaires métissés en littérature pour la jeunesse*. Quebec: Presses de l'Université de Québec, 2006.

– 'Le métissage culturel: Confrontation ou mélange.' In Sorin, ed., *Imaginaires métissés en littérature pour la jeunesse*, 38–48.

Spadoni, Carl, and Judy Donnelly. *A Bibliography of McClelland and Stewart Imprints, 1901–1985: A Publisher's Legacy*. Toronto: ECW, 1994.

Speller, Randall. 'Book Design in English Canada.' In Gerson and Michon, eds, *HBIC*, vol. 3, 378–85.

– 'Frank Newfeld and McClelland and Stewart's Design for Poetry Series.' *DA: A Journal of the Printing Arts*, no. 56 (2005): 3–36.

– 'Frank Newfeld and the Visual Awakening of the Canadian Book.' *DA: A Journal of the Printing Arts* 45 (1999): 5–6.

– 'Hidden Collections: The Invisible World of English Canadian Book Illustration and Design.' In *Essays in the History of Art Librarianship in Canada*. ARLIS Canada. http://www.arliscanada.ca/hal/Arlis%20online_28_06_06.pdf.

St John, Judith. 'About Miss Howard-Gibbon and Her Illustrated Comic Alphabet.' In *An Illustrated Comic Alphabet* by Amelia Frances Howard-Gibbon. Toronto: Oxford University Press, 1966, n.p.

– 'Early Canadiana in the Osborne Collection.' *CCL*, no. 4 (1976): 9–10.

– 'A Peep at the Esquimaux.' *Beaver: Magazine of the North*, no. 296 (Winter 1965): 38–44.

Stacey, Robert. *C.W. Jefferys*. Canadian Artists Series, no. 10. Ottawa: National Gallery of Canada and National Museums of Canada, 1985.

– *Charles William Jefferys 1869–1951*. Kingston: Agnes Etherington Art Centre. Queen's University, 1976.

– *'Under Some Malignant Star': The Strange Adventures of Uncle Jim's Canadian Nursery Rhymes by David Boyle and C.W. Jefferys*. The Helen E. Stubbs Memorial Lectures, no. 4. Toronto: Toronto Public Library, 1992.

Stahl, J.D. 'The Theory and Artistry of Picture Books.' *CLE* 21, no. 2 (1990): 129–34.

Steig, Michael. 'The Importance of the Visual Text in "Architect of the Moon": Mothers, Teapots, et al.' *CCL*, no. 70 (1993): 22–33.

Stephens, John. 'Language, Discourse, and Picture Books.' *CLAQ* 14, no. 3 (1989): 106–10.

Sterritt, Neil J., Susan Marsden, Robert Galois, Peter R. Grant, and Richard Overstall. *Tribal Boundaries in the Nass Watershed*. Vancouver: UBC Press, 1998.

Stevenson, Robert Louis. 'Penny Plain and Twopence Coloured.' Chap. 13 in *Memories and Portraits*. London: Chatto and Windus, 1887.

Stewart, Gillian. 'When Little Guys Don't Count Anymore: New Patterns in Book Buying and Book Reviewing Could Spell Bad News for Some Authors.' *Media* 5, no. 3 (1998): 24.

Stewig, John W. *Looking at Picture Books*. Fort Atkinson, WI: Highsmith Press, 1995.

– 'Picture Books: What Do Reviews Really Review?' *Top of the News* 37, no. 1 (1980): 83–6.
– 'Reading Pictures, Reading Text: Some Similarities.' *New Advocate* 5, no. 1 (1992): 11–22.
Stillman, Terry A. 'Book Illustration by the Group of Seven.' *Antiques and Art* 6, no. 5 (1980): 32–6.
Stinson, Kathy. 'From Kathy Stinson.' *CCL*, no. 68 (1992): 136–7.
Stoler, Ann Laura, and Frederick Cooper. 'Between Metropole and Colony: Rethinking a Research Agenda.' In *Tensions of Empire: Colonial Cultures in a Bourgeois World*, ed. Frederick Cooper and Ann Laura Stoler, 1–56. Berkeley: University of California Press, 1997.
Story, Norah. *The Oxford Companion to Canadian History and Literature.* Toronto: Oxford University Press, 1967.
Stott, Jon C. 'A Conversation with Maria Campbell.' *CCL*, nos. 31–32 (1983): 15–22.
– 'Form, Content, and Cultural Values in Three Inuit (Eskimo) Survival Stories.' *American Indian Quarterly* 10, no. 3 (1986): 213–26.
– 'An Interview with John [*sic*; should be James] Houston.' *CCL*, no. 20 (1980): 3–16.
– 'The Marriage of Pictures and Text in Alligator Pie and Nicholas Knock.' *CCL*, nos. 39–40 (1985): 72–9.
– 'Profile: Ian Wallace.' *Language Arts* 66, no. 4 (1989): 443–9.
Stott, Jon C., and Raymond E. Jones. *Canadian Books for Children: A Guide to Authors and Illustrators.* Toronto: Harcourt, Brace, Jovanovich Canada, 1988.
Stuart-Stubbs, Basil. *Canadian Books in Public Libraries.* Ottawa: Department of Communications, 1984.
Stuewe, Paul. 'Rumblings on the Left: Two Political Presses.' *Canadian Forum* 55, no. 650 (1978): 58–9.
Sturges, Paul. 'The Public Library and Reading by the Masses: Historical Perspectives on the USA and Britain, 1850–1900.' Paper presented at the 60th IFLA General Conference, 21–7 August 1994. http://www.ifla.org/IV/ifla60/60-stup.htm.
Styles, Morag, and Eve Bearne, eds. *Art, Narrative and Childhood.* Stoke-on-Trent, UK: Trentham Books, 2003.
Sundmark, Björn. 'Hockey Fictions.' In *Literary Environments: Canada and the Old World*, ed. Brita Olinder, 119–30. Brussels: Peter Lang, 2006.
Sutherland, Neil. *Childhood in English Canada from the Great War to the Age of Television.* Toronto: University of Toronto Press, 1997.
– *Children in English-Canadian Society: Framing the Twentieth-Century Consensus.* Toronto: University of Toronto Press, 1976.
Sutherland, Zena, and Betsy Hearne. 'In Search of the Perfect Picture Book Definition.' *Wilson Library Bulletin* 52 (1977): 158–60.
Sybesma, Jetske. 'Illustrated Children's Books as Art: The Art of the Lobster Quadrille.' *CCL*, no. 60 (1990): 8–24.
Sybesma-Ironside, Jetske. 'Through a Glass Darkly: William Kurelek's Picture Books.' *CCL*, nos. 39–40 (1985): 8–20.
Tabbert, Reinbert. 'Approaches to the Translation of Children's Literature: A Review of Critical Studies Since 1960.' *Target* 14, no. 2 (2002): 303–41.
Tarasoff, Tamara. 'Roch Carrier and "The Hockey Sweater."' Section 'Capturing Customers.' *Before E-Commerce: A History of Canadian Mail Order Catalogues.* Canadian Museum of Civilization. http://www.civilization.ca/cmc/exhibitions/cpm/catalog/cat2208e.shtml.

Taxel, Joel 'Children's Literature at the Turn of the Century: Toward a Political Economy of the Publishing Industry.' *Research in the Teaching of English* 37 (November 2002): 159–62.

Temple, Elaine de. 'Profile: George Clutesi.' *IR* 4, no. 2 (Spring 1970): 14–15.

Thacker, Deborah. 'Disdain or Ignorance?: Literary Theory and the Absence of Children's Literature.' *LU* 24, no. 1 (2000): 1–17.

– 'Feminine Language and the Politics of Children's Literature.' *LU* 25 (2001): 3–16.

– 'Victorianism, Empire and the Paternal Voice.' In *Introducing Children's Literature: From Romanticism to Postmodernism*, ed. Deborah Cogan Thacker and Jean Webb, 41–55. New York: Routledge, 2002.

Thaler, Danielle. 'Métissage et acculturation: Le regard de l'Autre.' In Sorin, ed., *Imaginaires métissés en littérature pour la jeunesse*, 12–22.

Thistleton-Martin, Judith. 'How Can the Illustrations in Canadian Picture Books Introduce "Canadianness" into Australian Classrooms.' Paper presented at session 430, The Fun of Reading International Forum on Canadian Children's Literature, National Library of Canada, Ottawa, 26–9 June 2003.

Thompson, Hilary. 'The Pattern of Illustration in "Owl Magazine."' *CCL*, no. 60 (1990): 75–80.

– 'Topophilia: The Love of Place in Maritime Literature.' *CCL*, nos. 39–40 (1985): 45–54.

– 'Transformation and Puppetry in the Illustrations of Elizabeth Cleaver.' *CCL*, no. 70 (1993): 72–83.

Thorpe, Douglas. '"Why Don't We See Him?": Questioning the Frame in Illustrated Children's Stories.' *CCL*, no. 70 (1993): 5–21.

Thring, Sarah. 'This Little Book Goes to Market: A Cautionary Tale of Canadian Book Publishing and Pricing.' *Canadian Bookseller* 14, no. 3 (1992): 12, 14–16.

Tilley, Carol L., and Daniel Callison. 'Preparing School Library Media Specialists for the New Century: Results of a Survey.' *Journal of Education for Library and Information Science* 42, no. 3 (2001): 220–7.

Tippett, Maria. *Bill Reid: The Making of an Indian*. Toronto: Random House Canada, 2003.

– *Making Culture: English-Canadian Institutions and the Arts before the Massey Commission*. Toronto: University of Toronto Press, 1990.

Tompson, Ruth M. Fruin. 'Book Service for Children and Young People.' In *Librarianship in Canada, 1946 to 1967: Essays in Honour of Elizabeth Homer Morton*, ed. Bruce Peel, 112–21. Victoria: Printed for the Canadian Library Association by the Morriss Printing Company, 1968.

Toronto Board of Education. Work Group on Educational and Library Materials. *Canadian Books in Canadian Schools*. Toronto: Association of Canadian Publishers, 1977.

Toronto Public Libraries. Boys and Girls Services. *Books for Boys and Girls: Being a List of Two Thousand Books Which the Librarians of the Boys and Girls Division of the Toronto Public Library Deem to Be of Definite and Permanent Interest, with Annotations and Descriptions*, ed. Lillian Smith. Toronto: Boys and Girls House. Public Library of Toronto, 1927.

– Osborne Collection. *The Osborne Collection of Early Children's Books, 1476–1910: A Catalogue*. 2 vols. Prepared at Boys and Girls House by Judith St John; with the assistance of Dana Tenny and Hazel I. MacTaggart. Toronto: Toronto Public Library, 1975.

Townsend, John Rowe, ed. *John Newbery and His Books: Trade and Plumb-Cake For Ever, Huzza!* Metuchen, NJ: Scarecrow Press, 1994.

– *A Sense of Story: Essays on Contemporary Writers for Children*. London: Longman, 1971.
– 'Standards of Criticism for Children's Literature.' In *The Arbuthnot Lectures, 1970–1979*, 23–36. Chicago: American Library Association, 1980.
Toye, William. 'Book Design in Canada.' *CL*, no. 15 (1953): 52–63.
– 'Publishers Answer.' *Canadian Author and Bookman* 47 (Winter 1971): 1–2.
Trachtenbery, Jeffrey A. 'To Compete with Book Chains, Some Think Big.' *Publishing Research Quarterly* 21, no. 2 (2005): 35–38.
Travis, DeCook. 'The History of the Book, Literary History, and Identity Politics in Canada.' *Studies in Canadian Literature* 27, no. 2 (2002): 71–87.
Trotter, Frances W. 'Story-Telling in Canada.' *Ontario Library Review* 24, no. 3 (1940): 302–6.
Truchan-Tataryn, Maria, and Susan Gingell. 'Dances with Coyote: Narrative Voices in Thomas King's "One Good Story, That One."' *Postcolonial Text* 2, no. 3 (2006). http://www.postcolonial.org/index.php/pct/article/viewFile/485/323.
Tucker, Nicholas. 'Setting the Scene.' In Reynolds and Tucker, eds, *Children's Book Publishing in Britain*, 1–19.
Tufte, Edward R. *Visual Explanations: Images and Quantities, Evidence and Narrative*. Cheshire, CT: Graphics Press, 1997.
Turner, Kate, and Bill Freedman. 'Nature as a Theme in Canadian Literature.' *Environmental Reviews* 13, no. 4 (2005): 169–97.
Twyman, Michael. *Breaking the Mould: The First Hundred Years of Lithography*. The Panizzi Lectures, 2000. London: The British Library, 2001.
Tyler, Anna Cogswell. 'Library Reading Clubs for Young People.' Hazeltine, ed., *Library Work with Children*, 325–9. [Originally published in the *Library Journal*, 1912.]
Tyrrell, Bob. 'The School Library Market: A Canadian Publisher's Perspective.' *SLiC* 21, no. 1 (2001): 27–8.
Vandergrift, Kay E. 'Female Advocacy and Harmonious Voices: A History of Public Library Services and Publishing for Children in the United States.' *Library Trends* 44 (Spring 1996): 682–718.
Van Vliet, Virginia. 'Profile: Laszlo Gal.' *IR* 14, no. 5 (October 1980): 18–22.
Vidor, Constance. 'Inner Worlds Made Visible: Metaphor and Image.' *JYS* 7, no. 2 (1994): 149–56.
Vincent, David. *Literacy and Popular Culture: England 1750–1914*. Cambridge: Cambridge University Press, 1989.
– 'The Progress of Literacy.' *Victorian Studies* 45, no. 3 (2003): 405–31.
Wadsworth, Sarah. *In the Company of Books: Literature and Its 'Classes' in Nineteenth Century America*. Amherst: University of Massachusetts Press, 2006.
Walker, Paul 'C.W. Jefferys and Images of Canadian Identity in School Textbooks.' Master's thesis, Queen's University, 1990.
Wallace, Ian. 'The Emotional Link.' *New Advocate* 2, no. 2 (1989): 75–82.
Walz, Gene. 'The PGA Connection.' *Animation World Magazine* 2, no. 2 (1997). http://mag.awn.com/?article_no=778.
Waterston, Elizabeth. *Children's Literature in Canada*. New York: Twayne Publishers; Toronto: Maxwell Macmillan Canada, 1992.
– 'Lucy Maud Montgomery, 1874–1942.' In *The Clear Spirit: Twenty Canadian Women and Their Times*, ed. Mary Quayle Innis, 198–219. Toronto: University of Toronto Press, 1966.
– 'Margaret Marshall Saunders: A Voice for the Silent.' In *Silenced Sextet: Six Nineteenth-*

Century Canadian Women Novelists, ed. Carrie MacMillan, Lorraine McMullen, and Elizabeth Waterston, 137–68. Montreal and Kingston: McGill-Queen's University Press, 1992.

Watson, Victor, and Morag Styles, eds. *Talking Pictures: Pictorial Texts and Young Readers*. London: Hodder and Stoughton, 1996.

Whalen-Levitt, Peggy. 'Picture Play in Children's Books: A Celebration of Visual Awareness.' *Wilson Library Bulletin* 55 (1980): 102–7.

Whalley, Joyce Irene, and Tessa Rose Chester. *A History of Children's Book Illustration*. London: John Murray with the Victoria and Albert Museum, 1988.

Whitaker, Muriel. 'Child in the Wilderness: The Romantic View.' *CCL*, nos. 5–6 (1976): 23–30.

– 'Editorial: On Illustrating Canadian Children's Books.' *CCL*, no. 60 (1990): 2–3.

– 'Guest Editorial: Illustrating Children's Books.' *CCL*, nos. 39–40 (1985): 2–3.

– 'Monsters from Native Canadian Mythologies.' *CCL*, nos. 15–16 (1980): 57–66.

– 'Perceiving Prairie Landscapes: The Young Person's View of a Western Frontier.' *CLAQ* 8, no. 4 (1983): 30–2.

– 'The Raven Cycle: Mythology in Process.' *CCL*, nos. 31–32 (1983): 46–52.

– 'Tales of the Wilderness: The Canadian Animal Story.' *CCL*, no. 2 (1975): 38–46.

Whitaker, Muriel, and Jetske Sybesma-Ironside. 'On Reviewing Picture Books.' *CCL*, no. 21 (1981): 58–65.

White, Jean. 'New Perspectives on Feminist Publishing.' *Canadian Author and Bookman* 65, no. 2 (1990): 3–4, 23.

Whitehead, Jane. '"This Is Not What I Wrote": The Americanization of British Children's Books'. Part 1. *HB* 72, no. 6 (1996): 687–93; Part 2. *HB* 73, no. 1 (1997): 27–34.

Whiteman, Edna. 'Storytelling as a Method of Directing the Reading of Children.' In American Library Association, Committee on Library Work with Children, *Children's Library Yearbook*, no. 1. Chicago: American Library Association, 1929.

Wild, Leanne. 'Franklin: Ideal Children's Literary Idol or Flavourless Turtle of Privilege.' *CCL*, no. 90 (1998): 38–44.

Wilkinson, John P. *Canadian Juvenile Fiction and the Library Market*. Ottawa: Canadian Library Association, 1976.

Wilks, Rick. 'The Economics of Canadian Children's Book Publishing.' *CM* 13, no. 6 (1985). http://www.umanitoba.ca/cm/cmarchive/vol13no6/economicsofchildrenspublis.html.

Willats, John. *Art and Representation: New Principles in the Analysis of Pictures*. Princeton: Princeton University Press, 1997.

Williams, Jean. 'Profile: Janet Lunn.' *IR* 7, no. 1 (Winter 1973): 5–6.

Williams, Raymond. *The Country and the City*. London: Chatto and Windus, 1973.

Willinsky, John. 'Frye among (Postcolonial) Schoolchildren: The Educated Imagination.' *CCL*, no. 79 (1995): 6–24.

Winearls, Joan. 'Illustrations for Books and Periodicals.' In Fleming, Gallichan, and Lamonde, eds, *HBIC*, vol. 1, 103–9.

Winham, Linda. '1987 Notable Canadian Non-Fiction for Children.' *CM* 16, no. 6 (1988). http://www.umanitoba.ca/cm/cmarchive/vol16no6/notenonfictionchildren1987.html.

Wolf, Doris, and Paul DePasquale. 'Home and Native Land: A Study of Canadian Aboriginal Picture Books by Aboriginal Authors.' In Reimer, eds, *Home Words*, 87–105.

Wolfenbarger, Carol Driggs, and Lawrence R. Sipe. 'A Unique Visual and Literary Art Form: Recent Research on Picturebooks.' *Language Arts* 84, no. 2 (2007): 273–80.

Wollman-Bonilla, Julie E. 'Outrageous Viewpoints: Teachers' Criteria for Rejecting Works of Children's Literature.' *Language Arts* 75, no. 4 (1998): 287–95.

Woodcock, George. 'Face of a River.' *CL,* no. 2 (1959): 89–90.

Wright, Robert. *Hip and Trivial: Youth Culture, Book Publishing, and the Greying of Canadian Nationalism.* Toronto: Canadian Scholars' Press, 2001.

Wyatt, Val. 'Publishers in Profile: Annick Press.' *IR* 14, no. 5 (October 1980): 24–5.

– 'Publishers in Profile: Greey de Pencier Books.' *IR* 14, no. 1 (February 1980): 12–13.

– 'Publishers in Profile: PMA Books.' *IR* 15, no. 3 (July 1981): 23–5.

Wyile, Andrea Schwenke. 'The Drama of Potentiality in Metafictive Picturebooks: Engaging Pictorialization in "Shortcut," "Ooh-la-la," and "Voices in the Park" (with Occasional Assistance from A. Wolf's "True Story").' *CLAQ* 31, no. 2 (2006): 176–96.

Wynne-Jones, Tim. 'The Adult Writing for Children.' In Fasick, Johnston, and Osler, eds, *Lands of Pleasure,* 97–109.

Xie, Shaobo. 'Rethinking the Identity of Cultural Otherness: The Discourse of Difference as an Unfinished Project.' In McGillis, ed., *Voices of the Other,* 1–16.

Yaffe, Phyllis. 'Another Look at Non-Sexist Canadian Children's Books.' *IR* 9, no. 1 (Winter 1975): 10–11.

– 'The Children's Book Centre: Canadian Books for Kids.' *IR* 12, no. 2 (Spring 1978): 5–7.

– 'Double Jeopardy: Books and Culture in Canada.' *Library Journal* 115, no. 13 (1990): 56–7.

Yamakami, Brenda. 'Little Fingerling: An Analysis of a Picture Book Illustration.' Paper for LIBR 522E, Children's Illustrated Books, School of Library, Archival and Information Studies, University of British Columbia, December 2006.

Yamazaki, Akiko. 'Why Change Names? On the Translation of Children's Books.' *CLE* 33, no. 1 (2002): 53–62.

Young, David. 'The Macmillan Company of Canada in the 1930s.' *Journal of Canadian Studies* 30, no. 3 (1995): 117–33.

Young, Judy. 'No Longer "Apart": Multiculturalism Policy and Canadian Literature.' *Canadian Ethnic Studies* 33, no. 2 (2001): 88–116.

Zipes, Jack. *Sticks and Stones: The Troublesome Success of Children's Literature from Slovenly Peter to Harry Potter.* New York: Routledge, 2001.

Zola, Meguido. 'Publishers in Profile: Douglas and McIntyre.' *IR* 13, no. 2 (April 1979): 19–20.

Zornado, Joseph. *Inventing the Child Culture: Ideology and the Story of Childhood.* New York: Garland Press, 2001.

Index

STUDIES IN BOOK AND PRINT CULTURE

General Editor: Leslie Howsam

Hazel Bell, *Indexers and Indexes in Fact and Fiction*

Heather Murray, *Come, bright Improvement! The Literary Societies of Nineteenth-Century Ontario*

Joseph A. Dane, *The Myth of Print Culture: Essays on Evidence, Textuality, and Bibliographical Method*

Christopher J. Knight, *Uncommon Readers: Denis Donoghue, Frank Kermode, George Steiner, and the Tradition of the Common Reader*

Eva Hemmungs Wirtén, *No Trespassing: Authorship, Intellectual Property Rights, and the Boundaries of Globalization*

William A. Johnson, *Bookrolls and Scribes in Oxyrhynchus*

Siân Echard and Stephen Partridge, eds, *The Book Unbound: Editing and Reading Medieval Manuscripts and Texts*

Bronwen Wilson, *The World in Venice: Print, the City, and Early Modern Identity*

Peter Stoicheff and Andrew Taylor, eds, *The Future of the Page*

Jennifer Phegley and Janet Badia, eds, *Reading Women: Literary Figures and Cultural Icons from the Victorian Age to the Present*

Elizabeth Sauer, *'Paper-contestations' and Textual Communities in England, 1640–1675*

Nick Mount, *When Canadian Literature Moved to New York*

Jonathan Earl Carlyon, *Andrés González de Barcia and the Creation of the Colonial Spanish American Library*

Leslie Howsam, *Old Books and New Histories: An Orientation to Studies in Book and Print Culture*

Deborah McGrady, *Controlling Readers: Guillaume de Machaut and His Late Medieval Audience*

David Finkelstein, ed., *Print Culture and the Blackwood Tradition*

Bart Beaty, *Unpopular Culture: Transforming the European Comic Book in the 1990s*

Elizabeth Driver, *Culinary Landmarks: A Bibliography of Canadian Cookbooks, 1825–1949*

Benjamin C. Withers, *The Illustrated Old English Hexateuch, Cotton Ms. Claudius B.iv: The Frontier of Seeing and Reading in Anglo-Saxon England*

Mary Ann Gillies, *The Professional Literary Agent in Britain, 1880–1920*

Willa Z. Silverman, *The New Bibliopolis: French Book-Collectors and the Culture of Print, 1880–1914*

Lisa Surwillo, *The Stages of Property: Copyrighting Theatre in Spain*

Dean Irvine, *Editing Modernity: Women and Little-Magazine Cultures in Canada, 1916–1956*

Janet Friskney, *New Canadian Library: The Ross-McClelland Years, 1952–1978*

Janice Cavell, *Tracing the Connected Narrative: Arctic Exploration in British Print Culture, 1818-1860*

Elspeth Jajdelska, *Silent Reading and the Birth of the Narrator*

Martyn Lyons, *Reading Culture and Writing Practices in Nineteenth-Century France*

Robert A. Davidson, *Jazz Age Barcelona*

Gail Edwards and Judith Saltman, *Picturing Canada: A History of Canadian Children's Illustrated Books and Publishing*